ROUTLEDGE LIBRARY EDITIONS:
LORD BYRON

Volume 3

BYRON, SULLY, AND THE POWER OF PORTRAITURE

BYRON, SULLY, AND THE POWER OF PORTRAITURE

JOHN CLUBBE

Routledge
Taylor & Francis Group
LONDON AND NEW YORK

First published in 2005 by Ashgate Publishing Limited

This edition first published in 2016
by Routledge
4 Park Square, Milton Park, Abingdon, Oxon OX14 4RN
605 Third Avenue, New York, NY 10017

Routledge is an imprint of the Taylor & Francis Group, an informa business

British Library Cataloguing in Publication Data
A catalogue record for this book is available from the British Library

ISBN: 978-1-138-67557-5 (Set)
ISBN: 978-1-315-56060-1 (Set) (ebk)
ISBN: 978-1-138-65967-4 (Volume 3) (hbk)
ISBN: 978-1-138-66563-7 (Volume 3) (pbk)
ISBN: 978-1-315-61979-8 (Volume 3) (ebk)

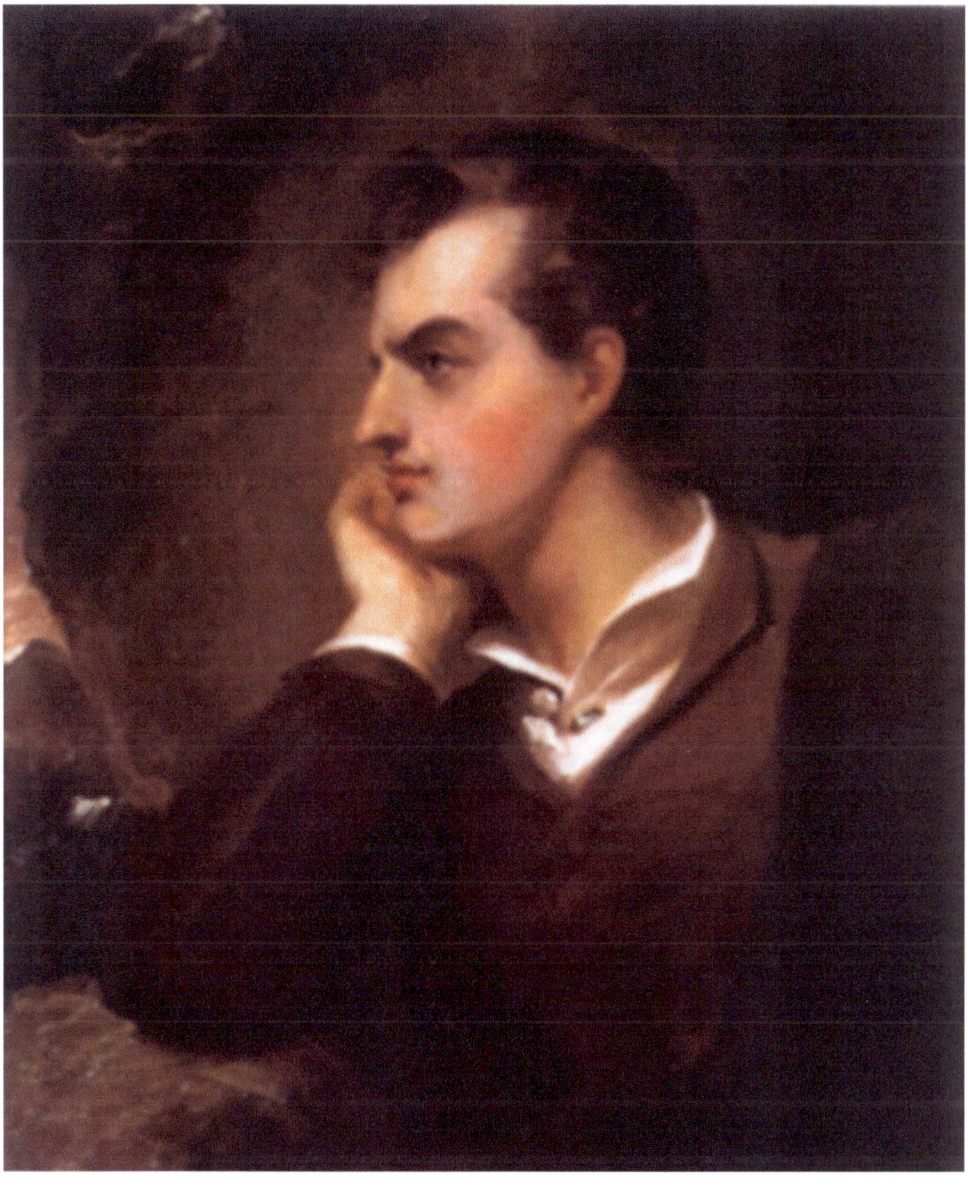

Thomas Sully, *Lord Byron*, 1826–1828. Private Collection, USA.

Byron, Sully, and the Power of Portraiture

JOHN CLUBBE

ASHGATE

Published by

Ashgate Publishing Limited
Gower House
Croft Road
Aldershot
Hants GU11 3HR
England

Ashgate Publishing Company
Suite 420
101 Cherry Street
Burlington
Vermont, 05401–4405
USA

Ashgate website: http://www.ashgate.com

British Library Cataloguing in Publication Data
Clubbe, John, 1938–
Byron, Sully, and the Power of Portraiture. – (The Nineteenth Century Series)
1. Sully, Thomas, 1783–1872 – Criticism and interpretation. 2. Byron, George Gordon Byron, Baron, 1788–1824 – Portraits. 3. Portrait painting, American. 4. Portrait painting – 19th century. I. Title.
759.1'3

US Library of Congress Cataloging in Publication Data
Clubbe, John
Byron, Sully, and the Power of Portraiture
p. cm. – (The Nineteenth Century Series)
Includes bibliographical references and index.
1. Sully, Thomas, 1783—1872. Lord Byron. 2. Byron, George Gordon Byron, 1788–1824 – Portraits. 3. Sully, Thomas 1783–1872 – Criticism and interpretation. I. Title. II. Series: The Nineteenth Century Series (Aldershot, England)
ND1329.S84A65 2005
759.13–dc22 2004006791

ISBN 0 7546 3814 6

This book is printed on acid free paper.

Typeset by Bournemouth Colour Press, Parkstone

Printed and bound in Great Britain by MPG Books, Bodmin, Cornwall.

To Joan

Contents

Illustrations

Color Plates

Black-and-white Illustrations

Preface

There is no greater work of art than a great portrait.
Henry James[1]

I was struck as if by a flaming arrow. It was April 4, 1999, and I was back in my hometown of New York, taking in as is my wont as many as I could of Manhattan's museums and art galleries. I had mounted the stairs to the second floor of the Owen Gallery on 75th Street, just off Madison Avenue. As I turned into the showroom, I gasped involuntarily, "That's Byron!" There in front of me was a large, utterly gorgeous portrait of Lord Byron. I had never seen it before. I was transfixed. Keats's famous lines about "stout Cortez," his eagle eyes seeing the Pacific Ocean for the first time, rushed to mind. As Cortez and his men stared "at each other with a wild surmise— / Silent, upon a peak in Darien," so I stared at this portrait. Cortez's astonishment could hardly have surpassed mine. How could I, a Byron scholar for 40 years, come upon a major portrait of Byron that was completely unknown? Here before me, I sensed, stretched my Pacific.[2]

Approaching the painting, I noted a plaque below. It indicated the artist: Thomas Sully. A further surprise. Sully I knew as the leading American portraitist of his generation. Most major American museums display works by him, and being an inveterate museum-goer I had long admired his artistry. Even an initial glance told me that *Byron* ranked among his finest portraits. Decades of scholarly work along with visits to museums and historic houses had made me familiar with the main portraits of Byron. Indeed, they had become a major part of my awareness of him. The ways I visualized Byron affected my understanding of the man and his writings. But a portrait of Byron by Thomas Sully? That was, again to cite Keats's sonnet, "a shadow of a magnitude." How could Sully have painted Byron without any Byron scholar knowing of it?

The pose of Sully's painting, I realized instantly, resembled that of Richard Westall's 1813 portrait of Byron. Appearing in numerous books and on dustjackets, Westall's brooding likeness ranks as one of the best-known representations of the poet. But I sensed also that Sully's portrait, despite outward similarities to Westall's, differed from it greatly. How and why it differed would take me longer to understand.

In her novel *Girl in Hyacinth Blue* Susan Vreeland explores the possibility of an individual discovering he had a Vermeer. An unknown Vermeer passing through a number of private owners, most but not all ignorant of its true worth, makes for an intriguing tale. People hold on to a painting because they like it or, possibly, because they regard it as an object they can part with if financial circumstances require. A Vermeer unknown to the world remains a possibility; in fact one appeared in 2004. Byron scholars hope against hope that a copy of the poet's infamous *Memoirs*, burned after his death in 1824, will turn up somewhere, sometime. With the Sully I had found my "Vermeer," or the closest to a Vermeer that this Byron scholar might hope to stumble upon. The portrait was not merely a splendid one; it was by a major artist.

Good portrait painters are about as rare as good poets. The best artists, like the best poets, open up for us imaginative realms. Their oeuvre deserves study in itself and for what it can tell us about human nature or about the era in which it was created. Once I had gotten over the excitement of finding the portrait, I knew I had to understand it better. It was virtually unknown to Sully scholars, unknown to literary scholars, and I had much to learn. The first and obvious question is that explored in Chapter 1 – where had the portrait been for nearly two centuries? Paintings have a life of their own; often that life is interesting in itself. Though *Byron* seemed to have left few traces, I discovered, paradoxically, that more could be learned about it than about many other better-known paintings of its era.

The history of Sully's portrait, as I have reconstructed it, serves as an intriguing prelude to the larger and even more interesting story of the painting itself. The questions soon multiplied. Why does the portrait look the way it does? What had brought it into existence? Why did Sully paint it? What does it reveal about his art? About Byron? The hunt to find answers never lost its excitement. From the first sighting of the portrait on that fateful day in April 1999, the investigation brought a full array of challenges. Often it went in directions other than I had anticipated. In time many things did come together, though a few puzzles remained. The questions also led to larger issues. By setting the portrait within a more encompassing framework, the book takes up Byron's place in America's early history and culture, his role in the American imagination. Almost inevitably, it raises issues about art and the nature of portraiture.

Byron's elusive genius, flamboyant personal life, and impressive poetic achievement inspire as much controversy today as in his lifetime. If no portrait quite captures his essence, perhaps that goal is itself unrealizable. But some efforts succeed better than others. The most gifted artist ever to render Byron's features, Sully created what may be the most accomplished of all portraits of the poet. His interpretation of Byron enables us to "read" that enigmatic figure, yet once again, anew.

For nearly two hundred years Sully's portrait of Byron has remained virtually unknown. There are no known preliminary sketches. Never exhibited, never engraved, never copied by the artist, the portrait has also never been discussed, either by scholars of Sully or of Byron.[3] For these reasons Sully's *Byron* does not hold the iconic status of several other portraits of the poet. As it begins to make its way into our awareness of Byron, its merit should become apparent. The most beautiful, arguably even the most verifiably accurate, of all the many representations of the Noble Poet, Sully's *Byron* may in time achieve iconic status of its own.

Acknowledgments

Art has intrigued me all my life. I grew up not far from New York's Metropolitan Museum. Though later trained as a historian and literary scholar, I have gawped at pictures since youth. Over the years, along with my literary scholarship, I developed interests in cities, in art and architecture, and in landscape, and I went on to publish articles and books on these subjects. As my awareness of art developed, my interest in portraiture grew. In the 1960s I wrote about Thomas Carlyle's dazzling word portraits of his contemporaries, including that of the Scottish artist Archibald Skirving, himself a fine portraitist; in the 1970s I published essays on William Edward West's portraits of Byron and his last attachment, Teresa Guiccioli; in the 1980s, writing *Cincinnati Observed: Architecture and History* (1992), I took up the city's long artistic traditions and the many artists associated with it. More recently, I have explored the work of Henry Farny and Joseph Henry Sharp, two artists of the American West who depicted Native Americans with sympathy and insight. Learning about Sully's portrait of Byron has allowed me to combine my interests in art with those in literature.

Sully spent over sixty years of a long life in Philadelphia, and to understand him I had to familiarize myself with the city and its rich artistic traditions. Philadelphia provided a nourishing environment for this study. Its pride of cultural institutions must be the most extraordinary in America, and in almost every one of them reside Sully portraits. Seeing and studying them as I wandered about the city put *Byron* into its cultural context.

The search to learn more about Sully and his portrait of Byron took me to libraries and depositories in Britain and America. Almost all key materials for this artist, I learned quickly enough, remain unpublished. If I were to understand Sully's artistry, his manuscripts, letters, and scrapbooks required careful examination. I thank the friendly and professional staff of various East Coast repositories for their help: in Washington, the Archives of American Art; in New York, the Frick Art Reference Library, the New York Historical Society, and the New York Public Library; in New Haven, Yale's Beinecke Library; in Delaware, the Winterthur Museum outside Wilmington (Jeanne Solenski); and in Philadelphia and its environs, a cornucopia of institutions. These include the Historical Society of Pennsylvania, the Library Company of Philadelphia, the Union League Club (particularly James G. Mundy, Jr), the American Philosophical Society (Roy E. Goodman), the Rosenbach Museum, the Pennsylvania Academy of the Fine Arts, the Stephen Girard Collection at Girard College (Elizabeth Laurent), the Lancaster Historical Society (Tom Ryan), the Philadelphia Museum of Art (Madeleine Viljoen), and the Schwarz Gallery (Robert Schwarz and David Cassedy), whose superb catalogues are an education in themselves. Heather Vaughan at Philipse Manor Hall confirmed one of my hypotheses regarding the painting's provenance. James Biddle kindly allowed me to visit Andalusia, the Biddle family home, in order to study Sully's portraits of Nicholas and Jane Craig Biddle *in situ*. Examination of the Sully scrapbooks in the Philadelphia Museum of Art – full of the artist's sketches and engravings he had collected for reference and instruction – heightened my awareness of the sources of his creativity.

Sully's *Byron* came into existence within an artistic context that included a host of painters influential or alive during his formative years: in Federal America, Gilbert Stuart and various Peale family members, especially Rembrandt Peale; in Georgian England, Joshua Reynolds, Henry Fuseli, Thomas Lawrence, and the transplanted American, Benjamin West. West whose art and life, like Stuart's, straddled the Atlantic took charge of Sully when he came to London in 1809 to study portrait painting. But if the English-born Sully learned from British artists, he had spent his years of apprenticeship in America. Later, the maturing republic – during the crucial decade of the 1820s – powerfully influenced both the conception and the artistry behind *Byron*.

What began as an investigation into a new portrait of Byron necessarily came to encompass other works by Sully. Studying them introduced me to a bevy of Sully's famous sitters. Portraits by him of the Shakespearean actors George Frederick Cooke and Fanny Kemble, the young Queen Victoria, the Byronic financier Nicholas Biddle, the "hero of two worlds" Lafayette, presidents Washington and Jefferson and Jackson, play key roles in the story of *Byron*.

The early nineteenth century marks the climax of the golden age of Anglo-American portraiture. In London, where he had studied under West and Lawrence, the youthful Sully had sought out this wealth of work and had learned from it. Two centuries later, I feasted on the fabulous examples of British portraiture on display there. Unpublished information about Richard Westall came chiefly from the library of London's National Portrait Gallery. A long tube ride brought me to the Gallery's off-site storage depository in South Wimbledon, where Westall's Byron portrait is usually housed. In All Souls Church, Langham Place, I sought out Westall's *Ecce Homo*, the face of whose central figure may bear a similarity to that in his *Byron*. Nearby, in the Wallace Collection, hangs Sully's superb three-quarter-length *Queen Victoria*. That painting, along with his full-length *Victoria* in New York's Metropolitan Museum of Art, became the focus of a special exhibit at the Wallace early in 2001. The exhibit's prior venue had been at the Metropolitan. Both exhibits, along with a concurrent one at the Metropolitan of its exceptional Sully holdings, shed new light on *Byron*.

Serendipitous discoveries of works needed for my research occurred in secondhand bookshops chiefly in Santa Fe, Albuquerque, Cincinnati, and Philadelphia. In Santa Fe, I thank particularly Nicholas Potter and Helen Macleod; in Albuquerque, Jerry Lane and Eric Patterson; in Cincinnati, Jim Fallon and Dick Baringhaus, Tom Brengelman, Sam Jenicke and Phil Metz; and in Philadelphia, John F. Warren, Clarence Wolf, and Sallie van Merkensteijn.

James Biddle kindly read my Chapter 7, as did Patrick Snadon. Both made helpful suggestions. I am particularly indebted to the Press's anonymous critic who read the manuscript with genuine empathy for my quest and came up with valuable insights about portraiture and prose. From the international fraternity/sorority of Byron scholars, with whom I have long shared interests, I thank especially among those who have written about Byron portraiture Peter W. Graham, Suzanne Hyman, Christine Kenyon Jones, Doris Langley Moore, and David Piper. Michael Rees, now Brother Teilo, has for years generously encouraged my work on Byron. The array of information that Annette Peach has assembled with impeccable attention to detail in *Portraits of Byron* (2000) has provided useful perspectives. Sully scholars are fewer and less known to me, but no less dedicated, and I have learned much from the labors of Steven Bronson, Philipp Fehl, Christopher Johns, and, among the pioneers, Edward Biddle, Mantle Fielding, Nicholas Wainwright, and Monroe Fabian. I thank them all.

During Saturday forays to the University of New Mexico's excellent Art Library in Albuquerque Dave Herzel and Kyle Nelson went beyond the call of duty in making my time fruitful. My research assistants at the University of Kentucky, Jenny and Ron Pitcock and Jessica Hollis, trawled with almost invariable success for obscure articles and books. Computer technology can be a trial as well as a blessing, and more than once Jim Cornelius rode to the rescue to solve foul-ups with customary aplomb and unerring success. Erika Gaffney of Ashgate expressed enthusiasm in my discovery and the tale I proposed to tell; subsequently, Ann Donahue inherited and seconded her enthusiasm. Working with both has been a pleasure, as has been the support given by the series editors, Joanne Shattock and Vincent Newey. Such specific debts I acknowledge gratefully; if others who have helped or have patiently answered queries remain unnamed, I hope they will excuse my negligence. Foremost I thank Joan Blythe, my severest critic. With unfailing good humor she has patiently honed often recalcitrant prose and sharpened imperfect insights. In sharing with me her own fascination about art, she has vastly stimulated mine.

John Clubbe

Casa Gabrielle
Santa Fe, New Mexico

Introduction
The Importance of Portraiture

> Nothing, in the whole circle of human vanities, takes stronger hold of the imagination, than this affair of having a portrait painted. Yet why should this be so?
>
> Nathaniel Hawthorne[1]

> Historical understanding is like a vision, or rather like an evocation of images.
>
> Johann Huizinga[2]

> We're made so that we love
> First when we see them painted, things we have passed
> Perhaps a hundred times nor cared to see;
> And so they are better, painted – better to us,
> Which is the same thing. Art was given for that.
>
> Browning[3]

Why a book on one painting? Studies dealing with the history of a single work of art are few. Usually only major works receive such amplitude of treatment. Peter Watson's *Wisdom and Strength: The Biography of a Renaissance Masterpiece* (1989) investigates the long and adventure-filled history of Veronese's allegorical *Wisdom and Strength*, painted in 1576, before it entered Henry Frick's collection in 1912. Cynthia Saltzman's *Portrait of Dr Gachet: The Story of a Van Gogh Masterpiece* (1998) explores the equally various if briefer career of Van Gogh's famous last portrait before it ended up in a warehouse in Japan.

The Veronese and Van Gogh are well known and in monetary terms very valuable. When sold in 1991, the Van Gogh achieved the record price for a painting (until surpassed in 2004) of $82,500,000. Prices for art works change with the times and are always arbitrary. Sometimes, not always, market value correlates with a work's intrinsic worth. Interest in Federal era portraits – Sully's *Byron* is one – peaked in the 1920s, a time when one could buy a Van Gogh for a pittance. The market for Federal portraits has, in relative terms, declined ever since. But the situation may be changing. Early in 2001 a private foundation bought Gilbert Stuart's "Lansdowne" *Washington*, still owned by the British family that commissioned it, for $20 million. Another $10 million went to sponsor a national tour for the painting, long an American icon, along with its reinstallation in the Smithsonian's National Portrait Gallery.[4] Like the Veronese, the Van Gogh, and the Stuart, Sully's *Byron* is a major work of art. It may never command the impressive sums they did, but for some – Byron and Sully aficionados but also admirers of good portraiture – it may be no less important. Unlike the Veronese or the Van Gogh or the "Lansdowne" *Washington*, art historians have not brought Sully's *Byron* to the attention of a wider audience.[5] The reasons are not hard to fathom. Sully in his "Account of Pictures" noted that he began a portrait of Byron in 1826 and completed it in 1828. Apart from this document (not published until the twentieth century), only a few scattered comments in out-of-the-way publications mention the portrait.

Byron ranks as a major poet of the English language and one of the outstanding figures of world literature. People all over the world have responded to his writings and the drama of his life. An archetypal Romantic, a defender of political liberty wherever he lived, Byron died in Greece a hero in the cause of freedom, his name revered there even more than in Britain, Europe, and America. Each generation has formed its own conception of Byron. His name continues to resonate around the globe, and the International Byron Society, with an ardent non-academic as well as academic membership, has branches in over thirty countries. When Sully painted him, Byron was the most famous – and enigmatic – poet in the world. He remains famous and enigmatic today. Americans of Sully's era, from Boston to the "the banks of the Ohio," devoured edition after edition of his poems. Byron delighted in every manifestation of his American fame.

Portraits of the famous tend to attract more attention than portraits of those less known. Portraits of the Romantic poets – Washington Allston's *Coleridge*, Henry Inman's *Wordsworth*, Joseph Severn's *Keats*, the several *Byrons* of Thomas Phillips, even the inset portraits of Keats, Hazlitt, and Wordsworth in Benjamin Robert Haydon's *Christ's Entry into Jerusalem* have become icons, recognized by the general public as well as academics. Contemporaries often tell us much about these portraits; scholarship has filled in gaps. Unfortunately, we lack such commentary for Sully's *Byron*. No one in Byron's circle knew of it; likewise, aside from Sully's family and a few friends and admirers, no one in Philadelphia. For the next two centuries the portrait existed amidst a silence almost total.

In contrast, a rich contemporary commentary surrounds Veronese's *Wisdom and Strength* and Van Gogh's *Portrait of Dr Gachet*. *Wisdom and Strength* came into being in a mythical city during one of its most colorful periods. The popularity of *Dr Gachet* draws upon the legend of Van Gogh, created and shaped almost entirely after his death but compelling in its tragedy and almost unbearable poignancy. No dramatic stories attach to Thomas Sully. A devoted husband, a conscientious father, he worked for over sixty years in Philadelphia, sometimes considered the least romantic of America's great cities. Sully's *Byron* is also an American painting, and American art, at least until recent decades, has not attracted the critical attention accorded European masters.

Visual images can exert almost irresistible power. The most famous painting in the world – the *Mona Lisa* – is a portrait, one which enthralls but whose meaning puzzles and eludes our scrutiny. Images can induce fear – and hope – as well. "Portraits," wrote the Renaissance theorist Alberti, "were believed to have the power to bring the dead back to life, make the absent present, and present the portrayed's features to posterity."[6] Russian authorities in 1826 forbade individuals sent to Siberia from having their portraits sketched. They worried that others might use the images to make prints, and that the prints would become icons. Similarly, the Bourbon monarchy in France banned visual images of the now-exiled Emperor Napoleon after 1815. They feared that too many of their subjects would thrill to the power inherent in such images. Theodore K. Raab and Jonathan Brown suggest that images exert such a hold on people because "painters, sculptors, and architects are able to give us clues (and sometimes answers) about the universe that they inhabit that are available nowhere else."[7]

Images even briefly glimpsed can haunt us over a lifetime: the Virgin of Guadalupe, Martin Luther King preaching, the death of a Loyalist soldier, Elvis gyrating, Marilyn Monroe smilingly holding down her skirt standing in the updraft vent of a Manhattan subway. Icons need not be people: St Paul's Cathedral in the Blitz, the raising of the American flag at Iwo Jima, the Statue of Liberty. Some figures or structures – James Dean, the World Trade Center – become icons posthumously, understood better or valued more after they have gone. Images also last longer. Few recall the details of the frigate *Medusa*'s last voyage in July 1816 but who, looking at Géricault's *Raft of the Medusa*, cannot feel the anguish of the survivors, the artist, and his contemporaries? We carry such images with us wherever we go. They exert unimaginable impact upon our daily lives as well as form a vital part of our culture.[8]

Why do we seek out portraits of individuals we admire? Shouldn't appreciation of their work or achievement suffice? Perhaps, but often we long for more. We hunger, we thirst, for images of the great creative figures whom we venerate or love. We strain to visualize the individual – whether musician, painter, author, political figure or other hero or heroine of history who has created what we care about. We may read these images as expressions of personal qualities or evidence of cultural history, or, as often with twentieth-century works, for other reasons, expressions of composition and color, for example. We may read ourselves into such images, imagine ourselves in relation to them. The desire to *see* persists. The need to gaze upon relics of the holy and the great may be inherent in the human condition. Images shape our responses to the work of the individual in question. We read *Hamlet*, but yearn to visualize Shakespeare.

Art elicits in us powerful emotional responses. Painted portraits may engage our minds more intensely and at deeper levels of personal involvement than sculpture or photographs. They are more fully products of a living hand. Unlike many sculptures and most photographs, portraits render color and recreate the illusion of flesh and blood. The living hand sketched and interpreted the individual according to the artist's gifts and insight. A good portrait should contribute something indispensable to the way we look at – and understand – artists or their subjects. It's quite possible to misread everything in front of our eyes – perception is after all many-layered, individual, and often deceptive – but a portrait of someone we care about can afford us an intense feeling of joy.

Byron makes a noteworthy instance here, one whose known portraits I explore in Chapter 2. Beethoven makes another.[9] The portrait record for Beethoven is as spotty, inconsistent, and as frustrating as Byron's. Many Beethoven enthusiasts execrate the best-known portrait of the composer, that by Waldmüller. Most of the others are by nonentities. We scan them hopefully, but with little success, for clues that will illuminate for us what we understand by "Beethoven," the man who created that overwhelming music. Does not, after all, *seeing* the man imply the possibility that we may know and understand him better? It might seem so. Amusingly, both Beethoven and Byron posed a similar problem for those who drew or painted them: neither the impatient composer nor the restless poet would sit still for long.

With Bach we face a different quandary. As with Beethoven and Byron, we are curious to know more about the individual who created such glorious works. "Why is it so necessary to know Bach the man?" asks George B. Stauffer; "Isn't his music enough?" Stauffer answers his own question: "One suspects that it is the consummate nature of the works that drives us to understand their maker." The only authentic contemporary portrait of Bach is a modest effort done in 1746 by a local artist named Elias Gottlof Haussmann. Two years later Haussmann made a copy. Both versions show Bach as "the dutiful cantor, professional composer and upright middle-class citizen, but no more than that." Nothing in either version suggests the composer of the *St Matthew Passion*, the *Mass in B minor*, *The Art of the Fugue*, or other masterpieces equally transcendent.[10]

Lovers of Bach yearned for more, and in 1894 they got it. Gravediggers working in the cemetery attached to St John's Church in Leipzig unearthed a skeleton assumed to be Bach's. A sculptor, asked to recreate Bach's features from the skull, responded (in 1908) with a statue. Standing beside St Thomas's Church in Leipzig, this statue has since become an object of veneration for Bach pilgrims everywhere. If this sculptural "Bach" bears more of a resemblance to Bismarck than to the cantor of St Thomas's Church, comments Stauffer, "it is only because of the tendency of every age to recreate Bach in its own image." Compared to Bach, Byron poses the different problem of excess. With Bach the written record is scant, and unrevealing of the person; with Byron, it is vast, and exceedingly revealing of the person, so much so that we have to evaluate carefully to which representations, written and visual, we give credence. But, as with Bach, every generation recreates Byron in its own image.

Bach is not the only major genius for whom we have a paucity of surviving portraits. We have nothing certain of Spenser or Marlowe or, for that matter, of Crazy Horse or the Buddha or Sappho or Teresa of Avila or John Harvard. (Whereas the Buddha's interpreters are legion, Harvard University, commissioning a statue of its benefactor in the 1880s, solved the problem by having Daniel Chester French model his sculpture upon a suitably handsome young man.) Of Shakespeare, three images, all posthumous, have some claim to having been created with the awareness of people who knew the poet.[11] That is all, yet to those who care about Shakespeare's works an image of the man can assume tremendous importance.

Keats was one who did care, passionately. Touring the Isle of Wight in 1817, he came upon, in the hallway of his inn in Carisbrooke, an engraving of Shakespeare, probably of the Chandos portrait. To Keats this image came "nearer to my idea of him than any I have seen."[12] He considered finding it a good omen. He asked his landlady if he might hang it in his room. She agreed. When he left, he asked if he might take it with him to Margate, his next stop, and again she agreed. The portrait later hung in his rooms in Well Walk, Hampstead, where it stimulated Keats to develop his identity within a Shakespearean vision of the poet and of the self. To create great poetry Keats felt he needed "the blessing of the past."[13] His portrait of Shakespeare helped give him that blessing.

The quest for authentic images of Jane Austen illustrates the passion that lies behind our response to portraits. The recent controversy over a possible second portrait of her also illustrates how desperately we want – and want to keep in mind – valid images of those we love. Only one reasonably certain portrait from life exists of Jane Austen: a small oval miniature painted by her sister Cassandra about 1810. It came to London's National Portrait Gallery in 1948 and *faute de mieux* has become "the face of Jane Austen throughout the reading world." Her niece Caroline Austen wrote of it that "there is a *look* which I recognize as *hers* – and though the general resemblance is *not* strong, yet as it represents a pleasing countenance it is so far a truth." We have to accept the portrait's dour expression as Jane Austen's, wondering all the while in what ways "the general resemblance is *not* strong." The National Portrait Gallery in London admits its portrait lacks "conventional aesthetic merit" but touts its transcendent "iconic significance."[14]

Recently scholars have challenged the reign of Cassandra's miniature as the single authentic representation of Jane Austen. Advocates of the charming Rice portrait – which depicts a winsome but hard-eyed 14- or 15-year-old girl holding in her right hand an unfurled parasol – have put forth claims that it too represents Jane. Until the last half-century its authenticity was not questioned. Claudia L. Johnson argued in the *Times Literary Supplement* for its acceptance and wanted it put on a basis of equality with Cassandra's portrait.[15] Letters for or against the portrait's authenticity deluged the *TLS* for months and years afterward. The arguments convinced few others than those putting them forth. John Cooper in the *National Portrait Gallery. A Visitor's Guide* (2000) cites as authentic only Cassandra's miniature. The Rice portrait's status remains in dispute.

Johnson ponders how a portrait can arouse in us such intense emotions, how any image can be commensurate to what we think and feel about Jane Austen. "How could so momentous and yet so intimate a figure, one who becomes the site of such different and such contradictory visions and fantasies . . . survive figuration without arousing disappointment or anger?" Jane Austen means as much to those who deny the portrait's validity as to those who accept it. The skeptics understandably want the portrait authenticated beyond reasonable doubt before they give credence to a second icon of their heroine.

Not long after the controversy over the Rice portrait, a debate arose over a representation of Emily Dickinson. Only one documented photograph exists of Dickinson, a daguerreotype showing her at about seventeen. Thin and dark, she appears with an overbite and a serious expression. A 1999 *New Yorker* piece considered the possibility of another image, "a slightly faded photograph of a dark-haired, dark-eyed woman who may or may not be the poet in her early thirties, at the height of her creativity, when she was turning out an average of a poem a day."[16] Found on the Internet by a professor at Chapel Hill, it seemed to match up well to what we know of the poet. A new portrait of Dickinson, particularly of her in her maturity, would if authentic be inexpressively meaningful to those who care about her life and poetry. But again the evidence seems inconclusive.

What happens when a sitter dislikes a portrait, finds the artist's insights into his or her character, even if true, repellent? In *Tales from the Art Crypt* Richard Feigen tells of Mary Block, whose not overly pleasant personality Ivan Albright "uncannily captured" in his 1950s portrait of her. Mary Block so hated it that the moment it was finished she gave it to the Art Institute of Chicago.[17] There the detested image hangs – for all posterity to savor.

One recalls Picasso, half a century earlier, fielding negative comments that Gertrude Stein did not look like the initial version of his portrait of her. And Picasso's ineffable response: "that does not make any difference, she will."[18] Not how we are, but how we are portrayed, may be what ultimately survives. But Picasso's gnomic words imply something more: that the artist divines how time will affect our features, even our character, that a portrait may anticipate the future perception of our being. As Whistler remarked, "it takes a long time for a man to look like his portrait."[19]

An extreme form of distaste occurs in Winston Churchill's response to Graham Sutherland's portrait of him. Done in 1954, it was intended as a gift from Parliament to its most eminent living member. "Are you going to paint me as a cherub or a bulldog?" Churchill asked Sutherland. "It depends on what you show me" was the reply. Later, the artist reported, "He showed me a bulldog so I painted a bulldog." "The Sutherland portrait," comments Richard Hough, "showed a bowed, belligerent figure, deeply lined and aged, lower lip thrust forward – a real warrior and a brilliant rendering of the man as the public knew him best."[20] But Winston, after initial satisfaction, came to think the portrait "malignant." Even more offended was his wife Clementine, who found it "a gross and cruel travesty." Sometime in 1955 or 1956 she had the portrait destroyed.[21] "I painted the man I saw," said Sutherland. That was his offence.

The Times, when the news broke, asserted that "a portrait of the greatest Englishman of his time by an artist who is arguably the best English portraitist is an object of outstanding historical importance." The loss of a "work of honesty and force" it termed "a great misfortune."[22] That loss can still cause pain, though of a kind different than that given the Churchills. Sutherland's ill-fated portrait shows a great spirit stranded in the indignities of old age; it may well embody the negative traits the Churchills thought it did, though the surviving oil sketch, brilliant in its suggestiveness, stirs no controversy today.[23] Clementine Churchill by her act foreclosed the future.

By denying generations to come the possibility of seeing the finished portrait, she diminished her husband – and our understanding of him. It was not the intent of her act, only its disastrous result. Sutherland's portrait offered an interpretation of Churchill's character that, however harsh and insensitive it seemed to the statesman and his family, was by a gifted artist who had the chance to observe him closely and to read his being. He read it, it seems, all too well.

Portraits can affect our lives, even change them irrevocably – as the Chandos Shakespeare did Keats's. A portrait can also make us rethink our attitude toward an individual. James Fenimore Cooper detested Thomas Jefferson. A staunch Federalist and in maturity perhaps America's most illustrious curmudgeon, Cooper admitted he would "have gone twice as far to see the picture of almost any other man." In 1823 he visited West Point in the company of Charles Mathews, the popular English comic actor then touring America. The novelist learned that in the Library, newly hung, was Thomas Sully's full-length portrait of ex-President Jefferson (Figure 1). He was persuaded to look at it. Sully's achievement stunned him. Cooper asked Mathews – whom he deemed a "collector" and rated a "very respectable" art critic – to take a look also. Mathews did. Impressed, he "pronounced it one of the finest portraits he had ever beheld." He told Cooper "that he would never have forgiven me if I had let it escape his notice." Sully's portrait had an even more formidable impact upon Cooper.

> You will smile when I tell you its effects on myself. There was a dignity, a repose, I will go further, and say a loveliness, about this painting, that I never have seen in any other portrait . . . . I saw . . . Jefferson, standing before me, not in red breeches and slovenly attire, but a gentleman, appearing in all republican simplicity, with a grace and ease on the canvas, that to me seem unrivalled. It has really shaken my opinion of Jefferson as a man, if not as a politician; and when his image occurs to me now, it is in the simple robes of Sully, sans red breeches, or even without any of the repulsive accompaniments of a political "sans culotte."[24]

What has happened? Seeing Sully's *Jefferson* was for Cooper an overwhelmingly positive experience. The portrait changed utterly his opinion of Jefferson the man. Cooper's response reminds us that a good portrait can provide us with new insight into an individual's character or achievement. A careful study of Sully's *Byron* may do the same.

How Sully came to paint *Byron* – the portrait's history, its sources, its context, its significance – is a story told here for the first time. I originally conceived this study as an extended essay, each section dependent on the others, the whole constituting a meditation on a remarkable work of art. It can still be regarded as such an essay, though for the convenience of readers I have adopted a conventional arrangement by chapters. Each explores the portrait in its context by focusing on a particular facet of the larger subject. The argument evolves slowly and deliberately, and is throughout

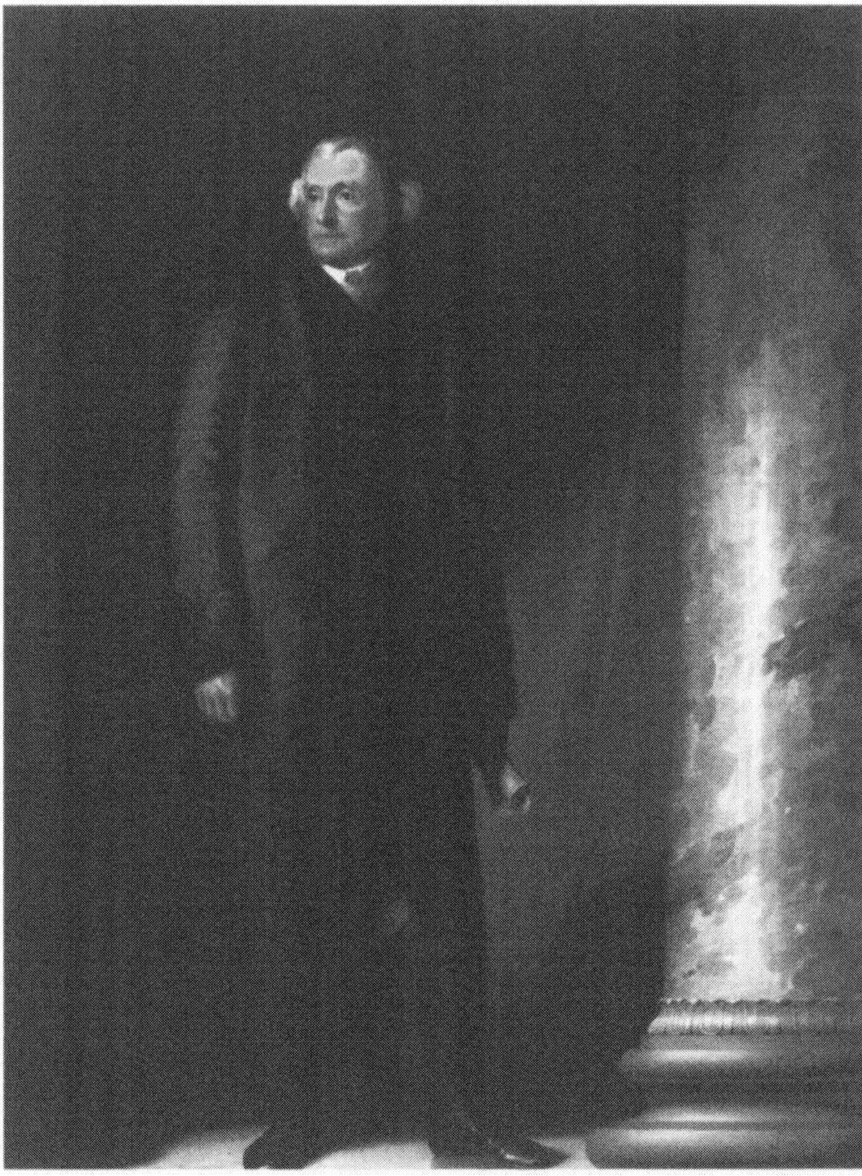

1 Thomas Sully, *Thomas Jefferson*, 1822. West Point Museum Art Collection, United States Military Academy

interlocking, each chapter building on those preceding. What may initially seem tangential when first encountered is part of an overall design whose purpose is to reveal the portrait in its context. The interconnections between Byron and Sully, between Britain and America, between Sully's other portraits and that of Byron, are meant to illumine the artist no less than the poet.

We can explore in depth the context of Sully's portrait of Byron as we cannot any other portrait of the poet. Sully is perhaps the only artist who painted Byron for whom a great deal of information, most of it in unpublished manuscripts, is available. We can establish not only Sully's life circumstances but also make reasonable conjectures about his awareness of Byron. Such a context is often complex, and I take you, dear reader, upon several rambles. Sometimes I leap ahead, sometimes I circle back, always with the goal in mind of illuminating, in some new way, Sully's *Byron*. What may seem detours will, I trust, like the digressions in *Don Juan*, lead us back with renewed appreciation to the matter at hand. The journey has fascinated me, and I hope my account of it will fascinate you. If this book is about how a portrait came to be, it is about that magical, magnetic figure, Lord Byron, of whom we can never know enough – or too much. It is about that fine artist, Thomas Sully, the finest portraitist of his era and a major figure in the history of American art. It is about art, British as well as American, about an era, about a city and a culture, and not least about the nature and traditions of portraiture.

CHAPTER ONE

Provenance of a Painting

Who are you? said he. Don't puzzle me said I.
Tristram Shandy[1]

Like the Veronese chronicled in Watson's *Wisdom and Strength* and the Van Gogh in Saltzman's *Portrait of Dr Gachet*, Sully's *Byron* has had its fair share of adventures. Though the painting has been virtually unknown for nearly two centuries, the artist who created it has left behind numerous traces in the historical record. My investigation took me down many unexpected byways, as I sought out information about the portrait's owners, several of whom played a part on the national scene, and tried to understand what had prompted them to acquire – and relinquish – *Byron*.

A work of art's provenance can help us understand it; it can also illumine a nation's social history. By knowing who created an art work, where it was made, who purchased it, who knew about it, our knowledge of an era – its tastes, styles, consumption preferences, enthusiasms, collecting trends – is deepened. The trajectory of *Byron* through time and space allows us to enter, if briefly and tantalizingly, into the lives of its owners, to explore who they were, where they lived, what idiosyncrasies they possessed. Interesting in itself, *Byron*'s history also encapsulates fluctuations of taste in the art market, public attitudes in America toward Federal era paintings, and Sully's evolving reputation as a portraitist and American master. It also tells us much about Byron's appeal in the United States for nearly two centuries.

*

During most of his working life Sully kept an account book of his paintings. As published in an edition of 110 copies by Charles Henry Hart in 1909, the account book lists Sully's portraits in alphabetical order by sitter. The first public mention of *Byron* described it as a "bust," a "copy begun in 1826," and dated it "1828."[2] That is all. In 1921 Edward Biddle and Mantle Fielding reedited the account book in preparing their *Life and Works of Thomas Sully*, whenever possible bringing the entries up to date. Their research yielded the names of *Byron*'s owners to that time. Along with Hart's earlier volume (and scattered references in turn-of-the-century publications), Biddle and Fielding's still standard work provides virtually the only published documentation for Sully's *Byron*.[3] Under August 10, 1828, Sully wrote in his Journal: "Last Monday, 4th, I finished a copy I had begun some time ago of Westall's Byron. – Sent it to the Gallery."[4] The Journal notes the completion of few paintings. That it mentions *Byron* may be happenstance, or it may indicate that the artist valued it more than many of his other works.

The "Gallery" was Earle and Sully's Gallery in the artist's adopted city of Philadelphia. A carver and gilder of picture frames, James Earle framed Sully's work and like other carvers and gilders probably displayed paintings in his shop. He had opened the gallery in 1810, at the southeast corner of Third and Market, and by 1819, the year Sully came on board (he became a full partner the next year), he had moved it to 5th and Chestnut. James McMurtrie describes its location "nearly opposite the State house" as being in "the most central part of the city. It is a lighted by a sky-light. The room is about 20 by 40 feet."[5] The year 1819 was a bad one for business and especially bad for portrait painters; the years that followed proved no better. Yet Sully and Earle's survived and prospered. Earle appears to have handled the Gallery's business end; Sully, with his extensive connections in the art world, supplied the pictures, his own as well as those by others. In the financial review with which he closed each year's entries in his Journal, Sully invariably mentioned the Gallery's financial status. He was himself an astute businessman (a talent increasingly recognized), and he often complained in his Journal about Earle's slack bookkeeping. His arrangement with Earle is documented as continuing until the end of 1846 and probably lasted until about 1860. The Gallery, in existence under varying names as late as May 1896, had an exceptionally long run.[6] It remained a force in the city's art life for nearly a century.

The modern art gallery was then in its infancy. Such venues as Earle and Sully's were among the few where the public could see works by contemporary artists. Without public spaces to show their paintings established artists often maintained their own galleries. In them prospective clients contemplating a commission could examine representative works. Galleries might also be rented to colleagues or to traveling exhibitions. Contemporary artists in letters or recollections often mention Earle and Sully's Gallery or, as it became known after 1840, Sully and Earle's. Most paintings the partners owned jointly. The Gallery displayed Old Masters, some authentic, many later regarded as dubious. John Sartain, the engraver, remembered it "filled with pictures of fairly good quality," including a large, spectacular work by James Ward of a man on horseback in the coils of an anaconda. Along with two undistinguished early portraits by Reynolds as well as framed prints from Boydell's folio edition of Shakespeare, Sartain (sometime after 1832) noted works by the Philadelphians Shaw, Birch, and Doughty.[7] In 1823 the Gallery exhibited Lawrence's famous portrait of Benjamin West. Earle and Sully's also handled the sale of paintings by James Peale. Sully placed his completed paintings in the Gallery until they sold or a purchaser picked them up. Here he put *Byron* on display until its first owner came for it.

Artists often painted portraits of famous people for the purpose of making an engraving. Engravings that sold in large numbers could be remunerative. Since engravings also spread the renown of both artist and subject, it may seem surprising that Sully never commissioned one of *Byron*. The portrait not being from life, he may have felt an engraving inappropriate, or the painting may no longer have been easily accessible, or he may have realized that only a very skillful engraver could have captured the distinctiveness of his rendering. We do not know. Nor was *Byron* publicly exhibited elsewhere during Sully's lifetime. Portraits were mainly intended for domestic settings, not public venues. Except for its brief stint in Earle and Sully's Gallery in 1828, Byron quickly passed into private hands, where it has remained.

*

Artists occasionally portrayed actors and actresses, sometimes literary figures, without a formal commission. They hoped the subject's fame would sell the painting. We do not know whether or not *Byron* was commissioned, but we do know its first owner. He is John R. Murray (1774–1851), a leading member of a wealthy New York landholding and merchant family.

Murray's background was Quaker. His father, John Murray (1738–1806), along with his brother Robert, moved in 1753 from Lancaster, Pennsylvania, to New York City where they formed a mercantile partnership. It prospered, and the Murrays became the chief shipowners in the colonies. Importing on a large scale, Robert not only owned more ships than anybody else but was also one of five persons in New York rich enough to keep a coach. As a Quaker, a "Friend," he called his carriage "my leather conveniency."[8] But success was precarious. The brothers' failure in mid-1772 sent shock waves through the city. The Murrays must have soon recouped their fortunes, for they owned several of the 21 vessels seized by the Revolutionary Committee of 60 from November 1774 to February 1775 for violating the trade embargo with Britain.[9] After the Revolution the Murrays reestablished their reputations. A director of the United States Branch Bank in New York and president of the city's Chamber of Commerce from 1798 to 1806, John Murray also took a leading part in the city's philanthropic activities. At his death his estate was estimated at half a million dollars, a huge sum for the time.[10]

John's son, John R. Murray – the "R." presumably for uncle Robert – received a formal education in New York City that included training in art.[11] In 1799 young Murray, like other wealthy male Americans of the era, set off on a Grand Tour. Monarchic Europe – chiefly Britain, Prussia, Russia, and Austria – then waged almost continual war with republican France. On November 9, Eighteenth Brumaire in the revolutionary calendar, young General Napoleon Bonaparte toppled the Directory and became First Consul. Because of the turmoil Murray visited neither Paris nor London but did take in Berlin, Potsdam, Prague, Vienna, Warsaw, and St Petersburg. Old Master pieces by Correggio, Rubens, Van Dyck, Lorrain, Murillo, Titian perhaps most of all, intoxicated – and educated – him.[12] By late 1800 he was back in his native city. Gilbert Stuart's portrait of Murray, *c.* 1800, depicts an inquisitive young patrician with receding hairline, arms crossed, about to take his place in the privileged world into which he had been born.[13]

New York, having outdistanced its competitors in commercial activity, had become the nation's most flourishing city. Young Murray played a role both in its mercantile prosperity and in its cultural life. In 1801 Robert Livingston, minister to France, along with his brother Edward, mayor of New York, wished to establish in the city an art school and academy. The time seemed propitious. Among the 79 public-spirited citizens who answered the call was Murray. Although the Academy did not receive a charter until 1808, Murray in 1804 was corresponding with John Vanderlyn, in Paris, about obtaining plaster casts of antique statues in the Louvre. Along with Vanderlyn's copies of Old Master paintings they would "form the basis" of the new academy.[14]

In 1808 the Academy opened, with Robert Livingston as president and John Trumbull as vice-president. John R. Murray was one of five directors. In 1816, when the Academy was reorganized, Trumbull became president, Murray vice-president. By then the Academy had acquired Benjamin West's *Lear* and *Ophelia and Laertes*. Murray was heavily involved in its first exhibit, organized "around copies of European paintings and likenesses of illustrious local benefactors and military heroes."[15] He may even have shown several of the paintings he owned. Surviving correspondence shows Murray working closely with other artists, including the Academy president Trumbull. Unlike the autocratic Trumbull, Murray possessed an accommodating disposition. He served as vice-president until 1823; from 1825 to 1828 he was on its board of directors.[16] The Academy, controlled by its mercantile patrons, became a stronghold of old New York families. Its fortunes waned. When Samuel Morse and others in 1826 established the breakaway National Academy of Design, the new organization was controlled by artists, not businessmen. Murray became an honorary member.

Like other culturally inclined New Yorkers of established social position, Murray wished to bring home the benefits of European culture. He early began to collect Old Masters, many of them copies, a few "originals." Some he may have acquired in Europe, others from New York's premier art dealer, the notorious Michael Paff.[17] In time Murray put together one of best-documented art collections of the day, with works reportedly by Correggio, Gaspar Poussin, Nicholas Poussin, Andrea del Sarto, Rembrandt, and Teniers. He especially favored religious scenes or classical landscapes in which arcadian shepherds cavorted amidst fountains and villas.[18] Mrs Trollope, in New York in 1830, denounced "the utter ignorance respecting pictures to be found among persons of the *first standing* in society."[19] But she did not see Murray's collection.

When Sully's *Byron* arrived in New York, most likely in 1828, the year it was completed, it would have entered one of the city's most discriminating art collections. Murray owned few American paintings, only a half-length portrait by Copley and *Birds* by James Wilson.[20] Another source mentions works by Stuart (presumably Murray's own portrait) and Vanderlyn.[21] Such paucity of native work was not unusual. Murray, like most art-lovers at this time, considered the American product insufficiently venerable and avoided buying it. Among early New York collectors, only Philip Hone and Luman Reed patronized American artists.[22]

We can only speculate why Murray bought Sully's *Byron*. Perhaps he had seen an engraving of Westall's *Byron* and wished for himself a portrait of the great and spectacular poet of the age. As a young man he had admired Titian's heroic figures, and the larger-than-life protagonists of Byron's poems may have appealed to him. Nothing more natural for a wealthy merchant with artistic leanings like Murray than to enthuse over a poet who enjoyed vast contemporary renown in America and commission a representation of him from America's first portraitist.

Sully knew New York well. He lived in the city for a year as a youngster and again as an up-and-coming artist in 1806–07. Given his sociable nature, he would have become acquainted with the movers and shakers in New York's closely knit literary, theatrical, and art worlds. In Philadelphia after 1810, Sully returned to New York frequently. Over the decades in extended trips, north to Boston and south as far as Charleston, he met many of the great American collectors of the day: Thomas Handysyd Perkins of Boston, Dr David Hosack and Philip Hone of New York, Robert Gilmor, Jr of Baltimore, Daniel Wadsworth of Hartford, even Thomas Jefferson at Monticello. Often he painted their portraits. Likely enough on one of his trips to or through New York Sully encountered Murray.

Murray presumably acquired *Byron* because he responded positively to Sully or to the poet, or to both. Byron's death in Greece in 1824 burst upon astonished Americans with a tremendous *éclat*. The poet was everywhere in the news. But by decade's end the fashion for Byron may have waned somewhat; many who had enthused over *Childe Harold* found *Don Juan* disquieting. As in Britain, publication in America of its early cantos had provoked angry criticism. Though the attacks gradually ceased, Leigh Hunt's *Lord Byron and Some of His Contemporaries* (1828) presented the poet as an epigone of immorality and besmirched Byron's reputation on both sides of the Atlantic. Did Hunt's acidulous comments diminish Murray's enthusiasm? There are grounds for thinking that owning a portrait of the author of the notorious *Don Juan* made Murray squeamish.

Two decades before, Murray had asked John Vanderlyn to choose a painting in the Louvre and copy it for him. In 1809 Vanderlyn offered him Correggio's nude *Antiope*. William Dunlap, who liked the painting, mentions seeing it in the Murray home. "Murray admired it, but he said 'What can I do with it? It is altogether indecent. I cannot hang it up in my house, and my family reprobate it.'"[23] A voluptuous nude in a upper-class New York parlor? – it gave Murray, of Quaker background, second thoughts. Presumably Mrs Murray was not amused.

Few New Yorkers of this era had ever seen a competently rendered figure, much less a nude woman apparently in postcoital repose. Several years after copying *Antiope*, Vanderlyn painted *Ariadne Asleep on the Island of Naxos*, one of the earliest female nudes by an American artist. Adolph-Ulric Wertmüller's *Danaë and the Shower of Gold* (1787), which the artist brought with him from Sweden to Philadelphia, caused much controversy when exhibited publicly in the US. When Vanderlyn displayed *Ariadne* in 1814, the lush flesh tones and frank sensuality astounded many. Collectors were wary of nudes, and it took Vanderlyn 12 years to sell his painting. In 1891, after *Ariadne* had entered the collection of the Pennsylvania Academy, its "flagrant indelicacy" made several women so uncomfortable they asked to have it removed from public view.

Did Sully's *Byron* arouse in Murray a sniff of impropriety? Not in itself surely, and surely not as a work of art. But *Byron* did, after all, depict the author of the ribald and irreverent *Don Juan* and the apparently heretical *Cain*. Though the poet spoke like no one else to receptive female readers like Jane Welsh Carlyle, Harriet Beecher Stowe, and Fanny Kemble, they too quailed before *Don Juan*. The Murrays may also have quailed. Murray as a Quaker, a member of a sect that avoided ostentation, thought portraits, of oneself especially, a sign of undue pride. Displaying the prurient author amidst Old Master scenes and religious and biblical allegories certainly made for a startling juxtaposition. Whatever his reasons, Murray kept *Byron* no more than a year or two.

*

Byron's next owner was George Munday of Philadelphia. City directories list Munday, like James Earle, as a carver and a gilder. He did business at 64 South 4th Street and had a "dwelling house" at 5 Boyles Court. Like James Earle, he kept paintings on consignment and gave them wall or window space in his shop. He owned at least two other Sullys, portraits of Lafayette and Napoleon. In addition to his work as an artisan framemaker, Munday wandered about Philadelphia as an itinerant street-preacher, known to contemporaries as the "hatless prophet." Eighty years ago, recalled William U. Hensel in 1912, proper Philadelphia had a lively Bohemian colony of artists, writers, and assorted nonconformists. Amidst this lively scene Munday more than held his own.

Munday's doings have left traces in the public record. Several surviving letters date from prison. In one of 1836 to Edward S. Burd, listed in that year's city directory as a counselor at law, Munday implored Burd to help him in his current "difficulties": otherwise, he had "to find some other friend to whom I *must be at the mortification* of telling the Story of my Sufferings and who may be induced to *hear* it, and *extend relief*."[24] Munday does not specify his "Sufferings," nor do we know whether Burd bailed him out. Things got worse. In an 1841 letter from the new model prison, Moyamensing's Tombs, to his "Esteemed and Respected Friend," Henry M. Phillips, an attorney and counselor at law who was also an inspector at the prison, Munday complained that "my unmitigated sufferings and persecution for upwards of 'Four Months' now past" compelled him "as a . . . last resort to intrude myself on your notice." Munday was "committed to this place upon the 'Humbug' charge of 'Disorderly conduct' in the State House and on 'Independence,' Square," for which he was being "held to the enormous Bail of 'one Thousand Dollars' *without any Hearing*."[25] Whether Phillips responded or not is unknown, but Munday eventually gained his release. But his troubles were not nearly at an end.

In 1847 the escapades of the "hatless prophet" amused US troops invading Mexico. The *Flag of Freedom*, the army's newspaper published in Puebla, Mexico, commented on

> the last adventures of the "Baptist Watchman," as he sometimes styles himself, the "converted thief" of Philadelphia. George is a man of some ability and preaches against the clergy with considerable force, if his arguments are a little crazed. It is a pity that his fun should cost him so much suffering, as it was certainly witty, although not very decorous or good natured. [26]

On this occasion Munday had railed against organized religion; on others his targets were political injustice and social customs. Even if he was unbalanced, Munday's intelligence and charm impressed even those who did not share his radical views. Small wonder he looked up to (and owned portraits of) Lafayette, Napoleon, and Byron, rebels all, as models to emulate.

Munday died in 1865. One obituary speaks of his "kindly heart" and his being "loving and trustful and unsuspicious in his earlier intercourse with his fellows." Munday "was but imperfectly understood and was of[t]en misjudged . . . He was consistent, even in his peculiarities, and was singularly free from guile. Of an active, nervous temperament, he pursued with energy and perseverance anything he undertook." "Death of an Eccentric Character," another obituary, referred to him with only slight irony as "one of the notabilities of the city." It provides a clue regarding the cause of Munday's difficulties:

> He fell into habits of dissipation, and after squandering all he possessed, he suddenly reformed and ran into the opposite extreme of becoming an ardent advocate of temperance. He lectured frequently, generally in the open street, and most of his addresses were marked by ready wit, a keen and sharp logic, a detestation of shams, and no mean degree of reasoning power.

In Munday's "detestation of shams" we sense Byron's appeal for him.[27]

This second notice mentions that Munday put out occasionally a newspaper called *The Voice of the Prophet; or, The Pioneer of Truth*, which he hawked about the streets:

> He was particularly severe upon the fashion of wearing artificial flowers in bonnets, and throwing off his own hat he declared he would never resume it until the ladies ceased to wear the floral abominations. The ladies did not cease to wear flowers, and as Mr. Munday was a man of his word . . . he never after wore a hat, and went through storm and sunshine, winter and summer, without any shelter for his head, except such as nature gave him.

Temperance came hard for Munday, as it might for any man who detested shams, who warred with the ways of the world, and who campaigned against artificial flowers in ladies' hats. By explaining the sobriquet of the "hatless prophet," the obit reminds us that every prophet, hatless or not, has at least one bee in his bonnet. Although Munday had moments of backsliding, the man's inner integrity shone forth:

> Our own belief is that despite all Mr. Munday's faults and eccentricities, he was a man of no mean ability, honest in his convictions, and well-meaning, and kind at heart, a quality that was shown by his frequent successful efforts to get up holiday treats for the pauper children at the alms-houses.

Such was George H. Munday, clearly an American original: of *Byron*'s owners, the most independent and arresting, and, in his savage wrestlings with an imperfect world, the most appealing.

Murray and Munday, the New York blueblood and the "hatless prophet," may seem an unlikely pair. Yet both counted among Sully's patrons. Perhaps it was through the artist's intercession that *Byron* made its way from Murray to Munday. But the portrait did not stay in Munday's possession much longer than it did in Murray's.

*

In 1831 Munday, in repayment of a debt, pledged his Sully portraits of Byron, Lafayette, and Napoleon to Jacob Eichholtz.[28] Eichholtz (1776–1842), originally of Lancaster, was one of Munday's familiars in Philadelphia. He now became the proud owner of *Byron*.

A painter of distinction, Eichholtz knew Sully for over thirty years. We know more about him than about Murray and Munday, and he will reappear in our story as the artist who repeatedly portrayed Nicholas Biddle, in youth and in age, but never to the happiness of that distinguished individual. Lancaster, where Eichholtz lived most of his life, is about seventy miles west of Philadelphia. Largely populated by German immigrants, the city lies in the heart of Pennsylvania's Amish country. One of its earliest settlers was Eichholtz's grandfather. In the war for independence Eichholtz's father and two older brothers fought on the side of the colonies. Jacob, born just months *after* the signing of the Declaration of Independence, took fierce pride in never having lived under British rule.[29]

Sully first met Eichholtz when he arrived in Lancaster, then the state capital, early in 1808 to paint newly elected Governor Simon Snyder. Eichholtz was then struggling to learn the rudiments of portrait painting. A tinsmith and coppersmith by trade who also did tavern signs, he invited Sully, already a name to be reckoned with, to use "his painting room." Sully, usually a model of tact, was not impressed by Eichholtz's initial efforts at portraiture. He characterized them to Dunlap as "hideous": a "Tin man," he adds uncharitably, "attempting to paint pictures very miserably."[30] Nonetheless Sully generously passed on to Eichholtz "all the professional information [he] could impart." The next year he obligingly gave Eichholtz his cast-off brushes. "This was a great feast to me," recalled the grateful Eichholtz, "and enabled me to go on until others were to be had."[31]

Eichholtz got better. Like Sully before him, he went, in 1811, to Boston to learn what he could from Gilbert Stuart. There Stuart, as part of his instruction, painted Eichholtz's portrait. Sully, when he saw the improvement in Eichholtz's work, "was much surprised and gratified."[32] In 1817, to gain more sitters, Eichholtz moved from provincial Lancaster to Philadelphia, where he achieved modest renown. In 1820, seeking clients in Baltimore, he engaged in friendly competition with Sully and Rembrandt Peale, all three there to drum up the business Philadelphia no longer provided. It was Eichholtz, chiefly because he charged only $30 a portrait against Sully's $75 or $100, who came off best.[33] Such financial success in the face of keen competition indicates that contemporaries thought well of his talent. Back in Philadelphia the next year, Eichholtz resided in the city until early 1832.

Sometimes labeled a folk artist, one working in the naive tradition, Eichholtz became with Sully's and Stuart's aid a competent if somewhat stilted and mechanical painter. "His work," comments E. P. Richardson, "always retained the flavor of slightly archaic simplicity and severe honesty that we associate with the untrained professional."[34] Sully admired Eichholtz as "a man of frank, simple, unpretending manners, whose conversation marked his good sense, and whose conduct evinced that propriety which has led to his success and ultimate independence."[35] Compelled like most artists of this era to paint portraits, Eichholtz never achieved – perhaps never sought – Sully's more polished technique. Stylistically and temperamentally his mode of portraiture is closer to Charles Willson Peale's than to Sully's. Whereas Eichholtz's dour expressions and stiff poses recall Peale's, his livelier palette reflects Sully's influence. Like Sully, he yearned to do historical and allegorical paintings. Seven years older than Sully, Eichholtz yet regarded him as his master. He was nowhere near being in Sully's league as a portraitist and knew it. Though he adopted Sully's poses, Eichholtz lacked the younger artist's flair, energy, and suavity. His admiration for Sully lasted throughout his life.[36]

Eichholtz realized that *Byron* represented Sully at his best. In 1831 he made a copy, possibly several, and sold one to George W. McAllister of South Carolina for $20.[37] From Sully, who had helped him at a critical early stage, he learned much. Describing himself about 1832 as having "a mind urging [him] on for further improvement," he felt he had much still to learn. Although he never attained Sully's fluency, he had *Byron* at hand for inspiration and guidance. That his Sully portrait was of Byron must have thrilled the staunchly democratic Eichholtz. Byron, though an English nobleman, believed in republics, spoke enthusiastically of America, and died fighting for Greece's independence. His poetry stirred the national soul. Here was a man whom Eichholtz could admire.[38]

In late 1831 Eichholtz acquired title to a house on South Lime St in Lancaster and early the next year moved back to his native city. At a testimonial dinner after his return, it was said of him that "the skill of the artist is only equalled by the moral excellence of the man."[39] Sully's *Byron* came with him, a treasured memento of the painter who had largely formed his art. When Eichholtz died in 1842, he left *Byron* in his studio along with the equally valued portrait Stuart had done of him. While all of America talked of Byron, Sully's portrait slumbered there for eighty years, admired perhaps by Eichholtz's sons and grandchildren but unknown to a wider public.

*

Our next clear sighting of Sully's *Byron* occurs in 1919. On January 7 of that year the American Art Association in New York auctioned off the portrait as one of 40 from the Thomas Benedict Clarke collection. Except for *Byron*, Clarke's paintings were almost entirely of American subjects. "A collection of canvases of this character has not before been offered to the public," proclaims Dana H. Carroll, somewhat grandiloquently, in the catalogue preface. Carroll hardly exaggerates. The collection, mostly of Federal portraits, featured five of Washington, one by Stuart, two by Rembrandt Peale, and others by Charles Willson Peale and Charles Peale Polk; portraits of Revolutionary worthies; of Jackson and Grant, Webster and Clay, and Edwin M. Stanton. Among non-political portraits, Poe, John Howard Payne (author of *The Star Spangled Banner*), Whistler's military father, Major George Washington Whistler, and Irving's Ichabod Crane stand out. Along with several works of dubious authenticity, the collection included paintings by Copley, Vanderlyn, Jarvis, Inman, Elliott, Morse, Harding, Allston, and Trumbull. The catalogue reproduces *Byron* in a full-page sepia photograph.

Clarke's 1919 sale realized $78,000 and set several price records for early American portraits. The Stuart *Washington* for which Clarke had paid $16,000 in 1912 went to Duveen Brothers for $21,000.[40] Compared to the sums paid by the likes of Frick, Morgan, and Huntington for portraits by Reynolds, Raeburn, Romney, and Gainsborough, the amount may seem paltry, for a few years later Huntington paid $771,000 for *The Blue Boy* alone. But American portraits had begun to rise in collectors' esteem. In a few years – thanks in part to the sale's success – they would bring far higher prices.

Clarke was born in 1848 to middle-class parents in New York's Washington Square. In Chinatown one day the 14-year-old youngster saw in a shop window a black jar decorated with white hawthorn blossoms and a flock of birds. Some youngsters fixate on their new bicycle; Clarke yearned for this Chinese jar. "He felt he had never seen anything in his life before he saw that jar." Hoarding his 50-cents-a-week allowance, Clarke gradually managed to buy it. Other pieces followed. His collection of porcelains grew. With it came the need to form others. Fanatic collectors are monomaniacs. Aline Bernstein remembered Clarke as one who "lived under the spell of whatever" then interested him. "He told me he was obsessed," she remembered. "He would get up in the night to touch his treasures, to pass his hands over them in the dark."[41] So fabulous and famous did Clarke's porcelain collection become that he eventually advised J. P. Morgan and catalogued his collection.

Art-collectors in America in the decades after the Civil War often viewed American art as socially inferior to European. The market for it at times stagnated. The passion for European masters, particularly among the newly affluent, seemed inexhaustible, as collectors bid record prices for Old Master works and contemporary Barbizon school landscapes. American *nouveaux riches*, intellectually uncertain of their taste, felt more secure buying artists who belonged to long-established cultural traditions. The rage of the Anglophilic élite became "British art, British books, even British aristocratic sons-in-law."[42]

Clarke was the exception. In 1869, when 21, he bought his first painting by George Inness. Stimulated by Inness's artistry, he began three years later to collect seriously the less fashionable American art.[43] In this enthusiasm Clarke had few predecessors. The major pioneer collector, Luman Reed, had died in 1836. Support of native art had grown quietly until the Civil War. Initially, the War, which had destroyed so much, stimulated interest in art that recorded what had been lost. A decade afterwards, the Centennial Exhibition of 1876 reminded Americans that their artistic traditions had a respectable history. But American contributions to the Paris World's Fair of 1867 had failed to impress European taste, and after the Centennial Exhibition interest in American art languished. The moneyed collectors of the Gilded Age – H. O. Havemeyer, Mrs A. T. Stewart, Catharine Lorillard Wolfe, August Belmont, William T. Walters – filled their chateauesque and neo-Gothic palaces with European masters. Similarly, the new museums of these decades collected plaster casts of Classical and European sculptures; the paintings chosen were no less European.

Clarke became the era's major collector of American art. He bought avidly and with discretion as no other man of his time did. In *The Art Treasures of America* (1880) Edward Strahan noted Clarke's "most refined collection, intending especially to demonstrate the essential attainment of American art in its best representation."[44] Other than Clarke's, no major art collection had in it more American than European paintings. Not bad – and not bad company – for a man only 32. When in late 1884 Clarke exhibited 140 of his paintings at the American Art Galleries, it marked the first showing of privately owned contemporary works by American artists. Buying against the taste for European masters, Clarke among his American contemporaries came across as a man with an eye for quality. He corresponded with artists, helped sell their pictures, arranged exhibitions for them. Whenever possible, he purchased directly from the artists themselves and encouraged his wealthy friends to do likewise.

Clarke invariably sought out the work of living men, some hardly known. He liked the tonalists – Wyant, Martin, Tryon – though in his personal collection Inness, Winslow Homer, and Albert Pinkham Ryder held pride of place. Inness had begun to attract attention when Clarke collected him, Homer less so, Ryder not at all. Clarke established all three in the public mind as great and desirable talents and significantly influenced their lives.[45]

Inness regarded meeting Clarke in 1878 as a turning point in his life. He took him as his agent, and Clarke became a lifelong patron – he eventually acquired 39 canvases by Inness – and a devoted friend.[46] Clarke also became, with Lawson Valentine, one of Homer's two chief patrons. Over the years he bought 31 works by Homer, including several now recognized as among his greatest, and at one time wished to establish in his house a "Homer Gallery."[47] In 1890 Clarke purchased his *The Two Guides*, probably for little more than $500. Homer was pleased when Clarke told him that John Singer Sargent had visited his collection especially to see works by him. After the artist's brother Charles, Clarke had the strongest influence on Homer's career. Ryder, the third of Clarke's contemporary painters, assumed importance for him when in 1885 he acquired two major works, *The Temple of the Mind* and *Christ Appearing to Mary*. Surviving correspondence indicates a relationship of considerable and increasing cordiality.[48]

As a young girl Aline Bernstein, later famous for her theatrical designs and for being the mistress of Thomas Wolfe, lived near Clarke's lace-curtained house on West 44th St. In *An Actor's Daughter* (1941) she left an unforgettable portrait of Clarke in the 1880s and 1890s.[49] Recent scholars have described this omnivorous and indefatigable collector as a ruthless high-stakes, deal-driven businessman, but in her pages he emerges as passionate in his interests but generous. Clarke, who appears, transparently, as "Mr. Watson," was "a good friend" to young Aline, who pictures his life "caught in two passions, first and foremost a love of art, second the pursuit of pleasure" imaged as "a handsome yacht riding a blue and wavy sea." Part of that pleasure was Clarke's fascination with Nana, Aline's beautiful but troubled aunt who lived with the family. His tastes ran "not only for the ladies, but for food and wine, flowers and rides in the country, and wonderful parties at Claremont or Delmonico's."[50] But Clarke kindly paid for Aline to attend the New York School of Applied Design.

A manufacturer of linen collars and cuffs, Clarke had the resources to finance his collections, not only of Homer, Inness, and Ryder but of oriental art and Greek vases and sculptures. By way of justifying the enormity of his collecting, Clarke in 1891 set himself up as a full-time connoisseur, a kind of gentleman art dealer with his own vast gallery. "His energy and avidity," it was said, constituted "one of the wonders of the world's metropolis."[51] Until his death in 1931 he was involved with virtually every major event in New York's art world.

In 1899, for reasons not entirely clear, Clarke sold off his collection of American paintings, then numbering 372. This celebrated auction, at Chickering Hall in New York, marked an epoch in the appreciation of American art. It achieved the then unheard-of sum of $234,495 and established record prices for contemporary artists. Inness's *Gray Lowering Day*, which Clarke had bought for less than $3000, was knocked down for $10,150. His *Delaware Valley* went to the Metropolitan for $8,100. Homer's *Eight Bells* brought $4,500; *The Life Line*, almost as much. Ryder's *Temple of the Mind* fetched $2,250, *Christ Appearing to Mary*, $1,000.[52]

Compared to Inness and Homer, the stars of the sale, the prices for Ryder were more modest, but they established that in financial terms his paintings could compete.[53]

The Clarke sale forever altered the American art world. Collecting American art now became respectable. A few years before, of recent artists only the Academicians Gérôme and Meissonier, or the Barbizon painters Corot and Daubigny, Millet and Rousseau, would have brought such prices. No better proof that American art had arrived was the appearance on the scene of forgers and swindlers. A happier result was that museums began to consider American art worth acquiring.

Fanatical collectors often lose interest in completed collections. Even before Clarke sold his American moderns in 1899, he had developed another passion: early American portraits. The choice of field is unexplained. Aside from the artists he had championed, he had shown little enthusiasm for most others, whether Hudson River School landscapists, whose popularity had faded, or American Impressionists, whose star was now rising. Clarke did not deign to notice the urban realists (later dubbed the "Ashcan School") led by Robert Henri. Instead, he went back a century or more. Like many a savvy collector, he bought against the market, and early American portraits were still cheap. Our story – the history of *Byron*'s provenance – now becomes complicated and more speculative.

*

Among the collectors whom Clarke advised was Alexander Smith Cochran (1874–1929), a member of a wealthy and philanthropic family of Yonkers, New York, on the Hudson upriver from Manhattan. Manufacturer, sportsman, and philanthropist, Cochran inherited his money from his parents and uncle, whose Alexander Smith and Sons Carpet Company established the family fortune. Journalists smilingly designated Cochran "the world's most eligible bachelor." He donated to the Metropolitan his collection of illuminated manuscripts of Persian poetry, and in 1911 he established the Elizabethan Club at Yale, providing it with a house, a generous endowment, and a library consisting of his own magnificent collection of rare editions of Elizabethan and Jacobean literature.[54] And he may – or may not – have bought *Byron*.

In 1907 Cochran's mother, Mrs Eve Smith Cochran, purchased Philipse Manor Hall in Yonkers for $50,000. Built by the Philipse family in 1682, the Hall attained its present form in about 1745.[55] In 1779 the royalist Philipse family abandoned both the Hall and its vast land holdings and fled to British-occupied New York City, subsequently to England. Philipse Manor Hall then went through half a dozen owners and in the process lost its grounds. In 1868 it came into the hands of Yonkers, which used it as a village hall until 1872, afterwards as City Hall. Mrs Cochran, the new owner, deeded Manor Hall in 1908 to the American Scenic and Historic Preservation Society, but stipulated that the house, which had fallen into disrepair, be restored and appropriately furnished. Her son Alexander set up the Manor Hall Association to raise funds for the renovation and himself donated $25,000. In July 1911 the city of Yonkers vacated the Hall for a new building, and in 1912 Manor Hall reopened to the public.[56]

Thomas B. Clarke, one of the supporters of the Manor Hall Association, now reenters the scene. When in 1907 Cochran asked him how he might best restore Manor Hall as a center of patriotic interest, Clarke suggested he fill it with portraits of American presidents, military leaders, statesmen, educators, and other worthies of Revolutionary and Federal America.[57] Cochran energetically sought out such pictures along with furniture of the era. Within a few years he had with Clarke's help put together a splendid collection. From descendants, auction sales, the artists themselves, or from Clarke's scouring the land, Cochran had the paintings he needed when the Hall reopened in 1912.[58]

Cochran in his choices also benefited from the aid of Charles Henry Hart (1847–1918). Almost an exact contemporary of Clarke's, Hart is the third of our wealthy collectors whose path crossed Sully's *Byron*. He too may have briefly owned the portrait. A Philadelphia lawyer, Hart turned to art during the 1880s. The Pennsylvania Academy's portrait exhibitions during that decade owed much to his energy.[59] Early American portraits had become his passion, and his expertise in a then virtually untouched field gained him national recognition.[60] Gilbert Stuart was his specialty, and numerous articles and monographs testify to acute scholarship. Able, outspoken, possessed of a discerning eye, he waged constant war against spurious attributions. He turned up many little-known portraits, some major, others now considered of doubtful authenticity.[61] Like Clarke, Hart bought and sold paintings, and like Clarke's, his reputation for probity has suffered in recent decades.[62]

It is Hart who in 1909 first published Sully's register of paintings. Aware, perhaps through William U. Hensel's articles, of the location of Sully's *Byron* in the Eichholtz family home in Lancaster, Hart may have put Clarke in contact with Eichholtz's descendants. It is he, presumably, who arranged *Byron*'s sale in 1912 (in which year Hensel recorded seeing it in Eichholtz's old studio) or soon afterwards.[63] Possibly Hart bought it himself, then sold it to Clarke directly – or possibly he sold it to Cochran. Cochran, for reasons discussed below, may have sold it to Clarke (or back to Clarke). We do not know. Hart had sold Cochran his first paintings in 1907. Of the 68 works Cochran acquired for Philipse Manor Hall, more – at least 15 – came from Hart than from any other source. For many of them Hart provided no provenance.[64]

Having put together the only complete set of American presidential portraits outside of the National Capitol, Cochran by 1912 may have considered his collection sufficiently complete to turn down Clarke's latest purchases, *Byron* among them.[65] Heather Vaughan, curator at Philipse Manor Hall, found no documentation of *Byron*'s presence in the Collection. Many of these other works, however, were suitable for the Philipse Manor Hall collection of presidential portraits (still in existence and intermittently on display). Cochran may well have admired the painting, but a portrait of a young English nobleman would hardly have bedded down comfortably amidst venerable American patriarchs. Or would it? Many Americans, as had their ancestors in the 1820s, still considered the man who fought and died for liberty in Greece, whose poetry took America by storm in his lifetime and long after, an *American* hero.

*

Unable to persuade Cochran to accept or keep *Byron*, Clarke presumably retained it himself; then in 1919, along with 39 other portraits, he sold it at auction. Cochran may never have owned the painting. When Dana H. Carroll writes in the catalogue introduction that the task of choosing art for Manor Hall "made possible the discovery and acquisition of the forty portraits of the present collection," he discreetly implies this. If the 40 contain a number not judged suitable for Manor Hall, they nonetheless comprised a distinguished lot. What Clarke sold at auction compares favorably in quality to what Cochran bought for Manor Hall.

Ultimately, the location of Sully's *Byron* after it left Eichholtz's studio in or after 1912 until its sale in 1919 remains uncertain. Clarke may have acquired the painting directly from the Eichholtz family or he may have acquired it through Hart. It is probably Clarke who put on the frame a plaque (which remains) that, besides indicating Byron's birth and death dates along with Sully's, salutes "George Gordon Noel Byron" as "England[']s Poet." A member of several New York clubs full of wealthy anglophiles, Clarke might well have unearthed a potential buyer happy to have a lord – a lord also "Englands poet" – above his mantel.

But, just possibly, Clarke bought *Byron* for himself. This complex, brilliant, probably unscrupulous man may have acquired the portrait because he thought Sully a major American artist or the portrait a good investment or because he liked Byron's poetry. There may be still another reason. Most photographs of Clarke derive from later years and show him almost totally bald. But in his young maturity, Aline Bernstein remembered, he was "pure blond, so rare in a man, gold hair and white skin; his eyes were sapphire blue and always sparkling and there was sweetness and humour in the curve of his mouth, particularly in the deep corners." But this inordinately handsome man had, like Byron, a physical handicap: he limped. Though he handled his lameness wonderfully, Clarke found walking painful.[66] Byron, even handsomer, had, like Clarke, a deformed foot. As he hobbled along, Byron never ceased to excoriate the curse of lameness placed on him at birth. Perhaps Clarke, similarly handicapped, purchased *Byron* out of awareness of the elective affinities he shared with the poet.

The emotional upheaval caused by the First World War stirred interest in American ancestors. Federal portraits, mostly forgotten for a century, came back into vogue. Perhaps they had to become lost, speculates Wesley Towner, and be "found again before they could become chic and expensive as collectors' items."[67] In the decade after Clarke had purchased *Byron* big spenders like Astor, Frick, and Mellon each bought a copy of Stuart's

"Vaughan" *Washington*. After selling his collection in 1919, Clarke continued to acquire early American portraits and in 1921–22 showed them at New York's Union League Club.[68] Two years later, in November 1924, the Metropolitan Museum opened its American Wing, the first permanent exhibition of colonial and early Federal decorative arts in an American art museum. Other institutions followed suit.

The Philadelphia Museum of Art, when it inaugurated its splendid new building on March 26, 1928, had on display Clarke's new gathering of 164 portraits. Termed "the most important collection of American historical portraits ever made," they hung there for three years, the only native paintings in evidence. Clarke wrote the catalogue himself.[69] In 1929 or 1930 he sold the collection not to the Museum but to the dealer Knoedler for a price said to be around one million dollars.[70] On January 29, 1936, the Andrew W. Mellon Educational and Charitable Trust bought it *en bloc* from Knoedler. Mellon wished to incorporate a number of the portraits – among them, Sully's own copy of his *Major Thomas Biddle* – in the new National Gallery in Washington, a project he had had in mind since the 1920s but whose new building did not open until 1941. Other portraits, including Sully's *John Quincy Adams*, the Gallery held as a nucleus for a future National Portrait Gallery.

*

By then *Byron* had long since found a new owner. He was Arthur W. Meeker of Chicago, who either bought the painting at the 1919 Clarke sale or, more likely, acquired it shortly afterwards from Frank Bayley, a Boston art dealer.[71]

Of *Byron*'s owners, Meeker (1866–1946) rivals Clarke in flamboyance. Meeker's ancestors had emigrated to America three hundred years before. His mother, *née* Maria L. Griggs, arrived in Chicago in September 1845, only ten years after the Pottawatomies had massacred settlers fleeing Fort Dearborn on the Chicago River. The voyage from New England to Chicago by coach, canal boat, and lake steamer took nearly three weeks. Her Chicago was almost unimaginably different from that encountered today. Then the "green, sloping banks" of residences on the Chicago River "ran down to the sedge-grown water's edge"; the community's "greatest excitement" was the arrival of the weekly Buffalo packet.[72] In 1855 Maria married Arthur Burr Meeker. When their son Arthur was born 11 years later, the city was well on its way to becoming the Midwestern metropolis.

Young Meeker was five when the disastrous fire of 1871 changed Chicago forever. The early families, like the devastated city, vigorously remade themselves. In 1885, aged 19, Arthur left the Sheffield Scientific School at Yale to work for Philip Danforth Armour ("P. D." to his intimates), president of the already gigantic meatpacking company. Meeker over the next six decades had a major role in Armour's growth. In addition, he served as chairman of the board of Arcady Farms Manufacturing Company and of the National Aluminate Corporation. In 1892 he married the former Grace Murray. The Meekers had four children. Arthur, the only son, long hoped for, arrived last, in 1902. The chapter "Mr. and Mrs. Chicago" in his *Chicago, With Love. A Polite and Personal History* (1955) records the intensely active role his father and mother played in the city's social life for over half a century.

The Meekers frequented a privileged milieu that centered on Prairie Avenue, that once-fabled street on Chicago's South Side. They lived at number 1815. Their next-door neighbors, the Samuel Insulls, owned the city's utilities. Nearby were such business titans as George Pullman and Marshall Field – names that still resonate in Chicago lore – as well as Armour, neighbor and family friend as well as Meeker's employer. Arthur Jr recalled P. D. as "perhaps the strongest of Prairie Avenue's tough old roosters." As the South Side became less fashionable, the Meekers moved in the autumn of 1914, just after the war broke out, to the still largely undeveloped North Side. The previous year Meeker had built at 3030 Lake Shore Drive a Georgian mansion "the size of a small hotel."[73] The house stood at Barney Avenue and the Outer Drive. So isolated was it that the neighborhood, when it caught up with them, became known locally as "Meekerville."

"Not for nothing have I called him Mr. Chicago," wrote Arthur, Jr; "he was typical of the city that gave him birth, first of all in his marvelous courage." This courage was moral no less than physical. "A big and strongly masculine man," Meeker had a "passion for practicality and quick impatience with stupidity or shyness." Energetic as well as immensely social, he had definite likes and dislikes – Biedermeier furniture was a dislike. Neither parent was "especially literary"; in fact, father professed "a genuine horror of poetry as well, and those who made it."[74] But he was not as culturally inert as his clever son, scornful of the tastes of an earlier generation, implied. Arthur Sr had a more serious engagement with art than Arthur Jr gave him credit for.

The National Art Committee, formed in 1919, consisted of 11 of the country's most prominent art collectors and patrons. Meeker was one. In an attempt to counter postwar isolationist tendencies, the Committee commissioned portraits honoring American and allied leaders of the First World War – among them Pershing, Wilson, Foch, Clemenceau. It launched a national campaign in support of the project, with art patrons in different cities subscribing for particular portraits, which were then presented as a gift from that city to the Smithsonian Institution, to be included in a future National Portrait Gallery. According to William H. Gerdts, these paintings represented "the last instance in American history when portraits were considered the principal means of permanently recording the identities of great heroes."[75]

It was while living at 3030 Lake Shore Drive that Arthur Meeker bought Sully's *Byron*. It formed part of a considerable art collection. After beginning with French Impressionists, Meeker moved on to early American portraits and miniatures. The collection, at one time "rather famous," Arthur Jr flippantly concedes, "included rows of genteelly stodgy Copleys and Trumbulls and Peales, a renowned right-side-of-the-face of George Washington by Stuart, and other prizes of note."[76] Again, as with several of *Byron*'s previous owners, we may speculate why Meeker might have acquired the painting. An extrovert, outgoing and genial by nature but (according to his son) not a reader or thinker, Meeker presumably responded to Byron less for his writings than for the image of manliness he conveyed. "What he liked he liked with all his strength," wrote Arthur Jr. Presumably Meeker liked Byron. The poet's unquestioned courage, his determination to fight for the causes he believed in, his commitment to republican ideas, his liking for America and Americans – in all these qualities the vigorously opinionated Meeker would have delighted.

An anecdote recounted by Arthur Jr of another painting offers a clue how Meeker came to own *Byron*. He tells of

> an English portrait of a handsome man posed in a rich golden light against a dark background, which to my mind was the gem of the lot; it escaped the dead-and-stuffed prissiness of the Americana. Artists came to rave over it; I remember Cecil Clark Davis crying ecstatically: "What genius! What luminosity! Ah, there's no-one like Raeburn!"

Alas, "the gem of the lot" turned out after a cleaning not to be by the Scottish master. "It rubbed off, disclosing to our scandalized eyes the innocuous likeness of some portly Victorian dame." Mrs Meeker was pained, Meeker Sr vastly "upset," and Arthur? – well, Arthur was amused. Mr Bayley of Boston, their advisor in art matters who had sold them the *faux* Raeburn, found himself chastised.[77]

Arthur Jr does not say, but it seems likely that Mr Bayley made amends for the portly but evanescent Victorian dame by offering the Meekers a comparable replacement. The "rich golden light" of Sully's *Byron* recalls Raeburn, and *Byron*, more than many other portraits of its era, looks like the work of an Old Master. Its authenticity had been certified by inclusion in Biddle and Fielding's 1921 *Life and Works of Thomas Sully*, which lists Arthur Meeker Sr as the portrait's new owner. If Meeker Sr had succumbed to the *faux* Raeburn with its shining male figure against a tenebrous background, the *vrai* (and presumably even more dazzling) *Byron* of Sully may have pleased him more. A famous American artist's depiction of a famous English poet could hardly not have appealed to the manly entrepreneur. Why Arthur Jr, in retailing this episode of the *faux* Raeburn, stops short, for reasons unknown, of mentioning what I take to be Sully's *Byron* is puzzling. Nor does he, it appears, speak elsewhere of the painting.

During the 1920s both Sully and Byron achieved new heights of posthumous renown. In 1922 the Pennsylvania Academy of the Fine Arts put on display 235 of Sully's paintings, the most extensive show he has ever received. Widely noticed in the press, the show garnered the artist much acclaim.[78] Likewise, a flurry of books, newspaper articles, and exhibitions upon the centenary of Byron's death in 1924 enthusiastically reassessed the poet and the man.

In the mid-1920s Alexander Smith Cochran reenters our story. If he did not purchase Sully's *Byron* for Philipse Manor Hall, he knew well Arthur Meeker, the man who did. In 1924 Cochran, "the world's most eligible bachelor," had finally succumbed to a Madame Ganna Walska, an opera singer, whom a dazzled Arthur Jr described as "so radiantly lovely that everybody gasped when they saw her." But she sported a long train of ex-husbands prior to Cochran, and their marriage was not a success. Officially separated from him, Madame Walska showed up in Chicago, where she readied herself for a role in Leoncavallo's today-forgotten *Zazà*. The months she spent in the city evoked emotional mayhem among the millionaire males on the Chicago Lyric Opera board. It took longer than it should have to discover that Madame Walska could hardly sing. The Lyric's board finally had to cancel – to great *éclat* – her Chicago engagement.[79]

During the 11 years the Meekers lived in "Meekerville" the family fortunes prospered. Flush with Armour's wartime profits, Meeker now owned the eleventh largest private yacht afloat, the *SS Arcady*.[80] In 1925 he took an apartment closer to downtown, at 1100 Lake Shore Drive, an eight-story building on the aptly named Gold Coast immediately south of Lincoln Park, at the intersection with Cedar.[81] Though limited to 12 rooms and five baths, Meeker could console himself that the apparently even wealthier Samuel Insulls deigned to occupy one of the building's seven other flats. But in 1932, at the height of the Depression, Insulls's immense utilities empire collapsed and he precipitously departed 1100 Lake Shore Drive. The Depression also affected Meeker, who, "at the stroke of a pen . . . lost three million dollars."[82] Still, he came out better than did the firm he worked for, now run by Odgen Armour, P. D.'s successor and Meeker's closest business associate. Armour and Company (so *Ripley's Believe It or Not*) lost a million dollars a day for 130 straight days.

Art has always been intimately tied to power. Collectors from the Medicis to Napoleon to American industrial barons have recognized that having art in their houses confers prestige and renown upon their other accomplishments. Wealthy, conservative collectors of the postwar era often favored portraits, preferably English or American, preferably of the great by the great. Men of Arthur Meeker's wealth and social class, who could afford to collect on an impressive scale, avidly sought out portraits of well-born, distinguished, stylishly attired individuals. Purchase of paintings like Sully's *Byron* was expected of them.

Anglo-Saxon ideals, at least among the native-born, underwent a revival in the America of the 1920s and 1930s. The "gentry," resentful of the teeming tides of immigration from Southern and Eastern Europe, uncurtailed until 1924, reasserted what they took to be Old English or Old American values. As the newly minted megarich sought to create an aristocracy in the English mold, Neoclassical and Tudor Revival palaces became fashionable, and to fill them with Old Masters and Georgian portraits their occupants gladly paid the increasingly high prices asked by Duveen and other dealers. Displaying such works enhanced one's social cachet. The phenomenon was not exactly new. Tuckerman, speaking of

Copley in 1867, observed, "it has been said that the possession of one of these ancestral portraits is an American's best title of nobility."[83] What was new was the scale of the acquisition. The interwar mania for portraits – in which *Byron* plays a small but representative role – constitutes a distinct phase in the nation's collecting history.

Duveen died in 1939, just before the onset of the Second World War. In the postwar decades, Old Master portraits, English and American, lost their aura. Dark palettes did not go well in bright new modernist interiors. Prices dropped and have not yet recovered fully. The art market also evolved. Old Masters became harder to find, thus more expensive. Along with the Impressionists and Post-Impressionists – Monet, Van Gogh, and Picasso – modern and contemporary artists now command greater interest and higher prices. Multiculturalism has also pushed the market in new directions.

Byron remained in Arthur Meeker's possession about a quarter of a century, first in his North Side mansion, subsequently in his luxurious Gold Coast flat. Several generations of Chicago's social élite must have seen the painting. Whatever their impressions, they have not devolved to posterity. Neither they, nor Meeker himself, left behind surviving comments. Nor, it must be said, had any of the portrait's previous owners – Murray, Munday, Eichholtz, or Clarke – set down their thoughts. Wherever *Byron* has found itself billeted, it has apparently never elicited a recorded word of praise or dispraise. That silence is part of the mystery surrounding the portrait.

*

Upon the senior Meeker's death in 1946, two months short of 80, the portrait passed to Arthur Jr.[84] He had spent his first years on Chicago's fabled Prairie Avenue, and on that elm-shaded street in the 1880s, several decades before he was born, he set his best-remembered novel *Prairie Avenue* (1949). After study at Princeton and Harvard, Arthur joined the staff of the *Chicago Herald and Examiner* and later became a freelance writer, contributing to newspapers and magazines in the intervals between books, articles, stories, and reviews. Arthur enjoyed the good life that family wealth made possible. Without losing touch with Chicago, he spent many of the interwar years in foreign travel, with headquarters in a Swiss chalet on the Bürgenstock, above Lucerne. A francophile fluent in French, he wrote historical novels about seventeenth-century France that brought him a measure of fame. For *The Ivory Mischief* (1941), set in the time of Louis XIV, Arthur happily soaked himself in Parisian lore.

To Fanny Butcher, one of the grandes dames of Chicago letters, Arthur was "like a young brother." Often accompanying Fanny and her husband to Europe, "young Arthur Meeker" (as she invariably referred to him) flits in and out of her entertaining memoir of the era, *Many Lives – One Love* (1972). The older married woman and the precocious *littérateur*, both enthralled by language, established a friendship that lasted their lives. Well off, widely travelled, a pleasant and witty presence, Arthur never troubled himself with a wife or excessive responsibility, yet did serve as president of the Society of Midland Authors and co-founded the Chicago P.E.N. chapter.

With André Maurois, her "dear friend of most of my adult life," Butcher often exchanged visits. In the late 1920s Maurois was working on his brilliant biography of Byron, a bestseller in France, England, and America. Butcher recalls a dinner with Maurois in Chicago attended by "young Arthur Meeker."[85] Most likely Arthur responded to the suave Maurois and read his Byron biography; most likely, too, Maurois saw in the Meeker home Sully's *Byron*. But if he did he left no record of his impressions.

After his parents died Arthur took a small flat on nearby Bellevue Place. Though increasingly ill at ease in his native city, he wished to keep a Chicago *pied-à-terre*. But the next year he moved back to Switzerland and in 1951 gave up his Bellevue Place flat for one in New York, at 4 Gramercy Park, a fashionable address, where he lived "surrounded by souvenirs of my youth." *Byron*, inherited from his parents but never mentioned, presumably hung upon a wall.[86] By 1955, when Arthur published *Chicago, With Love*, he was dividing his time between New York and Switzerland. He could not bear to be in Chicago, the city whose earlier social scene he had lovingly chronicled. His sisters had moved away, and he no doubt missed the patient and loving parents to whom he had always remained close and the home they had provided for him. Arthur Meeker Jr died in 1971 deeply disillusioned with his home town.

Byron's trajectory during the later twentieth century is the least-documented period in its existence. The portrait drops out of sight the year of Arthur Jr's death, not to reemerge until a Christie's sale of American Masters in New York (May 29, 1987).[87] My inquiries to the firm seeking information about seller and buyer turned up no information, though the painting seems to have spent some time after 1987 in New Orleans. Early in 1999 the art dealer Michael Owen acquired *Byron*, and at the Owen Gallery on April 4 of that year, to my enormous and continuing surprise, I came upon it. Shortly afterwards, the painting made its way, once again, into a private collection (the owner prefers to remain anonymous), one that happily for me is in Santa Fe, where I now live. To the painting itself, and its position in Byron portraiture, we now turn.

CHAPTER TWO

Portraits of Byron

This fullness of life . . . the man instilled into the things that came into contact with him. . . . Byron is an atmosphere, a climate of feeling, a trend of the spirit. . . . When we think of Byron, the first thing that comes before our eyes is a physical presence, a profile.
Mario Praz[1]

The chameleon-like character of Byron makes it difficult to portray him.
Lady Blessington[2]

What, if anything, does a portrait actually reveal about a person?
Michael Kimmelman[3]

If only Lawrence had painted Byron, sighs the connoisseur of portraiture, all too aware that Britain's greatest portrait painter never had a go at the age's most celebrated poet. Representations of Byron – pictures, sketches, busts, medallions – proliferated during his lifetime and long after. They continue to this day. With his auburn curls, luminous, bewitching eyes, and full, voluptuous lips, Byron, in Trelawny's dramatic juxtaposition, had "the form and features of an Apollo, with the feet and legs of a sylvan satyr."[4] From 1812, when the author of *Childe Harold's Pilgrimage* woke up to find himself famous, to 1816, when he exiled himself from his native land, Thomas Lawrence stood at the height of his powers.

Byron's was a face to faint for, and faint the ladies did. "*That pale face is my fate*," sighed the discarded Caroline Lamb, *toute entière à sa proie attachée*.[5] "It was one of those faces," she wrote in her novel *Glenarvon* (1816), "which, having once beheld, we never afterwards forget. It seemed as if the soul of passion had been stamped and printed upon every feature."[6] Claire Clairmont, rejected even more brutally than Lady Caroline, mooned over the "wild originality" of Byron's countenance.[7]

Not all or most surviving descriptions of Byron are by women. In numbers and in passionate enthusiasm the men have it. The Byron they describe often appears otherworldly. The first and only time Coleridge saw Byron occurred during a magical half-hour on March 10, 1816: "he was the sweetest Countenance I ever beheld – his eyes are really Portals of the Sun." A few days later the sun still shone. "If you had seen Lord Byron," Coleridge wrote,

> you could scarcely disbelieve him – so beautiful a countenance I scarcely ever saw – his teeth so many stationary smiles – his eyes the open portals of the sun – things of light, and for light – and his forehead so ample,

> and yet so flexible, passing from marble smoothness into a hundred wreathes and lines and dimples correspondent to the feelings and sentiments he is uttering.[8]

"A brother poet," Walter Scott recalled in 1816, compared Byron's features "to the sculpture of a beautiful alabaster vase, only seen to perfection when lighted up from within." Most likely the "brother poet" was Coleridge.[9] The available engravings, thought Scott, "give one no impression of him – the lustre is there, . . . but is not lighted up. Byron's countenance *is a thing to dream of*."[10] For Scott, Byron's extraordinary personal beauty lay as much in the observer's mind and imagination as in reality. No representation adequately captured it. "Lord Byron's head," wrote Scott's son-in-law John Gibson Lockhart, "is, without doubt, the finest in our time – I think it better, on the whole, than either Napoleon's, or Göethe's, or Canova's, or Wordsworth's."[11] Testimony from sources so varied – several not otherwise friendly to Byron – indicates the degree to which the poet's physical appearance mesmerized contemporaries.

This of course is the younger Byron. In Italy after 1816, older and grayer, alternately bloated and lean, Byron nevertheless continued to dazzle onlookers. The Countess Albrizzi, a big fan, sighed in 1819, "It would be to little purpose to dwell upon the mere beauty of a countenance in which the expression of an extraordinary mind was so conspicuous." But like all the others she could not resist temptation: she details the forehead, the hair, the eyes ("expressive," "azure"), the teeth, cheeks, neck, hands, figure.[12] Trelawny, no fan at all, looking back in 1858, said that "in external appearance Byron realised the ideal standard with which imagination adorns genius."[13] James Hamilton Browne, who traveled with Byron to Cephalonia in 1823, portrayed the older Byron in words that evoke the younger:

> The contour of his countenance was noble and striking; the forehead, particularly so, was nearly white as alabaster. His delicately formed features were cast rather in an effeminate mould, but their soft expression was in some degree relieved by the moustaches of a light chestnut, and a small tuft "à la houssard," which he at that time sported. His eyes were rather prominent and full, of a dark blue, having that melting character which I have frequently observed in females, said to be proof of extreme sensibility. The texture of his skin was so fine and transparent, that the blue veins, rising like small threads around his temples, were clearly discernible.[14]

This is the man Lawrence never painted. Queried in old age why he hadn't, Lawrence recalled "that a communication had once passed between himself and Byron on the subject of a portrait but as his engagements prevented him from acceding to the time of the Noble Bard's appointment, the opportunity was broken off and never resumed."[15]

The missed opportunity probably occurred during the early months of 1813. Lawrence painted most figures of note in Regency England: Wellington, Southey, Rogers, Nash, the Prince Regent, Campbell, Sir John

Soane, and Scott. But not Byron. It is one of the great failures to connect. And it could so easily have happened. Had Byron stayed in England perhaps it would have happened. Both knew well, and from within, the intensely political, cosmopolitan world of Regency England, and a portrait of Byron would have redounded to the fame of each. Furthermore, Lawrence held Byron the poet in the greatest esteem. Upon visiting Rome, he read *Childe Harold* 4, which prompted him to comment that "only Lord Byron has feeling and capacity to describe" Rome. Perusing *Cain*, Lawrence was appalled, yet awed: it was by "Lord Byron, the first poet and (with this unanswerable proof of it) the first philosopher of the age.[16] Lawrence almost certainly would have painted the most probing – I hesitate to say definitive – portrait of the age's most spectacular poet. And Byron would have had his elusive features captured by its master portraitist.

There are rumors of a sketch. In 1815 Lawrence finally completed a dazzling rendering of Mrs Jens Wolff, English wife of the Danish ambassador. Mrs Wolff adored Byron, and Lawrence adored her. Elegantly posed (after the Erythraean Sibyl in Michelangelo's fresco on the Sistine Chapel ceiling), she looks bemused, book in hand. One would like to think she is perusing Byron's poems but the volume, more appropriately, is of Michelangelo's drawings. To gratify his *inamorata*, Lawrence "dashed off with his pen the head of the poet, but with somewhat too dark coloring."[17]

But if Lawrence never did a full-scale *Byron* he set down for Mrs Wolff, probably sometime in the summer of 1814, a remarkable pen portrait. He glimpsed Byron fleetingly at a social event, but even this limited exposure enabled him to seize something of the complexities of Byron's character. Where Coleridge found beauty in Byron's face, Lawrence saw conflict:

> its keen and rapid genius – its pale Intelligence – its profligacy and its bitterness, its original symmetry distorted by the Passions, his laugh of mingled merriment and scorn. The forehead clear and open, the brow boldly prominent, the Eyes bright and *dissimilar*, – the Nose finely cut and the Nostril *acutely* formed – the Mouth well-form'd but wide, and contemptuous even in its smile; falling singularly at the corners, and its vindictive and disdainful expression, heightened by the massive firmness of the Chin, which springs at once from the centre of the full under-lip, – the Hair dark and curling, but irregular in its growth.
>
> All this presents to you the Poet and the Man. . . .[18]

In its detailed observation, perspicacious insight, and intuitive analysis, Lawrence's verbal sketch rivals Byron's own magnificent pen portraits of Gibbon, Voltaire, Rousseau, Sheridan, and Napoleon. Lawrence's phenomenally sharp and probing vision must have equalled Byron's own.[19] Few details escaped his scrutiny. But perception involves the mind as well as the eye, and in Lawrence's words eyesight becomes insight. Nothing inspired his imagination more than the human face. Clearly Byron rivetted his gaze, for he pounced on the man like a hawk and in a paragraph seized key traits of his being. To contemplate what he could have done in a portrait staggers the imagination.

Much painted, sometimes sculpted, often engraved, Byron greets us with a plethora of images, in a variety of poses. The portraits, done at most stages of his career, shape how we envisage him. We look for images that accord with our conception of the man. Few seize either the man or the imagination. When Thomas Lawrence missed his opportunity, he deprived posterity of an acutely rendered and imaginatively conceived *Byron*.

But could even Lawrence have captured the bundle of contradictory impulses that roiled within Byron? Most portraits of Byron lack the life energy of the best word pictures. To sketch Lincoln's portrait truly, Walt Whitman felt, it would take four different sorts of genius: that of Plutarch, Aeschylus, Michelangelo and Rabelais.[20] Only one was an artist. How many different kinds of genius would it take to sketch Byron's? The poet's *mobilité* (his own term) challenges even the finest portraitist. So greatly did his countenance vary "at every moment as different ideas suggested themselves to his powerful mind" that we may, with Hamilton Browne, doubt whether any artist could have caught its expression fully.[21] Byron never seems to have appeared the same twice to anyone. How to depict Coleridge's sun-god?

The painter to have captured Byron, thinks Doris Langley Moore, was Ingres, whose portraits connoisseurs value no less for their magnificently detailed costume than for their psychological acuity.[22] Presumably Ingres would have rendered Byron's face in marmoreal splendor; certainly he would have done justice to his attire. For David Piper, Delacroix was the man. Piper offers no reasons, but presumably he valued the early Delacroix's probing of being, his Oriental imagination, his exuberant sense of spectacle. Leigh Hunt had noted "succinctness and gentlemanliness" in Byron's appearance. "If Lawrence had drawn Byron," conjectures Piper, "he would probably have caught more of this 'succinctness and gentlemanliness.'"[23] Piper may underestimate Lawrence here. Though Lawrence could render "succinctness and gentlemanliness" well enough, he was, like Byron himself, capable of penetrating insight into character. As his verbal sketch indicates, he yielded to no one in his psychological intuition of Byron's being.

That Lawrence would probably have obliterated the competition, whatever its merits, Caroline Lamb grasped intuitively. She reveals herself a discerning critic of portraiture. In despair over Byron's rejection of her, she wrote the painter on May 1, 1814:

> had I brought one I hate [Byron] to you – Good heavens, what a head you had painted – I see it now – all that others exaggerate you would have softened off – and a beauty would have arisen that sometimes for a moment exists, and that none have attempted even to seize that I remember – .[24]

Who but Lawrence could have captured the poet's ironic brilliance, the controlled Romantic flair, and that momentary, fleeting, but irresistible beauty that enthralled Caroline?

*

Portrait painters hovered about Byron. On the whole, they did not serve him well. Except for the (undiscovered) Lawrence sketch and possibly Thorwaldsen's marble bust a few years later, no hitherto known representation of Byron among the forty-odd done during his lifetime is by an artist judged, either then or now, first rate.

There are five artists who created significant portraits of Byron during his years in England: George Sanders, Thomas Phillips, Richard Westall, James Holmes, and George Henry Harlow. Sanders depicts the 19- or 21-year-old Byron accompanied by his page debarking from a boat.[25] The only illustration in the English edition of Moore's biography, Sanders's portrait defined for a generation the young Byron.[26] Despite recent speculation about whether it drew upon naval iconography, including portraits of Nelson, or mimicked a Napoleonic pose, Sanders's portrait of Byron before he became Byronic falls short as a representation of the mature poet.[27]

Phillips (1770–1845) and Westall (1765–1836) were the two best-known artists to paint Byron. Unable to work things out with Lawrence in 1813, Byron turned to them. Phillips had studied with Lawrence, and Westall had once shared a house with him in London. Though neither would achieve more than a small fraction of Lawrence's renown as a portraitist, they created what have become the best-known images of Byron. Byron "stood" to Phillips, presumably at John Murray's request, in June and July 1813. Phillips portrayed Byron both in a dark blue cloak and in a colorful Albanian costume that Byron had acquired on his travels (Figure 2). The Albanian Byron sports a moustache; the cloaked Byron is clean-shaven. Otherwise, the faces closely resemble each other. Phillips depicts Byron with light blue eyes, brown hair (hidden in the Albanian version), and a pale complexion with bluish jowls. He completed the two paintings by mid-March 1814, in time for the annual Royal Academy exhibition. Each entitled *Portrait of a Nobleman*, Phillips's renderings left no doubt regarding their subject.[28]

A fashionable, accomplished academician, Phillips did competent work, no more. Skilled but soulless, he lacked insight into his sitters' inner being. In 1813 Owen, Shee, Beechey, Lawrence preeminently, ranked as the top portrait painters in London. No one would have thought to put Phillips in their company. Yet he was a hard worker, a self-promoter who cultivated his connections as he widened his clientele. At Murray's request he petitioned in 1818 several literary men to do their portraits. With Byron (and Blake) in the bag, he snared Scott, Southey, Lamb, Crabbe, Campbell, and the next year Coleridge. The Redgraves in the 1860s thought his portraits "faithful," "marked by soberness and propriety, by negative rather than positive qualities"; "generally good as to likeness, solid and careful in execution, free from meretricious color, and truthful as to character. He takes no rank as a

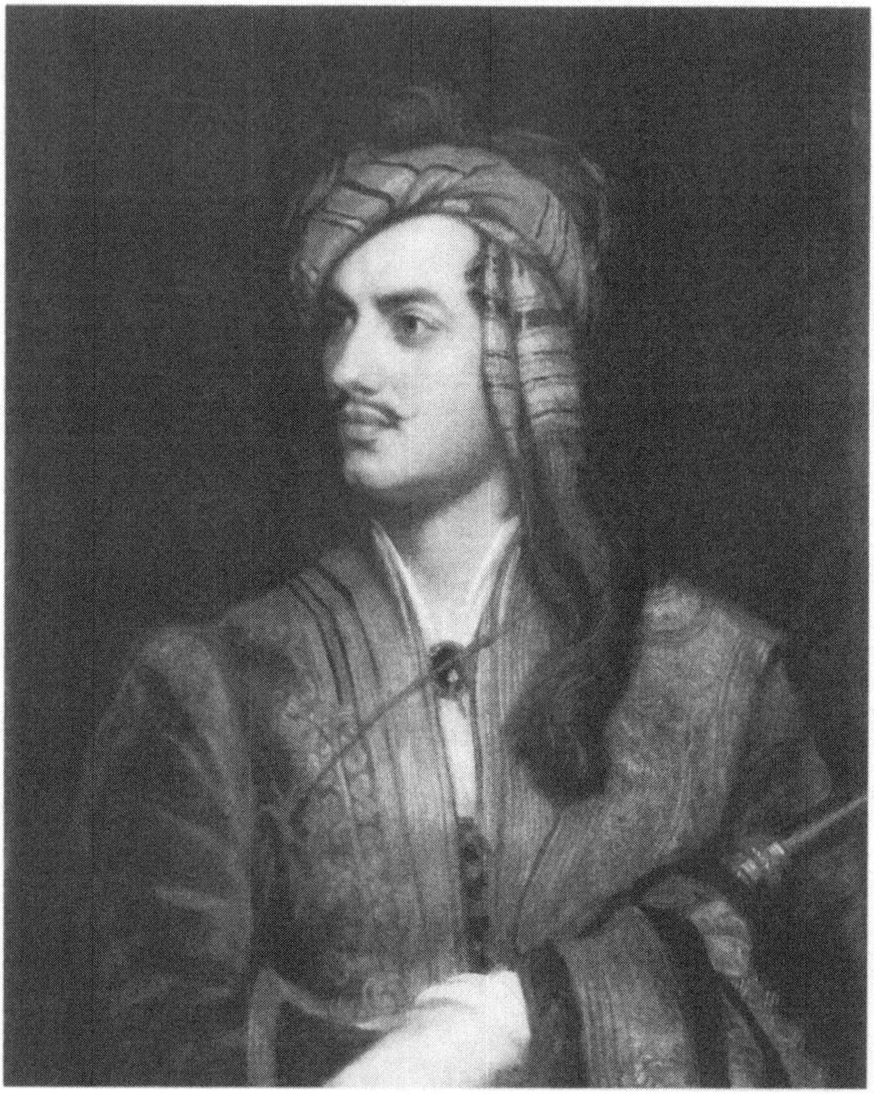

2 Thomas Phillips, *Byron in Albanian Dress*, 1813–14. National Portrait Gallery, London

colourist, but a pleasant tone pervades his works."[29] Surface polish is there; the depths remain unplumbed.

During Lawrence's lifetime Phillips toiled in his huge shadow. After Lawrence's death in 1830 competitors were few. Wordsworth, asked to choose for his portrait between Phillips and Pickersgill, chose the latter. Phillips, the poet opined in 1831, "has made Coxcombs of all the Poets, save only Crabbe, that have come under his hands, and I am rather afraid he might play that trick with me, grey-headed as I am."[30] The thought of Pickersgill did not thrill him, but worse was Phillips.

Phillips's Byron portraits puzzled most of the poet's friends. Dallas described the expression in the cloaked version as "one of haughtiness and affected dignity never once visible to those who ever saw him."[31] Hobhouse viewed both portraits as unfaithful: "I see no resemblance in either one."[32] Lady Caroline Lamb could not understand how Phillips botched Byron's hand or ear.[33] "One is never satisfied with a portrait of a person that one knows," wrote Goethe in *Elective Affinities*, and of Byron more than most others this may hold true.[34] But even for Hazlitt, less familiar with Byron's features than Hobhouse or Caroline Lamb, the portraits were "too smooth, and seem, as it were, 'barbered ten times o'er,' both in the face and the expression."[35] Hazlitt doesn't say the portraits don't look like Byron, only that he found in them that which "conveys the idea" of a certain popular poet identified with Eastern subjects. A modern observer, Morton Paley, concurs. He sees in the Albanian portrait "dash"; it is "Byron as his own Corsair," but it does not go beyond surface illusion and lacks "imaginative life."[36] Since Byron bought the costume and most likely chose the pose, we have him as creator of his own image rather than as his friends knew him.[37]

Other portraitists hardly fared better. Byron liked most, for reasons no one has convincingly given, James Holmes's miniature of a curly headed, vacuous young man.[38] Twice, in 1814–15 and again in 1818, G. H. Harlow, the most brilliant of Lawrence's pupils, sketched what Piper calls "the romantic but highly controlled glamour of the Regency man of the world."[39] The first sketch captures Byron aloof, disdainful; the second, contemplative, troubled. Though appealing to modern taste, these elegant sketches represent only tiny facets of Byron's being.

After 1816, with Byron away from England, the number of portraits drops sharply. His relative inaccessibility, his dislike of British visitors, his lack of interest in having his portrait taken, leave large gaps in the iconographical record. It is a major loss for posterity. Thorwaldsen's sculpted bust of Byron, commissioned by Hobhouse, denies "all character to one of the most vivid personalities the world has known."[40] It reminds us that even a major artist can fail to do justice to his subject. In 1822 the American William Edward West broke through Byron's self-imposed reclusiveness to paint his portrait and one of Teresa Guiccioli. Byron, virtually for the first time, looks at the viewer directly, if somewhat blandly.[41] West, better with women, rendered Teresa with more flair.[42]

Byron actively involved himself in shaping both his portraits and the engravings made from them. He knew how he appeared to the public would help sell his poems. Murray told him that his "portrait is engraved & painted & sold in every town throughout the Kingdom."[43] The news would have gratified him. He identified with these images, comments Frances Wilson, and felt "his reflection to be more finished and complete than the fragmented figure he expressed himself as being."[44] At least twice when

Murray proposed engravings as frontispieces to editions of his poems Byron reacted furiously, believing they did his appearance injustice.[45]

If Byron doesn't look much like his portraits, he yet enjoyed the idea of others portraying him, by both brush and pen. Who knows? – the portraits might help him understand who he was. "One will represent me as a sort of sublime misanthrope . . . Another will portray me as a modern Don Juan"; a third "as an *amiable*, ill-used gentleman."[46] Stendhal saw him as Lovelace, a predatory male, but younger and a thousand times more appealing than Richardson's glib protagonist.[47] Lady Blessington took the measure of the situation. "I am sure that if ten individuals undertook the task of describing Byron, no two, of the ten, would agree in their verdict respecting him." Byron "will always appear different from the hand of each limner."[48] Written and visual descriptions of Byron rarely overlap. Yet most portraits, whether in words or in paint, offer some insight into his being, have some validity.

Sully's *Byron* has a familiar look. In 1813, the year of Lawrence's missed opportunity and the commissioning of Phillips's two iconic likenesses, Richard Westall also painted Byron (see color plate section). The composition of Sully's *Byron* derives, most obviously, from Westall's portrait of 1813. It is this portrait, or rather engravings of it, that the American artist drew upon in creating his own.

Byron's publisher John Murray wished to have an engraving of his bestselling poet to preface a revised seventh edition of cantos 1 and 2 of *Childe Harold's Pilgrimage*. He chose Westall for the job. Though better known for his history paintings and book illustrations, Westall had achieved some renown as a portraitist, exhibiting over sixty at the Royal Academy between 1784 and 1836.[49] Westall's *Byron* is a controversial work by a controversial painter, one whose niche in the history of British art remains undefined.[50] It tells us much about Westall and his art, rather less about Byron.

The circles of Westall and Byron overlapped. Byron knew Westall's patrons, Richard Payne Knight and Thomas Hope, and he spent the 1812–13 winter at Bowood enamored of the seasoned Lady Oxford, a friend of both. Knight, a disciple of Charles James Fox and an MP from 1780 to 1806, admired Lady Oxford greatly.[51] Earlier she had become "the prey" of Sir Francis Burdett, Byron's valued friend, who later became the purchaser, in about 1825, of Westall's *Byron*.[52] James Holmes, the miniaturist, was Westall's lifelong acquaintance and possibly steered the painter to the poet.

"I am to sit to [Westall] for a picture at the request of a friend of mine," Byron noted on April 21, 1813.[53] But not until June, shortly before he sat for Phillips, did the first sitting occur. Westall found Byron "a very singular character," the diarist Farington observed; "he is animated & cheerful while speaking, but when not so occupied His look is grave and settled."[54] Westall painted Byron in profile, without cheer, melancholy, the mind seemingly occupied less with large thoughts than with personal traumas. Brown eye(s) look straight ahead; the hair is curly black, the complexion pinkly pale. A cameo brooch ties a white open-collared shirt; over it is a crimson waistcoat and a black cape.[55] The pose, head resting on hand, derives from Dürer and is, as Piper says, a "variation on the classic topos of poetic melancholy."[56]

*

Born in 1765, Westall attended the Royal Academy school in London, where he met Thomas Lawrence, already a recognized child prodigy. He first exhibited at the Academy in 1784. From 1790 to 1794 he shared a house with Lawrence at 57 Greek Street, fronting Soho Square. In the latter year he, along with Lawrence, became a royal academician. Lawrence's black chalk drawing of his lifelong friend reveals a brooding young man.[57] Others characterize Westall as malleable and polite. His artistry falls between two periods: idealizing classicism in his youth, emergent Victorian prettiness in his maturity. The Romantic energy and vitality evident in Turner, Constable, and Lawrence never touched Westall. He chose instead sentiment and fancy.

One who admired and supported Westall's work from the first was the noted aesthete, Richard Payne Knight. He helped found the Society of Dilettanti, a club for the fashionable interested in the arts and whose members had visited Italy; later he served as its president. A controversial figure in his day, Knight wrote extensively on art and on the picturesque and collected antique busts. He knew his own mind and he enjoyed controversy. Horace Walpole, who disliked him intensely, referred to him as the "Knight of the Brazen Milkpot."[58] Knight's *Discourse on the Worship of Priapus* (1786), a relatively inaccessible tome because of its homoerotic plates, is his most famous work.

Knight served London society as an *arbiter elegantiarum*. His writing was influential, even more so his huge reputation as a man knowledgeable about art. "His cultural power was prodigious," comments John Brewer; "contemporary painters much feared his acidulous criticism and rigorous connoisseurship."[59] At the parliamentary hearings on acquiring the Elgin Marbles in 1816, Knight almost alone fiercely denounced them as crude and inelegant, copies of later Roman works, unworthy of purchase by the nation.[60] Knight's refusal to acknowledge the merits of the Marbles, along with a lifelong arrogance, cost him much credibility.

Of living artists, Knight patronized Westall most extensively. One of the early practitioners of watercolor in England, Westall embodied in this medium Knight's idea of what art should be. He is first recorded as Knight's dinner guest in 1796 though the two men may have met, possibly through Lawrence, before. Knight's subsequent treatment of the artist could "almost be described as paternal."[61] The two lifelong bachelors, Westall 14 years Knight's junior, shared an aesthetic rapport. In time Knight came to own nine major paintings by Westall and at least 13 drawings – more than by any other individual. Poet as well as painter, Westall, encouraged by Knight, published with John Murray *A Day in Spring and Other Poems* in 1808. A recent critic, deeming the volume "slight," concludes that Westall was "not an intellectual" but someone who "seems to have been willing to turn his hand to what was asked of him."[62]

Knight considered Westall's *Storm in a Harvest*, an oil originally a watercolor, one of the three "most interesting and affecting pictures, that the art [of painting] has produced."[63] Westall depicted the harsh realities of peasant life in sentimental, idealized fashion. His unnaturally graceful and surprisingly elegant laborers posture in stage poses expressive of terror before the oncoming storm. The rococo cuteness of *Storm in a Harvest* flirts with the Delicate Sublime; it did accord, however, with Knight's notions of aesthetic beauty. But if Knight liked Westall's fearful but stylized laborers, others criticized them, not unfairly, for having "the air of persons in a higher rank in life."[64]

This presumably was Hazlitt's opinion. The most outspoken as well as the most literate art critic of the era, he fought a lifelong and lonely battle against contemporary popular taste. "I confess I never liked Westall," he told James Northcote. "It was one of the errors of my youth that I did not think him equal to Raphael and Rubens united, as Payne Knight contended."[65] One reason for Hazlitt's dislike was Joshua Reynolds's praise of art that focused on the general and avoided the specific. "On Sir Joshua's theory of the *beau ideal*, Mr. Westall's pictures are perhaps the best that ever were painted, and on any other theory, the worst; for they exhibit an absolute negation of all experience, character, and discrimination of form and color." Westall's art, as Hazlitt understood it, fostered misguided principles.[66] His was

> the elegant antithesis to the style of Hogarth, where, instead of that originality of character which excluded a nice attention to general forms, we have all that beauty of form which excludes the possibility of character; the refined essence and volatilized spirit of art, without any of the *caput mortuum* of nature; and where, instead of her endless variety, peculiarities and defects, we constantly meet with the same classical purity and undeviating simplicity of idea – one sweet smile, one heightened bloom diffused over all.[67]

That the public did not always agree with him did not bother Hazlitt overly. Westall's *Christ in the Temple* and *Margaret of Anjou* brought out Hazlitt's laconic wit: "Of this artist's works we always wish to speak well from our respect to the public taste, and are only sorry that we cannot, consistently with any regard for our own."[68]

Westall's work struck Hazlitt as unmanly. "Where shall we stop in the easy down-hill pass of effeminate, unmeaning insipidity?" he asked. And again: "Are we to confound the difference of sex in a sort of hermaphroditic softness, as Mr. Westall, Angelica Kauffmann, and others have done in their effeminate performances?"[69] The questions Hazlitt asked have remained unanswered. By his repeated use of "effeminate" he seems to imply that Westall was homosexual and his art homosexual in nature. Westall's few modern commentators touch upon, but do not deal directly with, this possibility. Ballantyne comes closest, when in an acute discussion of Knight's admiration of the artist and the man he refers to Westall's relationship with

Knight as "homosocial."[70] "Curiously," remarks Ballantyne, "Knight's appreciation of Richard Westall's work would not have worried his readers at the time. There were members of the artistic elite of the day who had misgivings about Westall's work, but it was generally accepted as being of the highest calibre."[71] This is about as flattering as evaluations of Westall come. Although many contemporary artists – Sandby, Constable, Leslie, as well as the art patron Beaumont – cared little for Westall's paintings, he did indeed have admirers.

Another of his patrons was Thomas Hope, a contemporary aesthete infatuated with the Greek ideal and later author of *Anastasius* (1819). Like Knight, Hope defended neoclassical values and ideals. In 1804 he commissioned from Westall – for the dazzling sum of 450 guineas – two paintings of Greek mythological scenes, with lithe youths and floating maidens, to adorn his London mansion.[72] Collectors with enthusiasms comparable to Knight and Hope found in Westall an artist who could paint the world of their desires.

John Boydell (1719–1804) employed Westall for his Shakespeare Gallery. A wealthy printmaker, publisher, and a dealer of international renown, Boydell wished to encourage a nationalistic school of history painting in Britain based on Shakespeare. Boydell's Gallery spearheaded the era's widespread Bardolatry, and in Shakespeare painters of the era found a usable past. Shakespeare influenced every aspect of the visual arts. Equal parts aesthetic theory, adulation of Shakespeare, and Boydell himself, the Gallery became a center of London's artistic life. By determining how people visualized Shakespeare's characters, in paintings as well as in dramatic productions, it influenced public taste. Among the 35 artists who received commissions from Boydell were Reynolds, Romney, West, Fuseli, Opie, and Northcote. The Gallery opened in Pall Mall in 1789 with 34 paintings; by 1802 Boydell had about 170.[73]

"Forgettable mediocrities" like Westall, Richard D. Altick informs us, produced half the 170.[74] In fact, Westall is now chiefly remembered for his work for Boydell from 1795 to 1802. Prints of the paintings, reissued by nineteenth-century publishers, often surpassed the originals in quality of detail and enjoyed sustained popularity. In America Shakespeare had perhaps a still greater vogue. Sully's portraits of the Shakespearean actors George Frederick Cooke and Fanny Kemble (both discussed in Chapter 5) drew upon the widespread Bardolatry stimulated by Boydell.

In addition to his Shakespeare work, Westall collaborated with Henry Fuseli in the latter's short-lived Gallery of the Miltonic Sublime (1799–1800).[75] Earlier he had contributed 28 copperplate engravings to Hayley's *Life of Milton*.[76] He also worked with Fuseli on an edition of *Paradise Lost*. Although preserving his independence from that forceful individual and artist, Westall's flaccid renderings of Miltonic scenes hardly elicit more than a sentimental response.[77] If admired by some contemporaries, they misread Milton and misled his readers.

*

Westall's experiences with Boydell proved instructive, and he may have sensed early that whatever fame he might achieve would derive from engravings made of his work. As opportunities to illustrate books multiplied after 1814, his career as a painter waned. Westall's sentimentalism carried over to his illustrations, and he seems to have had as much work as he wished. Early commissions included the second edition of Sotheby's translation of Wieland's *Oberon* (1805); Scott's *Lay of the Last Minstrel* (1808) and *Lady of the Lake* (1810), later that author's *Guy Mannering* and *Ivanhoe*. Westall also illustrated Goldsmith, Thomson, and Cowper, *Don Quixote* and *The Arabian Nights*, Goethe's *Faust* and Milman's *Fall of Jerusalem*; poems by Burns, Crabbe, Campbell, and Southey; and the 1824 London edition of Irving's *Sketch-Book*. His designs for the Bible and the Prayer Book pleased religious tastes.[78] The *New Monthly* opined that Westall's work gave to illustrated books "a higher character than they had before obtained in this country."[79] Some contemporaries rated him as an illustrator second only to Thomas Stothard.

Expectedly, Hazlitt found Westall's engraved work, as he had the paintings, insipid. Scott could not abide it, and Benjamin Robert Haydon, ever opinionated, decried "Westall's vicious stuff."[80] Westall's idealized subjects and graceful if mawkish poses may have suited the Victorians better. In the 1860s, with sentimentality in full flower, Richard and Samuel Redgrave found in "his female ideal" both "great sameness" and "great prettiness."[81] The *DNB*, in considering the artistic merit of Westall's illustrations, concluded that "there is not very much to be said." Conventionally melodramatic, they "soon degenerated into mannerism, and in the female types especially there is great monotony."

Undeterred by Westall's detractors, John Murray commissioned from him 21 illustrations of Byron's poems. Engraved by the fashionable Charles Heath, they appeared in Murray's four-volume *Works of Lord Byron* (1819).[82] Westall's compositions usually avoid action. Languishing maidens consort lifelessly with weak-kneed males who, the Redgraves opined, "sadly lacked the manliness of the heroes they represented." Women fared worse. As with the men, "the mannerism of the artist was always apparent."[83] Westall liked to portray women suffering. For *The Corsair* he has Medora in despair over Conrad's departure; then dead, a suicide. Similarly for *Lara*: Kaled consoles the wounded Lara; then Lara, dying, looks up at the grieving Kaled.[84]

Westall reused his poses again and again. His male protagonist usually looks like his *Byron* portrait. Having painted a half-imaginary Byron in 1813, Westall illustrated the poems with its features.[85] This unprepossessing individual – long-necked, eye wildly staring, face invariably in profile, in short a caricature – parodies Byron's words. In his poem *Alfred* (1823) Westall defended Byron's recently published and immediately notorious *Cain*; he claimed the "noble poet . . . has squandered more talent than most others ever possessed."[86] His illustrations of Byron's poems, however, imply vice rather than exalt nobility. Contemporaries understandably identified the often reprehensible-looking Byronic hero Westall drew with Byron himself.

Competing with other illustrators, most of whom catered to a mawkishly sentimental public taste, Westall may have been following more than creating a style.[87] Byron deemed his designs for *Don Juan* "quite beautiful" and "superb" and professed to believe "the brush has beat the poetry."[88] If it had, he saw in them something his more discerning contemporaries missed. In this view he was almost alone.

History has not judged Westall's reputation kindly. John Neal, delightfully opinionated as always, termed him in 1829 "the feeblest of all masters" and "that most insipid of English painters."[89] Westall, noted the Redgraves, "has been characterized as 'great in little things.'"[90] Neoclassical or early Victorian, but hardly Regency, Westall's foppish males and languishing females anticipate Victorian collections of "beauties." Ballantyne speaks generously of his "briefly brilliant career," but Kerry Downes, reviewing Ballantyne, calls him "a pretty painter . . . of whom nobody since Hazlitt has had much to say, good or bad."[91]

*

After Murray published *Childe Harold's Pilgrimage* in March 1812, Byron became the lion everyone wished to meet, and the ladies to tame. In 1813, when Westall first met him, Byron rode his notoriety hard and well. Despite his disclaimers, most contemporaries associated him with *Childe Harold*'s dissolute but appealing hero. For Annette Peach, Westall embodies the romantic hero of *Childe Harold*'s first cantos, the youth who "'spent his days in riot most uncouth.'"[92] If Phillips (in Hazlitt's phrase) "'barbered [Byron] ten times o'er,' both in the face and the expression," Westall cleaned, rinsed, and towelled the man.[93] His rendering is fastidious, even overly so. "It seems to me that if the refinement of a portrait is carried too far," wrote Sully in *Hints to Young Painters*, "the identify of the sitter may be lost."[94] Though intended generally, Sully's insight helps us gauge why Westall's epicene *Byron* limits and finally emasculates Byron's powerful being.

Westall completed his Byron portrait late in 1813 (see color plate section). Normally he would have shown it at the next May's Royal Academy exhibition, but he did not. That year Phillips displayed his cloaked *Byron* and *Byron in Albanian Dress*. Reviews of RA shows often matched one painting against another, and set against Phillips's shallow but flamboyant work, Westall's effort would not have fared well. Instead, at Knight's instigation, he launched a gigantic exhibition solely of his own work. Held at the New Gallery, Pall Mall, the exhibition included 312 paintings, 240 of which Westall had not shown before. Many – including *Storm in a Harvest* (owned by Knight) and *Dionysus and Damocles* (owned by Thomas Hope) – had already found purchasers. Admission was one shilling. The *Catalogue of the Exhibition of a Selection of the Works of Richard Westall*, also one shilling, listed as no. 98 "Portrait of a Nobleman." This work, transparently of Byron, attracted the public's attention.

Westall may have intended the "hermaphroditic softness" that Hazlitt noted (and disliked) in his work. As contemporaries wondered about

Westall's sexuality, so he may have wondered about Byron's. Farington, whose diary of the years between 1793 and 1821 retails much delicious art gossip, recalled a dinner conversation with Westall and his brother at which it was said in regard to Byron that "in his still earlier youth He made himself remarkable by some acts, deviations from propriety which would not have been excused at another period of life."[95] Meaning, phrasing, and speaker are ambiguous, but Farington does imply that a hot topic of conversation in Regency London was the history and nature of Byron's sexuality.[96]

Only a few visitors to the exhibition seem to have liked Westall's Byron portrait. The author of the two-part review in the fashionable *New Monthly Magazine* did not comment specifically on *Byron* but he did reveal his taste when he praised *The Last Parting* for "the pathetic feeling, and affectionate regard of the dying wife to her distracted husband."[97] The reviewer for Ackermann's *Repository*, which also catered to the well-to-do, predictably puffed the "extraordinary talents" of the "prolific genius" that was Westall.[98] Byron's fawning cousin Robert Charles Dallas contemplated the portrait "with calm delight, and at times with rapture." He claimed to have seen Byron "in the very position represented in Mr. Westall's picture."[99] Teresa Guiccioli, who did not meet Byron until 1819, perhaps glimpsed Westall's portrait on a later trip to England. She found it "superior to the others" but not "up to the original."[100] But what, for her, could rival the reality? Dallas and possibly Teresa excepted, few others looked kindly on Westall's *Byron*.

Byron may have been among the few. "I happen to know that this portrait was not a flatterer, but dark and stern," he commented, most likely about Westall's attempt, " – even black as the mood in which my mind was scorching last July, when I sat for it."[101] As often happens with pictures of a personal nature, the subject sees in them what he wishes to see, and perhaps the portrait recalled for Byron passionate moments with his half-sister Augusta. The poet responded to Westall's sentimental charm. It was Westall whom he chose to do the portrait of Lady Charlotte Harley, 11-year-old daughter of his then current *inamorata* Lady Oxford, a girl whose youthful beauty on the verge of womanhood he memorialized in the stanzas "To Ianthe" added to *Childe Harold*'s seventh edition (1814).[102]

The 1814 exhibition was Westall's bid for public and professional acclaim. He positioned himself for widespread recognition as a major artist, spent heavily on it, but the exhibition failed and recognition did not come. Knight sympathized, but the next year Westall, deeply in debt, moved in with his brother William, also an artist. He gradually gave up original work.[103]

Engravings based on Westall's *Byron* appeared as early as February 1814, but the portrait's mixed reception may have decided the artist to keep it by him. The news of Byron's death at Missolonghi on April 19, 1824, reached London too late for Westall to show his portrait at that year's Royal Academy exhibition. In 1825, with the Academy show again beckoning and no competing portraits of the poet announced, Westall must have felt confident of success. By then Byron, his renown expanding in death, was the talk of

Europe and America. But if Westall's *Byron* did not have to go up against Phillips's portraits, it encountered competition even more formidable. It had the misfortune, at least for the artist, to be hung near Lawrence's masterful *Julia, Lady Peel*. The *New Monthly* reviewer compared the two to illustrate "what a portrait should and what it should not be." Whereas Lawrence in a pose borrowed from Rubens created a *Mrs Peel* that was "lovely" and almost "perfect," Westall's *Byron* lacked conviction and failed the test of verisimilitude. The poet had absented himself from England in 1816, and Westall may have hoped that few attending the exhibition retained accurate or recent memory of his features – thus could not dispute or refute his portrayal of them. But if such was his hope, it was disappointed. "The portrait of Byron is as much an *ideal* work as any of Mr. Westall's historical ones," intoned the *New Monthly* critic. "The features, the general expression, the hair of the head, and even the colour of the eyes, are all Mr. Westall's and none of them Lord Byron's." He chided Westall for his usual faults. He found *Mary Magdalen, & c. at the Sepulchre of Christ* "striking and powerful" but rated "the character and expression of all the figures sadly inferior and ineffective . . . His profiles (and he delights in profile) are all alike; and what is worse, they are all unnatural." The form and character of his mouths, in particular, "are never to be observed in nature." The reviewer came down even harder on Westall's *Christ appearing to Mary Magdalen*: "subjects of this nature are wholly unsuited to the powers and acquirements of this elegant mannerist. They demand a simplicity of style which it is (if we may so speak) his express merit to be without."[104]

"Elegant mannerist" may seem harsh, but modern critics have not been kinder. Doris Langley Moore saw in Westall's *Byron* "something exaggerated . . . , especially the neck, which must have been done without a model."[105] Richard Walker thought Byron's distorted appearance related less to the poet's accepted iconography than to Westall's *Ecce Homo* at All Souls Church, Langham Place. Was Westall, he asks, there portraying Christ as Byron? An amusing speculation, but not too likely.[106] Few of Byron's many biographers engage visually with the poet or deal responsibly with images of him. Recent lives, undeterred by the portrait's reputation for dubious verisimilitude, have reversed the image when reproducing it or left it unidentified.

Portraits constitute a minor part of Westall's *oeuvre*. Like most British painters, he looked to them for reliable income. They are not what he did best. His figures often appear generic; his faces, composites. He seems not to have troubled himself with live models, and his landscapes seldom depict an actual view. How carefully did he look at Byron? Byron's eye color in portraits varies considerably (I return to the subject later), but only Westall paints them amber or brown. Which leaves us with a question: was he rendering the man before him, someone he imagined, or someone he wished him to be? Westall maintained a close association with the theater all his life, and he would have known that contemporary stage manuals recommended that actors, at key moments in a play, present the body in contorted poses, the facial expressions agitated. If we did not know the subject of Westall's portrait, might we not take it to be of one of Shakespeare's melancholy, brooding characters, Hamlet perhaps?[107]

Westall used profiles early and often. The *New Monthly* reviewer found them "all alike" and, worse still, "unnatural." The elderly man in full profile of *Storm in a Harvest* has a highly irregular physiognomy. Other figures appear, somewhat oddly, in full or partial profile. Both his portraits and his Byron illustrations reveal Westall hesitant to adopt frontal views. The other Romantics usually chose a frontal view for their portraits, but in few of his does Byron (Piper reminds us) gaze directly at the spectator.[108] In the Phillips portraits and most others he faces the viewer's left. Westall's *Byron*, head on chin, looks left in full profile.

Profile poses may have been Byron's choice. He would have been familiar with portraits by Kneller and Van Loo of his favorite Pope that posed him in profile. One of Byron's eyes, as Lawrence noted, was slightly larger than the other, and a frontal pose would have revealed this asymmetry. With "his eyes set close together and a contracted brow," opined Lady Stanhope, Byron had "a great deal of vice in his looks."[109] If Byron agreed with this assessment, better go down to posterity in virtuous profile.

Profiles, partial or full, are among the oldest and most enduring forms of portraiture. Their ancestors include Egyptian bas-relief figures and Greek and Roman coins. Profile portraits modelled upon the coins enjoyed a vogue in Renaissance medals. Artists followed suit. Paolo Ucello's *Profile Portrait of a Young Man*, Piero della Francesca's *Federico da Montefeltro, Duke of Urbino*, and Titian's *Pietro Aretino* rank among the greatest of all portraits. Outside Italy fewer profiles were undertaken, but north of the Alps Holbein the Younger's *Thomas Cromwell* and *Erasmus* and Rubens's *Portrait of a Gentleman* testify to the profile's popularity. Many Annunciations present the angel Gabriel, sometimes also the Virgin Mary, in profile.

Profiles became popular again during the Enlightenment. The neoclassical style, which exerted a broad impact in Europe and America from 1760 to 1820, developed as a consequence of a revived interest in classical Greek and Roman art. Enlightenment thinkers valued profile portraits, which had ties to a distant past and epitomized belief in reason and order, as particularly truthful representations. Ingres experimented with profiles in drawings of the 1790s. Lawrence's best *George IV*, an incomplete sketch in the National Portrait Gallery, is a profile. An acknowledged masterpiece, *Mrs Jens Wolff* is in stunning profile as she ponders her book. In France, David d'Angers's portrait medallions in high and low relief, in marble, wax, and paste, kept alive the profile tradition, as did, in vastly different ways, Daumier and other caricaturists.

*

Byron, commented Keats, "cut a figure."[110] What kind of figure did he cut? Byron portrayed himself in poems as frequently as Rembrandt did in self-portraits. Most of his protagonists, from Childe Harold to *Cain*'s Lucifer, bear some resemblance to their creator. Repeated poetic self-portraits may suggest vanity; they may also suggest frustration at limitations in self-knowledge. When the mood took him, Byron could dismiss likenesses, particularly his sculpted busts, as unnecessary, but before leaving England in 1809 he commissioned miniatures of Harrow classmates.[111] There are also the word-Byrons by, among others, Wordsworth, Shelley, Goethe, Arnold, Mazzini, Grillparzer, and Joyce. Like the visual portraits, these word pictures cut different figures, each contradicting the others in some way. Visual and verbal portraits present Byron variously because the man himself was various. Biographers explore that variety in the breadth and friendships of an extraordinary life. Critics find the poetry subtle, rhetorical, inspiring, topographical, witty. No less for the portraitists than for the biographers and critics, Byron remains complex, puzzling, a challenge, larger than any depiction of him can be.

"I cannot see the man for the likeness," Roger Fry once quipped regarding Sargent's rendering of General Sir Ian Hamilton.[112] Likewise, many find the portraits of Byron superficial, defective, otherwise flawed. Though Sanders, Phillips, Westall, Harlow, William Edward West et al. transcribed Byron's image for posterity, their efforts largely perpetuate contemporary stereotypes. Their insights into the man are limited. They had inadequate skills, or, more often, lacked a vision, or even psychological understanding, of their subject. Sanders and West are known almost exclusively for their Byron portraits; without them, their work would command the attention of few. Although Phillips and Westall left behind a sizable *oeuvre*, paintings by them rarely appear in museum displays. Their *Byron*s remain their best-known works.

Each generation exalts or reduces genius within its own terms and finds in it what it wants. As with the man and his writings, so the reputation of Byron's portraits has waxed and waned. A portrait's fame may depend less on its intrinsic merit than on what the public of the time thinks of its subject. Sanders's youthful *Byron*, thanks to the Findens' engraving, encapsulated Byron for much of the nineteenth century.[113] For most of the twentieth Phillips's cloaked portrait held sway. Westall's *Byron* early achieved considerable currency through engravings. Entering the National Portrait Gallery's collection in 1961 increased its renown and it now ranks as one of the iconic images of Byron.[114]

Most post-1813 portraits of Byron take their cue either from Westall's *Byron* or from Phillips's cloaked version. Both feature the poet in an open-necked shirt. Byron, at least in portraiture, liberated the male neck nearly two hundred years ago. Those who came to maturity chained to the compulsory jacket and tie gratefully acknowledge that liberation. Every wannabe cowboy or cowgirl in the American West, collar open and bolo tie prominent, owes a (usually unconscious) debt to the sartorial boldness of Byron in his portraits. The early copyists of Westall amd Phillips often altered the head or gave the poet a different body or attire. Such changes can make the copies interesting in themselves. If the knock-off *Byron* presents the poet in partial profile with blue cloak and red-brocade vest underneath, the artist has leaned upon Phillips; if Byron appears in full profile with hand on chin and open collar, the artist has borrowed from Westall.

It took 150 years for Phillips's glitzy *Byron in Albanian Dress* to achieve its iconic status as the poet's best-known portrait.[115] After being shown in 1814, it disappeared from public view for a generation. Popularized by William Finden's engraving of 1841, it emerged at mid-century a rival to the romantic Sanders and the brooding Westall. Shown at the 1969 Victoria & Albert exhibition "Berlioz and the Romantics," *Byron in Albanian Dress* launched Byron for a new generation.[116] Byron as Corsair, Byron as Oriental hero, Byron (suggests David Piper) as Errol Flynn, even Byron (if I may add) as androgynous, exotic pop star: it is one of the most recognized images of a poet, the only portrait on the cover of the National Portrait Gallery's recent *Visitor's Guide* (2000). Byron as Other – sartorially lavish, excessive, unreal even – offers something to many.

Which portrait will best embody Byron in the twenty-first century? The question cannot yet be answered. Byron portraiture remains alive and well, and several of the newer portraits are of considerable skill and power. (I discuss a few briefly in Chapter 10.) A new contender, however, one that is yet an Old Master, has entered the lists. Its rivals are many and varied, but the merits of Sully's *Byron* are, I think, strong enough to contest the ground. We turn now to the career and development of its creator.

CHAPTER THREE

First Portraitist of Philadelphia

The greatest portrait-painters are the greatest painters.
Delacroix[1]

In the decades before and after 1826, when he began *Byron*, Sully gained wide recognition as the nation's leading portraitist.[2] Among contemporary American artists, only Gilbert Stuart (b. 1755), who worked in Boston and whose fame depended largely on copies of his *Washington*, rivalled Sully in reputation. Even the gifted Charles Willson Peale (b. 1741) gracefully yielded as a portraitist to Sully after the younger man moved to Philadelphia late in 1807. Peale and Stuart, who both came to artistic maturity in the 1770s, had studied in the England of Joshua Reynolds and Benjamin West. Characteristic of an older generation that spent most of its life in the eighteenth century, their work reflected earlier styles and theories about art. By 1826 Stuart had two years to live, Peale one. What Copley had been to portraiture in America in the middle and Stuart at the end of the eighteenth century, Sully became to portraiture during the first half of the nineteenth century.

Sully brought a new level of sophistication and cosmopolitanism to his portraits of Americans. Well aware of Lawrence's career in England, he incorporated into his art Regency – and Romantic – ideals. His long career as a painter envelops Byron's as a poet. As Byron reinvigorated poetry for his generation, so Sully introduced into American portraiture a Romantic sensibility, a livelier palette, a heightened energy and flair, a sense of drama.

Sully painted his first portrait at 19. When he died 71 years later a half-finished sketch lay on his easel. Over the course of his long and immensely productive life he painted over two thousand portraits. Many rank among the glories of American art. His psychological insights and vibrant palette led contemporaries to dub him the "Sir Thomas Lawrence" of America.[3] It is a great compliment, the greatest perhaps to which an American portraitist of the time could aspire, but like most labels it applies but partially. Lawrence's American successor in Grand Manner portraiture, Sully yet stands on his own as a artist of uncommon skill, varied achievement, and stalwart reputation. Examining the stages of his education in art enables us to comprehend how he became his generation's preeminent portraitist.

*

Born in Horncastle, Lincolnshire, in 1783, Sully was the fourth of nine children (and the youngest son) of Matthew and Sarah Chester Sully. His parents, provincial actors, led unsettled lives, and for much of his childhood

Thomas lived in Birmingham with his maternal grandmother. In 1792 this theatrical family emigrated to America to improve its fortunes. Landing in Norfolk, Virginia, they moved inland to Richmond, where they engaged with the West and Bignall Company (Thomas Wade West was Matthew Sully's brother-in-law). The parents, perhaps thinking of an alternate career for young Thomas, sent him to William Sanford's school in New York. At his mother's death in 1793 he returned post-haste to Richmond. That year West offered Matthew Sully and his family employment in Charleston, where on February 11 West and Bignall had opened the Charleston, or Broad Street, Theater.

As actor-manager West engaged, often for several seasons, the best actors, singers, and musicians, including Mrs Whitlock, born a Kemble and sister to Sarah Siddons.[4] West and Bignall specialized in comedy. Matthew had a fine voice and excelled in comic roles and pantomimes. A celebrated harlequin – and harlequins were the joy of the times – he had, as did all his sons, impressive gymnastic and tumbling skills. Several female Sullys had roles in the inaugural season. In fact, nearly all the Sullys, including Thomas, performed on the stage.

Federal Charleston ranked as one of the largest American cities. With a population only slightly smaller than Boston and Baltimore, it had long been connected commercially and socially with them and with Philadelphia. Planters and merchants shared banking and trade interests. Young Sully grew up amidst a sophisticated group of French and British refugees. The echoes of English life he encountered in his daily rambles must have reminded him of the land he had left behind. All his sisters, including his favorite, Betsey, married and remained in Charleston. In later years the artist returned to the city on several occasions seeking portrait commissions.

In Charleston young Sully attended the Rev. Robert Smith's School. Showing an inclination to doodle, he received instruction in drawing. He also learned from his artistically inclined schoolmate contemporary Charles Fraser (1782–1860).[5] The Charleston theater not only catalyzed Thomas's passion for actors and acting but also awakened in him an interest in stage design.[6] Although his parents apprenticed him to an insurance broker when he was 12, young Sully did not respond to a business career. Fraser had introduced Sully to miniatures, for which a ready market existed; and Sully learned further basics in art from his French brother-in-law, Jean Belzons, who designed sets and who also, from about 1794 to 1812, worked in the city as a miniaturist and drawing teacher.[7] After a violent altercation with Belzons in 1799, however, Sully abruptly left Charleston for Richmond, where his much older brother Lawrence (1769–1804) had achieved success as a miniaturist. He was 16, and he was on his own. The peripatetic life of his parents had now, perhaps inevitably, become his.

Thomas gained from his brother further knowledge of art. In Norfolk, where Lawrence took the family, the portraitist Henry Benbridge (1743–1812) also gave Thomas "useful and kind instruction."[8] His first independent work, in 1801, an oval miniature, watercolor on ivory, 1¾" x 1¾" (4.4cm x 4.4cm), depicted his mother with an angel hovering over her tomb. Mourning miniatures were common in an age which acknowledged death more openly than today. His mother and father being itinerant actors, young Sully must have often yearned for the mother who had died when he was only ten.[9] As a mature artist, he kept his own family close about him.

Sully began as a painter of miniatures. Though overshadowed today by portraits, miniatures often demonstrate close observation of character and superlative craftsmanship. Usually but not always watercolor on ivory, they were relatively cheap and, for the skilled, quick to execute. The most numerous kind of portraits then produced, miniatures enjoyed immense popularity in the Federal period. Intended as symbols of a shared emotional bond – love, friendship, filial piety, grief – they functioned as private keepsakes, worn about the body as bracelets, lockets, on a chain around the neck, or placed on the lids of snuff-boxes. As an art form the miniature underwent a final flowering before daguerreotypes gradually replaced them. Initially daguerreotypes, invented in 1839, copied miniatures, assuming their small size and oval or rectangular shape.

In 1804 Sully planned to go to Europe "for the purpose of improvement," but that year Lawrence Sully died in Richmond.[10] Thomas, then 21, altered his plans and undertook the support of Sarah Annis Sully (known as "Sally"), Lawrence's widow, and their three children. Two years later, on June 27, 1806, he married her. Now responsible for four lives in addition to his own, Sully, like most American painters at this time, found what work he could wherever he could but chiefly in Richmond, Norfolk, and Petersburg. In 1807 Washington Irving recalled seeing in front of a Richmond hostelry an eight-by-five foot signboard of a golden eagle. Sully had painted it for a generous $50.[11]

By 1806 Sully had completed about sixty miniatures, but he had higher aspirations. In 1802 after copying *Telemachus at the Court of Menelaus*, a historical painting by Angelica Kauffmann, he determined to attempt a different medium and larger format.[12] Though a few artists managed careers as miniaturists and portraitists, the two specialties drew on different materials and artistic skills. Miniaturists had to master a more exacting, largely irreversible technique. Sully's early training in miniatures taught him how to render the facial details in easel portraits in oils carefully, painstakingly. Skillful technique distinguishes even his first portraits; no less evident are insight and penetration into character.

*

In Richmond Sully painted Thomas Abthorpe Cooper, actor, manager, and now owner of New York's Park Theatre, one of several English players who became stars in America. Though Sully did not follow his parents onto the stage, he maintained his interest in the theater. Cooper was also a family friend, and impressed by Sully's skill he urged the young artist to come to New York, where he guaranteed him a thousand dollars' worth of business. Cooper put up the money in advance. It was an offer Sully could hardly refuse. He moved to New York in November 1806 and set up his studio in the theater lobby.[13] Through Cooper Sully gained introductions to leading actors and actresses. Numerous commissions followed. In addition to portraits he did sketches of theatrical scenes. Not surprisingly, Sully's income jumped in New York.[14]

To hone his artistic skills Sully consulted the city's leading portraitists, John Wesley Jarvis (1780–1840) and John Trumbull (1756–1843). No two figures could have been more dissimilar than the eccentric Jarvis – sometimes called "New York's first real Bohemian," a wag, raconteur, and, despite his hard drinking and notorious private life, the darling of society – and the patrician Trumbull. Jarvis freely communicated to Sully "whatever information he could."[15] To Trumbull Sully paid $100 – a large sum for a fledgling painter with a new family to support – for the privilege of watching him paint Sarah Sully's portrait.[16] The experience was beneficial; it was not determining. Sully admired Trumbull's skill in composition and design but recognized that in technique Trumbull was already of the past. His was a "hard" style, by which adjective Sully also characterized works by Benjamin West and John Singleton Copley. He wished to develop a style other than hard. His relationship with Trumbull, if never warm, continued cordial during Trumbull's lifetime. Sully was adaptable. To succeed, aspiring portrait painters had to learn early to deal with life's variety. Sully got along with the autocratic Trumbull no less well than with the *bon vivant* Jarvis.

On July 27, 1807, Sully left for Hartford and Boston. Trumbull had provided an introduction to his uncle-in-law, the wealthy Hartford merchant Daniel Wadsworth. In Hartford Sully painted several portraits. One depicts Wadsworth in a nonchalant pose, hair dishevelled; at the merchant's request, Sully also painted a self-portrait, the first of at least twenty. From Hartford the artist went to Boston. He had Thomas Cooper's letter of introduction to Andrew Allen, and through it the means to seek counsel from Gilbert Stuart, who at the nineteenth century's dawn commanded the greatest respect as a portraitist. Over the next three weeks Sully observed Stuart at work. "I had the privilege of standing by the artist's chair during the sitting," he recalled, with his usual generosity, "a situation I valued more, at that moment, than I shall ever again appreciate any station on earth."[17] Although Sully had already developed his characteristic style prior to studying with Stuart, he admired the older man's work immensely. Stuart asked Sully to paint the head of Isaac P. Davis, to whom Sully had also carried a letter of introduction. Impressed by the result, Stuart took a long look, then told Sully tersely: "Keep what you have got, and get as much more as you can."[18] It was the best advice Sully would ever receive.[19]

The artist returned to New York in the autumn of 1807. Commissions had dried up. Britain, at war with Napoleonic France, seized American vessels on the high seas. The Embargo Act, imposed by President Jefferson, closed American ports to foreign merchants. This controversial Act bolstered manufactures somewhat but paralyzed trade. Opportunities for portraits – luxury items sensitive to economic downturns – declined. Vanderlyn and Samuel Waldo were already in Europe; Trumbull and Rembrandt Peale soon joined them. With little competition Jarvis had come to the fore among New

York's portraitists. Lack of business led Sully to offer his services to Jarvis, who remarked, "It is a great shame that it should be so," but took him on as his assistant to help with backgrounds and draperies and employed him generously.[20] But Sully was 24, with a growing family, and he needed to establish himself on his own.

Philadelphia beckoned. Sully had grown to maturity in East Coast cities, but in Philadelphia, still America's cultural capital, he had not yet tested the waters. His friend, the merchant Benjamin Chew Wilcocks, invited him to visit and arranged commissions. Washington Irving dashed off letters of recommendation. "I hardly need introduce the bearer, Mr Sully, to you," wrote Irving on November 4, 1807, to Rebecca Gratz, "as I trust you recollect him perfectly."[21] Rebecca Gratz was a member of one of the city's leading Jewish merchant families. Disappointed in love, she never married, but instead devoted her life to raising her sister's children and to Jewish and other charities. A vastly respected and admired woman, she reputedly served as the model for the self-sacrificing Rebecca in Scott's *Ivanhoe*.[22] Her brother Hyman helped found the Pennsylvania Academy of the Fine Arts in 1805. Sully, Irving went on, "is a gentleman for whom I have a great regard, not merely on account of his professional abilities, which are highly promising, but for his amiable character and engaging manners."[23]

With such introductions in hand, Sully in December 1807 moved to Philadelphia. There he shared a studio with the miniaturist Benjamin Trott (1778–1843). Rebecca Gratz lost no time in recommending him. Among the numerous portraits of Jews listed in Sully's Register of Paintings occur the names of Michael Gratz, her father, and other family members and friends. He painted several of Rebecca, of which the most charming, deriving from Vermeer, depicts her in a picture-hat. He needed all the help he could get. "Embargo stopt S's first business at 50$," recalled William Dunlap.[24] On Rembrandt Peale's advice, Sully, in order to drum up work, reduced his asking price, offering to paint 30 portraits at $30 per head. The tactic succeeded. Modest prosperity followed. One of Sully's reduced-price commissions is a dazzling portrait of Samson Levy, lawyer, patron of the arts, and supporter of the new Pennsylvania Academy, on whose board sat his father Moses. Six months after Sully's arrival Rebecca Gratz wrote Irving that Sully "has at length got established here and is every day gaining friends and reputation. I think he has improved greatly since I saw him in New York," she told Irving, "and is generally preferred to Peale, who is a favorite here." She had no doubt that Sully would be "successful in his profession."[25] Sully remembered Irving, Rebecca Gratz, and those early commissions fondly: "The best sitters I had when I came to Philadelphia from New York were from Irving. They were t[w]o ladies, and they were of great service to me."[26]

Sully realized that to excel in his profession he needed further training. "Get as much more as you can," Stuart had urged, and by that he meant study in England. Many Americans felt they lived on the periphery of a civilization whose center was London. For decades after the Revolution English standards determined American taste. Study in London gave any professional reputation in America additional cachet, for in that artistic mecca an ambitious, energetic, and resourceful painter could hone skills that would enable him to scale the heights at home.

Sully first petitioned the Pennsylvania Academy for $3000 to support him while abroad he painted Old Masters for the collection. When that proposal did not meet approval, his Philadelphia patron, Benjamin Chew Wilcocks, arranged for him a subscription by friends and lovers of art.[27] Supporters, along with Wilcocks himself, included James McMurtrie and Charles Biddle, father of the Nicholas who later loomed large in Sully's life.[28] Sully in turn agreed to supply his backers with copies of Old Masters. Of the $1400 raised, Sully left $1000 for Sarah and his growing family and with the remaining $400 (and $200 from Trott for artists' supplies) embarked on June 10 for England. Two weeks earlier, perhaps wishing to avoid the risk of impressment into the British navy, he had become an American citizen.[29] For portraiture London was the place to be: such was Sully's opinion at the time, and such it remained.[30] Before he left, he began, at Benjamin Rush's suggestion, to keep the detailed journal from which we derive much of our knowledge of his time abroad and subsequently.

*

After landing in Liverpool on July 13, 1809, Sully enjoyed a brief but satisfying reunion with his 90-year-old grandmother in Birmingham. By July 18 he was in London, where he fell in with a young American painter, Charles Bird King. King, resident in the city since 1806, agreed to share digs and expenses. They lodged at Mrs Bridgen's at 2 Cleveland Street, Buckingham Place.[31] Two weeks before Sully arrived in Liverpool, Byron, on June 29, aged 21, had set off from Falmouth via Portugal and Spain for the Orient. He would be away from England for two years.

Like other aspiring American artists before him, Sully came armed with a recommendation for Benjamin West. His was written by Charles Willson Peale, once a West student. West had left Philadelphia in 1760 at the age of 22, initially to study in Italy. In 1763 he went to London, where he settled and had a golden career. One of the founders of the Royal Academy, West succeeded Reynolds as its president in 1792 and, except for 1805–6, served until his own death in 1820. He ranked as the most famous American expatriate since Benjamin Franklin, as well known across the Atlantic as in Britain. In 1809 he was 71.

West proffered a helping hand to three generations of American artists. Before the Revolution he had mentored Copley and Peale, in the late 1770s he befriended an initially reluctant Stuart, and in the 1780s and 1790s Trumbull and William Dunlap came under his wing. With the new century, a new generation – King, Rembrandt Peale, Washington Allston, Samuel F. B. Morse, and C. R. Leslie – learned under his tutelage. History painting was then considered the highest achievement in the realm of art, and West, its foremost advocate and practitioner, imbued his students with an elevated notion not only of its significance but of the profession of artist. All his students benefited from his gifts, his generosity, and his kindness.

West, somewhat to the consternation of his English friends, remained staunchly American. "West certainly has not an *English mind*," commented Farington. In 1804 West told the diarist "that were He 10 years younger *He wd. go to America.*"[32] In 1805 the directors of the Pennsylvania Academy elected him its first honorary member, and from 1806 on West lent works to the Academy, where Sully would have seen them. Later, Robert Fulton brought back with him to America two of West's major paintings, *Lear in the Storm* and *Ophelia and Laertes*.[33]

Under West's watchful eye Sully worked to improve his art. Although West had a reputation as a portraitist, by 1810 he had largely abandoned portraits for history painting.[34] To ascertain the level of Sully's skills he asked him to paint a portrait. Sully painted King. After looking at it, West judged his drawing and modeling weak; to improve Sully's understanding of human bone structure he advised him to study anatomy and osteology by taking Sir Anthony Carlisle's lectures at the Royal Academy, which Sully dutifully did.[35]

Like John Vanderlyn and Rembrandt Peale, Sully had thought to further his studies in Paris. He had promised his Philadelphia patrons copies of Old Masters, and Napoleon's Louvre had them in abundance. But West dissuaded him. In 1802, during the Peace of Amiens, that shaky truce of 15 months between England and France, West had dashed over to Paris. The unsurpassed collection of Old Masters assembled by Napoleon enraptured him. But, he told Sully, for portraiture London was the place. He generously allowed Sully to copy Old Masters from his own collection. In the same breath he urged him "to abandon *copying*; and to begin manufacturing for himself."[36] Too busy with his huge historical canvases to spend much time with the young American, West recommended that he seek guidance in portraiture from others, especially Thomas Lawrence.

"I need not say how much benefit I reaped from the services of this good man," Sully recalled of his time with West; "he treated me as if I had been his son."[37] Meaningful words from a man who does not appear to have been close to (and rarely mentioned) his own father. Sully does not say much about West's artistic influence on him, and it may have been minimal. As with Copley, he found West's drawing too "hard." But West's counsel and support gave Sully confidence. The younger man's progress pleased West. "I find him every way worthy and promising," he wrote a Philadelphia friend in November 1809.[38] The relationship remained cordial to the end. "It affords me daily pleasure," West wrote Sully in March 1819, the year before he died, "in hearing your name and Paintings, highly mentioned by all those from that Country."[39]

With West's support Sully made haste to meet the English luminaries that comprised the tight little London art world: Lawrence foremost, but also William Beechey, John Hoppner, Martin Archer Shee – all of whom, he noted circumspectly, "received me with profession of kindness."[40] He does not mention Copley, who was ill and whose star was declining.[41] He missed

Raeburn, Lawrence's great rival, who after testing the waters in London in 1810 decided his chances for success were not strong enough and returned home to Edinburgh.

While abroad Sully also met Thomas Phillips and Richard Westall, both of whom would paint Byron in 1813. Sully (we know from Leslie's *Memoirs*) visited Westall at his home; with Phillips, he gained at least a nodding acquaintance. Not mentioned is David Wilkie. Even younger than Sully and in London since 1805, Wilkie later became one of Sully's closest Scottish friends. Though his genre scenes made him famous, Wilkie also achieved renown as a portraitist. Only the gouty, temperamental Hoppner, who was to die in January 1810, disappointed Sully. On being asked by the American what sort of yellow he used in flesh tones Hoppner replied testily, "There is no yellow in flesh, sir."[42]

Sully revelled in the artistic treasures on display in London. Reynolds, Gainsborough, Fuseli, Stubbs, West, and Lawrence had after election to the Royal Academy given examples of their best work, which were displayed in the Council Chamber. Sully also admired the paintings at the Guildhall.[43] The English aristocracy kept many prized art works in their London town houses. John Hare Powel, secretary to the United States legation in London, took Sully to see Sir Francis Baring's collection of Old Masters, and Lawrence arranged for Sully to view the Old Master paintings of John James Angerstein, prominent financier, a founder of Lloyd's – and one of Lawrence's main patrons. Angerstein's collection at his house at 100 Pall Mall became in 1824, with Sir George Beaumont's, the core of London's National Gallery. At Angerstein's Hogarth's *Marriage à la Mode* sequence amazed Sully. "Gerontius by Vandyke" he regarded as unsurpassed. Lawrence also showed him his own fine collection, of drawings especially, which Coleridge and Wordsworth had admired a few months before, in March 1809.[44] Sully responded favorably to works by Owen and Gainsborough, West and Shee; less favorably to Opie, Copley, and Beechey.[45]

In addition to Carlisle's often lively lectures on anatomy, Sully, probably at Lawrence's suggestion, also attended those by Henry Fuseli on the Antique School. Fuseli's approach to anatomical instruction involved drawing casts of classical sculpture. Fuseli's lectures have survived, though only a few had been published when Sully arrived in London. From Fuseli Sully would have learned that in portraiture "the deeper nobler aim is the personification of character."[46] Although Sully shied away from Fuseli's dramatic, confrontational portraiture, he responded to its emotional power. An important concept in Fuseli's system, Steven Bronson has argued, was the need to capture in paint the "pregnant moment," a moment which "combines the traces of the past, the energy of the present, and a glimpse of the future."[47] The idea of the "pregnant moment" helped shaped Sully's Grand Manner portraits, as we shall see. Although Reynolds and Lawrence exerted a lifelong hold upon Sully, Fuseli's Romantic aesthetic offered him an alternative to Reynolds's neoclassical vision.[48] Sully also responded strongly to Fuseli's eclecticism and to his beliefs about physiognomy, subjects examined in later chapters. Late in life Sully recalled Fuseli's belief that "the arts are travelling westward" and that men of Sully's generation would "live to see the day when American art will attain the highest round in the ladder."[49]

England exerted well into the 1830s a strong artistic influence in the United States. Yet the interaction went both ways. For a good part of the last three centuries the British portrait tradition has been an Anglo-American affair. For instance, accomplished American artists painted several of the best-known portraits of the major English Romantic poets. The first of Washington Allston's two depictions of Coleridge is for Richard Holmes "probably the finest portrait from life that Allston ever executed."[50] Wordsworth told a friend he found Henry Inman's portrait of him "the best likeness of them all." Mary Wordsworth concurred.[51] In addition to these images, Sully and William Edward West rendered Byron.

*

All his life Sully debated within himself the respective merits of Reynolds and Lawrence. He admired Reynolds, who had died in 1792, for his skill and for the aesthetic precepts he gleaned from his *Discourses*. These seminal lectures, a massive and insightful reinterpretation of art history, established the credentials of British art. Reynolds's precepts served as a gospel for many contemporary artists during the eighteenth century's last decades and well into the nineteenth century. The *Discourses* were so much in the air, observes Frances Blanshard, "that even an artist or critic who had not read them could not escape their pervading power."[52] Not all artists responded positively, but Sully was one who did. But Reynolds's hold upon Sully preceded London and went beyond theory. The English artist deemed a warm palette essential to Grand Manner portraiture, and Sully's soft browns, ambers, and greens in his 1808 portrait of *Samson Levy* already reflected this counsel.[53] In London, where Sully found abundant works by the master to study, he experienced Reynolds's art first hand. Impressed, he chose to copy for one of his Philadelphia patrons a Reynolds *Holy Family* owned by West.

Then there was Lawrence. He had burst upon the scene in 1790 with a pair of spectacular full-length portraits, *Elizabeth Farren* and *Queen Charlotte*. The aged Reynolds, hardly able to hold brush in hand, thought him the artist who would accomplish "all that I have failed to achieve."[54] Enjoying success immediate and overwhelming, Lawrence went on to dominate British portraiture for the next forty years. Edward Miles, a painter of miniatures in Philadelphia and a friend of Lawrence's, had given Sully a letter of introduction to Lawrence. He "received me very warmly," wrote Sully, shortly after arriving in London. Yet he gauged the master's work shrewdly. "Lawrence's too much loaded with paint," he noted, "and the red and yellow overpowering."[55] Though "English taste" was decidedly "in favour of strong effects, & brilliant colouring," Lawrence's bravura style left Sully uneasy.[56] Yet the reds and yellows, however "overpowering," could not have offended overly. John Neagle, later Sully's son-in-law, recorded that

Sully copied "color samples from Sir Thomas Lawrence's palette."[57] Actually, Lawrence by his example and precepts influenced Sully more than anyone else. And why not? As a portraitist Lawrence, with Hoppner's death in January 1810, had no major rivals in London. Lawrence represented success.

During his return trip to London in 1838 Sully revisited Sir Francis Baring's collection. Again he expressed his admiration for Reynolds, again he criticized Lawrence. This time it was for more than an overbright palette.

> On examination I found much to admire in Lawrence as he appeared at Barings[:] fine flowing outline – force and richness – but in his flesh he is rather often harsh, either falling into the brick dust hue, or the charcoal. Reynolds on the contrary whether his tone be warm or cold, is always true to nature, but his breadth is very [*often* partly crossed out] apt to have the fault of being vague or cold. Lawrence defines better, but I cannot like the figures and heads being larger than life. Reynolds made them exact, and I find it better in every respect.[58]

The dignified and enlightened looks of Reynolds's sitters pleased Sully and led others to compare his work to that of the English master. One of Sully's former students, the Charleston portrait painter James De Veaux, in comparing him to Allston, both native sons, exclaimed "SULLY is our REYNOLDS, and ALLSTON our wonder."[59]

Yet in 1809–10 it was Lawrence, even more than Reynolds, who left upon Sully's art the deepest imprint. "It was a predictable but, nevertheless, wise choice," writes William Gerdts. "Lawrence continued the tradition of Grand Manner portraiture in England, unbroken from the time of Van Dyck and, arguably, from that of Holbein."[60] In revisiting Lawrence's work in 1838, Sully also commended the English painter (who had died in 1830) for his "dignity, elegance and taste." His

> may be a little too much of conventional taste, bordering on theatrical strut; but there is always vice in the excess of excellence. Van Dyke's simple dignity is allied to insipidity, Reynolds' brea[d]th and boldness degenerates often into a mysterious boldness – I feel the beauties and excellent qualities of all these great men, but if I were forced to choose between Lawrence and Reynolds, I should prefer Lawrence.[61]

Sully got along well with the man. If occasionally questioning Lawrence's opinions and artistic practice, he valued his personal integrity and the image of the artist he projected. "Lawrence was one of the most finished gentlemen I ever met . . . He made a good deal of money, but was too generous to grow rich, for if a beggar asked him for five pounds he would give him fifty."[62] He was kind as well as generous. Though "extravagant in purchasing pictures & scarce prints," Lawrence, said Sully, "was not a gambler, lived in style, was a religious man & told anecdotes of going & reading [sermons] to an old sick servant &c."[63]

Though never Lawrence's disciple or slavish imitator, Sully took heart in finding in Lawrence's art affinities with his own and a confirmation of his practice. On occasion he drew directly upon Lawrence. He copied portraits by Lawrence of Robert Gilmor and John Hare Powel, and he modeled several compositions upon works by Lawrence. In *Mrs Katherine Matthews* (1813) he translated Lawrence's rather sensual image of *Elizabeth Farren* into a suitably genteel likeness of a Philadelphia lady; in *Mrs Hughes* (1831) he fashioned a three-quarter-length portrait after Lawrence's *Julia, Lady Peel*.[64]

Upon returning to America Sully kept up with Lawrence's work through engravings. Though in his writings he rarely mentioned the English painter, his *Hints to Young Painters* included Lawrence's long letter of 1820 to Robert Gilmor, the Baltimore collector and a mutual friend, in which Lawrence told Gilmor how to care for a fine painting, how to hang it, how to enjoy it.[65] For Sully, endorsement by Lawrence constituted the final word. Sully's best portraits have the unusual pose, the vibrant palette, the psychological insight, the flair, the drama, the romanticism of Lawrence. The loosely brushed style, coloristic and idealizing, even the careful craftsmanship of Sully's best work, draws upon the English master. His control of his medium in his mature art is as evident as it is in Lawrence.[66]

*

For most Americans Lawrence set the standard for portraiture. But not for James Fenimore Cooper. At New York's Academy of the Fine Arts he had seen on display in 1823 Lawrence's full-length *Benjamin West*. Cooper was impressed, but when he came upon Sully's *Jefferson* at West Point shortly afterwards he was overwhelmed. "With respect to its merit as a painting, to me it seemed more easy and natural by far than Lawrence's West, though the colouring might not, possibly, be so splendid."[67] Setting the American against the English artist, Cooper awarded the palm to the American.

Most painters learn by studying other painters and constantly rethinking what they see. Sully is no exception. He had no choice. Formal education in art did not then exist in America. Ever practical, Sully learned from many artists; no single one ever satisfied him fully. "That artist who can unite in himself the excellencies of the various great painters," Reynolds wrote in his sixth *Discourse*, "will approach nearer to perfection than any one of his masters."[68] Sully, in self-imposed discipline, took Reynolds's admonition to heart. "Great painters," he wrote in 1838, in a discussion of Horace Vernet, a French history painter he admired, "belong to no *school*."[69] This was Sully's belief all along. Aware of the history of art and often echoing in his own work earlier artists, he became over time a very allusive painter. Unceasing curiosity and a willingness to try out the new helped raise his art above that of his contemporaries. Ever learning from those whose work he valued, he yet became no man's disciple.

In youth Sully had received instruction from Fraser and Belzons, Benbridge a little, more from brother Lawrence. Later, Jarvis and Trumbull, then Stuart, had a hand in shaping him. Though as praising of Stuart as he is silent about Trumbull, Sully learned from both. In England it was chiefly Reynolds and Fuseli and, it seems, often and always Lawrence. Sully also learned from conversations with other artists, from reading books about art, from intense study of work by painters who interested him and whom he respected, and most of all from the challenges incurred over a lifetime's hard work painting over two thousand portraits.

He never stopped learning. If in youth Sully sought out the talented of his day, in maturity he indulged in incessant experimentation and speculation. He was interested in both the process of painting and the theory, and his scrapbooks and sketchbooks indicate he studied Old as well as new Masters. Always interested in expanding the range of his skills, he constantly made experiments in the preparation of color and canvas. It is often difficult, at this distance, to say among contemporaries who owed what to whom, but it is certain Sully owed much to many. Journal entries overflow with comments about the painters he had met and the methods they used. His talent for assimilation early manifest, he made himself into a self-teaching eclectic. He possessed an insatiable desire to master the technical aspects of his work, to experiment, to improve his skills in portraiture, to become a true and possibly a great artist.

By spring 1810 Sully sensed he could no longer neglect wife and family. West, Copley, and Leslie did not go back to America; Stuart stayed away nearly two decades; but Sully, like Dunlap and Trumbull before him, knew he would return. Initially he had thought of three years abroad. What he could not know then was how short – and how harried – his time in London would be. Habitually industrious, he never worked harder than in his eight months abroad. If he did few portraits of his own in London, he soaked in the art scene and fulfilled his obligations to his patrons. On March 10, 1810, he sailed for New York and by April 16 was back in Philadelphia. Hoping to emulate Lawrence's success in London, he set out to make his mark in his adopted city. In a thorough but less spectacular way he succeeded.

Assessing his London experience upon his return, Sully wondered how far he had progressed in his knowledge of portrait-painting.[70] Copies for his patrons as well as attendance at Royal Academy lectures had siphoned off time from his own work. Perhaps he had not learned all he might have in Carlisle's anatomy course. Bone structure and anatomy were less important to him than handling pigment, and in after years his sense of human proportions was not always perfect. Yet he had accomplished much: he had met, listened to, and talked with almost all the major artists then active; he had experienced the pullulating life of the great metropolis; above all, he had seen – and responded to – an immensity of paintings from all eras. He now knew, from the evidence of his own eyes, the best that had been done in portraiture. If Sully estimated his improvement negligible, Philadelphians disagreed. Commissions flowed in. In Philadelphia, culturally still America's richest city, he found himself its most sought-after portrait painter.

*

Philadelphia from 1750 to 1800 was the wealthiest, most cosmopolitan, and most centrally located American city. With nearly 70,000 inhabitants in 1800, it was also the largest. It had long cherished Benjamin Franklin's spectacular career; after Franklin's death in 1791 Benjamin West upheld the city's prestige internationally. Philadelphia was the center of the American Enlightenment and of American culture but also, from 1790 to 1800, the nation's political capital. Portrait painters settled in to capture the luminaries. Gilbert Stuart, who had returned to America hoping to portray Washington, worked in Philadelphia from 1794 until 1805.

The city greeted the new century with a burst of energy, both economic and cultural. Long the richest trading center on the Continent, it remained America's financial center until the mid-1830s. It seemed likely to retain its role as the "Athens of America." English-born Benjamin Latrobe, the country's first professionally trained architect, created in Philadelphia America's earliest fully conceived neoclassical buildings; native son William Rush, arguably the country's finest professional sculptor, carved wooden ships' figureheads and other allegorical subjects. The continued presence of the multi-talented Charles Willson Peale, along with his gifted siblings and progeny, reminded Philadelphians of their city's long and illustrious cultural history. In science and medicine the achievements of David Rittenhouse and Benjamin Rush were impressive. In fact science and technology were to Philadelphia what theology and literature were to Boston. Even though the transfer of the capital to the District of Columbia in 1800 lessened Philadelphia's attractiveness for portraitists, the city's prospects remained sound.

American cities had since colonial days engaged in ongoing rivalries. After 1800 New York was Philadelphia's chief competitor. With its magnificent natural harbor, New York in the new century underwent rapid growth. The opening of the Erie Canal in 1825 clinched its position as the nation's commercial center. Hindsight makes New York's victory inevitable, but in 1810, the year Sully returned from London, the winner was by no means certain. Yet as the Federal period drew to a close about 1815, a change was felt in Philadelphia. As fast as Philadelphia grew, New York grew faster. Imperceptibly, the Golden Age of Franklin yielded to the Silver Age of Girard and Biddle. Though Philadelphia retained its artistic and cultural prestige, it no longer seemed destined to become the nation's top city.

Philadelphia fostered commercial and social links with the Southern states. Prominent Philadelphia families like the Biddles often went south for brides. Historians even speak of Philadelphia, the first big city above the Mason–Dixon line, "as the high tide of the South."[71] Many Philadelphians supported the continued presence of slavery. When the Civil War came, however, Philadelphia sided with the Union, though at first reluctantly.[72]

The publishing hub of the former colonies, Philadelphia remained a national center for printing and bookmaking. *The Port Folio*, founded in the city in 1801 and capably edited by Joseph Dennie until his death in 1811, was Federal America's leading forum of political and literary opinion. The interest in graphic arts was equally lively. In 1805 art patrons founded the Pennsylvania Academy of the Fine Arts. With casts chosen and sent from Paris by young Nicholas Biddle, Benjamin West's loan of major paintings, and plans for a building taking shape (it opened in 1807), the Academy soon exerted a major influence on the city's cultural life. It also provided opportunities for patronage, a training ground for students, a forum for the exchange of ideas, and a venue for exhibitions.[73] Artists could admire on its premises three late masterpieces by West: the "improved" second version of *Christ Healing the Sick* (1815), *Christ Rejected* (1814), and *Death on the Pale Horse* (1817). The presence in the city of prominent artists like the Peales and Sully reinforced the Academy's leadership role.

*

Sully had spent his youth in Charleston, Richmond, Norfolk, and Petersburg. Philadelphia, filled with pretty red brick houses, was half-southern in appearance. Compared to bustling Manhattan, its building style was plainer, its grid street plan more regular. Its quietly genteel atmosphere – in part reflecting its Quaker origins – would have appealed to Sully. Given his temperament and talent, he must have realized that the match between him and his adopted city was good. Commissions rolled in, his earnings soared. Even in 1810, partly spent in England, he took in $3610. For each of the next seven years his income topped $4000. For ten years he rarely left the city.

Aged 27 in 1810, Sully achieved eminence in the city's art world almost immediately. Joining most professional arts organizations, he served on the Pennsylvania Academy's board of directors and became a founder of the Society of Artists and an honorary member of the Franklin Institute.[74] He was a founding member of the United Bowmen of Philadelphia, the first (and still existing) archery organization in the country. His reputation soon became national. Sully developed excellent relationships with virtually every notable painter in America including Trumbull, Morse, Asher B. Durand, Matthew Harris Jouett, Dunlap, Samuel Waldo, G. P. A. Healy, John James Audubon, and Thomas Doughty. In Philadelphia Rembrandt Peale quickly became his closest friend and professional colleague, and John Neagle, by marrying a daughter of Lawrence Sully, became his de facto son-in-law. Washington Allston in an 1841 letter indicates the high esteem in which he and others held the artist: "Remember me to Sully; he is a man I have great regard for."[75]

Sully entered enthusiastically into a broad spectrum of Philadelphia cultural life. He attended, at least occasionally, the Wistar Parties. Peculiar to Philadelphia, they were founded in 1818 as a memorial to Dr Caspar Wistar, a distinguished physician at whose home intellectually inclined Philadelphians, men and women alike, often accompanied by notable visitors, had met in the twenty years preceding Wistar's death. After 1818 the meetings continued on Saturday evenings at members' houses where participants engaged in lively, often probing, discussions about literature, science, philosophy, and the arts. The only topics forbidden were politics and religion.[76] Sully, like Gainsborough, but unlike Reynolds, was a gifted amateur musician who sang and played both the piano and the flute and who delighted to participate in and attend musical performances. In 1820 he helped organize the Musical Fund Society of Philadelphia, upon which the city's musical life centered until the Civil War and in whose orchestra he played the flute.[77] His Journal mentions the luxury of treating himself to a "second flute." Audubon, writing from Edinburgh in 1829, regretted he could not hear the voices of Sully's children "and your sweet flute."[78]

Sully had his work rooms, or studio, in Charles Willson Peale's former quarters in Philosophical Hall at 5th St, virtually adjoining the old City Hall, today Independence Hall.[79] He rented the rooms in 1812 from the American Philosophical Society for five years at $300 per annum and in 1817 renewed the lease. Here meetings of the Sketch Club were held. In April 1818 the Society agreed to rent Sully the two north rooms, where, after 1819, in partnership with James Earle, he maintained "a gallery of pictures to which the public was admitted at a charge of 25 cents."[80] The American Philosophical Society, the leading intellectual organization in the fledgling United States, now occupies the premises. Jefferson had been a past president. John Vaughan, who lived on the premises until his death in 1841 and held the offices of treasurer and librarian, was Sully's good friend and fellow Unitarian as well as cicerone to all the distinguished visitors who came to the city.[81]

The Sullys lived at various addresses in Philadelphia. For most of the period before 1828 they lodged at 530 Spruce Street, an attractive red brick Federal townhouse three stories high and three windows across. A wall plaque identifies the building as Sully's only surviving residence. In October 1828 he rented 11 South 5th Street, near the corner of Chestnut and 5th, where Ramstead St goes off, a stone's throw from Independence Hall. The house was owned by Stephen Girard, the city's leading financier who, at Sully's request, built for him a "painting room" (the word "studio" did not replace work room or "painting room" until the 1850s) behind and attached to the main dwelling. Sully's residence lay smack in the city's heart. Urban energy swirled around him. He remained at Chestnut and 5th until his death more than forty years later.

Compact physically as well as close-knit socially, Philadelphia when Sully settled in it hardly extended past 9th Street. Strolling around Old Philadelphia today we still experience that compactness. Sully, who liked to walk, could reach most parts of the city within twenty minutes. A few blocks east of his residence, the city's harbor fronting the Delaware teemed with vessels from as near as Bordentown, upriver on the Delaware, and as far as Canton. Gazing upon the departing sails, he could waft himself in imagination to the ends of the earth. A few blocks west of his home stood (after 1812) the Pennsylvania Academy at 10th and Chestnut. On the west side of Broad virtually rural countryside stretched before him. If Philadelphia left its imprint on Sully, he – the portraitist most commonly identified with the city's Silver Age – left his on Philadelphia. Personages active in Federal and Jacksonian Philadelphia come alive for us in Sully's portraits.

Philadelphia today is virtually a living museum of three hundred years of American life, politics, and culture. City organizations hold the bulk of Sully's *oeuvre*. Although the Philadelphia Museum of Art has (and displays) a number of its Sully portraits, the Pennsylvania Academy of the Fine Arts has the largest collection, well over forty works, of which a few are usually are on display. Most of the city's eighty-odd local museums, historic houses, and private clubs own Sullys. The Pennsylvania Hospital, which has West's *Christ Healing the Sick*, also displays Sully's splendid full-lengths of *Samuel Coates* and *Benjamin Rush*.[82] Philosophical Hall has among its Sullys a half-length portrait of the aged Jefferson and one of John Vaughan. The Library Company on Locust has his portrait of its longtime librarian Zachariah Poulsen. The Historical Society of Pennsylvania next door has transferred its 43 Sullys to the Atwater Kent Museum for eventual display. Among the Rosenbach Museum's four Sullys is his splendid portrait of Rebecca Gratz, his early patron. At the top of the grand entrance stairs of the Union League Club on Broad Street Sully's huge *Washington at the Battle of Trenton* inspires heroic thoughts.

To a portraitist of Sully's talent and ambition Federal Philadelphia offered excellent opportunities. In 1807, when he first arrived in Philadelphia, the Peales chiefly occupied the field, but more as presences than as active portraitists. Charles Willson, notable Philadelphian and nationally known leading citizen, hovered formidably over the city's cultural scene. Patriarch, polymath, naturalist, founder of museums, inventor and entrepreneur, and a portraitist of distinction, he devoted after 1810 more of his enormous energy to improving Belfield, his country estate, than to portraiture. Several among his 17 children became artists. His son Rembrandt, immensely capable but lacking his father's drive, steadiness, and focus, is the best known.

*

Portraiture dominated American art in Peale's lifetime (he died in 1827) and for several decades afterwards. Along with the rise of biography and autobiography, both essentially eighteenth-century developments, portraiture in the early Republic became a preferred technique for self-expression. In 1805 Aaron Burr advised John Vanderlyn, successful in Paris as a history painter, that "if you are to spend some years in portrait painting, this is the best country for here is the rage for portraits."[83] Visitors from abroad deemed America's rage for portraits an expression of obnoxious national characteristics, notably flagrant vanity, and self-confidence.[84] This obsession, whatever it may say about national character, had one undeniable benefit: it registers upon the consciousness of later generations images of those who shaped a historical epoch. In hindsight we've come to esteem certain artists as prime portraitists of their eras: Holbein, for Henry VIII's England; Tintoretto, for the patricians of cinquecento Venice; Velázquez, for the court of Philip IV; Egon Schiele and Gustav Klimt, for Jugendstil Vienna;

David Hockney, for 1960s California – and for Federal Philadelphia, Thomas Sully.[85]

Portraiture had its detractors. Benjamin Robert Haydon, the eccentric English history painter, contemptuously dismissed the lowly portrait, and the German critic Lessing wished to banish it from art's domain.[86] Few first-rate American painters alive in 1800 endorsed such radical stances, yet even eminent artists like West, Charles Willson Peale, and Trumbull had reservations about the portrait-mania. For Trumbull, it was (he wrote Thomas Jefferson) a frivolous endeavor, "little useful to Society, and unworthy of a man who has talents for more serious pursuits."[87] Americans who trained in Europe imbibed lofty artistic ideals from the masters of history painting and from seeing examples of Grand Manner portraiture, but upon returning home they found scant use for those ideals. Society in Federal America rarely held portraitists in high esteem, regarding portraits less as likenesses than as elements in a decorative scheme, utilitarian rather than aesthetic. Most established American portraitists had no illusions about their modest status. To survive, aspiring artists had to conform to market conditions: inevitably, they jettisoned idealism and took to the "business" of portrait-making.

Portraiture's lowly status in America galled John Neal. The portrait-painter has his subjects determined for him, makes appointments that are casually broken, and "is obliged to preserve the likeness, and make a pleasant picture nevertheless," all this in a trade "always overcrowded with adventurers, and cheap workmen."[88] Henry Inman, despite success in New York, found portraiture "a precarious and sometimes humiliating occupation."[89] Even Gilbert Stuart, who worked almost exclusively as a portraitist, deplored the number of others who did as he did and may have nursed a closet wish to become a history painter.[90] Not everyone decried portraiture. The self-taught Chester Harding, who as a youth "thought sign painting the highest branch of painting in the world," aspired to success in portraiture, nothing more.[91]

Commemorative volumes of portraits of the illustrious go back to 1546, when Paolo Giovio published a collection of them with biographies of the sitters.[92] The collection is housed in the Museo Gioviano on Lake Como. The first publication of this kind in America, Joseph Delaplaine's *Delaplaine's Repository of the Lives and Portraits of Distinguished American Characters* (3 vols, Philadelphia, 1815–18) announces the encyclopedic spirit of the century. As the War of Independence receded into the past, interest in the Founding Fathers, particularly in signers of the Declaration of Independence, grew markedly. John Sanderson's illustrated *Biographies of the Signers of the Declaration of Independence* (9 vols, Philadelphia, 1820–27) helped satisfy this curiosity. The title pages of the four volumes of *The National Portrait Gallery of Distinguished Americans* (1834, 1835, 1837, 1839), edited by James Barton Longacre of New York and James Herring of Philadelphia, quoted Byron's *Childe Harold*:

There are deeds which should not pass away
And names that must not wither though the earth
Forgets her empires with a just decay,
The enslavers and the enslaved, their death and birth.[93]

Byron's lines epitomized the editors' aims. Engraved portraits accompanied by laudatory biographical essays of the nation's leading figures constituted a pictorial repository suggestive of its greatness. Longacre and Herring's publication was intended to accompany a permanent collection of portraits at the American Academy of Fine Arts in New York. That did not happen, but numerous other collections of engraved portraits, later of photographs, accompanied by biographies, appeared across the land. Their popularity indicates that citizens identified portraits with the growing American republic – and that they thought portraiture important.[94]

Despite this interest, a national repository of American paintings and sculptures of its great was slow to come about. The idea for such a repository went back almost two centuries. One of its earliest proponents, Charles Willson Peale, hoped to have his collection, begun in 1783 and designed to promote American identity, form the nucleus of a national portrait museum. He would have had a long wait. Washington's National Portrait Gallery may today look like a venerable institution since the building that houses it (the Old Patent Office) was built in 1836. But Congress did not establish the Gallery until 1962, and its first exhibition dates only from 1968.

*

Like Lawrence in England, Sully painted the great and well known of his day. He early gained the patronage of Philadelphia's social, economic, intellectual, and political élite, its movers and shakers. Working up and down the Eastern seaboard from Charleston to Boston as well as in Philadelphia, he captured most leading personages active in the decades from 1810 to 1840. The names of his sitters read like a *Who's Who* of American life. On February 7, 1831, prominent Bostonian William H. Eliot wrote to Harvard classmate Jared Sparks, telling his friend that he could not do a greater favor to him and his wife "than sitting for your portrait to Sully, now decidedly the first portrait painter in the country. As a production of his pencil it will have great value to me, but as a souvenir of its subject I will not attempt to say how dear it will be to us both."[95]

Sully's roster of sitters includes leading physicians, among them Philadelphia's Benjamin Rush (the portrait executed shortly after his death), along with Rush's distinguished former student, New York's David Hosack; a bevy of naval heroes, not least Stephen Decatur; Charles Carroll of Carrolton, the distinguished revolutionary leader and (at the time of Sully's portrait) the last surviving signer of the Declaration of Independence; every president but one from John Adams (term of office, 1796–1800) to James Polk (1844–48), including Jefferson, Madison, Monroe, John Quincy

Adams, Jackson, Harrison, and Tyler (Van Buren the odd man out; Washington from portraits by others, Lincoln later from photographs); Philadelphia Biddles and Hopkinsons, Baltimore Gilmors and Pattersons; Washington Irving, maybe Edgar Allan Poe (unlocated), Gouverneur Morris, Robert Morris, General Winfield Scott, Lydia Sigourney, Ralph Waldo Emerson, Lafayette (during his triumphant American tour in 1824), the English actor Charles Kemble, and (13 times!) Kemble's talented daughter Fanny. This list of the great and near great who sat for him could easily be extended.

No one on the scene in 1810 matched Sully in energy and sheer competence. The obvious successor to Peale and Stuart in the line of Philadelphia "First Portraitists," Sully consolidated and carried on in portraiture what Gerdts has called "the" Philadelphia style.[96] Characterized by "loose brushwork, brilliant coloring, and romantic backgrounds filled with swirling clouds and billowing drapery," the Philadelphia style was a variant of European and especially British Grand Manner portraiture.[97] Gainsborough and after him Lawrence practiced for forty years earlier versions of this style. The *sine qua non* of English portrait painting was that those portrayed look like ladies and gentlemen. Philadelphia fashions aped London fashions, and except during the Revolution the city retained close ties with London. London's criteria became Philadelphia's. Gilbert Stuart, 11 years a resident, gave the Philadelphia style American roots. In 1809 Sully, upon first seeing Gainsborough's work at the Royal Academy, quickly perceived "some resemblance" in it to "Stuart's manner, only that Stuart is firmer in his handling." Gainsborough's skin tones "at a distance . . . appeared to me the most natural flesh in the room."[98]

Commissioned portraits constitute Sully's major, but by no means his only, activity. In other genres he demonstrated a range rarely acknowledged and less explored. Drawn to history painting as well as to portraiture, Sully was yet a realist: in America few history painters earned a decent living. If portraits did for him, they did not preempt his painting other subjects. Work drove Sully, challenged him, steadied him. No job for which a client would pay was beneath the dignity of this working artist. Sully copied or retouched or added to the works of other artists, he hand-colored engravings, he painted at least one tavern sign. In 1836 Sully sketched a seated Liberty for newly minted coins. Nineteenth-century banknotes reproduce his painting of Dr Alfred L. Elwyn. Today's 20-dollar bill, including the revised version of 2003, uses one of Sully's portraits of Andrew Jackson. He did a coat of arms for the State of Georgia and another for Philadelphia, abstract subjects, Indian subjects, numerous portraits of George Washington after other artists, illustrations for *Robinson Crusoe* and Cooper's *The Pilot*, and *Dancing Doll*, occasionally on display at the Pennsylvania Academy, an oil on paper with cloth flowers and sequins made up for a friend's young daughter. In 1826, the year he began *Byron*, he added hands to a portrait attributed to Sir Peter Lely.[99] Also that year, along with Morse, Vanderlyn, and Doughty he painted historical murals on canvas, including a *Mother and Child* (after Allston) and a copy of C. Lawrence's *Passage of the Delaware* for cabins in a steamboat, the *Albany*, commissioned by the enterprising Colonel Stevens, and then under construction in Philadelphia.[100] Working in watercolor as well as oil, he did landscapes of scenes in Pennsylvania, New Jersey, and New York, including "two moonlight studies" and, inevitably, Niagara; several historical, religious, and mythological paintings; and, later in his career, numerous "fancy pictures," capriccios, studies of children, and idealized women that anticipate the *fin de siècle* aesthetization of Woman in Dewing, Alexander, and Frieseke. The range of historical, biblical, literary, and everyday subjects considered by Sully is astonishing. They include Joan of Arc, Ophelia, Alexander the Great, Hagar and the angel, "a mother bathing her infant," "an argument at the brook" – and for many of them Sully speculated on a possible composition.[101] Hundreds of ink-and-wash drawings, many copied from prints – one is of David's *Napoleon Crossing the Alps* – fill his sketchbooks. All these works, generally ignored by scholars, can – even more than the portraits – be revealing of Sully's range, interests, tastes, and artistic evolution.

Sully placed in his account book a valuation on every painting he did. It indicates what he thought it was worth, not necessarily what he received for it. Even a successful portrait painter could not depend on being paid. Reynolds had a roomful of unsold portraits that sitters had not liked or did not wish to pay for.[102] Sully's situation was almost certainly comparable. Whereas in England (and on the Continent from 1818 to 1820) Lawrence moved from triumph to triumph, Sully in the New World, like painters in America generally, had to content himself with a less worldly and more financially modest success. Despite the rage for portraits, portrait painting in America did not have the cachet – or remuneration – it had in England. The bachelor Lawrence went through money like a tornado, but the frugal Sully, the mainstay of a large family, struggled to make ends meet. Despite his talent, he never achieved Lawrence's fees. No painter in America did; none even came close. Lawrence in 1806 charged for a bust-sized portrait 50 guineas; in 1810, 100 guineas; after 1820, 200 guineas.[103] Sully in the 1820s received for a bust $75 or $100.[104]

There is nothing provincial about Sully's long career. By the late 1820s, with Stuart and Peale gone, his work gained greater recognition than ever. He had known Stuart in his prime, and in decades to come he watched the passing of the three generations of Americans who had studied under West. He witnessed the rise in the 1830s of the Hudson River School of landscape painters. In the 1870s Winslow Homer, Frank Duveneck, and Thomas Eakins inaugurated a new realism in painting. When Sully died in 1872, in his ninetieth year, he was the last survivor of West's students. For several of the intervening decades he had been America's – and probably the English-speaking world's – master of the portrait.

*

A portrait is a luxury, and luxuries, in adverse economic conditions, tend to be sacrificed. The Embargo of 1807 (which lasted until 1809), the folding of the First Bank of the United States in 1811, and the War of 1812 (which did not end until early 1815), left the economy precarious for nearly a decade. Sully weathered these crises and for several years prospered, but toward the end of 1816 and especially after the Panic of 1819 the demand for portraits plummeted. "Sully has not had a portrait to paint for Philadelphia since May last," Dunlap noted in October 1819, "& but four for Strangers."[105] The artist reduced his fees, but to no avail. His fortunes declined. What to do?

Europe was a possibility. With the Philadelphia market having dried up, a venture abroad may have tempted Sully. In 1819 he applied to the Pennsylvania Academy for several thousand dollars, "offering in return copies of European art treasures." The Academy turned him down.[106] The next year his former student, William Edward West, wrote Sully from Florence that, with the American economy stagnant, Sully could triple his income abroad and live more cheaply to boot. "No Painter in Italy equal to Lawrence," thought West; in fact, "there is not a Portrait Painter here that is even tolerable."[107] The thought of Italy was tempting, but for a man with a wife and large family to support, uprooting himself for the Paradise of Exiles had perforce to remain a dream.

It was easier for Sully to go to Baltimore and Washington, where he had friends with whom he could stay, and test the waters there for commissions. In seven extended trips away from Philadelphia during the early 1820s Sully attempted to recoup his fortunes. An artist on the road, instead of spending weeks idly waiting in his studio for clients, benefitted from the novelty of his presence. During a brief visit to a "new" city, he might squeeze in a dozen orders.[108] When in 1821 a commission for a full-length *Jefferson* necessitated his traveling to Monticello, Sully's financial situation looked up, but only momentarily. In the 1810s he had usually earned over $4000 a year, a splendid income for the times. Now he and his family lived on less than half that. In 1824 – the year of Byron's death – Sully earned $1750, a five-year low, in fact, an income a good deal less than at any time since his London stay. But if Sully lamented his lot, his journal leaves no trace.

Sully's embarrassments became by 1824 so onerous, Dunlap recalled, that he had "determined on a plan of subscription for portraits of Eminent men in England originals & Copies of portraits of Locke Newton &c." He began to take portrait commissions for London.[109] After all, Chester Harding, an artist of less skill than he, had set out for the English capital in 1823 and in spite of Lawrence's dominance had garnered from the fashionable dozens of commissions. Edinburgh was also a possibility, Boston still another. But, as in 1809, benefactors came to Sully's rescue. To discourage his move to Boston, three Philadelphia engravers – Gideon Fairman, Cephas G. Childs, and Gilbert Fox – commissioned their own portraits.[110] Sully abandoned plans to leave. Other requests began to trickle in. The year 1825 was better than 1824, 1826 than 1825. As the economy revived, so did Sully's fortunes. Over the next few years he painted many of the portraits for which he is best remembered.

Sully's decision to remain in Philadelphia did not mean that life in the city did not occasionally exasperate him. Comparing rough-hewn America with cosmopolitan Europe was an old refrain, voiced by natives who had traveled abroad as well as by foreign travellers. "In comparison with the people [of England]," Copley, safely ensconced in London, had lamented, "we Americans are not half-removed from a state of nature."[111] At times Sully might have agreed. "I shall proceed in a few months to Boston," he informed Audubon, now living in Britain, in February 1829; "how that may answer, I know not. You need not feel surprized to see me in London in a short time, perhaps before next autumn. London with all its difficulties, is the only place for a *white man* to live in, the only place possessing the least congeniality to the fine arts, and above all, the only place for improvement."[112] Racial tensions, a powerful undercurrent in Philadelphia's life, had gradually intensified in the pre-Civil War decades as Blacks moved north and competed for jobs with new immigrants from Ireland and Germany. The situation made Sully uneasy. He was also well aware that many Philadelphians (like Americans generally) felt a deep suspicion toward the arts. With New York the nation's undisputed art capital by 1830, residence in America's second city meant for Sully loss of lucrative commissions. It may also have lessened his professional stature. American indifference to the arts was not confined to his adopted Philadelphia. During the Jacksonian decades a tide of utility seemed to engulf the nation. "I am not the painter I should have been had there been a higher taste," Thomas Cole lamented in 1841.[113] Sully probably felt the same. But in Boston in 1829 he secured the commission for what became a spectacular full-length portrait of Thomas Handasyd Perkins, a leading merchant and philanthropist of the city. Pleased by his reception and by his success, Sully abandoned thoughts of London or Boston and returned to Philadelphia in better spirits. The next year, the young English engraver John Sartain, wondering whether to settle in New York or the Quaker city, recalled that "Mr. Sully was warm in his commendation of Philadelphia as a place of residence, and advised me by all means to settle in it."[114] We hear no more of Sully's unhappiness with the city or of plans to leave it permanently.

*

Throughout his life Sully was generous with what money he had, always lending small sums to needful friends or family members; and generous with his time, aiding younger artists as West and Lawrence had aided him. Aspiring artists were told to go and seek him out. One who did was Charles Robert Leslie, born in London to American parents. When that youthful prodigy subsequently returned to England in December 1811, he took with him, along with Sully's instruction in oils, invaluable letters of introduction. Thomas Doughty, the landscapist, also benefitted from Sully's tutelage.[115] Sully furthered the career of the German-born Philadelphian, America's first important genre painter, John Lewis Krimmel.[116] In 1831 he encouraged the young portraitist, G. P. A. Healy.[117] That year the 21-year-old Alfred J. Miller of Baltimore, later to gain fame for his Indian portrayals and Western scenes, studied with Sully.[118] Along with Rembrandt Peale, Sully befriended during his Philadelphia sojourn George Catlin, another painter of Indians and subsequently a master showman.[119]

Others whom Sully helped included Edward F. Peticolas and Samuel Morse.[120] James Reid Lambkin, aged 16, arrived on his doorstep one day seeking instruction from the acknowledged master. Trumbull in 1828 wrote to Joseph Hopkinson that he had recommended a Mr Chapman to Sully. He told Sully he was "confident you will take pleasure in giving him [Chapman] your advice & assistance in his pursuit."[121] Sully did, and Chapman was grateful. "S. Sloan" Sully aided financially.[122] Sometimes artists arrived in groups. On August 1, 1825, three – "Mr. Moore from Kentucky, a Mr. Weaton of North Carolina," and "a gentleman of Carlisle" – knocked on Sully's door. With such multiple requests upon his time, no wonder an overwhelmed Sully exclaimed, "Students of painting multiply – . . . !!"[123]

Help or instruction might ripen into lasting friendship. From April to August 1824 John James Audubon had taken lessons in portraiture from Sully. The straightforward neoclassicism of Audubon's portraits, inspired by David, moved under Sully's tutelage toward a Romantic, even Byronic conception of pose and presentation. As with others whom he aided, Sully refused Audubon's offer of payment.[124] In 1826 Sully's letter of introduction to Lawrence opened doors for Audubon in London. Lawrence "rose and shook hands with me the moment I pronounced my good friend Sully's name," Audubon wrote his mentor. Lawrence made every effort to help Audubon, praising his work and finding him patrons.[125] A Sully letter of 1833 introduced Audubon to Allston, who delighted in the acquaintance.[126] Audubon's published writings frequently mention, and with good reason, "my old Friend Sully."

Cincinnati, until the Civil War the largest city in the trans-Appalachian West, was but one of several inland metropolises that sent its most promising artists to Sully. Some, like Hiram Powers, "the young sculptor of Cincinnatti [*sic*]," Europe-bound, stopped to pay their respects. Sully also welcomed Cincinnatians "Mr. [James] Beard" and Godfrey Frankenstein and helped train the gifted, tragically short-lived Aaron Houghton Corwine (1802–30).[127] Across the Ohio, Kentuckians who came east to study with Sully include William Edward West (1788–1857), after 1808; Joseph H. Bush (1794–1865) in 1817; Oliver Frazer (1808–64) in 1828; and, the finest talent of them all, Matthew Harris Jouett (1788–1827), probably in 1823.[128] Jouett, after four months of study under Stuart in Boston in 1816, had developed a sophisticated yet somber technique, but after 1823 he adopted, almost certainly a result of Sully's tutelage, a more colorful palette.[129]

*

Like Sully, William Edward West, from Lexington, Kentucky, was to portray Byron. Living in Philadelphia on and off after 1808, West studied informally with Sully.[130] By 1816 he had definitely become a student, for an entry of 1815 in Sully's account of pictures notes that "my pupil West" had begun a replica of his portrait of West Point's influential first superintendent,

Jonathan Williams.[131] As surviving examples of West's work indicate, Sully's technique – thin layers of paint, light brush strokes, bright palette – strongly influenced West's own. In 1817 West was working in New Orleans and in Natchez, and by 1819 he was in Italy, where he met Lawrence and saw many of his "best paintings" that, done abroad at the Prince Regent's request, depict the great European potentates of the post-Napoleonic world.

In 1822 West asked Byron, then in Pisa, to do his portrait. Byron agreed. "Whenever an American requests to see me – (which is *not* unfrequently) I comply," he wrote, "1stly. because I respect a people who acquired their freedom by firmness without excess – and 2dly. because these transatlantic visits 'few and far between' make me feel as if talking with Posterity from the other side of the Styx."[132] West's nationality gained him the commission of a lifetime. His *Byron* (Figure 3) constitutes one of the few late portraits of the poet. Engravings made of this somewhat adipose *Byron* enjoyed wide distribution in America as well as in Britain. That by T. A. Dean became the frontispiece to Galt's *Life of Byron* (London, 1830), while J. B. Longacre adapted Dean's work for the Philadelphia edition. West's portrait was the single illustration chosen for the American edition of Moore's *Letters and Journals of Byron*. Over the next thirty years West made at least ten copies of his portrait, all the while dining well off its renown and his connection with Byron. The only work by West to become well known, *Byron* holds its own as an indicator of Byron's appearance at age 34.[133]

It is to New Yorkers that we owe the creation of two major portraits of Byron: Sully represents the poet near the beginning of his career, West near the end. George W. Bruen, who had commissioned West in 1822 to paint Byron for the American Academy of Fine Arts, was a New York merchant temporarily based in Livorno. Three years later, Bruen noticed in a New York shop window a lovely landscape by an unknown painter. Impressed, he bought the painting for $10, sought out the young artist, and financed him to a study trip along the Hudson. Three paintings resulted from that trip. When John Trumbull saw them, he immediately bought one, *The Falls of the Caterskill*, and persuaded his friends, Asher B. Durand and William Cullen Bryant, to buy the other two.[134] Thus was launched the career of Thomas Cole, who became the foremost landscapist of his generation. The first owner of Sully's *Byron*, we remember, was John R. Murray, also like Bruen a leading New York merchant. Thus did art and commerce conjoin in Gotham.[135]

It is unlikely Sully ever saw West's original or a copy, or was influenced by any of the engravings made from it.[136] If he had, he would have recognized in his former student's work lessons well learned, for West adapted to his own more modest talent aspects of Sully's style and technique. Whereas many of Sully's portraits are valued as major works of American art, West never duplicated his success with *Byron*. In American art Sully has a national reputation, West a provincial one. West depicted Byron at a particular moment, about a year before he left for Greece, but Sully depicted him for the ages.

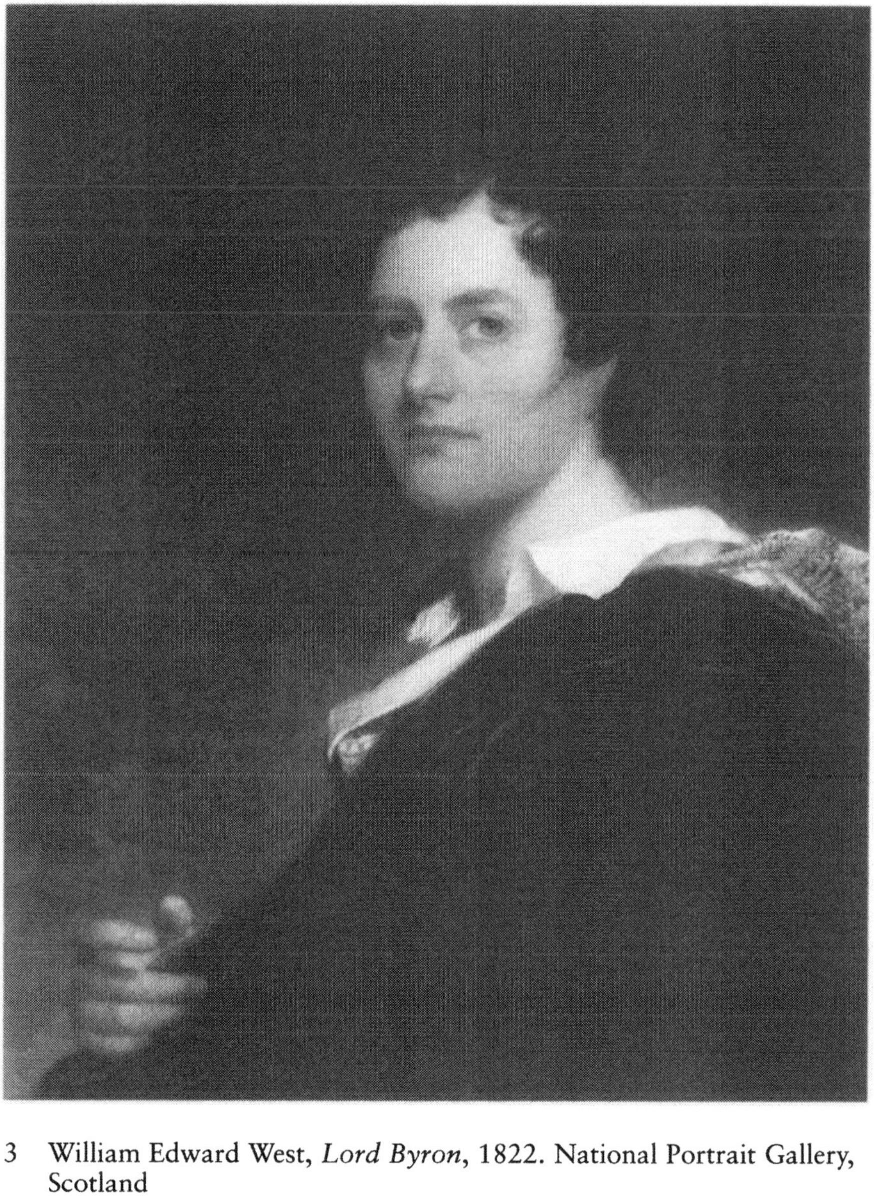

3 William Edward West, *Lord Byron*, 1822. National Portrait Gallery, Scotland

CHAPTER FOUR

Dramatic and Historic Portraiture:
George Frederick Cooke and George Washington's Passage of the Delaware

So long as men can breathe and eyes can see
So long lives this, and this gives life to thee.
Shakespeare[1]

Hazlitt's elevation of [portrait-painting] to the rank of a bona fide art – which echoed throughout the Romantic period from Lavater to Baudelaire – reflected his century's philosophy that truth resides in the specific rather than the universal and that the individual peculiarities of nature, far from being fantastic, are the constituents of reality.
Nadia Tscherny[2]

How Sully conceived dramatic and historic portraiture determined the nature of his achievement in *Byron*. The theater ran in Sully's blood, and helped shaped the drama, interior no less than exterior, of his portrait. Rethinking and reworking Westall's *Byron*, he made his own both a dramatic and a historical performance. He set Byron upon a stage, a stage both mental and physical. The poet performs, not on the boards of a Philadelphia playhouse, but in the natural world, or so his public (sometimes) thought and so Sully wished us to think. Sully's *Byron* is the Romantic Poet, of Nature and in Nature. Amidst waterfalls, caverns, mountains, he contemplates, composes, creates. Unusual in Sully's *oeuvre* in being of a major literary figure – *the* major literary figure active in Sully's lifetime – *Byron* can best be understood within a context of the artist's portraits of leading actors and major historic personages. The meticulous care Sully took to establish truth of figure and scene in them will be equally manifest in *Byron*.

This chapter focuses on *George Frederick Cooke as Richard III* (1811), Sully's finest theatrical portrait, and *Washington's Passage of the Delaware* (1819), his best-known history painting. Related works – *William Burke Wood in the Role of Charles de Moor* (1810-11) and *Washington at the Battle of Trenton* (1842) – are brought in to support the argument. The chapter following concentrates on Sully's portraits of Fanny Kemble, specifically of her as Beatrice (1833), and his culminating dramatic portrait, *Queen Victoria* (1838). Though perhaps best known for idealized, somewhat sentimentalized depictions of society women, Sully was no less adept at painting virile men. *Cooke as Richard III* and his several *Washingtons* embody power and dynamism. To individuals of both sexes he imparted a lifelike quality both engaging and convincing. In the context of these portraits, *Byron* emerges in sharper perspective. We begin with the era's most esteemed theatrical portrait, Reynolds's *Mrs Siddons as the Tragic Muse* (1784).

*

Reynolds's fifth *Discourse* established a special category of "historical portrait." A portrait "painted in the Historical Style . . . is neither an exact minute representation of an individual, nor completely ideal."[3] Instead of a mere bust-length record of someone, such a portrait was intended to exalt art no less than the sitter. Through his *Discourses*, his long presidency of the Royal Academy, and his artistic practice, Reynolds elevated the status of British portraiture virtually to that of history painting. Like major works of tragedy, epic, or history, "historical and poetic portraiture" was designed to educate and improve its audience.

Reynolds challenged contemporaries to combine portraiture with history painting, but as his student James Northcote observed, "portrait often runs into history and history into portrait, without our knowing it."[4] If few artists could pull off portraits both "historical and poetic," they remained an elusive goal to strive for. Grand Manner portraits by Reynolds and others depict individuals, often idealized, in historical and mythological roles. At their best these portraits are brilliant, powerful, compelling.

Late eighteenth-century society celebrated actors and actresses, acknowledged their importance, debated their professional and personal qualities. Of the actresses none was more renowned than Mrs Sarah Siddons, and her portrait by Reynolds pervasively influenced the development of portraiture. Contemporaries enthused over *Mrs Siddons as the Tragic Muse* from the beginning. Lawrence spoke of it as "indisputably the finest female portrait in the world."[5] Widely known through engravings, it exemplifies Reynolds's ideal of portraiture. Profoundly aware of his artistic heritage, Reynolds constantly referred to his predecessors. He based Mrs Siddons's regal pose, as contemporaries recognized, upon Michelangelo's prophets on the Sistine Ceiling. Siddons's companions, shrouded in darkness on either side of her massive throne, also draw upon Michelangelo. They personify Pity and Terror. Thus did Reynolds link Grand Manner British portraiture to the long tradition of history painting of classical and religious themes. Sully, who venerated the *Discourses*, knew *Mrs Siddons* through engravings and may even have seen the original during his London stay.[6] The influence of *Mrs Siddons* upon his portrait of Byron is unquestionable.[7]

The practice of Lawrence must also have impressed Sully. Fired by *Mrs Siddons*, Lawrence melded theatrical portraiture with history painting though, unlike Reynolds, he avoided allegorical allusions. Lawrence took as subject Mrs Siddons's almost equally famous brother, John Philip Kemble. In a letter of 1798 he referred to his *John Philip Kemble as Coriolanus* (Figure 4) as "a sort of half-history picture."[8] Strong lighting accents the theatrical pose of the

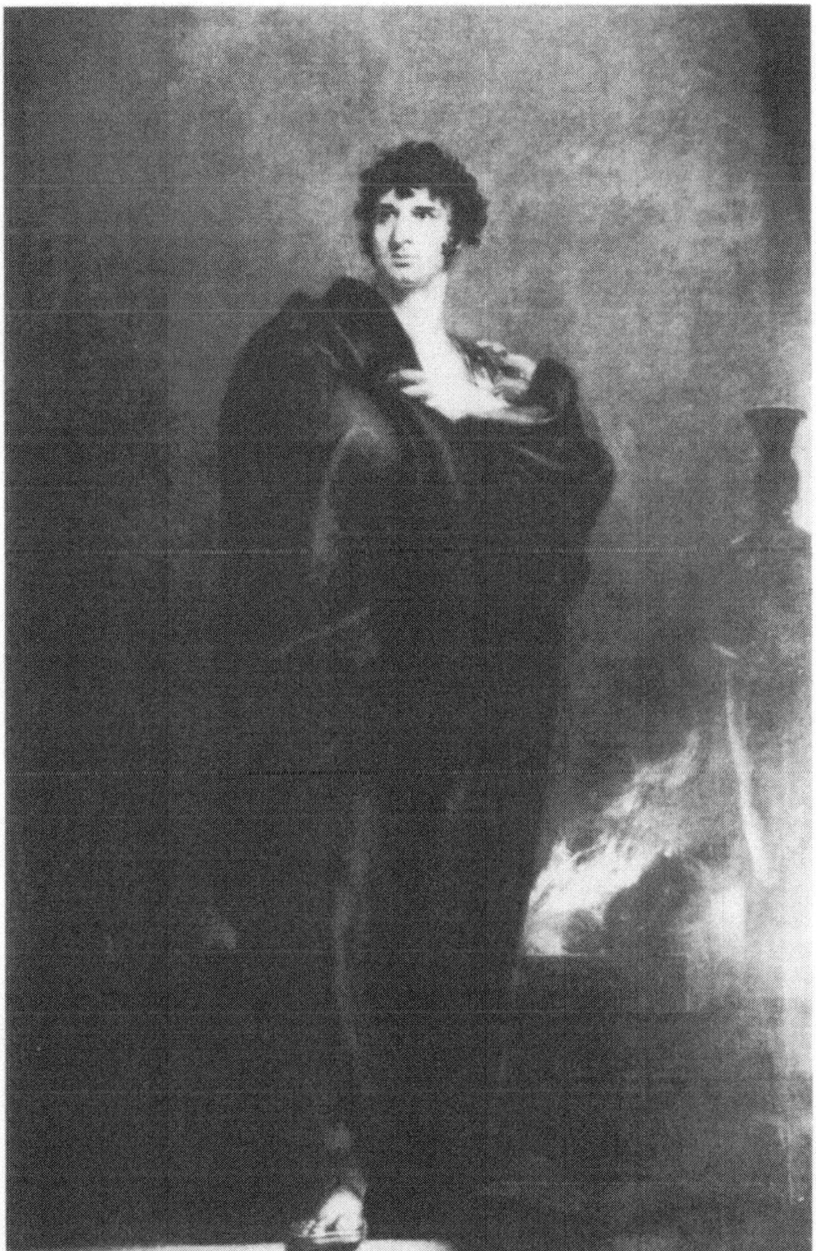

4 Thomas Lawrence, *John Philip Kemble as Coriolanus*, 1798. Guildhall Art Gallery, London

single heroic figure, now cognizant of his fate; he steps up to what seems the edge of the stage, and from the observer's low viewpoint he looms majestic, forbidding. Lawrence also depicted Kemble as Hamlet, Brutus, Cato (in Addison's once-famous play), and Rolla in Sheridan's *Pizarro*. Though none of his "half-history" *Kemble*s succeeds entirely and his one acknowledged history painting, *Satan Summoning his Legions* (1796–97), failed to impress contemporaries, Lawrence believed they validated his ambition to become a history painter. Besides, "half-history" portraits made good economic sense, for engravings and later lithographs of them sold well. Lawrence acknowledged that history painting was a superior art but sensibly recognized his limitations.[9] He had achieved fabulous success as a portraitist, and a portraitist he remained. Sully found Lawrence's concept of "half-history" paintings congenial, and Philadelphia provided an artistic environment responsive to British Grand Manner portraiture.

All his life Sully soaked himself in the theater and its personages. His parents and siblings performed on the stage. He grew up in theaters, imbibed their traditions, knew the managers, worked in the companies, was backstage, onstage, in the audience. Dramas came to vivid life before his eyes; he recreated scenes and characters in his imagination. Stage sets were among the first paintings he saw. The move to New York in 1806 intensified his connection with the drama. With his studio literally inside the Park Theatre, he experienced to the full the city's vibrant theatrical life. In London, much occupied with commissions for patrons and dedicated attendance at RA lectures, he may not have had time to attend performances, but he would have heard much talk about Kemble and Sarah Siddons, the earlier shooting star fame of Master Betty, "Young Roscius," and the volatile behavior of George Frederick Cooke.[10]

In Philadelphia Sully saw John Howard Payne and Edwin Forrest as well as the English thespians Edmund Kean and Charles Mathews on their American tours. A close friend was the ubiquitous actor, theater manager, playwright, novelist, diarist, conversationalist *extraordinaire* and sometime portrait painter William Dunlap (1766–1839), "the Father of the American Theater." Chronicler of both its theatrical and art scenes, Dunlap could have told Sully anything he wanted to know.[11] Theatrical portraits ranked higher than society portraits because of their literary and historical associations, and Sully frequently painted actors and actresses, including Charles and Fanny Kemble. When elected an honorary member of the Garrick Club in London in 1837–38, he admired its celebrated portrait collection of "theatrical worthies" and vowed upon his return to "paint them one" of Forrest.[12] Charlotte Cushman, the leading dramatic actress of the 1840s, sought out Sully in 1843 for her portrait. In his ninth decade Sully, working from an engraving of the Chandos portrait, twice depicted Shakespeare. This lifetime immersion in the theater inevitably complemented and reinforced Sully's natural theatricality. Indeed, given the interaction between artist and subject – the artist performing in paint before the sitter, the sitter posing for the artist – theatricality might almost seem a requisite for success in portraiture.

*

In Sully's America the theater loomed large in public awareness. Shakespeare was the most popular playwright. Stage versions of the Bard's plays had even greater impact than the numerous printed editions.[13] Bowdlerized, expurgated, cut down, added to, the plays on stage were still Shakespeare. In East Coast cities Shakespeare dominated in number of performances given, and almost all the chief professional actors were Englishmen. They had learned their skills in British provincial theaters, and Americans deemed it right and natural for them to have the leads. They flocked enthusiastically to see them declaim the great scenes for all they were worth. Overwrought gesture and emotive facial expression accompanied passionately spoken words. Spectators expected – and enjoyed – an emotional orgy.

Among Philadelphia's theaters the Chestnut, known as "Old Drury" after London's famed Drury Lane, was preeminent. Located on the northwest corner of 6th and Chestnut, it housed what many considered America's finest company. Built in 1794, renovated in 1805 by Benjamin Latrobe with assistance from William Strickland, both leading architects of the Greek Revival, the Chestnut was a stunning building. Sculptures by William Rush adorned the interior. A noted actor, William Burke Wood, managed the Chestnut with William Warren. Until 1826, when Wood and Warren dissolved their partnership, they brought to Philadelphia the best productions from Drury Lane and Covent Garden.

Shakespeare formed the staple of the Chestnut's repertory. During the 1809–10 season the house presented nine of the Bard's plays; during 1810–11 Shakespeare accounted for 22 of 88 performances given; in the season following, 27 of 108. Philadelphians alive during the century's first third could have seen 21 of Shakespeare's 37 plays.[14] Sully, steeped in this Shakespearean ethos, knew and loved the plays, portrayed actors and actresses in familiar roles, and in scrapbooks drew dozens of sketches of Shakespearean scenes and characters.[15] Although his non-theatrical portraits often exude a quiet drama, the vigor in his portraits of actresses and actors is unmistakable.

Sully's first major dramatic portrait, *William Burke Wood in the Role of Charles de Moor*, derives from his friendship with Wood. Begun in August 1810 and completed by the following June, the painting depicts Karl Moor, the bandit hero of Schiller's *Sturm und Drang* drama, *The Robbers* (1781). Stories and plays celebrating noble outcasts like Moor loomed large in the popular imagination. Moor, falsely accused of criminal activity by his younger brother, was seen as a victim of social circumstances beyond his control. Uncaring society having soured his noble nature, he flees his home to become the leader of a vicious band of robbers. Advocating political, social, even linguistic revolt, *The Robbers* quickly became, in its many adaptations, a staple of Romantic drama. Though absolutist Vienna banned it until 1808, it flourished on European stages. Its first performance in Federal America was in New York in 1795.

Versions of absolute rule prevailed throughout Europe, Switzerland and

Venice (until 1797) excepted. The exploits of messianic heroes like Moor, Wallenstein, and Count Egmont fascinated readers of Schiller and Goethe. The late Enlightenment public evinced mesmerized curiosity about flesh-and-blood bandits. The clerical physiognomist, Johann Caspar Lavater, read nothing as a youth "but accounts of banditti, their chiefs, and awful exploits" and dreamed "of becoming the chief of a group of robbers."[16] Similarly, Conrad's exploits in Byron's *The Corsair* (1814) thrilled a generation thirsting for exotic heroism. Childe Harold's disconsolate wanderings across Europe inspired the wanderings in the Abruzzi amidst primitive societies of Berlioz's egocentric rebel in *Harold in Italy* (1834).

Sully's painting reveals Moor half-prone upon a hillock above the Danube (Figure 5). He has just defeated the forces of the law. Hitherto impetuous and quick-tempered but now pensive, he ponders the misery his depredations have caused. Looking over a bountiful landscape – fertile fields, fruit trees, heavy vines – he extends his right arm toward the setting sun and exclaims, "So stirbt ein Held! – Anbetungswürdig" – "Like the death of a hero. I could kneel before it in adoration!"[17] In Sully's painting the evening sky complements the pensive protagonist. The scene is a turning point in the drama. A fundamentally good and potentially great man, Moor had found inspiration in the Plutarchian ideal of great men.[18] But his brother's treachery and an indifferent society drove him to a life of crime. By skilful use of diagonals, Sully implies the dilemma of Schiller's robber chief: emotionally exhausted, distraught, his future uncertain, but still heroic.

Moor's languid pose reflects that of Adam in Michelangelo's Sistine Ceiling. John Hamilton Mortimer's painting *Bandit Taking up His Post* (*c.* 1778), itself influenced by banditti and soldier pictures by Salvator Rosa and his English imitators, provided a further model.[19] Sully had probably seen engravings of Hogarth's *David Garrick as Richard III* (1745), where the startled king, betrayed by his half-dreaming mind, confronts the ghosts of those whom he has slain. Closer at hand were Benjamin West's canvases in Philadelphia where figures writhe in theatrical poses. *William Burke Wood in the Role of Charles de Moor*, an intriguing work, at once a dramatic portrait (the best done of Wood) and a history painting, led to an acknowledged and undisputed triumph, *George Frederick Cooke as Richard III* (see color plate section). Like *Wood in the Role of Moor*, *Cooke as Richard* represents a hugely flawed individual whose exploits thrilled as they shocked Romantic hearts.

*

Cooke led a star-crossed life. After several decades working English provincial houses to mixed success, he opened on October 31, 1800, at Covent Garden as Richard III. His triumph was so complete that Kemble, the leading actor of the day, gave up the part after a brief period of competition. Cooke performed the Shakespearean villains Richard, Shylock, and especially Iago, with great brilliance. His rich, deep voice gave him an unforgettable stage presence. James Boaden, Kemble's early biographer,

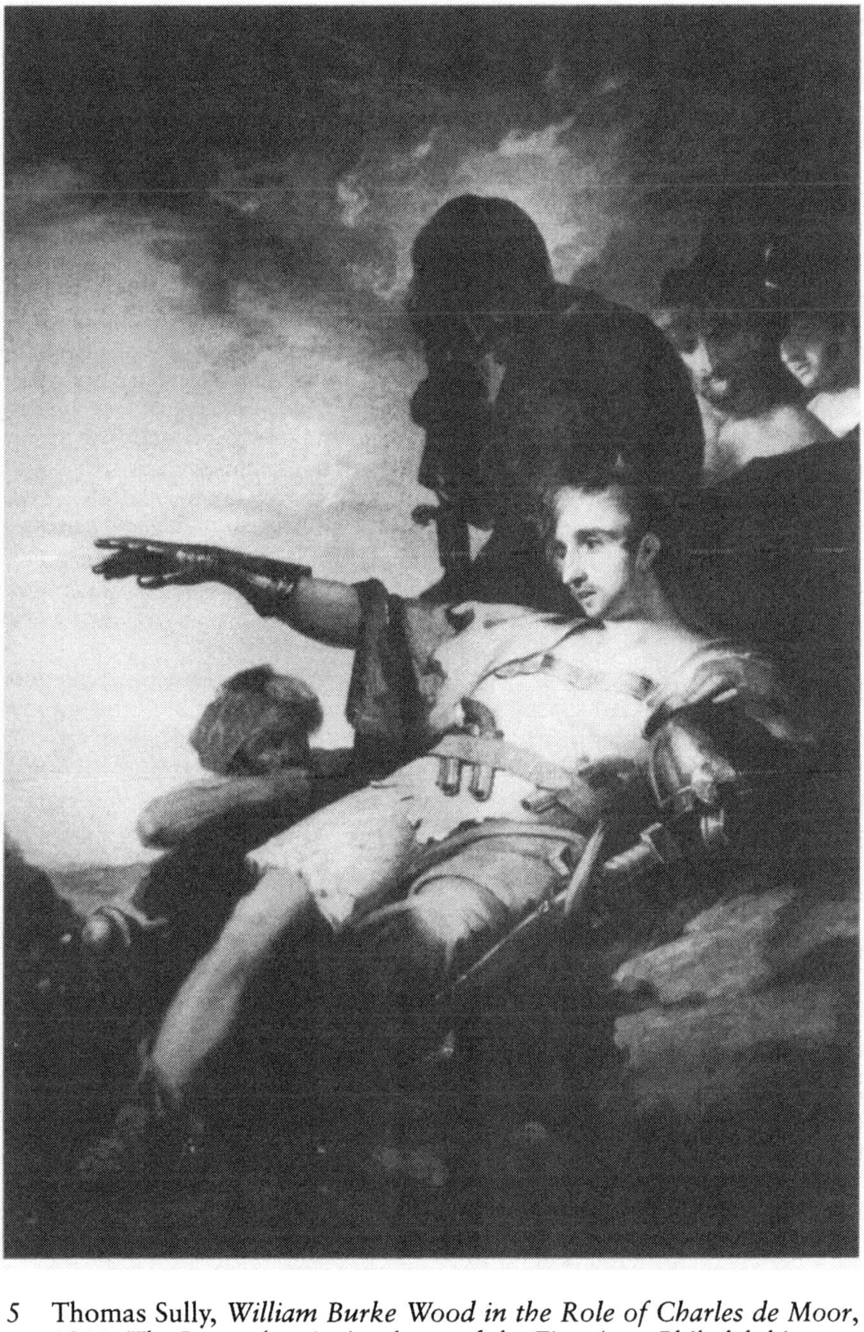

5 Thomas Sully, *William Burke Wood in the Role of Charles de Moor*, 1811. The Pennsylvania Academy of the Fine Arts, Philadelphia.

observed that Cooke "spoke with two voices, one of which was harsh and acrimonious, the other mild and caressing. The great secret of his *effect* in speaking, was a rapid transition from one of these sounds to the other: He used the first either to control or convince – the second to soothe or betray."[20]

Cooke's performances moved the young Byron to ecstasy. In 1813, reading William Dunlap's biography of Cooke, he exulted, "Such a book! – I believe, since Drunken Barnaby's Journal, nothing like it has drenched the press."[21] Byron's verbal exuberance echoes Dunlap's account of Cooke's alcoholic excesses. Cooke offered Byron new evidence of his transatlantic fame: in a reading-room in Albany, near Washington, he pronounced *English Bards, and Scotch Reviewers* "well written."[22] Cooke was among the actors Byron could imitate exactly.[23] He regarded him as a natural. "Sufficiently studied to appear to lack study," Cooke gave the appearance of playing intuitively. Regency audiences – and Byron – prized such dramatic *sprezzatura*. Cooke's style was closer to that of Edmund Kean, an actor whose performances of Shylock and Richard III astonished an audience that included Byron in 1814, than either's was to Kemble's. While Kean's Richard electrified Byron, Cooke's he never forgot. "I think Kean is a great man," he told William Parry in Greece in 1824, "but Cooke was very much his superior."[24] If Byron thought Cooke's Richard "superior" to Kean's, he thought highly of him indeed.

Generous and witty, a good friend, Cooke always retained the affection of audiences, but periodic episodes of alcoholic debauchery resulted in evenings when he could not act. Such erratic behavior lessened his popularity with British management. In 1810 Thomas Abthorpe Cooper, the theatrical impresario who had brought Sully to New York, managed to shanghai a not altogether sober Cooke on board a New-York-bound ship.[25] He would be Cooper's star for the coming season. No English actor of such dazzling reputation as Cooke's had arrived on American shores before. *Richard III*, despite depicting an outlaw from mankind, was easily the most popular of Shakespeare's plays in the United States. When Cooke opened on November 21, 1810, at New York's Park Theatre in Cibber's clever, stagy adaptation, he amazed both critics and the pit.[26] Theater-goers stampeded the box office. Debuting as Richard in Philadelphia on March 25, 1811, Cooke took the city by storm.[27] Crowds fought to see him perform and besieged the stage door. During three separate engagements in Philadelphia, totalling 39 nights, Cooke failed to appear but once. He won the city's heart.

Theatrical portraiture was as popular in America as in Britain. *Richard III* in England alone had inspired over fifty artists, among them Nathaniel Dance and Gainsborough.[28] While Cooke was performing in Philadelphia, a group of his supporters, led by the wildly enthusiastic China trade merchant (and Sully patron and friend) Benjamin Chew Wilcocks commissioned from Sully, for $300, a full-length Grand Manner portrait of *Cooke as Richard III* (see color plate section). Intended as a gift to the Pennsylvania Academy of the Fine Arts, the portrait would honor an actor the city adored.

Sully depicted Cooke reciting lines spliced into *Richard* from the third *Henry VI*:

> Why, I can smile, and murder whiles I smile,
> And cry 'Content' to that which grieves my heart,
> And wet my cheeks with artificial tears,
> And frame my face to all occasions.[29]

Cooke's Richard stands before us in the pride of his villainy. His blue-gray eyes, hooded under heavy brows, are large and penetrating; his nose, long and a trifle beak-like, is well shaped. For the role Cooke apparently assumed a moustache and close-trimmed Vandyke. His features have a "heroic scowl" that implies cunning and a spiteful intensity. Sully did the clothing to perfection: purple-plumed hat (in a church!), doublet and breeches trimmed with fur, boots of buff leather turned down just below the knee, the Order of the Garter visible on the left leg. By placing Richard in a Gothic church Sully has the king exercise his villainy on sanctified ground, in defiance of God as well as of man. The broken column base, right foreground, prefigures his eventual fall.[30] Whereas Hogarth displayed Richard III in a histrionic pose, Sully focused on the heroic villain's psychological subtleties.

Cooke as Richard III reveals Sully a master fully formed. The painting stands in his career as *The Skater* (1782) does in Stuart's or *Elizabeth Farren* and *Queen Charlotte* (both 1790) in Lawrence's. Sully was 28, Stuart 27, when they did their breakthrough works. Nothing hitherto in Sully's *oeuvre* prepares us for *Cooke as Richard III*. Stuart before *The Skater* had never done a full-length portrait, and Sully before *Cooke* only a small one of James Madison and *William Burke Wood in the Role of Charles de Moor*. Stuart, after six years of study abroad, could achieve (so a contemporary) "a tolerable likeness of the face, but as to the figure he could not get below the fifth button." *The Skater* lifted him into fame.[31] With *Cooke* Sully rose to the challenge of full-length portraits. Over time he painted more of them and painted them better than any of his American contemporaries.[32]

Cooke as Richard III inhabits the realm of Lawrence's "half-history" portraiture. Sully's painting is more subtle, less overtly dramatic than comparable works by Fuseli, West, even Lawrence. Over his career Sully did about twenty Shakespearean subjects, but *Cooke as Richard III* is his most highly wrought Grand Manner theatrical composition.[33] Upon Cooke's death in New York in September 1812, Philadelphia on October 5 paid tribute "to his extraordinary dramatic genius." While an actor recited a monody to Cooke's memory, Sully's *Cooke as Richard III*, arrayed in mourning, dominated the Chestnut's stage.[34]

*

Like *Cooke*, Sully's *Washington's Passage of the Delaware* combines historical portraiture with history painting. Paintings of historical scenes had almost as great a vogue in America as in Britain. Even today these works can still impress, and the best – West's *Death of General Wolfe* or Sully's *Washington's Passage of the Delaware* – are magnificent theater. *Washington's Passage* draws upon a long tradition of history painting, and to understand its manifestation in Federal America we explore first the European background out of which it emerged.

Late Enlightenment Europe inaugurated a great age of historical writing. For over a century, from Gibbon to Spengler, a heightened awareness of history haunted the European imagination. During the French Revolution Plutarchian examples of rectitude fostered hero-worship. Historical figures loomed large in Romantic sensibilities. Herder and Schiller, Voss in his magnificent translations of Homer, Carlyle in his fiery *French Revolution*, Macaulay and Froude in their great multi-volume epic histories of England, dynamically recreated the past within a contemporary context. Novelists – Scott, Bulwer-Lytton, Dickens, Thackeray, George Eliot – brought earlier epochs to vivid life. Artists who took up historical subjects tackled the ethical and political issues that agitated their time under the guise of themes from the Bible or Greek and Roman mythology.

Reynolds made people rethink art in relation to history. By the 1780s, artists and art critics, connoisseurs and patrons, all influenced by his *Discourses*, agreed that historical or biblical subjects constituted the highest form of art. French arguments for the primacy of history painting went back a century to André Felibien's lecture of 1667.[35] Diderot, like Reynolds, established a hierarchy of categories for art in which history paintings, "les grandes machines" he called them, stood at the summit.[36]

David with his great canvases of classical, usually Roman, subjects was the very type of history painter Diderot called for. The artist preferred episodes from ancient history, but during the Empire (1804–15) he commemorated Napoleon's triumphs in monumental history paintings. The Greek and Roman works he considered his true art; works consecrated to Napoleon's glory he valued less. They were an obligatory career detour. Today we regard both classical and contemporary works as historical, but David did not.[37]

Reynolds wanted history painters to animate and dignify historical figures "with intellectual grandeur." Their works should give "the appearance of philosophick wisdom, or heroick virtue." Only by enlarging "the sphere of his understanding by a variety of knowledge" can an artist acquire awareness of such high qualities. He must warm "his imagination with the best productions of antient and modern poetry."[38] Connoisseurs believed that to treat important historical and literary subjects imaginatively and convincingly required artists of great gifts and mind, artists who had educated themselves and traveled abroad. The history painter was expected to know (and be able to talk about) not only history but biography, classical literature and antiquity, geography, climate, social customs and habits, costume, and architecture. Furthermore, he had to understand psychology, physiology and (as Chapter 9 will indicate) physiognomy.[39] Between 1772 and 1805 Benjamin West drew £1000 per year as "History Painter to the King." By his example and prestige West, and later Copley, raised history painting in England to a height never before reached. West based his works on classical themes, on the Bible, and on British history. His *Death of General Wolfe* (1771) made the didactic point that heroic deeds were as possible for modern as for ancient man. Biblical subjects encouraged the faithful. *Death on the Pale Horse*, the 1817 version in the Pennsylvania Academy of the Fine Arts, superimposed upon neoclassical restraint a sublime vision. The gigantic *Christ Rejected* (1814), also in the Pennsylvania Academy, rivaled in complex composition and monumental scale popular dioramas and panoramas. Contemporaries acclaimed it enthusiastically. "I have seen West's famous painting," opined Jane Austen, "and prefer it to anything of the kind I ever saw before. [It] is the first representation of our Savior which ever at all converted [?] me."[40] The public looked upon such works, Austen's comment implies, not just as aesthetic statement but as revelation.

Benjamin Robert Haydon intended his *Christ's Entry into Jerusalem* (1814–20), as West had *Christ Rejected*, to be a major religious–historical statement. Wordsworth's sonnet beginning "High is our calling, Friend" expressed respect both for the poetical "high art" of history painting and for Haydon's achievement. Today the painting's fame rests, however, on its inset portraits of Wordsworth, Keats, and Hazlitt. Both capable of immense theatricality, West and Haydon yet reveal generational differences in sensibility. Whereas West (b. 1738) drew upon the neoclassical acting styles of Kemble and Mrs Siddons, Haydon (b. 1786) responded to the Romantic *élan* of Cooke and Kean. Sully, worshipping Reynolds but tutored by Lawrence and Fuseli, leaned toward Haydon.

*

In 1827 an American art critic ranked the artistic genres on a scale of one to ten. He placed history painting first. Just after it came "Historical or Poetic Portraiture" – that is, "those portraits that come closest to the most valuable painting of all, history painting." Such a portrait would be *Mrs Siddons*, while David's *The Death of Socrates* or Sully's *Washington's Passage of the Delaware* would be examples of history painting worthy of emulation. History painting occupied art's pinnacle; everything else came in more or less lower down. "Landscape views and common portraits," lumped together, placed for this critic a lowly sixth.[41]

America's victory in the War of Independence engendered intense self-consciousness and hero-worship. Proud of their new nationhood, Americans became obsessed with portraits of the historic great. Painters rose to the challenge. Often they adopted the new, painterly English manner, the *dolce stil nuovo* that Gilbert Stuart in 1793, and Sully after him, brought back from England. Foreign as well as native heroes engaged the attention of artists. Napoleon had died in exile in 1821, a giant to many, and three years later the self-exiled Byron perished in Greece. Glory accrued to both the solitary Prometheus chained to his rock on St Helena and the would-be savior of the sacred land of democracy. Among native heroes none surpassed

Washington. The father of his country, Washington was revered in Europe by a generation that included Napoleon and Byron. In his historical portraits of Washington, Gilbert Stuart aspired beyond mere physical verisimilitude: he hoped to enshrine Washington in the national consciousness as "an icon for posterity."[42]

American artists who studied in England, or (less often) in France or Italy, experienced the high esteem in which Europeans held history painting. Upon returning they found they had to modify high-flying theory. Ancient epics, the mists and shadows of dimly remembered events, the rich tapestry of European history: all fair game for artists abroad, but not for Americans.[43] Urged to think historically, the would-be American history painter found that he had less history to draw upon. His nation's past was brief. Lurking in the back of his mind might be the possibility that America would never come into its own as a cultural nation, or that a republic might not provide a suitable environment for the arts.

The career of John Vanderlyn illustrates one artist's frustration in transferring European modes of art to American soil. A gifted portrait painter, Vanderlyn yet sought renown for his historical canvases. *Marius Amidst the Ruins of Carthage*, exhibited at the Paris Salon in 1808, won a gold medal. Napoleon wished to purchase it for the state. Vanderlyn refused. But when shown in Republican America, *Marius* failed to impress. Vanderlyn's voluptuous *Ariadne* fared no better, waiting nearly two decades for a buyer. Nor did Vanderlyn find lasting success with his vast panoramas. His *View of the Palace and Gardens of Versailles* (1818–19) did not gain him the larger public he expected.[44] Later efforts of this kind were no more successful. Vanderlyn stubbornly resisted caving in to market forces. In 1850, two years before he died, he fumed over the age's hypocrisy and money-grubbing vulgarity.[45] Vanderlyn "was made to realize in a painful manner," Tuckerman pointed out in 1867, "the antagonism between an essentially practical community and the spirit of trade, and artistic enthusiasm."[46] For Vanderlyn, success in art came down, as it often did (and does) in America, to money.

The new nation lacked a tradition of state or church patronage of the arts. Opportunities for large-scale history paintings were limited. There were few major public buildings to adorn, and even for those, city, state, and national governments were reluctant to fund the kind of art typically found in European civic and religious structures. Several of the Founding Fathers – John Adams notoriously – deeply distrusted the sensuous and emotional appeal of art. History paintings created laboriously and with great hopes rarely found suitable venues. Yet history painters, if often unsuccessful in marketing their works, enjoyed considerable cultural esteem. Both the American Academy of the Fine Arts and the Pennsylvania Academy were founded in part to promote the painting of historical works.

If Vanderlyn's is an extreme case, consider John Trumbull, easily the most successful American artist entranced by the siren song of history painting. His *Capture of the Hessians at Trenton* and *General George Washington at the Battle of Trenton* capitalized on the nation's growing fascination with the

Revolution and with Washington. He adopted the modern attitude toward history painting popularized by West and Copley, but avoided their conservative rhetoric by giving his scenes the illusion of events actually happening.[47] Believing the establishment of the American republic an event of great historic significance, Trumbull hoped later generations would compare the Revolution and the resultant Republic with the great achievements of Greek and Roman civilization.

Even if American artists had to focus on the near past, they could invest their historical recreations with timeless significance. In emulating the "grand style" of the masters through history paintings, artists as diverse as Washington Allston and Samuel Morse aspired, despite discouragements, to high achievement in that exalted sphere. Allston had studied under West, and sought, like him, religious subjects. His *The Dead Man Restored to Life by Touching the Bones of the Prophet Elisha* (1811–14) powerfully recreates the biblical story in II Kings 13:21 through facial expression, gesture, and posture. In 1817 he began a vastly ambitious work entitled *Belshazzar's Feast*. Belshazzar was a popular European theme and the subject of one of Byron's *Hebrew Melodies*, but at his death 26 years later Allston had not completed his biblical epic. His failure to do so serves as a paradigm of the failure of American artists generally to achieve success in history painting.

Vanderlyn and Allston may have failed, but Samuel Morse, a better businessman than either, attempted in such works as *The Dying Hercules*, *The Gallery of the Louvre*, and *The Old House of Representatives* to capture a public for history. Morse knew that people would pay to see paintings on exhibit, and artists often organized a multi-city tour to show off their works. They accompanied them with texts that explained in detail the import of the historical event depicted. *The Old House*, neither a "pregnant moment" nor a victory in battle, focused on the public, essentially abstract, nature of American democracy in progress. But, though full of interesting details of legislators communicating among themselves and thus demonstrating democracy in action, *The Old House* lacks a central focus. It and the gigantic *Gallery of the Louvre* are often admired today but few at the time wanted to pay to see them. Like so many of the era's artists, Morse overestimated the visual sophistication of his audience.

For about a decade, from 1811 to 1822, Rembrandt Peale concentrated on history painting. Like Vanderlyn he began with foreign subjects, like Morse he ended up with domestic. Two trips to Paris during 1808–10 helped free Peale from eighteenth-century portraitist conventions learned from his father. His *Napoleon* (1810) is unusual in its idealistic candor.[48] Back in Philadelphia, Rembrandt had little luck with his historical efforts. The now unlocated *Bonaparte on Horseback* (1811), huge at 13' x 11' (396 cm x 335 cm), did not attract visitors when displayed. Pavel Petrovitch Svinin, a Russian *émigré*, attacked *The Roman Daughter* (1811) as a plagiarism. Accompanied by Thomas Sully, Peale challenged Svinin to prove his case. He could not. The Russian retracted his charges, though with ill grace.[49] Rembrandt's even more enormous (11 ½' x 23 ½' – 350 cm x 716 cm) historical allegory *The Court of Death*, worked on from 1817 to 1824, had clearer sailing. Its remunerative tours of the Republic's principal cities made it Rembrandt's best-known history painting. Exceptional in its success, it took in $8886 over the course of a year.[50] He hoped the US Congress would purchase for the Capitol rotunda his *Washington before Yorktown* (1824–25). He hoped in vain. The House did not appropriate funds, and the painting remained in his studio.

Most Americans found history painting too grand, too pompous and aristocratic, too distant perhaps from American realities. Portraitists, initially less well regarded, acquired increasing respect well into the 1830s. History painting gradually yielded to portraiture. Even in Sully's heyday – the 1820s and early 1830s – Grand Manner portraiture had begun to lose its cachet in America. The Hudson River landscape painters assumed in part the mantle of historical portraiture and of history painting. By introducing epic, dramatic, and historic themes into his works, Thomas Cole believed that artists would discover an endless variety of subjects in the rich American landscape. As history painters had sought to instruct through past events, so landscape painters could employ nature, argued Cole, to impart moral lessons comparable to those in history paintings.[51] Genre painting also rose in popularity during the 1830s. It too taught history of a kind, usually contemporary history, history with subjects from everyday life, history with an identifiably American character to which ordinary people could relate. In a suitably American compromise, William Sidney Mount's genre paintings came to occupy a place in the nation's artistic pantheon not too far below the sublime landscapes of Cole and Church.

Time has reversed Reynolds's ranking of the genres. Today our fundamentally non-hierarchial conception of art leaves us reluctant to categorize, but few artists now active – Germany's Anselm Kiefer is a stunning exception – practice history painting. While specialist art historians plumb the Federal era's history paintings for insights they offer into how an earlier age conceived ages still earlier, museum-goers accustomed to the fast-paced imagery of film and television often regard them as curiosities, period pieces, ponderous, awkward, static. Yet history paintings, often marvelously well composed, tell us about the values and ideas current when they were created. Since the 1970s museum-goers may be giving them a more sympathetic look.

It is primarily through portraits rather than history paintings that the life of earlier times comes alive. Except for the relatively few works presenting contemporary events, the portraits have become the history paintings. Benjamin West, rare for his generation, understood the distinction. Commenting on Lawrence's portraits, West urged his contemporaries not to "confound his pictures with mere portraits: painted as his are, they cease to be portraits in the ordinary sense; they rise to the dignity of history, and, like similar works by Titian and Vandyke, they may be said to be painted not alone to gratify friends and admirers in the present day, but rather for posterity."[52] Few at the time grasped the prescience of West's magnificent compliment. Two centuries later his perspective has become ours. As

Lawrence brings to life the leading personages of Regency Britain, so does Sully those of Federal America.

Like West, Trumbull, Allston, Vanderlyn, Peale, Haydon, Lawrence even, Sully aspired to greatness as a history painter. His first work in oils, we remember, was a copy of a *Telemachus* by Angelica Kauffmann, who saw herself as a history painter. During much of Sully's active professional life Philadelphia directories listed him as "History and Portrait Painter."[53] Compared to Vanderlyn, he had a less checkered experience, in part because he attempted fewer historical works. His *Gil Blas scaring the Cook in the Robbers' Cave* (1812), based on the popular French novel *Gil Blas de Santillane* and drawing on a painting by John Opie, relates closely to theatrical portraits like *William B. Wood in the Role of Charles de Moor* and *Cooke as Richard III*. In its dramatic lighting and exaggerated gestures, it owes much to West, even more to Fuseli. *Byron* combines superbly, if subtly, history with theater.

Sully left behind a listing of his paintings, a number of journals and letters, and several versions of his Hints for Pictures. But about matters close to him he can be singularly unrevealing. If he yearned to become a history painter, he almost never articulated that yearning. Instead, it is Sully's fellow artists who inform us of it. From Italy William Edward West wrote his former teacher, "there is no Painter in Italy equal to Lawrence, if that is what we are after."[54] West presumably implied that what he and Sully were "after" was something else, something more than portraiture, namely history painting. If a painter sought greatness, he emulated the Old Masters by painting historical compositions. That was the accepted wisdom. Portraits limped in a poor second, if that. One did them for a living. Connoisseurs often regarded portrait painters less as creative artists than as artisans, superior tradesmen, practitioners of a craft.

In 1817 Jacob Eichholtz, commenting on a forthcoming exhibition of Sully's work, observed that "it is not to be, merely, an exhibition of portraits. No, your historical powers will now be called into action. What exquisite pleasure it would give to know you were engaged in some large work . . . If it were a subject taken from sacred scripture," Eichholtz, a man of religion, goes on, he would be even more pleased. "It is certainly the wish of many of your friends that your talents be devoted to nobler subjects than portraits. I am aware that it is your wish also, and hope the time near which will realise these prospects."[55] Also in 1817, another artist-friend of Sully's echoed Eichholtz's sentiments from far-off England: "I hope you have got a good liberal commission to paint a historical picture," Charles Robert Leslie wrote his former teacher.[56] Sully had. The year before, he had begun negotiations for what became his best-known history painting, *Washington's Passage of the Delaware*.[57]

Sully had hitherto shied away from the sacred subjects urged by his old friend Eichholtz and the historical subjects attempted by West, Haydon, Allston, Vanderlyn, and Trumbull. Nonetheless, he kept before him the idea of a major history painting. The events and personages of the Revolution, the defining event in the United States' not overlong history, seem to have riveted Sully. Eichholtz had painted in 1809 *The Capture of Major André*; Sully's 1812 picture of the same title was widely exhibited, then engraved. Both he and Eichholtz depicted episodes from Cooper's revolutionary war novel, *The Pilot*. Often artists invested emotionally or psychically in their historical paintings.[58] Eichholtz, born in 1776 and of German descent, delighted that he had been born *after* the colonies declared their independence from Britain; Sully, born in England the year the Treaty of Paris officially ended hostilities and since 1809 an American citizen, lived in a Philadelphia not far from where the battles of Trenton, Princeton, and Germantown had been fought. The fabled winter encampment of Valley Forge lay nearby.

*

Late in 1816 the North Carolina legislature commissioned two portraits of Washington from Sully. One was a copy of Stuart's full-length "Lansdowne" portrait. Sully suggested for the second a scene illustrative of one of the general's many actions. By 1819, when he got around to it, the Panic of that year had caused portrait commissions in Philadelphia to evaporate. With time on his hands and no doubt visions in mind of Trumbull's success with the Revolutionary subjects recently installed in the Capitol Rotunda, he ventured into history. The moment had arrived, states the hyperbolic John Neal (who knew Sully well), when he "could loosen the bands that bound him, and unfetter his genius." Sully was, according to this source, "passionately desirous . . . to employ his power upon the historical department."[59] What better subject, the artist must have thought, than a large-scale history painting based on the nation's founding father.[60] Almost every painter in America – Vanderlyn, Trumbull, Charles Willson and Rembrandt Peale, and Durand, among them – had had a go at Washington. The market for portraits of the national leader, already great, would only increase.

Sully placed his *Washington's Passage of the Delaware* at McKonkey's Ferry some miles upstream from Philadelphia (see color plate section). There Washington and his troops had crossed the ice-choked river during the night of December 25–26, 1776. Early the next day they won the battle of Trenton. The artist began work in August 1819. Trumbull's huge 12' x 18' (370 cm x 550 cm) historical paintings probably influenced the unusually large size, 12' 4" x 17' 5" (380 cm x 530 cm), of *Washington's Passage of the Delaware*. By December 15 Sully had completed work.

Mason Locke Weems in his eulogistic and enormously popular biography of Washington had apotheosized him as the great man of the age. Published the year after the president's death in 1799, by 1850 it had gone through 59 editions and many changes in text. Full of dubious but winning moral tales about Washington's inimitable virtues, including (in the 1806 edition and subsequently) that of the cherry tree and the hatchet, Weems's life fostered the image of Washington as superhero, an American demigod.[61] Though in many ways a deeply democratic man, Washington was in his bearing enormously majestic.[62] He posed a tremendous challenge for the era's painters. How to render him? Sully chose the moment just before his most audacious military triumph. "The first business of an historical painter," he observed in his Hints, "is to make his picture tell its story clearly, distinctly and quietly."[63] This Sully did in *Washington's Passage of the Delaware*. The painting's "story," however, is still imperfectly understood.

Late on Christmas day 1776 Washington crossed the Delaware with about 2400 men and 18 cannon. His intention was to launch a night attack on 1200 Hessians encamped at Trenton, ten miles down river. The conscripted Hessians were as good as any soldiers in Europe, and this regiment of grenadiers, commanded by Colonel Johann Gottlieb Rall, had the dubious distinction of having killed more Americans than any other foreign unit.[64] Hitherto American forces had retreated before the British and their Hessian allies. Washington's army was in rags and unpaid; many enlistments ran out at year's end. Morale was low. It was even lower among partisans of the Republic.

Sully recreated the scene skillfully and in essence accurately. Washington, in a blue uniform with buff breeches, bestrides a white charger atop a snow-covered hill (see color plate section). Below, boatloads of troops cross the gray river perilous with ice floes. In the left foreground men in gray and brown uniforms maneuver a cannon up the bank. To Washington's right several officers, in partial or full profile, clothed in gray and blue uniforms and mounted on brown horses, try to calm their wild-eyed mounts. A full moon shown on December 25, 1776, but the looming night sky has become overcast. Snow has begun to fall, and visibility is uncertain. On the far horizon a pink glow heralds the dawn.

Drawing upon his acute theatrical sense, Sully infuses into *Washington's Passage of the Delaware* the lessons of pose, gesture, and expression that he had demonstrated earlier in his portraits of Wood and Cooke. Right hand on hip, left not visible, Washington masters the prancing horse with his knees. What may look like a debonair pose is proper equestrian behavior. The pose contrasts with Washington's pensive, patient look. The composition of horse and rider, which John Neal thought borrowed from Van Dyck's *William of Orange*, actually derives from Sully's own close observation of people on horseback.[65] Washington, just right of the compositional center, dominates the scene. A shattered tree juts out from the embankment behind him. A frequent symbol in art and literature of the evanescence of life, blasted trees appear in landscapists from Ruisdael to Sully's contemporaries Allston and Cole. Evocative descriptions of blasted or enduring conifers in Byron's *Childe Harold* and Alpine Journal influenced Sully's contemporaries. Possibly the tree here symbolizes the eventual collapse of English colonial power.

Sully believed the dedicated student of portraiture must make every effort to establish the features of his subject. Sully had never contemplated Washington in the flesh, and so from portraits, sculptures, prints, literature, and oral traditions he took great care to authenticate Washington's face and figure and then to recreate an image of Washington's likeness. Washington appears, as in reality he was in 1776, a vigorous man in mid-life. Stuart and Trumbull and the two Peales, Charles Willson and Rembrandt, had known and painted the great man while alive. Even so, relatively few portraits emerged directly from life sittings. After Washington's death in 1799 the copying industry, already active during his lifetime, went into overdrive. Besides portraits by Stuart, Trumbull, and the elder Peale, Sully studied closely busts by Ceracchi and Houdon.[66] His figure of Washington, as Fehl has well said, celebrates "the *gentilezza* which necessarily distinguishes the finest of heroes."[67] Sully's depiction convinces by its integrity, its civility, its quiet grandeur.

The scene of the crossing Sully recreated from his own on-the-spot observation and sketch. He explained in a broadside of *c.* 1820 that he based his painting's historical accuracy upon the *Memoirs of General Wilkinson*, "chapter 3, page 128." "The portraits I have meant to introduce," he went on, "besides Washington, are General Knox, crossing the bank in the second ground; [and] General Greane, about to mount his horse."[68]

Of nearly equal importance to the figures is the unfolding scene. As with the portraits, Sully made every effort to depict it authentically. Here is no imaginary landscape but an actual historical site. Instead of conjuring up an already almost mythic endeavor, Sully went straight to the spot, observed it closely, sketched it, and recreated accurately the topography. As his 1820 broadside indicates, truth to reality was his primary concern:

> The place of embarkation [*sic*] is M'Konkey's ferry, about twelve miles above Trenton, although the histories of the event generally call it four. I was attended there by the son, or some near relative, of Mr. Belenger, who was the person that piloted the boat across the river in which Washington was; therefore I cannot have made any mistake in the spot. I was there on the twenty-third of December, and made my drawing during a snow storm, therefore have been able to give much accuracy to the representation.[69]

The distance between the ferry crossing and Trenton is actually about ten miles, but Sully established the scene with the same meticulous research and care he gave to Washington's face. The painting is no less a topographical than a figural reconstruction. Anyone who visits the site of Washington's Crossing today has to admire Sully's effort to achieve authenticity of locale.

If *Cooke as Richard III* qualifies as a "half-history" picture, then *Washington's Passage of the Delaware* could rate as a "full" history. But is it? Neal, who praises the painting's "*dramatick individuality*," claims it "was never meant for a downright historical picture." Sully, "without actually invading the great territories of history," has painted a "portrait of Washington."[70] Sully himself in an 1819 letter spoke of his work as "an Historical Portrait."[71] He directs our eyes to Washington's person, particularly his expression. Thoughtful yet determined, it haunts us. On this man fell the burden of the war, of dealing with an often indecisive and penurious Congress, of caring for men who trusted him. Sully intended

Washington's face to be the painting's focus, and in this regard *Washington's Passage of the Delaware* qualifies as a "half-history" portrait. But it is more than that.

Washington did not command from afar. He had the virtue of staying close to his men. His imposing presence at the end of the crossing enabled him to inspire his army with confidence and a sense of sacrifice. A staff officer's diary, dated December 26, 3 a.m., describes Washington's leadership at that moment:

> I have never seen Washington so determined as he is now. He stands on the bank of the river, wrapped in his cloak, superintending the landing of his troops. He is calm and collected, but very determined. The storm is changing to sleet, and cuts like a knife. The last cannon is being landed, and we are ready to mount our horses.[72]

Washington has staked everything on a surprise attack. It is getting late, and the weather is ominous. But if anxious, Washington is also calm and resolute, and Sully's painting depicts him thus. With nearly all his troops on the Jersey side, the general has achieved the most difficult part of his endeavor. The army can now reassemble. It was nearly 4 a.m. before it began to march on Trenton. The delay led Washington to adjust his plans. The attack will take place, not at dawn, but early on the day after Christmas.

Washington's strategy succeeded brilliantly. The American assault resulted in a Hessian rout. Few enemy soldiers were killed or wounded, but Washington took over 900 prisoners. There were, amazingly, almost no American casualties.[73] Washington's raw troops had surprised and defeated highly disciplined and trained mercenaries. In a protracted retreat from Long Island, to Brooklyn, to Manhattan, to New Jersey, his men hadn't won a battle in over a year. They had lost New York and would soon lose Philadelphia. The victory at Trenton revived their spirits and those of the nation. Sully chose his moment well. Washington, perhaps alone of the American commanders, had realized that a decisive victory was urgently needed. The time to strike had come, and he had struck.

For Henry Fuseli, an informed history painter chooses to depict the "pregnant moment" because it encapsulates, or illuminates, the larger train of events. Sully's decision to focus on the crossing of the Delaware on the night of December 25–26, 1776, reflects a Fuselian "pregnant moment." But Sully hardly needed Fuseli to tell him that the crossing was a "pregnant moment." His choice reveals both his awareness of history and his keen sense of theater. Likewise, Hazlitt, writing of the contemporary stage, speaks of a "dramatic hit," when at a moment carefully built up the actor, playing the scene for all he or she is worth, startles or overwhelms the audience.[74] Sully, in depicting Cooke reciting lines borrowed from *Henry VI*, achieved such a "dramatic hit." In having Washington poised to strike the enemy he achieved another.

*

Washington's Passage of the Delaware has from the beginning caused problems of interpretation. It does not yield its meaning easily or quickly. Commentators from Neal onwards have divided the painting into halves: the right given over to Washington (secondarily to his officers); the left, to the crossing itself. The halves, it is claimed, do not fuse perfectly. However, once we view *Washington's Passage* as Sully intended it to be viewed – within the context of the actual site – the painting coheres superbly. Most book-sized reproductions shrink this dark, gigantic work to postcard size. We see the general astride his horse, but details – e.g., the big Durham iron ore boats filled with soldiers – we make out only with difficulty. But Sully intended in *Washington's Passage* to commemorate the passage of the men as well as of their general.

Every significant work is open to diverse interpretation, but a recent analysis of *Washington's Passage* by Alex Nemerov is so fundamentally misleading that it deserves comment. Nemerov grounds his analysis of Sully's painting on a flawed understanding of the historical event, the setting, and of the crossing itself. He has Washington going to the battle of Princeton, fought about a week later, not to the far more significant Trenton, a turning point in the history of the Revolution and indeed in the fortunes of the America-to-be.[75]

The crossing of the Delaware took almost nine hours, from 6 p.m. to nearly 3 a.m. Nemerov assumes Washington to be on the Pennsylvania shore supervising a crossing just beginning. Actually, Sully depicts Washington on the Jersey shore, with the crossing nearly over. After his Virginia troops had established a beachhead, Washington crossed early, at about 8 or 8.30 p.m.[76] The Pennsylvania shore is flat for a mile or two inland; only the Jersey side provides the high ground necessary to achieve the perspective in which Sully placed Washington. Nemerov's basic misreading of the time-frame skews his analysis. Washington, for him, "turns partly away from the river crossing, looking at it over his right shoulder only glancingly or perhaps not at all." Actually, Washington, instead of looking away from his troops, looks forward to leading them into battle. He stands there, as the commanding general, in front of his army, anxiously awaiting the crossing's completion. Too good a dramatist to have his hero face away from the crossing while his men toiled to get over, Sully presents Washington and the army going in the same, not opposite, directions. Additionally, Nemerov wonders why the figures on the right "show no sign of moving toward that perilous zone."[77] Why should they? They have already crossed. Like Washington himself, his officers await impatiently the march ahead.

The crossing of the icy Delaware has taken longer than anticipated. Washington is eager to get going and his horse senses his impatience. If he were still on the Pennsylvania side, his right arm, hand on hip, might be understood as a dismissive gesture. Actually, the pose reflects his restlessness. If only it could control the situation as well as he does his horse – and bring his remaining troops across the river more quickly! The position of

Washington's arm is also a gesture of pride: pride in his men, pride that they have successfully crossed a wide river filled with ice floes. The gesture recognizes their heroism, their toughness. "Look what men are these," it says.

Sully depicted the soldiers and their boats on the river; we dimly see the far shore through the fog. The light on the horizon, which Nemerov assumes to be the sunset, is actually the sunrise. Sully in his "one moment of major poetic license" has anticipated 'its rising by an hour or two.[78] The pink horizon, a foretaste of the death – and rebirth – to come, suggests freedom's dawn. Once we understand that Sully has depicted the crossing as virtually complete and a success, the painting possesses the unity that Neal and Nemerov failed to recognize in it. Sully's brilliantly composed scene well merits Dunlap's encomium of "sublime."[79]

The expression on Washington's face has aroused debate. Nemerov speaks of him as "a soulful younger man," "a kinder, softer leader."[80] Sully may well imply Washington's own modest conception of himself during the Revolution's early years when he had doubts about his military abilities. The artist had even warned his prospective patrons in North Carolina that they might not recognize *his* Washington.[81] Nemerov wonders if Washington's regard reflects Sully's anxiety in attempting a history painting. He cites John Neal's claim that "it was putting [Sully's] very existence at hazard, even to trespass, for a day, upon the historical department"; in focusing on portraying Washington, Sully could tackle the general "without actually invading the great territories of history." Nemerov, following Neal, has Sully thinking "ambivalently about a foray abroad [as a history painter], a 'hazardous ordeal.'" As Washington anxiously faced an uncertain future, so Sully feared to tread on the "historical department."[82] If (as Oscar Wilde once claimed) portraits are in effect self-portraits, does Washington express something of Sully's emotional state and, if so, what might that something be?

Shortly after he finished *Washington's Passage of the Delaware*, Sully went to Baltimore desperately seeking commissions. His journals almost never speak of his emotional state, but once in Baltimore he painted a remarkable *Self-Portrait* (1821, Figure 6).[83] It depicts the artist, blue eyes verging towards gray, hair curly brown, gazing directly at the viewer. Unlike a number of Rembrandt's self-portraits, Sully presents himself in his working clothes. He assumes no fictional identity. Brush in hand, both pointing toward his face, he appears confident in his powers. The no-nonsense regard implies that someone has just entered his studio. "Why are you interrupting me?" the artist appears to ask. "I hope you have important business." The gaze is direct, self-aware, apparently self-assured, hardly inquisitive. The artist neither smiles nor doesn't smile. He does not flatter himself. "I am a painter," he seems to say, "first and foremost. Judge me by my work."

The straightforward gaze indicates a man in command of himself and of his *métier*, a man of determination and will, steady, persevering, committed to the task. Sully held a vision of his career, one that embodied strength, courage, discipline, a clear-eyed pursuit of his goal to become the finest

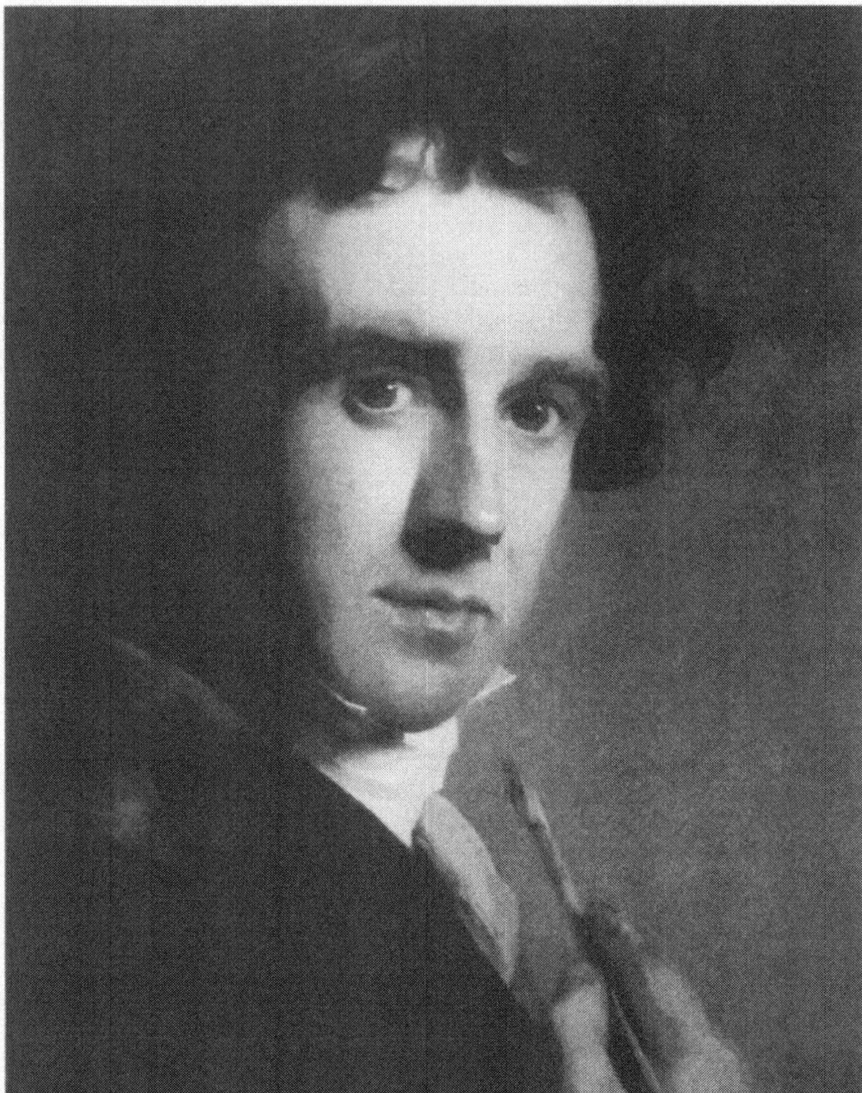

6 Thomas Sully, *Self-Portrait*, 1821. The Metropolitan Museum of Art, New York.

portraitist in America. He is not, as Nemerov claims, a man wallowing in self-doubt, but an artist of rare vigor who seldom faltered and who (as his writings reveal) almost never complained, a man of quiet self-confidence. Reading the face of Washington as expressive of self-doubt, Nemerov superimposes upon Sully a modernist *Angst* totally alien to his being.

*

Cooke as Richard III and *Washington's Passage of the Delaware* reveal Sully a master of dramatic portraiture. The balance may differ – *Cooke* leans more toward historical portraiture, *Washington's Passage* toward history painting – but Sully's integration of theater and history demonstrates his capacity for complex representation. The choice of episode for *Washington* seems, in historical retrospect, inevitable. But most depictions of the Revolution had shown the signing of the Declaration of Independence or an actual battle. No one before Sully had focused on the crossing. Years before anyone else Sully had picked out *the* crucial moment in Washington's long struggle. Though the general was to endure many reverses, at Trenton he succeeded superbly. Crossing the Delaware on Christmas day made Trenton possible.

Unfortunately, Sully and the North Carolina legislature had not agreed beforehand about *Washington*'s size. The huge canvas did not fit the space intended, and so the legislature rejected it. Sully, with *Washington* on his hands, put it on exhibit, then on tour, where it had moderate success. His income precarious at this time, Sully sold *Washington's Passage* in 1823 to John Doggett, "a wealthy framemaker of Boston," for $500.[84] Doggett, also an art dealer, had spotted *Washington's Passage* at Earle and Sully's Gallery. He exhibited it at Doggett's Repository, no. 16 Market Street, Boston, but soon disposed of it to a Mr Greenwood, keeper of the New England Museum in Boston. Sully, visiting the city in 1829, thought the museum a "dirty hole." He was even more dismayed to find the *Passage* "rolled up."[85] He considered repurchasing it and in April 1833 wrote one Robinson at Boston, via a Miss Lamb, "to learn the price which the Museum is willing to dispose of my larger picture of the Delaware."[86] Negotiations failed, but happily the situation improved. Sully, in Boston in 1836, found his painting "in excellent condition, and if it were my own could much improve it."[87] But such an opportunity would not be his.

Five years later, the painting passed to the Boston Museum and Gallery of the Fine Arts. A theater as well as a haven for assorted collections of oddities, the Boston Museum opened on June 14, 1841. It offered onlookers stuffed tropical birds and animals, including two elephants and a giraffe, as well as over a hundred cabinets of Chinese curios. Of the nearly two hundred paintings on display, Sully's *Washington's Passage of the Delaware* was easily the largest and most spectacular. An 1840s illustration of the museum's main room shows it filling an end wall. The giraffe looks inquiringly in its direction while a couple eyes the giraffe. When in 1846 the Museum moved to Tremont and School Streets, Sully's painting hung over the staircase at the far end of the main hall.[88] When the Boston Museum closed in 1903, it gave *Washington's Passage* to the city's Museum of Fine Arts.

Despite a checkered history, *Washington's Passage* achieved considerable fame in the nineteenth century. Through engravings and lithographs, copies by others, and reproductions in books and periodicals it made its way into the public consciousness. Of the engravings, that done by George S. Lang in

Philadelphia in 1825, was the first and long the best known; the lithograph by Kelloggs and Thayer, made in New York, *c.* 1847–48, furthered the painting's renown, as did that of Joseph Napoleon Gimbrede in 1861. Edward Hicks, artist of *The Peaceable Kingdom*, used one of the engravings to paint at least six versions of his own, which he usually called *Washington Crossed Here.*[89]

Contemporaries ranked *Washington's Passage of the Delaware* among the era's finest historical paintings. Neal, if sometimes wrongheaded about details, recognized greatness when he saw it. Expectedly enthusiastic, he found *Washington* "a spirited and beautiful conception, rapidly and confidently wrought out." Dunlap regarded "the whole composition grand." Allston in 1830 judged Sully's "historical powers" to be "of no common order." James Jackson Jarves in *The Art-Idea* (1864) deemed *Washington's Passage* "both in sentiment and composition . . . of a high order of merit. . . . In view of much of what has been done since in this line" – surely a reference to Emanuel Leutze's grandiose (and more recent) *Washington Crossing the Delaware* – "it may justly be termed a masterpiece."[90]

Leutze would have seen engravings, if perhaps not the original, of *Washington's Passage*. A native of Germany, he had grown up in Philadelphia and was no doubt aware of his older contemporary, the city's best-known artist. His *Washington Crossing the Delaware* (1850) developed a subject first attempted by Sully thirty years before. Leutze's colossal canvas, when first displayed, caused a sensation, but Sully's painting had paved the way. Part of the enduring popularity of Leutze's epic work derives from its prominent position as the centerpiece of the Metropolitan's American Wing, whereas Sully's *Washington's Passage*, in Boston's Museum of Fine Arts, is not currently on exhibit.[91]

Leutze's work, painted in Düsseldorf, was begun in 1849. It came into being during a time of turmoil and repression in Europe. The democratic revolutions that had broken out in the German states the year before had been savagely crushed by the forces of reaction.[92] Leutze depicted the commander-in-chief, heroic in strong profile, leading his troops across the half-frozen river.

Washington Crossing the Delaware (Figure 7) catches well the spirit of a great moment in which everyone gave his best. The near-photographic illusionism gives the appearance of verisimilitude. The prestigious and influential Düsseldorf Academy, where Leutze had studied and now taught, promulgated a hybrid style of genre and history painting that combined precise detail with idealized figures set within dramatic scenes. But the composition of *Washington Crossing the Delaware* belies the reality of history. Leutze took great and deliberate liberties with historical evidence. The crossing took place during a snowy night, not in Leutze's early dawn; the river Leutze depicted is the Rhine at Düsseldorf, not the Delaware above Philadelphia; his boats are dories or large rowboats, not the much larger Durham ore boats the army actually used and which Sully depicted accurately. Washington would have been crazy to stand up in any of Leutze's

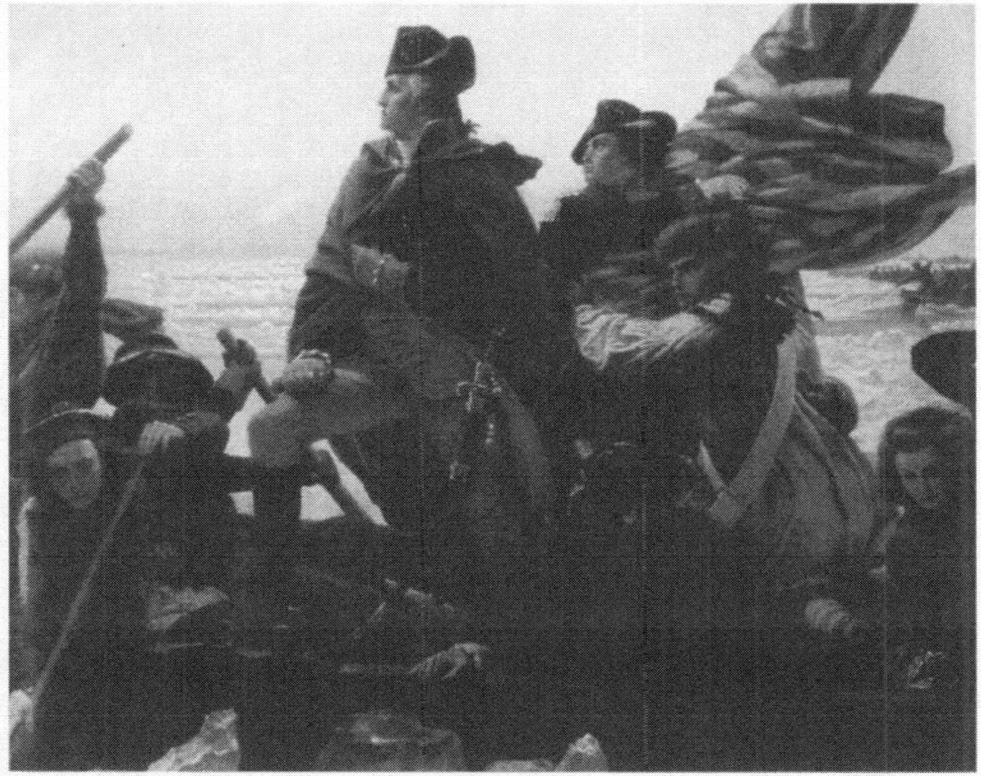

7 Emanuel Leutze, *Washington Crossing the Delaware* (detail), 1851. The Metropolitan Museum of Art, New York

craft, much less transport horses in them. Congress only adopted the design of Leutze's flag six months after the crossing. He based Washington's visage on only one source – a cast of Houdon's full-length sculpture – and dressed in a reasonable facsimile of Washington's clothing his friend and fellow artist at Düsseldorf, Worthington Whittredge, also the model for the steersman.[93]

Notwithstanding its dubious reconstruction of a past event, Leutze's heroic canvas thrilled mid-nineteenth-century spectators. Embodying the public's reverential attitude toward the general and the America he had fought for and helped found, it clinched Washington's renown as the chief Founding Father. The young Henry James in *A Small Boy and Others* (1913) recalled his awe upon seeing at Goupil's Gallery in New York "the epoch-making masterpiece of Mr. Leutze, which showed us Washington crossing the Delaware in a wondrous flare of projected gaslight."[94] As the nation in the decades on either side of 1850 rapidly expanded its territory at Mexico's expense, Leutze's *Washington Crossing the Delaware* came to epitomize for the rest of the world not only American super-patriotism but also the might of onrushing Manifest Destiny. As a symbolic projection of the heroic spirit Leutze's painting succeeds brilliantly. His *Westward the Course of Empire* (1861–62) becomes the almost inevitable sequel.

Historical fantasy was not usually Sully's way. After the mid-century, Leutze's melodramatic *Washington Crossing the Delaware* overshadowed *Washington's Passage of the Delaware*. Sully's pioneering interpretation of the crossing failed to hold its own against Leutze's inaccurate but undeniably powerful rendering as the image most Americans associated with the event. Yet Sully's *Washington's Passage*, if less prophetic, remains the more subtle work. Sully's thoughtful Washington, less ostentatiously assertive than Leutze's, is equally his own man. Different in conception and feeling from the brazen heroism evident in Leutze's *Washington Crossing*, Sully's painting offers a nuanced reading of Washington's character at an early stage of his military career. His portrayal of the scene, when grasped in all its significant detail, is both accurate and imaginatively convincing. Sully's Washington, for all his doubts, may even embody a more substantive heroism than Leutze's conventionally resolute hero. Sully painted *Washington's Passage* in 1819 in a less expansionist era. The nation was still taking stock of itself. Its history was short, and Manifest Destiny (the term was coined in 1845) lay several decades in the future. In the twenty-first century, with the methods and human costs of the conquest of the continent increasingly questioned, Sully's *Washington's Passage of the Delaware* should gain deserved recognition as a masterful interpretation of America's greatest hero and a work of understated power and insight. At least one distinguished modern art historian, Milton W. Brown, has spoken of it as "perhaps the finest painting in the Washington iconography."[95]

*

A Philadelphian in 1844, an admirer of *Washington's Passage*, urged Sully to "paint grand historical subjects oftener." Given the *Passage*'s popularity, "it is really surprising that he has not." The author mentioned a "late equestrian portrait of Washington" by Sully as "a magnificent affair," a work that "ought to be bought by some state capital or placed in the legislative halls, or the President's mansion at the seat of government of the United States."[96] Our author refers to Sully's second major history painting of Washington, one even less known than *Washington's Passage*, namely *Washington at the Battle of Trenton* (1842, Figure 8). Although Sully never had the opportunity to "improve" his *Passage*, he had had ample time since completing it in 1819 to rethink both heroism and Washington himself. In 1841, as commissions had again dried up, Sully began a study for "a whole length equestrian portrait" of Washington. A year later, his journal records, he "rode to McCauley's factory to order a large enough canvas."[97] Work, once commenced, proceeded rapidly.

Washington at the Battle of Trenton, a vertical composition, 11' x 7' (360 cm x 210 cm), is smaller than the first *Washington.* As does *Cooke as Richard III*, *Washington at Trenton* focuses on the single actor who dominates the scene. Sully sets the general, astride a spirited bay, in the winter snow against a vast ominous sky. Hero and steed fill the canvas. Keeping his horse under tight control, Washington exudes power. With his right hand he doffs his hat – the gesture recalls Washington's extended arm in Stuart's "Lansdowne" portrait – as if in acceptance of the recognition accorded his achievement. Although the general's face draws upon Stuart's "Athenaeum" *Washington*, it is that of a much younger man. The eyes are shaded by full eyebrows. In the distance Lilliputian cannoneers work their weapons; cannons puff smoke. That is all. We are hardly aware a battle is taking place. Having successfully crossed the Delaware and achieved the stunning victory at Trenton, Washington is apotheosized as his country's savior. With such a captain the new nation's fate is secure.

The hero's quiet confidence in the earlier *Washington's Passage of the Delaware* has deepened in *Washington at Trenton.* He appears pensive, weary of death and tragedy. His triumph gives him no joy, and nowhere does the painting suggest jubilation. Charles Willson Peale, who served at Trenton, recalled the battlefield as "the most hellish scene I have ever beheld."[98] Aware of the human cost, Sully's hero turns his back upon the violent fray, his countenance grim. *Washington at Trenton* is not an iconic *pater patriae*, but a suffering yet strong Romantic hero.

Equestrian portraits by Titian, Rubens, Van Dyck, Lawrence in his 1817 *Wellington*, often came with distinguished pedigrees. But a comparatively recent work – David's *Napoleon Crossing the Alps* (1801) – influenced *Washington at Trenton* more decisively. An original of this magnificent historical fantasy was at Joseph Bonaparte's home in Bordentown, New Jersey, where Sully would have seen it. An early Sully sketchbook includes a drawing of it, and for the steamboat *Albany* he copied C. Lawrence's version. Numerous engravings had made David's work familiar.[99] Controlling a rearing stallion, David's idealized General Bonaparte conveys an image of bravura energy. In actuality, a peasant led Napoleon, mounted on a sturdy mule, across the Alps.[100] In David's rendering, the troops, seen

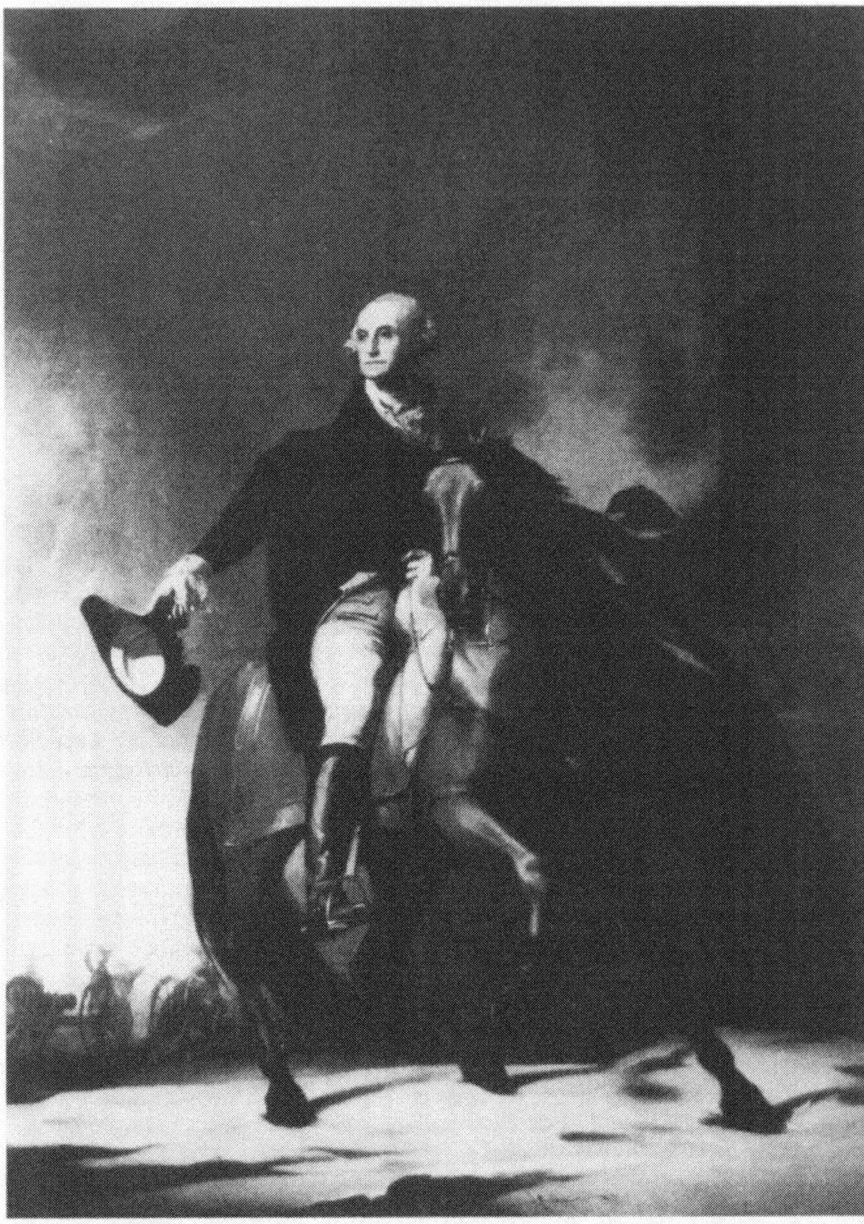

8 Thomas Sully, *Washington at the Battle of Trenton*, 1842. Union League Club, Philadelphia

through the legs of Napoleon's horse, laboriously pull cannon up the mountain path. With such a leader, the artist implies, the campaign can have no other outcome than the triumph at Marengo in June 1800.

Several months after beginning *Washington at Trenton*, Sully entered, as he had a quarter of a century before, into negotiations with the North Carolina legislature. The work would be both a portrait and a history painting – and presumably this time of the desired size. It was not to be. Once more Sully experienced disappointment: "Letter from Wheeler," he lamented; "the authorities of Raleigh decline purchasing my picture." Hoping for better luck in Washington, Sully offered it to Congress for $2200. But Congress, as so often with the endeavors of artists, did not appropriate the funds: the long a-building Capitol lacks a Sully. Once again, the artist concluded with quiet resignation, "my equestrian portrait will be *lumber* to me."[101]

Washington at Trenton remained in Sully's studio for two decades. In 1863, the decisive year of the Civil War, Frederick J. Dreer, a member of Philadelphia's newly founded Union League Club, persuaded the Club, then at 1118 Chestnut, to purchase the painting for $750.[102] When the Union League later moved to its present location on South Broad, *Washington* moved with it. Once frequently reproduced in school history texts, *Washington at Trenton* is today virtually unknown.[103]

*

Drawn to history painting, Sully yet knew the risks involved. He was responsible for a wife and nine children, and he was a realist. In America few history painters earned a living. Portraits earned Sully his. Although portraiture did not preempt his attempting other genres, he had to plan his career with practical considerations in mind. *Hints to Young Portrait Painters* (1873), as well as the larger Hints for Pictures out of which it was quarried, contain his long-maturing thoughts about art. Neither version has much to say about history painting. By contrast, both include many pages of Sully's intense, detailed speculations about the whys and wherefores of portrait painting, the primary focus of his career.

Cooke as Richard III and Sully's two magnificent "historical portraits" of Washington depict the "pregnant moments" of which Fuseli spoke, moments that Hazlitt, in another context, defined as "dramatic hits." They were also moments that Sully's native genius instinctively realized. *Cooke* skillfully discloses the inner machinations of Richard's crafty mind; both *Washingtons* reveal the majestic, yet pensive, hero. Though Sully did not become a history painter, he drew on the concepts of the "pregnant moment" and "dramatic hits" in several of his most successful portraits – of women as well as of men.

CHAPTER FIVE

Dramatic and Historic Portraiture
Fanny Kemble and Queen Victoria

> There must be varieties of lovely touches and surprising Effects to make the Heart dance . . . so in Portrait painting there must be a Lustre and finishing to bring it up to individual life.
>
> Gainsborough to Reynolds.[1]

Some portraitists do men better, others women. Gainsborough – and Sully after him – were renowned for their women. Other artists – Reynolds, Stuart, Neagle – may have done better with men. Writers on portraiture, while acknowledging Sully's undeniable skill in rendering men, single out his women. Like Byron, Fanny Kemble and Queen Victoria are among the nineteenth century's best-known figures, and to Sully's portraits of these celebrated females *Byron* serves as a kind of male escort.

The American poet and critic Henry Tuckerman thought Sully sympathized "with the fair and lovely, rather than the grand and comic." His *forte* was "the graceful."[2] The ladies liked him, he liked them. In Sully's era many believed "that female portraiture, being concerned necessarily with beauty, should be generalized; whereas male portraiture could be more individualized."[3] A modern scholar observes that "portraits of women tended to be much more idealized, allegorized, historicized or otherwise falsified than portraits of men."[4] John Neal termed Sully's portraits of women "oftentimes poems, – full of grace and tenderness, lithe, flexible, and emotional."[5] Such poem–portraits grew out of the era's values, its conception of womanhood, and Sully's females, beautiful and idealized, can be utterly magical. But along with delicacy and refinement Sully imbued his women with warmth and vitality and power, even hints of passion. They engage us by their savvy and intelligence no less than by their beauty.

Byron combined in his being masculine and feminine. Hazlitt, presciently sensitive to sexuality in art, was well aware that Byron's feminine side often came to the fore in his portraits. He noted in Westall "a sort of hermaphrodite softness"; Phillips "conveys the idea of the softness and the wildness of the character of the popular poet of the East."[6]

Sully gave Byron womanly beauty and masculine handsomeness. He *generalized* Byron, as he did many of his women subjects; he *individualized* him, as he often did in his male portraits. Both by temperament and genius Sully was ideally suited to render the sexually elusive poet, for inherent in his artistry is an androgynous, even bisexual, quality.[7] The decidedly heterosexual Sully may not have known that the hero of Greece engaged in amorous encounters with males as well as with females, but he rendered Byron integrated within a kind of dual sexuality.

Byron would not have taken offense. "My brain is feminine," he once claimed.[8] George Finlay, who met the poet in Greece, recalled that Byron exuded unusual ambivalence in his sexuality: "It seemed as if two different souls occupied his body alternatively. One was feminine, and full of sympathy; the other masculine. . . . When one arrived the other departed."[9] Modern observers concur. For G. Wilson Knight, Byron is "our greatest recorded example of bisexuality. He and others often saw himself as a fallen angel, a Lucifer, Milton's Satan; but he as often gave the impression of sweetness, radiating such beauty and power that ladies fell before him and strong men gave him their souls' allegiance." Though Knight found Byron's "powers as a man of action . . . as male as his prose," he granted that to his friends Byron could appear half feminine.[10] Contemporaries – Isaac D'Israeli, Scrope Davies, Thomas Moore, Lady Blessington among them – commented on what they perceived as Byron's effeminacy. Later biographers have delved insistently into his sexuality, with the most recent claiming his essential attraction was to males. In my view, such a claim falsifies the basic orientation of Byron's admittedly complex sexuality. His long-term attachments were not to males but to females, his half-sister Augusta and to Teresa Guiccioli. Somewhat like Nijinsky, Byron had male lovers but the primary stimulus to his libido remained female.[11]

In Sully's *Byron* feminine softness tames or complements masculine wildness. In rendering the poet as a bi-gendered being the artist allowed himself an interpretative freedom he rarely permitted himself in portraying either men or women. As well as drawing upon Sully's innate theatricality, his keen awareness of the traditions behind both historical and poetical portraiture, *Byron* in its regal self-possession draws upon Sully's female portraits. Imperious females such as Fanny Kemble and Queen Victoria vied with strong-minded males – George Frederick Cooke and Washington – in determining Sully's conception of the poet. I have taken my examples here from works later than *Byron*, for Sully's portraits of Fanny Kemble and Victoria not only underscore superbly his artistry with women subjects but open up intriguing interactions between Sully and Byron.

*

On October 5, 1829, Frances Anne Kemble (known to intimates and to posterity as "Fanny") debuted at Covent Garden as Juliet. She triumphed, completely, and a month short of twenty became the toast of London. Fanny's spectacular performance saved her actor father Charles from immediate bankruptcy. Upon John Philip Kemble's death in 1823, Charles, 18 years younger than his brother, had inherited the management of Covent Garden. Intoxicated with Shakespeare, infatuated with Byron, Fanny professed never to have wanted to go on the stage. She hated the thought of declaiming the poetry she passionately loved before lowbrow audiences. But from the first her appealing physical presence and electrifying personality captivated the public. Like her almost exact contemporary in France, Maria Malibran, she stunned audiences with her performances. Talent stuck Fanny, if briefly, with an unwanted career.

To strengthen the still precarious family fortunes Charles and Fanny decided to tour America. Since the heady days of Cooke, other British thespians – notably Edmund Kean and Charles Mathews – had triumphed in the New World. Less than two weeks after their arrival in New York in September 1832 Charles opened at the Park Theatre to impressive success as Hamlet. The next evening Fanny shone as Bianca in Milman's *Fazio*. The Kembles' fame in Britain had preceded them, and American audiences acclaimed the daughter even more than the father. Philip Hone, noted diarist and once briefly mayor of New York, remembered that he had "never seen an audience so moved, astonished, and delighted. Her display of the strong feelings which belong to the part was great beyond description, and the expression of her wonderful face would have been a rich treat if her tongue had uttered no sound."[12]

On October 10 the Kembles conquered Philadelphia. Then, after a successful engagement in Baltimore, they moved on to Washington where the aged John Marshall, long Chief Justice of the United States, wept at her performances. Associate Justice Story, being reminded that his Puritan ancestors would not have approved of his theatergoing, replied, "I only thank God I'm alive in an era with such a woman." Back up the coast went the Kembles to Boston, where each night Wendell Phillips and his Harvard classmates trooped in "to see Fanny perform."[13]

Her popularity increased with each American engagement. Overnight she became the most fêted actress in America, and to have seen her on stage marked an epoch in one's life. Fanny enchanted young and old, from the veteran Daniel Webster to the teenaged Walt Whitman. Whitman, recalling her as Bianca, waxed poetic: "Fanny Kemble! Name to conjure up great mimic scenes withal – perhaps the greatest! . . . She came to give America that young maturity and roseate power in all their noon, or rather forenoon, flush."[14] Theater stars then reigned supreme as attention-getters. People gazed at Fanny onstage and off, besieged her in hotels, scanned the crowds for her at public venues, bought souvenir plates, scarves, and trinkets inscribed with her image. In an era when Shakespeare, however bowdlerized, set the standard, she became, at 23, the best-known Shakespearean interpreter in America.

In the summer of 1833 Fanny, with her father and her beloved Aunt Adelaide ("Dall"), made the obligatory pilgrimage to Niagara Falls. Taking a steamer up the wasp-waisted Hudson, they savored the beauty of the Catskills, whose mountains, lakes, and waterfalls Thomas Cole was then imprinting upon the nation's consciousness. Accompanying the party was Pierce Butler, a wealthy Philadelphian whose income derived from plantations on Georgia's Sea Islands. Butler made no secret of his wish to make Fanny his bride. Also on board was dashing Edward John Trelawny, traveler, adventurer, fabulist, and self-aggrandizing friend of Shelley and Fanny's adored Byron.[15] At a stopover at West Point the Kembles enjoyed a dinner with Sully. If the artist met Trelawny, his opinion went unrecorded.

Dark-complexioned, a giant of a man who lorded it over the party, including and especially the diminutive and dull Butler, Trelawny for Fanny was Byron's Corsair manifest in the flesh. His presence charged the air. Two years before Trelawny had published *Adventures of a Younger Son*, a novel whose hair-raising adventures set in exotic locales most readers regarded as autobiographical. Acting came as naturally to Trelawny as to any Kemble, and he had tales to tell of the notorious poet whom he had known in Pisa and accompanied to Greece. Once in upstate New York he "burst forth" into a passionate rendition of "The Isles of Greece."[16] If most people today regard *Don Juan* as Byron's masterpiece, many of Fanny's contemporaries looked askance at its ribald satire, its bold sexuality, its aspersions against religion. All the same, Byron enjoyed vast popularity in America. At Trenton Falls, then considered a wonder scarcely less impressive than Niagara, Fanny recorded in her journal that their guide "said he had read all Byron's works – this pleased me."[17]

Fanny starred on the American stage for only two seasons, from 1832 to 1834, a brief interlude in a long, rich, complex life. Like Lafayette's triumphal tour in 1824–25 (discussed in Chapter 7), Dickens's controversial visit of 1842, and Jenny Lind's singing engagements in the early 1850s, her two seasons were national events. They placed Fanny in the American imagination forever.

During her girlhood Fanny had developed a deep love for Byron's poetry. *Parisina*, that juicy treatment of eroticism, she devoured at age ten. Oriental tales about Corsairs, Giaours, and Brides of Abydos sent thrills down her spine. *Childe Harold*, *Manfred*, and *Cain* exalted and terrified her. "How wildly I did, how deeply I do still worship his might, majesty and loveliness," she wrote of Byron in her mid-twenties.[18] The stormy being depicted in Moore's *Life*, which she read during the long transatlantic voyage, worked upon her imagination like an unsettling drug. Female readers in England as in America writhed under Byron's powerful spell. Harriet Beecher Stowe, unlike Fanny, saw no essential contradiction between her feverish longings for immersion in the world of the adventurous and sinful Byron and female virtue.[19] In an age that fostered emotional self-expression, Byron empowered the often sobbing Fanny to wear her feelings on her sleeve.

Like Byron, Fanny was an iconoclast, fearless in conversation and opinion; like Byron, she yearned for exercise that stimulated and exhausted her. Horseback-riding, the poet's favorite exercise, was no less hers. The way to die, she thought, was to "break my neck off the back of my horse at a full gallop on a fine day."[20] Her devotion to Byron had in it an element of rivalry. Possessing deeply felt artistic and literary inclinations, Fanny at heart wanted fame as an author. This Byron had achieved, and so, she felt, could she.

*

In 1835 Fanny published a journal recording her American experiences. It offers acute but acerbic commentary on the theatrical, national, and social scene. Her vigorous and (for many readers) unladylike language recalled that of her hero whose brooding *Childe Harold*, still scandalous to some, she openly praised.[21] But even Fanny balked before the ineffable *Don Juan*. The poem was beyond the pale in Jacksonian America. In publishing her thoughts about the new republic Fanny followed in the tumultuous wake of other independent-minded British travelers who included Frances Wright, Basil Hall, and, most notoriously, Frances Trollope. The last-named's *Domestic Manners of the Americans* (1832) came out the year of Fanny's arrival in America. Later, Harriet Martineau, Captain Marryat, and Dickens weighed in with their own disillusioned tomes. None of these literary pilgrims flattered the new republic. In fact, they caused immense outrage. So did Fanny. Young, beautiful, and talented, the most celebrated actress in America, Fanny, like Byron, woke to find herself the center of a storm. An admired celebrity had become a controversial author. "The city is in an uproar," wrote her Boston friend Catharine Sedgwick upon publication of Fanny's *Journal*. "Nothing else is talked of."[22] Even though elisions concealed the names of people she mentioned, in Philadelphia, where Fanny now lived and where she published her book, the response was even more violent. Fanny by her mid-twenties had garnered a Byronic reputation of her own.

In June 1834 Fanny had married Pierce Butler. A life as an actress was not deemed entirely proper, and after marriage an actress, unless married to an actor, invariably left her profession. Fanny bowed to accepted custom. The newly marrieds settled on Butler Farm, on the Old York Road in Germantown, then a village outside Philadelphia. Compared to bustling New York, Philadelphia impressed Fanny with its "greater air of age" and its "perfect silence and solitude."[23] She felt isolated. In nineteenth-century America married women came under their husband's jurisdiction and gave up their property and most legal rights. Fanny found her new dependency constricting and irksome. Almost from the beginning her marriage began to unravel.

Most English actors came from nonconformist backgrounds. Fanny's family was originally Catholic and as a schoolgirl she attended a dissenters' chapel.[24] In America she went to services of diverse denominations. By 1836, influenced by her meeting with the Bostonian William Ellery Channing, the main expounder of Unitarianism in America, and an admirer of William Howard Furness, she became a committed member of Philadelphia's First Unitarian Church of which Furness was minister and Sully a member. There she taught Sunday school. "Just think of her," commented Furness, "as a Sunday School teacher."[25]

Furness's outspoken anti-slavery position split parishioners after 1839. Fanny, who by then had seen the grim reality of slavery on her husband's Sea Islands plantations off Georgia, supported Furness with enthusiasm. Living on them in 1838–39, she recorded at first hand and vividly the slave and planter life she saw. Her *Journal of a Residence on a Georgian Plantation in 1838–1839* was not published until 1863, with the United States in the throes of its Civil War. The only English woman to describe her experiences in the slave-holding South, Fanny helped tilt British public opinion towards the Union.[26]

Abolitionists in Philadelphia were widely viewed as extremist. Sully was not an extremist. Most of the time he was hardly a political being. A Federalist, later a Whig, he distanced himself from Furness's position. Like the vast majority of Philadelphia's citizens, he was opposed to abolition.[27] He valued his minister, but he had grown up in the Britain of the 1780s, a conservative decade in which the slave trade prospered; had come to maturity in Virginia and South Carolina, where his sisters continued to reside; and in 1838 had watched Furness marry his daughter Ellen to a Southern plantation owner. Along with many other parishioners, including Pierce Butler, the artist absented himself for some years from Furness's services. Butler kept his distance, but Sully returned to the congregation on April 25, 1847, when Furness conducted the funeral service for his son, Thomas Wilcocks Sully. Sully advocated ecumenical tolerance regarding disputes among the various Christian sects. For him, Pope's "The Universal Prayer" was "a complete compendium of moral and religious belief."[28]

Sully joined the pro-Federalist Washington Benevolent Society of Pennsylvania. He also served as vice president of the Pennsylvania Colonization Society, whose mission, supported by many white Americans, was to return freed Blacks to Liberia. Abraham Lincoln was a nearly lifelong supporter of colonization, as was Harriet Beecher Stowe. Like a number of other artists, including Jacob Eichholtz, Sully contributed portraits of the Society's officers and supporters. His 18 portraits between 1846 and 1865 made him the best-represented artist in the Society's Portrait Gallery.[29]

In the mid-1840s an unhappy Fanny left her uncongenial husband and their two children. Although she still found performing distasteful, financial need compelled her to reembark on a stage career in America and England. Her first Shakespearean readings date from 1848. Longfellow, much impressed, wrote an admiring sonnet, "On Mrs. Kemble's Readings from Shakespeare."[30] "She was so saturated with Shakespeare," reminisced Henry James, "that she made him the air she lived in. . . . He was indeed her utterance, the language she spoke most from herself."[31] For some years Fanny based herself in Lenox, Massachusetts, in the Berkshires, where her presence helped promote its popularity as a resort.

Not everyone responded positively to Fanny. Some contemporaries viewed her less charitably than did James. They found her self-centered, hard-edged, difficult to deal with. Several who knew both her and her husband thought their marital problems more her fault than his. Fanny spoke her mind, spoke it freely, spoke it well. At many a turn she offended propriety. Even the imperial Lady Holland winced before her words. All the Kembles had an innate sense of theatricality, and as a style of behavior the theatrical worked less well in America than in England. Even her stage skills did not escape criticism. In 1848 the acerbic William Charles Macready, a rival for the public's attention, rated her "*ignorant of the very first rudiments of her art.*" (She evaluated his talent with equal candor.[32]) Philadelphia's indefatigable diarist Sidney George Fisher initially judged Fanny as artificial. She nevertheless fascinated Fisher, and over the years he came to view her more positively. Once married, Fanny could receive visitors, and in 1839

Fisher encountered a changed Fanny, "a very gifted person" but now one whose "qualities of heart & character are as excellent as those of her intellect." Each time Fisher met her he understood her a little better. "She is more agreeable in tête a tête than in society," he wrote in 1844, "because she is simple & natural then, whereas she exhibits too great a desire to shine, her conversation and manners are too exaggerated & theatrical[,] in company." In 1860 Fisher spoke of her as "a woman of genius & noble impulses & kind feelings. Too much will & vitality & force of character, however, to be very happy in domestic life, more especially with such a man as Butler, her inferior far in all intellectual endowments." In 1867, in an extended tribute, he praised her as "a person of overwhelming vitality," whose magnetic presence it was not easy to resist.[33]

Later years Mrs Kemble (as she became known) spent in England. James valued her "deep, rich human nature" and thought her "the first woman in London." A force of nature, a manifestation of genius, possessed of a resonant capacity for friendship, Fanny was unlikely to be tamed or controlled. The more James saw of her, the more he admired. Fanny is "the elegant and unyielding older woman" who accompanied him on the first leg of the voyage written up in that most charming of travel narratives, *A Little Tour in France*.[34] Summers Fanny often spent in the company of her other great love besides Shakespeare, the Alps, which Byron's sojourn and his Alpine arias in *Childe Harold* III and *Manfred* had made meaningful to her and whose heights she loved to scale.[35] Until death came in 1893 she lived life to the fullest. James, who recalled her in a tribute of heartfelt eloquence, remembered particularly the "extraordinary mixture of incongruous things, of England and France in her blood, of America and England in her relationships, of the footlights and the glaciers in her activity, of conformity and contumacy in her character, and tragedy and comedy in her talk."[36]

*

Portraiture and the theater had long linked arms. Actresses and actors performed, painters painted them. Illusionists all, they frequently interacted. Sully, passionate about the stage, loved beauty no less than drama. His unbridled enthusiasm for watching Fanny Kemble perform developed into one for painting her.

It is not unknown for male portraitists to form attachments to their female sitters, particularly when they are attractive. In the 1780s the statuesque Emma Hart, model and celebrated beauty, captivated George Romney. A woman who played many roles to many men, the much-coveted Emma had lovers, including Charles Greville and William Hamilton, became Lady Hamilton, and eventually formed a notorious liaison with Admiral Nelson. Meeting Emma in 1782, Romney painted her at least 23, possibly 50 times in portraits of seductive sweetness.[37] Emma had evidently a genius for "sitting" and for striking poses, and Romney rendered her innocent-looking loveliness in a bewildering variety of attitudes, often as the model for subjects of virtue. In his worshipful obsession for the unobtainable he rivalled Dante.

Actresses exerted powerful sway over Thomas Lawrence. His 1790 portrait of the actress Elizabeth Fadden was his first great triumph. Sarah Siddons, whom he had met as a youngster, drew him to her as into a magnetic field. He executed many drawings and paintings of Sir Joshua's Tragic Muse and for most of his life remained quietly enamored, on stage and off, of her. Mrs Siddons stirred him to odd emotional capers. To her attractive daughters, Sally and Maria, he transferred in the 1790s a portion of his romantic devotion to the mother. He paid court, successively and at the same time, to both. They were in delicate health. Maria died of consumption in 1798; in 1803, Sally followed.[38] Lawrence, heartbroken, wore black all his life. Though he developed other attachments, Mrs Wolff the most compelling, he never married and stayed close to Mrs Siddons and her family. Such emotional experience gave insight and depth to his portraits of women. Flawless in technique, fluid in handling, each captures in its seemingly unstudied brilliance an individual soul.[39]

In 1829 Mrs Siddons's niece Fanny debuted at Covent Garden. Lawrence, now nearly sixty, found himself intensely moved. Two years before he had drawn her at 18, a sketch she termed the "likest thing you can have of me."[40] Enchanted once again by a female Kemble, Lawrence saw in her the reincarnation of his youth.[41] Her stage presence left him mesmerized. He wrote up his observations of her performances and sent them to her the next morning. Fanny admired the intelligence behind the perception: "Lawrence was the only man I ever heard speak about the stage with understanding and accuracy."[42] He intended to paint her as Juliet, but death intervened in 1830. It would have taken little for an attachment to develop, but theirs remained an *amitié amoureuse*. Shortly after his death Fanny wrote a friend:

> The elegant distinction of his person, the exquisite refined gentleness of his voice and manner – had I sat to him for the projected portrait of Juliet, in spite of the forty years' difference in our ages and my knowledge of his disastrous relations with my cousins, I should have become in love with him myself and have become the fourth member of my family whose life he had disturbed and embittered.[43]

In America actors and actresses stood more apart from polite society than in Britain. Because they possessed astonishing gifts, they were superior to ordinary mortals; because they led (maybe) tainted lives, inferior. To survive financially, theaters had to present widely varying bills of fare to please the different socioeconomic groups that made up the audience. As in Regency England, the well-to-do in Federal America viewed uneasily this mixing of classes. The wonder, thought William Dunlap, was that, given their precarious existence, many actresses remained virtuous.[44] Sarah Siddons, unusual in her time, maintained an unsullied reputation. She was an exception. Her niece would prove another.

When Fanny first arrived in Philadelphia in 1832, no one knew what her morals were – or would become. The Kembles, as Britain's leading acting family, were welcome in London's fashionable circles, but in America the reception was less favorable. Actors were not social pariahs, but prominent Philadelphians looked down upon them. Much as they enjoyed the Kembles on stage, few invited them into their homes. Fanny in Washington was introduced to President Andrew Jackson and at dinner sat between John Quincy Adams and Daniel Webster; she spent time with Washington Irving there and in New York met Fenimore Cooper. But well-born admirers believed that by calling upon her they would compromise their social position.

A few Philadelphians remained unfazed. Nicholas and Jane Biddle accompanied their eldest son Edward to meet Fanny. "They are the only inhabitants of this good city," she wrote, "who have done us that honour." Soon Edward, "with a nosegay as big as himself in his hand," came calling on his own.[45] Dinner at the Biddles followed. It was not enough for Fanny. She remarked coolly: "'One exception makes a rule,' say the scholars, and by that same token the Philadelphians are among the most inhospitable set of people it has ever been my good fortune to fall with." Puzzled by "the want of courtesy" she and her father encountered in the City of Brotherly Love, Fanny shrewdly attributed it "to the greater prevalence of that very small spirit of dignity which is always afraid of committing itself."[46]

The Sullys proved a second exception. Through the offices of a mutual friend, possibly Washington Irving, Sully met Fanny and her father in early November 1832. The son of traveling actors and himself a longtime theater buff, Sully got along with people in all walks of life. Scoffing at the national unease before stage morality, he and his family soon became intimate with the Kembles. Seemingly in anticipation of their arrival, but more likely in admiration of Reynolds's Tragic Muse, he had named a daughter, born in 1818, Rosalie Kemble Sully.[47] Fanny's *Journal* records numerous instances of to-and-froing between Head's Hotel, on 3rd near Spruce St, where she and her father stayed, and the artist's home a few blocks away at 5th and Chestnut. The Kembles pleased the Sullys; the Sullys pleased them.

Now it was Sully's turn to become bewitched. "I must gratify my vanity in telling you that I have had the good fortune to paint a very successful likeness of Fanny Kemble from memory," he enthused to Audubon, then in London. "She has paid me two visits; but I was not able to induce her to sit for a portrait; as she had assured me that she has made a solemn vow never to sit again."[48] Charles Kemble came by to see the sketch Sully had made of his daughter.[49] Did Sully bring back to Fanny memories of Lawrence? Did her unwillingness to sit recall to her the potentially dangerous infatuation of that admired artist? Sully too was a handsome man. Neal describes him as always "a favorite with the better part of mankind." In 1833, the year he first sketched Fanny, Sully was 50 but looked "as if he were still a young man."[50] During Fanny's Philadelphia engagements he seized every opportunity, in society and on stage, to observe her.[51]

Fanny's American *Journal* often mentions Sully. He was one of the few Philadelphians whose company she genuinely enjoyed, and her reluctance to pose did not diminish her liking for him. "How we English folk do cling to our own habits," she wrote in her American *Journal*, "our own views, our own things, our own people."[52] In Sully, who admitted a preference for "old-fashioned things," she relished the company of another exile.[53] Besides, Fanny was a woman of whom (said Henry James) "music was in her blood," and Sully breathed music.[54] Most of all, she admired Sully's artistic talent. "Called in on my way to Mr. Sulley's who is painting a portrait of my father," she commented on December 18 about the work now known as *Charles Kemble as Fazio*. "Saw one or two lovely women's pictures. I wish he would go to England. I think it would answer his purposes very well." "Called at Mr. Sully's," she wrote two weeks later, "and spent half an hour delightfully in his studio. His picture of my father is very like and very agreeable. 'Tis too youthful by a good deal, but the expression of his face is extremely good, and 'tis the likest thing I have seen of him. We had a long discussion about the stage." An able, intelligent conversationalist like Lawrence, Sully may have rivalled the English artist in acuteness of observation. On February 2 Fanny "spent a delightful hour with Mr. Sully and his family. He is a most agreeable person, but he thinks too well of acting."[55] With the artist's family, including wife Sarah and the daughters, Fanny got along swimmingly. They responded with equal warmth to her.

Did Byron enter the conversations? Who in America better, after all, with whom to discuss her favorite poet than the artist who had painted his portrait? That portrait, now owned by Jacob Eichholtz, had left Philadelphia earlier in the year. Sully had never met Byron, but he knew people who had or like Irving admired him greatly, and such was his curiosity about him that in England several years later he sought out everyone with a connection to Byron.

*

Sully had asked Fanny in November to sit for a portrait. Her refusal did not deter him from asking again. The happy day she accepted took its time coming. If memories of Lawrence's rapt attention lay behind her initial hesitation, she need not have worried. This artist was emotionally rooted. The charismatic young actress obviously felt comfortable with the handsome older painter. "F. Kemble has at last offered to sit to me," a gleeful Sully confided to his journal on March 17, 1833. Working at white-hot speed he finished the portrait in four days. He gave it, he tells 'us, "to my wife."[56] Was this his way of keeping Fanny's likeness in the household?[57] Of the 13 portraits Sully did of Fanny, it remains one of the more engaging.

Nine of these portraits date from 1832 to 1834. Three – all of Fanny as herself – emerged from the initial sitting on March 10, 1833, and those that followed. The others Sully did from memory or from sketches he made watching her perform. Two portraits – *Fanny as Beatrice* and *Fanny as Isabella* – he later took with him to England. He painted Fanny in her Shakespearean roles – Beatrice in *Much Ado about Nothing*, Juliet in *Romeo and Juliet*, Lady Macbeth – as well as Bianca in Milman's *Fazio* and, one of her signature roles, Julia in Sheridan Knowles's popular melodrama *The Hunchback*.[58]

Multiple portraits allowed Sully to seize multiple facets of Fanny. None quite satisfied him. Medwin, whose best-selling *Conversations of Lord Byron* (1824) Sully may well have read, thought the poet "would have made the finest actor in the world" for "his countenance was capable of expressing the tenderest, as well as the strongest emotions."[59] Medwin's words apply equally to Fanny. She, like Byron, never seemed twice the same person. As with the poet, artists had difficulty portraying her, and the quintessential Fanny may well have eluded Sully. No portrait of her much resembles the others. Decades later, upon meeting protean Fanny, Fredrika Bremer, whose intelligence rivaled hers, commented shrewdly, "I do not know that I ought to see *so many people as you are*."[60]

If Byron obsessed Fanny Kemble, Fanny obsessed Sully. Offerings to the goddess, his portraits pay homage to a woman he found enormously appealing. Like Lawrence before him, Sully may have been half in love with Fanny, or with her face, or with her as an incarnation of someone else. His reaction was not unusual. During Fanny's lifetime her admirers treated her to a kind of fetishistic devotion that transcended circumstances and age differences. Thomas Lawrence in the 1820s, Edward Biddle and Pierce Butler in the 1830s, Sidney Smith in the 1840s, Henry James in her later decades – all succumbed. The public hungered for images of the former actress now married (but unhappily), who had written a candid (but controversial) book about America, and whose stage readings of Shakespeare kept her in the public eye. Engravings and lithographs of several of Sully's portraits – including one as herself (1833), as *Julia* (1833), and as *Beatrice* (1833) – helped feed the hunger. Sully usually details only Fanny's face, neck, and hair, loosely sketching the rest. What drew him to her was the face – and in that face, the eyes: eyes that glowed with a fierce intensity of being.

"Nobody ever painted more beautiful eyes," claimed Neal of Sully; "not even Gainsborough, nor Sir Thomas Lawrence." Sully's women, for Neal, have "the eyes of poetry, deep and melancholy, or patient and timid; but always, whatever be their expression, looking as if copied at the critical moment of their extremest beauty."[61] In all Sully's portraits of her Fanny's preternaturally large brown eyes, apparently inherited from her beloved Aunt Dall, stare out at the viewer.[62]

Of the portraits, Fanny liked best *Fanny Kemble as Beatrice*. Henry James remembered an impromptu Beatrice of Fanny's that rang "like a silver bell": Fanny embodied that "charming creature" with "all rapidity and resonance of wit."[63] Intelligence and sensuality conjoin in what she considered "one of the best likenesses ever taken of me."[64] Sully's *Fanny as Beatrice* (see color plate section), worked on from September 22 to October 7, 1833, is his only portrait of her as a stage figure painted from life sittings.[65] Fanny looks back over a bare left shoulder, a pose Sully later adapted, and reversed, for his several *Victorias*. *Fanny Kemble as Beatrice* joins his full-length *Victoria* as one of Sully's few portraits that shows the subject with parted lips. Fanny possessed beauty, sensuality, and brains in abundance. Sully evoked her beauty, implied her sensuality (the shoulder), and brought out her intelligence (the eyes). The eyes indicate mental toughness. Imperious, occasionally disdainful, sometimes hinting at anger held in reserve, her eyes shielded by raised eyebrows, Fanny radiates confidence and command, mystery and passion.

Passionate women fascinated Sully. Stage figures allowed him greater liberty than his more usual portrait subjects. Sully delighted in painting sensuous flesh; he savored particularly *des épaules impertinentes*. Aware of Wertmüller's *Danaë* and Vanderlyn's *Ariadne*, he attempted in 1813 a nude, *Musidora*, a bathing nymph whose lover has come upon her unexpectedly. The subject derives from Ovid as retold in Thomson's *Seasons*, a poem that long influenced the sensibilities of British and American artists.[66] Sully's painting has an interesting genealogy. It copied Charles Robert Leslie's copy of Benjamin West's 1802 original, entitled *Arethusa*, which was exhibited at the Pennsylvania Academy.[67] West's *Arethusa* has not been seen since 1829, and Leslie's copy may not have survived. Sully's first version, with Musidora looking at the viewer, was exhibited in Baltimore and perhaps Philadelphia in 1820.[68] In 1835, the year after he completed the last of his Fanny Kemble portraits, Sully rethought *Musidora*. In his new version she still displays an enticing shoulder but now turns away from the viewer.[69] She is shorter, fuller, more voluptuous. Study of the nude was limited for Sully and other artists of the time to copying paintings and prints. Transcending these limitations in his training, Sully developed an original and compelling interpretation. His revised *Musidora* (Figure 9) is one of the most voluptuous nudes painted in America during the nineteenth century.

Besides the shoulder, might there be a further connection between *Fanny Kemble as Beatrice* and the second *Musidora*? We can, I think, consider *Musidora* as a portrait of sorts of Fanny. The shoulder is indeed enticingly rendered, but so is much else, and Musidora's anatomy is such as one might imagine Fanny Kemble's to have been. She did not pose in this way for Sully, but the artist who had so often recreated her face from memory was surely capable of recreating the rest. Musidora's story – and chastely erotic pose – appealed greatly to contemporaries. Bare-shouldered Fanny in *Fanny Kemble as Beatrice* looks forward to (and likely is) the revised *Musidora*. Sully's *Victoria* will owe something to both.[70]

While Fanny admired herself as *Beatrice*, the portrait Sully did of her in 1835 left her uneasy (Figure 10).[71] She feared that Sully might have idealized her. "Sully's forte," she thought, "lay in delineating the softness and charm of female character." She did not wish to be thought soft and charming. "I do not feel very sanguine about it," she wrote, "for Sully's characteristic is delicacy rather than power, and mine may not be power, but it is certainly not delicacy."[72] She was right on both counts regarding herself, but regarding Sully, right only partially.

Sully once asked his friend and fellow artist, C. R. Leslie, to tell him what was his "leading fault" as a portraitist. "Your pictures," Leslie told him, "'look as if you could blow them away.' 'Ah,' I replied, 'you mean that they

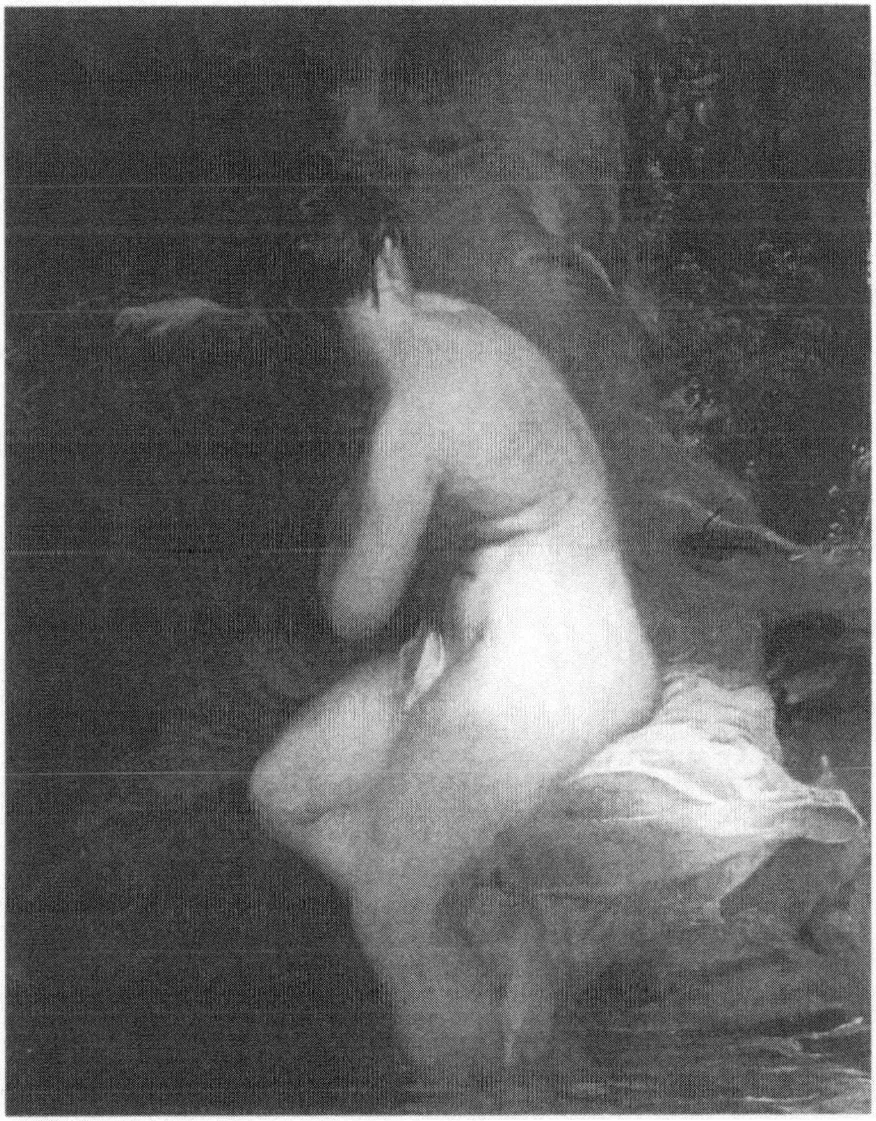

9 Thomas Sully, *Musidora* (revised version, 1835). The Metropolitan Museum of Art, New York

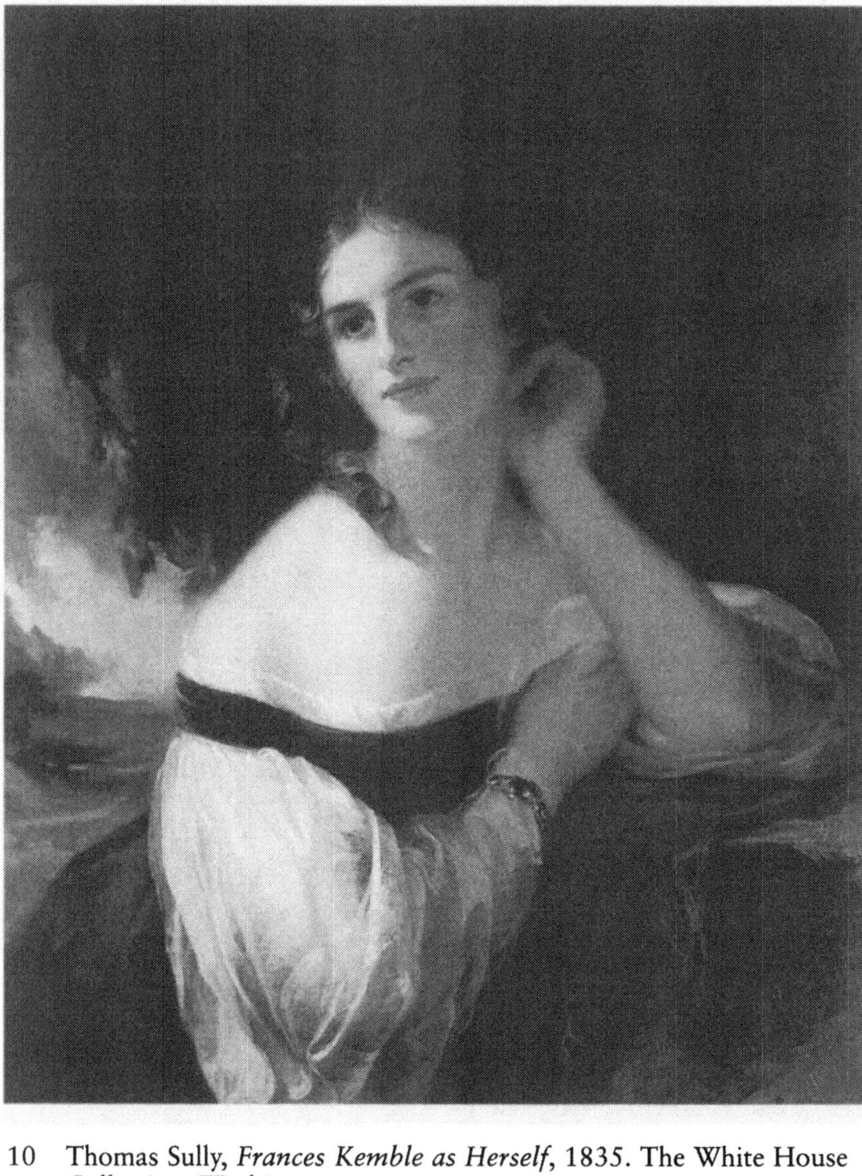

10 Thomas Sully, *Frances Kemble as Herself*, 1835. The White House Collection, Washington

lack strength.' 'Yes,' said he, 'that is it.'"[73] Leslie's criticism echoes Fanny's: lacking "strength" is another name for "delicacy." "Sully's own imagination," recalled Henry Budd, who knew the artist in high old age, "was of the gentle rather than of the robust character, and yet not effeminate."[74] Even Neal, who knew Sully in his prime, agreed: "His characteristicks are elegance and taste. He is not so remarkable for strength, or fidelity, or workmanship."[75] These criticisms have a limited validity, but hardly apply to Sully's major depictions of men, including Cooke as Richard III and Washington, or of women, including most of his portraits of Fanny Kemble.

But Fanny has a point. However gracefully and delicately he portrayed her, Sully could lack "strength." Several likenesses of Fanny are what we may call "floating heads," a mode of portraiture Sully occasionally practiced from the 1820s on. In these oval-shaped vignettes, a disembodied face emerges from cloud-like swirls set within a red, pink, cream, or brown background. Neither clothing nor background distracts our gaze from the features.

Surprisingly, Fanny expressed unease not about a "floating head" but about a larger, later portrait of herself done in 1834. Elegantly attired, her visage as thoughtful as it is beautiful, she looks out half-defiantly. Sully has rendered her power no less than her delicacy. Perhaps she and Sully had had a talk. His portrait reflects a woman who had a mind of her own. He knew it, and she knew it. Intelligent women were after all something of a Sully specialty. The year before Fanny's arrival in Philadelphia, he had painted Rebecca Gratz (Figure 11), the distinguished lady who had secured Sully several of his early Philadelphia commissions. Still beautiful at 51, intelligence emanating from every feature, she continued her interest in his career. Sully responded to Fanny's brains no less than to her beauty. Four years later Sully depicted another young woman whose bearing also embodied delicacy and power. This was Queen Victoria.

*

Sully had long wished to make a second study trip to England. He did not, as he had hoped, go abroad in 1824, or in 1829 when his lingering dissatisfaction with Philadelphia peaked. Upward turns in his fortunes cancelled both schemes. In the late summer of 1837 he sensed the time had come. The Panic of that year had reduced the demand for portraits, and a change of venue would improve his health. His friend, admirer and patron, Edward Carey, generously advanced him $1000 on commissions for copies of subject paintings by Sir Joshua Reynolds.[76] Other Philadelphians – Nicholas Biddle among them – placed similar commissions. Soon Sully had sufficient funds with his savings to cover household expenses in Philadelphia and for a stay of some months abroad.

Literally at the last moment, the Society of the Sons of St George in Philadelphia, aware of Sully's imminent trip to London, sent him a hand-delivered letter on October 9 – the day before his departure – asking him to paint Britain's new queen, Victoria. The Society, which provided relief for

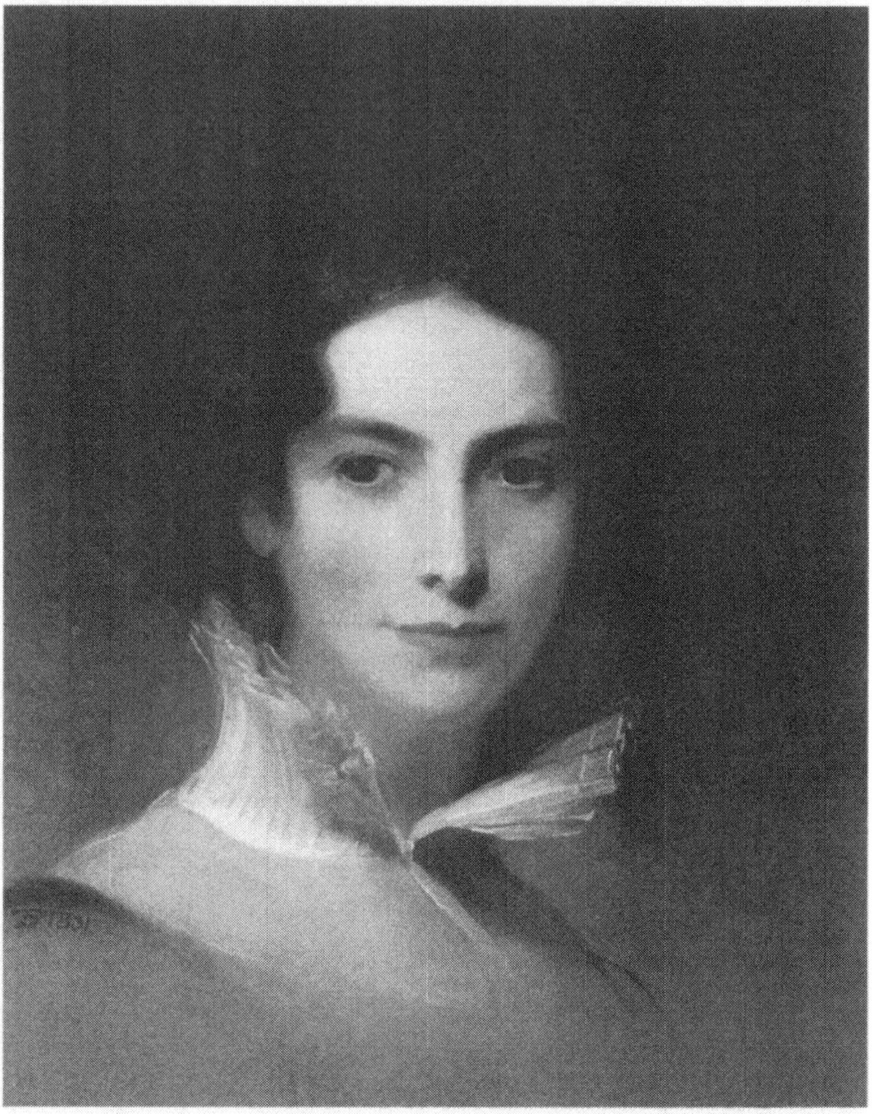

11 Thomas Sully, *Rebecca Gratz*, 1831. The Rosenbach Museum, Philadelphia

down-on-their-luck English immigrants, wished to adorn its meeting room with a full-length portrait of the queen. Surprised by the request and even more by the timing, Sully agreed immediately.[77] The Society's commission of $1000 would further underpin his trip. Accompanied by his 23-year-old daughter Blanche, the artist left for New York on the 10th. Upon arrival in Portsmouth on November 3, father and daughter went up to London. They took rooms first in Howland Street, then rented a three-room flat at 46 Great Marlborough Street. Thanks to unusually detailed entries in Sully's journal and the preservation of his and Blanche's detailed letters home, we know more about Sully's doings during the next eight months than for any other period.[78] From these documents it is clear that the artist regarded his sojourn abroad as a high point of his life.

London soon became a major attraction for the Sullys. Hoping for a lengthy stay but finding the city "*enormously* expensive," Sully realized he needed to seek commissions.[79] The city's wonders unfolded before wide-eyed Blanche like scenes from the *Arabian Nights*. Awed by the "mixture of splendour and misery," Blanche yet found misery exceeding splendor.[80] When by themselves, she and her father talked "of dear home and our now twice valued Philadelphia and the many kind friends we have there."[81] Almost immediately they entered into a lively social round. Their letters and journals record constant leaving and receiving of cards, of dinner invitations and parties. With Joseph Bonaparte, Napoleon's elder brother, whose fabulous art collection in his home outside Philadelphia Sully had studied, the artist "spent a delightful evening" admiring the paintings in his London home. Dining "at the fashionable hour of half past seven," Sully savored "grouse from Norway and apples from Philadelphia."[82] Father and daughter spent several evenings with Harriet Martineau, a fellow Unitarian now back from her American adventure. They had met her during her six weeks' residence in Philadelphia in 1834.[83]

Sully passed happy hours with old friends Leslie and Audubon and with a newer acquaintance, the portraitist G. P. A. Healy.[84] He met Greenough and Doughty, he called upon Martin Archer Shee and David Wilkie; he got to know Landseer, whose animal paintings he admired, and the portraitists Cattermole and Pickersgill.[85] He developed tremendous enthusiasm for Turner's landscapes, especially those in "his new gorgeous style."[86] Most valuable perhaps, given that the original purpose for his trip was to educate himself further about art, Sully looked hard at paintings in both public and private collections. Reynolds and Lawrence again vied for his fervent approbation, with the palm going – just – to Lawrence.[87] He even went to school again, reporting home on November 27 that he had "attended one Lecture on Anatomy at the Royal Academy – I shall go through the course – as also those on Statuary – Architecture & other subjects."[88]

Sully met many of Byron's acquaintances, including Rogers, Moore, Hunt, Lockhart, and the publisher John Murray. It seems he made a special effort to seek out those who had known the poet. Murray he had called on during his first week in London. Washington Irving, who like Byron published with Murray and who admired the poet immensely, may have written a letter of introduction. Though Sully did not record his initial impression of Murray, he spoke of him later as "friendly and agreeable." Several times Murray invited him to dine with him and his family. The company on January 28 included "the great Captain Back – Moore the poet – his son – Landseer and a Mr. [James] Smith an author."[89] Sully was excited at being placed next to "T. Moore and son!!!" Moore, whom hostesses eagerly sought out as a dinner guest, thoroughly enchanted the artist. Sully's account of the evening suggests why. "Altho' unwell," Byron's biographer "shewed himself to be that joyous, sparkling mortal I have always thought him to be. [H]is wit, his short stories were so *pat* to the occasion – and the cause of wit in others that he proved to be indeed the soul of the company."[90] In mid-March, again at the Murrays, Sully and Blanche met "*the* M*r* Lockhart," Scott's formidable son-in-law and biographer-to-be. Blanche, not present at the first dinner, had "pictured M*r* L rather an old man." She was delighted to find him "youngish and somewhat handsome – very entertaining and of course highly intellectual."[91]

A few days later Sully called at Murray's offices at 50 Albemarle Street to thank him for the dinner. The publisher, "with a pleasant freedom," showed him his fine collection of literary portraits.[92] Just two years before, Murray had commissioned from Thomas Phillips a copy of his cloaked *Byron* of 1813–14. The copy now hung at 50 Albemarle Street, but Sully does not mention it. Did he observe to Murray that he had done a portrait of Byron himself? We do not know, though it would be surprising if he had not. Subsequently, the Murrays called on Sully and Blanche; Blanche "like[d] vastly" the Murray daughters, who went out of their way to make her stay pleasant, taking her around the city and to the Zoological Gardens.[93]

Everywhere he went in London Sully assiduously noted Byronic echoes. Letters home and journal entries detail his interest in the poet whose portrait he had painted ten years before. That interest had increased, not diminished. The day before Sully first met Murray (November 9) he had called upon Cattermole, who occupied Byron's rooms in the Albany.[94] Sully may also have met Leigh Hunt.[95] One night at the opera Blanche was thrilled "to think we were so near the Countess Blessington and D'Orsay . . . and never knew it."[96] Lady Blessington had in 1834 published her *Conversations of Lord Byron*, and she and D'Orsay were a well-known and often commented-upon London pair. Sully and Blanche breakfasted with the everlasting Rogers, in whose library "he has many a time entertained Walter Scott – Lord Byron and M*rs* Siddons." Whereas Sully stood agape before Rogers's Old Masters, particularly Titian's *Noli mi tangere*, the fame of the assembled guests overwhelmed Blanche.[97] They heard John Braham, the tenor for whom Byron had written the lyrics for *Hebrew Melodies*. Braham did not impress the normally easy-to-please Blanche. "Heard him sing," she exclaimed; "never want to hear him again – you cannot imagine worse – still he is a great favourite and every song *encored*."[98] Blanche also met Allan Cunningham, "the author, and intimate friend of Sir Walter Scott – [who] told me innumerable anecdotes of Sir W."[99] Murray had published Cunningham's six-volume *Lives of the Most Eminent British Painters*,

Sculptors, and Artists (1829–33), which Sully had read with interest, as well he might, for during his first London venture he had met many of the individuals whose careers Cunningham chronicled. Dining with the Egertons in March, father and daughter encountered Charles Babbage, "well known to science." With Ada, Countess of Lovelace, Byron's only legitimate child, as gifted for mathematics as her father had been for poetry, Babbage would develop the first proto-computer.[100]

At a gathering in December Blanche mentioned that she had sat next to "a nice old man – and friend of Lord Byron."[101] This was John Wright, whom Sully spoke with at the fabled January 28 dinner at Murray's. Wright had done yeoman's work editing Byron, chiefly overseeing Murray's seventeen-volume set of the works (1832–33). He wished now to prepare an edition of Byron's "correspondence and other memoranda."[102] As a result of his conversation with Wright, Sully on February 14 wrote to Mrs Catherine Potter Stith. Mrs Stith had encountered Byron on May 21, 1822, on board the *USS Constitution*, anchored off the Italian coast, and had subsequently corresponded with him. Sully had known her in Philadelphia and painted her husband's portrait. He told her that at Murray's table he had "happened to mention the circumstance of your meeting the famous Poet, when on your way to Gibraltar – his wit on board the [ship?] you were, with your husband – the affair of the rose and his subsequent note to you and presentation of Goethe[']s Faust with his marginal notes." Wright had requested Sully to ask Mrs Stith if he might include in his forthcoming volume her reminiscences of Byron; better yet, Sully went on, if "your written account" of the meeting could include "a copy of his Lordship's note; and any thing besides that you think novel."[103] The encounter sketched in Sully's letter to Mrs Stith is worth pausing over, for it provides important clues for understanding the depth of his response to Byron and why he had painted the poet as he did.

*

The *Constitution*, the most fabled ship in the American navy, was in May 1822 anchored off Leghorn. Byron lived at Montenero nearby. Its commander, Commodore Jacob Jones, invited the poet to pay him and his ship an official visit. George Bancroft, the future historian, one of the guests invited, recorded the response of the Americans to Byron – and his to them:

> Finding all present to be Americans, his manner became easy, frank and cheerful . . . Every one who came near him held that day a happy one. One lady, of great personal beauty, put out her hand, and saying 'When I return to Philadelphia, my friends will ask for some token that I have spoken with Lord Byron,' she gently took a rose which he wore in the button-hole of his black frock-coat. He was pleased with her unaffected boldness.[104]

The lady was the wife of the American consul at Tunis, Major Townsend Stith. Catherine Potter Stith, her biographer states without exaggeration, was "a woman of rare physical charm, twenty-seven years old, an accomplished musician on the piano, guitar, and harp, a linguist and student of considerable ability, and a person who possessed exceptionally broad intellectual attainment and interests."[105]

Also present on board the *Constitution* that morning was William Edward West. West, Sully's former student, must also have impressed the poet, for that summer Byron granted him the rare privilege of painting his portrait and that of his *amante*, Teresa Guiccioli. West forms a link in the chain of relationship between Sully and Byron; the talented Mrs Stith forms another; Trelawny, whose presence aboard the *Constitution* has usually not been noted, a third. Byron was in exceptionally good humor that day. He gave the *Constitution* "a thorough examination" and was, he recalled, "treated with all possible honour and ceremony."[106] The time on board went by happily. The occasion meant much to those present, not least to Byron himself.

From the *Constitution* Captain Chauncey took Byron to look over the *Ontario*, where the welcome was if possible even more enthusiastic. In the quarters of the junior officers the poet came upon – perhaps deliberately placed! – "a New York edition of his poems." He "took it up with every appearance of pleasure, and seemed to interpret it as an earnest of his fame."[107] American frigates much impressed Byron. "I found them finer ships than your own of the same class, well manned & officered," he wrote Murray, nicely separating his pro-American perspective from that of his Tory publisher.[108]

The *Constitution* formed part of America's small Mediterranean-based squadron. Despite a treaty requiring tribute, pirates from the Barbary States (Algiers, Morocco, Tripoli, and Tunis) had long preyed on American merchantmen plying the trade routes, stealing their cargoes and selling their crews into slavery or holding them to ransom. In 1805 the United States signed a new treaty with the Pasha of Tripoli but not with the other states. The attacks continued until 1815 when Commodore Stephen Decatur led a squadron that captured and destroyed the pirate fleet. Shortly afterward, a treaty with the Bey of Algiers ended both tribute and conflict.

Byron was extremely well versed in the annals of the American navy. He knew, for example, which American frigates had fought British ships during the War of 1812, which American naval officers had duels and their outcome. That a first cousin, Sir Peter Parker, had died in 1814 in a British attempt to storm Baltimore did not prevent Byron from admiring American naval resourcefulness. During the War of 1812 American frigates had gained the victory in 14 of 18 engagements with British ships. Byron was aware of this. "It is to be observed that the manly prowess and marine nerve" of Britain, he told Isaac Nathan, "is very rapidly taking wing to America."[109] No less than the ships they sailed, Byron had good reason to admire the officers and crews who greeted him on board the *Constitution* and the *Ontario*.

Launched in 1794, the *Constitution* was meant to be a frigate powerful enough to fight any other frigate afloat, quick enough to flee anything bigger. It had a frigate's speed, but in size and stoutness – its heavy oak frame was in fact virtually impenetrable – it was comparable to a small ship-of-the-line. During the War of 1812 the ship had stood invincible against the Royal Navy.[110] In its celebrated encounter with the British frigate *Guerrière*, the first naval battle of the war, the crew cried out after a cannonball bounced off, "Huzza! her sides are made of iron." Thus the ship's nickname of "Old Ironsides." The *Constitution*'s success in this and later encounters disturbed British national pride in its navy. Byron was thrilled to be on board so famous a ship.

If the War of 1812 did not change much between Britain and America, it did produce a bevy of American naval heroes. Depictions of them and of naval scenes became fashionable. Sully was as familiar (and presumably as impressed) as Byron with the officers and their victories. He painted Charles Stewart (who had commanded the *Constitution* in the War of 1812) in 1812, Stephen Decatur (famous as well for blowing up the captured *Philadelphia* in Tripoli harbor – and later for "our country, right or wrong") in 1814, Commodore Jones in 1816 and 1817, James Biddle (whose naval career we touch upon in Chapter 6) in 1839, Admiral Samuel Phillips Lee in 1845. He also designed many of the commemorative medals of war heroes cast at the US Mint in Philadelphia.[111]

Byron had gladly relinquished his *boutonnière* to Mrs Stith. She evidently charmed him. As well as talk (and no doubt compliments) about Byron's poetry, German literature entered the conversation, particularly the merits of the great Goethe, to whom Byron had dedicated *Sardanapalus* in 1822, then when Murray inexplicably omitted the dedication, reattached it to *Werner*. The next day he sent her his prized edition of *Faust* with engravings based on Morris Retzsch's designs. It came with a note reflecting his pleasure in encountering so many congenial Americans: "I have also been ever a Well wisher to your Country and Countrymen – in common with all unprejudiced minds amongst my own."[112]

Byron tended to regard America and Americans idealistically. Although individual Yankees had sought him out in the past, his visits to the *Constitution* and *Ontario* were probably his first sustained encounter with a people for whom he had often expressed admiration. By "unprejudiced minds" among his countrymen Byron meant minds that judged people and nations not from political bias but openly, objectively. Tories like Sidney Smith had sneeringly dismissed American culture: "In the four quarters of the globe, who reads an American book? – or goes to an American play? – or looks at an American picture or statue?"[113] Such Blakean single vision was not Byron's. His awareness of Americans, hitherto largely confined to educated young male New Englanders, was now grounded in a broader spectrum of individuals. His encounters aboard the *Constitution* and *Ontario* delivered solid evidence that a republic could produce men and women of high caliber.

In Philadelphia Mrs Stith achieved the status of a minor celebrity. In an era when every detail of Byron's notorious personal life aroused intense curiosity, anyone who had known the great man achieved virtually instant renown. Mrs Stith's brief but memorable encounter with the famous poet became a general topic of conversation, and when Sully painted her husband's portrait late in 1825 she most likely told him of it. Publishers pressured Mrs Stith to write up her recollections of the poet. A gushing L. Gaylord Clark actively courted her favor on behalf of his brother's New York firm, Clark and Edson, telling her that she "must make your own terms," to which he would gladly accede. "You are, I believe," he wrote, not quite accurately, "the only lady and probably the only individual in the United States, who has ever had a personal acquaintance with the noble author of *Childe Harold*."[114]

Alas, Mrs Stith did not wish to leave written reminiscences of Byron for posterity. Catherine Stith sensibly realized that her fleeting association with the poet would live longest not in the sober reality of prose but in glorious legend. But her first-hand impressions of her day with the poet, in whatever form Sully received them, undoubtedly gave him additional insights into Byron, not least a sense of the poet at his relaxed best: congenial, witty, curious, questioning, desirous of pleasing, considerate, and generous. The meditative poet of Sully's portrait (begun the year after he met Mrs Stith) may owe more than we realize to that glorious day aboard the *Constitution*.

*

While writing to Mrs Stith in February 1838 about her reminiscences of Byron, Sully was pondering the significant task at hand: how to gain permission to paint Victoria? Though she sat frequently for artists, sometimes twice a day, competition to portray the Queen was fierce. "Poor little thing," lamented Blanche, herself only a few years older than the monarch; "she has already sat twenty seven times – she must be quite tired of it."[115] She probably was, but sitting for one's portrait was for royalty a necessary task, and Victoria's sense of her public image, even in her early years, was acute.

Seeing George Hayter's official portrait of an enthroned Victoria left Sully unimpressed. True, it blended queenly presence with pageantry, but the nose was wrong, the expression unappealing. "Hayter's portrait is too large, too old, & to my judgement rather vulgar," Sully wrote his son-in-law James Darley. "I do not fear to enter into competition with it."[116] Hayter's effort benefitted Sully, for it led him to formulate in his mind how he might improve upon it.

Shortly after his arrival in London Sully had, on November 9, unexpectedly glimpsed the Queen during the Lord Mayor's Procession. "We had a perfect sight of the Pageant," he wrote, "and for the first time saw the young Queen of England. She was everywhere greeted with bursts of rapture."[117] They had, Blanche added, "an excellent view of her majesty." Victoria wore "her hair quite plain, a tiara of diamonds her only ornament."[118] Blanche initially thought Victoria resembled Fanny Kemble's sister-in-law, but after seeing a portrait of Victoria in David Wilkie's studio she soon recognized in the Queen the features of Fanny herself. Later, at the "Opera buffa," Blanche spotted Victoria: "the little I saw of her gave me the idea of a good-natured, fat face – ugly likeness of M*rs* Butler."[119] Victoria's resemblance to Fanny struck Sully no less forcefully. Again and again both Sullys compared her to the absent Fanny. Seeing the Queen pass before them strengthened Sully's resolve. "I have set myself a task which I will perform if I can," he wrote home, "and my great reward will be improvement in my profession and future advantage to my family."[120]

Fanny exerted a potent spell over Sully. Her presence haunted Blanche hardly less. Letters home from both mention her frequently and ask to be remembered to her. Sully had brought to England his portraits of her as *Beatrice* (borrowed from Edward Carey) and as *Isabella*. The portraits, which served as commission-gaining examples of his work, adorned their London apartment. Fanny in effect lived in their midst.

Early in December Charles Kemble called to ascertain whether the Sullys were really in London.[121] He was pleasantly surprised, and soon the two families were again intimate. Sully and Blanche met Fanny's younger sister, Adelaide, who reminded them uncannily of their absent friend. "Saturday," wrote Blanche, "we spent a delightful evening at the Kembles – quite a party, but not a handsome woman in the room, save Miss A Kemble, who is quite like Fanny[;] with the exception of large nose and small mouth, her voice and manner so reminded me of her, that several times I was on the point of calling her M*rs* Butler."[122] Adelaide, who gained fame as an opera singer, was not the only London lady to bring Fanny to mind: a "Mrs. Langley" Blanche found "the image of Fanny Butler."[123]

Fanny's days on the London stage had brought her well-connected admirers, and from Philadelphia she wrote them about Sully. Her efforts gained Sully entry into several private collections. When Lord Francis Egerton stopped by, he and Sully "talked much of the Arts, America, and M*rs* Butler."[124] Egerton invited Sully to come and look over his paintings whenever he wished. On one visit "Lady E[gerton] frequently engaged me in conversation about Fanny Butler to whom she seems much attached."[125] After hearing from Fanny Lord Lansdowne also opened his collection to Sully's attentive gaze. "Lady L[ansdowne] is not old, nor remarkably handsome," wrote the artist, inevitably almost, "but . . . her pleasant manner and sweet voice . . . put me in mind of dear Fanny Butler."[126] Fanny, it seems, was everywhere.

Sully had first sought permission to paint Victoria through official channels. Four long months rolled by. "Had I been able to have guessed that it would have caused me so much delay & bother," he moaned on March 1, "I would not have hampered myself with this commission." When efforts by the American Legation proved unavailing, Sully appealed directly to Lord Melbourne. To no avail. Then Lord Francis Egerton stepped in. "I find as I expected that it has been principally through his aiding my claim with Lord Melbourne (Prime Minister) that the business has been brought to a conclusion . . . is he not kind?"[127] Egerton had saved the day. If he was kind, Fanny Kemble had been kinder. Indirectly, it was her friendship with Egerton and her letter of introduction to him for Sully that finally made possible his portrait of Victoria.

*

On the evening of March 21 Sully received from Egerton a hand-delivered communication telling him he was expected at Buckingham Palace the next day at noon. Shortly before the hour appointed Sully and Blanche arrived at the Palace. With his easy social grace Sully quickly hit it off with the young Queen, then not yet 19. David Wilkie had advised him on protocol in addressing the monarch. For all his fame in America Sully knew how fortunate he was to be among those chosen to portray Victoria. His name would have been familiar to her. Fanny Kemble's American *Journal*, which Victoria had read avidly, often mentions Sully. *The Juvenile Forget Me Not* for 1835, also in her library, included a tale "Country Lodgings in America," in which a Mrs Pownsey expressed her admiration for the painter. "I know Mr. Sully very well . . . He painted my portrait, and a most delightful man he is, only rather obstinate."[128] Victoria found the artist before her quite other than obstinate.

Sully described their first meeting through the eyes of an acutely observant portraitist:

> She is short – 5 feet 1 & 1/4 of an inch – of good form – particularly the neck and bosom – plump, but not fat. Neatly formed head, perhaps rather infantine in the contour of the face. Forehead well proportioned – eyes a *little* prominent but kind and intelligent. Her nose well formed and such as I have frequently seen in persons of wit and intellect. A lovely, artless mouth when at rest – and when so, it is a little open, showing her teeth – eyes light blue and large – hair light brown, smoothly braided from the front.[129]

Victoria, in sum, was "quite pretty." Blanche, about four years older, helped make the all-important first sitting a success. Sully was delighted: "I had the rare opportunity of seeing the Queen throw off all constraint and talk and laugh like a happy girl of eighteen – long! long may she have that light and happy heart."[130]

The Times on March 26, 1838, briefly noted that Sully was painting the Queen. One of the Finden brothers, meeting Sully in the street, told him "such a paragraph was to be considered a mark of respect." He advised the artist "to procure a paper and send it home – not I."[131] "Paul Pry," who also encountered him, exclaimed, "Oh my dear Mr. Sully are you not pleased to see your name in all the papers in town?"[132] A surprised Sully replied that he did not read the papers.

Four other sittings followed that of March 21, the last on May 14. On the following day Blanche posed for her father bearing Victoria's crown and heavy regalia. Victoria in the company of several ladies-in-waiting appeared unexpectedly. The spectacle of Blanche in *her* state costume amused her vastly. "She was looking so kindly" on us, recorded sweet-natured Blanche of the Queen's response to her and her father, "that you can hardly help loving her yourself."[133]

Victoria already conducted herself like a queen. Upon the death of her uncle, William IV, the previous year, she had inherited the crown. Her Hanoverian predecessors had rarely endeared themselves to the people, and in the decades preceding her ascension regard for the monarchy had waned. The long-lived George III, king from 1760, ended up mad, blind, and deaf. His scapegrace successor, the Prince Regent, later George IV (1820–30), had charm but was extravagant and tactless; "Sailor Billy," the naval brother who succeeded him, had stolid virtues, but was blustery and boorish. Victoria came upon the scene like a breath of fresh air. With her all seemed possible.

At her first Council in June 1837 Victoria presided over a grand assembly of lords, notables, generals, and ministers of state. Her regal bearing astonished those present. The Duke of Wellington observed, "She not merely filled the chair, she filled the room."[134] Possibly, feared some, she might become too regal, too assertive. Sully's initial study captures Victoria's radiant young womanhood and also that self-confidence (Figure 12). The study has a freshness, life, and spontaneity the larger versions somewhat lack; in it the Queen's features, crisply delineated, appear a little hard-edged, imperious even. Her mouth is closed, her eyes less open than in the full-length portrait. "If one might judge by the [Queen's] manner," commented Sully shrewdly, "I should conclude that in governing, she will have much her own way."[135] He evidently treasured this study, for it remained in his studio until his death.

After completing the sittings and with the Queen approving his work, Sully at the request of the royal booksellers Hodgson & Greaves did a three-quarter length, or "Bishop's half-length," for the purpose of an engraving. The commission garnered him a needed two hundred pounds. Victoria had liked both the portrait and the artist who did it, but Sully found dealings with Hodgson & Greaves difficult and he did not care for Charles Edward Wagstaff's engraving. Nonetheless, it was from it that contemporaries in England knew Sully's *Victoria*. Back in Philadelphia that autumn, Sully used his initial study for two large-scale, full-length portraits of Victoria. One he began on September 30, the second on October 2. He finished both on January 14, 1839.

Victoria in the full-length portrait (see color plate section) appears more wide-eyed, idealized, full of wonderment than in the study. By posing the Queen as she ascends the steps leading to the throne, Sully conveys the prevailing sense of expectancy. Victoria looks back over her shoulder and glances at and beyond the viewer. Leaving youth behind, she moves toward the awesome responsibilities of her mature destiny. The study angles the head more to the right, accenting the chin – and Victoria's determination. The full-length portrait, tilting the head more to the left, makes Victoria appear more accommodating.

The scene possesses high drama. Victoria wears the diadem; the Order of the Garter hangs across the back of her robe; the imperial crown and scepter rest on the table. The massive classical column, a standard stage prop, suggests order and tradition, as do the flowing robe and billowing drapery.

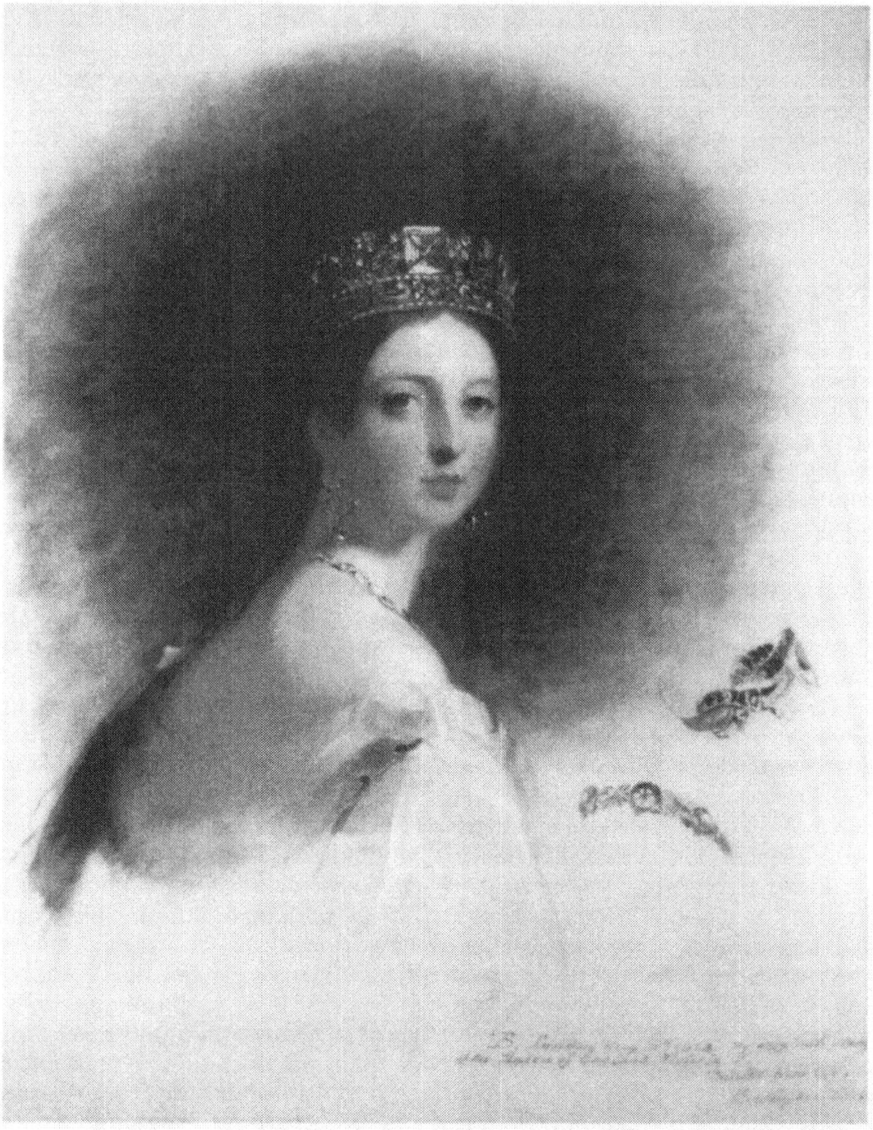

12 Thomas Sully, *Queen Victoria* (original study), 1838. The Metropolitan Museum of Art, New York

Typical of Grand Manner portraiture, these trappings were initially reserved for royalty or for military heroes and statesmen. Sully builds contrasts through light and dark. Light from the upper right leaves much of the robe in shadow but illumines the face. As Victoria approaches the throne, her left foot is about to alight on the top step while the right is planted on the middle step. By stretching her scant height Sully not only made Victoria seem taller but gave a sense of her in movement from head to toe. Her left hand touches the arm rest, but she has not yet reached the throne. (The coronation did not take place until June 22, 1838.) The calm demeanor and confident pose suggest Victoria's high hopes regarding the grand adventure ahead. The seat of the massive throne – seemingly too big for its new occupant – Sully leaves in shadow, possibly to symbolize the new reign's attendant uncertainties. Victoria will fill the throne and the room, as Wellington had divined, and give her name to one of Britain's greatest eras. Sully's masterly dramatic sense once again served him well.

The Queen's mouth, noted Sallie Stevenson, wife to the American ambassador, was "generally a little open."[136] This characteristic Mrs Stevenson thought "her worst feature," but Sully, also observant, took brilliant advantage of it. In contrast to Hayter's tight-lipped queen, Sully's full-length leaves Victoria's mouth slightly open. Either Victoria is expressing surprise or she is responding to someone who has just spoken to her. The irony of course is that in British etiquette no one addresses the Queen without first being addressed by her. It is she who begins a conversation. Victoria's open mouth may be Sully's finest touch as a dramatic portraitist.

And that shoulder! We have already seen it. It is Fanny Kemble's, posing as Beatrice. It is Musidora's, the Kemble like nymph caught unawares while bathing. Now it is Victoria's. When Sully came to paint *his Victoria*, reminiscences of Fanny determined Victoria's pose and influenced his depiction of her features. The parallels extend beyond pose and appearance to language. "I often think," Sully wrote home, "there is a mixture of character in this personage resembling Fanny Kemble – she calls Lord Melbourne 'Mel' and the Duke of Wellington 'Well.'" Thus "Lord Palmerston is called 'Pall' by the Queen, so she has Pall, Mell, and Well."[137] Victoria had read Fanny Kemble's *Journal* in 1835, as had Sully, and like Victoria the artist viewed Fanny through the *Journal*'s idiomatic, bold language and his own recollections of her lively conversation. What Henry James called the "innocent impertinences" of Fanny's "girlish" American *Journal* delighted the young Queen.[138] Initially put off by the *Journal*'s seemingly "vulgar" language, Victoria soon found herself caught up in its "fine feelings." The heroine's outspoken, courageous attitude toward life both amused and enlightened her, and the *Journal*'s glimpses into how a lively young woman thought, felt, and behaved gave Victoria ideas about how she might live her own life.[139]

Fanny had come up in conversation during the first sitting. The Baroness Lehzen, the Queen's secretary, had asked Sully, "'You are acquainted with Mrs. Buttler [*sic*] perhaps' – Yes, I replied, intimately; she is to me almost as one of my children – The Queen observed – 'She is not so pretty as her sister,

I believe' – I gave my opinion in favour of her expression and exquisite eyes. 'I think,' said the Queen, 'Miss Kemble is rather thin.'"[140] Victoria had seen Fanny Kemble perform; she may even have sensed in her a rival – she is one of the very few who ever found Fanny "thin" – but it is unlikely she ever realized that Sully drew upon *Fanny Kemble as Beatrice* for his pose of her.

The full-length *Victoria* works through contrasts, not only between light and dark but also between youth and age, the youth of the queen and the age of the British monarchy; between Victoria's buoyant energies and her weighty responsibilities; between her momentary surprise at being addressed and her poise in response; between the statue-like setting and the implied kinetic movement; between the sensual shoulder and the formal robes; between the words unheard and heard. *Victoria* may be a consummate instance of Fuseli's "pregnant moment," but it is no less a consummate instance of Sully's rich talent for dramatic portraiture.[141]

*

Victoria became Sully's greatest professional triumph. It was, however, a triumph tinged with frustration. The Society of the Sons of St George unchivalrously refused Sully's right to benefit from the copy of the full-length portrait that he had made. A lawsuit ensued, through which Sully, in what proved a pioneering case regarding the claim of an artist to his work, successfully established this right.[142] The Society retained legal title to the original full-length portrait, which it exhibited in Philadelphia and Montreal. Sully showed his copy in New York, Boston, and Washington. *Victoria* enhanced Sully's already sterling reputation. It competed against renderings of the young Queen by Hayter, David Wilkie, Edwin Landseer, the famous Austrian F. X. Winterhalter, and the transplanted American C. R. Leslie. Matched against work by the finest portraitists of England and Europe, Sully's *Victoria* more than holds its own.

One reason why Sully undertook *Victoria* was that, as he confided to his journal, if successful in his task, he would enhance his reputation both "in my adopted country and home."[143] His adopted country was the United States. Though he had lived in Philadelphia for thirty years and enjoyed a "firm reputation" there, English he remained. When he spoke of "the obstinacy of his countrymen" he meant the English, not his fellow Philadelphians.[144] Sully did not view the English uncritically. He regarded them as "a humane people – some instances to the contrary notwithstanding." To the aristocrats who had helped him he awarded the palm: "Of a truth nothing can exceed the perfection of manner of the English nobility – it is impossible to be more at your ease than their kindness and attention is calculated to place you."[145]

British portraiture in its greatest ages is essentially an Anglo-American affair, though few art critics on either side of the ocean have adopted this perspective.[146] Once West arrived in the 1760s, followed by Peale, Copley, and Stuart, English art developed a strong American component. "David asked me," recalled Rembrandt Peale of a meeting in 1808 with France's great master, "'why it was that all the best painters in London were Americans.'"[147] David was not being facetious. He may not have known of the work of Rembrandt's father, Charles Willson Peale, who had studied with West in 1766–69; but he would have known of Stuart and Trumbull, probably of Allston, most certainly of Copley and of West himself.

In the 1780s the successor to Gainsborough and Reynolds was thought to be not John Hoppner or the unforeseen Lawrence, but Gilbert Stuart, who spent 18 years in London and five in Dublin before returning to become the creator of the iconic Washington. Some American artists, Sully and Jarvis among them, were born in Britain and worked in America. Others, like Leslie, born in London of American parents, worked chiefly in Britain. West and Copley are Britain's greatest history painters; a century after them, Whistler and Sargent revitalized British portraiture. Anglo-American portraiture is in effect an international style, two branches of the same tree. Resemblances outweigh differences. Without major changes in technique but often reflecting a national perspective, Americans like Stuart and West, Sully and Chester Harding, later Whistler and Sargent, gained renown on two continents.

Professionally as well as culturally Sully thought of himself as English, the heir of a tradition that extended through Reynolds and Lawrence back to Van Dyck. "England has never made any distinction between our artists and her own," Washington Allston had claimed, perhaps too generously.[148] Sully would probably have agreed. He picked and chose, from England and America, what suited his talent best. Though in the United States since age nine and an American citizen since 1809, he felt at one with Lawrence, who proved his greatest inspiration, as with Reynolds, whose *Discourses* constituted his artistic Bible, "the most valuable present you can make to a young man of real merit."[149] If Sully, living in America and a citizen of the Republic, thought himself English, West, working in Britain for nearly sixty years, thought himself American. Out of this joint Anglo-American tradition of dramatic portraiture emerged Sully's portrait of Byron. Painted by an artist neither fully English nor fully American, it combined traditions of both lands.

Byron also emerged from very specific historical circumstances. In 1826, when Sully began work on it, America had attained the half-century. It now celebrated the fiftieth anniversary of the beginning of the American Revolution. The year before had marked the fiftieth anniversary of the signing of the Declaration of Independence. These anniversaries portended a new self-awareness in America, a self-awareness that influenced *Byron*'s coming into being. In 1826 Sully also began a portrait of Nicholas Biddle. Biddle's career bore remarkable similarities to Byron's, and his portrait by Sully influenced *Byron*. To that individual we now turn.

CHAPTER SIX

Byronic Biddle

> Though he did not deserve to be called a *great* man, yet he had more of the elements of greatness & of the qualities allied to genius than any other prominent man in this city, or, Webster excepted, in this country, now living.
>
> Sidney Fisher on Nicholas Biddle[1]

Pairing Nicholas Biddle with Lord Byron may seem an odd thing to do, but as individuals and as subjects of portraits by Sully they make for a mutually illuminating comparison. In conception of subject no less than in composition, Sully's *Nicholas Biddle* (see color plate section) poses intriguing parallels with his *Byron*, parallels that derive ultimately from the many, often astonishing, points of contact between Biddle's career and Byron's. Sully began *Biddle* in July 1826; *Byron*, probably a month or two earlier. In life, contemporaries often compared Biddle to Byron; no one, it seems, thought to compare Byron to Biddle. Thus it is more likely that Sully interpreted *Biddle* in the light of *Byron* than the reverse. He worked on them at the same time, and each painting influenced the other. Neither left his studio for the last time until 1828. The artist presented Byron in a manner appealing to Americans, and juxtaposing *Byron* with *Biddle* we discover why. Biddle was a prominent, controversial figure in Federal and Jacksonian America. Painting him constitutes part of the process by which Sully transformed Byron from English lord into "American" icon. Being even tangentially part of Biddle's circle gave Sully opportunities – for example, to meet Joseph Bonaparte and study his magnificent art collection – that he might not otherwise have had.

In 1826, just before beginning *Byron* and *Biddle*, Sully completed *Lafayette* and *Napoleon*. Americans of 1826 considered Biddle a figure hardly less central than Lafayette, Napoleon, or Byron, and Byron and Biddle constitute no more unusual a pair than Lafayette and Napoleon. All four live as major figures of their era. They interacted in Sully's visual imagination and as subjects of his brush.

"Unquestionably a most important man; more questionably, a great one": thus Nathaniel Burt posed the dilemma of Biddle.[2] President of the Second Bank of the United States from 1822 to 1836, Biddle guided the nation's finances during a crucial period in its history. He wielded almost as much power as the successive presidents – Monroe, John Quincy Adams, Jackson – under whom he served. When painted by Sully, Biddle stood at the summit of his fame. In America's history, however, he occupies a vexed position. His actions, behavior, even personal character have come under attack. Scholarship has not served him well. His career has been misconstrued and undervalued, his character grossly misunderstood.

The United States spawned Byronic figures of varying personalities and achievements. Among prominent Americans who fancied themselves "Byronic" there was the eccentric, sexually undefined Senator John Randolph of Virginia, a "passionate admirer" of Byron, "moody and romantic, and flung upon the world";[3] the relentless explorer of the macabre and fantastic, Edgar Allan Poe, author of *Tamerlane* (1827), whose protagonist in his pride and gloom and remorse owes much to Byron, as Poe did in his life; the tortured homosexual poet, Fitz-Greene Halleck, who burst into tears upon hearing of Byron's death; the irrepressible John Neal, Sully's friend and admirer, obsessed with Byron. But in Sully's visual imagination it was Nicholas Biddle who seemed most like Byron. His portraits of Biddle and Byron interweave complexly. To understand the relationship between them we turn to the Byronic career of the charismatic Philadelphian.

*

Biddle may be Philadelphia's most famous name. For Burt, chronicler of the "perennial Philadelphians," Nicholas was "the paragon of all Biddles, certainly the man who gave the name its cachet, and certainly one of Philadelphia's essential and symbolic figures."[4] A William Biddle first settled in New Jersey in 1681 as a major landholder. His grandson, also William, moved to Philadelphia in the early eighteenth century. The family prospered, along with the city Penn founded, and became leading Quaker merchants.

Nicholas, born in 1786 to Charles and Hannah Biddle, gained early recognition as the family prodigy. Intelligent and serious beyond his years, he entered the University of Pennsylvania at ten and completed course work at 13. The family felt he needed more seasoning and sent him to Princeton, where studying everything he could, and studying hard, he drove himself impatiently and with determination. One who knew Nicholas then described him "a youth of dauntless and indomitable spirit."[5] He graduated, class valedictorian, at 15, then studied law for three years in Philadelphia. Byron, less focused in his studies at Harrow and Cambridge, also read omnivorously. Like Biddle, he soon revealed a "dauntless and indomitable spirit," one that demonstrated its own fiery impatience.

Contemporaries often compared Biddle's appearance to Byron's. Both were handsome – Biddle, "if the miniatures of him do not lie, a model of Byronic beauty."[6] A curly-headed darling in youth, inordinately handsome in maturity, Biddle possessed features both "regular & chiselled."[7] He had a remarkably high and ample forehead, a fair complexion, chestnut hair and eyebrows, an oval face, and a round chin. His eyes, like Byron's, were described variously by contemporaries: whether "chestnut," "blue," or "grey," they "reflected an eager and excited intelligence."[8] "He wore his hair very long, hanging around his face in silken curls, and he was very neat & recherché in his dress."[9] Although Biddle matured in appearance, the long hair in curls gave him a lifelong boyish look. The total effect, a contemporary claimed, earned him the epithet "the handsomest man in Philadelphia." "A noble man in every sense – ," recalled another, "beautiful

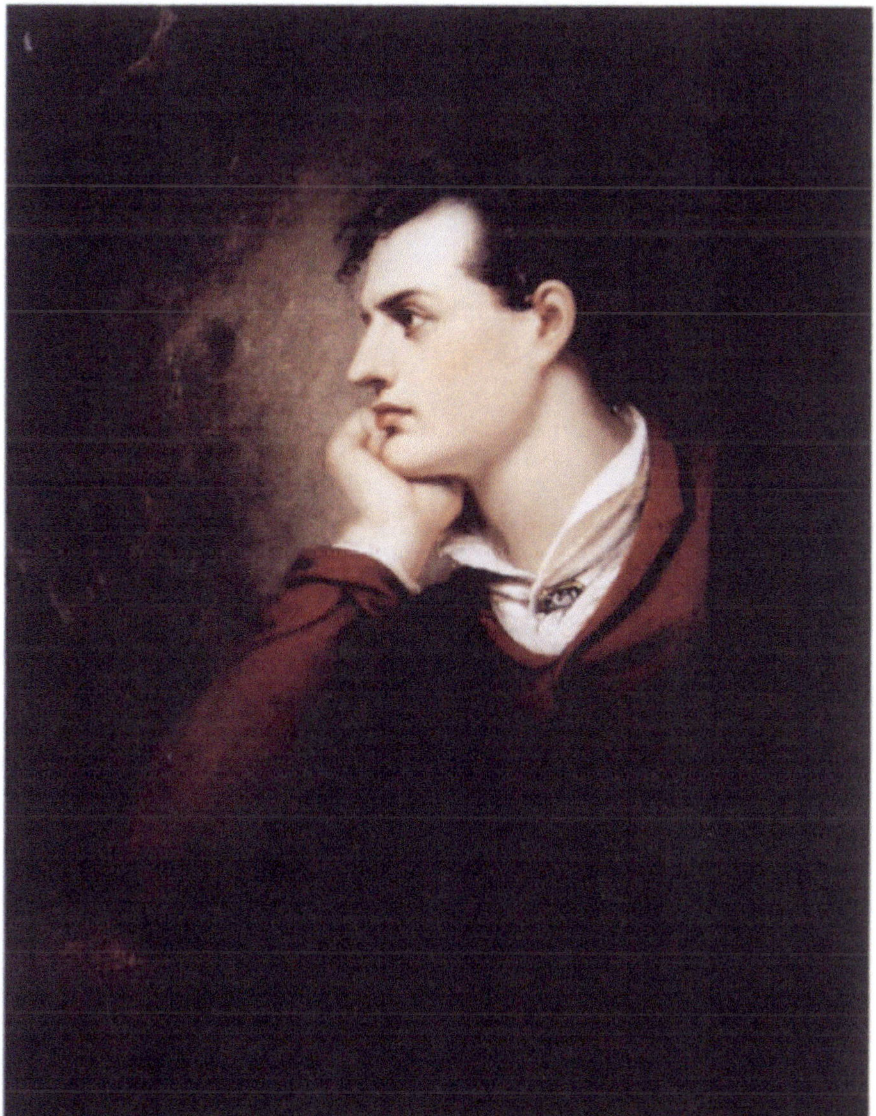

I. Richard Westall, *Lord Byron*, *1813*. National Portrait Gallery, London.

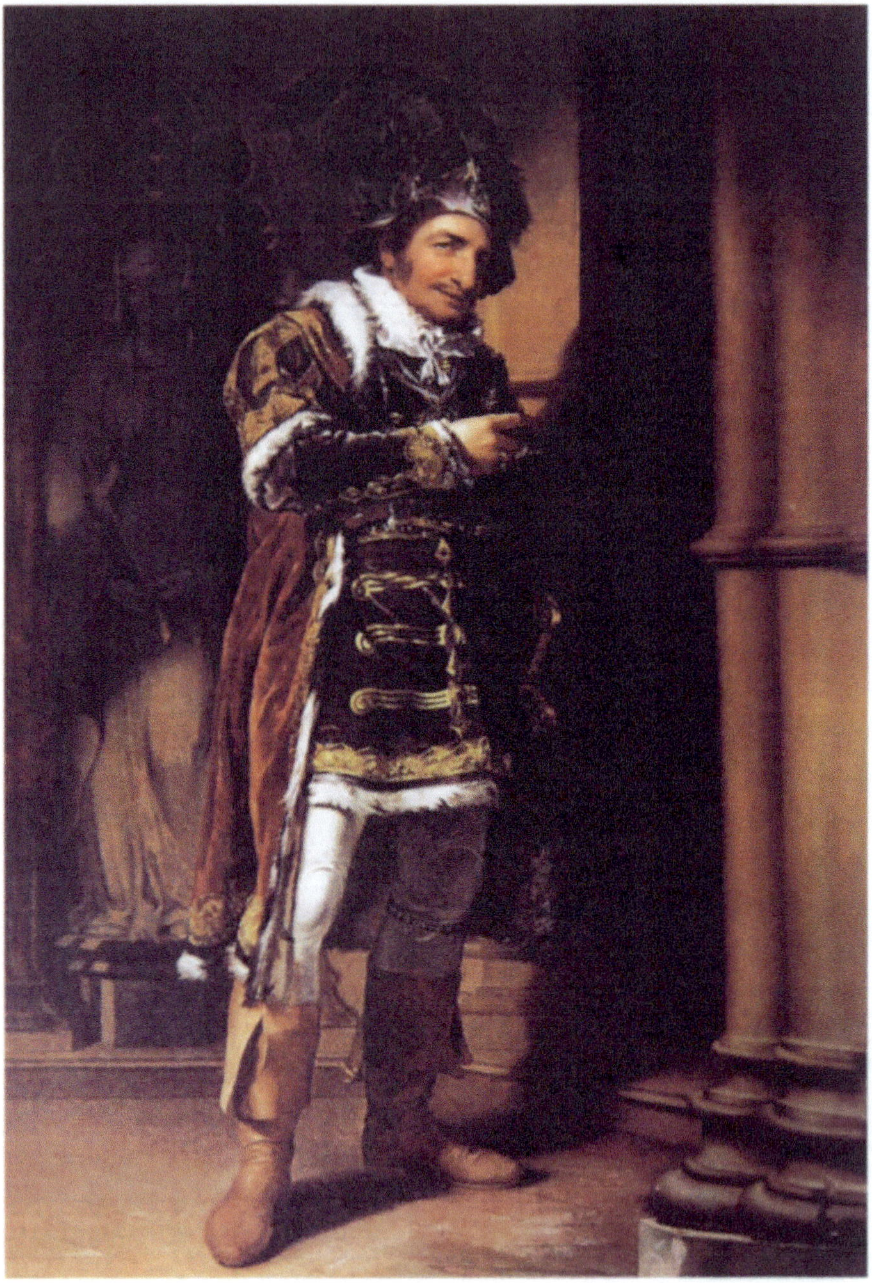

II. Thomas Sully, *George Frederick Cooke as Richard III, 1811–1812.* The Pennsylvania Academy of the Fine Arts, Philadelphia. Gift of friends and admirers of the artist.

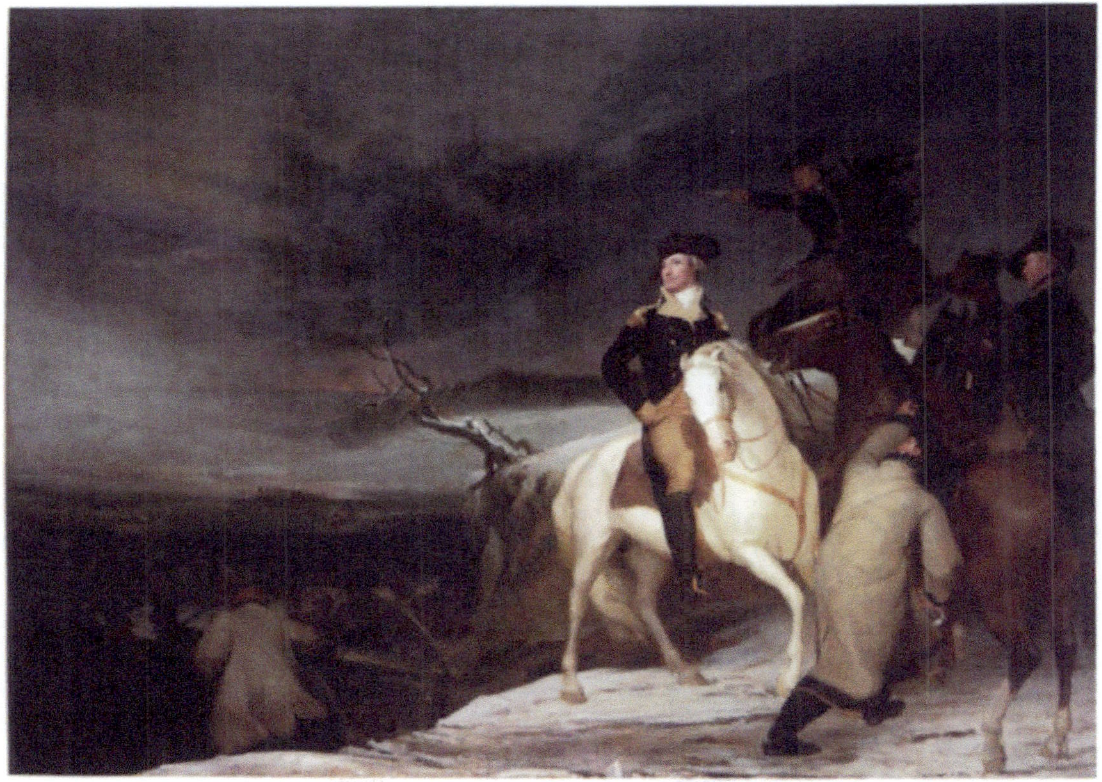

III. Thomas Sully, *The Passage of the Delaware*, 1819. Gift of the Owners of the old Boston Museum. Courtesy, Museum of Fine Arts, Boston.

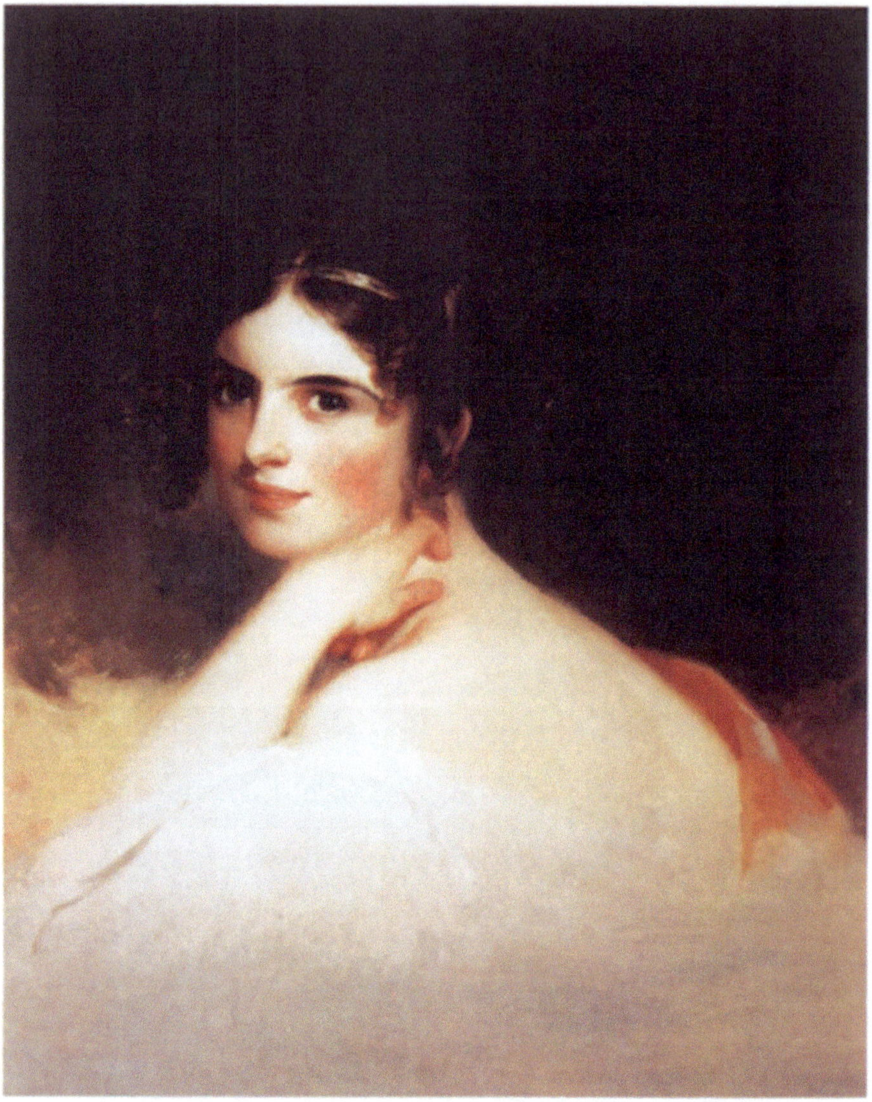

IV. Thomas Sully, *Fanny Kemble as Beatrice, 1833?*. The Pennsylvania Academy of the Fine Arts, Philadelphia. Bequest of Henry C. Carey (The Carey Collection).

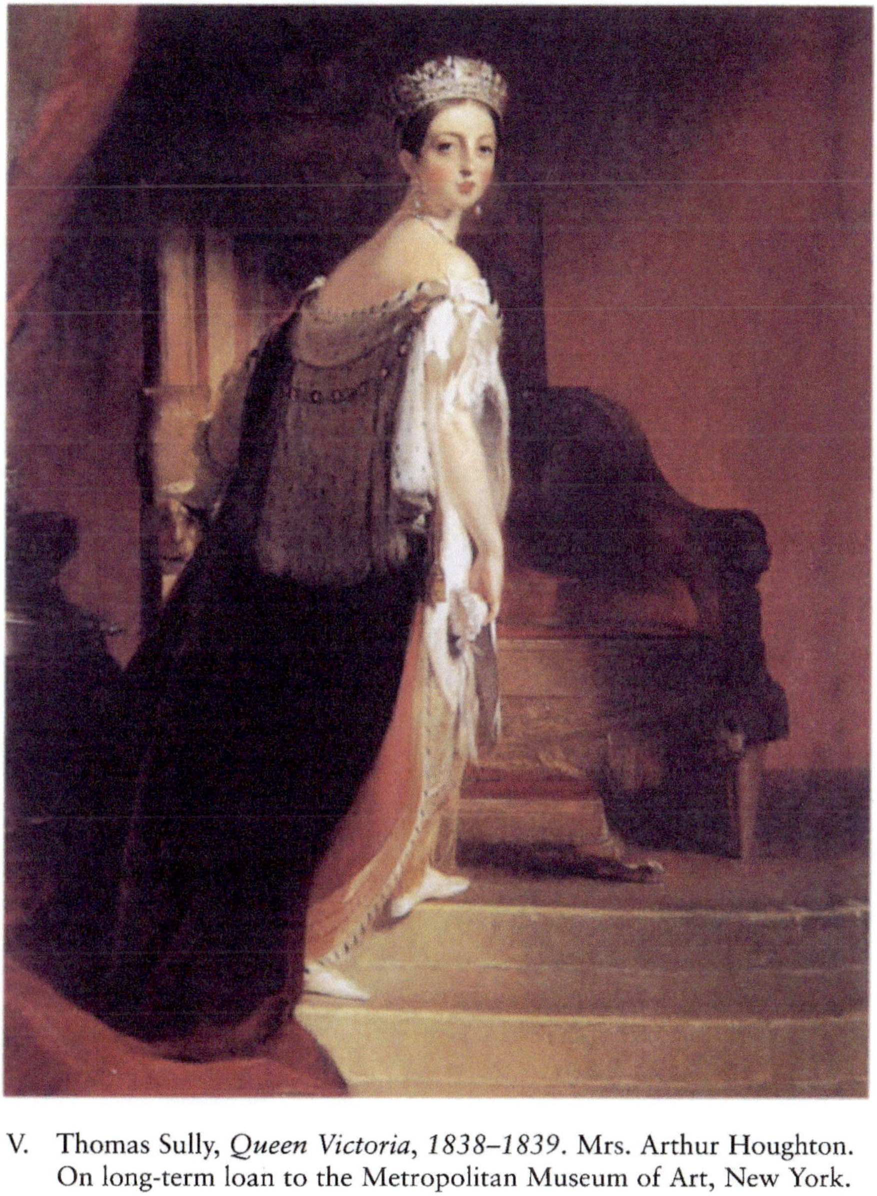

V. Thomas Sully, *Queen Victoria, 1838–1839*. Mrs. Arthur Houghton. On long-term loan to the Metropolitan Museum of Art, New York.

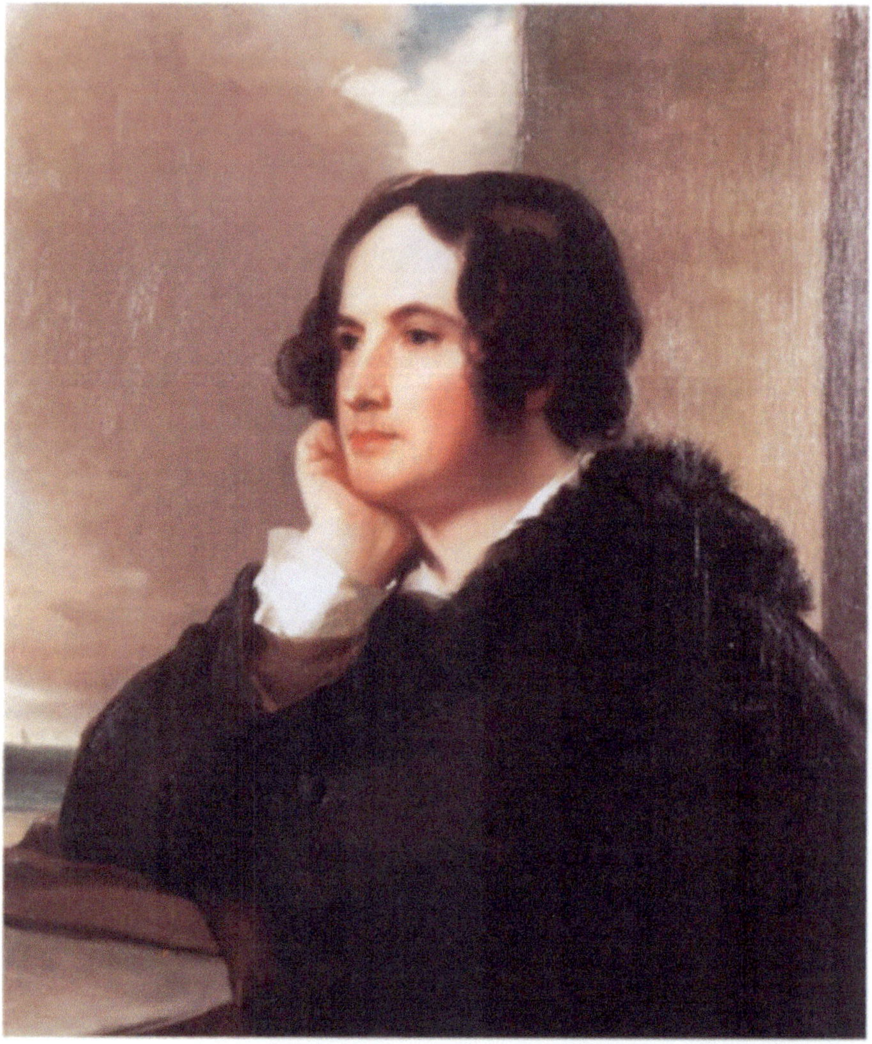

VI. Thomas Sully, *Nicholas Biddle, 1826–1828*. Andalusia, Bensalem, Pennsylvania. Courtesy of James Biddle.

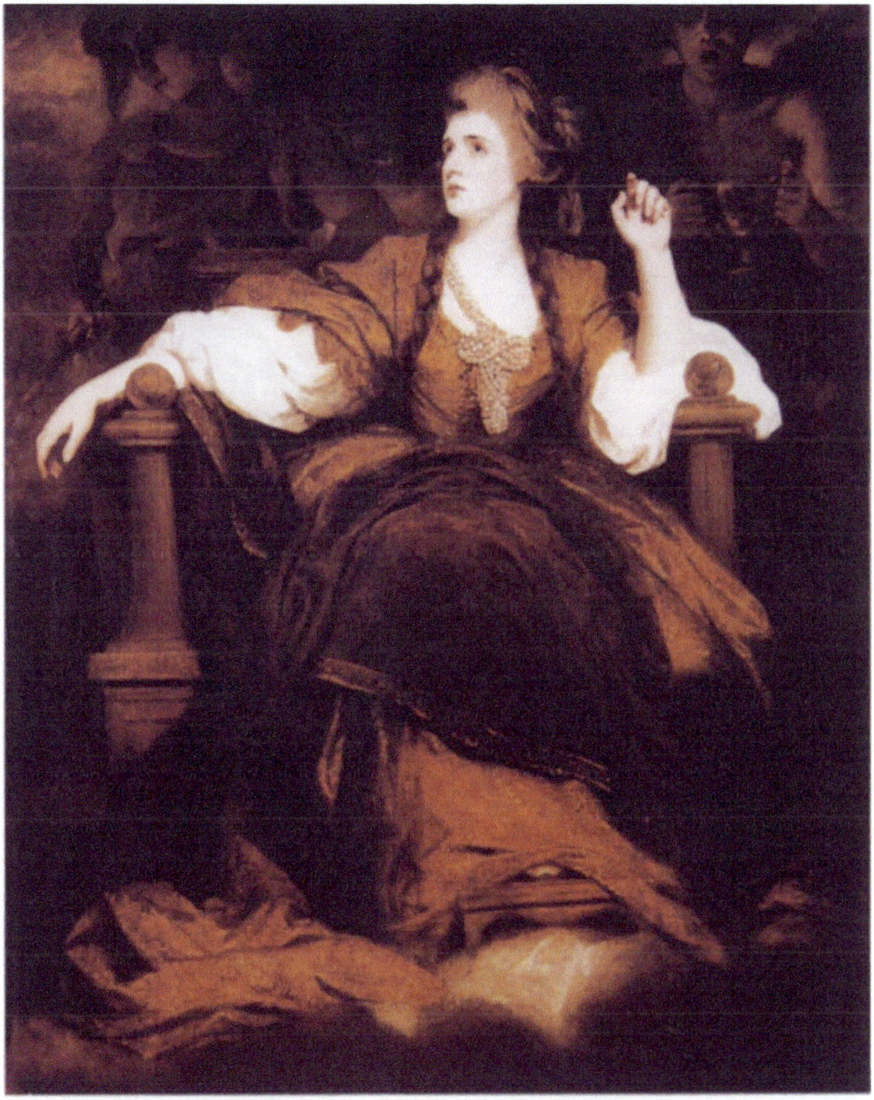

VII. Joshua Reynolds, *Mrs. Siddons as the Tragic Muse, 1783–1784.* The Henry E. Huntington Library and Art Gallery, San Marino, California.

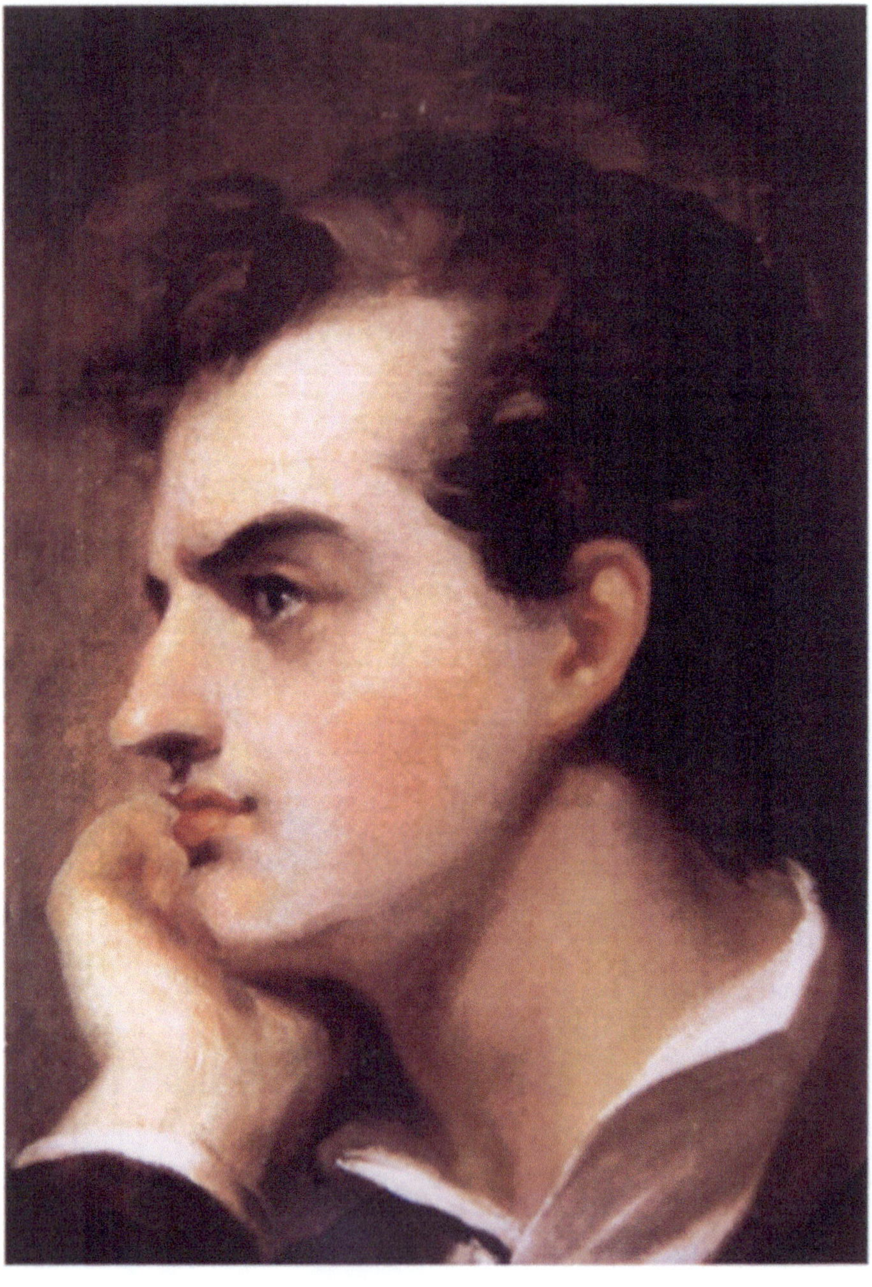

VIII. Thomas Sully, *Lord Byron, 1826–1828* (detail). Private Collection, USA.

in person as Apollo; highly educated, polished in his manners, and gifted with all the grace that ever adorned the most refined court of Europe."[10] Byronic indeed!

Even more than in appearance, parallels to the English poet in career are significant. Each aspired to political greatness. Eloquence, Nicholas declared in Greece in 1806, was at once "the engine of power the road to fame and the means of fortune." To govern a free citizenry "by means of eloquence seems to me the object most worthy of ambition."[11] Throughout his life Biddle in key speeches spelled out the citizen's responsibilities to the state. Byron, too, early recognized the power of the spoken word to move others. Harrow set speeches prepared him for the three carefully crafted orations he delivered before the House of Lords in eloquent support of liberal causes. Initially of no party, Byron gave his allegiance to the Whig faction favoring compromise with Napoleon. But with the Conservatives in seemingly interminable dominance, a significant political role for him in England was ruled out. In 1816 Byron forsook his native land for self-chosen exile. But Biddle, in part through his eloquence, achieved the position of power in his native land that eluded Byron.

Biddle may have regarded Byron as a kind of *alter ego*. He was Byronic in the spectacular arc of his career, his eloquence, his deeply political nature, his epic vision, his lifelong desire for greatness. Both men liked show, designed uniforms, loved books, wrote and translated poetry (though compared to Byron, Biddle wrote little).[12] Biddle shared with Byron a passionate love for the landscapes and people of Greece, a land both knew well. Republicans in spirit but emperors in imagination, Byron and Biddle could behave autocratically, but in thinking ancient institutions the best models for present and future republics they were one.

Opportunity beckoned early to the young Philadelphian. In 1804 Jefferson asked General John Armstrong, newly appointed minister to France and a Biddle family friend, to negotiate French claims in Louisiana. Armstrong wondered if 18-year-old Nicholas would like to join him in Paris as unpaid secretary. He would. Auditing and paying French claims against the United States resulting from the recent purchase of Louisiana from Napoleon, Biddle acquired valuable first-hand experience in financial affairs. French dignitaries marveled at his youth and ability. Nor was settling the French claims Biddle's only task. The fledgling Pennsylvania Academy of the Fine Arts, founded in 1805, commissioned him to acquire for its collection plaster casts of antique statuary. Guided by Jean-Antoine Houdon, Biddle chose well.[13] Upon completing his work in Paris, he decided to explore Napoleon-dominated Europe.

Biddle's *Wanderjahre*, from 1805 to 1807, counterpoint Byron's from 1809 to 1811. Like Byron, Biddle toured Europe sporting military credentials. Both had uniforms made for the trip. Biddle, appointed a colonel in the New Jersey militia by Governor Joseph Bloomfield, designed his own. General James Wilkinson, a kinsman by marriage, procured Nicholas a brevet captaincy in the United States Artillery. Byron also designed his own uniforms. Army officers in Britain were almost always noble born, and

Byron's uniforms announced his rank and citizenship in a nation in active combat against Napoleon. Biddle's military uniform indicated birth but, since the United States had thus far remained uninvolved in Europe's conflicts, implied neutrality.

Byron had to plan a route across lands not controlled by Napoleon; Biddle traveled more freely. Wherever a theater of war did not prevent him going, he went. He began in northern France, looked around Switzerland, then voyaged down Italy to Sicily. Whereas Biddle traveled with only a single servant, Byron, as well as servants, had a companion in John Cam Hobhouse. As Byron's early reading influenced his itinerary, so Biddle sought cicerones among past authors. In France, he attempted to follow Laurence Sterne in his *Sentimental Journey through France and Italy*; in Switzerland, he marveled with Thomas Gray before the sublime but terrifying Alps; in Geneva, Rousseau shaped his impressions of that strict Protestant bastion; in Italy, Cicero's *Orations* became his "compagnon de voyage."[14] Natives supplemented literary guides; he questioned older travelers about their experiences. Whereas Byron detested Geneva, Biddle found it "the most comfortable society I have seen."[15] Did it remind him of Quaker Philadelphia?

The trip not only educated Biddle, it educated others. Already he saw himself as a transmitter of European culture to an American audience. A letter he published in *The Port Folio* in 1806 described Florence and its inhabitants. In Rome he met Coleridge. His only comment was "Il parle bien, mais il parle trop." Washington Allston and Vanderlyn showed him the city's wonders. Vanderlyn also introduced him to the genius of Henry Fuseli, and from him Biddle borrowed that *summa* of artistic counsel, Reynolds's *Discourses*.[16]

From Sicily Biddle went to Malta, where he found the *Constitution* in port. He dined almost daily with Commodore John Rodgers and his officers, many of them friends or former shipmates of his naval brother James. When the *Philadelphia* was captured by the Bey of Algiers, James had endured 19 months of imprisonment. The peace treaty of 1805 ending tribute to Tripoli and freeing American captives was drawn up in Commodore Rodgers's cabin. Nicholas's visits foreshadowed that memorable day in May, 17 years later, when the *Constitution*'s officers fêted Byron. But to our knowledge no lovely lady plucked a rose from Nicholas's *boutonnière*.

*

Biddle, like Byron fascinated by Greece, decided in 1806 to see for himself that classical land. Greece, since 1456 part of the Ottoman Empire, was then an unusual destination. Excavations in southern Italy, chiefly at Herculaneum and Pompeii, had unearthed Greek statues: thus did the Enlightenment rediscover the glory of classical Greece. Drawn by the lure of fabled ancient monuments, early nineteenth-century travelers sought to encounter first hand in Greece the art and values of classical civilization. Many came away disillusioned. "Well, Monsieur, I have seen Greece!"

lamented Chateaubriand to a friend in 1806. "I visited Sparta, Argos, Mycenae, Corinth, Athens; beautiful names, alas nothing more. . . . Never see Greece, Monsieur, except in Homer. It is the best way."[17] But it was not Nicholas Biddle's way. He wanted to experience this new world with his own eyes. "The wider the horizon of our view," he wrote in a reflective passage, "the more we have seen of man."[18]

Travel in Greece daunted all but the bravest of heart. "Blest is the man! who dares approach the bower," wrote undaunted Byron in *English Bards*, "where dwelt the Muses at their natal hour."[19] Despite the dangers, hardy cultural tourists had begun to arrive in the home of the Muses. As did Byron three years later, Biddle first experienced western Greece, a land a more recent traveler has described as so remote "from the conventional Grand Tour and as adventurous and rare (so wide an ocean seemed the Adriatic, and so daunting a barrier seemed the Acroceraunian Mountains) as a journey today from Athens to the Hindu Kush . . . It was a world of strife, ambush, revenge, burning villages, massacre, impaling and severed heads."[20]

Biddle was only the second American to go to Greece.[21] Few travelers from other countries had preceded him. Though a precocious student at Penn and a graduate of Princeton, a practiced diplomat in Paris, and a seasoned traveler across Europe, he was but 20. Biddle's Greek journals allow us to follow him around. Not a casual tourist, Biddle took his sightseeing no less seriously than he had his studies. The trip was for him a turning-point in a larger educational program. Interested in all before him, Biddle subscribed to the idea, inherited from ancient Greece and Rome, that the citizen should serve his country to the best of his ability. His time in Greece would prepare him for the public career to which he aspired.

Travel also broadened Byron. A year older than Biddle when he first visited Greece, he too had in mind a political mission. "A few years knowledge of other countries than our own," he wrote his mother in November 1808, would provide a worthwhile apprenticeship for a political career.[22] Inspired by Enlightenment ideals, Byron, like Biddle, refused to be bound by the limited intellectual horizons of his country. Each looked for instruction beyond his own land and, as Bacon counseled, took the world for his province. Byron read voraciously in Greek and Turkish history. Biddle's chief guide in Greece, the Abbé Barthélemy's famous *Voyage du jeune Anacharsis en Grèce* (1788), Byron also devoured.[23] Both valued Homer's breadth of vision. Biddle in Greece envisaged himself the hero of an epic adventure; Byron in *Childe Harold* and *Don Juan* tellingly echoes Homeric epic.

Byron early proclaimed himself not English but cosmopolitan. Greece reinforced the claim. Lines from Fougeret de Monbron's *Le Cosmopolite, ou le Citoyen du Monde* (1753) preface *Childe Harold's Pilgrimage* (1812).[24] The poem opened up the exotic, strangely compelling land that was Greece to the European – and American – imagination. Melville and Twain in American letters, Frederic Church among her artists; Chateaubriand, Lamartine, and Gautier in France; Disraeli and Eastlake in Britain – all undertook, along with countless voyagers of the later nineteenth and twentieth centuries, to travel to Greece in Byron's wake.[25] Whereas Byron dreamed of Greece all his life and returned in 1823 to free the land from Ottoman oppression, Biddle, the public-figure-to-be, dreamed of recreating a new Greece in America. Believing the Greek Revival style of architecture that best suited for a republic, he became its foremost advocate in America. With three of its chief monuments – the Second Bank of the United States, Girard College, and his country estate Andalusia – his name is irrevocably linked. However great America's debt to Greece, a Greece-inspired America had in its form of government as in its buildings even more to offer the world.[26]

"I had long felt an ardent desire to visit Greece." With these stirring words Biddle begins his Greek journal. After a stop at Zante, one of the Ionian islands (then in possession of the French), he reached the Peloponnese mainland at Chiarenza (ancient Kyllene). He was intensely moved: "I have at last touched the holy soil of Greece." His seemingly carefree months on that soil strengthened an already vibrant interest in the country's language and history. Zigzagging his way to Athens, he took in Elis, Patras, and Delphi; Chryso (Crissa), Livadia, Thermopylae, Moli, Cheronea; Leuctra, Plataea, and Thebes. His first letter home from Athens vibrates with excitement: "My heart beats as I date my letter from the venerable presence of the mistress of the world." Measuring and drawing classical buildings strengthened in Biddle the enthusiasm for Greek architecture that proved lifelong. The French consul Fauvel, "an amiable Frenchman of the old school of manners," showed him around as, four years later, he did Byron.[27] Once settled in Athens, Biddle visited Marathon and the famous temples at Sunium and on the island of Aegina.

Through Fauvel Biddle met Lusieri, the painter supervising Lord Elgin's removal of the Parthenon Marbles to Britain. Shocked by the damage that time and neglect had done to the statuary known to posterity as the "Elgin Marbles," Biddle four years before Byron expressed outrage over the actions of the "Scotch vandal." Compared to Elgin's ravages, Biddle exclaimed, the destruction in classical times of the Temple of Ephesus was a high and honorable deed: "some indignant historian of Grecian misery may one day do him justice by declaring that [what] Herostratus burnt for glory, Elgin robbed for gold."[28] Later philhellenes who savaged Elgin would be many, but none more eloquent than Byron. In *Childe Harold*'s second canto and *The Curse of Minerva* he denounced Elgin as "the last, the worst, dull spoiler."[29]

Biddle like Byron detested Turkish tyranny, deplored Greek servility, and compared ancient grandeur with the present decay of fallen buildings and beaten-down inhabitants. The plight of the Greeks engaged him totally. "They have sense enough to feel their misfortunes," he believed, "but not spirit enough to remedy them." Yet like Byron Biddle also perceived hope in squalor: "The spirit of the Greeks is bowed but not broken. Tho' oppressed cruelly by their masters they remember, that they were *men*." The situation, he noted percipiently, could change rapidly: "The slightest spark (either foreign assistance or a favorable moment) is all that is wanted to inflame the whole nation into rebellion." Nearing his departure from Greece, Biddle exulted, "I think I learnt more during these last two months than in any other of my life."[30]

Biddle continued his travels – Venice, Vienna, Bavaria, the Rhine, Holland – and in March 1807 turned up in London. There he served the American envoy James Monroe, another family friend, as unofficial secretary. His adventures, his maturity, and his financial acumen impressed the future president. Benjamin West, president of the Royal Academy, opened doors for Biddle as, two years later, he did for Sully. Thanks to West, Biddle gained entry to the Marquis of Stafford's art gallery, rich in French paintings from the Orléans collection. Discussing the state of art with West he honed his perception of aesthetic merit. He recorded, with obvious approval, West's prediction that "in a century America will be above all the world in the arts."[31]

*

Biddle returned to Philadelphia in July 1807. Four years later he married Jane Craig, daughter of a wealthy Philadelphia merchant. The couple settled at the Craig family seat, Andalusia, which fronted the Delaware River in Bucks County.[32] Andalusia lay within easy reach of Philadelphia, 14 miles north by road, three hours upstream by boat. Elected as a Federalist to the State Legislature, Biddle began to make a name for himself as a public-spirited citizen. He maintained his interest in literature. He wrote and translated poetry. He admired works of art. He attended meetings of the Tuesday Club, organized by Joseph Dennie, at which well-born young professionals like himself gathered to discuss painting, music, and poetry. The conversation could sparkle. Thomas Moore, not pleased by his American experiences in 1805, conceded that he passed "in the society of Mr. Dennie and his friends at Philadelphia . . . the only agreeable moments which my tour through the States afforded me."[33]

Dennie was the gifted founder and eccentric editor of *The Port Folio*, based in Philadelphia and the nation's principal literary journal. Federalist in origin and bias, it was the dominant intellectual presence in the early republic. Biddle, with his strong literary and artistic inclinations, soon became a contributor (sometimes under the *nom de plume* "Oliver Oldschool") and served as assistant editor. When Dennie died unexpectedly in January 1812, Biddle, taking over the editorship, announced new permanent sections on the fine arts and on developments in Europe.[34]

The Philadelphian was well aware of Byron's burgeoning popularity in America. The poet's portrait was as familiar in shop windows as Washington's or Napoleon's.[35] The earliest American reference to Byron – a review of *Hours of Idleness* – appeared in the March 1809 *Port Folio*.[36] Biddle already found himself compared to the poet, and during his tenure as editor *The Port Folio* published lengthy extracts from Byron's poems. Under "Recent and intended English publications," the October 1812 number carried notices of Byron's *Hints from Horace* and *The Curse of Minerva*; the December 1813 and January 1814 *Port Folio* transcribed the entire

Giaour.[37] The July 1814 number noted that "the most fashionable writer now in England – and the fashion there is always sure to be the fashion here – is Lord Byron."[38] But challenge of another kind loomed in Biddle's life.

Jefferson during his presidency had sponsored the Lewis and Clark expedition. He asked Biddle to edit for publication the journals kept by the explorers. Meriwether Lewis had died in 1809, but William Clark was alive. Biddle first refused, then accepted the task. He knew that to educate the American people about the vast, newly acquired Louisiana purchase was of the greatest importance. For at least seven or eight hours a day over a year Biddle worked to tame Lewis and Clark's crude but invariably robust language – some passages so robust he put them into Latin. The journals came out in 1814 without Biddle's name on the title-page, but it was he who had edited, arranged, rewritten, and even composed parts of them.[39]

Among those whom Biddle's edition impressed was Byron. The poet who thrilled to the thought that his poems were "redde on the banks of the Ohio!" knew of that river as America's main road West.[40] But Lewis and Clark had penetrated far deeper into the Continent, had gone up the endless Missouri, across the Rockies, down the Columbia to the Pacific. "The sources of the Columbia and Missouri rivers," wrote Biddle, "which had eluded all former research, have been fully explored, and a line of intercourse – the future path of civilization – connects the Atlantic and Pacific oceans."[41] In contrast to constricted, populated England, America seemed immeasurable, its features unknown or hardly known. The idea of the place, the enormous potential of its seemingly infinite expanses, exhilarated Byron. Not only was the American West epic in itself, he thought; its exploration had resulted in a work of epic significance.

"The United States," Whitman would write later, "themselves are essentially the greatest poem." The Lewis and Clark journals, Larry McMurtry has suggested, may well be "our only really American Epic."[42] Byron sensed this earlier than anyone. He asked George Ticknor, a young Harvard graduate visiting England, whether any poet had yet captured the epic nature of the American Continent and whether Americans "looked upon Barlow as our Homer."[43] Byron refers here to Joel Barlow's patriotic epic, *The Columbiad, a Poem* (1807), but his question to Ticknor implies skepticism. Barlow in his preface rejected Homer as a model and condemned the *Iliad* for having "done more harm than good." Lewis and Clark's narrative seemed to capture better the new republic's size and grandeur. For Byron it was more than a historical document: it represented a new order of epic achievement. Lewis and Clark had lived a genuine epic and their words had created another. Upon reading their journals, Byron told Ticknor, he "never envied any men more than Lewis and Clarke."[44] Crossing the unknown Continent was indeed (as wrote a later editor) "our national epic of exploration, conceived by Thomas Jefferson, wrought out by Lewis and Clark, and given to the world by Nicholas Biddle."[45] In *Don Juan* Byron would reinterpret Homeric epic for a disillusioned post-Napoleonic world. He presents Daniel Boone, an American hero on the outermost frontier, as his Natural Man uneasily in Eden.[46] Like Boone, Byron felt constricted; like

Boone, he dreamed of worlds elsewhere. If Biddle admired Byron, so Byron admired, if not Biddle (of whose editorship he most likely would not have known), what Biddle had wrought.

*

The overwhelming presence of Napoleon in the imagination of Federal America limns out another perspective on epic achievement. Biddle acknowledged, as did Byron, Napoleon as the age's model of greatness. In fact, early nineteenth-century Americans often coupled Napoleon and Byron in the same breath. Alternately adulating and attacking the French Emperor, Byron attempted all his life to match himself against the man he considered his chief rival in genius. After Napoleon's exile to St Helena, he viewed himself as in some sort Napoleon's successor. Similarly, the French emperor loomed large in Biddle's life as a gigantic shadow, a being against whom to measure progress and possibilities.

When Biddle arrived in Paris on November 7, 1804, he found everyone talking of Napoleon. He had prepared himself for his mission well. His written French was accomplished, and before leaving America he had perused in the family library many works on French history and literature. He first observed Napoleon at a military review. "What a sight!!" he recorded in his journal.

> Not fifteen yards from me I beheld "the man before whom the world had trembled," the hero whose name has sounded in every quarter of the globe & who has rivaled if not excelled all that antiquity can produce of hardy valour and successful enterprise. I did not neglect this rare opportunity of seeing so wonderful a man & for upwards of an hour while 12,000 men passed before him my eyes scarcely for a moment left him.[47]

The young man who wrote these words was a convinced believer in the virtues and potential of the American republic whose interests in Paris he served faithfully and well. And yet he was mesmerized by Napoleon.

The Pope, summoned from Rome, attended Napoleon's coronation at Notre-Dame on December 2. David's great painting in the Louvre captures the moment in the *sacre*, or coronation, when Napoleon places the crown on Josephine's head. Dazzled by this brilliantly staged event, Biddle did not let its deeper significance escape him. "What a sight was this for a philosopher. A little second lieutenant now wielded the Bourbon sceptre, a woman now occupied the place of Antoinette." Like other self-made men of his era and after, Biddle identified almost *malgré lui* with the man whose initials he shared.

No less than Byron, he wrestled with the enigma of Napoleon's meteoric rise, his spectacular successes, his sudden fall, the continuing magnetism of his being. What did such a mixed achievement portend for the world – and for them? Like many Americans, Biddle admired the French emperor's genius, but regretted his policies. In 1811, in a Fourth of July oration, he "contrasted the condition of free Americans with that of the decadent Europeans, enslaved by the tyrant Napoleon." He attributed America's success "to the loyalty it had shown to the teachings and example of Washington."[48] Byron also compared Napoleon to Washington, and like Biddle found the balance lay all with Washington. Twice the American had possessed, and then relinquished, supreme power, whereas Napoleon, having seized power, kept it, relished it, and fought until the bitter end to keep it. But it was Napoleon, not Washington, who seized Byron's imagination – and Biddle's.

In politics, despite his ambivalence regarding Napoleon's rule, Biddle leaned toward France. He liked French ways, disliked English. Though Napoleonic France "was the enemy of free men everywhere," England posed an even greater danger. Britain, Biddle reminded his hearers in 1811, "by its disregard of American sensibilities and commercial rights, was steadily forcing the United States into a declaration of war."[49] "Incidents" – impressment of seamen, seizure of ships, embargoes of goods – kept relations between the two countries tense. War, long on the horizon, erupted the next year.

Fifteen years later, Biddle eulogized Jefferson, who had just died, in contrast to Napoleon, dead five years. America had made peace with Britain in 1815 and Biddle's own career now stood at its apogee. Of all Napoleon's "foreign triumphs," he said, "not one remained, and in his first military conquest, his own country . . . there is now no place for the tomb of this desolate exile." Whereas Napoleon died dethroned and exiled, Jefferson lived a life of "perpetual devotion, not to his own purposes, but to the pure and noble cause of public freedom."[50] Nine years later Biddle again contrasted the Virginian's fate with Napoleon's: he termed it "the great moral lesson of our age."[51] But he could not put Napoleon out of mind, nor (as he said) forget the glorious *sacre* when he "stood by the great master spirit of our age on the day when he was crowned Emperor."[52]

Jefferson had also pondered Napoleon. Young General Bonaparte's exploits in Italy and Egypt dazzled the world. They dazzled Jefferson too. But Napoleon's assumption of power on 18 Brumaire, November 9, 1799, disturbed him; his crowning himself emperor five years later disturbed him even more. Though Jefferson could no longer regard Napoleon as a defender of republics, he still viewed him, as did the young Byron and Biddle, as heir to the ideals of the French Revolution. European liberals looked upon Napoleon as their best hope to bring about an era free of kings. Though disliking his military and economic policies, Jefferson admired the man's brilliance. True, after Waterloo he thought France better off without Napoleon, but he deplored the callous treatment accorded him by Britain on St Helena. Chained to that barren isle like Prometheus to his rock – the comparison was worn threadbare on both sides of the Atlantic – Napoleon as martyr regained the world's sympathy. His death in 1821 dissipated Jefferson's lingering unease. With Napoleon no longer a political threat, Jefferson could again look on Napoleon as the embodiment of genius. A bust of the emperor adorns the library at Monticello to this day.

Biddle's heady experiences in France during the first flush of Napoleon's empire kept alive his initial enthusiasm for the man. Whatever his subsequent reservations about Napoleon's policies, the man never ceased to fascinate him. Even after Waterloo the now exiled emperor held Biddle in thrall. Puzzled how so great a figure could have risen, and fallen, so far, he, like Byron, devoured book upon book about him. And following in the path of Lord and Lady Holland, Wellington, Byron himself, and countless others, he avidly collected mementoes of Napoleon.

"Any remains of a great man are sacred": so Biddle, aged 20, in his Greek journal, adding, "a love for relicks is the most pardonable side of superstition, for the mind finds a relief at the most trifling monuments of things which were dear to us & which are lost forever."[53] After Napoleon's death "relicks" served Biddle, as they served Byron, as a means to keep the presence of the man of genius close, to stave off for a time the finality, and reality, of his mortality.

The star item in Biddle's collection of Napoleonic memorabilia was a statue of the emperor in his coronation robes. It still adorns the library at Andalusia, Biddle's country home, that was also his retreat, his Malmaison. Other mementoes include a medallion of Josephine; the well-known engraving of Napoleon on a sofa reading to a blond child asleep next to him, presumably the son born to him and his second wife Marie Louise; an engraving of Paul Delaroche's powerful *Napoleon at Fontainebleau* showing a dejected emperor pondering his abdication in 1814; another of Benjamin Robert Haydon's painting of *Napoleon at St Helena* staring out over the endless ocean with, pasted on the back, Wordsworth's sonnet to Haydon.[54] The present Biddle heir to Andalusia sleeps in the bed of Joseph Bonaparte, Napoleon's elder brother. Nicholas Biddle had George Catlin copy a miniature of Napoleon once owned by Joseph that the ex-king of Spain considered the best likeness of his famous brother.[55] Biddle also commissioned from the Philadelphia painter, Bass Otis, a copy of the version owned by Joseph of David's heroic *Napoleon Crossing the Alps*.[56] The original canvas was in Joseph's house.

*

That house was not in France but across the Delaware, in Bordentown, New Jersey, an attractive village a few miles upriver from Andalusia and a transfer point in the busy route between Philadelphia and New York. After the débâcle at Waterloo Napoleon had sought refuge aboard a British warship. Hoping for a comfortable retreat in Britain, he underwent instead exile to the faraway island of St Helena. Joseph – escaping across the Atlantic to America on another ship – had better luck.

In September 1815 Joseph reached Philadelphia, where Stephen Girard found him a place to stay. The following July, Joseph, who went under the name of Count of Survilliers, bought a Bordentown estate named Point Breeze. On a high bluff overlooking the Delaware, the house came with 211 acres of parkland that Joseph gradually increased to 1800.[57] There for the next 16 years Joseph lived and entertained royally. He had, after all, ruled Naples from 1806 to 1808, then for five stressful years (1808–13) Spain. At Point Breeze, beautifully decorated and full of art work, he held court with liveried servants, a French chef, and gourmet dinners.

The genial ex-king mixed easily with Philadelphia gentry and soon became fast friends with Charles Ingersoll, Joseph Hopkinson – and Nicholas Biddle. He came to know and like Thomas Sully. Stephen Girard, who helped many French exiles and facilitated the transfer of Joseph's funds to America, served as his banker. Sidney Fisher looked Joseph over "with interest from the scenes thro which he had passed, & from his connection with the master-spirit of the age."[58] Joseph benefited from the high opinion Americans held of Napoleon. Endlessly curious about Napoleon's life, fascinated by his public career, sympathetic to his fate, they viewed him as a self-made man who abolished old ways and had new ideas, who challenged the absolutist monarchs of old Europe, who professed support for movements of national independence, and, especially important for Americans just emerging from a war of their own with Britain, who had long kept the British lion at bay.

Americans also sympathized with the Napoleonic exiles who sought refuge in the New World. Among those who fled the Bourbon repression and joined Joseph in America were Generals LeFebvre-Desnouettes, Vandamme, Clausel, Lallemand, and, not least, Marshal Grouchy, who famously did not show up at Waterloo to help Napoleon. Charles-Lucien Bonaparte, Joseph's nephew (and husband of his daughter Zénaïde), lived for five years in the mid-1820s at Point Breeze, where he wrote his four-volume *American Ornithology*, an important forerunner of Audubon's more famous *Birds of America*.

Joseph fascinated Nicholas Biddle. The banker found him "by far the most interesting stranger that I have ever known in this country. He is free and communicative and talks of all the great events and the great persons of his day with a frankness which assures you of his good nature as well as [of] his veracity."[59] Whenever Biddle found himself in Joseph's company, which was often enough, he led the conversation around to Napoleon. His journal records many anecdotes about the emperor. On July 7, 1818, at the Ingersolls, Joseph had "a great many interesting things" to say about his difficult experiences in Spain. He believed in the ideas spawned by the French Revolution and supported republics. Biddle marvelled at Grouchy's claim that during the retreat from Moscow, when Napoleon left his troops to attend to affairs of state in Paris, "not a man in the French Army complained."[60] Biddle's interest in the most famous man of the age increased over the years. Joseph's stories, of which he never tired, stimulated his already acute sense of Napoleon's greatness. At a dinner at the Cadwalladers (an occasion when Joseph was absent) Biddle expressed admiration for Napoleon's steadfastness. "The great Art of Bonaparte," he wrote, "was the firmness and determination that accompanied all that he undertook, and which commanded the same sentiments throughout his army. He desired absolutely to carry out such and such a thing and in the end he accomplished it."[61] "J'ai repoussé les limites de la volonté et de la liberté," Napoleon had once claimed, not without justice, and many Americans believed him. For them, Napoleon represented the triumph of will in pursuit of determined-upon goals. Napoleon's steadfastness served Biddle as an example as he pursued his own career.

Joseph had brought together at Point Breeze an outstanding collection of Old Masters. In an era before public museums his collection easily ranked as the finest on American soil. French Empire furniture complemented more than two hundred paintings, including five Rubens, seven Murillos, two Canalettos, a Leonardo, a Velázquez, and many Dutch works. In the foyer guests encountered David's *Napoleon Crossing the Alps*, once sketched by Sully and much admired by Nicholas Biddle. In the central salon visitors found *Napoleon* by François Gérard, another Gérard of Joseph as king of Spain, seascapes by Joseph Vernet, Neapolitan scenes by Simon-Joseph Denis.[62] Everywhere there were sculptures, in different poses and various sizes, of Napoleon himself.

Joseph opened Point Breeze and its grounds to the public on Sundays. A steady stream of visitors came up from Philadelphia. Not only were the paintings and sculpture on view, but the "king" himself often greeted visitors and talked about the history and importance of his treasures. A few Philadelphians found Joseph's oils of nude young women risqué.[63] One proper soul wondered about "all the young females with less clothing than they or you would have found comfortable in our cold climate."[64] Joseph generously lent his paintings to public institutions, including the Pennsylvania Academy and the American Philosophical Society, of which he was a member. After New York's National Academy of Design opened in 1826, Joseph sent art works to its annual exhibitions.[65]

Lafayette stopped at Point Breeze twice during his triumphal American tour of 1824–25. The emperor in his will had not minced words about the "Hero of Two Worlds": "The unhappy results of the two invasions of France . . . are due to the treason of Marmont, Augereau, Talleyrand and Lafayette."[66] Though not always treated gently by Napoleon, Joseph yet felt immense pride in his imperial brother's achievement. Tirelessly he refuted books that posthumously attacked Napoleon. For him, "there never was but one Napoleon."[67] Lafayette had kept his distance from Napoleon during the Empire and, as Napoleon implied, turned against him after Waterloo. Yet Joseph received Lafayette warmly. He tried to interest him in establishing Napoleon's son, the young duke of Reichstadt, on the French throne. But Joseph could not fully trust Lafayette and, unsurprisingly, the discussions went nowhere. The "Hero of Two Worlds" remained firmly committed to his republican ideals.

Thomas Sully, who like Joseph participated actively in Philadelphia's cultural and intellectual life, came to know Joseph well. His journal of April 30, 1826, details a visit, probably not the first, to the count at Point Breeze. Ostensibly Sully went to select paintings for an upcoming exhibition at the Pennsylvania Academy. The artist, an early riser, was amused by what he assumed were Joseph's leisurely habits. "We found the Count with his family at Breakfast – 11 o'clock! partook with him and afterwards the buildings and grounds until one o'clock."[68] To have European artworks the quality of Joseph's a short boat or carriage ride away, even occasionally on exhibit in Philadelphia, was for Sully, who worshipped the Old Masters, a great joy. His journal analyzes in detail, invariably within the context of technique, works he saw at Point Breeze by Titian, Velázquez, Murillo, Guido Reni, and Rubens.[69] They were his masters too, and he wished to learn from them all he could. This particular visit to Joseph's collection, taking place about the time Sully began *Byron*, enabled him to envision the poet within the context of European as well as Anglo-American portraiture.

Other visitors to Point Breeze included the English traveler Captain Basil Hall, RN, and his high-stepping wife Margaret. Hall praised the "suavity" of Joseph's "personal address and the generous hospitality of his princely establishment."[70] The Halls, returning from India, had met the exiled Napoleon on St Helena. Hall thought Joseph looked "extremely like" his brother; Margaret, less certain, thought that between Napoleon and Joseph there was "no comparison." She is one of the few to fail to acknowledge the remarkable facial resemblance between the two. "Still," she added, "any relation of so wonderful a man cannot be looked upon without considerable curiosity."[71]

Hall came to Philadelphia armed with an introduction to Sully from Audubon. Already at work on a travel book about America, he asked Sully to enlighten him about the art scene in America. "We have seen Mr [Charles] Carroll several times since we came here," the captain wrote the artist from his next stop, Baltimore, "& have no hesitation in saying that your picture of him is most excellent." Hall refers to Sully's full-length portrait of 1826 of the aged Carroll. "It is strikingly like," Hall went on unctuously, " – & it has that strong air of character & force of conception about it which I think, after all, is the chief merit in a portrait – & gives to that department of the art, in the hands of a man of genius, a fair title to the praise of Historical excellence." Hall signs off, "with the disposition and the power to follow the grand style of your art."[72]

Hall's *Travels in North America*, published in 1829, caused much outrage in America. From H. B. Fearon in 1818 to Dickens in 1842, English travelers happily denounced America's democratic ways. Worse, Americans drank too much and trumpeted national greatness, present and to be, non-stop. Irving's eloquent essay in *The Sketch-Book* (1819) had condemned British misrepresentations, but to little avail. That Hall's criticisms had a grain of truth to them – more than a grain perhaps – did not deter American indignation.[73] But *Travels in North America* does not discuss the American art scene. Sully, most likely put off by Hall's lordly ways and awkward flattery, had sensibly refused his aid.

The July revolution of 1830 in Paris – a three-day uprising, "*les trois glorieuses*" – turned Joseph's mind once again to Europe. Delacroix's gigantic *Liberty Leading the People* captures the excitement. The repressive Bourbon monarch Charles X went into exile and Louis-Philippe, the citizen-king, now ruled. In 1832 Joseph decided to return to Europe to press the cause of the duke of Reichstadt, Napoleon's son by Marie Louise. He left America reluctantly, for he had enjoyed his life at Point Breeze. Only upon his arrival in England did Joseph learn that, two days after he had sailed, the duke had died, aged 21.[74] When Sully next saw Joseph, it would be as his dinner guest in London.

*

We have anticipated events. Nicholas Biddle, whom we left enjoying the rich cultural ambience at his famous friend's house across the Delaware River, was not destined to be an editor or a literary man. His stint on *The Port Folio* lasted about two years. In London Biddle had impressed James Monroe with his financial acumen. A higher duty was now in prospect. The Second Bank of the United States, chartered by Congress in 1816, was in its early years plagued by political influence, mismanagement, and corruption. In 1819, in an attempt at reform, Monroe, now president, nominated Biddle to serve as one of the Bank's government directors. Biddle accepted. Three years later, in 1822, aged 36, he became the Bank's president.

Though a private institution with private stockholders, the Bank received all government funds and served as the nation's real treasury. By his astute management of the Bank and its 18 branches around the country, Biddle gradually steered the American economy out of the depression resulting from the Panic of 1819. By the mid-1820s the country had righted itself. In Philadelphia Biddle ranked as the city's most prominent citizen; his peers in Washington, New York, and Boston counted him among the nation's most influential leaders. The mature man had realized his initial promise. "Brilliant, impetuous, and daring" – not the usual adjectives attributed to bankers, but so Govan, Biddle's biographer, characterizes his work at the Bank.[75] Andalusia, his country estate, became one of the nation's centers of power. To Biddle's domain resorted "the intellect of the country," among them John Quincy Adams, Henry Clay, and Daniel Webster. "Coruscations of wit, and bright sallies abounding with anecdote and information were continually occurring to enliven these festive gatherings," observed John Jay Smith; "never did I leave his society without admiration of his talents and superior social powers."[76] But on the horizon loomed a cloud.

Upon becoming president in 1828 Andrew Jackson had expressed his contempt for all banks but especially for the one most powerful, the Second Bank of the United States. Jackson, who distrusted a national bank and believed it unconstitutional, saw the Bank as an impediment to democracy. In addition, New York – with its magnificent natural harbor and its economy bolstered by the Erie Canal opening in 1825 – had long resented Philadelphia's financial position and wished to supplant it as the nation's monetary capital. Biddle attempted, but failed, to justify to Jackson the Bank's importance in regulating the nation's economy. The President determined to reduce the Bank's power and, if possible, destroy it.

Personal as well as political motives may have determined Jackson's hostility to Biddle and the Bank. This self-made man was in nearly every respect Biddle's antithesis. Orphaned and penniless by the age of 14, he had had few advantages. With little education he achieved much. He became a frontier lawyer, a prosecutor, a state judge, a congressman from Tennessee, eventually a major-general who defeated the British at New Orleans and the Spanish in Florida. The aristocratic Biddle, a francophile and now Jeffersonian Republican, had voted for Jackson when he first ran for president in 1824. Jackson lost that race, but won four years later, the first Westerner to become president. Biddle applied to Congress in January 1832 for a new charter for the Bank. Both Houses passed the necessary bill, but Jackson vetoed it, and the Bank's supporters could not muster the two-thirds majority needed to override the veto. In the presidential election later that year the Bank became a main issue. Jackson, after defeating Clay, further undercut the Bank's power by ordering government deposits withdrawn. With his secretary of state, now vice president, Martin Van Buren, a New Yorker, it seemed as if both West and East had combined against the Bank. In 1836, when its charter expired, Biddle at great cost reorganized the Bank as the Bank of the United States of Pennsylvania.

After the Panic of 1837 the institution limped along, seemingly stable. The nation momentarily recovered its prosperity. Biddle, health failing, resigned as president in March 1839. The timing seemed right. Later that year, however, came the Panic of 1839. The Bank reeled and early in 1841 failed. Many blamed Biddle. His reputation perished with the Bank. A convenient scapegoat, he moved overnight in his native city from most admired to most hated.[77]

What proved a turning-point in Biddle's fortunes also proved one in Sully's. For Biddle, the Panic of 1837 led to the Bank's eventual collapse; for Sully, the Panic sent him on his way to England. A year later, as a result of portraying Victoria, he returned to Philadelphia to find his career revived, his fortunes renewed, sitters eager to have portraits done by the American who had painted the British queen. Biddle's fortunes, however, never recovered.

When Sully painted him in 1826, the banker was known internationally as well as nationally. "'No American had such European repute,'" one of his political opponents later wrote of him; "'Jackson's was the only one comparable, and that far inferior to it. . . . Biddle was . . . respected in Europe as the most sagacious and successful banker in the world.'"[78] Sidney Fisher, shrewdly observant about Fanny Kemble and Joseph Bonaparte, regarded Biddle with muted admiration. How Biddle "was followed, praised, worshipped, can scarcely be conceived by those who did not witness the scenes in which he was an actor."[79]

Byron in 1816 appeared to have reached the zenith of a spectacular career. He possessed *sprezzatura*, that essential attribute for Castiglione of the courtier, that which gives the appearance of doing with ease and effortlessly anything one wishes to do. But in the spring Byron underwent a dramatic, much-publicized separation from his wife. Rumors swirled about London of a sexual liaison with his half-sister Augusta. Cut by the society that once adulated him, Byron determined upon self-exile. He retired to the

Continent, first to Switzerland, then to Italy, "the Paradise of Exiles." He never returned to England.

Like Byron, Biddle achieved a great contemporary splash; like Byron, he experienced a spectacular fall, exiled from the world that now rejected him. As Nathaniel Burt puts it, "the darling of the gods . . . at the very height of his glory, at the top of his pride, his hubris, is struck down by the lightning of Nemesis."[80] From international repute to near-universal obloquy: it is the stuff of Greek tragedy. Discredited and reviled, Biddle retired to Andalusia. His Malmaison became his St Helena. As isolated in his exile as the emperor had been in his, Biddle now relished more than ever his Napoleonic memorabilia, much of it acquired at this time. He maintained an outward buoyancy, but the Bank's failure ruined him financially. His fall did not affect Andalusia, held in his wife's name. Whereas Byron underwent a brief glorious finale in Greece, Biddle died quietly at home in 1844, one year before Old Hickory. Still in disgrace, he was already half-forgotten by the public.

Admirers of Biddle defended his integrity. Biddle, wrote Philip Hone, had been "indicted for high crimes and vulgar misdemeanors by a secret conclave of greasy householders!"[81] John Quincy Adams summed him up as a man of attributes antithetically mixed: "Biddle broods with smiling face and stifled groans over the wreck of splendid genius, blasted expectations and ruined hopes. A fair mind, a brilliant genius, a generous temper, an honest heart, waylaid and led astray by prosperity, suffering the penalty of scarcely voluntary error." Even Martin Van Buren, Jackson's chosen successor as president and no friend to Biddle, conceded "that his private and personal character has never, to my knowledge, been successfully impeached."[82]

Biddle had aspired to become a statesman of Periclean greatness: what the Greek leader had meant to Athens, he would become for Americans. He had prepared himself well, and he had worked untiringly in pursuit of his vision. But to say that Biddle failed catastrophically is to scant his other chief legacy: that in America, in large part through his efforts, a new Greece had arisen.

*

All his life Biddle looked back longingly to the glory that was Greece. Burt envisions him, picturesquely, "with one hand on a Greek bust and the other on the country's finances."[83] Biddle was, after all, one of the very few Americans of his era to have actually seen in Italy as well as in Greece the timeless monuments of antiquity or what remained of them. Regarding ancient Greece as the cradle of democracy, Biddle wanted a new American architecture to replicate the Greek style. Public buildings, even private residences, were to look like temples. As a sponsor, inspirer, and patron of Greek Revival architecture in America, he was popularly known in Philadelphia during his lifetime as "Nick the Greek."[84]

Biddle knew William Strickland, who had won the competition to design in the Greek Revival style Philadelphia's still-standing Second Bank of the United States (1818–24). The directors had explicitly stated the style they wished, and Biddle followed the progress of the competition closely. When Strickland's design won, his father Charles Biddle sent a special messenger to Andalusia to inform Nicholas.[85] Biddle did not join the Bank board until 1819, when he immediately became chairman of the building committee, oversaw the Bank's construction, and possibly influenced aspects of its design.[86] He certainly took pride in its magnificent Doric exterior based (via the illustrations in Stuart and Revett's *Antiquities of Athens*) upon the Parthenon. Architectural historians regard the Second Bank as the first major Greek Revival building in America. After becoming the Bank's president, Biddle worked every day in Strickland's interior. He also had the Bank's branch offices around the country built in the Greek style. So lasting was his influence on bank design that not until well into the twentieth century did banks in America cease looking like Greek temples. Biddle's experience with the Second Bank whetted his ambition to put his own stamp on a major building.

In 1831 Stephen Girard died. Easily the richest man in America, Philadelphia's most famous merchant and patriot-banker, and incidentally Sully's current landlord, Girard left at his death a $7.5 million dollar estate. His will decreed that a large portion of it go to establish a school for orphans, Girard College. Although Girard dictated the basic plan and structural layout of the huge central building, he did not prescribe a specific architectural style. In a well-publicized competition, every major architect in the Northeast, with the exception of Robert Mills, submitted a design – among them, Philadelphians Strickland and John Haviland, the latter the architect of the nearby neo-Gothic Eastern State Penitentiary (1823–29), already a famous landmark, and of another prison, the infamous Egyptian Revival "Tombs" in New York, setting of Melville's tale "Bartleby the Scrivener." But the committee passed over Strickland and Haviland and instead chose Thomas Ustick Walter, a 28-year-old Philadelphian, a former student of Strickland's, who had submitted a Greek Revival design. Nicholas Biddle, the committee's new president and the city's best-known grecophile, almost certainly influenced the decision to choose Walter. With Walter only in his twenties, Biddle may have felt that he could exercise more control over the building than with an older architect. Once Walter's design had been chosen, Biddle persuaded the architect to alter it to reflect *his* notion of how a Greek Revival building should look.

Biddle, like John Ruskin and Andrew Jackson Downing after him, thought architecture should contain a significant ethical dimension. Architecture, in effect, reflects character, to such an extent that those of poor character who move into a perfectly well-designed, well-built house will turn it into a shabby, ugly dwelling.[87] For Biddle, there were two great truths in the world, the Bible and Greek architecture. Architecture's "highest glory" for him consisted of "a refined simplicity," and so Girard College would become a model for Americans, a building that would "at once gratify the honourable pride of every citizen of the United States, and form the best study for all the branches of industry connected with architecture."[88] Biddle succeeded in his hope: Founders' Hall, the huge Corinthian temple-form building that began to rise in north Philadelphia, is as much his as Walter's. Whereas Walter's interior conforms to the specifications of Girard's will, Biddle's long-held vision of Greek-inspired architecture resulted in the impressive colonnade of huge Corinthian columns.[89] Although professing to simulate what Poe called "the glory that was Greece," Girard College's gigantic proportions achieve "the grandeur that was Rome."

Founders' Hall, outside of the US Capitol then under construction in Washington, was the largest building in the United States. With a $2 million budget, it was also America's most expensive building to date. It went up during the years Biddle fought his long losing battle with Jackson over the Second Bank. Such a structure, in effect, the biggest public works project in America, gave Jacksonians a "perfect target" toward which to launch partisan attacks against the banker. If Biddle lost the Bank war against the old warrior president, he hung on long enough at Girard College to achieve an architectural triumph.[90] At least one modern observer has termed Founders' Hall, not without justice, Philadelphia's "single greatest building."[91]

In 1833 Biddle rewarded the compliant Walter with a commission to remodel and enlarge Andalusia into an imposing Greek Revival country house. Benjamin Latrobe had redesigned an older house in 1807–8; to it Walter added a library at the rear with bookcases sporting Grecian pediments, rooms at the front, and before them proud Doric columns – modeled upon those before the Theseum – that overlook the Delaware (Figure 13). Andalusia today remains largely as it was remade then, "one of the most beautiful of America's Greek temple mansions."[92]

Walter also designed at Andalusia gigantic forcing-houses, or greenhouses, in which the banker cultivated the grape. One wonders if the idea came to him after Biddle saw or heard about the *Grande Serre Chaude* (1805) that Josephine Bonaparte had built at Malmaison, outside Paris, the largest and most advanced heated greenhouse in Europe.[93] Always interested in agricultural pursuits and a frequent lecturer on them, Biddle during his foreign travels had noted soil conditions, crops, and the raising of livestock. A sometime gentleman farmer upon his return, he used the original hundred-acre grounds at Andalusia, which he increased, for agricultural experiments. New artificial and animal fertilizer, strains of seed, irrigation, crop rotation, new farming technology: he tried it all. The land produced for city markets corn, wheat, barley, oats, buckwheat, rye, and vegetables; beef cattle and dairy cows grazed in his meadows.[94] From 1831 to 1844 Biddle served as president of the Philadelphia Society for the Promotion of Agriculture. Biddle "raises fine grapes and gets a good price for them in the Philadelphia market," noted an admiring Philip Hone.[95] Though storms wrecked Biddle's greenhouses after his death, the high walls still stand. Covered with wistaria and now enclosing a boxwood garden, they recall Biddle's lifelong enthusiasm for agricultural pursuits.

*

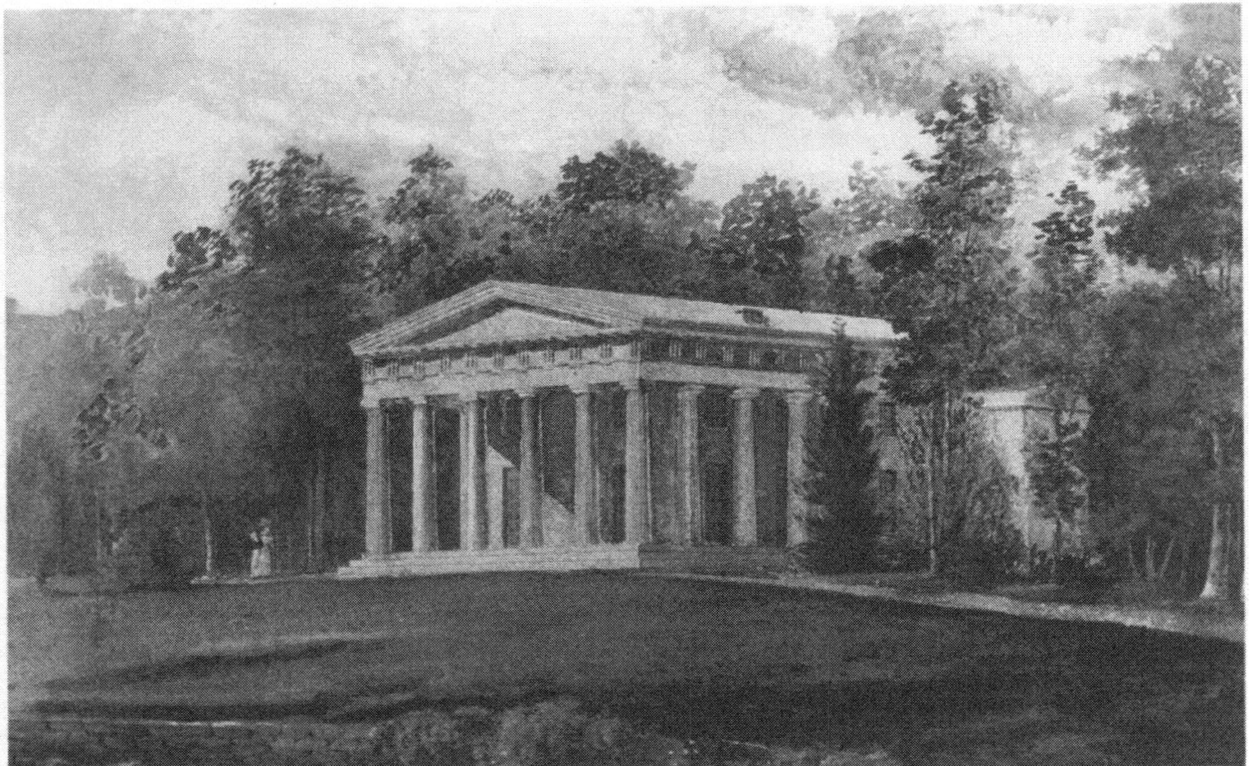

13 Thomas U. Walter, *Andalusia* (watercolor), 1834. Andalusia, Bensalem, Pennsylvania. Courtesy of James Biddle

Conscious from an early age of the need to craft a public persona, Biddle often had himself painted and sculpted. He understood well the power of images: upon taking over the editorship of *The Port Folio*, he introduced a department of fine arts and subsequently increased the number of illustrations. Americans of this era who aspired to public service took care to commission portraits and have engravings made of them. Such works served as "a kind of teaching device, a way of inculcating the lessons of political virtue by illustration."[96] Citizens looked at the physiognomies depicted in the portraits and engravings in hope of discerning signs of individual merit. From the first Biddle was aware that he needed to commission images that would reflect his accomplishments and disseminate his fame. Ellen Miles counted 22 representations of him done between 1805 and 1843: seven miniatures, one drawing, one silhouette, five marble busts, eight oil paintings.[97] At least three of the portraits Biddle had engraved for wider distribution. The variety of formats and poses in which he is depicted suggests that, like Byron, he presented a challenge to artists.

The beauty Biddle projected was more in the face, the mind, the manner than in the form. "His figure," observed Fisher, "was short, round & fat." Biddle at 5' 7" stood an inch and a half shorter than Byron. The portraits and, even more, a silhouette of 1843, a year before Biddle's death, indicate a large head atop a stocky body of noticeable, though contained, girth. Like the occasionally rotund Byron, Biddle had trouble keeping his weight down.

One artist whose portraits of Biddle did not please his subject was Jacob Eichholtz. In February 1811 Biddle, then a state legislator in Lancaster, sat for Eichholtz not once but twice. Eichholtz, just beginning his artistic career, had much to learn. "All I can say of it," commented Biddle's witty new bride of this portrait, "is that I hope you do not suppose you resemble it; such thick lips, such dead eyes. . . ."[98] Nothing daunted, Biddle gave Eichholtz a second try the next month. He could be as witty as his wife about the injustices inflicted upon his physiognomy. Eichholtz's second effort elicited the following drollery:

> It is a melancholy satisfaction to know that in making an ugly picture the worthy painter has not made a very strong likeness; and yet if the portrait be dull & heavy the whole fault must not rest on him, for dullness is very contagious and I am willing to believe that like a man of the world I have accommodated my looks to the Lancaster standard.[99]

Biddle liked Eichholtz, and in 1837 gave him a commission for a third portrait. He should have known better. "I have been sadly traduced into the very lowest low Dutch by a well meaning friend, Mr. Eichholtz," he lamented, "and I hope to recover my equilibrium by Mr. Sully's means."[100] He did not purchase Eichholtz's portrait. Presumably he recovered his equilibrium with Sully.[101]

One may wonder why "Nicholas the Great," president of the Second Bank and one of America's most influential men, waited until 1826 to engage Sully. Over his career the artist painted 26 portraits of members of the Biddle family, and by 1826 he had already painted Nicholas's brothers Thomas, John, and James, as well as his wife Jane. Even more surprising, no Sully portrait of Nicholas is full-length. Although bust- and waist-length portraits had largely replaced the knee- and full-length portraits of Colonial America, Sully, unlike Stuart, had made full-length portraits a specialty. In these years he had on his easel full-lengths of Jefferson, Jackson, Lafayette, and Carroll. But in such portraits the eye usually goes first to the belly rather than to the head. By focusing on Biddle's head (which was splendid) rather than on his body (which was not), Sully averted potential embarrassment. No doubt he would not have been adverse to attempting a full-length portrait of Biddle, but the choice was the patron's, not the artist's. Biddle had good reason to choose the smaller format.[102]

Sully began his portrait on July 26 and by October 31 had completed it, recording (on November 22) that he "sent home the portrait of Nicholas Biddle, Esqr." When he painted Biddle, the gathering storm of Jacksonian hostility had not yet affected the Second Bank, and Sully himself may have felt personal gratitude to Biddle for his astute management of the nation's finances. As the economy recovered from the Panic of 1819, the artist had regained modest prosperity. He had already begun a portrait of Jane Craig Biddle on April 22, in which her hat and attire, if less fanciful, is comparable to that in Lawrence's contemporaneous *Lady Peel*, itself derivative of Rubens's *Chapeau de Paille*.[103] Double portraits of American couples were common. Now Andalusia would have a pair. But the portrait of Biddle came back to Sully. Biddle, who knew much about art, may have found it unsatisfactory, or Jane, who had definite opinions about her husband's appearance, may have wished it otherwise. We know only that in 1828 Sully reworked the portrait extensively.[104]

The 1826 *Biddle*, approximately 30" x 25" (76.2 cm x 63.5 cm), is the same size as *Byron*. It is not only contemporaneous with *Byron*; it shares with it a similar pose: the subject deep in thought, chin resting on right hand, light falling on face, eyes reflective. Biddle's jacket – deep green, with open collar and fur ruff – compares in style if not in color with Byron's. Columns, standard props of neoclassical and Romantic Grand Manner portraiture, often imply, as in Sully's full-length portraits of *Victoria* and *Jefferson*, strong character and leadership.[105] The column behind Biddle alludes to his statesmanship but also to his interest in classical architecture, whether found in Athens, Aegina, Philadelphia, in the new national capital of Washington or, in time, Andalusia. The Greek Revival buildings rising in Philadelphia supplied Sully with ample evidence of Biddle's enthusiasm.

As with Byron, Sully portrays Biddle looking over an ideal landscape that both complements and characterizes the sitter. Behind him loom dark clouds; out at sea are two sloops. The open water, a much broader expanse than the Delaware that flows before Andalusia, may evoke thoughts of the Ionian or Aegean. Biddle may have looked eternally young, but Sully captures as well the mature man of sensibility, the wise banker, the sometime poet and creative editor, the lifetime lover of art and architecture, the man of far vision, even the dreamer.

Why did Sully depict Biddle looking like Byron? In Sully's portraits of males, theirs is not a usual pose. Did Biddle, noticing *Byron* in the artist's studio, request the pose? – or did Sully choose it himself? Like everyone in Philadelphia, he was aware of the banker's Byronic good looks and intellectual brilliance. Aware too of Byron's involvement with Greece, Sully consciously associated the banker with the poet.

Artists often rendered political leaders in a neoclassical style intended to indicate high-minded purpose and dedication; theatrical and literary figures were often posed in more Romantic fashion.[106] *Jefferson* reflects Sully's neoclassical style; *Cooke as Richard III*, his Romantic. *Biddle*, both statesman and man of wide culture, combines the two. By giving Biddle and Byron virtually identical poses Sully suggests worldly achievement, but also romance. Both portraits interacted with each other in conception and creation, but *Byron*, I shall argue, renders a still more complex individual than *Biddle*.

Heroism fired Sully's imagination no less than his palette. In the 1820s the artist, if more subdued than the combative youth of 16, was viewed as a man, in Neal's words, capable "of the most heroick, unostentatious, and truly noble acts, that I have ever heard of."[107] Neal does not specify what these heroic acts might be, but he implies that Sully faced life with courage. For many Americans, Biddle and Byron stood out as heroes: Biddle had restored the nation's finances; Byron had died for Greece. *Biddle* thus echoes *Byron*, possibly even the untraced *Napoleon*. It captures heroic traits even skeptical contemporaries like Fisher recognized in Biddle: that the banker partook of "the elements of greatness & of the qualities allied to genius." For Fisher, Biddle's "schemes were visionary, not founded on reality, & too grand to be accomplished by even the immense power which he wielded."[108] He could be writing Byron's epitaph in Greece. The poet posed an even greater challenge than the banker for Sully. Greatness and genius and heroism were part of it, but creativity was there as well.

CHAPTER SEVEN

The Heroic Decade:
Lafayette to Byron

To most of those whom he passed, his form must have worn the air of some image drawn from the pages of history. Half a century had carried all of his contemporary actors of the Revolution into the great abyss of time, and he now stood like an imposing column that had been reared to commemorate deeds and principles that a whole people had been taught to reverence.
James Fenimore Cooper on Lafayette[1]

While Lafayette supplied her with a hero, no one captured the romantic mood of 1826 quite like the impassioned British poet George Gordon Byron.
Andrew Burstein, on Eliza Foster's *Yorktown*[2]

He asked me once who was the favorite poet of America – I told him he was – he seemed to think I meant to compliment him.
William Edward West, in conversation with Byron[3]

Byron never touches Greece but he blazes.
John Neal[4]

The 1820s proved to be a heady time in the national consciousness. As the nation began to identify its historical image, Americans came to a more confident awareness of themselves as a people. "Home, Sweet Home," first performed publicly in 1823, struck a responsive chord as Americans were now more than ever aware they had a home.[5] A series of public anniversaries signaled the nation's coming of age. 1824 marked the fiftieth anniversary of the creation of the Continental Congress; 1825, of the battles of Lexington and Concord. In August 1824 Lafayette, invited by President Monroe to become "the Nation's Guest," began a memorable visit that lasted until September 1825. Hardly had he left than Americans cheered the opening of the Erie Canal, the all-water route between New York City and Lake Erie that soon rivaled the Ohio as the nation's main path West. The Continent first traversed by Lewis and Clark captured the imagination not just of Byron but also of millions in America and in Europe who envisaged in this vast new land a better life than from whence they had come.

Americans celebrated July 4, 1826, the fiftieth anniversary of the signing of the Declaration of Independence, with a splendid jubilee. The bitter and divisive struggle for freedom that was the Revolution had united them. Fifty years had passed, and it was felt that the nation had a sufficiently long history. A new political entity had come into place, utterly distinct from anything Europe had known, and Americans realized how much they owed to the heroic generation that had created their still young country. Hero-worship of revolutionary leaders and first statesmen extended no less vibrantly to the foreign great, chief among them Lafayette, now the only surviving general of the Revolution; Napoleon, the mighty shatterer of kingly regimes and feudal ways, now dead five years; and Byron, the immortal poet and martyr for Greece, dead only two.

The year 1826 was also the year in which Greeks trapped in besieged Missolonghi attempted a desperate, only partially successful, break through Turkish lines. Mathew Carey, Philadelphia's leading publisher and a noted philhellene, wrote that "the annals of the world, since ruthless warfare began to devour the human race, present nothing of patriotism and bravery more honourable to our nature than the defense of Missolonghi."[6] Delacroix's powerful *Greece Expiring on the Ruins of Missolonghi* (1827) depicts a full-figured female "Greece" bearing the sufferings of her country, her arms outstretched over the ruined city. In an operatic gesture of protest she supplicates the world for redress in the unequal combat. Below Greece a white male arm extends up from the ruins – an arm one observer deems Byron's.[7] The painting is at once a wake-up trumpet blast to Greek philhellenes and a homage to Byron. It was in this year of national and international self-awareness that Thomas Sully began his portrait of the poet.

On October 20, 1827, a combined British, French and Russian fleet defeated a larger Turkish–Egyptian fleet in a major sea battle in the bay of Navarino in the Peloponnese. The victory turned the war around. The Greeks, close to defeat, rallied their forces and spirits. Victor Hugo's poem "Navarin" addressed two Greeces, modern and ancient, as the "Grèces de Byron et d'Homère." Well before Byron's death at Missolonghi, Westerners had formed their conception of modern Greece on him and his poems. Near the end of "Navarin" Hugo wrote, "La Grèce est libre, et dans sa tombe / Byron applaudit Navarin."[8] Most historians end the Greek Revolution in 1828, by which time America's protracted jubilee was over, and the nation had completed a preliminary assessment of herself and of her participation in the larger world. In that year Sully put the finishing touches on *Byron*. Byron's extraordinary impact upon the New World helped shape the context in which Sully conceived heroism and heroic individuals. That impact and those individuals – particularly Jackson, Napoleon, and Lafayette – enable us to comprehend better what Sully attempted to do in his portrait.[9]

*

The cult of the great man had impressed itself no less upon American than upon European civilization. Unsurprisingly, Americans of the 1820s wanted representations of the heroes who had made their nation. In addition to a national portraiture, this hero-worship also called forth biographies. A few men and women even began to write not simply memoirs of their public careers but autobiographies (a new word at this time) that assessed their country as they explored their inner lives. Aware that the nation now had a history, however brief, Americans evinced increased interest in knowing about and visualizing the people, past and present, great and small, who had contributed to the nation's coming into being, particularly the unsurpassed Washington.

Rembrandt Peale created his large-scale *trompe l'oeil* Washington, *Patriae Pater* (1823), perhaps the decade's most famous portrait, at a time when nostalgia for the Revolutionary past had begun to peak. The *Patriae Pater*, as later its smaller "porthole" versions, became a national icon. Samuel F. B. Morse's full-length *Marquis de Lafayette* (1825) commemorated a man whose name many Americans invoked in the same breath as Washington's. Morse's *The Old House of Representatives* (1822), with its embedded portraits of the nation's current leaders, reminded Americans they lived in a republic, a noble experiment in democracy. John Neagle's brawny *Pat Lyon at the Forge* (1826) vaunted confident, democratic self-reliance no less than personal independence. Charles Willson Peale's *The Artist in His Museum* (1822) portrayed an artist sure of himself but equally sure of his role in a society seeking enlightenment.

The West contributed its share of heroes. John Vanderlyn in two full-length portraits of 1820 and 1824 commemorated the man many considered Washington's military heir, Andrew Jackson. Byron, imaginatively awed by far-questers like Newton and Columbus, idealized in *Don Juan* the pastoral existence of Daniel Boone, but Chester Harding had followed America's most famous frontiersman deep into the Missouri forest to paint his portrait (1820), an experience that left the aged frontiersman "much astonished."[10] Two years later, caravans of wagons full of traders launched themselves from the Missouri Territory across the uncharted, dangerous Plains for fabled Santa Fe. Alert Americans were aware that the frontier was shrinking as quickly as it was expanding.[11]

Sully took an active role in honoring heroes near and far. The Panic of 1819 had inaugurated several difficult years for him, but as the nation recovered financially he entered upon a second, even more productive period in which he depicted surviving members of the Revolutionary generation and their successors. Major commissions included portraits of Lafayette, Jefferson, Jackson, John Quincy Adams, and Charles Carroll of Carrollton. Of these figures, Carroll (1737–1832) is the least known today, but as delegate to the Continental Congress, signer of the Declaration of Independence, later senator from Maryland, he outlived almost all his contemporaries and in old age was revered as a national hero. The English traveler Basil Hall professed himself amazed by Sully's full-length portrait of the long-lived Carroll, done in May 1826. Four years before, Sully had captured the aged Jefferson at Monticello. Seeing the portrait the next year at West Point left Fenimore Cooper agape. Sully also did a small (25" x 33" – 63.5cm x 83.8cm) full-length portrait (1825) – small, because for an engraving – of John Quincy Adams. Precocious son of the second president and in 1825 the compromise winner over Jackson and Clay as president, the younger Adams represented the successor generation to Washington and Jefferson and to his own father, a generation for whom the Revolution existed as little more than a fond and distant memory.[12] Besides his bust-sized portraits of Biddle and Byron, Sully completed one of Napoleon Bonaparte.

Lafayette and Napoleon, Jefferson and Jackson, Adams and Carroll, Byron and Biddle: their lives were the stuff of drama and history, their deeds the inspiration of enthusiastic and endless commentary. The portraits were destined for public places, engravings of them for private homes. Although mostly commissioned, the portraits reveal to us (as Neal claimed) a "heroick" Sully, an artist who relished the challenge of capturing greatness on canvas. This challenge shaped in subtle and largely intangible ways his *Byron*. The portrait emerged from engravings, from his reading, and from his imaginative conception of his subject, but it also emerged from Sully's understanding of heroism and of heroic figures.

When Andrew Jackson defeated the British, spectacularly if belatedly, at the Battle of New Orleans early in January 1815, he became overnight America's most popular military man. Three years later, in a controversial campaign, he curbed the Seminoles and helped evict the Spanish from Florida. An enthusiastic nation awarded him a triumphal tour, the longest and most elaborate such celebration in its history until Lafayette's five years later.

Philadelphia merchants commissioned Sully to do a portrait of the victorious general. The initial sitting took place on February 17, 1819. The three-quarter-length portrait, painted between March 26 and April 15, 1819, has the martial Jackson standing in full uniform before his steed (Figure 14). Various copies of this portrait earned Sully more than $1400 during his lifetime. J. B. Longacre's engraving of 1820 furthered its renown.[13] The full-length portrait of 1845, the most widely recognized portrait of Jackson, was the inspiration of the three-cent stamp in 1902, the ten-cent stamp in 1985, and currency of various denominations, including the present $20 bill in its earlier manifestation as well as in its revised, colorful new version of 2003.[14] The Peales, Charles Willson and Rembrandt, also portrayed Jackson early in 1819, as did the sculptor William Rush, but posterity has responded to Sully's dramatically vigorous interpretation.[15]

Jackson dominated American politics in the 1820s. In 1824 he ran for the presidency, his candidacy immeasurably strengthened by his distinguished war record. Although the hero of New Orleans lost a contested election to John Quincy Adams, he remained the man to watch. Sully evidently established a cordial relationship with the general, for when in Washington to paint Lafayette in December 1824 Jackson invited him to dine.[16] Ten years later, once again in Washington, Sully received from Jackson, now president, another dinner invitation, this time to the White House.[17]

The general personified qualities – "courageous honor, the *appearance* of utter honesty, homeliness, bluntness, a desirable inelegance, cordiality, familiarity" – that many Americans professed to cherish. Additionally, "those who saw the worth, or thought they heard the heartbeat, of the democratic masses identified with Jackson."[18] Determination and being

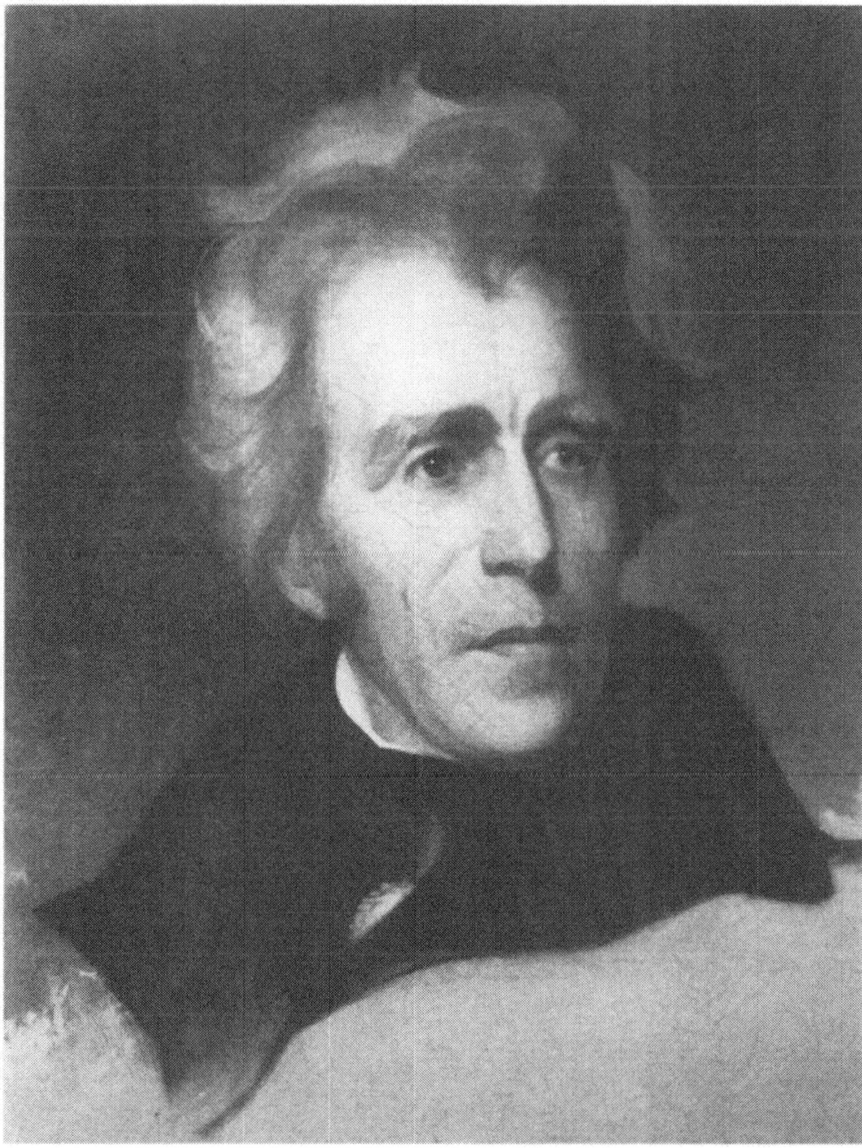

14 Thomas Sully, *Andrew Jackson*, *c.* 1824. National Gallery of Art, Washington, DC

reputedly "tough as hickory" had given him the familiar nickname of "Old Hickory." Political propaganda linked the general with Washington, and Americans considered him, in light of his military successes, as Washington's successor.

More surprisingly, they linked Jackson with Napoleon. His sudden celebrity after the victory at New Orleans occurred just two months before the dramatic reappearance in Paris of Napoleon, who had escaped from Elba. Portraits of Jackson at this time are modeled unmistakably on the French leader.[19] A popular diorama of the mid-1820s pictured Jackson, Washington, and Napoleon "'in the center of the American stars of freedom.'"[20] An unflattering engraving of 1828 of Jackson as Richard III probably derived from an 1813 caricature of Napoleon surrounded by corpses.[21] Unlike Washington's, Napoleon's achievements had taken place on a European scale and within more recent memory. Jackson's supporters elevated his exploits to make him out, as some had made Napoleon out to be, "a champion of the people." Americans perceived Jackson, like Napoleon, as a self-made man. A French official even dubbed the rugged Tennessean "*Napoléon des bois*," Napoleon of the woods.[22] After Lafayette had triumphantly toured America in 1824–25, the trio surrounding the Hero of New Orleans expanded to a quartet. In recalling Washington and Napoleon when celebrating the new hero Jackson, the nation bathed itself in nostalgia and reflected glory in greeting the old war hero Lafayette.

*

Unusual as it might seem in hindsight to include Napoleon in a diorama with Jackson and Washington "in the center of the American stars of freedom," Napoleon's presence there indicates how vibrantly he appealed to Americans. Anti-British feeling was rife after two wars with Napoleon's main antagonist. Most fashionable houses had a bust or portrait of Napoleon; at Andalusia Nicholas Biddle had both. The bust of Napoleon in Jackson's Hermitage is prominently displayed to this day. Though Washington and Lafayette were greatly admired, Napoleon appealed to Americans because he incarnated heroism *and* genius – and both on a grand scale.

Himself self-made, the emperor exemplified his own credo, "*la carrière ouverte aux talents.*" Visionary no less than pragmatic, he jettisoned tired absolutist dogmas, restructured and modernized France, chose leaders on the basis of ability not rank, redistributed power in favor of the young and enterprising, and by energy and skill dominated Europe for 15 years. Additionally, in selling the vast territory of Louisiana to the United States he had participated in the formation of the American nation, by that single stroke doubling the size of the fledgling republic. A man who had risen largely on his merits, who had genuine achievements to his credit, Americans found worth thinking about.

Nineteenth-century authors of American schoolbooks regarded Napoleon, without exception, "as the greatest general of the contemporary era."[23] Asked each year to name the man they most admired, Harvard students always chose, and by a large majority, Napoleon.[24] Sidney Fisher, no hero-worshipper, referred to him as "the soul which governed the world."[25] George McClellan, Civil War Union general, relished (but did not merit) his nickname as "The Young Napoleon." The US Post Office directory of 1859 listed 15 towns or villages named Napoleon. They joined ten Lodis, four Arcoles, and eight Marengos, clear indication that Americans regarded both the man and his spectacular early victories in Italy as stepping-stones along mankind's path to political freedom.[26]

Men of imagination and liberal views responded positively to Napoleon. Most artists, in Britain as in America, felt the same. Hazlitt remained all his life enamored of the man; likewise, Benjamin Robert Haydon could not stop painting an emperor he had never seen. In 1802 Benjamin West, in Paris to see the Louvre's treasures, was much impressed when he met Napoleon. West applauded his initiative in opening the Musée Napoléon, as the Louvre was then known, to the public. In an era before public museums the Louvre displayed the largest and finest concentration of masterpieces ever to be assembled. Characteristically West, even in an England soon at war with France, did not hide his admiration for the emperor. George III, when he heard how vocal West was in praise, fired him from his lucrative position as Court History Painter. West's "French principles" also forced him, reluctantly, in 1805 to resign the presidency of the Royal Academy. Reinstated the next year, he continued to express esteem for Napoleon.[27]

The French emperor impressed Thomas Lawrence no less. Though his adored Nelson's death at Trafalgar caused him to refer to Napoleon as "the Reptile of France," the longer Lawrence contemplated Napoleon the more he admired "the daring frankness of His mind."[28] Napoleon possessed "a power which enabled Him instantaneously to see into the nature of every character & person who might be brought before Him."[29] The heroic scale of Napoleon's achievements dazzled Lawrence. "The '*Tiger*' is indeed gone," he wrote, somewhat prematurely, in January 1814, "but with him that exciting power that has so rous'd one's faculties, and seem'd indeed to have shot new activity into the human Mind." A few months later, Napoleon abdicated at Fontainebleau and went into exile on Elba. Lawrence, revisiting the Louvre, feared, rightly it turned out, the probable "breaking up and dispersing the most magnificent Collection . . . of all Arts that the World has ever seen."[30] Looking about him in the city, however, he found an even more impressive exhibit. "No man can see France and Paris," he exclaimed, "without bowing to the greatness and extent of this man's conceptions. . . . I speak of him as present, and every where he is; and it is as impossible that he can ever be separated from the past greatness of his country, as for human efforts to blot out the sun."[31]

American artists admired Napoleon virtually without reserve. In 1808 Rembrandt Peale, lured to Paris by the Louvre, was amazed by the festivities surrounding Napoleon's birthday on August 15.[32] Back again in Paris during 1809–10 he did a portrait study of Napoleon, which David, Napoleon's favorite artist, praised. David offered to appoint Rembrandt one of

Napoleon's court painters, but the American refused.[33] In America he took inordinate pride in his heroic, large-scaled equestrian *Bonaparte on Horseback*.[34] John Neal praised it glowingly as "a distinct, single, and vigorous picture, with a sublimity in the countenance of Napoleon, that I never saw excelled – it is absolutely articulate and preternatural."[35]

Despite his English birth and ways, Sully, like Jefferson, Biddle, and artists on both sides of the Atlantic, admired the French emperor's genius. Napoleon's brother Joseph received him kindly, both at Point Breeze and in London. Like West, Lawrence, and Rembrandt Peale, Sully valued Napoleon's support of the arts. In London in 1838 he often referred to, and may have owned, the multi-volume folio catalogue of the Louvre's huge collection.[36] The catalogue whetted his appetite to see the collection for himself. The chance came at the end of his London stay. The Louvre, now with its holdings much reduced, still had more and finer works on display than any other public venue, and early in July Sully crossed the Channel for a brief visit to Paris – and to the Louvre. His favorable response to the Napoleonic vision that had brought the collection into being extended to the man. "Last week," he wrote in March 1834, "Hare Powel presented me a medal of Napoleon."[37]

Before Sully left England for good he paid a visit to Lord and Lady Holland at Holland House in Kensington. Lady Holland, wife of a leading Whig grandee, had adored Napoleon. To soften his exile on St Helena she had sent him packages of food and nearly five hundred books. In return the emperor left her in his will a snuffbox. After his death, two of his companions on St Helena, Generals Bertrand and Montholon, arrived at Holland House, in full dress uniform, to deliver the snuffbox. Enclosed within Lady Holland found a note: "L'Empereur Napoléon à Lady Holland, témoignage de satisfaction et d'estime."[38] Napoleon's terse yet eloquent acknowledgment of her many kindnesses moved Lady Holland greatly. The snuffbox and its note became the most precious of her many mementoes of the deceased emperor, and she had facsimiles made of both. One set she gave to Sully. She would not have done so without cause. Sully, a visitor from America, a man she hardly knew, must have expressed his enthusiasm for the emperor sufficiently for Lady Holland to sense in him a kindred spirit.[39]

In 1826, the year he completed *Lafayette* and *Carroll* and began *Biddle* and *Byron*, Sully executed a portrait of Napoleon. Painting it would have made him conscious of that famous face, its much-admired physiognomy often compared to Byron's. The buyer of *Napoleon* was William Alston of the Georgetown District, South Carolina.[40] His brother, John Ashe Alston, had previously purchased Sully's "original study" for *Washington's Passage of the Delaware*.[41] Presumably, like so many Americans, the Alston brothers associated the Titan of France with the Titan of America. Unfortunately, Sully's *Napoleon* has proved even more elusive than his *Byron*. Until it surfaces its likely significance for *Byron* cannot be adequately assessed.

But another hero whose career nudges Byron's at several points reappeared on the scene in 1824. This is Gilbert du Motier de Lafayette.

*

Liberal France recognized the marquis de Lafayette's prominent role in its Revolution; in 1824 Americans hailed him as the only surviving general of its War of Independence, an honored associate of Washington and other early leaders of the American republic. Had Lafayette not served Washington as a major general from 1777 through the decisive Virginia campaign of 1781? Had he not fought bravely and endured with him the dark days of Valley Forge? Important in the history of both nations, "the Hero of Two Worlds" (so he was early known) achieved in his lifetime historic stature. European Liberals had invested large hopes for America, and Lafayette, an outspoken standard-bearer of the American mission, helped spread republican principles and the meaning of American liberty.[42] The visit of the aged Frenchman gave the nation's jubilee a symbolic center.[43]

Lafayette arrived in New York in August 1824. Initially conceived as a four-month stay, the tour became a 13-month extravaganza full of pageantry. It garnered worldwide publicity. Everywhere Lafayette went, civic dignitaries accorded him honors, and the public lavished adulation. He spent time with the nation's leaders – the two Adams, Jefferson, Madison, Monroe, Jackson – but also held receptions open to anyone who wished to talk with him.[44] The extended opportunity for celebration and nostalgia heightened Americans' interest in their Revolutionary past. It also led to a burst of portraiture.

Speeches and toasts cited Lafayette's devotion to Washington, most revered of the Founding Fathers. The public considered him Washington's companion, friend, disciple. The virtually adopted son of the childless hero, Lafayette had become "an integral part of the national creation story."[45] Regarded as almost the last of the Founding Fathers, most now dead or, like Jefferson and Adams, in precarious health, Americans held him in scarcely less reverence than Washington himself.

All his life Lafayette steadfastly championed freedom. In America he had fought for liberty; in France, he advocated "America as a paragon of freedom and the model of how to sustain it."[46] Lafayette's was essentially a Romantic vision. For him, as for Thomas Paine, "America was a far off Arcadian land, an unspoiled environment where a whole host of Cincinnati had left their plows for a glory-filled struggle against tyranny and despotism."[47] Paine had written of the struggle, but Lafayette had lived it. In speeches, published writings, and private correspondence, he elevated the fight for independence in the American Revolutionary cause to a fight for human liberty everywhere.

During the early stages of the French Revolution Lafayette achieved symbolic prominence. As leader of the Paris National Guard, he promoted the republican principles he had imbibed in the American War for Independence, but as the Jacobins increased in power he lost favor and fortune. Forced to flee France, he was captured in 1792 by the Austrians, who considered him a revolutionary and thrust him into prison. Josephine Beauharnais, later to become Josephine Bonaparte, intrigued for his release, and for her help he remained lastingly grateful.[48] Lafayette, thanks to the influence of Josephine's new husband, Napoleon Bonaparte, emerged from prison in 1797, but did not return to France until two years later. By then young General Bonaparte, having escaped from Egypt, had become First Consul following the *coup d'état* of *18 Brumaire*, November 9, 1799.

Ever a convinced republican, Lafayette could not sanction Napoleon's increasingly absolutist rule. He ostentatiously rejected the legitimacy of the emperor's regime and refused to serve under him.[49] Napoleon, for his part, left Lafayette alone. During the Empire, which lasted until 1815, Lafayette lived quietly at his family home, La Grange, not far from Paris. His opposition to Napoleon encouraged others to use his name without his knowledge: he was more often suspected than actually involved in plots against the emperor.[50] Upon Napoleon's defeat and exile in 1814 Lafayette refused, out of his love of liberty, to join the restored Bourbons. The next year Napoleon effected a dramatic return from Elba. With the government now based on a new "liberal" constitution, Lafayette accepted election to the Chamber of Deputies. After the 100 Days ended in Waterloo (June 18, 1815), he led the call in the Chamber of Deputies for Napoleon to abdicate. Believing that "a people in arms would expel the occupying forces and bar the return of the hated Bourbons," Lafayette proposed reviving the National Guard.[51] It was a utopian belief. Napoleon abdicated, but the National Guard did not form, the people did not rise, and the Allies reinstated Louis XVIII upon the throne of France.

Lafayette never lost faith in republics. In wide-ranging correspondence he supported liberal revolutions everywhere they broke out. In 1818 he returned to the Chamber of Deputies and in 1823 he opposed French intervention in Spain on behalf of its reactionary monarch, Ferdinand VII. That year, in a personal letter to President James Monroe, he urged the American government to support, directly and indirectly, revolutions in Latin America – and in Greece.[52] He told Monroe that he would feel "delight" in returning to "the Beloved Land of which it Has Been My Happy Lot to Become an Early Soldier and an Adopted son."[53] Congress extended an official invitation. Lafayette, almost 70, gratefully accepted.

The general arrived in New York near the end of the near-regal presidency of Monroe. His landing at the Battery, a contemporary remembered, "his reception by the military under General Martin, his triumphant progress through Broadway, his first visit to City Hall, awakened emotions which cannot be described."[54] Pomp and ceremony, heartfelt emotion even more, greeted Lafayette wherever he went. Over his still-living presence a wave of commemorative sentiment crested. As Lafayette himself suspected, the enthusiastic welcome he received – without parallel or precedent in American history – was partly a response to his symbolic role.[55] Lafayette visited all 24 of the states that then made up the nation. Grown men like William Wirt, the Attorney-General, reading newspaper accounts of the general's welcome, admitted to weeping "like a child."[56] Layfayette had expected a friendly reception from his second country, but the plaudits he received from the day he stepped ashore until the day he reembarked for

France caught him and everyone else by surprise.[57] For Charles Sumner the tour belonged to "the poetry of history."[58] It served Americans as a tangible reminder of their past, Romantic and mythic at once. "The Hero of Two Worlds" had become a legend in his lifetime.

In 1824 the Corporation of New York announced a competition for what became the most coveted commission in America: a portrait of Lafayette. It was won by a young but promising artist, Samuel F. B. Morse. Having studied for four years in London with West, Morse knew how to mix realism, classicism, and moody Romanticism in a style owing much to Thomas Lawrence. By the time of the Lafayette commission he had made a name for himself.[59] States and cities often awarded commissions to their own, and Morse was prominent in the New York art scene. A founder of the city's National Academy of Design, he served as its first president. Sully, among the artists who applied unsuccessfully for the Lafayette commission, was impressed. "Mem, – the corporation of New York," he noted in his journal, "is to pay Morse $1000 for a whole length of La Fayette!"[60]

Morse's *Lafayette*, attired in a black cape with a scarlet lining and posed against a lurid sunset, looks magnificently dyspeptic. Eschewing idealization, Morse adopted "a kind of physiognomic expressionism."[61] Physiognomists believed a person's features and the shape of his head revealed his character. (In Chapter 9 I examine physiognomy's significant impact on Sully's *Byron*.) Physiognomically inclined artists needed to study their subjects carefully. In practice such an approach, departing only minimally from realism, facilitates bringing out favorable aspects of an individual's character. Physiognomy worked better with some subjects than with others. Rembrandt Peale's "porthole" *Lafayette* (1825) and Horatio Greenough's sculptured likeness of the general (1831–34) both reflect physiognomical theory, as do numerous representations, in oil and in stone, of Washington.[62]

On September 28, 1824, "The Nation's Guest" reached Philadelphia. His entry into America's most culturally sophisticated metropolis constituted a high point of his tour. Plans for the parade and ceremony had begun two months before. In front of the Pennsylvania State House, now Independence Hall, William Strickland had designed a 45-foot-high civic arch modelled on that of Septimus Severus in Rome. William Rush's statues of Justice and Wisdom crowned the arch. Between them stood Thomas Sully's painted rendering of Philadelphia's coat of arms.[63]

A group of eminent Philadelphians commissioned from Sully a portrait of the general. So rapid was Lafayette's progress that several of his portraitists, Sully among them, only caught up with him in Washington, where he had settled in for the winter months. Sully had done an initial pencil study of the head in Philadelphia; in Washington in December 1824 he did a life sketch in oil. Despite this preliminary work, Sully only began his *Lafayette* on September 9, 1826, in part because his initial group of subscribers had reneged on their promise. He completed the full-length portrait on November 25 (Figure 15).[64]

Sully attired the general in civilian costume, with gray gloves and a cane. The top coat is thrown open, exposing a rose silk lining; a silken tie

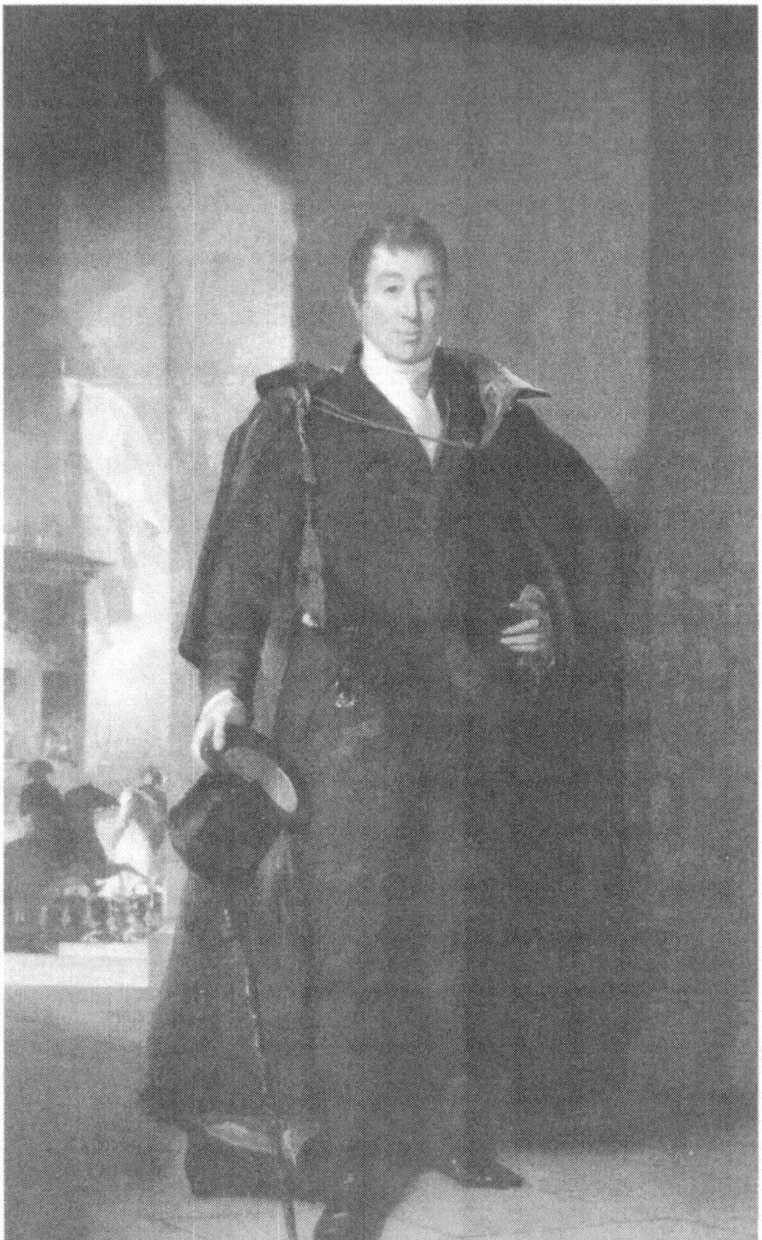

15 Thomas Sully, *The Marquis de Lafayette*, 1824–26. Independence Hall National Park, Philadelphia

cord of the same hue loosely crosses his chest. The general's visage is keenly humorous; black bead-like eyes miss nothing of what is going on. Sully reduced Lafayette's years, regularized his nose, mouth, and chin, eliminated wrinkles, and gave his toupee an illusion of reality. The oddly shaped head in Morse's *Lafayette* attains in Sully, as classical canons recommended, the geometric purity of a perfect oval. Slimmer and taller than in reality, his complexion roseate, the idealized general appears altogether rejuvenated.[65]

The portrait unites past with present. If the present is the striking marquis, the background recalls the past. An escort of troops stands at arms below; cheering folk on balconies welcome the returning hero. But no, they cheer personages wearing old-fashioned cocked hats: Washington calmly astride a white horse; Lafayette half in shadow nearby, on a rearing roan stallion. Sully depicts, not Lafayette's reception in Philadelphia in 1824, but an earlier visit to the city at the side of Washington, his adoptive father. Artists in the mid-1820s were forging new modes of commemorative art. Portraits were to recreate physical appearance, but also to render subjects ideal and inspiring. They were intended to express gratitude for deeds well done or fame justly earned.[66] In *Lafayette* Sully sought to perpetuate the general's heroic career for future generations.

Lafayette's triumphal tour coincided broadly with preparations for the fiftieth anniversary of American independence. When members of the Continental Congress approved the Declaration of Independence on July 4, 1776, they launched the American Republic. The jubilee celebrations fifty years later inspired sadness as well as joy, for on July 4 of 1826 Jefferson and Adams, the nation's third and second presidents, died within hours of each other. Aged war veterans, like Rip Van Winkles awakened from a long sleep, helped by their mere presence to bring about a new awareness among Americans: there had been giants on the earth and they had done great deeds. An era had ended; a new era had begun.

*

The jubilee years also became a protracted funeral for Byron.[67] In the minds and hearts of Americans he played a role scarcely less important than Lafayette. Americans responded to his love of freedom and liberal views, his expressions of regard for their country and for their republican government. They valued his support of revolutions. Had he not participated in the failed uprising of the Carbonari in 1821? When one of the Italian revolutionaries left that year for Greece, an English lady gave him not a Bible but a handsome edition of *Childe Harold*.[68] Byron died in Greece the year Lafayette arrived in America. "I can understand and enter into the feelings of . . . La Fayette," he had written Hobhouse earlier.[69] Symbolically at least he entered with Lafayette into the jubilee celebrating America's independence.

The New World looked favorably upon Byron. The poet relished the enthusiastic young Americans who visited him in England and on the

Continent. George Bancroft, Edward Everett, and George Ticknor left behind records of their impressions, but such figures as Catherine Stith, who did not, also influenced Americans' conception of Byron. All spoke invariably of Byron's courtesy and affability, his genuine pleasure in their company. Abroad after 1816, Byron professed to shun his countrymen, yet welcomed Americans. Once, after a visit by Joseph Coolidge, aged 21, Byron claimed he "was more flattered by this young enthusiasm of a solitary transatlantic traveller than if they had decreed me a Statue in the Paris Pantheon."[70] "Americans are the only people to whom I never refused to shew myself," he told Medwin; "the Yankees are individually great friends of mine."[71] Interesting in themselves, they represented a nation whose government he valued. Byron came to own about thirty books on American history, politics, travel, and literature.[72] Although he never met the nation's best-known man of letters, Washington Irving, he delighted in Irving's writings and held the man in great esteem.[73] Irving, whose reputation stood high in England, shared Byron's publisher, John Murray and was a member of Murray's literary circle. Later he arranged the American rights for Thomas Moore's biography and so helped shape Byron's American reputation. Irving valued Byron no less than Byron did him.

Byron often quizzed American visitors about his transatlantic fame. When shown "an American copy of his works," in two "small and very shabby volumes" printed at Philadelphia, Byron (noted Ticknor) expressed "evident pleasure."[74] In "Ode to Venice," *The Age of Bronze*, and *Don Juan*, he voiced his admiration for American life and institutions, and at various times after 1819 he contemplated a voyage to America, South or North. Byron, let us admit, was more enthused with the ideal of democracy than with its messy practice, but he genuinely envied Americans their good fortune in living in a free land. And the ideal had export potential. The new government of Greece should take as its inspiration a republic – "I will not say a federation of republics; but a federation of states" – based on the American model.[75] America's government was a model for people everywhere.

Americans first encountered Byron's poetry when the Philadelphia firm of Branner and Morford reissued *English Bards* in 1811. That publication heralded an avalanche: between 1811 and 1830 American publishers put out at least 99 editions of works by Byron.[76] Thirty additional bits of Byroniana – parodies, travelogues, fictional representations, memoirs of the poet – appeared as well. Editions of Byron came out in eight American cities: Boston, 14; New York, 34; and Philadelphia, where Sully lived, an astounding 39. In 1814, at the height of Byron's initial popularity, publishers in four American cities brought out *The Corsair*. The year before, Moses Thomas – who dominated Philadelphia's reprint market for years and published more works by Byron than did anyone else – issued the first collected edition of the poet's works. By 1830, 12 other collected editions had followed it. "In all," according to Peter X. Accardo, indefatigable recorder of Byron's American publication history, "nearly one hundred and fifty publishers, printers, booksellers, artists, and engravers were engaged in the Byron reprint trade."[77] Such a bare recital of publishing data only begins to indicate the enormous excitement that Byron's name and works generated in America.

After his death, editions of his poems, articles about him, engravings of his portraits, testify to Byron's accruing renown in the New World no less than in Britain and Europe. R. C. Dallas's *Recollections of Lord Byron* (1824), Medwin's *Conversations of Lord Byron* (1824), Pietro Gamba's *Narrative of Lord Byron's Last Journey to Greece* (1825), and William Parry's *The Last Days of Byron* (1825) are among the better known of the numerous books spawned by this enthusiasm. Through London and European editions or by cheap reprints at home, Americans soon read the books and articles, often illustrated by American artists, that poured forth from presses. With much information at hand, Sully had ample opportunity to educate himself. That he had done so is indicated by the vibrant interest he continued to display in Byron long after he had completed his portrait.

In 1821 the Greeks began a revolt against the Turkish yoke. Two years later, wishing to aid so worthy a cause, Byron left for Greece. All Europe – and America – knew he had put his life on the line. On April 19, 1824, he died miserably, not in the battle he had sought but of fever and medical malpractice. The circumstances hardly matter. The perceived martyrdom did. "He died for the Greeks like another Jesus," exclaimed Alexander Dumas.[78] Death placed an imperishable crown on his memory. Henceforth Byron's name would be inextricably linked with Greece.

News of the Greek uprising touched mystic chords of memory in America. In 1785 Jefferson had hoped that he might once again "see the language of Homer and Demosthenes flow with purity, from the lips of a free and ingenious people."[79] Their Revolution over, Americans named over three thousand "cities" after those in classical antiquity.[80] Names like Athens, Sparta, Cincinnati, Troy, Utica, Syracuse, Ithaca, and Corinth both legitimized America's special destiny and stressed the nation's continuity with the heroic legacy of Greece and Rome.[81] Revolutions prior to 1821 – in Italy, Mexico, and in Spain's South American colonies, Argentina, Chile, Colombia, Venezuela, Peru – had not captured the American imagination or aroused its sympathy and charity. That in Greece did.[82] It brought home to Americans now dim memories of their own Revolution, of a time when they had struggled to achieve a democratic utopia. They made the Greek cause their own.[83] Greek-quoting students likened Ypsilantis, the Greek leader who initiated the revolt, to Washington. A Philadelphia newspaper advocated the "Romantic project" of sending an American fleet to help the Greeks. "Since the days of the American war of independence," George Bancroft mused in his journal on July 4, 1821, "there has been no scene of exertion so pure and so glorious as this."[84]

Lafayette was known to sympathize with the plight of the Greeks. Their envoys in London had written him in "great friendship and trust," and Lafayette in a personal letter to Monroe, an old friend, suggested that America send the Greeks "a few friendly ships and a trifling loan of money."[85] Most Americans, however, preferred to remain uninvolved. The

United States should stand as an example or model of republican government, one other nations or peoples might adopt if they chose; but Monroe's Doctrine promulgated in 1823, while warning against European involvement in the Americas, advocated non-intervention in European affairs. America should provide only moral support for the cause of liberty abroad. Among those opposing active support of the Greeks was Congress and Secretary of State (and soon-to-be President) John Quincy Adams. Congress, deciding in favor of non-interference, refused both material assistance and recognition. Boston merchants who traded in the eastern Mediterranean also questioned supporting the Greeks. To counter the forces of non-involvement, various philhellenic societies sprang into existence in the fall of 1823.[86]

That modern Greeks hoped to establish a government based on democratic principles – and were professed Christians to boot – only enhanced the worthiness of their cause to American philanthropists. In promoting Greek Revival architecture, Nicholas Biddle reflected the widespread belief that Greece was the cradle of liberty in which the earliest republics were rocked. Other prominent Americans – Jefferson, Madison, Albert Gallatin, Webster, Clay – actively championed the Greeks and spoke eloquently in favor of their achieving independence.

Foremost among enthusiastic American philhellenes was Edward Everett, professor of Greek at Harvard and editor of the influential *North American Review*. Inspired by Byron, whom he had met, Everett himself made the pilgrimage to Greece in 1819. Upon returning to America his articles in the *Review* swayed American opinion toward actively supporting the Greeks. Second only to Everett in his influence as a philhellene was Mathew Carey, author, philanthropist, human dynamo, publisher of Byron, and friend of Sully. Samuel Gridley Howe, an American physician who organized medical facilities in Greece, dedicated his *Historical Sketch of the Greek Revolution* (1828) to both Carey and Everett.[87] Carey helped set up the Committee of Philadelphians, on which Nicholas Biddle served as an honorary member, to solicit aid for the Greeks. In monies raised it ranked only behind New York's.[88] With such aid, Greece had a viable chance to become a new America.

Lafayette's American tour renewed America's sense of mission. Inevitably, it intensified interest in things Greek.[89] American philhellenes proclaimed that America (via Europe) owed its civilization to the ancient Greeks, that their modern descendants (however debased their current state) came from the heroes of old, and that in driving out the Turks Greece would regenerate itself. Empathetic Americans felt compelled to help the land they deemed democracy's birthplace. Sometimes they solicited money and goods at receptions for Lafayette. Only a few, motivated by Byron's example, actually went to Greece. "They were more Byronic than Byron," one observer has said of those who took ship, "trying to find in Greece the exoticism which they loved, thinking they were copying Byron but actually behaving in a way which Byron himself never did."[90] Many of those who inspired by Byron volunteered set sail for Greece with a copy of *Childe Harold* in their pockets.

*

Byron's death at Missolonghi in 1824 was an event of major import in the history of the age. A gifted genius, a spectacular career, and now, in the great and honorable cause of freedom, glorious death. In the Britain that he had rejected and that had rejected him, the shock of that death was still great. Jane Welsh, upon learning the news, cried out to her future husband, Thomas Carlyle, "My God if they had said that the sun or the moon had gone out of the heavens it could not have struck me with the idea of a more awful and dreary blank in the creation than the words Byron is dead[.]" The previous day, Carlyle had written her, "Poor Byron! Alas poor Byron! The news of his death came down upon my heart like a mass of lead; and yet, the thought of it sends a painful twinge thro' all my being, as if I had lost a Brother!"[91] For the young Tennyson, aged 14, the day Byron died "the whole earth seemed to be darkened." He went out and carved on a rock "Byron is dead."[92] "Never," declared Bulwer-Lytton, looking back in 1833, "shall I forget the singular, the stunning sensation, which the intelligence produced. . . . We could not believe that the bright race was run. So much of us died with him."[93] The loss was felt for decades. Eliot's heroine in *Felix Holt* (1866), Esther Lyon, defends her favorite poet against the sarcasms of the titular hero, himself unconsciously Byronic. She exclaims, "I have a great admiration for Byron" (ch. 5). Several generations in England and America defiantly echoed her sentiment.

When Walter Scott, Byron's admired friend and rival poet, heard the news, he dictated the next day at James Ballantyne's printing office an eloquent tribute, "Character of Lord Byron." "The voice of just blame, and that of malignant censure," said Scott, "are at once silenced; and we felt almost as if the great luminary of Heaven had suddenly disappeared from the sky, at the moment when every telescope was levelled for the examination of the spots which dimmed its brightness."[94] Byron's errors, he claimed, "arose neither from depravity of heart – for nature had not committed the anomaly of uniting to such extraordinary talents an imperfect moral sense – nor from feelings dead to the admiration of virtue. . . . Lord Byron was totally free from the curse and degradation of literature – its jealousies we mean, and its envy." Comparing Byron favorably with Shakespeare, Scott praised *Don Juan*'s infinite variety, its breadth of vision. The poem, whose worth he was among the few to recognize, "embraced every topic of human life, and sounded every string on the divine harp, from its slightest to its most powerful and heart-astounding tones."[95]

Byron, for Scott, was an active hero, a fighter. "His foot was always in the arena, his shield always hung in the lists." Like the champions of old he never quit, "and came always off with distinction, almost always with complete triumph."[96] Scott paid tribute to Lafayette and Napoleon, but only Byron, in fighting for freedom, achieved a martyr's grave. His death shook Scott profoundly. A year after first hearing the news, he wrote Thomas Moore of Byron: "I very often think of him almost with tears."[97]

In Europe Byron's death symbolized unfulfilled genius. In France, where he shaped a generation of writers, 14 books about him appeared within six months of his death.[98] For Mazzini, Byron was an Anglo-Greek Washington. "I know of no more beautiful symbol of the future destiny and mission of art than the death of Byron in Greece," he wrote in 1839.[99] The myth of heroic genius created by Byron and Napoleon, the Dioscuri of Romanticism, shaped a century. Its power resonates to this day.

Word of Byron's death reached the United States in late June 1824. Newspapers and journals accorded it even more space than Lafayette's farewell trip. Many picked up Scott's laudatory tribute. The heartfelt words of the most famous surviving English writer moved Americans. No one carved on a rock "Byron is dead," but grief was no less sincere.

Harriet Beecher, aged 13, never forgot the day her father, the estimable Dr Lyman Beecher, told his wife, "with a sorrowful countenance, as if announcing the death of some one very interesting to him, 'My dear, Byron is dead – gone.'"[100] The future author of *Uncle Tom's Cabin* felt a sense of overwhelming loss and retired to a nearby hill to brood. Byron's impact upon her reverberated over a lifetime. His poems, along with the Bible, exerted upon her writings "the single greatest literary and imaginative influence."[101]

For Americans, Byron in death symbolized an age's aspirations. He embodied the romantic appeal of an individual who cherished great ideals. Preparing a trip to Europe, the poet Fitz-Greene Halleck obtained a letter of introduction to Byron. But when Halleck left New York Byron had already sailed for Greece. Upon hearing of Byron's death, Halleck was stunned. "Byron dead, and I did not see him!" he cried out. Such an "uncharacteristic display of emotion startled his friends." For Halleck, allegiance to Byron may have been erotic as well as literary. Halleck, a homosexual, viewed the bisexual Byron (so Halleck's latest biographer) as "an icon of sexual and literary liberation."[102] Byron spurred Halleck to write "Marco Bozzaris" (1825), in which the American expressed his admiration for the struggling Greeks. Botsaris (a modern spelling), one of the ablest Greek leaders, had planned to meet and discuss strategy with Byron. But on August 20, 1823, a few days before Byron arrived in Cephalonia, he died in a night sortie against the Turks. Halleck conceived of Botsaris's heroism in terms that imply Byron's:

> Thy voice sounds like a prophet's word;
> And in its hollow tones are heard
>   The thanks of millions yet to be. . . .
> For thou art Freedom's now, and Fame's;
> One of the few, the immortal names
> That were not born to die.[103]

In hymning Botsaris's death Halleck hymned Byron's, which soon followed. Botsaris's daring sortie on a sleeping enemy may well have reminded Americans of Washington's strategy at Trenton when on a snowy Christmas night in 1776 he led his ragged troops across the Delaware. Richard H. Dana considered "Marco Bozzaris" America's finest lyric; Cooper prefaced lines from it to a chapter of *The Last of the Mohicans*.[104] Byron's American fame stimulated the poem's immense contemporary *éclat*. Thanks to Halleck's threnody Botsaris became in the New World almost as famous as the heroes of the American Revolution.[105]

William Cullen Bryant admired Byron's poetry no less fervently than Halleck. As a boy, Bryant had devoted his "whole soul to the study of Greek," and the grown man supported the Greek cause with enthusiasm equal to Halleck's.[106] News of the massacre of the Greeks on Chios (Scio) in 1822 – the Turks executed the island's male population and sold surviving women and children into slavery – fanned American indignation. Bryant began thus "The Massacre at Scio":

> Weep not for Scio's children slain;
> Their blood, by Turkish falchions shed,
> Sends not its cry to Heaven in vain
> For vengeance on the murderer's head.

With such effusions, little wonder that American public opinion turned violently anti-Turk. Few doubted that this was now a war for survival.

Poems and plays linked Greece and Byron. John Howard Payne's *Ali Pacha; or, the Signet Ring* (1825) features Ali as "the terrible Turk" who, predictably, lusts after a Greek captive. As Longfellow remarked ironically, "every village had its little Byron."[107] Legions of the young learned how to curl the lip, shadow the brow, and turn themselves, like the notorious Lara, into "a thing of dark imaginings."

After Byron's death one-volume editions of his works, replacing the multi-volumed pocket editions of the 1810s, flooded the American market, multiplying his readership. Best and most comprehensive of them was the hefty tome edited anonymously by Halleck in 1832. With 74 letters and a number of poems not in Moore's great edition being published by John Murray, it was, so its American publisher, "the first *complete* edition." It does contain almost all the poems, along with many letters, prose writings, essays, and extracts from reviews. Halleck's 13-page introduction reveals his sympathetic, detailed awareness of Byron's career. One-volume editions proliferated into the 1830s and well into the 1840s.

Byron was omnipresent. Touring America during the mid-1830s, Harriet Martineau doubted if many Americans read Byron.[108] Frederick Marryat, encountering Byron's poems everywhere a few years later, disagreed. "I believe that in nine drawing rooms out of ten," he wrote in *A Diary in America* (1839), Martineau "must have seen a copy of Byron lying on the table."[109] In the log cabins of Sault Ste Marie, the deepest backwoods of America, Marryat came upon "complete editions of Lord Byron's works."[110] In 1840 N. P. Willis named his new periodical *The Corsair* after Byron's poem. In seeking to have himself painted in Byronic fashion Attorney-General William Wirt was not alone.[111] Nicholas Biddle had done the same before him, and Webster in his early portraits often assumed a Byronic air.

Popular novels like Eliza Foster's *Yorktown* (1826) drew heavily on the potent Byronic myth.[112]

Byron inspired art no less than literature. Thomas Cole appended lines from Byron's poetry to at least three major paintings of the 1830s, of which *Manfred* (1833) is the most spectacular. Byron influenced Cole's attraction to moonlight imagery – witness *Desolation* (1836), the last of his *Course of Empire* sequence. Cole adopted the cyclic view of history developed in *Childe Harold*'s fourth canto, which evoked in melancholy fashion the ruins of Rome. By the 1830s the poem had become so popular that travelers used it as a guidebook. When Cole encountered the Apollo Belvedere in Rome, he exclaimed, unsurprisingly, "I can conceive of no description finer than Byron's in his *Childe Harold*."[113] Hawthorne in *The Marble Faun* could mock, but not dissuade, the literary tourists who inspired by Byron's *Manfred* made the mandatory pilgrimage to the Colosseum at midnight, "exalting themselves with raptures that were Byron's, not their own."[114] American artists immersed themselves in the Prometheus of Aeschylus's *Prometheus Bound*, the myth of the heroic Titan Byron had drawn upon all his life. Cole in a powerful rendering of *Prometheus Bound* (1847), recognized the myth's vital relevance for Americans. As William Page, another artist, put it, "Prometheus is not a dead Greek fable but to us a living type."[115] One of his modern descendants might even be a certain English poet.

Greek-inspired sculptures based on Byron's poems that hymned Greek freedom may have been even better known than the paintings. Robert Gilmor, the Baltimore art collector, commissioned a *Medora* (1832) from Horatio Greenough. Based on *The Corsair*'s domestic heroine, it presents her supine on her deathbed. Oddly, the work most influenced by the Greek Revolution – if we exclude the Greek Revival temples sprouting across the land – did not appear until nearly twenty years after the war ended. Cincinnatian Hiram Powers, influenced by Byron, created in dazzling white marble *The Greek Slave* (1843). Presumably Powers meant viewers to imagine the demure nude young woman standing dejectedly in chains being eyed by lustful Turks. The subject, and even more the nudity, of Powers's sentimental sculpture caused a sensation. Touring America from 1847 to 1849, *The Greek Slave* inspired unprecedented numbers of poems, engravings, pottery. It gained in the decade preceding the Civil War additional meaning as viewers associated the figure with violated mulatto and black slaves.

Byron's fame in the United States lasted longer than in Britain or on the Continent. Until the Civil War, indeed well beyond, he embodied genius. For his American Museum, that savvy showman, P. T. Barnum, offered in the 1850s five hundred pounds to Colonel Wildman, owner of Newstead Abbey, for a tree on which Byron had carved his name. Wildman, however, flew into a rage at Barnum's Yankee impudence.[116] In the 1860s James Jackson Jarves saluted George Inness, the brooding, mystical painter of the national scene, as "the Byron of our landscapists."[117] In 1879 S. G. W. Benjamin described Emanuel Leutze, of *Washington Crossing the Delaware* fame, as totally

"Byronic in the impetus of his genius, the rugged incompleteness of his style, the magnificent fervor and rush of his fancy, the epic grandeur and energy, dash and daring, of his creations."[118] Clearly the audience Jarves and Benjamin wrote for knew well Byron and his poetry.

Notable dissenters like Thackeray apart, hero-worship pervaded the century. The Greeks and Romans whose exploits Plutarch recounted in his parallel *Lives* encouraged Americans to draw analogies between them and the heroes of their Republic. America, unlike Rome, had not regressed. It had rejected the trappings of royalty; it had no king or emperor; it resisted corruption and discouraged Rome's extremes of wealth and poverty.[119] In the 1780s Charles Willson Peale had launched a museum devoted to portraiture of the great. Gilbert Stuart, in depictions of Plutarchian rectitude, enshrined in the national pantheon the heroic character of Washington. The paintings of famous men displayed in the homes of collectors like Jefferson served them as daily sources of inspiration.[120] Lafayette and Napoleon, as later Jackson, were acknowledged among the lasting great. Byron as the would-be savior of Greece, the sacred land of democracy, lived for Americans as a major poet and a martyr. Around his flawed but magnificent achievement hovered the halo of the final sacrifice.

Little of the adulation Americans accorded Byron escaped that keen-eyed observer of national life, Thomas Sully.

CHAPTER EIGHT

A Portrait for Americans:
Sully's *Byron*

I tried to assess Byron as if he were a mountain, but I was wrong, Byron is a volcano. . . . There is in him a kind of warmth which makes one feel that his life still endures and is still, as it were, present in the places where he was.
Mario Praz[1]

Le visage est le théâtre de la pensée
Adolphe Thiers[2]

The most popular, famous, and influential poet of his generation, Byron was also its most dramatic personality. For Sully as for other Americans Byron by the mid-1820s was "more a name than a figure of mortal flesh"; he had become, in fact, "an actor in a pageant of national awakening."[3] America's response to Byron charts the fitful but steady evolution of its culture. Byron, though an English poet, featured prominently in the fervent patriotism of America's Jubilee. Interest ran high in the man and in his poetry. After his sacrifice for the Greek cause, Americans no less than Europeans clamored for representations of the fallen hero. Artists capitalized on the public's enthusiasm. Perhaps the best known of the images is "Baron" Adam Friedel's depiction of Byron in Greece in 1823. It presents the exotically clad poet, a Homeric helmet at his feet, in a pose that could be associated as much with Napoleon on St Helena as with Byron in Greece.[4]

Prints of popular paintings depicting national heroes or political figures furthered a sense of national purpose. Given the country's vast size and few public places, most nineteenth-century Americans could not view portraits or sculptures first hand. Prints became America's most influential art form. New engravings proliferated and enterprising publishers recycled older ones. Americans snapped them up enthusiastically. Engraving was a highly skillful art form closely related to painting, which it complemented. Like portraits and sculptures, engravings represented different levels of skill. The best are independent works of art; the worst travesty their subjects. If the engraver were highly competent or familiar with the subject, an engraving might have authority of its own.

Lithography, established in America by the mid-1820s, permitted still more reproductions. For his first lithograph of 1825–26, among the earliest done in America, Rembrandt Peale chose Byron as his subject. In mid-1826, a year after Peale's lithograph and about the time he began to portray "Byronic" Biddle, Sully undertook *Byron*. He liked challenges, and interpreting visually a creative, dynamic spirit like Byron gave him one. He seized opportunity by the forelock. This chapter analyzes why Sully depicted Byron as he did; the chapter following interprets the portrait from the perspective of Lavaterian physiognomy; and the last considers in relation to *Byron* some problems inherent to portraiture.

*

Like most artists of his generation in England as in America, Sully had to educate himself. Fiercely dedicated to his chosen career, he sought constantly to learn more about art, its techniques and its practitioners. Those who attempted Grand Manner painting should ideally have taught themselves much, and Sully was predisposed to acquire knowledge of history, literature and drama, of ancient sculpture and of Old Master art since the Renaissance. His journals reveal intensive study of writers on art from Reynolds to Allan Cunningham. The self-portraits, of which at least twenty exist, indicate a thoughtful man, intelligent and knowledgeable, but reserved, a man who kept his innermost thoughts to himself.

To survive as a painter Sully had no choice but to become a highly literate man. His library has been deemed extensive.[5] His literary tastes may have been conventional, but they were not superficial. Painters in early nineteenth-century America drew chiefly upon British authors, sometimes upon continental, and rarely on American authors. Illustrating Shakespeare, Cervantes, Le Sage, Burns, Goldsmith, Irving, and Byron, they made characters and incidents in their works come alive.[6]

The 1820s were lean years for the American Muse. The nation retained a restless cultural dependency on Britain. Prospects at home were improving, however. Cooper and Bryant began to make names for themselves in this decade; and Poe, now on the scene, published his first volume in 1827, the year after Sully began *Byron*. Sully knew and liked Irving, his friend since at least 1807, and had Irving lived in America during these decades Sully could have learned much from him about Byron. Though Sully professed the study of Milton beyond him, he did, at Irving's request, a vignette of the blind Milton listening to his daughters read to him.[7] In the 1860s he painted two portraits of Shakespeare and in the previous decade ten oils, adapted from Thomas Stothard's designs, for an illustrated *Robinson Crusoe*.[8]

Sully's sketchbooks in the Philadelphia Museum of Art reveal him adept at imagining characters in Shakespeare but also in Byron, including those in the scandalous *Don Juan*. Haidée he drew plump and fully clothed, most unlike the poet's slender if voluptuous heroine. Gulnare of *The Corsair* emerges in Sully's sketch not imperious but sedate, restrained; Medora, consort of the pirate Conrad, stares blankly out of the window, pensive about his fate. Sully may have been reluctant to depict Byron's women as sensual, but his sketches indicate sustained interest in Byron's works. Sully also inserted in his scrapbooks numerous Byron-related prints. He owned William Finden's engraving of "Theresa, the Maid of Athens," fancifully attired and coyly demure in her elaborate headdress. He also had engraved portraits of Scott, Moore, and Byron, but apparently not of Wordsworth, Coleridge, Shelley or Keats. These engravings (several acquired after completing *Byron*) argue for an ongoing fascination with the poet and his circle.

Of Byron, said Scott, "the prints [engravings] . . . give one no impression."[9] Medwin agreed, as did Ticknor.[10] Those Ticknor had seen in America led him to expect a troubled soul. In truth, engravings of Byron rarely captured the man. In 1815, when Ticknor met the poet in London, he registered surprise that "instead of having a thin and rather sharp and anxious face, as he has in his pictures, it is round, open, and smiling."[11] Unsurprisingly perhaps, the living poet did not resemble his "pictures." Teresa Guiccioli, even more shocked than Ticknor, condemned as caricatures the engravings that came her way.[12]

English engravings often served as the basis for American. T. Blood's engraving of Westall's portrait, issued in the February 1814 *European Magazine*, reached America within months of its London publication. Quickly copied by English-born David Edwin, it came out in the July 1814 *Analectic Magazine*.[13] The two works differ, yet the latter clearly derives from the former. Westall had initially objected to engravings of his portrait (perhaps because he had not sold it), but after his big 1814 exhibition failed he needed money and soon came around. Walker's *Regency Portraits* lists seven engravings of Westall's portrait; others may remain unrecorded.[14] Blood's was the first, but by May 20, 1814, Charles Turner's mezzotint engraving was out (Figure 16). Westall had requested "to have the picture engraved of a large size and under my own direction."[15] Presumably Turner's satisfied him.[16] Both Walker and Peach speak of it as "romanticised," but overall and in detail it renders Westall's portrait faithfully.[17] The engravings made Westall's *Byron*, David Piper conjectures, even more influential an image than Phillips's cloaked rendering.[18] Most of them bear, however, but token resemblance to Byron, a criticism also made of Westall's portrait. The poet, who often denounced engravings of his portraits, seems to have liked what he saw of Westall's.[19] Sully presumably never viewed Westall's original, but his portrait shows similarities with it. Byron's pose, face, and attire indicate Sully had studied several engravings based on it. One was almost certainly Turner's.

A second visual source may have been Rembrandt Peale's lithograph of Byron. Lithography was a new art. Invented in 1796 and soon popularized in England and in France, it arrived in America by the late 1810s. Lithographs, easier and cheaper to produce than engravings, soon became popular. John Neal prophesied a great future for them.[20] Lithographs (as photographs later) could engage the vast realms of the illiterate, a group larger then than now. Pervading all levels of society, lithography became for visually minded Americans "the democratic art." Like engravings, lithographs depended on the artist's skill: they can improve or utterly debase a portrait.

Rembrandt Peale was among the more skillful early lithographers. Peale placed Byron, a national hero for America, among the great with Napoleon and Washington. His lithograph of Byron, issued through the Boston firm of

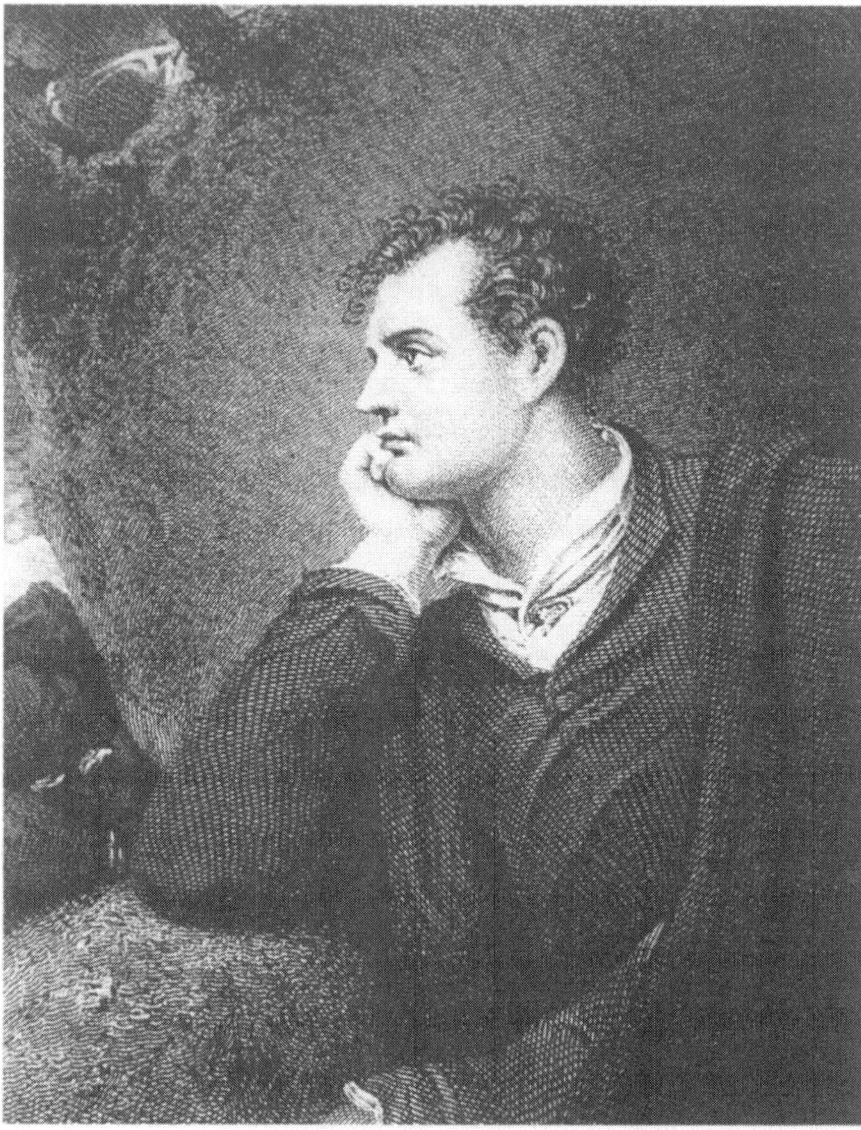

16 Charles Turner, *Lord Byron* (engraving), 1813. National Portrait Gallery, London

John and William Pendleton, appeared in 1825 or early 1826.[21] It exists in two states. The first, with the figure in reverse, puts Byron in the natural background sketched in Westall's original painting and developed in Turner's engraving (Figure 17). The second has Byron with elbow resting on what appears to be the manuscript of *Childe Harold* (Figure 18).[22]

For both Peale drew upon Nicolas-Eustache Maurin's memorial lithograph of 1825, *Lord Byron – la Grèce Reconnaissante*.[23] Although Maurin reproduced Westall's portrait with reasonable fidelity, he introduced his own background. Influenced by the ongoing war in Greece, he set Byron against a dark, lightning-streaked sky, below which roils a sea full of sailing-ships. One, presumably Turkish, set afire by Greek fire-ships, seems about to explode in a blaze.[24] Byron's left elbow rests on manuscript pages on which we make out "*Childe Harold.*" To the right of Byron's elbow lie broken-off temple columns that, in the sculptural symbolism of the day, imply a life cut off before its natural term. Peale rejected Maurin's sea-and-sky background, but his lithograph's second state did depict the pages from *Childe Harold*. In the studio of Peale, his friend and close professional colleague, Sully may well have encountered Maurin's engraving with its naval background; but, for reasons discussed later, he chose not to use it.

Sully for his *Byron* did not limit himself to depictions of Westall. By 1826, when he began work, a huge mass of information had accrued around Byron: reports by travellers, memoirs and books, articles in newspapers and journals, poems commemorating the martyr for Greece. Visual as well as verbal, these depictions include engravings from other portraits, most often those by Phillips or Harlow or that by William Edward West. So much was Byron in the news in America that Sully, if so inclined, could have immersed himself in Byron to whatever degree he wished.

Peale's lithograph and, even more, Charles Turner's engraving convey Westall's pose and profile, the shape of his lips, chin, and nose and, loosely, the dress and background. Although these works influenced the composition of Sully's *Byron*, they do so more as framework than inspiration. Outwardly similar, inwardly opposed, Westall's and Sully's portraits differ more than they resemble each other. Sully's conception departs radically from Westall's. Even considered only as a work of artistic skill, his portrait improves vastly upon Westall's. It may also offer, as this chapter and the last will argue, a truer likeness of Byron.

*

Sully had come to artistic maturity in Lawrence's heyday. Cognizant of changes in portraiture in the decades since Reynolds, he knew that portraits had to indicate character and mind as well as status and physical appearance. Though he never ceased to value Reynolds's precepts, he realized that in neoclassical portraiture the range of facial expression was limited. By the late eighteenth century painters concerned themselves less with ideal traits, more with interpreting the sitter's psychology. If the Old Master tones of the clothing and background of *Byron* recall Reynolds, the

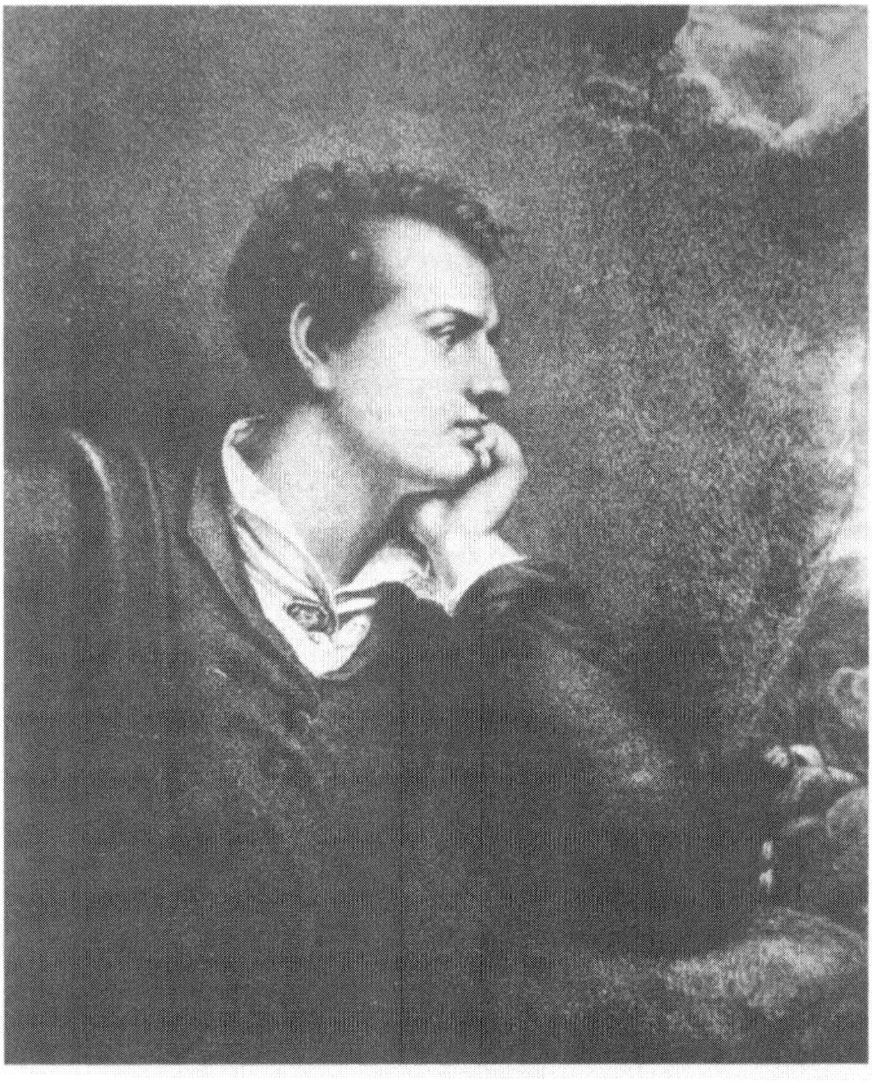

17 Rembrandt Peale, *Lord Byron* (lithograph, first version), 1825 or 1826. National Portrait Gallery, London

face recalls Lawrence. "By imparting to the features an expression of thought," wrote Sully of Lawrence's *Walter Scott*, the artist "has given a countenance worthy of the reputation of Scott. . . . The portrait of a talented person," Sully believed, "should be so treated as to express to the spectator an elevation of character, no matter how stolid may the features be by nature."[25] Sully represented Byron as both real and ideal, as if, in Blake's fine phrase, "eternity [were] in love with the productions of time."[26]

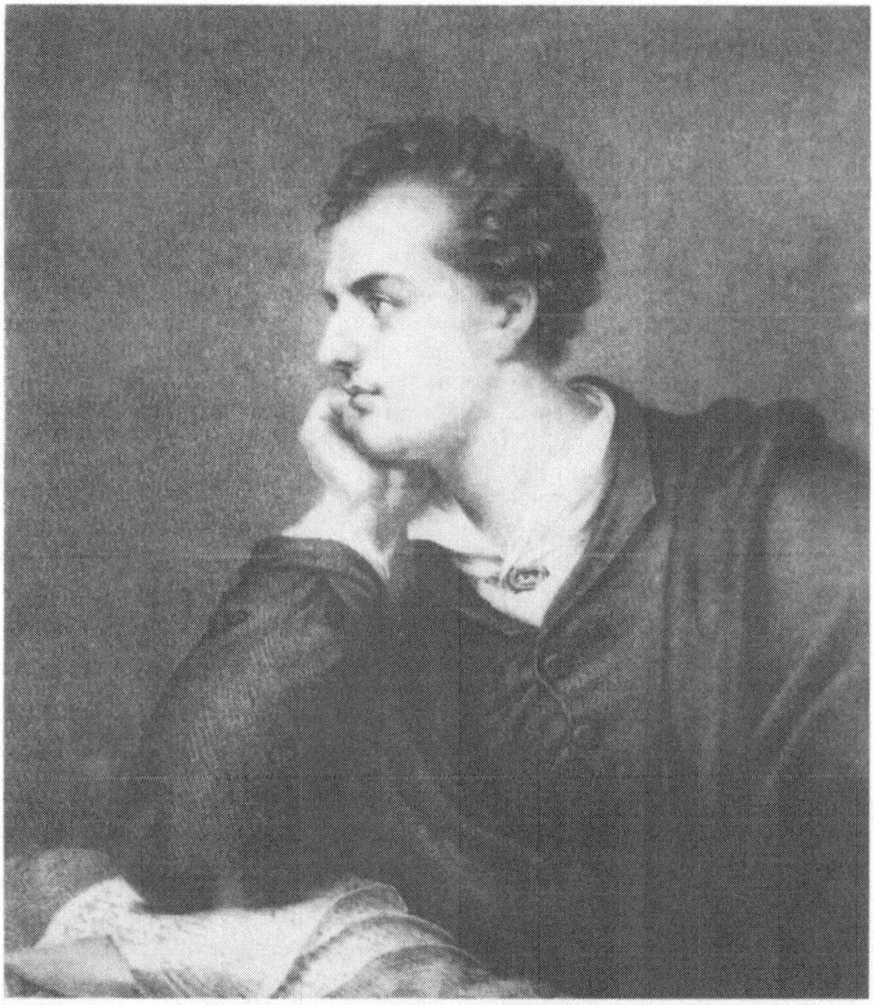

18 Rembrandt Peale, *Lord Byron* (lithograph, second version), 1825 or 1826. Courtesy of Marsha M. Manns and the Byron society Collection, University of Delaware

Chemistry between painter and subject cannot be predicted. Sully's long and productive career indicates that he managed sitters well, but not being distracted by the restless, chattering poet face to face may have facilitated work on *Byron*, for it gave him opportunity to interpret the poet in his own way and develop an image of Byron unmistakably his.[27] In Westall's original (as in most of the engraved versions) Byron's countenance appears self-absorbed; in Sully's *Byron* it is confident, engaging, pregnant with creative thought. The artist has evoked Byron's elusive *mobilité* of expression.

Perhaps it was Westall's years of work for Boydell's Shakespeare Gallery that led him to interpret Byron in essentially neoclassical terms. His is a static, almost formulaic late eighteenth-century stage pose. Westall's portrait sucks up energy; Sully's radiates it. Instead of Westall's brooding, half-scowling misanthrope, Sully melds with grace and distinction Old Masterly precepts with Lawrentian bravura to create a dynamic vision of a poet in creation.

We know little about how Byron actually looked. Although contemporaries contemplated his physical being, there are, amazingly, few depictions of indisputable authenticity that tell us in words, line, or paint how, at most points in his career, he looked. His appearance will always remain debatable. Even about basic features of his physiognomy controversy swirls. More than a long-familiar portrait, a "new" portrait like Sully's *Byron* – one not known before – should make us rethink Byron. Does Sully's bring us any closer to understanding Byron? If so, why – and how? Sully had trained as a miniaturist, and miniatures – besides patience, close observation, and attention to detail – require tremendous discipline. How do these qualities manifest themselves in *Byron*?

First of all, Sully rendered Byron's features with exquisite skill. Even for Sully the face exhibits an exceptional level of artistry. *Cooke as Richard III* and *Washington's Passage of the Delaware* demonstrate careful use of facial detail to interpret character. *Byron*, among the finest of his male portraits, interprets no less subtly that individual's being. By 1826 Sully's contemporaries in England and America, indeed all over Europe, were praising Byron's achievement as they lamented his passing. The painter faced a dilemma: how to do justice to that fabled countenance, now immortalized through death? How to come to terms visually with the man behind the achievement?

The portrait celebrates Byron as an icon of freedom. Westall painted Byron at the onset of a brilliant career; Sully, in the first flush of his posthumous renown. In the Jubilee year of 1826 Byron was confirmed as an American hero, a great poet, a martyr who died for the liberation of a country not his own but mankind's. The portrait implies poetic inspiration, present glory, future fame. The Byron of *Byron* has accomplished his goals. Though the man represented is dead, his achievement lives on.

If some Americans thought Byron an imperfect man, few doubted his greatness as a poet. In an America still largely without major writers of its own he was easily the age's most talked-about figure. When Sully painted him, Byron's reputation stood at its highest. Sully's stood no less high. A posthumous portrait, in bringing a flesh-and-blood individual back to seeming life, seeks to defy mortality. Instead of mere likeness, Sully in *Byron* attempted through facial expression to suggest essence. Such portraits, wrote an unidentified American critic in 1813, are paintings of the "*Soul* as well as *Body.*" They "*exhibit human nature dignified.*"[28] Sully searched for Byron's inner being, the soul beneath the surface. It was a soul Americans could identify with.

If Byron's English contemporaries had known of Sully's portrait, what might they have thought of it? It is tempting to speculate. John Murray,

Byron's publisher, might have enjoyed seeing his best-selling author depicted as romantic, glamorous, ethereal: the creator of *Childe Harold*, not the satirist of *Don Juan*, which Murray had ceased to publish. Murray's "senate," his cenacle of advisors, had observed Byron carefully and would have evaluated the portrait shrewdly. If Sully's *Byron* had swum into the ken of Thomas Moore, the portrait might well have pleased him, for the dapper Irishman would have instantly seen that the features Sully gave Byron resemble closely the description of Byron's physical appearance in his biography. (I explore these parallels in Chapter 10.) Less pleased might have been John Cam Hobhouse. Hobby-O, a thin-skinned but equally devoted friend of even longer standing, expressed dissatisfaction with almost every likeness of Byron that came his way.

In Wordsworth's life it was the women who gave his portraits their enthusiastic approbation; in Byron's the women were another story. Lady Noel, mother of Byron's wife Annabella, worried that Phillips's *Byron in Albanian Dress*, which she had bought in 1815, might have a deleterious effect upon Ada, Byron and Annabella's daughter. Might Ada, seeing it every day, not come to adore her absent father, a man of whom all Europe sang the praises but whom her mother considered a renegade "born for my desolation"? To foreclose this possibility Lady Noel had the portrait placed behind a green curtain. At her death in 1822, she decreed that the portrait be put in a box and Ada not allowed to see it until she turned 21. Of course what Lady Noel feared happened. Ada, when finally allowed to see the portrait, adored it – and the father she had never known. If Lady Noel had owned Sully's *Byron*, what might have been its fate? The question is moot, for neither she nor anyone else in Byron's circle knew the portrait existed.

*

Profile portraits have a long history, but were uncommon in the American colonies. The ideals and virtues attributed to ancient Rome infatuated the republic that gradually came into being after the Revolution. Profiles, which reminded Americans of heroes on ancient and Renaissance coins, conveyed an apt look for citizens of a new nation. They now became no less popular in the United States than in Britain.[29] Most artists – the elder Peale and Allston, among them – did profiles, but the chalk sketches of Charles Balthazar Julien Févret de Saint-Mémin (1770–1851) represent the high point of the profile portrait in America. A French *émigré* artist, Saint-Mémin possessed a keen draughtman's skill and turned out profile sketches quickly and inexpensively. His list of sitters was distinguished, and his profiles are still deservedly admired. Saint-Mémin's success spawned many imitators, among them, John James Audubon, who working throughout the Midwest between 1819 and 1826 drew several hundred chalk profile sketches.[30]

Silhouettes, even less expensive and readily mass-produced, were even more popular. The choice of the less affluent, they simplified further the profile portrait.[31] Lavater, discussed in the next chapter, used silhouettes to illustrate his subjects' physiognomical probity. Sully, no stranger to profile portraits, did them early and late. In addition, 19 surviving cut-outs by him in the Philadelphia Museum of Art indicate his interest in silhouettes. Profile portraits must have come easily to him, for even when portraying subjects straight on he, like Lawrence, often had his sitters – Nicholas Biddle, for one – face to one side, usually to the viewer's left.[32]

Westall's *Byron* impressed few of Byron's contemporaries. The *New Monthly*'s critic questioned its verisimilitude in 1825, and like many British journals the *New Monthly* was reprinted in America. Its critique may well have come Sully's way. It may even have impelled him to attempt his own interpretation. We do not know. If Sully chose not to follow Westall slavishly, he retained Westall's composition (as realized chiefly in Turner's engraving and Peale's lithograph) in creating his own "Byron."

Whereas Lawrence often placed his sitters above eye level, Sully places us at Byron's. The poet's expression suggests drama, interior no less than exterior. The drama takes place on a stage, actual or historical, but also in Byron's mind. We try to fathom what it is about. Less obvious than that in *Cooke as Richard III* or in *Washington's Passage of the Delaware*, the drama may also be more subtle. We experience it, as we often do Byron's poems and plays, as mental drama.

"I have a portrait of Dr. Gachet," wrote Vincent Van Gogh to his brother Theo, "with the heartbroken expression of our time."[33] Sully's *Byron* does not look heartbroken, but here Sully hints at the "sensibility" that was so much a part of the age. *Tristram Shandy* and Mackenzie's *The Man of Feeling* (1771) remained enormously popular in America well into the nineteenth century. The hero of the latter, an emblematic novel of sentiment often reprinted, is Harley, the man of feeling. Mackenzie implies that he is a true hero. The *Byron* of Sully is a man of the Romantic stage but also a man of feeling. His feelings are sincere. Stimulated by Rousseau, "sincerity" became prominent in the European and American imagination.[34] Whereas sensibility can seem solipsistic, sincerity implies integrity and conduct within a social and moral code. Placed within the natural world in which he appears at home, *Byron* embodies the new world of the responsible self.

Before the eighteenth century ended, the head had more than before become the focus of portraits. Stuart, who often used "the head alone as a vehicle of moral expression," felt that by removing or diminishing the body in relation to the face he could better express a person's interiority.[35] Sully often did the same. In *Byron* the poet, lost in reverie, is center stage. The pose goes back at least to Dürer's influential *Melencolia* (1514), a symbolic image of artistic genius. Later artists characterized sitters known for intellectual pursuits with similar contemplative poses; Reynolds's *Sterne*, Severn's *Keats*, Inman's *Wordsworth* come to mind. The *Byron* of Sully is, as John Galt described the poet on board ship to Greece, "strangely rapt."[36] He meditates within yet detached from the natural world. Calm, relaxed, entranced, the poet awaits the Muse. Reflection is in progress; creation may be imminent. In Phillips's *Blake* the inspirational pose – eyes bulging, the glance heavenward – is exaggerated, contrived. In *Byron* the poet looks not upward, but inward and outward. The fresh face, rosy-cheeked like a youth's (like many of Lawrence's sitters), suggests that happiness may dwell within. The expression negates the frequent contemporary view of Byron as a kind of predatory free spirit out for himself. Sully's portrait calls to mind the "roseate power" Whitman admired in Fanny Kemble. Ticknor, knowing only the engravings, was, we remember, amazed to discover in England Byron's "round, open, and smiling" face. Sully's *Byron* captures a man in bloom (see color plate section).

An aureole of half-light bathes the visage of *Byron*. The time is no longer day, nor yet night, but dusk – a time for meditation. "In large pictures," wrote Sully in his unpublished Hints, "very sober colours may be employed to produce richness of effect."[37] Sully's light here, curiously palpable, comes close to what Braque would call "tactile." Westall's portrait contrasts an even more dramatically dark background with the pale face. Christine Kenyon Jones has recently argued that the Apollo Belvedere, brought to Paris by Napoleon and widely known through engravings, influenced Westall's pose.[38] That may well be, but Westall's juxtaposition of black and red also has about it an almost Gothic luridity, Dracula-like, Satanic even. Sully, by contrast, achieves his desired "richness of effect" through somber earth tones. Against the universals of golden browns (a color Sully referred to as "Vandyke brown" or "brown from Holland"), the face radiates with the promise of youthful genius. The glow of the flesh tones, more metaphysical than natural, appears to come from some far-off spiritual world.

In 1824 Byron, prematurely old and gray, had died in Greece. But Sully portrays Byron in the prime of life. His expression hints at innocence. Byron had died a young master, but for Sully he is already an Old Master. The portrait's elaborate sculpted frame, presumably determined by the artist, enhances the impression of venerability. The brown tonalities evoke Rembrandt and other Dutch masters. Likewise, *Byron*'s dramatic use of light recalls the mysteries of chiaroscuro we associate with them. Sully painted Byron as if he, the artist, had become an Old Master. The browns also hark back to a famous work Sully may well have seen in England, Reynolds's *Mrs Siddons as the Tragic Muse* (see color plate section). Reynolds had recommended dark tones for portraits, for by making them appear less ornamental and more somber the artist projected onto them the noble and timeless character of history painting. One of the keys to the success of *Mrs Siddons*, as its subject herself recognized, was its extremely limited palette. "The sober grandeur of the colouring – almost an absence of colour," claimed the actress, "contributed to the sublimity of that noble composition."[39] Brown is Reynolds's primary color in *Mrs Siddons*, and it is Sully's in *Byron*. Besides the illuminated rosy countenance given the poet, only a few isolated spots of color – among them, the turquoise brooch, the white open-collared shirt, the clouds and waterfall – emerge from the brown sobriety. Sully's sober palette may have suggested something more. Stuart, observes Dorinda Evans, experienced color in his portraits, "probably as early as 1782, as creating feeling much the way music does."[40] Sully, an accomplished musician, may have sought through *Byron*'s shades of brown to achieve the tonal harmony of music. The chiaroscuro also nicely recalls the more immediate past: one in which Byron, recently dead, stood ready to take his place among the Immortals.

Lawrence's *Master Charles William Lambton* (1825) may also have contributed to Sully's Byron in composition and palette. It portrays young Lambton in a relaxed, pensive pose, the looming cliffs bathed in harmonies of brown, the distant evening landscape on the left loosely sketched. The painting's appearance in the 1827 Paris Salon excited French critics. Gautier recalled in 1856 "the portrait of young Lambton, by Lawrence, which . . . caused a prodigious sensation; that camillia carnation, those eyes so silky and so brilliant, that pearly visage so sombre and clear it conjures the look of the young Byron."[41] A mezzotint of Lawrence's portrait was soon available, and it is possible that one of Sully's friends then in London – Leslie, Audubon, Neal, his nephew Robert Sully – sent it to him in Philadelphia or that it made its way to him by other means.

Sully's was also an American light. Americans of the Revolutionary generation often pictured their country as "the Land of Light and Liberty." "The sun never shined on a cause of greater worth," exclaimed Tom Paine of the Revolution. In 1826, when Sully began work, Jubilee oratory about the past and present great – about the "bright star" of America shining and "enlightening" the globe – resonated across the land.[42] The glowing countenance in Sully's portrait implies that Byron was now part of the American pantheon.

*

Can we say of Sully's *Byron*, as Coleridge cryptically said of Chantrey's bust of Wordsworth, that it is "more like Wordsworth than Wordsworth was like himself."[43] Are we looking at Byron, a Byronic hero, or some combination of the two? At a pastiche of technical brilliance and aristocratic expression? Byron's head, as Lady Blessington described it, "is finely shaped, and the forehead open, high, and noble."[44] *Byron* possesses Rembrandtian chiaroscuro, American luminosity, an almost ideal beauty, even symbolic messages, but also a plethora of significant detail. In what ways does the detail enable Sully to achieve his simulacrum of reality? If we examine closely face, complexion, eyes, hair, lips, nose, ears, throat, clothing, even landscape, what can we learn about *Byron* – and about its subject?

Accounts of Byron's appearance, as we have seen, often commented on his pallor. It seemed to radiate with a refined life force. "A beautiful alabaster vase . . . lighted up from within," said Coleridge; Jane Porter, author of *The Scottish Chiefs*, noted Byron's "moonlight paleness";[45] for Caroline Lamb, "*that pale face is my fate*."[46] Many at this time found such a face attractive, "an enhancement of good looks."[47] Understandably, Byron wished portraits to highlight his almost translucent skin.

"The complexion should be exact," wrote Sully in his Hints; "it is that part of the likeness which keeps to show the temper of the subject."[48] He captured Byron's flesh superbly. Westall, aiming for a cool, muted effect, painted his skin bisque and gave the cheeks a hint of pink. His *Byron* looks ashen (even more so in photographs), its "coolness" accentuated by the glass covering the portrait's smooth surface. Sully's *Byron*, on a canvas of coarser weave and with discernible impasto, achieves a "warmer" effect. More than in other portraits of Byron, Sully's shows the fair skin with the blue veins noted by observers.[49] Unlike Westall's marmoreal visage, Sully's is of flesh and blood.

Those alive at Romanticism's dawn paid attention to the eye and gaze of poets.[50] Along with the new interest in biography and the beginning of "autobiography" came a belief in the inspired poet as a breed apart. The Romantics equated creativity with genius and assumed poets had more genius than other people. Wordsworth in his famous Preface of 1800 compared the sensibilities of poets with ordinary mortals. He claimed differences in degree, but implied differences in kind.[51] Blake believed that genius was not teachable or acquirable, but "born within us." With both we have moved far from the *Discourses* of Reynolds. Phillips with *Blake* (1806) and Moses Herrington with *Coleridge* (1832) expressed the genius of their subjects through the eyes. Sight as a means of perception was vital to Byron. He put, thought Nathan, "more faith" in the eye "than all the fallacious rules of Lavater, Gall, or Spurzheim."[52] Byron had phenomenal eyesight, in low light no less than in bright, and could see detail that most others missed. From the "power of his gaze" Nathan extrapolated Byron into "a man of the greatest discernment."[53] How artists depicted Byron's eyes is crucial.

Eyes test a portraitist. They were a Sully specialty. John Neal, admirer of Sully's artistry and Byron's, thought no one ever painted more beautiful eyes.[54] Everyone agreed that Byron was a genius and that he had expressive eyes. After that, controversy. One of Byron's eyes was "visibly larger" than the other. Byron thought them, viewed together, unsightly, so he preferred profile portraits that showed only one eye.[55] Many artists, Sully included, obliged. Contemporaries disagreed markedly about the color of Byron's eyes. Shades of blue or gray, even brown – what color were they? A vexed subject, to which I shall return, but let it be said that Westall is the only artist to paint Byron's eye(s) dark brown. Sully did not follow Westall here.[56] One observer found Byron's eyes "somewhat of a light blue and grey."[57] Engravings of a painting cannot render eye color. So what color does Sully paint them? Perhaps gray, or light blue, or hazel. We are meant to think less of the physical color than of the mind's eye, even of Byron's "mobility" of eye.

"The eye-brows, being raised, give a grave and noble air," opined Sully in his Hints; "but if arched, an air of astonishment."[58] Byron's eyebrows are both raised and arched. A "grave and noble air" is his, and the arched eyebrow in *Byron*, wavy and peaked, soft and lustrous like the hair, may indeed express "astonishment." Melancholy and brooding in Westall, the hooded eye in Sully looks inward but also implies engagement with the exterior world. Whereas Westall's petulant *Byron* ponders dark matters, Sully's *Byron* gazes beyond the frame. Unconcerned about the viewer, personally distanced, the Pilgrim of Externity appears to reflect upon people and places and the words that will bring them to life.

Enough of eyes! Let us consider hair. Sully was famed for his skill with hair no less than with eyes. One of the most distinctive features of Byron's appearance was an artificially raised hairline with peaked indentations. To achieve this effect Byron, alleged Moore, shaved his forehead.[59] Sully captured through almost imperceptible shading and gradation of color the shaven hair over Byron's temples. Originally "black or rather very dark brown," its color had become (the poet tells us) by age 19 "a *light Chesnut*."[60] Byron was certainly pleased with his hair. Scrope Davies claimed he once caught the young poet with his hair *en papillote*, that is, in curlers, at which Byron reportedly said, no doubt with a smile, "I am as vain of my curls as a girl of sixteen."[61] Those who observed Byron's hair in maturity remember it as thick and curly, in color auburn or, more precisely, burnt sienna. Phillips in his cloaked portrait paints it nearly black (the Albanian turban conceals the hair), and Moore speaks of "glossy, dark-brown curls."[62] Byron oiled his hair with macassar oil – Rowland's was his brand of choice – to make it appear darker and set off his pale complexion.[63] Paintings darken and varnish certainly darkens. Did Byron have lighter-colored hair than in his portraits?

Artists differed in depicting Byron's hair color. Westall painted it raven, somewhat greasy, the forelock a tight spiral curl. Sully took Westall's (and Charles Turner's) curlicued hair, curled it even more, and returned it closer to the youthful Byron's "*light Chesnut*." Toward the back the hair shades toward burnt sienna, then deep brown. Sully fluffed it out on the head and at the nape of the neck. Neal thought the hair in Sully's portraits "wonderfully fine," "always shining and luxuriant."[64] Its vibrant silky texture in *Byron*, soft as well as fine, energizes the face. *Byron* receives perhaps the most vibrant hair of any of Sully's male subjects. Several portraits of Andrew Jackson are the poet's only rival. Along with the halo of light, the glowing curls of *Byron* heighten the dynamism of Sully's conception. Hair has long been associated with sexual power. Like Belinda's eager suitors in Pope's *Rape*, we yearn to snip off a Byronic lock. Delilah knew what she was about.

What facial feature is the most important? Portrait painters disagreed among themselves. Benjamin Trott, Sully noted in his manuscript Hints, "says that he considered the nose the most important feature in portrait painting."[65] Behind Trott lay the considerable authority of Stuart, who, Dorinda Evans claims, "had always maintained that a likeness depended chiefly on a careful transcription of the nose."[66] John Neagle, Sully's son-in-law, also found the nose revelatory of character.[67] So did Hazlitt, at least by implication, when he described the nose as "the rudder of the face, the index of the will." Coleridge's – "small, feeble, nothing – like what he has done" – disappointed him.[68]

Most portraitists of Byron have focused on his much-praised eyes and hair. Few made a comparable effort with his nose. His nose, for Byron, was like his eyes: a problematic feature. He thought it too long. The sensitive poet asked Phillips, at work on the cloaked portrait, to "retouch" it "as it is a feature of some importance."[69] Later in life, finding his nose "a little *too thick*," Byron preferred to see it, like his eyes, in profile.[70] Sully thought Queen Victoria's nose "well formed and such as I have frequently seen in persons of wit and intellect."[71] Presumably he also saw wit and intellect in Byron's well-formed nose. In a profile portrait the nose's thickness disappears; in Sully the nose, slightly aquiline, denotes sovereignty.

Although several of his contemporaries favored the nose, Sully believed the mouth "the most important feature."[72] De Quincey thought Wordsworth's mouth his "strongest feature," and Lady Blessington thought the same for Byron.[73] For *Byron* Sully rounds the lips, parts them slightly, and renders them full, soft, and voluptuous. Along with the mysterious eyes, the lips hint at a Gioconda smile. The chin is less prominent, softer than in Westall.

Byron liked his ears. Ali Pasha, purred the poet in Albania, "said he was certain I was a man of birth because I had small ears, curling hair, & little white hands."[74] Caroline Lamb liked them too. "In all England I know but of two that have ears similar."[75] She had in mind less their size or shape than that they came without lobes. Presumably she did not know that in Chinese culture ears without lobes denote a short life. Ears interested Sully less than other facial features for in both the study and the full-length *Victoria* he painted them in lightly. Not unusually among Byron's portraitists, he followed Westall in leaving out the lobes.

And that throat! A long throat corresponded to the era's ideal of feminine beauty. "At the splendour of his throat women are said to have grown pale," comments Piper.[76] Byron had in reality what society women longed to have, and did – in their portraits. Doris Langley Moore once professed delight that Byron lacked "that masculine blemish, an Adam's apple."[77] "I rather suspect," an unknown observer confirmed in 1827, "he piqued himself on the beauty of his throat."[78] He probably did. Sully, aware that the ideal of female beauty in Federal America favored extravagantly long necks, elongates the throat and shapes and shades it more fully than does Westall. *Byron*'s male throat may indeed merit a swoon. It arose from a muscular neck in which, according to Medwin and Trelawny, the poet took great pride.[79]

Pleased with his fine throat, Byron liked to have himself portrayed in an open-necked shirt, sans cravat. So Phillips and Westall depicted him, and so Sully after them. Actually, this famous open-collar pose, it has been suggested, may have been vanity on Byron's part.[80] It was a pose adopted for portraits. In ordinary life, it is disheartening to learn, the poet observed "scrupulous propriety" and "never wore an open-necked shirt."[81] Few knew the sad truth. The open collar fascinated a generation. Throughout the nineteenth century, in America no less than in Europe, brooding would-be Byronic heroes presented themselves to the world in open-necked glory, *à la Byron*. Dickens in *American Notes* (1842), observing the clerks in fashionable New York shops, termed them "Byrons of the desk and counter."[82]

Most contemporary portraitists concentrated on the face; clothing and background were brushed in loosely. Westall and Sully worked in this tradition. In Westall the left sleeve is rolled up; the left hand, invisible. Westall and Sully in their respective portraits, as Reynolds in *Mrs Siddons*, chose generalized timeless attire. Baudelaire had in mind paintings like *Byron* when he opposed to David and Ingres the example of Reynolds and Lawrence who made of every portrait "*un poème avec ses accessoires, plein d'espace et de rêverie.*"[83] Westall painted Byron's lounging jacket blood red, which suggests, not the impeccable Brummell in buff and blue, but a feckless reprobate. Sully paints the jacket brown. Even if he had known of Westall's red, he might have chosen brown. The cloak or toga about the shoulders, suggestive of a cape, was a bow to convention, for in Roman sculpture the toga endows the sitter with overtones of civic virtue. Sully also paints the cloak brown, but of a deeper hue. In addition to the timeless Old Master browns of *Mrs Siddons*, Sully may also have chosen brown to recall St Francis, the martyred Franciscan Savonarola, even the frontiersman Andrew Jackson. The browns keeps our eyes on the luminous face.

Westall fastens the shirt with a cameo brooch, white on a black onyx background, possibly Wedgwood. Such a traditional ornament was popular among the wealthy. Byron's brooch appears to depict a reclining woman: Venus at her toilet? Madame Récamier after David? Pauline Bonaparte on her *méridienne* gazing at Cupid after Canova? We do not know. Sully kept *Voluptas* at bay. Exercising artistic license, he painted the brooch turquoise. Turquoise sets off the throat, echoes the veins, complements the neutral eyes.

One senses in Phillips's *Byron in Albanian Dress* the player in the part rather than the part in the player. The flamboyant attire, presumably chosen by Byron, mitigates our appreciation of the subject. We look upon a prototype Sultan rather than Byron's inner being. A "rather vapid portrait" Richard Brilliant terms Phillips's effort, "the romantic, Byronic hero" only superficially realized. As an attempt "to fabricate Byron's identity," Brilliant adds, the portrait "hardly satisfies because . . . nothing" in it connects "the passionate poet and adventurer with his own splendid achievements, or with the persona he was so actively creating at the time, except the token of exotic dress."[84] By contrast, Sully's restrained attire leads the eye directly to Byron. Complementing the poet is a carefully chosen background.

*

Backgrounds tell tales. They can indicate a sitter's possessions, profession, or passion. Each national school fostered a different tradition: the French had their portraits done in the salon; the English preferred the garden.[85] The personality of sitters might be inseparable from their societal role. Copley's *Thomas Greene* (1758), papers in hand and an inset merchantman hovering above, tells us of the sitter's devotion to trade. The musical instruments in Gainsborough's *Portrait of Ann Ford (later Mrs Philip Thicknesse)* (1760) indicate her (and the artist's) vibrant love of music. In other portraits of the time the natural scene – often nature domesticated – is not unusual. Well-born or wealthy subjects the artist might put on the grounds of the family estate. The background could be topographically accurate or imagined. The complex *mise-en-scène* of Reynolds's full-length *Richard Peers Symons* (1769–70) is a *mélange* of classical and painterly echoes. Reynolds posed Symons against the Farnese Hercules, a favorite classical sculpture much admired for its massive rhomboids; the Temple of Vesta at Tivoli, outside Rome, is in the distance. The foreground dog comes from a Van Dyck. But Symons never left England. This most artful composition is entirely fictitious.[86] Even though Sully only sketched in the landscape of *Byron*, that does not mean he thought it insignificant.[87] The slightly out-of-focus natural phenomena complement the finely detailed head. Byron exists both in and out of the setting. If the chief drama takes place in his mind, the landscape provides interest of its own.

Maurin in *Lord Byron – La Grèce Reconnaissante* posed Byron against a sea battle in Greek waters. By underscoring Byron's sacrifice, Maurin both promoted the Greek cause and gave to Byron's death context and immediacy. The naval vessels in action imply the hero, even the martyr. But Maurin's battle tied Byron to a place, Greece, and to an activity, one traditionally limited to males, the fight for freedom. By associating Byron with a particular conflict, however glorious, he sidelined the man of letters, the creator. Though Byron often expressed his love for Greece, he was less a warrior than a poet. His words have stirred mankind more than his deeds. Westall's portrait barely indicates background: mountain but no waterfall, clouds that may (or may not) reflect the moon. From such hints Charles Turner supplied further details.

And Sully? Where was he to set *his Byron*? Contemporary portraitists often depicted men in their studies, women in or close to nature. Society women often led cloistered lives, the heightened sensitivity attributed to the female sex represented by a generalized landscape, pleasantly domesticated. For males, a closeted environment indicated thought, Faust in his study perhaps, a pile of books at hand as in several Sully portraits. Would not such a presentation have confined the roving Byron? Sully must have thought so. Whereas his portrait's chin-on-hand pose, elbow on convenient boulder, does recall the scholar in his study, this active contemplator lives and creates out of doors, where the wind sweeps through his hair and the moon shines brightly. Poets had to look profound – just in case someone coming by, say (in Byron's case) a Harriette Wilson, observed them.[88] So Sully rejected both the heroics and the narrowing particularity of a Greek naval battle. Taking hints from Charles Turner's engraving, he set a reflective Byron within wild and undomesticated nature, timeless and everlasting, universal yet particular to Byron's poetry. Amidst its wonders – sky, moon, mountains, waterfall – the poet mentally composes the poem-to-be.

Gulian Verplanck, the Knickerbocker critic, defined the historical portrait in 1824 as "a medium between portrait and history, in which . . . a likeness was combined with a subject's characteristic action."[89] *Byron*, by this definition, is both a historical and a poetic portrait. Recognizably heroic, it may be more poetic than historical. By placing Byron amidst elemental nature, the landscape hymned in his poems, Sully creates a setting evocative of his "characteristic action." The dark background, by shortening the distance between subject and viewer, provides a more one-on-one relationship.

The natural world is the poet's unconscious as well as conscious inspiration. It strengthens the mood of reflection, hints at mystery. Why is Byron here? He sits, hermit-like, perhaps under a cliff, more likely near the entrance to a grotto or cave. Fuseli in *Milton, When a Youth* portrayed the poet at the entrance to a dark cave. Sully, Fuseli's student, may have responded to the Swiss artist's cave-like scenes no less than to his Turneresque skies.[90] Caverns were often mysterious places, tantalizingly dangerous, the haunt of banditti. Putting Byron in one recalls cavern scenes in contemporary dramas and Romantic operas, from Schiller's *The Robbers* (1781) to Weber's *Der Freischütz* (1821), not to mention innumerable novels of the period. Caves are no less frequent in Coleridge and Shelley. For them as for Byron they carried symbolic weight as places of refuge. In *Don Juan* Haidée shelters Juan in one, and Neuha in *The Island* leads Torquil under the sea to another. Recall Pope's lines: "But o'er the twilight groves, and dusky caves, / Long-sounding isles, and intermingled graves, / Black Melancholy sits. . . ."[91] Sully's *Byron* is not melancholic, but he has found a comfortable place in which to sit.

Caves had gender associations. Artists placed women in them more often than men. Here is a description of *Portrait of a Woman*, c. 1805–06, by Sully's older French contemporary, Louis-Léopold Boilly: "The woman is situated in a dark and mysterious cave, near agitated, rushing rapids – sexually symbolic forms that are coupled with an idea of inaccessibility – as she looks away, her arm raised in an antique gesture of meditation. Woman here is characterized as unfathomable, reflective, dreamy."[92] Sully probably never saw this painting, but parallels between it and *Byron* include a varied palette of browns, a meditative gesture, a mysterious cave lit from within, a powerful waterfall outside, and the subject's dreamy gaze. Against a cavern wall Sully's vulnerable, somewhat feminine Byron – protected, secluded, isolated from human communion – sits in meditation. The woman in Boilly's painting looks away from the viewer, but Sully's *plein-air* Byron, amidst a landscape also subtly and sexually charged, gazes into the distance as well as into himself, at one with the scene.

Westall's portrait predated Byron's most famous depictions of landscape. One observer counterpoints "the rocky background and stormy sky" in Westall with Byron's description of his hero in *Childe Harold* 1:

> For Meditation fix'd at times on him;
> And conscious Reason whisper'd to despise
> His early youth, misspent in maddest whim;
> But as he gazed on truth his aching eyes grew dim.[93]

These lines indeed hint at the scene depicted in Westall's portrait and in several of its engravings. For David Piper, the "dark, craggy background swirls into undefined mist" more Ossianic than Byronic.[94] Possibly so. As in other of Westall's depictions of landscape, the scene seems more of the mind than of any physical reality.

By 1826, when he began work, Sully could draw upon almost all of Byron's poems. His generation knew best the "Romantic" Byron, the poet of *The Corsair* and *Lara*, of *Childe Harold* and *Manfred* – not that of *Don Juan*, and not yet that of the writer of the most scintillating letters in English. Sully's sketches in the Philadelphia Museum indicate he had read at least the first cantos of *Don Juan*, but the dramatic landscape *Byron* recalls less that poem than the energy of sublime Nature of Canto 3 of *Childe Harold*. Written largely in Switzerland during the creative summer of 1816, when Byron lived in close proximity to Shelley and Mary Shelley, the canto embodies Byron's excited perusal of Rousseau's *La nouvelle Héloïse*, the heady impact of Shelley's conversation, and his rereadings of Wordsworth mediated through his enthusiastic friend. All these experiences intertwined as they bore fruit in Byron's imagination. Ostensibly the Childe is the poem's hero, but Byron's public, viewing the poem as autobiographical, imagined Byron the Childe. The public was not in essence wrong: Byron consciously exploited the popular image of himself as one of his poetic creations. Swiss mountain scenery was often favored for drama and opera, and the Alps were inhabited by descendants of the Swiss mountaineers of yore famed for their love of freedom. The Swiss scene thus symbolized political no less than personal liberty. Having escaped the "mind-forg'd manacles" of London, Byron breathes the Alpine air of those born free.

Above the poet's head in Sully's *Byron*, precariously rooted in the hill or cliffside, loom two tree trunks. Sharply angled, the trees fight to survive; Sully's impasto outlines their roots. Clinging precariously to the cliff, the trees recall the blasted, destroyed pines of Canto 3 and the "Alpine Journal," even more the hardy *Tannenbäume* of Canto 4 which survive sustained onslaughts from the elements.[95] On the left stands a distant mountain; below it, a waterfall gleams in the fading light, a likely echo of the Falls of Terni in *Childe Harold* 4, stanzas 69–72. A boulder, impasto heavy to indicate roughness, supports the poet's right arm.

Sully turns Westall's overcast bluish-gray sky into a rose brown. Moonlight – or possibly a lightning bolt – breaks through the clouds. Moonlight scenes are common in Romantic poetry of all nations and in painting from Fuseli to Friedrich. The moonlight on the waterfall, the tree trunks, the mountaintop, and the bright green foliage below suggest nature's fertility. If "lightning," it may recall the "mightiest" thunderstorm in *Childe Harold* 3, based on storms Byron had experienced. "I have seen . . . several more terrible," he observed, "but none more beautiful."[96] Lightning bolts for the Romantics – as paintings by Turner and John Martin (and engravings of them) attest – often evoked other than physical phenomena. In *Childe Harold* 3 lightning embodies the poet's spark of genius, a powerful creativity awaiting its dramatic release. Sensitive, imaginative souls experienced a more intense emotional response to nature than did lesser mortals. In *Frankenstein*, begun during the Swiss summer of 1816, an electrical storm (very likely one also witnessed by Byron) inspired Mary Shelley to turn young Victor Frankenstein into a scientist determined to create a sentient being.

Byron, Sully implies in his portrait, responded strongly to nature, refracted it through his imagination, lived fully in its presence. Behind Sully's Grand Manner *Cooke as Richard III* lay eighteenth-century theatrical portraiture and Shakespearean illustration. But *Cooke*, impressive achievement that it is, tells us more about the actor than about the man. In *Byron*, the subject is more than a stage actor, the natural world more than a backdrop or stage set. Being a poet in nature is not a role to assume or take off but part of his essence.

In *Childe Harold* and *Manfred* Byron celebrated the Sublime in nature: mountains, thunderstorms, lightning, waterfalls, powerful phenomena that impress upon us feelings of awe, even terror. Faust, invoking Nature's Sublime in Berlioz's *Damnation of Faust*, cries out, "Forêts, rochers, torrents, je vous adore!" The Romantic imagination adored the Sublime. Inaugurated by Longinus, codified by Burke, recreated imaginatively in Radcliffe's Gothic novels, rendered dramatically by Byron in semi-autobiographical verse, Nature's Sublime both inspired and complemented the poet's sublimity of thought. "High mountains are to me a feeling," exulted Byron in *Childe Harold* (3: 72). The Sublime at its loftiest comprehends thoughts of pain and fear, of vastness and infinity; it manifests itself in greatness of conception, in nobility of expression. Byron's landscapes live both in themselves and within the imaginations of his often-tortured personae. As he had with *Washington's Passage*, Sully in his symbiosis of hero, situation, and place created a sublime landscape in which the soul lives and acts.

Throughout the second quarter of the nineteenth century and indeed long after, travel accounts and tourist guides to European sights frequently invoked Byron. His impassioned descriptions of the Rhine and Alps in *Childe Harold* (Canto 3), of Italy's fabled landscapes and storied cities (Canto 4), guided generations of Europeans and Americans abroad. Indirectly, his poetry fostered the dawning appreciation by Americans of the natural beauty of their continent. When Sully began *Byron* in 1826, Thomas Cole had begun painting the lakes, falls, and vistas of the Catskills. The spirit of the Romantic poets, Byron above all, imbued Cole's landscapes.[97] Sully, who admired Cole intensely, responded to the poetry behind his landscapes, as did Cole's great disciple Frederic Church. "What 'Childe Harold' did for the scenery of the Old World," commented a writer in *Harper's* in 1879, "the art of [Cole and] Church has done for that of the New."[98] Byron became for Americans, as Tuckerman observed in 1848, "an intellectual and ideal *cicerone*."[99]

Sully had an abiding love of landscape.[100] In 1828, traveling in New England, he admired the vista below Mount Holyoke over the Connecticut River's famous ox-bow. A few years after his visit, Cole chose the same viewpoint for his famous *Ox-Bow* of 1836. Sully regarded Cole's *Niagara* as "the only poetical representation of that place that I have seen" and one that "would have honored Salvator Rosa."[101] Later on this trip he stopped at the already famed Catskill Mountain House. Opened in 1824, it was located on a high ridge. Below, the Hudson stretched out for nearly seventy miles. This "sublime perspective" thrilled the artist whom we know today chiefly as a portraitist.[102]

*

A portrait will not come to life without the artist having a controlling vision of his subject. Westall's *Byron* spawned many derivatives, quite diverse, in effect many "Byrons" from a single template. During his first London stay of 1809–10 Sully had come to know Westall well enough to visit him at his home. Though he later urged his student Leslie to call upon Westall, Sully, like Hazlitt and Haydon, appeared to have harbored few illusions about Westall's artistic worth. "I have been to Westall's house to look at his pictures," Leslie wrote his sister Betsey on September 14, 1812; "you recollect Sully told me I should find some clever things amongst them." Leslie looked hard at what he saw. The "gaudiness" of Westall's coloring dazzled him at first, but further viewing exposed a "want of real science." "His style of painting is showy," Leslie went on, "and perhaps pleasing to those who are not in the habit of thinking when they look at a picture." To an observer who thought, however, "his pictures must seem meretricious."[103] Leslie did not rate the academician highly. Sully didn't either ("some clever things amongst them") but expressed himself more tactfully. Westall, if not always the mediocrity claimed by Hazlitt and Haydon or the "nonentity" described by a later commentator (William A. Shaw), hardly ranks as a major artist.[104]

More than on engravings or written accounts, Sully drew for *Byron* upon his own innate painterly gift. The imaginative insight into human beings acquired during 25 years of painting portraits stood him in good stead. Byron's absence forced him to conceive and to create on his own terms an artistic whole. *His Byron* reflected his understanding of the subject, not someone else's. Out of the diverse materials at his disposition, he developed his own interpretation – not Westall's, or anybody else's – of the elusive poet.

As we think Samuel Johnson old, so we think Byron young. Most portraits depict the poet as he was before he left England in 1816; representations after are fewer. To gain a sense of how Byron affected onlookers we need to consider both the physical descriptions in word or paint and, equally, the less tangible, almost impossible- to-imagine aura that Byron conveyed to contemporaries. The features themselves, if imperfect, were splendid. Housed in the vibrant physical being we imagine as Byron, they produced in combination the individual whose presence magnetized contemporaries.

"I should prefer Mr. Sully, I think, to any other artist I have known, if I wanted the portrait of a youthful, passionate, enthusiast, male or female."[105] So John Neal, who is often perceptive on Sully. Himself an ardent propagandist for Byron and his poetry, Neal, if he had wished a portrait of Byron as a "youthful, passionate, enthusiast," might well have chosen Sully to paint it. *Byron* is, as this chapter has argued, less a copy than an essentially new interpretation. With assists from Charles Turner's engraving of Westall and Rembrandt Peale's lithograph and no doubt other sources, Sully's *Byron* transcends its origins.

CHAPTER NINE

Lavater's *Physiognomy* and Sully's *Byron*

Has he not a rogue's face? Speak, brother,
you understand physiognomy; a hanging look to me –
Congreve[1]

Nor is there a man to be found on earth, who is not daily
influenced by physiognomy.
Lavater[2]

Un peintre qui n'est pas physiognomiste est un pauvre
peintre.
Diderot[3]

I had become, in my own opinion, a kind of Lavater.
George Borrow[4]

Lavater's system never asserted its truth more forcibly than
in Lord Byron's Countenance, in which you see all the
character. Its keen and rapid genius – its pale Intelligence –
its profligacy and its bitterness, its original symmetry
distorted by the Passions, his laugh of mingled merriment and
scorn. The forehead clear and open, the brow boldly prominent,
the Eyes bright and *dissimilar*, – the Nose finely cut and the
Nostril *acutely* formed- the Mouth well-form'd but wide, and
contemptuous even in its smile; falling singularly at the
corners, and its vindictive and disdainful expression,
heightened by the massive firmness of the Chin, which springs
at once from the centre of the full under-lip, – the Hair dark
and curling, but irregular in its growth.
All this presents to you the Poet and the Man. . . .
Thomas Lawrence[5]

Lawrence's brilliant verbal sketch of Byron, already cited in Chapter 2, forms the last of this chapter's several epigraphs. Not included in the earlier citation, nor usually by others who quote the passage, are the words in which Lawrence claims that Lavater's system never asserted its truth more forcibly than in Byron's features.

Who was Lavater and what was the system that so impressed Lawrence? Johann Caspar Lavater (1741–1801), an eloquent preacher and distinguished theologian, is the once-famous author of *Essays on Physiognomy*, and his system is the science or pseudo-science of physiognomy, defined by the *OED* as "the art of judging character and disposition from the features of the face or the form and lineaments of the body generally." Most of Lawrence's contemporaries believed, as he did, in the truths of physiognomy as interpreted and elucidated by Lavater. Lavater looked hard at human countenances, and his detailed analyses of them stimulated dramatists and actors, novelists, poets, and artists to look as hard or harder. Among artists, portrait painters looked hardest of all. Although historians of science today tend to pass lightly over Lavater, study of physiognomy had far-reaching effects upon the cultural life of Europe and America well into the nineteenth century.

By 1814, when he described Byron's appearance, Lawrence, as Borrow after him, had become a confirmed physiognomist, "a kind of Lavater." He observed Byron closely and acutely, and what he saw he interpreted within the context of Lavater's discussion of facial features. To grasp how Lawrence perceived Byron, awareness of Lavaterian physiognomy is crucial. It is no less crucial for understanding how Lawrence's contemporaries – not least, Thomas Sully – understood portraiture. Though physiognomy hardly makes an appearance in scholarly discussions of Sully, its appealing if controversial interpretations of the human countenance exerted considerable impact not only upon Sully himself but upon the artistic, theatrical, and literary milieus in which he lived and worked.[6]

*

Lavater's search for demonstrable traces of the divine in humanity drove him to intense study of the human countenance. Understanding human physiognomy, he believed, could help people value and love each other. His monumental study *Physiognomische Fragmente* (4 vols, 1775–78), literally *Physiognomical Fragments*, launched the new science into the forefront of European and American intellectual discussion.[7] Lavater based it on a simple premise: one's outward appearance, in the whole or in part, manifests one's inner self. Interest in his ideas made Lavater one of the best-known men of the age. Not just intellectuals and artists but also the common man responded vigorously, if variously, to Lavaterian physiognomy. If people sometimes wondered out loud whether physiognomy were truly a science, most accepted Lavater's theories as a legitimate means of decoding humanity's puzzling multiplicity and behavior.

For Lavater the face indexed the soul. The face's bone structure and the permanent lines left by habitual facial expressions revealed the moral being. Contemporaries skeptical of *fronti nulla fides* (put no faith in appearances) abounded.[8] For them, Lavater indulged in "a jumble of speculation, unverified claim and undistilled hypothesis."[9] Others felt Lavater had charted a dangerous course, one that would lead eventually, as a dubious Hegel put it, to make a bone of the mind.[10] Still others feared that an experienced physiognomist might divine more of the truth about his subjects than they wished to reveal. The reformist Habsburg Emperor Joseph II exclaimed to Lavater, "Ah! you are a dangerous man! I do not know whether any one ought to suffer himself to be seen by you. You look into the hearts of men. We must be very cautious when we come into your company."[11] Believing national physiognomy reflected national character, Lavater outlined the physiognomical characteristics of Germans, French, Italians, English, even of his Swiss countrymen, whom he did not flatter.[12] Englishmen fared best. English faces may well differ from Swiss faces, but after a century of war in part based on unscientific generalizations of physiognomical stereotyping, Lavater's hypotheses may leave us uneasy. In the 1780s and 1790s, however, the infant study of physiognomy appeared to hold great promise. Although Lavater in theory believed anyone could be a physiognomist, he warned that less than one in ten thousand could become "an excellent physiognomist."[13] Such warnings discouraged no one. If few became expert, many drew upon physiognomy's multi-layered psychological and ideological complexities for what they needed and eagerly applied to their own and others' lives what they wished or understood of Lavater's ideas. Lavater's work, translated into many languages, captivated Blake and Fuseli, Goethe and George Eliot, Goya and Girodet. Responses hardly differed from nation to nation, ranging from unqualified enthusiasm to utter contempt. Napoleon on St Helena dismissed Lavater to Las Cases as "cet insigne charlatan," but Madame de Staël spoke warmly of him in *De l'Allemagne* (1813).[14]

Physiognomy anticipated a crucial focus of Romanticism: that every created entity is unique. "Each leaf a world," wrote Lavater, none identical with another.[15] Similarly, "no two men can be found, who, brought together, and accurately compared, will not appear to be very remarkably different." This concept is of particular relevance to study of Sully's *Byron*, for the portrait largely represents Sully's own idea of what Byron looked like. When Lavater spoke of the "ever open book of the human countenance" he implied humanity's organic nature. "The human body is a plant," he believed, "each part of which has the character of the stem."[16] Goethe put it more succinctly in *Faust*: "green is life's golden tree."[17]

Most people today, if they have heard of physiognomy, class it with phrenology, mesmerism, spiritualism, and homeopathy as one of the era's many "pseudo-sciences." As credence in traditional belief-systems waned in the later eighteenth century, these pseudo-sciences enjoyed Europe-wide vogues. Many regarded them as legitimate and looked with hope upon their claims to answer life's questions. Early in the nineteenth century physiognomy intertwined with phrenology, a theory of the brain advanced by the Austrian Franz Joseph Gall (1758–1828). Whereas Lavater deduced character from the countenance, Gall assessed the significance of "bumps" on the skull. He and his disciple Johann Kaspar Spurzheim published widely read works in the nineteenth century's first decades. Gall said sharp things about Lavater, but his theories actually reinforced Lavaterian physiognomy. Young Nicholas Biddle revealed himself an acute physiognomist on his European tour, but the phrenological teachings of Gall, whom he met while abroad, absorbed him equally.[18]

Physiognomical precepts have survived better than phrenological ones.

We still study visages; few of us tap skulls. Physiognomy, shorn of its associations with Lavaterian "pseudo-science," survives in common usage. The "meaning" of people may well lie below the surface, as psychology and its various offshoots imply, but most of us believe the surface can provide useful clues. Although professed advocates of Lavaterian physiognomy are now few, we all remain in some sense physiognomists. We attempt, for an almost infinite variety of reasons (of which we may remain unconscious), to fathom personality through facial expression and gesture. To "read" people, to gauge their being, to ascertain their mood (it may determine our response), even to protect ourselves when we come upon someone we have not met before, is our hope. Our lives might just possibly hinge upon an accurate assessment.

Opinion then as now blurred distinctions between the two "pseudo-sciences" of physiognomy and phrenology.[19] Occasionally they made converts together. Some believers in physiognomy like Lawrence and Gilbert Stuart and William Blake took to phrenology.[20] Hazlitt and Carlyle did not. Physiognomy but not phrenology made good sense to Hazlitt, for whom "the face, for the most part, tells what we have thought and felt – the rest is nothing." Wordsworth was his idea of physiognomical perfection.[21] Benjamin Robert Haydon judged the poet "in phrenological development . . . without constructiveness," whereas "imagination is as big as an egg."[22] Wordsworth's bulging forehead, as De Quincey too truly pointed out, could attract "caricature misrepresentations."[23] Carlyle, impatient with Gall and Spurzheim, lauded "worthy wonderful Lavater."[24] Likewise, Emerson, utterly convinced of physiognomy's truths, cast a critical eye upon phrenology.[25]

Physiognomy gradually achieved the wider applications it still retains. William Cullen Bryant, wishing to isolate the unique qualities of the American landscape, hymned "the physiognomy of our own woods and fields."[26] Berlioz in 1839 spoke of the intense concentration needed to compose his *Roméo et Juliette* until it achieved "the shape and the physiognomy that I intended."[27] An avid observer of the city's life, he declared, "Je n'oublierai jamais la physiognomie de Paris."[28] Whereas physiognomy caught on in America as early as the 1790s, phrenology exerted its deepest impact on American thought only in the 1840s and 1850s, twenty or more years after Sully painted *Byron*. During the artist's formative years half a century before, it was physiognomy, not phrenology, that captured men's minds.[29]

Most people, E. M. W. Tillyard once observed, take for granted the "genuine ruling ideas" of their own era, the functioning but rarely acknowledged behavioral substratum of society that forms an age's common ideology. Understood by all, few bother to write about these ideas and they fade away and tend to be forgotten.[30] As the contours of the scientific pantheon change, the criteria differentiating "true" from "pseudo-" science are hardly clearer today than they were two hundred years ago. Newer frameworks like Freudian psychoanalysis and Jungian psychology, apparently well established, have in recent decades spawned skeptics and unbelievers. Who dares predict their status a hundred years hence? Discovery of scientific "truths" yet undreamt of may leave their ultimate reputation no less uncertain than physiognomy's.

Amateur physiognomists still abound. In an essay entitled "About Face" (1980) Joseph Epstein noted that though physiognomy may "have been largely discredited, there may be more to it than an intelligent person is supposed to allow." As someone who grew up gazing with never-waning interest across the aisles of Manhattan subways, I agree with Epstein that all of us read faces, a hundred times a day. Proust, he notes, "a writer greatly fascinated by faces," filled his pages "with the subtlest observations upon the human face."[31] Proust wrote *A la recherche du temps perdu* nearly a century *after* physiognomy's heyday, well after the great nineteenth-century European storytellers whose use of physiognomical concepts Graeme Tytler has studied. Like Proust (and Hazlitt before him), V. S. Naipaul searches faces for clues: "We carry our life in our face. We carry our experiences in our face."[32] The books cited in Epstein's essay – and recent popular works like Jo-Ellan Dimitrius and Mark Mazzarella's *Reading People* – suggest that many continue to find the study of faces relevant, indeed essential.[33] On a more formal level, the distinguished art historian E. H. Gombrich insists upon a continued engagement with physiognomy: "There is such a thing as 'physiognomic perception' which carried strong and immediate conviction. We all experience this immediacy when we look into a human face."[34] Many cultures – Chinese, Indian, Gypsy, for example – believe different parts of the body offer clues about personality or the future. My poker-playing buddies try to read their opponents' faces to gauge a giveaway "tell" for what it might imply.[35]

We base our physiognomical readings in large part on our personal histories. The danger of physiognomic study of the Lavaterian kind is that it invests our readings with universal validity. Lavater thought otherwise: what most human beings throughout history have done instinctively he sought to codify. Lavaterian physiognomy as an idea, a concept, a system lingered in American as well as European consciousness for over a century.

*

Just as there is physiognomy after Lavater, there was physiognomy before Lavater. Lavater himself, inherently modest in his being as in his claims, acknowledged the work of Buffon, Herder, Kant, Winckelmann, Leibnitz, Le Brun, as well as his friend Fuseli, in offering testimony to correspondences between inner and outer states. Among earlier figures he cited Pliny, Cicero, Montaigne, and the authors of the Bible. For his illustrations he drew upon, among other artists, Raphael, Dürer, and Hogarth.

Physiognomy was "practiced by Pythagoras, defended by Socrates, approved by Plato, and treated by Aristotle," according to Thomas Cooper (or Cowper), whose learned and thoughtful estimate of Lavater's achievement appeared in 1790.[36] Aristotle had inaugurated the subject formally in his *Physiognomics*, which drew detailed analogies between human shapes and traits as well as analogies of congruences (and dissimilarities) between man and different animals.[37] Though few scholars now accept this work as Aristotle's, Cooper claimed the *Physiognomics* as the "foundation" for almost every physiognomical treatise written since.[38] Aristotle's vast reputation underlay and gave authority to Lavater's exposition. Admiring "ancient ideal beauty" in Greek and Roman statuary, the Swiss thinker wept when he considered "the present depravity of men and imitative art."[39]

After Aristotle, Theophrastus in his *Characters* associated emotions (e.g., anger) or character traits (e.g., meanness) with specific physical attributes. The numerous sculptured busts that have survived from Roman times, of often astonishing vividness of expression, indicate that among Romans study of physiognomic traits must have been hugely popular. Although belief in physiognomy may have waned in the Middle Ages, Chaucer's portraits of pilgrims in *The Canterbury Tales* utilize physiognomical thinking. With the renewed interest in portraiture during the Renaissance physiognomy revived. The human face fascinated both Leonardo and Dürer, artists Lavater drew upon. Skeptics remained, however. Shakespeare in *Macbeth*, as dubious about systems as Byron two centuries later, questions whether we can divine character through physiognomy. Thinking of the treacherous Thane of Cawdor, Duncan proclaims, "There's no art / To find the mind's construction in the face."[40] But characters in Shakespeare's plays deploy much "art" in reading faces.

Toward the end of the Renaissance the idea that facial expression could be codified became commonplace. Hall's *Characters* (1608) renewed interest in Theophrastan characters and endorsed the systematic study of faces. The full title of La Bruyère's great work is *Les caractères de Théophraste, traduits du grec, avec les caractères ou moeurs de ce siècle* (1688). That connoisseur of human foibles saw more deeply into humanity than all but the greatest portraitists. Charles Le Brun designed his *Conférence sur l'expression générale et particulière* (1668) specifically as a manual for artists. He illustrated it with engravings showing different human expressions that often connect humanity with the animal world. Through its various editions and translations this treatise influenced portraitists well into the nineteenth century. Both John Trumbull and Rembrandt Peale knew their Le Brun well. As biography and autobiography emerged as literary genres and assumed their modern forms, they moved increasingly toward psychological portraiture through awareness of physiognomy. Physiognomic countercurrents existed but became less insistent as the decades went by.

In the eighteenth century Shaftesbury's *Characteristicks* (1711), Le Sage's *Gil Blas* (1715–35), Fielding's novels and particularly his *Essay on the Characters of Men* (1749) focus on individuality of being. William Hogarth based his caricatures on physiognomic precepts, and his groundbreaking *Analysis of Beauty* (1753) provided a theoretical basis for seizing character both naturalistically and in exaggerated form.[41] By mid-century, comments Roy Porter, "looks had to speak true, and a new physiognomy was needed to tell the honest face and the heartfelt look."[42] Rousseau boldly began his

Confessions, "Je veux montrer à mes semblables un homme dans toute la verité de la nature; et cet homme ce sera moi."

One of Lavater's immediate predecessors was the Rev. John Clubbe, an oddball English antiquarian. *Physiognomy* (1763), a clever satirical pamphlet that is his best-known work, lightheartedly finds "the science of *Physiognomy*" resting upon "sandy and fallacious foundations."[43] Clubbe, rejecting "all physiognomical systems past and present," proposed tongue-in-cheek "a *new* system of *Physiognomy*" whereby one may estimate moral character by weighing heads on an ingenious "Mechanical *Apparatus*" of his own devising. Placed on it, the man of gravity sinks to the ground while "absolute levity, or stark fool" rises to the top.[44]

Clubbe dedicated his satire to Hogarth, but it is more in the tradition of Shaftesbury and Addison. Its genial, exaggerated humor echoes Fielding's, and the learned cleric's Latin tags and indulgence in homely folk wisdom recall Parson Adams in *Joseph Andrews*. Unlike Le Brun, Clubbe offered the artist little help: "His skill depends upon his seeing and feeling, accompanied with a certain happy sagacity arising from both."[45] He viewed the prospects for a true physiognomy slim, but even his reservations indicate that physiognomy was in the air: denying the need for physiognomy implies that the need was indeed there.

Tristram Shandy (1759–67), with its cult of sensibility and its almost Plutarchian reading of gesture and behavior, illustrated that need and helped set the stage for Lavater. Sterne was not exactly a physiognomist. Except for his famous disquisition on noses, he does not discuss facial features. But he was well aware of the need for a heightened perception. "There are a thousand unnoticed openings . . . which let a penetrating eye at once into a man's soul," he wrote, "and I maintain . . . that a man of sense who does not lay down his hat in coming into a room, – or taking it up in going out of it, but something escapes, which discovers him."[46] A decade after *Tristram Shandy*, Lavater charted, categorized, and set the study of physiognomy coursing in new channels.

*

Journal and newspaper articles brought Lavater's ideas before English readers well before the first London publication of *Essays* began in 1789. The *Monthly Review* had noted the initial volume of *Physiognomische Fragmente* in 1775 and greeted succeeding volumes with interest. A 17-page review of 1781 praised the French translation. Encyclopedia articles on physiognomy in Britain treated Lavater from the beginning with respect. Thomas Cooper, aware of the contemporary debate over the *Essays* and not uncritical himself, yet spoke of Lavater's in 1790 as "the most important book on the subject, since the days of Aristotle." "The magnificence of the work itself," Cooper added, "and the supposed visionary nature of the subject treated, has contributed not a little to make it generally known."[47]

Lavater's ideas quickly insinuated themselves into popular discourse. Those who rejected or remained neutral before his complex theory of human personality were in the minority. "Mr. [Benjamin] West has the expression and fine features said by Lavater's physiognomical work to characterize him," commented in 1786 Sophie von la Roche, a German visitor to England, obviously up on her Lavater.[48] For English travelers to Switzerland a visit to the sage, with if possible a physiognomical consultation, was a requisite rite. Among those who called upon Lavater in Zürich were William Coxe, Helen Maria Williams, Charles Fox, and young William Pitt. The popularity of his ideas outraged Hannah More, and Maria Edgeworth's father opined of him that "to some genius he adds a good deal of the mountebank."[49] But such negativism was unusual. Most responded favorably both to the man and his ideas.[50] William Cowper, having persuaded himself "that faces are as legible as books," found himself "very much of Lavater's opinion."[51]

By the 1790s talk of physiognomy in London's artistic and literary circles filled the air. The first volumes of both Hunter's and Holcroft's editions of Lavater's *Essays on Physiognomy* had appeared, lavish of text and adorned with hundreds of plates. When Lavater died early in 1801, *The Scots Magazine* commented that he had been for many years "one of the famous men in Europe."[52] His books, "studied and admired," were, another reviewer claimed, "thought necessary in every family as even the Bible itself."[53] Throughout most of the nineteenth century editions, abridgments, handbooks, and translations of Lavater, often adapted to the needs of the editor or publisher, disseminated his ideas widely. Reprinted, abridged, summarized, pirated, quoted, parodied, imitated, and reviewed, the *Essays* were impossible to avoid. The differing texts altered physiognomy's scope and substance, but few could help but acquire some knowledge of the man or his theories. By the 1840s Lavater's works had gone through forty editions in English translation. Holcroft's edition, completed in 1793 in collaboration with Mary Wollstonecraft and in abridged forms often reprinted, led the parade. Many encountered Lavater's ideas through some version of Holcroft.[54]

Nearly from the time of the *Essays*' initial publication, satires and parodies had also disseminated Lavater's ideas. Among the first in the field was Georg Christoph Lichtenberg. Analogies between human beings and animals in a profile or silhouette might make for some fun, and Lichtenberg's light-hearted skits on physiognomy included illustrations depicting various kinds of tails, of dogs and pigs but also the "pig-tails" of men, which he proceeded to analyze for their physiognomical properties.[55] Lichtenberg did not deny the possibility of understanding and interpreting physical expression – he was himself the author of the most detailed commentary on Hogarth's satirical sequences ever to appear and a scientist to boot – but he believed intensity of personal intuition was no measure of its correctness. Isaac D'Israeli's *Flim-Flams!* (1805), a clever and lively Shandean satire, focused on what it regarded as specific excesses in scientific investigation – physiognomy was one.[56] Appearing long after Lavater's initial publication, *Flim-Flams!* spoofs its subject as lightheartedly as Clubbe's *Physiognomy* had spoofed the idea of physiognomy fifty years before. Not surprisingly, caricature – in which artists often depicted individuals in profile and gave them animal features – enjoyed a great vogue during the Lavaterian decades: in England with Gillray, Rowlandson, and Cruikshank; in France with Daumier, Gavarni, and Grandville. We may even regard Marcel Marceau as Daumier's heir in the art of facial and bodily gesture.

Lavater's writings had an immediate impact on the contemporary stage and on contemporary letters. "The countenance is the theatre on which the soul exhibits itself," the Swiss had claimed; "here must its emanations be studied and caught."[57] For the expensive three-volume-in-five Hunter translation of the *Essays* (1789–98), issued in 41 parts, numerous performers and dramatists pledged the extraordinary sum of 30 guineas.[58] Depictions of actors and actresses in engravings, portraits, and word descriptions reveal the ubiquitous nature of Lavater's influence upon facial expression. In literature, in addition to Wollstonecraft and Holcroft, William Godwin, Charlotte Smith, John Moore, Ann Radcliffe, and "Monk" Lewis were among those excited by physiognomical thinking.[59] Although tracing specific borrowings is difficult, Lavater's descriptions in the *Essays* often influenced the facial details of characters in their fictions.

Byron himself was well aware of both physiognomy and phrenology. Phrenology, which became popular in Britain after the visit of Gall's disciple Spurzheim in 1808, gave renewed support and currency to Lavaterian ideas. Byron knew Lavater's friend and disciple, Henry Fuseli, who greatly admired his poems, in fact in old age read every work by Byron upon publication and owned more volumes by him than by any other author.[60] Byron was "mightily taken" by the "fine engraving" in Lavater of Fuseli's painting *The Ezzelin Bracciaferro and the Dead Meduna* (*c.* 1784). Related to his famous *Nightmare*, this composition depicts a gloomy male brooding over an elongated female corpse.[61] Understandably Byron wanted "to know the story." Upon asking Fuseli his source, he learned it came out of the artist's head.[62]

Although Byron mentioned Lavater several times and his incidental comments on his own portraits indicate an awareness of Lavaterian notions,[63] he found phrenology more relevant in understanding his own temperament. Byron does not mention Gall, but Spurzheim, a "*craniologist*," "a discoverer of faculties & dispositions from heads," enthralled British audiences with his lectures on phrenology. Sir William Knighton, the king's physician, introduced Spurzheim to Byron. The poet was one of the first in England to give the esteemed "*craniologist*" the opportunity to probe the bumps on his already famous cranium. He described the experience to his future wife Annabella:

> He passes his hand over the head & then tells you – curious things enough – for I own he has a little astonished me. – He says all mine are strongly marked – but very antithetical for every thing developed in & on this same skull of mine has its *opposite* in great force so that to believe him my good & evil are at perpetual war.

"Pray heaven," Byron added, "the last don't come off victorious."[64]

Byron accepted Spurzheim's diagnosis as valid. Experiencing phrenology at first hand stirred him to ponder the nature of human psychology. Spurzheim had found within Byron's skull an unstable mixture of opposites indicative of an exceptionally antithetical being. That similar qualities resided in Burns Byron discovered in reading his unpublished letters.[65] Though he does not mention Spurzheim again, phrenology had a significant impact upon his poetry. Napoleon and Rousseau, figures in *Childe Harold*'s third canto with whom Byron identified himself temperamentally, exist in as uneasy, unstable, and potentially explosive a combination of polarities as Byron himself.

Physiognomy taught a century how to look at and understand people. Like their eighteenth-century predecessors, nineteenth-century writers in Europe as well as Britain reveled in the possibilities physiognomic theory opened to them. The sentimental heroine, the Gothic villain, the Byronic hero: all lasted the century (and longer) and all drew on physiognomy to describe emotional states. Let novelists endow a character with a pale face, a pronounced forehead, or a dark complexion, and lo, they have conjured up a Lavaterian essence. Dickens and Thackeray and George Eliot, Balzac and George Sand, Gotthelf and Keller attribute to their characters physical attributes that often correlate to Lavaterian behavioral characteristics. Delightful in themselves, these long, elaborate descriptions also stimulated those with interest or training in physiognomy – that is, most of the reading public – to exercise their powers of analysis. Balzac, fascinated with "the characters of Paris," regarded himself as Lavater's' disciple, as did, in vastly different ways, Stendhal and Chateaubriand, Sand and Baudelaire. Like Balzac and Berlioz, Baudelaire wished to chart the "physiognomy of Paris." One scholar has called Darwin's *Expression of the Emotions in Man and Animals* (1872) "the most subtle work of physiognomic theory of the nineteenth century."[66] As that century waned, novelists like James, Gide, Joyce, and of course Proust turned inward. Detailed physiognomical descriptions are fewer, but physiognomical observations remain a subtle, powerful undercurrent.

*

After 1789 physiognomy exercised a pervasive influence on the visual arts, in particular portrait painting. Lavaterian physiognomy, if mentioned at all in scholarly discussions of Regency or Federal portraiture, receives a few throwaway sentences, yet Lavater was right to insist upon physiognomy's importance for portraitists, and portraiture in Britain and America developed within the encompassing embrace of his ideas. Reynolds's *Discourses* had formalized portraiture's relationship to history and literature, but it was Lavater's *Essays on Physiognomy* that introduced fresh ways for artists to look at the human countenance . Goethe, cited by Lavater, asserted that "the best text for a commentary on man is his presence, his countenance."[67] But a human text so varied and complex posed challenges.

As noted earlier, all the editions of the *Essays*, in whatever language, came with numerous illustrative plates. The Hunter edition had 174 engraved plates and many engraved vignettes.[68] Holcroft's four-volume edition of the *Essays* included 418 plates of physiognomic heads along with supplemental sketches of facial features. Portraits of a sort, they ensured the work's popularity. Lavater intended the *Essays* and their abundant illustrations as a moral and prudential guide to human features. Essential to the successful portraitist was an understanding of the precepts therein, which were meant to induce painterly excellence. He wanted them to serve artists as a source book to train the mind no less than the eye. The artists, sculptors, and engravers who consulted it, in whatever edition, benefited even more from his visual characterizations than from his text. Immersion in Lavater led portrait painters, as specialists in human features, to reinterpret the significance of detail. Studying his written descriptions of faces and taking his diagnostic illustrations as models, they deepened their knowledge of character. Thus armed with physiognomic analyses both verbal and visual, portraitists set out to record the physical lineaments of human personality. The prospect of creating portraits aesthetically attractive, analytically true, and "scientifically" accurate pleased both artists and patrons. Not surprisingly, then, physiognomy had a great, if gradual, impact on portraiture. Until academies of art fostered physiognomically trained artists, Lavater believed, "we shall at best but creep in the regions of physiognomy, when we might otherwise soar."[69] Actually, England had such a receptive institution. The Royal Academy of Art had among its members several physiognomically inclined artists, among them Lawrence and Fuseli.

Lavater considered painting "the mother and daughter of physiognomy"; drawing was the physiognomist's natural tool.[70] He frequently drew his analogies from art, portraits in particular. Nature being "uncertain, thus fugitive," he thought portraits provided "a better knowledge of man" than living physiognomies: "Each perfect portrait . . . displays the human mind with the peculiarities of personal character."[71] Art criticism in a physiognomical text before this time, Le Brun excepted, was unusual, but Lavater wanted to develop the visual power of artists by expanding the potential in their descriptive language. His accounts of facial features often partake of self-help exercises designed to encourage artists to examine comparable physiognomies and make appropriate deductions. In correlating word to image the *Essays* reveal what one scholar has called "a powerful, at times incredible, interplay."[72] Portrait painting, "the most natural, manly, useful, noble" of the arts, stood high for Lavater as an ideal.[73] He found even the greatest artists of the past wanting. None, however brilliant, achieved the ideal: "I know no painter, of whom I can say he has thoroughly studied the harmony of the human outline, not even Poussin, no, not even Raphael himself."[74] Even more lamentably imperfect were current portraitists. Lacking a philosophical or even a "just, intelligible, and universal knowledge of men," moderns failed to grasp the intricacies of human physiognomy. And without "accurate knowledge of the form, proportion, connection" and interdependence of the parts of the body, Lavater lamented, they "will paint portraits ill."[75]

Lavater preferred profiles over frontal views and (perhaps of necessity) engravings of portraits over oils, for their clean lines delineated the human countenance more precisely. Believing that one's inner, moral character shaped one's head, he felt profiles revealed the skull's shape better. Since the profile lacks the interaction between sitter and viewer introduced by eye contact, Lavater may have thought it provided a more "objective" view of the head. Given intellectual prestige by his work, the profile portrait enjoyed its greatest vogue since the Renaissance. It is thus not happenstance that Westall – and Sully after him – chose to paint Byron in profile.

*

Thomas Lawrence had an unerring eye, and when looking at a person's head he seized the proportions and the relations of the parts, the importance of each detail to every other. Interpreting the human face in his own work, he adhered to physiognomical principles that, he admitted candidly, owed much to Lavater. Byron he found a "most interesting subject for the exercise" of the physiognomist's art. Lawrence, who may have seen Byron only once, observed him with great concentration and insight. But without the prefatory sentence in his description, would we have recognized that Lawrence had grounded his pen portrait of Byron in Lavater? What in the Swiss thinker, we might ask, did Lawrence find useful in helping him understand Byron? And how does a Lavaterian reading of Byron differ from what we might term a "normal" reading?

Lawrence (in the epigraph to this chapter) interprets Byron as contradictory and paradoxical of feature, but also matches him, point by point, against Lavater's analyses of physiognomical features. The words he chose to describe Byron's features – the face full of "character," the "clear and open" forehead, the "prominent" brow, the "finely cut" nose, the "*acutely* formed" nostril, the "well-form'd but wide" mouth, the "massive firmness of the Chin" – comprise a distinctly physiognomical reading.[76]

Within a Lavaterian context, the "clear and open" forehead and "brow boldly prominent" that Lawrence saw in Byron implied great potentiality and suggested mental power. The skull's contours reveal poetic power. Lawrence speaks of Byron's "keen and rapid genius – its pale Intelligence – its profligacy and its bitterness, . . . his laugh of mingled merriment and scorn." When "distorted by the Passions," the "original symmetry" of Byron's countenance – that Spurzheimian mixture of unreconciled opposites – seemed ravaged from within. When Lawrence described the eyes as "bright and *dissimilar*," he noted, as had others, both intelligence and that one was larger than the other. His summation – "all this presents to you the Poet and the Man" – is, if we are up on our Lavater, almost superfluous. Such a countenance as Byron's could in Lavaterian terms *only* exemplify mental and poetic power.

Byron's mouth returns us to contested terrain. "Well-form'd but wide"

Lawrence found it, "contemptuous even in its smile"; "falling singularly at the corners," it possessed a "vindictive and disdainful expression." But "the massive firmness of the Chin, which springs at once from the centre of the full under-lip," made the face end well. Last for Lawrence came the hair: "dark and curling," it was "irregular in its growth." Sully would capture those tousled locks superbly.

Lawrence, an amateur but well-informed physiognomist, was not the only contemporary to find Byron's face worthy of study. His Lavaterian reading of the poet's features reminds us that others of those who described Byron – Ticknor, Medwin, James Hamilton Browne, Lady Blessington, Captain Forrester, among them – may have subscribed to physiognomical notions. The spectacle of Byron fascinated Walter Scott, who fancied himself a physiognomist. In 1815, a year after Lawrence's analysis, Scott described Byron's countenance as "exquisitely modeled to the expression of feeling and passion." In "the remarkable contrast of very dark hair and eye-brows, with light and expressive eyes, [Byron] presented to the physiognomist the most interesting subject for the exercise of his art."[77] Scott's language virtually replicates Lawrence's. No less willing to exercise his physiognomical bent was John Galt, who assessed Byron's "physiognomy [as] . . . prepossessing and intelligent." But there was a fly in the ointment: "ever and anon his brows lowered and gathered; a habit, as I then thought, with a degree of affectation in it."[78] From analysis of Byron's physiognomy Galt proceeded, inevitably it might seem, to evaluation of his temperament. Most Byron-watchers then as now did the same.

Lawrence's immersion in physiognomy came largely via Henry Fuseli. Lawrence, who had studied under Fuseli, admired his art – he eventually owned 21 of his paintings – and his intelligence. Contemporaries commented on the ease and accuracy with which Fuseli sketched the human figure.[79] C. R. Leslie, who arrived in London a year or two after Sully, took (no doubt on Sully's advice) Fuseli's course of lectures. He long remembered Fuseli's exceptionally "competent knowledge" of anatomical structure.[80]

Fuseli (whose influence on Sully is discussed below) was a main conduit in England for Lavaterian ideas. Lavater moved in and about Fuseli's imagination like some inner force. Born in Zürich the same year as Lavater, Fuseli had known him since student days. Both were republicans, ardently opposed to injustice and oppression.[81] Eccentric in behavior as in appearance, Fuseli was shy, aloof, quick-tempered, even uncouth; but his conversation was "striking and extravagant."[82] To England, where opportunity beckoned, he emigrated in 1764. From 1770, during eight years of study in Rome, Fuseli focused his art on biblical and literary themes. The human physiognomies he drew reveal Lavater's potent influence. Fuseli wanted to translate Michelangelo's heroic vision into his own idiosyncratic idiom. His passionate ideal as an artist was to render Shakespearean drama into Michelangelo's pictorial language, a goal he realized best, Gordon Ray has observed, not in his work for Boydell's Shakespeare but in his contributions to several editions of Lavater's *Essays on Physiognomy*.[83]

During the 1780s Fuseli, back in England, helped diffuse Lavater's ideas by working with him, long-distance, on German, French, and English editions of the *Essays*. He supervised the plates as well as the translation for Hunter's edition of the *Essays on Physiognomy* (1789–98), in which he is mentioned and to which his friend Blake contributed three designs; after Lavater died in 1801 Fuseli contemplated writing his biography, but in the end did not. In 1789 Fuseli had freely translated a collection of Lavater's physiognomical *obiter dicta* as *Aphorisms on Man*. A popular success, the volume quickly went through several editions.[84]

Blake, not normally a man to take kindly to the systems of others, contributed a frontispiece and spoke of the *Aphorisms* fondly. "In the painter's small library," claimed his biographer Gilchrist, "the *Aphorisms* became one of his most favourite volumes. On the title-page occurs a naive token of affection: below the name Lavater is inscribed 'Will. Blake,' and around the two names the outline of a heart."[85] Clearly Lavater touched Blake's emotions no less than his mind. Blake went on to annotate Lavater's words sympathetically. By one of the aphorisms he commented: "This is true Christian philosophy, far above all abstraction." "Gold," "All Gold," "Pure Gold" occur frequently in the margins. Sensing in Lavater a kindred spirit, Blake responded to his religious nature, the side the atheistical Holcroft had suppressed. Blake did not read Lavater's *Aphorisms* uncritically, but at the end he commented: "I write from the warmth of my heart, & cannot resist the impulse I feel to rectify what I think false in a book I love so much, & approve so generally." For Blake, "the name Lavater. is the amulet of those who purify the heart of man."[86]

Lavater's *Aphorisms on Man* also set Blake to composing aphorisms of his own in *The Marriage of Heaven and Hell.* Gilchrist, like most readers since, found them "of a more original and startling nature" than Lavater's.[87] Lavater's No. 63 – "The most stormy ebullitions of passion, from *blasphemy* to murder, are *less terrific than* one single act of cool *villany*" – Blake transformed into the more concise, more graphic "Sooner murder an infant in its cradle than nurse unacted desires."[88]

*

America responded enthusiastically to Lavater. Read with enthusiasm, interpreted by critics, adopted by artists, its ideas diffused by the popular press, the *Essays* penetrated all strata of society. An edition published in Boston in 1794 was soon followed by others. The entry on physiognomy in Thomas Dobson's *Encyclopedia, or Dictionary of Arts, Sciences and Miscellaneous Literature* (1798) urged Americans to accept "Lavater's theories, and those of other physiognomists . . . as a confirmed science."[89] To what degree these theories affected the development of portraiture in America we may never fully know, but beyond doubt they influenced how artists during the nineteenth century's first decades looked at their subjects. Most American painters knew of Lavater, believed in physiognomy, and drew upon his physiognomical pointers for their portraits.

Charles Willson Peale was among the earliest physiognomical portraitists in America. Familiar with translations of Lavater, Peale probably owned *The Pocket Lavater, or, the Science of Physiognomy* (1800), one of the many handbooks available.[90] Peale's Museum, located in Philadelphia's Independence Hall, displayed portraits of notable Americans. Installed above cases of stuffed birds and animals, they were intended to serve not only as exemplars of great achievement but also as symbols of evolutionary progress.[91]

Like Lavater himself, Peale collected profiles for use in studying the human face. Profiles, as discussed in Chapter 8, became increasingly popular in America and were the trademark style of the French *émigré* artist, Charles Balthazar de Saint-Mémin. To achieve his portraits, Saint-Mémin used the physiognotrace invented by Gilles-Louis Chrétien in 1786. This device measured the exact dimensions of the head and thus allowed artists to create physiologically as well as physiognomically accurate profiles. Americans, as Ellen Miles has pointed out, expected this result and evaluated Saint-Mémin's portraits by Lavaterian standards.[92] Through John Isaac Hawkins, then living in Philadelphia, Peale acquired the American rights to the physiognotrace. In gratitude to Peale, Hawkins allowed Peale's son Raphaelle to use the physiognotrace (or "facietrace" as Raphaelle called it) for portraits in Virginia, where he had considerable success.[93]

Gilbert Stuart, also a keen student of faces, initially ridiculed what he took to be the rigidity of Lavater's system. Yet he found the attempt to codify connections between outward appearance and inner character thought-provoking and, in time, prided himself on his physiognomical skills.[94] John Neal, after talking with Stuart in 1817, thought "he believed in Lavater, or at least in the leading principles of physiognomy."[95] Stuart spoke of Washington's appearance in language that one scholar finds "decidedly Lavateresque."[96] He modelled his "Athenaeum" *Washington* closely upon Houdon's 1785 life mask of Washington, itself influenced by physiognomy. Stuart knew his audience interpreted his *Washingtons* within a physiognomical framework.[97] Although his "Vaughan" *Washington* was engraved for the Hunter translation of the *Essays on Physiognomy*, Lavater gave it only a mixed review. He valued "its expression of probity, wisdom, and goodness" and for revealing "the character of a great soul," but found it too idealized.[98] Still, Stuart had interpreted Washington, or so Lavater thought, by *his* light. To retain a clientele portrait painters had to be up to date, and economics if nothing else compelled them to become physiognomists.

Audubon, who received instruction in portraiture from Sully, saw faces from within a Lavaterian context. Upon meeting a certain individual, he carefully "inspected his features by 'Lavater's directions.'" John Wesley Jarvis, Sully's friend and teacher in New York in 1807, also judged people by their craniums. "By heavens," exclaimed the jovial Jarvis upon first meeting talented young Henry Inman, "the very head for a painter!"[99]

From Lavater, observes Lillian Miller, Rembrandt Peale derived "a general system for dealing with the intersection of the physical and the moral."[100] In the early 1820s when Rembrandt determined to produce his

"Standard National Likeness" of Washington, the *Patriae Pater*, it was in part because prevailing theories of physiognomy (and phrenology) made the idea of such a likeness important. Carol Hevner observes that the more salient features of Rembrandt's *Patriae Pater* correspond to Lavaterian precepts:

> A space between the eyebrows keynoted uncommon activity and energy, quickness of conception, and a soul composed and tranquil. A compact forehead symbolized a firm and solid character, and a prominent eye bone, a singular aptitude for mental labor and an extraordinary sagacity for great enterprise. Proportion in the face suggested richness of judgment and dignity of character while a straight line of eyebrows could be equated with a character vigorous and manly. The firmly closed mouth could be read as courage.[101]

An apt student of physiognomy, Rembrandt nicely integrated physiognomical accuracy into his realistic portraits.

Sully came to professional maturity at a time when interest in Lavater's *Essays* was peaking. As the young artist pursued his career in New York, Hartford, Boston, and Philadelphia, exposure to intellectual currents inevitably brought him into contact with Lavaterian thinking. Physiognomy intrigued this increasingly acute student of the human face and influenced how he conceived his portraits. Like Saint-Mémin, Stuart, the two Peales, Audubon and Jarvis, indeed most other contemporary portraitists, Sully knew he painted for an informed public, many of whom scrutinized portraits for the degree to which they based their interpretations on Lavaterian physiognomy.

In England Lawrence told Sully to improve his knowledge of anatomy and advised him to attend Henry Fuseli's lectures at the Royal Academy, where in 1799 Fuseli had first been elected Professor of Painting. Fuseli probably knew more about physiognomy than anyone else in England, and Lawrence, in effect, was counseling Sully to study physiognomy. Even more than Lawrence, it was the Swiss artist who honed Sully's awareness of physiognomical precepts. In his own being Fuseli was something of a physiognomical study. "His ideas are gnarled, hard and distorted, like his features," commented Hazlitt; "his theories stalking and straddle-legged, like his gait – his projects aspiring and gigantic, like his gestures."[102] Calling upon him in 1805, Benjamin Robert Haydon, aged 19, expected to meet "a sort of gifted wild beast" and "fancied Fuseli himself to be a giant." Instead, he was greeted by "a little white-headed lion-faced man in an old flannel dressing-gown, tied round his waist with a piece of rope, and upon his head the bottom of Mrs. Fuseli's work-basket."[103] Despite personal eccentricities, Fuseli proved a remarkable teacher. "No man had the power like Fuzeli [*sic*] of rousing the dormant spirit of youth," reminisced Haydon, "of inspiring young minds with high and grand views."[104]

By July 1809, when Sully arrived in England, Fuseli had presented before the Royal Academy eight of his 12 *Lectures on Painting*. Those already published – on Expression (no. 5), Design (no. 10), and Portraiture (no. 12) – reveal his dependence on physiognomical theory.[105] Like Lavater, he believed the shape of the skull revealed character and the state of the soul.[106] In fact, one critic finds Fuseli carrying "Lavater's doctrines further than did Lavater himself."[107] Though he professed to disdain portrait painting and did few portraits himself, Fuseli's ideas about physiognomic portraiture influenced a generation of RA students.

During his months abroad Sully imbibed *viva voce* from Fuseli Lavaterian notions about the human countenance. Attendance at his lectures as well as tutelage from the avowed physiognomist Lawrence sharpened Sully's awareness of Lavater's precepts. What he learned in England reinforced what he had learned in America. In addition to his intuitive grasp of human nature and the technical skills needed to covey the human face in paint, he had prepared himself well for a career in physiognomic portraiture by the time he returned to Philadelphia in May 1810.

Whether expressed in the *Essays*, rendered second hand through the teaching of Lawrence or Fuseli, or acquired by other means, Sully learned his Lavater. Many of the physical attributes of his *Byron* – hand-on-chin pose, open forehead, inward-gazing eyes, shape of the nose – indicate close acquaintance with Lavater's ideas. Although Sully's journal yields no direct references to the Swiss thinker *per se*, that fascinating document reveals the artist's almost obsessive study of facial proportions and the language of physiognomy. "Some amusement in speculating on the Phiz of travelling companions on a steamboat," he remarked on seeing an Indian woman and child, accompanied by a white male, in 1829.[108] Three years later he noted the physiognomical exactitude of his distinguished portraitist colleague Henry Inman. Inman's practice, wrote Sully, "is to measure the face from the eyebrow to the chin. That as a general rule, to the end of the nose is one-half of the face from the brow to the chin. He observes carefully the distance of the eye from the brow and from the nose, as on these points much of the identity of the face depends."[109] Only a physiognomically aware artist would have written thus.

*

Lavater as noted earlier particularly admired English physiognomies. "Englishmen have the shortest and best arched foreheads"; "large, well defined, beautifully curved lips"; "a round full chin"; "they are peculiarly distinguished by the eyebrows and eyes, which are strong, open, liberal, and stedfast."[110] In the context of Lavater's descriptions, Sully's *Byron* embodies virtue; in physiognomical terms, it exemplifies an ideal. Sully grounded both the virtue and the ideal in Lavater.

"How much may the anatomist see in the mere scull of man! How much more the physiognomist!" Thus Lavater began his chapter on skulls. He thought the "circumference and form" of the head, particularly the forehead, expressed an individual's "intellectual life." Phrenology, it may be noted, also saw a high forehead as the seat of intellectual power. The forehead for Lavater was the key component in the face. It defined a man's nature: "The form, height, arching, proportion, obliquity, and position of the scull, or bone of the forehead, shew the propensity, degree of power, thought, and sensibility of man." "The longer the forehead," Lavater went on, "the more comprehension, and less activity." When there occurred "a happy union of strait [*sic*] and curved lines," the resultant well-designed forehead "expressed the most perfect character of wisdom."[111]

Byron did well by Lavaterian criteria, or perhaps Lavater's opinions about foreheads conformed with Byronic reality. Contemporaries often noted how nicely proportioned was Byron's head. Trelawny spoke of it as "small" and "highly-finished," Lady Blessington, cited earlier, "as finely shaped," "the forehead open, high, and noble."[112] For John Galt, Byron's "forehead was rather noble certainly, and the general cast of his physiognomy was genteel and Grecian."[113]

A number of the facial features of Sully's *Byron* conform to Lavater's precepts. Sully paints the poet with a high forehead, brow flaring upward. "The skin must be more clear in the forehead than in the other parts of the countenance," insisted Lavater.[114] As James Hamilton Browne – himself perhaps drawing upon a Lavaterian perspective – had noted, Byron's skin, with tiny blue veins visible beneath, was exceptionally clear, and so Sully painted it.

Size and contour of nose indicated for Lavater character and temperament. Sully gave his *Byron* a handsome nose. Smaller and more delicate than that in Westall, the ostensible model, it anchors the face. Noses have riveted the human imagination for centuries, and Sully in depicting Byron's could have drawn upon a bevy of poets, painters, and novelists. Everybody had an opinion. *Tristram Shandy*, preceding Lavater's *Essays* by about a decade, speculates at length on the importance of noses.[115] Before Sterne, there was Rabelais, whose Friar John remarked: "*ad formam nasi cognoscitur*" (by the shape of the nose shall he be known).[116] Hazlitt, we remember, was unhappy with Coleridge's non-nose. De Quincey judged Wordsworth's "a little arched" and "large"; a large nose, he opined, "has always been accounted an unequivocal expression of animal appetites organically strong."[117] Little did De Quincey know! Wordsworth's love letters written to his wife Mary in 1812, unpublished until 1981, confirmed that this poet's animal appetites were indeed nasal.[118] Not surprisingly, Lavater's friend Fuseli also liked large or otherwise impressive noses. All men of genius, thought Fuseli, had them. Rembrandt's amazed him ("What a nose! why his nose is as big as his face!"). In letters Fuseli refers frequently to noses and, indeed, suggested to Lavater in 1779 that "the marrow of the nose is the nerve centre of friendship!"[119] But a large nose might suggest characteristics other than amorous propensities or friendship. In contrast to De Quincey, Proust rated the nose "generally the organ in which stupidity is most readily displayed."[120]

One who anticipated Proust in this belief was Captain Fitz-Roy of HMS *Beagle*. He needed a scientist for his epic voyage around the world. "An ardent disciple of Lavater," Fitz-Roy "was convinced that he could judge of a man's character by the outline of his features." The wrong kind of nose, as Charles Darwin now learned, could make trouble for you. In Fitz-Roy's view, a man with Darwin's ill-favored nose could hardly "possess sufficient energy and determination for the voyage." The young scientist almost did not get picked because "of the shape of my nose!" Further acquaintance, Darwin was pleased to say, left Fitz-Roy "well-satisfied that my nose had spoken falsely."[121]

Noses likewise riveted Nathaniel Hawthorne. In 1828 he withdrew from the Salem Athenaeum all four volumes of Lavater's *Physiognomy*, presumably in Holcroft's translation. Although Hawthorne followed Lavater in believing facial features provided a valid index to character, he balked at precise schemata for analyzing the nose's shape.[122] But the noses in his tales tell us much about their bearers.

How might Lavater have influenced the nose of *Byron*? Often cited as a nasal authority, Lavater regarded "the nose as the foundation or abutment of the brain."[123] It was the seat of intrepid genius, the key to understanding the face. Likewise, Wellington's nose, thought Byron, was "the hook where he suspends the world."[124] Noses also had aesthetic significance: for Lavater "a beautiful nose will never be found accompanying an ugly countenance."[125] Such a nose as Byron's implied, for him, intellectual distinction. "Requisite to the perfectly beautiful nose," Henry Inman also believed, is that "its length should equal the length [height] of the forehead." Further, the bottom of the nose, when viewed in profile, "should not have more than one third of its length."[126] Noses interested Sully. He found Victoria's, we recall, "well formed," appropriate for someone witty and bright. He gave Byron a nose whose length equaled the height of the forehead and whose bottom, when seen in profile, was only a third its length. More aquiline than Westall's, Sully's representation of Byron's nose justified Lavater's high opinion of English physiognomies.

When Lavater contemplated the mouth, he went into ecstasies.

> Oh! wherefore can I only imperfectly and tremblingly declare all the honours of the mouth; the chief seat of wisdom and folly, power and debility, virtue and vice, beauty and deformity, of the human mind; the seat of all love, all hatred, all sincerity, all falsehood, all humility, all pride, all dissimulation, and all truth?

He pleaded with "painters and designers" to "study this sacred organ, in all its beauteous expressions, all its harmony and proportion." "The contents of the mind," he claimed, "are communicated to the mouth."[127]

But, admitted Lavater, there was a problem. The mouth was hard for portraitists to render. It was usually conveyed through the shape of the lips, and about the lips Lavater expostulated more than about other facial features. He offered basic rules for their depiction: "Distinguish in each mouth the upper lip singly; the under lip the same; the line formed by the union of both when tranquilly closed." His summary will not surprise: "As are the lips, so is the character." Englishmen, he thought, "have large, well defined, beautifully curved lips."[128] Sully may have taken Lavater to heart here. The lips of *Byron* are fine and full, nicely curved. Clearly the artist thought the poet's "character" worthy.

It must have been difficult for a man who savored the human countenance in all its infinite variety to resist raving about each feature, but eyes and eye color mattered to Lavater. "The light of the body is in the eye," he believed. "Blue eyes are generally more significant of weakness, effeminacy, and yielding, than brown and black."[129] In English fiction gentle characters – Jessie Brown in *Cranford*, Harriet Smith in *Emma* – often are blue-eyed.[130] There are exceptions, but for Lavater brown eyes, not blue, indicate "strength, manhood, and thought."[131] Sully as a professional portraitist had to look hard at eyes. Victoria's he found "a little prominent but kind and intelligent."[132] Byron's he renders reflective, poetic, and of uncertain color. The uncertain color (discussed in the following chapter) may be there for reasons other than Sully's uncertainty about it. Seen from a Lavaterian perspective, the eyes of *Byron* – of a color somewhat blue, gray, or even hazel – combine masculine and feminine.

Regarding eyebrows the Swiss physiognomist developed ingenious interpretations. Most relevant to *Byron* is Lavater's interest in eyebrows that have the "arched and the horizontal combined." Such eyebrows "denote masculine understanding, and feminine kindness."[133] This supports the possibility that in *Byron* Sully intended a somewhat androgynous portrait. The artist thought raised eyebrows denoted in sitters "a grave and noble air."[134] Sully rarely theorized but his *Byron* comes across as a poet strongly masculine yet possessing a feminine sensibility. Like Lavater, Sully perhaps thought that eyebrows, like lips, were an important indicator of a subject's "character." Among Chaucer's characters, Criseyde's thin, close-meeting eyebrows indicate her libidinousness. Likewise, Byron's lush full eyebrows imply his inner nobility.

Hair was another Lavaterian focus (Figure 19). Study of its length, quantity, texture, and color told a physiognomically inclined portraitist much about a sitter's temperament, energy, sensibility, even mental capacity.[135] "How congruous are here the hair and the countenance!" wrote Lavater of a portrait of someone not altogether unlike Byron. "From the hair alone we may know the man," he says of another.[136] Sully took Lavater to heart. He diverged markedly, as noted earlier, from Westall in rendering Byron's hair long, thick and glossy, lustrous and rich in texture. By such hair Sully associated with Byron a corresponding richness of being. The hair signs *Byron* as his.

If Sully had never heard of Lavaterian physiognomy, would he have painted *Byron* differently? It seems likely. Few artists escaped physiognomy's influence. It was part of the era's intellectual currency. Sully, like Byron, had a temperament more practical than theoretical and like him regarded systems skeptically. But overall as well as in specific physical attributes, *Byron* reflects Lavater's precepts about determining the inner meaning of the human countenance. *Byron*, in sum, is a physiognomical portrait.

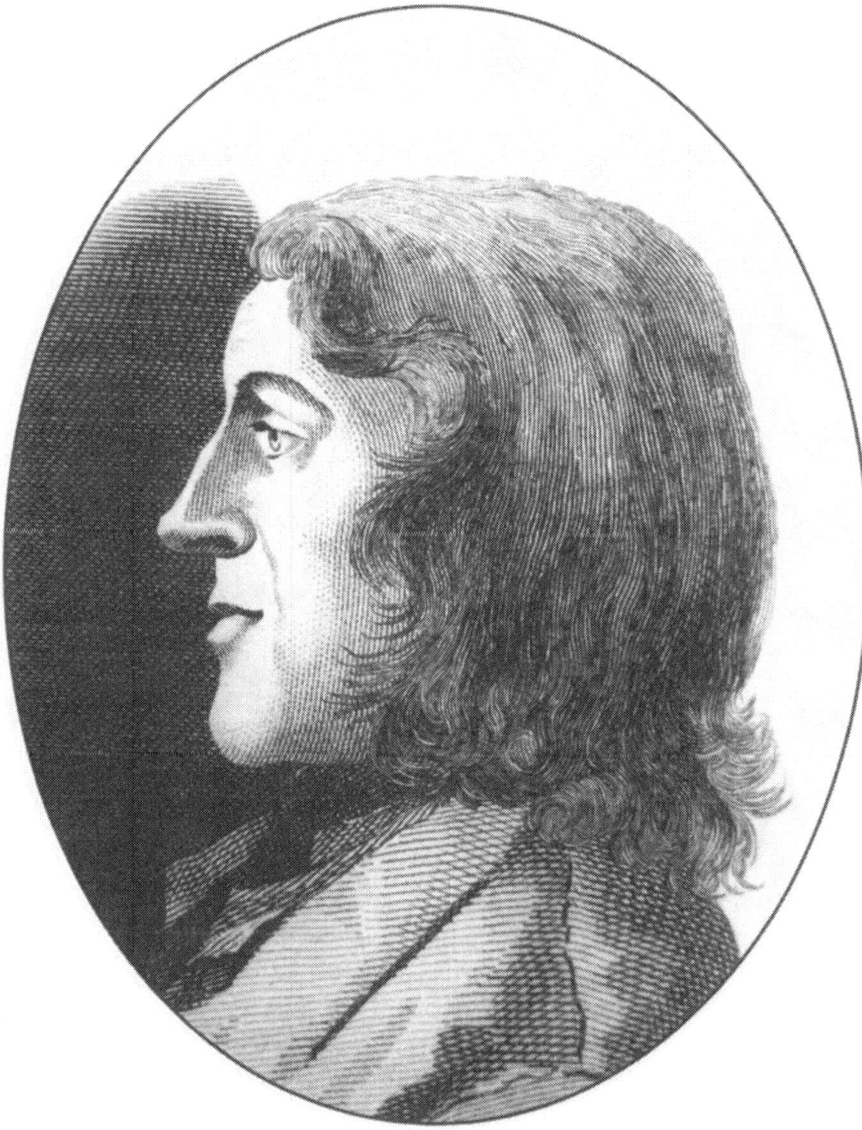

19 Lavater, [*Portrait of a Man with Hair*]. Reproduced from *Essays on Physiognomy* (1804) vol. 3, after p. 242

CHAPTER TEN

Sully's *Byron*: The Quest for Verisimilitude in Portraiture

I *should like* to do portraits which will appear a revelation to people in a hundred years' time.
Van Gogh[1]

For the greatest grace and life that a picture can have, is, that it expresse *Motion*: which the Painters call the spirite of a picture.
Hogarth[2]

His [Byron's] head was uncovered, and presented a fine model for the painter's art. He was unmasked, and his bright penetrating eyes seemed earnestly fixed, I could not discover on what. "Surely he sees beyond this gay scene into some other world, which is hidden from the rest of mankind," thought I, being impressed, for the first time in my life, with an idea that I was in the presence of a supernatural being. His attitude was graceful in the extreme. His whole countenance so bright, severe, and beautiful, that I should have been afraid to have loved him.
Harriette Wilson[3]

Mario Praz in his unusual book *The House of Life* claims that in the last of these passages, Harriette Wilson's description of Byron at a ball, "we have the image to which Byron liked to adapt his own life and that of his heroes." Praz asks a question that puzzles all those who have pondered Byron: "Where genuine exaltation ended and pose began, who shall say?"[4] What level of exaltation was "natural" for Byron? In what "pose" did he wish to present himself to others? The questions are insistent.

*

Most portraitists seek to determine which physical features most faithfully render their subject. If the artist wishes to capture the living being, the flux of life, how should this be attempted? Gainsborough for one felt acutely frustrated in seizing likeness in portraiture. "Had a picture Voice, Action, etc. to make itself known . . . but only a face, confined to one View, and not a muscle to move to say here I am, falls very hard upon the poor Painter who perhaps is not within a mile of the truth in painting the Face only."[5] R. G. Collingwood had this to say regarding verisimilitude: "When a portrait is said to be like the sitter, what is meant is that the spectator, when he looks at the portrait, 'feels as if' he were in the sitter's presence." Collingwood offered a solution. "The true definition of representative art is not that the artifact resembles an original . . . but that the feeling evoked by the artifact resembles the feeling evoked by the original (I call this emotional representation)."[6] To induce a state of "emotional representation," what Wendy Steiner interprets as the sympathy or empathy we feel for the subject, the artist "must make the perceiver feel as if he were in the referent's presence. Though this presence is only illusory, the creation of immediacy in portraiture, particularly painted portraiture, aims at diminishing the distinction between portrait and subject."[7]

Like the elusive Romanticism in which he plays so prominent and dazzling a part, Byron, famously chameleonic, was, he said, "every thing by turns and nothing long."[8] Others felt similarly about Coleridge. "Mobility," Byron's term, characterized Coleridge's countenance, which Southey deemed "the most variable that I have ever seen." Its expression, observes Morton Paley, "could vary dramatically within short periods."[9] Keats, after a walk "of near two miles" with Coleridge on Hampstead Heath, intuited the poet's essence aurally rather than visually and described him by his voice, not by his features.[10] Perhaps the age's most spoken-of man of mobility was Napoleon, whose ever-varying outward physiognomy, his secretary Bourrienne claimed, mirrored his inner being. No portraitist, said Bourrienne, had ever captured the mobility of Napoleon's face, "that quick and perceiving eye, that lightning glance, that expression now tender, now stern, now terrible, at times even caressing."[11] For Byron, Coleridge, and Napoleon, conversation often catalyzed changes in expression. Equally mercurial of being and speech was Beethoven. Johann Gabriel Seidl implies that the composer only revealed himself fully in talking: "For whoever heard him can also picture in his soul the noble master's image. No painter portrays him as he portrays himself."[12] Beethoven's lively physiognomy "reflected the inner man," writes a modern critic. "His 'two selves,' real and ideal, dark and light, inspirational and aspirational, were necessary the one to the other."[13] Courbet, frustrated in depicting Baudelaire in 1848, lamented, "I don't know how to finish it . . . Every day he has a different face."[14] Countless portrait painters must have felt the same about their subjects.

Portraiture reached a high level of sophistication in the early nineteenth century. "In those days before photography," Frances Blanshard comments, "any likeness may have seemed magical."[15] True enough. For the several decades subsequent to the invention of the daguerreotype in 1839, portraiture competed with the literalness of photography.[16] Miniaturists felt the impact first. With cheap daguerreotypes available by the 1850s for as little as 25 cents, people no longer wanted miniatures. Portrait commissions also declined, and portraiture again became the privilege of the rich. In contrast to the vigorous, richly toned, vibrant portraits earlier in the century, mid-century portraits are drier, less colorful, more literal. It took portraiture several decades to find its bearings again.

In the 1870s a new generation of American portraitists – Chase,

Duveneck, Sargent, and Whistler – came upon the scene. Recognizing that photography allowed them to approach portraiture more inventively, they overturned neoclassical conceptions of portraiture and made it into a dynamic exhibition of bravura skills and brushstrokes. Sully, in painting real individuals, kept the ideal in view; Whistler, less interested in accurate likeness, created carefully orchestrated compositions of color harmonies; Van Gogh, looking within, endowed his sitters with a searching, searing intensity. The actual individuals depicted in Lawrence's *Mrs Jens Wolff* or Sully's *Miss Elizabeth Ridgely* are no doubt imaginatively recreated, but would we even recognize, if they could appear before us, most of Whistler's subjects or Dr Gachet?

Chase, Duveneck, and Sargent continued variously active careers into the twentieth century's first decades. This period also witnessed the emergence of Robert Henri and the urban realists later denominated the "Ashcan" school. Recognition of that master interpreter of the human soul, Thomas Eakins, remained painfully slow. Henri and Eakins focused on portraiture, often choosing models from among their circle of acquaintance. Sargent died in 1925 and Henri in 1929 (Chase and Eakins had preceded them in 1916), and with the departure of this quartet American portraiture lost much of its cachet. In the 1930s artists often rejected the naturalistic, figurative depictions characteristic of earlier work. Instead, influenced by Picasso and other modernists, they reassembled the sitter's face (and body) according to their personal vision and/or current art theories. Warhol and Hockney evidence this trend later. Fascinating as are these reinterpretations, they usually forego claims to authenticity of likeness.

In the 1840s Samuel F. B. Morse had continued portraiture using the new medium of photography; one of his star pupils was the Civil War photographer, Matthew Brady. The photographic portrait is a subject unto itself, from the pioneers to Julia Margaret Cameron in England to August Sander in Germany to Diane Arbus, Annie Leibovitz, and Richard Avedon in present-day America. Their work challenges the eye and the understanding, though I find all but the greatest masters of the photographic portrait relatively superficial in achieving depth of insight into character. Film and later television have endowed portraiture with dimensions hitherto unimagined. "The concept of even continuous portraiture has become commonplace," observes Piper.[17] We may be approaching a new age of portraiture, when we compose on computers portraits of people as we wish them to be. Even live subjects may no longer be necessary. Indeed, as the *New York Times* has recently informed us, filmmakers have begun "to create photo-realistic computer characters that, at least in fleeting moments, will try to persuade the audience that actual humans are on the screen."[18]

Reports in the twentieth or twenty-first century of the demise of portraiture, whether figurative or abstract, have been (as Twain might say) greatly exaggerated. In a letter to his sister, Van Gogh explained that he was interested less in painting a photographic likeness of his subject than in "rendering our impassioned expressions."[19] He used shoes, boots, even an empty chair as emblems of the artist to create metaphorical self-portraits of himself as laborer. Although the artist's aspiration has often been exalted since Van Gogh and the sitter's importance correspondingly diminished, representations of the human face and form are not about to go away. Concerns about verisimilitude in portraiture continue. Pessimists like Robin Simon believe modern portraiture "has failed to discover a common language of expression (of which poses form such a vital point), to replace the traditional one that was successful for nearly four hundred years, and which it has chosen to ignore."[20] Valid enough, yet Simon sidesteps the new directions in which portraitists have engaged.

Portraiture, variously understood, has surged to the forefront of current debates about art, and a number of exhibitions have explored contemporary portraiture. Susan L. Stoops's *Mask or Mirror? (A Play of Portraits)* (2002), the catalogue for a show at the Worcester Museum of Art in 2002–3, offers a probing examination of avant-garde portraiture. Warning her readers/viewers to "beware the mask of realism," Stoops comments that, "in the early 20th century, artists like Picasso began to dismantle traditional portraiture with cubist portraits that did not rely on recognizable likenesses or distinguishing features." Portraiture was in effect reborn, under new auspices and new conditions, in the works of Van Gogh, Picasso, the Fauves and the Expressionists. "More recently," continues Stoops, "DNA profiles, professional attributes, clothing, biographical text, body fragments, and personal belongings also act as surrogates for the people portrayed."[21] Strictly figurative portraits – some of considerable power and impressive skill – continue to be made, but few art critics view them as significant. Most portraits today, less representational than their predecessors, challenge us as visual artifacts more than as physical depictions of an individual. Instant visual recognition may no longer be an absolute requirement for a portrait, yet in assessing how insightfully it reveals the sitter, physical resemblance remains a criterion for judgment – how important a criterion depends upon the viewer. Presumably even abstract or non-descriptive portraits have to have some relationship to their alleged subject. We still tend to evaluate portraitists by how much they value the exigency of rendering a likeness.

Our identities in life are never precisely fixed. After death what survives of us are "the memories of others" and – a big *and* – "those special portraits that have the authority to make predicative statements."[22] Byron left behind memories in the minds of those who knew or saw him, but few portraits of him are capable of making predicative statements. He had many selves. His friends loved him partly because he embodied, or seemed to embody, what they wished him to be. In Byron, too, seeming inconsistency sometimes resolves itself into underlying consistency: "Changeable too," he put it in *Don Juan*, "yet somehow '*Idem semper*.'"[23] How so?

*

Portraitists, we know, deemed Byron an extraordinarily challenging sitter. He moved, or he talked, all the time. Artists threw up their hands in despair at his refusal to sit still. Additionally, Byron held strong views about the pose and attire in which he wanted himself depicted, and in evaluating the finished work he could be caustic.

For figures from Byron's era and before we rely (when we have them) on verbal descriptions and paintings. Physical characteristics, as Byron himself knew well, change with age and respond to mood. Unbearable depression can shift within seconds to transcendent joy. Can a portrait ever seize someone at their very best? Accounts describing Byron cited earlier imply that no painter fully captured his elusive features.

During Byron's lifetime friends vigorously disputed his appearance. No single portrait captured the man; nor did any portrait please many. Even the best-known ones – Phillips's cloaked version, for example – convinced only a minority. Friends imagined Byron differently, described him differently. "If a man stands still and immobile," wrote Bernini, himself a master of the illusion of movement, "he is never as much like himself as when he moves about. His movement reveals all those personal qualities which are his and his alone."[24] But since a portrait fixes a moment in time or (as Bernini suggests) different "moments" in one image, how to make choices from Byron's vast repertory of expression, mood and movement?

Byron's portraits vary from historical documents to poetry. In most of them the poet looks a little stiff. Portraits cannot render the speaking or moving being, and Byron's notorious mobility of expression and mood made him difficult for contemporaries to pin down. We, two centuries removed, have difficulty resurrecting a mobile Byron. Except in the imaginations of others, his physical identity had passed beyond change. Thus we seek images that capture him in a characteristic pose or mood. Sully portrays a poet no longer living, no longer mobile. Yet he left to posterity an image of Byron, a "predicative statement" if you will, that can never be duplicated. The facial expression of Sully's *Byron* gives us a sense of the poet's inner life, an illusion of mobility. The artist achieved – it is a major achievement – what Collingwood has called "emotional representation."

Portrait painting is a demanding activity. Lawrence often pondered his commissions for years, and worked on one of his greatest portraits, that of *Mrs Jens Wolff*, from 1803 to 1815. For most portraits, from first sitting to final delivery, George Romney took between five and six months.[25] Like Sully, he asked six sittings of about two hours each. Reynolds could get by with three sittings of about an hour-and-a-half each.[26] Stuart, faster still, managed with four sittings of about an hour, but like Lawrence left many portraits unfinished at his death.[27] Sully completed more than two thousand portraits over his lifetime. With a large family to feed, he lacked the privilege of leisure. Some commissions he despatched in ten days, others in a week or less. This, for a portraitist, was quick work. Two years of intermittent work on *Byron* was for him both extraordinarily slow and unusually long.

Did Sully find working on *Byron* intriguing? It is hard to be certain, but it seems likely. He notes *Byron*'s completion both in his Register and in his Journal. Sully presumably painted the portrait for a specific client, John R. Murray, but possibly also for his own pleasure, or interest in understanding the subject, or even as a speculation. A portrait of a literary figure was rare for him. More than almost any other kind of sitter, a major poet offers complex psychological and artistic challenges. A poetic gift, a myriad being, cultural and historical records, the workings of the mind itself: all are involved. To think through so multifaceted a subject as Byron took time. Perhaps that is the simplest explanation for the two years and the exceptional effort. "For a painting to say something he held to be true," writes Susan Vreeland of Vermeer, "it took rumination, sometimes months of apparent inactivity."[28] The same may hold true of Sully's work on *Byron.*

*

"So few people look like themselves," lamented Beerbohm.[29] He was right. We don't look like ourselves, or perhaps we don't like looking at the selves we see. Subjects are not always the best judges of their portraits. Madame Récamier preferred Gérard's sentimental depiction of her as a coy beauty to David's more penetrating, psychologically arresting rendering. It is the David, not the Gérard (in the Musée Carnavalet), that hangs today in the Louvre. In another sense, Beerbohm is saying that portraits are artful fictions. Flattery in portraiture goes back at least as far as the Greeks. Where flattery often has a negative aura, idealizing tends to be regarded more positively. The concept of Ideal Forms was expounded by Plato and developed by Plotinus. It entered Western thinking about art through such Renaissance humanists as Ficino. People in the nineteenth century still expected an Ideal Form, that portraits portray them not as they were but as they should be. The hope for a Platonic "Ideal Form" in portraits is not extinct, nor probably ever will be.

What did people in the past look like? Is it even possible to ascertain whether a portrait flatters or not? Photographs (after 1839) tell us something but have limitations and also, deliberately or not, distort. The traditional English assumption, Andrew Wilton suggests, is that "portraiture should flatter only within the bounds suggested by common sense."[30] This holds true up to a point. Flattery came (and comes) in kinds and degrees. Reynolds, in telling portraitists to reveal general traits about human nature, defined the practice of a generation. Before photography "conditioned" our eyes to look at people through an apparently more objective perspective, the *Discourses* shaped the taste of portraitists. But though constrained by artistic decorum, Reynolds too had an interest in personality.[31] He believed a good likeness should capture physical appearance but also convey something of being and mind. Lawrence a few months before he died recalled the passage in the *Poetics* where Aristotle admonishes poets to imitate a good portrait painter: preserve the resemblance but keep the face beautiful.[32] Leslie admired Lawrence's skill in improving his subjects' "expression."[33] "The image he wanted to create," wrote a contemporary of Lawrence, was "something beyond mere likeness." He wished to show "the mind's construction in the face": "to leave the canvas permanently reverberating under the impact of a vitality not natural but artistic."[34] This is close to what Gombrich believes a great portraitist can give us: "the illusion of seeing the face behind the mask."[35]

Federal and Regency artists incorporated in their portraits their subjects' achievement or political or social status. They were expected to present a favorable image of an individual's life or character. Making people attractive may not make them more interesting, but it suggests that they are worth looking at and thinking about. Furthermore, distinguished sitters could be easily offended. Even Sargent, whom no one would accuse of objective realism, once said that every time he painted a portrait he lost a friend. Clients still usually expect artists to modify, refine, enhance what they see. They are not beyond endeavoring to look more handsome than they are. For Sully as for Lawrence portraiture was a fusion of real and ideal.

Byron thought much about flattery in portraiture. Lawrence's flattering tendency gave him pause. "Lawrence," he commented in *Hints from Horace*, was "skilled to grace / His classic canvass with each flatter'd face." That Benjamin West enhanced his subjects lessened his appeal to Byron. Upon hearing that West had urged the British Museum to acquire the Elgin Marbles, Byron, who thought they should never have left Greece, guyed "flattering, feeble dotard West, / Europe's worst dauber, and poor Britain's best."[36] Such comments may have arisen from Byron's sense of the futility of ever achieving truthful representation. His own portraits, he avowed in November 1813, "are, of course, more agreeable than nature."[37] He accepted flattery as part of portrait painting and when he was the sitter was not averse to it, but the idea left him deeply uncomfortable. Early in *Don Juan* he worried about "the end of fame," which was "to have, when the original is dust, / A name, a wretched picture, and worst bust."[38] The issues Byron raises here are worth pausing over. Flattery by a skilled artist may well distort the "truth" of appearance, but an ugly image by an unskilled or maliciously inclined artist is truly reprehensible. Byron had cause for worry. The wretched pictures done of him were many.

Not all artists felt as positively about flattery as did Lawrence. In contrast to Lawrentian enhancements, Gilbert Stuart professed to insist upon strict accuracy. Irked by the assumption of his English sitters that he would flatter them, Stuart claimed he painted them in his own way and "from [his] own vision and conception." Thus, observes Evans, he "incurred criticism fairly consistently for adhering too closely to what he saw."[39] Sully, more accommodating by nature than Stuart, admitted he flattered his subjects. In *Hints to Young Painters* he explained his perspective: "In speaking of likeness in portrait-painting, [Sir David] Wilkie once said to me that 'it was well to increase the beauty of the complexion and give the appearance of youth, as this in a measure compensates for the want of life and motion.'"[40]

The Reynoldsian tradition changed during Sully's lifetime. Lavaterian physiognomy reinterpreted the human face. Interest in personality grew. Lawrence responded to Lavater, grasped the new interest in personality, relished the development of a romanticized realism. Though Sully cited Wilkie (he could have cited Lawrence) to justify his own practice, he also believed in the need for flattery: "From long experience I know that resemblance in a portrait is essential; but no fault will be found with the artist, (at least by the sitter,) if he improve the appearance."[41] Trained in the English tradition exemplified by Reynolds, but Lawrence's younger contemporary and like him a good Aristotelian, Sully revealed his sitters not only as they were but as they might be. He never ceased to admire Reynoldsian precepts. In *Byron* did he generalize the individual into "the poet," the icon of freedom? – or attempt only a good likeness? On balance, it seems he did both. Well aware of Byronic *mobilité*, he also attempted what (in Gombrich's words) a proper portraitist should strive for: "the illusion of seeing the face behind the mask."

*

Every artist in Sully's day copied paintings, his own and those of others. Artists then did not accept the primacy of the original, nor consider replicas and variants inferior or lesser works. Jefferson, like other collectors of the time, filled Monticello with copies of Old Masters. "Portraiture," as Marcia Pointon has observed, "was the one genre in which copies increased rather than diminished the standing of the original."[42] If the artist painted a notable individual like Washington, he might (as Stuart did) anticipate the need to multiply the image and retain by him the "original" portrait. Or he might borrow back a portrait for the same purpose. Sully happily did multiple versions of several presidents, sometimes from his own "original," sometimes from that of others.

The practice of copying bothered no one. Copying was one way every portraitist made his living. An individual wished a copy or copies for friends or family, or was deceased and family members wished a memento. So the artist painted a copy from someone else's painting, or from an engraving or (after 1839) a daguerreotype or photograph, or tried to create a resemblance from descriptions by family members. Copying poses challenges of its own. A copy inevitably differs from the original. It may also reveal marks of the copyist's own painting style. There were copies intended as faithful renderings of originals and imitations based on originals. Had not Reynolds in his *Discourses* defended imitation that drew upon the works of others as a good thing and approved "the borrowing of a particular thought, an action, attitude, or figure, and transporting it into your own work."[43] Such imitation Reynolds regarded as "a perpetual exercise of the mind, a continual invention." It had nothing to do with "the servility of plagiarism." Michelangelo was "always imitating, and always original," Reynolds claimed, and "having taken so many models, . . . became himself a model for all succeeding painters." Coleridge explains why few people confuse a copy with an imitation: "an *Imitation* differs from a Copy in this, that it of necessity implies & demands *difference* – whereas a Copy aims at *identity*." Or as Carl Woodring phrases it: "a copy has sameness; an imitation has sameness with difference."[44]

In earlier eras portraits from life were not common. Often subjects lacked the time, or inclination, to give sittings. Gros, having encountered in 1797 young General Bonaparte in Milan, had – thanks to Josephine's beguilements – been allowed for an enchanting morning, possibly several, to paint him from life, full of Romantic fire and ardor. Virtually every representation of Napoleon subsequent to Gros's sketch is an artistic fabrication. Louis David did not get even a sitting. His physiognomical sketch of the hero of Italy, of 1797–98 and famously incomplete, was for a historical composition never executed, representing the conqueror holding the peace treaty with Austria. For *Napoleon Crossing the Alps* (1801), indeed for every subsequent portrait he did of Napoleon, the emperor refused David sittings. He told David to paint him in ideal fashion. "No one asks whether the portraits of great men are good resemblances," Napoleon claimed. "It is enough that their genius lives in them."[45] David did as he was told. Napoleon also refused Ingres sittings for his *Napoleon as First Consul* (1804). Ingres apparently caught only one brief glimpse of Napoleon, caught perhaps no glimpse at all. Like other artists who depicted Napoleon, he based his portrait on what his predecessors had done. Whatever their limitations, works by David and his contemporaries are what we have. Iconographic tradition has conditioned us to expect Napoleon to look like them. We "know" Napoleon from them. They have made him what he has become for us and history. The process continues to this day. For Tony Scherman, a modern portraitist fascinated by Napoleon, the artist is like a forensic pathologist: he must reconstruct a human being "through clues after the fact."[46]

Napoleon is not the only individual whose historical image is based chiefly on portraits made up from the works of others. Composite portraits are more common than we may suppose. Holbein's depiction of Erasmus, another composite, has always been much admired.[47] Lawrence's portrait of the younger Pitt is even more contrived than David's *Napoleon Crossing the Alps*. It was, Douglas Goldring tells us, "not painted from life, but partly from a bust chiselled by Nollekens from a post-mortem cast, and partly from a portrait by Hoppner." Such secondhand sources did not prevent Lawrence from creating "a remarkable *tour de force*" much admired by contemporary critics.[48] A generation earlier, Charles Willson Peale, unable to obtain sittings from the elder Pitt, carefully copied his likeness from a sculptured life bust by Wilton. Gérard's portrait of Madame de Staël as Corinne done in 1819, two years after her death, is considered an authentic image and graces many a dustjacket. Half a century later, Ford Maddox Brown based his *Shakespeare* on three portraits he believed authentic.[49]

Take the greatest of American icons, Washington himself. Gilbert Stuart returned to America in 1793 because he wanted to paint the definitive *Washington*. Not only would it guarantee him lasting fame but replicas and engravings would bring him a steady income. After gaining a sitting from Washington in late 1795, he produced a bust portrait known as the "Vaughan" type. He followed it with the full-length Grand Manner "Lansdowne" *Washington*, its majestic pose borrowed from Hyacinthe Rigaud's *Louis XIV*. This is the painting that the current Marquess of Lansdowne sold to the Smithsonian in 2001 for $20 million. The last and perhaps most famous of Stuart's *Washingtons* is the incomplete "Athenaeum" version. These three portraits are all deemed "originals," yet Stuart created the much-revered Vaughan portrait after only one sitting "and yet not from life." Failing to obtain additional sittings, he drew upon his imaginative memory to complete it.[50] Stuart's three versions established the norm by which we still visualize the first president. His "plurality of portraits" in effect provides us with a plurality of Washingtons, but they are all based on that one sitting.[51] The Washington project was successful beyond Stuart's wildest hopes. The more than one hundred copies he made between 1796 and his death in 1828, usually of the "Athenaeum," kept him in funds during lean times – he often referred to them as his "hundred-dollar bills" – and led to commissions from the great of the land. Painting the first president became a business for Stuart as a few decades later it became one for Rembrandt Peale.

Rembrandt, aged 17, had painted the President from life in 1795. In the 1820s, feeling keenly that none of the existing portraits fully captured Washington the man, he decided to create a "Standard National Likeness" of him. He meant his to become the definitive image. By then Washington was dead over twenty years, so Rembrandt, to excite and resuscitate fading memory, sought out every representation of Washington he could come up with. Out of them he created in 1824, after three months' labor, his *Patriae Pater* or "Porthole" portrait (Figure 20).[52] Made up of components from his varied sources, including Stuart's versions, this large-scaled (62" x 54" – 157 cm x 137 cm) *Washington* shows the hero enclosed in a painted "porthole" composed of *trompe l'oeil* "stone" casements. Using Lavater's physiognomical conventions, conventions widely understood at the time to indicate specific character traits, Rembrandt attempted an actual physical recreation.[53] Contemporaries judged his *Washington* a superior likeness, for it brought together bits from many other works and seemed to transcribe his features faithfully. Neither a portrait from life nor a copy of one, Rembrandt's effort has been termed by a recent critic "a fanciful invention made up of separate parts."[54] True enough, but the public received the *Patriae Pater* enthusiastically, the lithographs Rembrandt had made of it sold well, and its popularity led Congress in 1832 to purchase it – for a resounding $2000 – for the US Capitol. Sully, a good businessman, no less talented than Stuart or Rembrandt Peale, must have been impressed.

Beginning in the 1840s, Rembrandt churned out possibly as many as a hundred smaller-scaled replicas of his "Porthole" *Washington*. He was but doing what his father, with 25 copies of his *Washington at Princeton*, or Stuart, with over 60 copies of his "Athenaeum" portrait of Washington, had done, very profitably, before him. For a while Rembrandt's "Porthole" portraits rivaled in popularity Stuart's "Athenaeum" or "Vaughan" versions. Although they have not replaced Stuart's *Washingtons* for posterity, they hang in museums. Many people gain from them their visual notion of the first US president.[55]

"Original," as Ludmilla Jordanova has observed, is a word in most cases best seen in inverted commas.[56] As Stuart's and Peale's *Washingtons* imply, it

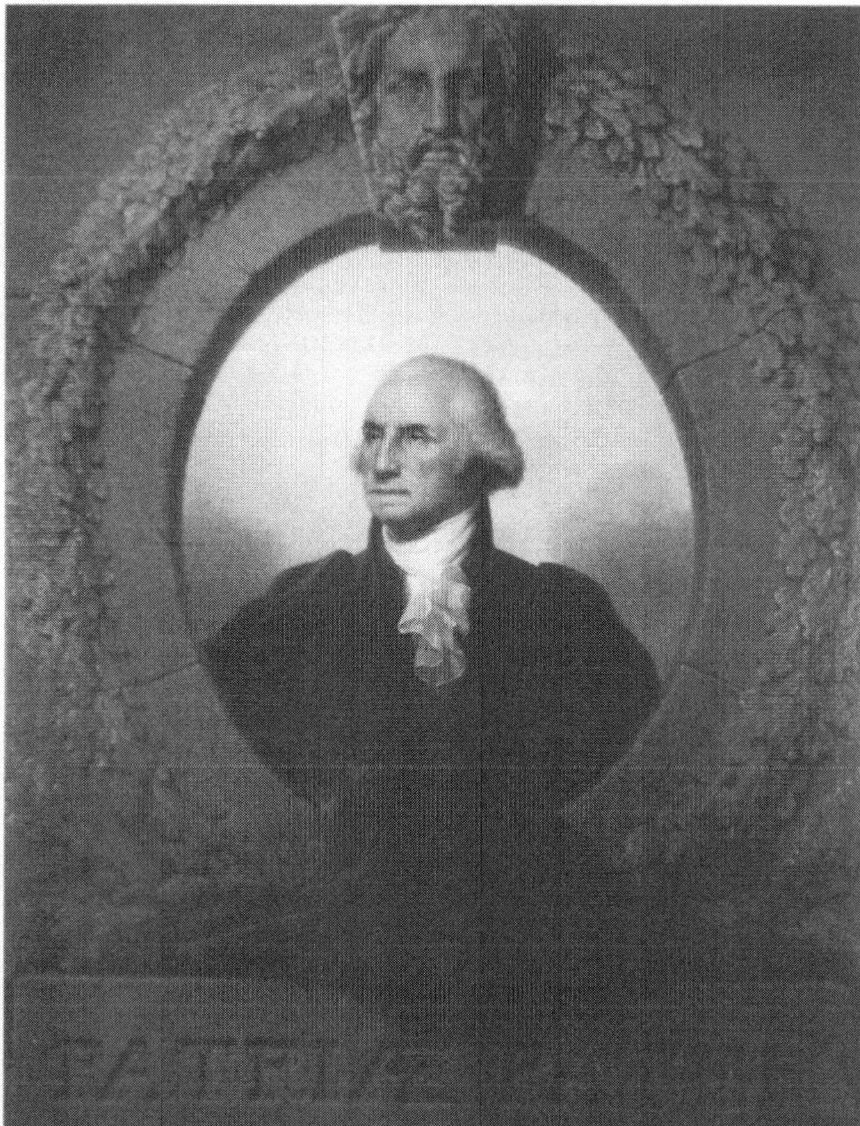

20 Rembrandt Peale, *Patriae Pater* (George Washington), 1824. United States Senate Collection, Washington, DC

can be extraordinarily difficult to tell (in Stuart's case) which of several works is *the* original or even (in Peale's) what the term means. Three centuries before, Titian had painted numerous portraits of the Holy Roman Emperor Charles V. The "original" he kept by him; the other versions copy its face. Contemporaries did not privilege that original; nor do later scholars. For certain historical personages – let us say, Jesus – the case is even more complex. No artist recorded his appearance, no chronicler described him in words, and we have thus no idea what he looked like. Innumerable artists have portrayed Jesus, but none from life. All re-creations stem from the artist's imagination or his awareness of tradition or from his reading of Jesus's character in the Gospels, which are themselves a pastiche.[57] Does it really matter when it comes to faith? We seem to know Jesus when we see him in paintings. In the world of spirit, of saints and their lives, of apparitions and miracles, portraits are less emblems of past reality than vehicles intended to carry the viewer to a higher realm of the spiritual, the enigmatic, the mystical, even the magical.

Leutze's *Washington Crossing the Delaware*, the most famous of American history paintings (and one considered in Chapter 5), is itself a copy of an earlier version destroyed in Bremen during the Second World War.[58] Are we overly bothered that Leutze modeled the figure of Washington on his friend Worthington Whittredge, that he painted it in Düsseldorf, that the river Washington crosses is the Rhine not the Delaware? Do we much care whether Shakespeare based his characters on "originals"? – which for some of them he did. (For example, some scholars think that for Shylock Shakespeare drew upon Elizabeth I's Jewish physician, Dr Lopez.) We ask rather, as with the figures in Leutze's painting, what life they have in them. Theater is artifice, and we accept that; but portraiture is also artifice. We should not ask for consistency. *Mont Sainte-Victoire*, painted by Renoir or Cézanne, could be two different places. Even when Cézanne painted Mont Sainte-Victoire, as he did many times, we find wide discrepancy of interpretation and representation.

Napoleon by David, the younger Pitt by Lawrence, the elder Pitt by the elder Peale, Charles V by Titian, Washington by Stuart and Rembrandt Peale and Leutze – these classic depictions did not benefit from numerous sittings from life, but the artists in question had all mastered the art of portraiture. Whether they had studied their subjects or glimpsed them or, as was sometimes the case, not seen them at all, they had thought hard about human physiognomy. Possessed of exceptional technical abilities and perceptual gifts, they bequeathed to posterity lasting insights into their subjects' inner beings.

Like other portrait painters, Sully copied his own paintings. He also copied works by other painters; other painters copied him. Copying others confers benefits. The artist learns the style and the technique of the artist copied. Copying teaches discipline. "The first picture I ever attempted in oil," Sully recalled in 1836, was "a copy of Angelica Kauffmann."[59] This was in 1802. Born in 1783, the year the Treaty of Ghent ended the American Revolution, Sully missed out on the initial portrait commissions of the nation's heroes and first statesmen that fell to the Peales, Stuart, and Trumbull. To fill an almost unceasing demand for portraits of the great, Washington foremost, Sully made, in all, 21 copies of portraits by Stuart and others of the first president. Copies are rarely mistaken for originals, and few would confuse a Sully copy of Washington with a Stuart original.

Sully copied paintings all his life: by Stubbs, of horses fighting; by Hoppner of Sarah Franke Bache (one copy in 1834, another in 1865); the Chandos Shakespeare (twice, in 1864 and 1865, both from an engraving); a "historic group" by Westall done in February 1808, and the same artist's *The Girl at the Well*, done the year Sully completed *Byron*.[60] Just before embarking on *Byron* Sully copied or created, from an unknown source or sources, a bust-sized *Napoleon* for William Alston of Georgetown, South Carolina. He copied twice removed: a portrait of Benjamin West, after Leslie's copy of Lawrence's portrait.[61]

Sully must have liked copying Lawrence. In 1810 Lawrence painted the portrait of Philadelphian John Hare Powel, Nicholas Biddle's chief local rival in good looks. Sully copied it in 1827, about the time he took on Byron and Biddle. Robert Gilmor, Jr, the Baltimore art patron, had with his wife sat for Lawrence in London in 1818. Impressed by Sully's interpretation of the Lawrentian style, Gilmor asked Sully in 1823 for two copies of his portrait by Lawrence. Sully even copied in 1830–31 a self-portrait by Lawrence.

For Sully, Lawrence was in his own league. No contemporary portraitist equaled him, and few in the past had surpassed him. Though Sully knew Lawrence's work intimately and in his own art retained it as a vital presence, he did not shy away from criticizing it. He introduced his students, Leslie and Audubon, to Lawrence; he cited him in his writings by precept and example; he followed the evolution of Lawrence's art through engravings. By the mid-1810s he had achieved imposing success in America working in the Lawrentian style. The most talented artist ever to paint Byron, Sully stands closer to the English master than to the "elegant mannerist" Westall, the academician Phillips, the romantic Sanders, the miniaturist Holmes, even the talented Harlow. Cosmopolitan and sophisticated, Sully became a master in his own right. It is an irreparable loss that we do not have a *Byron* from Lawrence. It is a great consolation that we do have one from Sully.

*

Ad vivam ("from life") portraits are sometimes preferred over others on the grounds that, more than other kinds, they give us a more accurate visual representation of the sitter. But do they? Sometimes they do; often they don't. Ideally, the best portraits from life, Goya's for example, draw powerfully upon the artist's skill and imagination. Contemporaries found them remarkable not only for their (often unflattering) accuracy of representation but also because they gave a compelling illusion of life.

No one will deny that portraits from life have a special value, but the authority they have they may possess more by default of other and better portraits than from intrinsic merit. Many famous portraits in Western art are not *ad vivam*, but copies by the artist of an earlier work with or without the "original" as *aide-mémoire*, copies by others, fanciful recreations like Rembrandt Peale's of Washington, or even totally original creations. A striking portrait by a greater artist may well present to posterity a more convincing image – and constitute a finer achievement – than a less successful *ad vivam* rendering. The presence of the sitter counts for much, but the genius of the portraitist counts for still more. Portraiture is at heart a grand fiction, and as in literary fiction we usually learn best and most from the exceptionally gifted and skilled, those who used their abilities to penetrate to the essence of their subject.

Artists are now creating portraits of Byron about as frequently as when the poet was alive. *Touched with Fire* (1993), Kay Redfield Jamison's study of manic-depressive illness, features Byron as one of its star exhibits. For the dustjacket Jamison commissioned a new portrait of the poet from Alan Moreau, who based it loosely on Westall and on Harlow's elegant drawing of 1815. Peter Graham, for his Twayne study *Lord Byron* (1998), drew upon a double portrait by Joni Pienkowski, "Byron East and West" ("West" draws mostly on Phillips, "East" on Pienkowski). The dustjacket of *Byromania* (1999), a volume of essays edited by Frances Wilson, juxtaposes Phillips's Albanian *Byron* with a still of Hugh Grant as Byron from the film *Rowing in the Wind*. The implication is that both images have equal authority, one for Byron's time, one for ours. We take our pick, and choose either or neither – or both. Most exotic of the recent portraits may be that reproduced on the cover of *The Newstead Byron Society Review* for January 2001 by the visionary Georgian artist Rusudan Petviashvili. Perhaps we should allow individuals to decide how Byron should look and let them choose (or paint) their own portrait of him. The individual on the cover of Jerome McGann's collection of essays, *Byron and Romanticism*, was once thought to be a portrait of Byron by Géricault, but it has long been known (as McGann is well aware) to be neither.[62] It may strike some, however, as looking somewhat like a seriously contemplative Professor McGann.[63]

New attempts to render Byron in visual terms appear at about the same frequency as new biographies. As with the biographies, so with the portraits: we can even argue (as Tony Scherman has for Napoleon) that only after death can we truly know the essence of a human being, only then make sense of what has been left behind. Visual recreations of an esteemed individual vie with (and complement) literary, and we may need new portraits as much as new books. Once we have no more of either, the individual fades away in cultural memory. For me, Antoine Bourdelle's sculptures capture Beethoven's visual presence better than any life portrait. Bourdelle fixated on the image of Beethoven for over forty years. From *Beethoven aux grands cheveux* (1889–91) to *Beethoven, dit La Pathétique* (1929), he pondered the composer in various media, chiefly in over two dozen sculptures that interpret different facets of Beethoven's being and genius (Figure 21). Leo Schrade suggests why these sculptures rivet us: "Bourdelle over and over again tries to get hold of and shape the face of the composer, but he never accomplishes this face 'definitely,' once for all. Each attempt shows a new secret, a new face of Beethoven."[64]

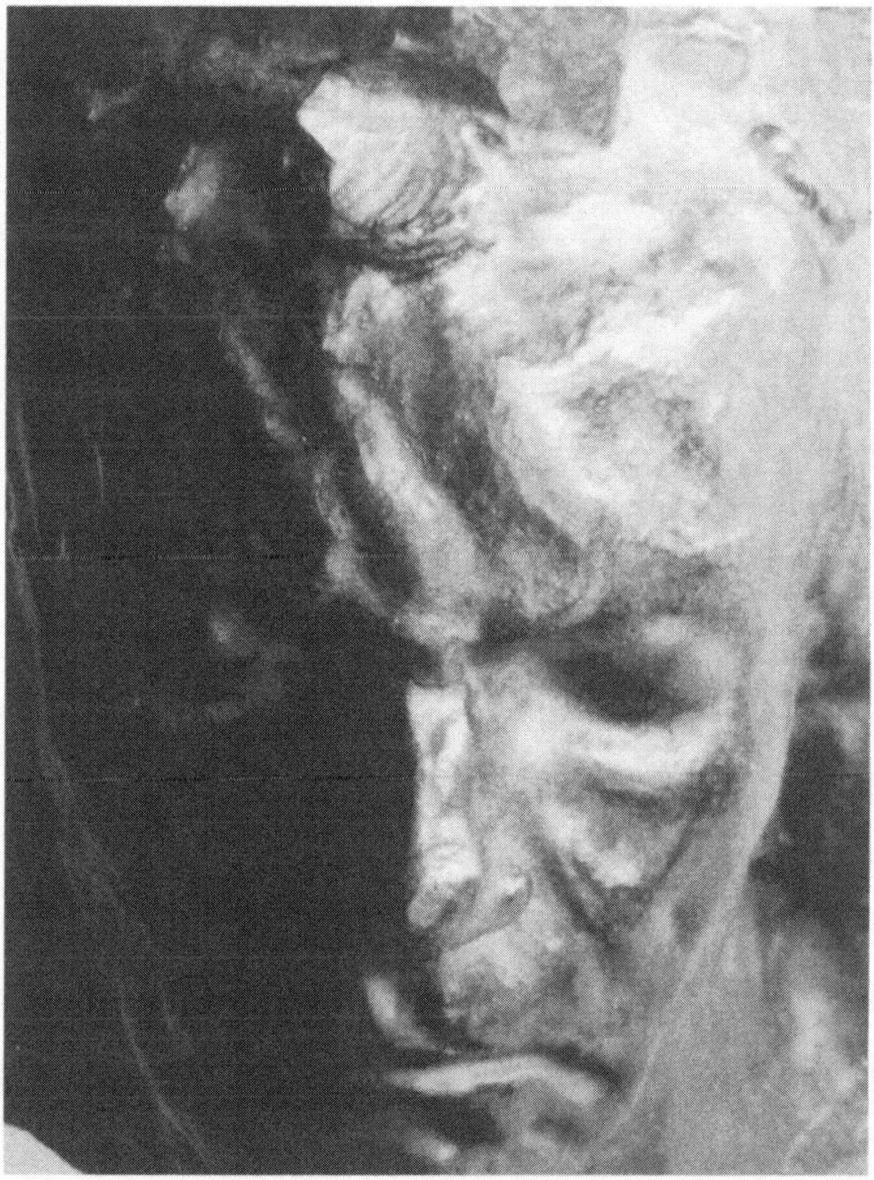

21 Antoine Bourdelle, *Beethoven dit Métropolitain*, 1891–1902. The Metropolitan Museum of Art, New York

The most convincing modern visual interpretation of Beethoven I know is a portrait by a young Santa Fe artist, Richard Potter (Figure 22). Like Sully with Byron, Potter draws upon varied sources – chiefly the 1812 life mask by Franz Klein and Joseph Karl Stieler's *ad vivam* portrait of 1819 – and like Sully he transformed them into something rich and rare. Potter's vibrant palette suggests Goya and Van Gogh; his dramatic brushwork, Kirchner and the German Expressionists. He realizes *Beethoven* in the anguish and ecstasy of composition. The magnificent head overflows the canvas: it is as if Dr Gachet had risen from the ashes of the *Disasters of War*. Potter's tortured but transcendent *Beethoven* glows with the energy – and ravages – of creation.

No more than painters are writers deterred from trying to recapture a being or an event. But word portraits, like brush portraits, pose challenges of their own. How to recreate a historical event as it happened? Like an able portraitist, a novelist of imagination and genius can make a person or an era come alive. Tolstoy did not know Napoleon or live through the Napoleonic era, yet *War and Peace* brilliantly recreates the emperor and his disastrous Russian campaign. Paul Britten Austin, drawing upon accounts by French survivors of 1812, has more recently recreated that campaign in a trilogy entitled *1812*.[65] Whereas Austin's survivors experience in gory detail the grisly horror below, Tolstoy's fictional narrative floats above the armies like a cloud. To which narrative do we give our credence? Either or both? The near-impossibility of putting Napoleon or his Russian campaign into words deterred neither Tolstoy nor Austin. It seems a safe bet, however, that *War and Peace* will last longer than *1812*. Yet words can deceive as well as illuminate, and perhaps we should evaluate portrait painters by criteria similar to those we use for historical novels. We like to think a portrait's rendering of character offers a reasonably truthful evocation of the subject, but in practice the question of authenticity is deeply problematic. Ingres's imaginary *Napoleon* – is it less worthy of attention (or useful to the historian) than an *ad vivam* portrait?

Byron in maturity preferred that artists portray the left side of his face. We rarely see the right side and almost never the face (and nose) head on. He was, in his portrait preferences, unique among the Romantics, but the notion of staged portraits, manipulated by the sitter, had a long history before Byron. Like Napoleon, Queen Elizabeth I is known to have sat for only a single portrait. She did not wish artists to paint her in ways that revealed her age, so an "authentic" contemporary portrait of her had to be a deceptive concoction, literally a "counterfeit" – to borrow the Elizabethan term for a portrait. The "Elizabeth" contemporaries saw in these images concealed more than revealed "truth."[66]

Basic questions keep rising up before us. What gives a likeness validity as a historical document? What are the visual conventions deployed by the artist? the desires of the sitter? How do they mesh? Can one define exactly where likeness ends and convention begins? Is not interpretative skill in a portrait more important than an attempt at physical accuracy? To convince, does not a portrait require active engagement on the part of the viewer, maybe even a willing suspension of disbelief? If we give that engagement,

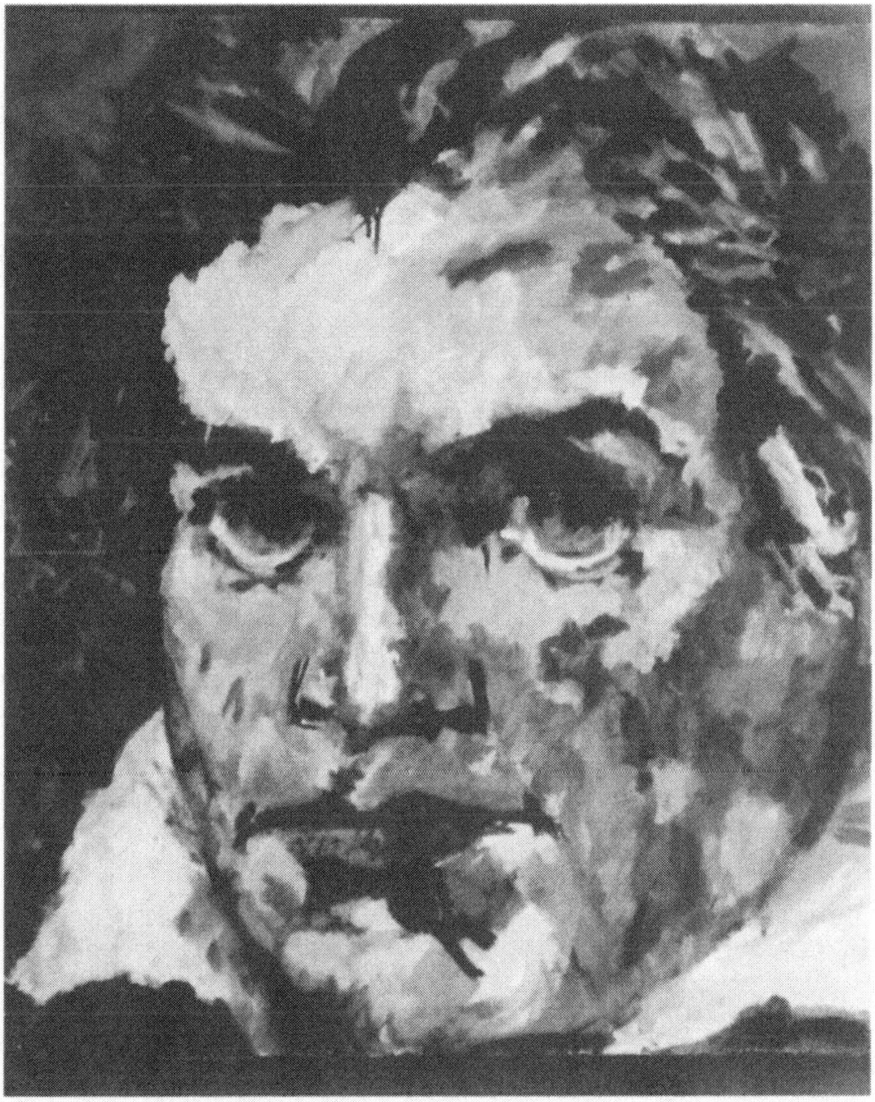

22 Richard Potter, *Beethoven*, *c.*1985. Private Collection, USA.

does the portrait deserve it?[67] Sully, a thoughtful man, a lifelong student of the human countenance, pondered such questions. He concluded, wisely, "It is not exactness of design in portraits that gives spirit and true air, so much as the agreement of parts at the very moment when the disposition and temperament of the sitter are to be hit off – it should strike us at first sight as true in likeness of character."[68]

*

Contemporaries often confused Byron the man with Byron the poet, a confusion Byron delighted in and helped perpetuate. Descriptions by diverse observers suggest that his appearance often dazzled them. That he incarnated mobility everyone agrees, but not everyone saw him as the sun incarnate, as did Coleridge, or as an alabaster vase lit from within. Which leads us to ask, to what degree does Sully's *Byron* render Byron? Can a portrait by a man who never saw Byron, one which draws its contours from engravings of another man's painting, lay claim to verisimilitude? The question raises issues both obvious and complex.

Take, yet once again, the color of Byron's eyes. What might seem a straightforward matter, easy to resolve, turns out to be exceedingly problematical. Reading Moore can be frustrating. He recalled an occasion when Byron abruptly turned and fixed upon him, for an instant, an angry look. He remembered Byron's eyes as "capable of all extremes of expression" and cited a line from Chatterton that "says that 'fire rolled at the bottom of them.'"[69] Byron, we presume, rolled his eyes expressively. But Moore looks at them through the eyes of Chatterton (who never saw Byron), not his own. He does not tell us what color Byron's were.

Regarding color, where we might expect some kind of agreement, we find instead confusion. Phillips painted Byron's eyes light blue, William Edward West, medium blue; James Hamilton Browne recalled them as dark blue; William A. Shaw, author of two articles on Byron's portraits, as "gray blue."[70] Moore remembered them elsewhere as "light gray," Ticknor as "light, and not black," Lady Blessington as "grey," Captain Forrester as "somewhat between a light blue and grey."[71] But we are not done. Richard Westall, who presumably had his chance to look hard at Byron, painted them brown.[72] All shades of blue and gray, sometimes in combination, even brown – how to explain such divergence?

Color can vary for different individuals and in different lights. Sometimes even the same artist or observer does not achieve consistency. The changing nature of color and expression in Wordsworth's eyes fascinated De Quincey.[73] In the cloaked portrait Phillips rendered Byron's eyes blue; in the Albanian dress, blue/gray.[74] I judge that William Edward West in his *Byron* painted Byron's eyes medium blue, but West *describes* them as "light blue, or grey." Another observer finds them "dark greenish blue-grey."[75] One begins to wonder about *ad vivam* descriptions and portraits. It is possible, admittedly, to imagine moments and lights in which blue might appear gray, and gray, blue. But Westall's brown? – that seems a stretch. Did the Coleridgean light emanating from Byron's orbs so dazzle contemporaries that they forgot to note their color?

With individuals of genius alive in Romanticism's great age, eyes apparently were perceived to change hues as emotions or physical state changed. In addition to Byron's, the eye colors of Coleridge and Wordsworth, Beethoven and Napoleon remain controversial. *Ad vivam* portraits, which should help here, muddle as often as they clarify. More than a dozen painters, notes Paley, failed to produce a clear consciousness of the color of Coleridge's famously expressive eyes, depicting them "blue, grey, hazel or brown."[76] De Quincey believed Wordsworth's eyes "varied exceedingly with the state of the stomach."[77] Beethoven's portraitists usually painted his eyes brown, even black, but one has them blue.[78] Napoleon's render his eyes variously, usually blue or gray, or a blend of the two, but no shortage of dark-eyed Napoleons exists. Even if color is determined, there can be other uncertainties. The exact shade of Hawthorne's eyes, admittedly gray, "has been remarkably elusive; they appear to be light gray in the Osgood [portrait], gray-green in the Thompson, dark gray in Healy's portrait, and blue-gray in Leutze's."[79]

The fullest and, I believe, most accurate contemporary physical description of Byron occurs late in Moore's classic life. By the end of volume 2 he is wrapping things up, and he stops to describe Byron as he looked during his years of fame in England, the time when Moore knew him best. Byron often described Moore as his closest friend, and of those who wrote about him Moore had probably the sharpest eyes and keenest mind. His discipline as a writer trained him to look at people closely. He describes Byron's appearance thus:

> His eyes [were] of a light gray. . . . But it was in the mouth and chin that the great beauty of his fine countenance lay. . . . His head was remarkably small. . . . The forehead was high, and appeared more so from his having his hair (to preserve it, as he said) shaved over his temples; while the glossy, dark brown curls, clustering over his head, gave the finish to its beauty. . . . [His] nose, though handsomely, was rather thickly shaped.[80]

If Sully had come upon Moore's account, he would have found his rendering of Byron startlingly confirmed. Always meticulous and careful, Sully caught the eyes of light color, the fine mouth and chin, the remarkably small head, the high forehead, the glossy and curly hair (Moore's "dark-brown" he renders more as other commentators describe it, auburn or burnt sienna). Upon the eye he used all his skill, and left its color for posterity to discern, possibly hazel, but more likely gray or gray-blue. One might note that Sully's own eyes were likewise of indeterminate color. Dunlap describes them as "grey, approaching to blue," and in self-portraits they sometimes appear blue, sometimes gray.[81]

Byron left the artist's hands in 1828 and, excepting a short stint in New York with John R. Murray, it soon returned to Philadelphia where it stayed with Sully's friends, first George Munday and then Jacob Eichholtz, until early 1832. The two volumes of Moore's biography of Byron came out at either end of 1830; an American edition was available by early 1831. The biography with its pen-portrait of the poet circulated widely in America, and Sully may well have read or dipped into it. It is possible, though not probable, that he borrowed his painting back from Eichholtz to bring Byron's features in line with Moore's description. Byron in later years,

Moore recalled elsewhere, had lost his earlier "refined and spiritualized look," but by technical skill, physiognomical study, and intuitive sympathy with his subject, Sully seized the earlier Byron's features unforgettably.[82]

*

Most portraits will have some truth. None can claim to be definitive. None necessarily excludes the others. We may not always know what we are looking for in a portrait of someone we care about, but when we see one not in sympathy with our conception of that individual we feel a loss. A good portrait makes the absent come to life, produces the impact of real presence. We hold in the mind's eye a composite image of Byron. This image is made up of how artists perceived him and how we imagine him. Built up over years through reading and thinking about Byron, our image is constantly tested against available portraits. The image changes as our conception of Byron changes, as time passes or knowledge increases. It is, to a degree, Byron as we might wish him to look or be. It may or may not resemble the historic Byron, but we like to think that it does.

I have set out to tell, within the available documentation, the story of one portrait. I have explored the genesis and history of Sully's *Byron*, placed it in the context of other artists' representations of the poet, and established its relationship to Sully's history paintings and theatrical portraits, of women as well as of men. Byron was and remains a literary figure of international stature, and he weaves in and out of this story as he did in Sully's life. I relate the portrait to its exact contemporary, that of Nicholas Biddle, and to the festivities surrounding America's Jubilee in 1826. The adulation the New World lavished upon Byron stemmed from his spectacular, controversial life, the excitement his poetry generated, and the shock Americans felt upon hearing of his death in Greece, a martyr for liberty. *Byron*, then, celebrates the English poet who meant most to Americans. Given Sully's study of portraiture in London and the informed awareness of Lavaterian physiognomy that shaped his sense of Byron's features, the portrait, inevitably, has a British and European context. What might seem initially like a relatively narrow subject – the story of Sully and his *Byron* – has, I hope, illuminated one much larger: it is how people respond to portraits, why they still move us intensely – in short, the power that portraiture exerts upon us.

Done in the succulent, rich, painterly style characteristic of his best work, Sully's *Byron* lets us divine, more than any other portrait, why Byron's face became Caroline Lamb's "*fate*," why Coleridge imagined he was looking at the sun, why Scott described Byron's countenance as "*a thing to dream of*," why Lockhart thought that none of Byron's famous contemporaries in England or Europe had a finer head than his. Lamb, Coleridge, Scott, and Lockhart imagined Byron less as a tangible being, captured in an immobile portrait, than in the mind's eye. Coleridge had tackled the issue with his usual perspicuity. A portrait reproduces one face but suggests another. "When you look upon a portrait," he wrote, "you must not compare it with the face when present, but with the recollection of the face." The portrait "refers not so much to the senses, as to the ideal sense of the friend not present."[83] So, in Coleridgean terms, stood Byron before his contemporaries: mocking their words and paint, near yet distant, ever-changing yet in their minds and memory the same, mobile yet refusing final definition.

Sully's *Byron* appears to be a work of astonishing verisimilitude. I say "appears," because verisimilitude in itself may be an illusion. Though we shall never know for sure what Byron looked like, some representations are more effective or valid than others. Sully's portrait is one such representation. Thanks to the artist's skill, the portrait gives us the illusion – and perhaps more than the illusion – that we have Byron as his gifted contemporaries visualized and understood him. For Sully he is Byron the Creator.

Quite wonderfully, Sully has captured the disturbing, mobile, and enigmatic being known as Byron. His *Byron*, though not *ad vivam*, may seize the poet's physical presence more faithfully than any representation that exists. But however well Sully's *Byron* corresponds to written descriptions by Moore and others, the case for its merit rests only in part on its resemblance, actual or assumed, to Byron. It rests even more on the artistic merit of the painting itself. Such was Sully's mastery of his art, he created an enduring image of the poet both as he presumably was and as others conceived him to be. Through an imaginative empathy, a conjuring magic, he felt his way into Byron's being to seize the essence of his appearance. Sully's portrait is, in Romantic terms, a work of beauty and vision as well as of verisimilitude. In looking at it we feel ourselves in the presence of the extraordinary human phenomenon that was Byron.

Abbreviations

Accardo (1998)	Accardo, Peter X. "Byron in America to 1830," *Harvard Library Bulletin*, N.S., 9.2 (Summer 1998): 5–60.
Accardo (1999)	Accardo, Peter X. "American Editions of Byron, 1811–1830." *Papers of the Bibliographical Society of America*, 93 (1999): 484–93.
Accardo (2001)	Accardo, Peter X. *Byron in Nineteenth-Century American Culture*. Byron Society of America and University of Delaware, 2001.
American Portraiture, ed. Quick	*American Portraiture in the Grand Manner: 1720–1920*, ed. Michael Quick. Los Angeles: Los Angeles County Museum of Art, 1981.
Barratt	Barratt, Carrie Rebora. *Queen Victoria and Thomas Sully*. Princeton, NJ: Princeton University Press/Metropolitan Museum of Art, 2000.
B & F	Edward Biddle and Mantle Fielding. *The Life and Works of Thomas Sully (1783–1872)*. Lancaster, PA: Wickersham Press, 1921.
Blessington	*Lady Blessington's Conversations of Lord Byron*, ed. Ernest J. Lovell, Jr. Princeton, NJ: Princeton University Press, 1969.
BLJ	*Byron's Letters and Journals*. 13 vols, ed. Leslie A. Marchand. London: John Murray, 1973–82, 1995.
Brilliant	Richard Brilliant, *Portraiture*.

	Cambridge, MA: Harvard University Press, 1991.
Bronson	Steven E. Bronson, "Thomas Sully: Style and Development in Masterworks of Portraiture 1783–1839." Ph.D. diss., University of Delaware, 1986.
Byromania	*Byromania. Portraits of the Artist in Nineteenth- and Twentieth-Century Culture*, ed. Frances Wilson. London: Macmillan, 1999.
Clubbe	John Clubbe, "Dramatic Hits. Napoleon and Shakespeare in Byron's 1813–1814 Journal." *British Romantics as Readers. Intertextualities, Maps of Misreading, Reinterpretations*, ed. Michael Gassenmeier, Petra Bridzun, Jens Martin Gurr, Frank Erik Pointer. Heidelberg: Universitäts Verlag C. Winter, 1998, pp. 271–94.
CPW	*Lord Byron. The Complete Poetical Works*. 7 vols, ed. Jerome J. McGann. Oxford: Clarendon Press, 1980–93.
Dunlap	William Dunlap, *A History of the Rise and Progress of the Arts of Design in the United States*, ed. Frank W. Bayley and Charles E. Goodspeed. 3 vols, Boston: C. E. Goodspeed & Co., 1918.
Fabian	Monroe H. Fabian, *Mr. Sully, Portrait Painter. The Works of Thomas Sully (1783–1872)*. Washington: Smithsonian Institution Press, 1983.
Furnas	Furnas, J. C. *Fanny Kemble. Leading Lady of the Nineteenth-Century Stage*. New York: Dial Press, 1982.

Garlick (1989)	Kenneth Garlick, *Sir Thomas Lawrence. A Complete Catalogue of the Oil Paintings*. Oxford: Phaidon, 1989.
Garlick (1992)	Kenneth Garlick, *Sir Thomas Lawrence. Portraits of an Age (1790–1830)*. Alexandria, VA: Art Services International, 1993.
Graham (1961a)	Graham, John. "Lavater's Physiognomy in England." *Journal of the History of Ideas*, 22 (Sept.–Dec., 1961): 561–72.
Graham (1961b)	Graham, John. "Lavater's *Physiognomy*: A Checklist." *Papers of the Bibliographical Society of America*, 55 (1961): 297–308.
Graham (1966)	Graham, John. "Character Description and Meaning in the Romantic Novel." *Studies in Romanticism*, 5 (1966): 208–18.
Hyman	Suzanne K. Hyman, "Contemporary Portraits of Byron," in *Lord Byron and His Contemporaries. Essays from the Sixth International Byron Seminar*, ed. Charles E. Robinson. East Brunswick, NJ: Associated University Press, 1982.
HSP	Historical Society of Pennsylvania
Lavater, *Essays* (abridged, 1800)	Lavater, Johann Caspar. *Essays on Physiognomy*, abridged from Mr Holcroft's translation. London: C. G. J. and J. Robinson (*c.* 1800).
Lavater, *Essays in Physiognomy* (1804)	Lavater, Johann Caspar. *Essays on Physiognomy*, trans. Thomas Holcroft. 2nd edn, 4 vols, London: H. D. Symonds et al., 1804.
Medwin	*Medwin's Conversations of Lord Byron*, ed. Ernest J. Lovell, Jr.

	Princeton, NJ: Princeton University Press, 1966.
MM	Metropolitan Museum
Moore	Thomas Moore, *Letters and Journals of Lord Byron: with Notices of His Life*, 2 vols. London: John Murray, 1830.
Moore, "Byronic Dress"	Doris Langley Moore, "Byronic Dress," *Costume*, 5 (1971), 1–13.
Neal	John Neal, *Observations on American Art. Selections from the Writings of John Neal (1793–1876)*, ed. Harold Edward Dickson. State College, PA: Pennsylvania State College, 1943.
NYHS	New York Historical Society
NYPL	New York Public Library
PAFA	Pennsylvania Academy of the Fine Arts
Peach	Annette Peach, *Portraits of Byron.* Reprinted from *The Walpole Society*, 62 (2000).
The Portrait, ed. Miles	*The Portrait in Eighteenth-Century America*, ed. Ellen G. Miles. Newark: University of Delaware Press, 1993.
Portrait Painting, ed. Miles	*Portrait Painting in America. The Nineteenth Century*, ed. Ellen Miles. New York: Universe Books, 1977.
Shortland	Shortland, Michael. "The Power of a Thousand Eyes: Johann Caspar Lavater's Science of Physiognomical Perception." *Criticism*, 28 (Fall 1986): 379–408.
Sully, *Hints*	Thomas Sully, *Hints to Young*

	Painters, intro. by Faber Birren. New York: Reinhold, 1965. Original edition 1873.
TLS	*Times Literary Supplement*
Tuckerman	Henry T. Tuckerman, *Book of the Artists*. New York: James F. Carr, 1966. Original edition 1867.
Walker	Richard Walker, *Regency Portraits*, 2 vols. London: National Portrait Gallery, 1985.

Notes

Preface

1. James, "John S. Sargent" (1887), reprinted in *The Painter's Eye*, ed. Sweeney, p. 227.
2. Keats apparently meant Cortez, not, as generations of literary scholars have surmised, Balboa. See Charles Rzepka, "Cortez – or Balboa, or Somebody like That: Form, Fact, and Forgetting in Keats's 'Chapman's Homer' Sonnet," *Keats–Shelley Journal*, LI (2002): 35–75.
3. The copy or copies Jacob Eichholtz made of Sully's *Byron* have not turned up (Beal, *Eichholtz*, p. 30).

Introduction

1. "The Prophetic Pictures," cited from *Nathaniel Hawthorne. Tales and Sketches* (New York: The Library of America, 1982), p. 461. Hawthorne rhetorically answers his own question: "It is the idea of duration – or earthly immortality – that gives such a mysterious interest to our own portraits."
2. Huizinga, *Dutch Civilization of the Seventeenth Century and Other Essays* (New York: Frederick Ungar, 1968), p. 269.
3. Browning, *Fra Lippo Lippi*, ll. 300–304.
4. Until the Catherine B. Reynolds Foundation purchased the portrait for the nation, few were aware that the "Lansdowne" *Washington*'s British owners had put it on long-term loan to the Smithsonian.
5. Peach in 2000 was the first art historian working on Byron to note the existence of a portrait of Byron "attributed to Thomas Sully" (pp. 41, 45).
6. Alberti, *On Painting*, cited from Verheyen, p. 131.
7. In *Art and History*, ed. Rotberg and Raab, p. 2.
8. Alma Lopez's computer portrait of the Virgin of Guadalupe in a flowered bikini, when it hung in Santa Fe's Museum of International Folk Art in 2001, caused virtually non-stop argument pro and con. Many denounced Lopez for interpreting a revered icon sacrilegiously; others supported the artist's right to express a personal vision.
9. "Introduction to a Beethoven Iconography," in H. C. Robbins Landon, *Beethoven. A Documentary Study* (New York: Macmillan, 1970) provides an overview.
10. Stauffer, "Beyond Bach the Monument, Who was Bach the Man?" *The New York Times*, April 2, 2000, AR, pp. 41, 42. Stauffer was reporting a major Bach conference in Kiev.
11. Cooper, *National Portrait Gallery*, pp. 26–7. The discovery in 2001 in Canada of a possible portrait of Shakespeare done in 1603 made national headlines. Of it, Verlyn Klinkenborg observed, "The resemblance we see in this portrait is not a resemblance to Shakespeare. It's a resemblance to what we would like to imagine that Shakespeare looked like" (*The New York Times*, May 27, 2001,

"Week in Review," p. 8). For the full story, see Stephanie Nolen, *Shakespeare's Face* (London: Piatkus, 2003). Though Nolen and her six scholarly collaborators prove that the portrait is undeniably of Shakespeare's era (and most of them would like to believe it authentic), they came up with no firm way to determine whether the portrait is of the Bard or of another man.

12. *Letters of Keats*, ed. Rollins, 1: 142.
13. Motion, *Keats*, pp. 168, 173, 174, 261. Keats also took trips with a small portrait of Shakespeare.
14. Cooper, *National Portrait Gallery*, pp. 67, 74.
15. Johnson, "Fair maid of Kent? The arguments for (and against) the Rice Portrait of Jane Austen," *Times Literary Supplement*, March 13, 1998, pp. 14–15.
16. Rebecca Mead, in *The New Yorker*, May 22, 2000, pp. 30–1.
17. Feigen, p. 192.
18. Stein, *The Autobiography of Alice B. Toklas* (1933; London: Penguin Books, 1966), p. 16; also pp. 51–3, 64.
19. Goldberg, '"A Physiognomic Reader,"' p. 14.
20. Hough, *Winston and Clementine*, pp. 494, 495.
21. Gilbert, '*Never Despair*,' pp. 1076, 1073, 1253.
22. Cited from Hough, p. 496; Soames, *Clementine Churchill*, p. 501.
23. Reproduced in John Hayes, *The Art of Graham Sutherland* (Oxford: Phaidon, 1980), plate 104 (p. 134). A photograph of the destroyed portrait appears on the next page. The only rival to Sutherland's portrait is Yousuf Karsh's famous 1941 photograph of a grimly smiling but appropriately bellicose Churchill. For further details, see John Richardson, *The Sorcerer's Apprentice* (New York: Knopf, 1999), pp. 165–7.
24. Cooper, *Letters and Journals*, ed. Beard (1960), 1: 95–6. See also Bush, *Life Portraits of Jefferson*, pp. 76–9.

Chapter One

1. *Tristram Shandy* (London and New York: Oxford University Press, 1983), p. 421. The hero, confronted by a French customs officer, responds thus.
2. Hart, *Register*, p. 38 (no. 254).
3. B & F, p. 114: item no. 262. I reverse their sequence of owners, arguing that Munday was the portrait's second owner, Eichholtz the third. For other early references to *Byron*, consult the notes in this chapter on Jacob Eichholtz.

   Sully describes *Byron* as a "bust," which indicates its size. Sizes were standardized, and a standard bust size was 20" x 24" (51 cm x 61 cm); a "half-length," 25" x 30" (63.5 cm x 76 cm). By these criteria *Byron* is a half-length; but Sully's "bust size" – differing from the contemporary norm – is 25" x 30". At 24¼" x 29" (61.6 cm x 73.6 cm) *Byron* is fractionally smaller. $50 was what Sully normally charged at this time for a "bust" portrait "without hands" (*Byron* has one hand sketched, the other implied). The sum is not necessarily the amount Sully received for the painting but rather the value he placed on it. In this case he may have received the sum indicated. Sully like Stuart usually made a preliminary colored sketch or a chalk study for a portrait, and some of these sketches survive, but *Byron*, not being an *ad vivam* portrait, may not have required a sketch.

   Many works Sully did not sign, including *Byron*. Signed works usually have a colophon "TS", sometimes "TSully" or "T. Sully." The signature, when it occurs, is followed by an inconspicuous date on the face of the canvas or on the back (B & F, p. 82; examples in Fabian, p. 122). Unsigned portraits were not unusual at this time. Stuart and Raeburn, for example, rarely signed or dated their pictures. Presumably Sully assumed that his signature lay in his distinctive style. Indeed, most Sullys – *Byron* is no exception – sign themselves.

Like many works in oil of its period, *Byron* displays occasional craquelure (irregular, hairline cracks, the result of age and brittleness), here noticeable on the face. Otherwise the painting is in excellent condition. Artists in Federal America had difficulty getting quality artists' supplies. Finely woven canvas was coveted but not always available. In order to achieve the smooth effect he preferred, Sully specially ordered his canvas from London. In 1827 he commented, "I find that the canvas I have lately prepared too coarse – I would much prefer [a] smooth surface to paint upon than so irregular a one" (Journal [NYPL], January 1, 1827). The next month he ordered new canvas from London. But he had already begun *Byron*, whose canvas is of relatively coarse weave. Coarse canvas was not limited to American artists. English portraits of the period – including a number of Raeburn's – are on no less coarsely woven canvas.

Frames often make a statement about the works they enclose. *Byron*'s appears original. The artist's longtime business partner, James S. Earle, or his son, James Jr, made frames for most Sully portraits. To keep up with developments in Europe, the carved and gilded rococo frames often seen before the Revolution – with their decorative motifs, scrollwork, and plant vegetation – yielded to the simpler neoclassical style in the Federal period, where frames were often black or of simple geometric design in gold. With its leaves and flowers, its fanciful curlicues and elaborate diamond cross-hatching, *Byron*'s frame harks back to an earlier time, perhaps that of sixteenth- and seventeenth-century Venice. An elaborate "Old Master" frame such as this one might cost the buyer as much as $40, a major portion of a painting's price (Fabian, pp. 20, 112). Sully later designed an ingeniously elaborate frame, full of symbolism, for his *Victoria*. The complex design of *Byron*'s suggests that he wished to set the poet within the tradition of Old Master portraiture. It suggests also that he thought his portrait an important work.

4. Journal (NYPL), Aug. 10, 1828, p. 62.
5. Sartain, *Reminiscences*, pp. 164–5; *Correspondence of Allston*, ed. Wright, p. 154. Sully's more precise measurements were "19 foot by 44 ft. 16 foot from floor to bottom of pitch" (Rebora, "Sir Thomas Lawrence," p. 46).
6. Later, James S. Earle & Sons and (in 1896) the Earles' Galleries (Fabian, p. 20; *Correspondence of Allston*, ed. Wright, p. 163; *Thomas Eakins and the Metropolitan Museum of Art*, p. 38).
7. Sartain, *Reminiscences*, pp. 163–5. Ward's painting was *Boa Serpent, Libya, Seizing his Prey* (1805).
8. Barrett, *The Old Merchants of New York City*, 1: 289.
9. Matson, *Merchants and Empire*, p. 305.
10. Barrett, *The Old Merchants*, 1: 294, 295. Trumbull, who knew the Murrays well, portrayed Murray in old age, hands clasped across ample girth (reproduction in *American Paintings in the MM*, 1: 221). He also painted Mrs John Murray (1746–1835), the former Hannah Lindley (reproduction, ibid., p. 222).
11. Murray took drawing lessons from a Scottish immigrant, Archibald Robertson

(1772–1841), who with his brother Alexander ran the Columbian Academy of Painting. Washington Allston and John Vanderlyn also studied there. Murray's sketch of New York Hospital, engraved by W. S. Leney in 1811, indicates talent (*American Paintings in the MM*, 1: 186). For an engraving of another drawing, *Lafayette Visiting Woodlawn Plantation* (1824–25), see Idzerda et al., *Lafayette, Hero*, p. 70.

12. Miller, *Patrons and Patriotism*, pp. 9, 275–6. Murray's "Travels in Europe" of 1799–1800 survives in manuscript in the NYHS.
13. *American Paintings in the MM*, 1: 186.
14. Miller, *Patrons and Patriotism*, pp. 92–3, 275, citing a letter from Vanderlyn to Murray, July 3, 1809. Napoleon, invited by Livingston to become the first Honorary Member of the fledgling American Academy, generously gave it books of drawings and 24 volumes of Piranesi prints.
15. Rebora, "Sir Thomas Lawrence," p. 20.
16. Cowdrey, *American Academy of Fine Arts*, 2: 264.
17. Paff's catalogue for 1812 lists Sully as one of three American artists (Goldstein, *Landscape with Figures*, p. 8). Knowing Paff long did not raise Sully's estimate of him. "Nothing could exceed the quackery of English picture dealers," the artist lamented in 1838, "unless it was M*r* Paff of New York" (Copybook 2, p. 82: Winterthur).
18. Miller, *Patrons and Patriotism*, p. 147.
19. Trollope, *Domestic Manners of the Americans*, p. 345. Toqueville blamed democracy for the low state of the fine arts in America (*Democracy in America*, ed. Phillips Bradley, 2 vols [New York: Knopf, 1963], 2: 50–51).
20. Miller, *Patrons and Patriotism*, p. 147.
21. *American Paintings in the MM*, 1: 186.
22. Foshay, *Mr. Luman Reed's Picture Gallery*, p. 17.
23. Dunlap 2: 162; but see Miller, *Patrons and Patriotism*, p. 276.
24. Munday-Edward S. Burd, March 13, 1836: HSP.
25. Munday-Henry M. Phillips, January 5, 1841: HSP.
26. Nov. 6, 1847, [p. 4] (copy in HSP); article reprinted from *The Pennsylvanian*.
27. "Obituary," February 9, 1865, possibly from the *Mercury* (written in ink on the printed clipping). The second obituary, according to identification on the clipping, derives from the [Philadelphia] *Bulletin*. Both obituaries are pasted into a pamphlet *Crazy Norah*, a brief disquisition on the life of Honora Power or Powers (1790–1865), another noted Philadelphia eccentric (copy in HSP). Munday was born in 1802 or 1803.
28. B & F say "1833" but 1831 makes more sense, being the year Eichholtz made a copy or copies of Sully's *Byron*.
29. Hensel, *Jacob Eichholtz, Painter. An Address*, pp. 48, 49.
30. Dunlap 2: 386; Dunlap, *Diary* 3: 704.
31. Dunlap 2: 386, 385. Brushes, canvas, and paints, all imported, cost more in the United States than in Europe and were not always available, even in Philadelphia.
32. Dunlap 2: 386.
33. Dunlap, *Diary* 2: 531; Dunlap 1: 328, 330.
34. Richardson, *Painting in America*, p. 124. A self-portrait in the Lancaster Historical Society reveals him blue-eyed, brown-haired, intense and earnest of gaze.
35. Dunlap 2: 386–387n.
36. Two letters, one from Eichholtz to Sully, January 19, 1817, and one from Sully to Eichholtz, November 4, 1832, indicate a long and cordial relationship (Beal,

Jacob Eichholtz, pp. 377, 379). Eichholtz covered many pages in his Commonplace Book "with summary sketches of how Thomas Sully posed the figures in his portraits" (p. xxiii).

37. Ibid., p. 30.
38. Eichholtz's presumed first attempt at portraiture, *c.* 1808, was inscribed on the reverse "Portrait of Lord Byron." It was given to the Lancaster Historical Society by Robert Lindsay, an Eichholtz descendant, in 1912. But Byron was hardly known at this time, and the resemblance appears tenuous to me.
39. Barker, *American Painting*, p. 274.
40. Saunders, in *The Portrait*, ed. Miles, p. 142.
41. Bernstein, *An Actor's Daughter*, p. 64.
42. *Velázquez in New York Museums*, p. 14.
43. Inness is already prominent, but Clarke also listed works by La Farge, Kensett, Gifford, Whittredge, and McEntee ("Private Art Collection of Thomas B. Clarke 1872–1879" [leather-bound volume, Winterthur]).
44. Strahan, alias Earl Shinn, *The Art Treasures of America*, lists representative works from Clarke's collection (2: 130–32).
45. Lynes, *The Art-Makers*, p. 404; Weinberg, "Thomas B. Clarke," p. 70; Gardner, *Homer*, p. 85.
46. Cikovsky, *George Inness*, p. 40.
47. Homer and Goodrich, *Albert Pinkham Ryder*, p. 89.
48. Ibid., pp. 36, 43, 68.
49. Bernstein, *An Actor's Daughter*, pp. 59ff. Aline Bernstein (1880–1955), *née* Frankau, lived at 217 W. 44th St; Clarke, at 203 W. 44th.
50. Ibid., p. 60.
51. Towner, *The Elegant Auctioneers*, pp. 46–7, 149.
52. Saarinen, *The Proud Possessors*, p. 257; Skalet, "Thomas B. Clarke," p. 6; Constable, *Art Collecting in the United States*, p. 142.
53. Homer and Goodrich, *Albert Pinkham Ryder*, p. 90.
54. *DAB*, "Cochran."
55. Torrey, "Philipse Manor Hall and the Cochran Art Collection," pp. 3–31.
56. Hansen, *North of Manhattan*, pp. 31–47, especially 43, 44.
57. Ibid., p. 41; Torrey, p. 20ff.
58. *Scenic and Historic America*, pp. 5–7; Torrey, p. 20; Hansen, pp. 41–2.
59. Danly, *Facing the Past*, p. 28.
60. Saunders, in *The Portrait*, ed. Miles, p. 140.
61. *Scenic and Historic America*, pp. 6–7.
62. E.g., Vose, "Boston's Vose Galleries," which conjectures that Hart "may have found an expensive lady friend" (p. 12).
63. Several of Eichholtz's other paintings entered the Lancaster Historical Society's collections about this time.
64. Scholars have questioned a number of Hart's attributions in his informal catalogue of Cochran's paintings. Hart emerges as an undercover dealer since 1875, one who "'primed the pump' for the colonial portraiture market beginning in the 1890s" (Saunders, in *The Portrait*, ed. Miles, pp. 144, 140). For Saunders the taint on Hart's integrity also rubs off on Clarke, another Janus-faced figure.
65. Heather Vaughan, curator at Philipse Manor Hall, found no documentation of *Byron*'s presence in the Collection. Many of these other works, however, *were* suitable for the Philipse Manor Hall collection of presidential portraits (still in existence and intermittently on display).

66. Bernstein, *An Actor's Daughter*, p. 68.
67. Towner, *The Elegant Auctioneers*, p. 151.
68. Winterthur holds a Union League Club scrapbook compiled by Clarke. Four portraits were by Sully.
69. *Portraits by Early American Artists*. Collected by Thomas B. Clarke. Fairmount: The Philadelphia Museum of Art, 1928.
70. Goldstein, *Landscape with Figures*, p. 172.
71. One individual who might have bought *Byron* but did not was Henry E. Huntington, the railroad magnate turned philanthropist. Huntington at this time was filling his newly established showpiece of British culture in San Marino, California, with eighteenth-century British (and a few American) portraits. In the early 1920s Huntington bought from Duveen Gainsborough's famous *Blue Boy*, widely touted in the press as the greatest picture in the world after the *Mona Lisa*. The Huntington Library owns a number of Byron manuscripts and rare editions, and Sully's *Byron* – a British poet painted by an American artist partially trained in London – combines in one artefact both British and American culture. But for Huntington "the important pictures in my collection are of the English School only" (Thorpe, *Huntington*, p. 440).
72. Mrs Arthur B. Meeker, pp. 41–46.
73. Meeker, *Chicago, With Love*, p. 70. The house stood at Barney Avenue and the Outer Drive.
74. Ibid., pp. 201, 204, 180, 204.
75. Gerdts, in *American Portraiture*, ed. Quick, pp. 73, 76; 206.
76. Meeker, *Chicago, With Love*, pp. 72–3.
77. Frank Bayley (1863–1932), whose less than exemplary career as an art dealer is chronicled by Saunders (in *The Portrait*, ed. Miles, especially pp. 146–50). Bayley shot himself in 1932.
78. See [Sully], *Memorial Exhibition of Portraits by Thomas Sully*.
79. Meeker, *Chicago, With Love*, pp. 244, 245–6; 248, 250–51.
80. Ibid., pp. 68–9, 114.
81. Ibid., pp. 121, 236. They lived there until 1936 (p. 80).
82. Ibid., pp. 267, 80–81.
83. Tuckerman, p. 72.
84. A faded label on the back of the frame attests to his possession. Slantwise across the label is written in pencil a name that appears to be "J. B. Foreman."
85. Butcher, *Many Lives – One Love*, p. 184.
86. Meeker, *Chicago, With Love*, pp. 281, 292.
87. Lot 6. Color reproduction p. 13.

Chapter Two

1. Praz, *House of Life*, pp. 146, 147.
2. Blessington, p. 72.
3. Kimmelman, *Portraits*, p. 171.
4. Trelawny, *Last Days*, ed. Morpurgo, p. 166.
5. Lockhart, *Memoirs of Scott*, p. 363. The French phrase is from Racine, *Phèdre* 1.3.
6. Lamb, *Glenarvon*, p. 120.
7. Piper, *Image of the Poet*, p. 132.
8. Coleridge, *Collected Letters*, ed. Griggs 4: 636, 641. Coleridge told Henry

Cary "that Byron's eyes were like the gates of heaven; they bewitched one in his favour" (Woof, *Romantic Icons*, p. xix, citing *Memoir of H. F. Cary* 2: 301). Coleridge may have had in mind the Apollo Belvedere.

9. *Quarterly Review*, 16 (1816): 177. Doris Langley Moore assumes the poet is Scott ("Byronic Dress," p. 6), as does Annette Peach. But Scott specifically says "a fellow poet," implying someone else, and Coleridge, whom Byron had just met, is the likeliest candidate.
10. Lockhart, *Memoirs of Scott*, p. 368.
11. Lockhart, *Peter's Letters to his Kinsfolk* 2: 338.
12. Moore 2: 255.
13. Trelawny, *Last Days*, ed. Morpurgo, p. 21.
14. Browne, "Voyage from Leghorn," p. 56.
15. Garlick (1989), p. 161, no. 150.
16. Williams, *Life of Lawrence* 3: 148, 69.
17. Garlick (1989), p. 161, citing J. Timbs, *Anecdotal Biography* (1860), p. 252. The sketch's present location is unknown.
18. *Sir Thomas Lawrence's Letter-Bag*, ed. Layard, p. 95. Layard believes this letter of "slightly later date" than the previous one of May 1, 1814. Differing versions appear in Williams, *Life of Lawrence* 3: 70–71, and Goldring, *Regency Portrait Painter* (1950), p. 264. Layard's version appears the most accurate.
19. Garlick (1993), p. 82.
20. Erica Da Costa, review of Roy Morris Jr, *The Better Angel. Walt Whitman in the Civil War*, in *The New York Times Sunday Book Section*, Sept. 17, 2000, p. 24.
21. Browne, "Voyage from Leghorn," p. 57.
22. Moore, "Byronic Dress," p. 13.
23. Piper, *The English Face*, p. 232.
24. *Thomas Lawrence's Letter-Bag*, ed. Layard, p. 94.
25. Sanders also painted miniatures of Byron in 1812 and 1814.
26. Piper, *Image of the Poet*, p. 127.
27. Bainbridge, in *Byron Journal*, pp. 13, 15, 16, 23. Peach suggests that the pose "is almost identical" to one adopted by Napoleon in a portrait by Gros (in *Lord Byron*, ed. Tessier, pp. 195–6). I find neither hypothesis convincing.
28. The National Portrait Gallery archive lists at least a dozen different copies of Phillips's cloaked portrait, several by Phillips himself (Walker 2: 81).
29. Redgrave and Redgrave, *A Century of British Painters*, p. 244.
30. Blanshard, *Portraits of Wordsworth*, p. 74.
31. Walker 1: 80. Woof notes that G. H. Harlow's portrait "has exactly that note of hauteur" (*Romantic Icons*, p. xix).
32. Broughton, *Recollections of a Long Life* 1: 98.
33. MS letter, n.d. [1815] (Murray collection), cited in Peach, p. 63.
34. Trans. James Anthony Froude and R. Dillon Boylan (New York: Ungar, 1962), p. 140 (Book II, ch. 2).
35. Hazlitt, *Complete Works*, ed. Howe, 18: 19.
36. Paley, *Portraits of Coleridge*, p. 7.
37. Peach, p. 61; Kenyon Jones, in *Byromania*, ed. Wilson, p. 130; Paley, *Portraits of Coleridge*, p. 7.
38. Byron praised Holmes in letters of 1821 and 1823 (*BLJ* 8: 95; 10: 176). Holmes's great admiration of Napoleon almost certainly influenced Byron's favorable impression.

39. Piper, *Image of the Poet*, p. 134.
40. John Walker, *Portraits*, p. 203.
41. Not everyone thought Byron beautiful. Perhaps reflecting his impressions of West's portrait, T. S. Eliot lamented "that pudgy face suggesting a tendency to corpulence, that weakly sensual mouth, that restless triviality of expression, and worst of all that blind look of the self-conscious beauty" ("Byron," in *On Poetry and Poets* [New York: Farrar, Straus, and Cudahy, 1957], pp. 224–5).
42. For detailed study of these portraits, see my articles in the *Byron Journal* of 1979 and 1980.
43. Murray–Byron, May 3, 1820, cited from MacCarthy, *Byron*, p. 352.
44. Wilson, Introduction to *Byromania*, ed. Wilson, p. 6.
45. Hyman, pp. 230–31; Kenyon Jones, in *Byromania*, pp. 128–9; MacCarthy, *Byron*, p. 237.
46. Blessington, p. 220.
47. *Correspondence de Stendhal (1800–1842)*, edited by Ad. Paupe and P.-A. Cheramy, 3 vols (Paris: Charles Bosse, 1908) 2: 13. Letter to Louis Crozet, Dec. 20, 1816.
48. Blessington, p. 72.
49. Walker 1: 82.
50. Richard J. Westall has attempted a modern revaluation ("The Westall Brothers").
51. Clarke and Penny, *The Arrogant Connoisseur*, pp. 11–12, 15. This book, along with Ballantyne's study, contains the fullest account of Knight's career.
52. Ibid., p. 16.
53. *BLJ* 3: 41. Marchand suggests Lady Oxford as "the friend" – and Peach agrees (p. 43); Walker thinks him Sir Francis Burdett (1: 82). The latter seems to me more likely. Another possibility for "the friend" is Richard Payne Knight, Westall's main patron, whom Byron also knew.
54. Farington, *Diary* 12: 4377. He is recording a dinner conversation on Sunday, June 20, 1813, at which Westall, his brother William, and J. Aytoun were present.
55. Westall's portrait, at 36½" x 28" (92.7 cm x 71 cm), is slightly larger than Sully's.
56. Piper, *Image of the Poet*, p. 133.
57. Reproduced in Westall, "The Westall Brothers," p. 24. Westall may have showed Lawrence his *Byron*, which remained in his possession from 1813 to about 1825.
58. Pevsner, "Richard Payne Knight," in *Studies in Art, Architecture, and Design* 1: 113.
59. Brewer, *Pleasures of the Imagination*, p. 265.
60. On Knight's infamous role in this controversy, see William St Clair, *Lord Elgin and the Marbles*, 3rd rev. ed (1967; Oxford and New York: Oxford University Press, 1998).
61. Clarke and Penny, *The Arrogant Connoisseur*, p. 107.
62. Ballantyne, *Architecture*, p. 172.
63. Ibid., p. 171.
64. Burke, *English Art, 1714–1800*, pp. 298–9; Ballantyne reproduces *Storm in a Harvest* under the more accurate title of *Harvesters in a Storm* (*Architecture*, p. 172).
65. Hazlitt, *Complete Works*, ed. Howe, 11: 144.
66. Ibid., 18: 79, 55, 152.
67. Ibid., 18: 29.

68. Ibid., 18:15. Hazlitt's remarks, for Ballantyne, are "fair-minded" (*Architecture*, p. 179).
69. Ibid., 18: 15, 152.
70. Ballantyne, *Architecture*, p. 173. Contemporaries gossiped about the sexuality of other artists who painted Byron, including G. H. Harlow, reputedly a cross-dresser, known to some as "Clarissa," and Lawrence, whose sexuality, despite his passion for successive female Siddons, appears to have been severely repressed.
71. Ballantyne, *Architecture*, pp. 307–8.
72. Watkin, *Thomas Hope*, pp. 43, 50, and plates 13 and 14; Clarke and Penny, *The Arrogant Connoisseur*, pp. 106–7.
73. Friedman, *Boydell's Shakespeare Gallery*, p. 3.
74. Altick, *The Shows of London*, p. 107.
75. Irwin, *English Neoclassical Art*, pp. 131–4.
76. *The Poetical Works of John Milton. With a Life of the Author by William Hayley*, 3 vols (London, 1794).
77. Pointon, *Milton in English Art*, p. 119.
78. Redgrave and Redgrave, *A Century of British Painters*, p. 187.
79. *New Monthly*, 2 (October 1814), 248.
80. "The Westall Brothers," p. 31; Haydon, *Diary*, ed. Pope, 1: 298 (week of March 3, 1813).
81. Redgrave and Redgrave, *A Century of British Painters*, p. 188.
82. Murray's four-volume edition was reissued in 1821 and 1823. I have used the 1823 edition.
83. Redgrave and Redgrave, *A Century of British Painters*, p. 188.
84. *The Works of Lord Byron*, 4 vols (London: John Murray, 1823): 3, opp. pp. 29 and 54 (*The Corsair*); opp. pp. 116, 156 (*Lara*).
85. Moore, "Byronic Dress," pp. 9, 11.
86. Clarke and Penny, *The Arrogant Connoisseur*, p. 17.
87. Westall's younger brother William also adopted his poses, e.g., "Childe Harold in Rome," reproduced in *Byromania*, ed. Wilson, after p. 116.
88. *BLJ* 7: 165, 168.
89. Neal, pp. 61, 64.
90. Redgrave and Redgrave, *A Century of British Painters*, p. 187.
91. Ballantyne, *Architecture*, p. 281; Downes, "The Pagan Deist of Downton Castle," *TLS*, May 1, 1998, p. 36.
92. Peach, p. 43; *CPW* 2: 9.
93. Hazlitt, *Complete Works*, ed. Howe, 18: 19.
94. Sully, *Hints*, p. 31.
95. Farington, *Diary* 12: 4377.
96. On this subject, see Crompton, *Byron and Greek Love*, especially ch. 5.
97. *New Monthly Magazine*, 2 (Sept., Oct. 1814): 141–2, 248–9. The quoted passage is from p. 142.
98. Ackermann's *Repository*, 11 (June 1814): 357, 358.
99. Dallas, *Recollections*, pp. 288–9.
100. Guiccioli, *My Recollections*, 1: 67.
101. *BLJ* 3: 224. Marchand thinks the portrait probably by Holmes, but for Walker it is a more realistic portrait by Westall underneath the present version (*Regency Portraits* 1: 82). I incline toward Walker.
102. *BLJ* 3: 33, 41. Byron's taste is closer to Westall's than to Hazlitt's. Westall later was deemed appropriate to give drawing lessons to young Princess Victoria.

103. Westall, "The Westall Brothers," pp. 29, 31; Clarke and Penny, *The Arrogant Connoisseur*, p. 107.
104. *New Monthly Magazine*, 2nd ser., 15 (1825): 253, 186.
105. Moore, "Byronic Dress," p. 9.
106. Walker 1: 82. If we accept Walker's view, worshippers at All Souls today, thinking themselves in the presence of the Lord, look up adoringly at Lord Byron. Sully in December 1837 saw the *Ecce Homo* at All Souls, "where it was dark enough to be twilight." He rated it "a tolerable picture" (Barratt, *Queen Victoria*, p. 95). The confrontation is memorable for what did not happen. Sully, in the dim light, neither recognized the *Ecce Homo* as Westall's nor made a connection between it and the artist's *Byron.*
107. Westall, spurred by Byron's death, may in 1825 have portrayed him a second time with face distorted, eyeballs staring wildly heavenward, neck elongated, that is, similarly to his *Childe Harold* illustrations. Peach thinks this 1825 portrait, not that of 1813, the one exhibited at the RA exhibition – and thus the subject of the *New Monthly*'s critique (pp. 44–5). I find the evidence for 1813 stronger. For doubts regarding the authenticity of 1825, see Piper and Walker (*Image of the Poet*, p. 133; Walker, 1: 82–83). If indeed by Westall, the portrait's vacuity of expression caps the downward spiral of his images of Byron.
108. Piper, *Image of the Poet*, p. 133.
109. Ibid., p. 132.
110. Keats, *Letters*, ed. Rollins, 2:27. See also Keats's poem "Sleep and Poetry," ll. 230–35.
111. Medwin, p. 7; *BLJ* 1: 197.
112. Brilliant, p. 26.
113. Peach, p. 28.
114. An engraved line version of Westall has since 1973 adorned the cover of the *Byron Journal.*
115. Peach, p. 63. The National Portrait Gallery usually has hanging *Byron in Albanian Dress*; Westall's *Byron* emerges only for special exhibitions.
116. Ibid., p. 64.

Chapter Three

1. *The Journal of Eugene Delacroix*, trans. Walter Pach (New York: Covici-Friede, 1934), p. 708.
2. The consensus view: e.g., "undoubtedly the best portrait painter of his generation" (Brown, *American Art*, p. 229); "the country's leading portraitist" (*American Paintings in the MM* 1: 358). Dunlap in 1834 commented that Sully "had long stood at the head of his profession as a portrait painter" (2: 234).
3. E.g., Neal, p. 29.
4. Willis, *The Charleston Stage*, p. 70.
5. Dunlap 2: 294; Severens, *Charles Fraser*, pp. 78–80 passim. Fraser later forged a successful career in Charleston as a painter of miniatures.
6. Severens, pp. 23, 27, 78.
7. Miller, *Rembrandt Peale*, p. 35; Bronson, pp. 23–4.
8. Dunlap 1: 166; Bronson, pp. 31–2. Benbridge, who worked principally in Philadelphia, may have set Sully to thinking about residence in that city.
9. Frank, *Love and Loss*, especially pp. 132–3, on which these paragraphs draw.

10. Sully, Journal (NYPL), September 1804, p. 4.
11. Irving, *Letters* 1: 242.
12. Sully, Journal (NYPL), October 20, 1802, p. 2.
13. Neal, p. 13. William Dunlap was assistant manager. Sully never forgot Cooper's generosity and repaid it in kind: "To-day sent to Mr. W. D. Lewis $100 for Cooper's Benefit" (Journal [NYPL], May 26, 1833, p. 93). Cooper in the 1830s had declined into alcoholism (Dunlap, *Diary*, passim).
14. Bronson, p. 42; *American Paintings in the MM* 1: 337.
15. Hennessey, *The American Portrait*, p. 9.
16. Sully's correspondence with Trumbull (preserved in the NYHS) is polite, if stiff. The portrait of Sarah Sully is now in the Amherst College Collection.
17. Dunlap 1: 250. Sully, who remained on good terms with Stuart, endeavored on a visit to Boston in 1828 "to see poor Stuart, but he was too ill to admit me" (Journal [NYPL], June 22, 1828, p. 60). Stuart died on July 11. See Sully's "Recollections of an Old Painter," *Hours at Home* (1869): 70.
18. Dunlap, *Diary* 3: 695. In 1832 Sully claimed "that one of Stuart's Boston heads was, without qualification, the *best portrait he ever saw*, and that while he was in England [1809–10], he saw nothing to compare it to . . . (Evans, *Genius of Stuart*, pp. 79, 102).
19. Sully left to his grandson Francis Darley "the silver snuff-box once the property of the late Gilbert Stuart, the celebrated portrait-painter" (Sully's will, manuscript in American Philosophical Society).
20. Bolton, "On a Portrait," p. 28.
21. Irving, *Letters* 1: 249 (Nov. 4, 1807). Irving, born in 1783, was Sully's age. Irving's love for Rebecca's friend Matilda Hoffman, who would die in 1809, endeared him to Rebecca. The same day Irving wrote another letter of introduction for Sully to William Meredith (pp. 249, 315). On Rebecca Gratz (and Irving's friendship with her) see Sartain, *Reminiscences*, pp. 183–5.
22. London, "Portraits of Rebecca Gratz by Thomas Sully," in *Portrait Painting*, ed. Miles, p. 162.
23. Irving, *Letters* 1: 249.
24. Dunlap, *Diary* 3: 695.
25. Wolf, *History of the Jews of Philadelphia*, p. 322.
26. Sully, "Recollections of an Old Painter," p. 74. The other lady has eluded identification.
27. Letter of Feb. 14, 1809. MS: PAFA. Dunlap, *Diary* 3: 696, 699. Wilcocks was an old China hand and an unabashed defender of the opium traffic (Goldstein, *Philadelphia and the China Trade, 1682–1846*, pp. 8, 50, 53).
28. Sully, Journal [NYPL], May 13, 1809, p. 10. The other two supporters were Mr Redwood and Mr Brinton.
29. Sully, Journal, May 17, 1809, p. 10.
30. In 1829 Aaron Corwine, a Sully student, asked him for advice on where in Europe he might best study portraiture and was told that if he wished to advance in his art he should go to England – advice Corwine followed (Dwight, "Aaron Houghton Corwine: Cincinnati Artist," in *Portrait Painting*, ed. Miles, p. 60).
31. In London since 1806, King had become strapped for funds. He later achieved a reputation for his depictions of American Indians. He and Sully became lifelong friends.
32. Farington, *Diary* 8: 2,908 (Nov. 16, 1806); 6: 2339 (May 31, 1804).
33. Staley, *Benjamin West in Pennsylvania Collections*, p. 22.

34. "Although I am friendly to portraying eminent men," West wrote Charles Willson Peale, "yet I am not friendly to the indiscriminate waste of genius in portrait painting" (Gerdts and Thistlethwaite, *Grand Illusions*, pp. 79–80).
35. B & F, p. 13; Alperts, *Benjamin West*, p. 357.
36. Neal, p. 16.
37. Dunlap 2: 257.
38. Ibid., 2: 260.
39. MS: NYHS (March 20, 1819).
40. Sully, Journal [NYHS], July 24, 1809, p. 11.
41. Sully later appreciated Copley more. In 1829 in the Harvard College Library he came upon a "fine collection of Copley's pictures, paintings and engravings from his work – great breadth of effect, and occasionally of colour – but too generally hard" (Journal [NYPL], August 17, 1829, p. 69–b). Three weeks later, he returned to Copley: "Copley was in all respects but one equal to West – he had not so great dispatch – but then he was more correct and did not so often repeat himself – his early portraits in Boston show the same style which he kept to the last – he had great force, breadth, but was hard in his terminations and color" (Journal [NYPL], Sept. 11, 1829, p. 70–g). Later in the century Henry James also found Copley "a trifle hard and rigid" (*The Painter's Eye*, ed. Sweeney, p. 107).
42. Dunlap 2: 257.
43. Sully considered the Guildhall's "Governor of Gibraltar, Elliot . . . the best picture of Reynolds that I could see in London" ("Hints" [Winterthur], 1812).
44. Holmes, *Coleridge* 2: 122–3.
45. "Hints" [Winterthur], 1809–1810.
46. Lecture of 1805, cited in Evans, *Genius of Stuart*, p. 72.
47. Bronson, p. 89. Along with Johns in "Theater and Theory," Bronson has brought to the fore Fuseli's importance for Sully (especially, pp. 87–9).
48. Johns, "Theater and Theory," p. 32.
49. Sully, "Recollections of an Old Painter," p. 74.
50. Holmes, *Coleridge* 2: 363.
51. Blanshard, *Portraits of Wordsworth*, pp. 94–6.
52. Ibid., p. 31.
53. On the Levy portrait, see Miles in *Three Hundred Years*, ed. Kushner et al., p. 24 (reproduction, p. 18).
54. Levey, *Lawrence*, pp. 6, 16.
55. Dunlap 2: 256, citing Sully's "Hints" [Winterthur], 1809.
56. Sully to Daniel Wadsworth, unpublished letter of June 17, 1810 (Connecticut State Library, Hartford, cited by Evans, *Benjamin West*, p. 154).
57. John Neagle papers, microfilm reel no. 23 (HSP). Sully's palette, with the colors identified, is reproduced in black and white in Faber Birren, *History of Color in Painting* (New York: Reinhold, 1965), p. 54.
58. Copybook 2, pp. 50–51 (March 4, 1838). MS: Winterthur.
59. *Correspondence of Allston*, ed. Wright, p. 546.
60. Gerdts, in *American Portraiture*, ed. Quick, p. 33.
61. Journal, June 17, 1838, in Barratt, *Queen Victoria*, p. 174.
62. Sully, "Recollections of an Old Painter," p. 69.
63. Dunlap, *Diary* 3: 703; Sully, "Recollections of an Old Painter," p. 70.
64. Information cited from captions (presumably by Carrie Rebora Barratt) for Sully exhibit, MM, 2000.
65. *Hints*, pp. 42–6.

66. Only Bronson downplays the importance of Lawrence's influence on Sully. He cites Sully's initially negative response, his few mentions of Lawrence in his Journal or the Hints for Pictures, and the "minimal" time he spent with him. Bronson admits there is an influence, but finds it less in brushwork than "in composition and the portrayal of the figure" (p. 64). Whereas Bronson sees Sully's admiration for Lawrence evolving slowly, I find it vibrantly present virtually from the beginning.
67. Cooper, *Letters*, 1: 96.
68. Reynolds, *Discourses*, ed. Wark, p. 103.
69. Journal, July 7, 1838, in Barratt, *Queen Victoria*, p. 187.
70. Dunlap 2: 265.
71. Burt, *Perennial Philadelphians*, p. 520.
72. Ibid., pp. 20–21.
73. In 1922 the Academy commemorated the fiftieth anniversary of Sully's death with a major exhibition.
74. Elected an Academician in 1812, Sully served on the board from 1816 to 1831. He declined PAFA's presidency in 1842.
75. *Correspondence of Allston*, ed. Wright, p. 471. For Morse's respect for Sully as man and artist, see his unpublished letter to Sully of Feb. 23, 1821 (Special Collections, Getty Research Center).
76. Govan, *Nicholas Biddle*, p. 73. On the Wistar parties, see Stevick, *Imagining Philadelphia*, pp. 111–13. The irascible Basil Hall, generally hostile to American ways, recalled with pleasure "these agreeable and instructive Wistar parties at Philadelphia" (*Travels in North America* [1829] 2: 339–40).
77. Journal [NYPL], Feb. 24, 1828, p. 57. See Budd, "Thomas Sully," p. 124, and, on the Musical Fund Society, Geffen, *Philadelphia Unitarianism*, pp. 103, 118–19. Dunlap acknowledged the "high authority" of Sully's "taste and knowledge of music" (1: 204).
78. MS: Beinecke Library, Yale.
79. His previous studio, in which he worked from April 1810 to 1812, was at 56 South 11th St (Geffen, *Philadelphia Unitarianism*, p. 102).
80. American Philosophical Society, *Catalogue of Portraits*, p. 90.
81. Geffen, *Philadelphia Unitarianism*, pp. 75, 167; *Philadelphia*, ed. Weigley, p. 221.
82. Dickens in his *American Notes* spoke of Sully as "a distinguished American artist." When visiting the Hospital, he praised his "very characteristic and life-like" portrait, presumably that of Rush (ch. 7).
83. Cited in Miles, in *Three Hundred Years*, ed. Kushner et al., p. 21.
84. E.g., Anna Jameson in 1837: "While in America I was struck by the manner in which the imaginative talent of the people had thrown itself forth into painting; the country seemed to swarm with painters" (cited from Richardson, *American Romantic Painting*, p. 6).
85. I draw here upon Pointon, *Hanging the Head*, p. 8.
86. Friedländer, *Landscape Portrait Still-Life*, p. 230.
87. Jaffe, *Trumbull*, p. 24.
88. Neal, pp. 50, 51.
89. Ibid., p. 69.
90. So Evans (*Genius of Stuart*, p. 120). But, reports Dunlap, Stuart "used to say that no man would paint history if he could find full employment in portrait" (2: 273).
91. Harris, *The Artist*, p. 57. Ch. 3, "The Burden of Portraiture," provides an excellent overview.

92. Miles, in *Portrait Painting*, ed. Miles, p. 13. The collection is housed in the Museo Gioviano on Lake Como.
93. The lines from *Childe Harold* are adapted from canto 3, stanza 67.
94. Miles, in *Portrait Painting*, ed. Miles, p. 13. Sully knew both Longacre and Herring, but contributed only a few portraits.
95. *American Originals. Selections from Reynolda House, Museum of American Art*. Essay by Charles C. Eldredge (New York: Abbeville Press, 1990), p. 36.
96. Gerdts, in *American Portraiture*, ed. Quick, p. 33.
97. Danly, *Facing the Past*, p. 17. She notes that Neagle, and Inman when working in Philadelphia, adopted versions of the style (p. 18).
98. Hints [Winterthur], 1809.
99. Fabian, pp. 13–14.
100. Hints [Winterthur], May 16, 1827.
101. Hints [Winterthur], February 9, 1812.
102. Pointon, "Portrait-Painting as a Business Enterprise," p. 200.
103. For a full-length portrait, Lawrence asked, even in 1790, 100 guineas; in 1806, 200; in 1810, 400 (Wilton, *The Swagger Portrait*, p. 162).
104. Sully's fees gradually went up over the years. For the 1830s see Hints [Winterthur], Nov. 5, 1835; March 1, 1837.
105. Dunlap 1: 328; *Diary* 2: 473 (Oct. 18, 1819). Today a "panic" is called a "crash."
106. Harris, *The Artist*, p. 79.
107. MS: HSP (Nov. 29, 1820).
108. Harris, *The Artist*, p. 69.
109. Dunlap 3: 703; Journal [NYPL], August 7, 1824, p. 32.
110. Dunlap 3: 703.
111. Ellis, *After the Revolution*, p. 11.
112. MS: Beinecke (Feb. 1, 1829). A restless Sully faced temptation from several directions. The Paradise of Exiles remained alluring. "None but those who have visited Italy," a recent student, John G. Chapman, wrote Sully on July 27, 1829, "can form any idea of the privileges any artist enjoys here" (Harris, *The Artist*, p. 78).
113. Noble, *Thomas Cole*, pp. 196, 220.
114. Sartain, *Reminiscences*, p. 142.
115. Lynes, *The Art-Makers*, pp. 193–4.
116. Krimmel (1786–1833), who immigrated to Philadelphia from Germany in 1809, became, along with Leslie, one of Sully's first students. Harding thinks "some small portraits in Krimmel's early sketchbooks are more like Sully's work in design" (*John Lewis Krimmel*, pp. 14, 199).
117. *American Portraiture*, ed. Quick, p. 164.
118. *Alfred Jacob Miller: Artist on the Oregon Trail*, ed. Ron Tyler (Fort Worth: Amon Carter Museum, 1982), p. 9.
119. Brooks, *World of Washington Irving*, p. 306. In addition to Sully's students (many not named here), four of Sully's children were at one time or another artists, and his stepdaughter Mary married John Neagle, with whom Sully maintained a warm and cordial relationship. He frequently helped his painter nephew Robert Matthew Sully, the son of his brother Matthew.
120. Barker, *American Painting*, p. 276 (Peticolas); Larkin, *Morse*, p. 52.
121. MS: Beinecke Library, Yale (Jan. 7, 1828). John Gadsby Chapman (1808–89) had a 45-year career in Italy.
122. Journal [NYPL], August 12, 1826, p. 43.

123. Sully, Journal [NYPL], August 4, 1825, p. 36.
124. Dunlap, *Diary* 3: 708; *History* 3: 205. Sully at one point considered charging for instruction, but I have found no evidence that he did (Journal [NYPL], Sept. 1, 1833, p. 94).
125. Goldring, *Lawrence*, pp. 314–16; *Audubon and His Times*, ed. Marie R. Audubon, 1: 252. Unpublished correspondence between Audubon and Sully in the Beinecke indicates that, as often happened with Audubon, his subsequent involvement with Lawrence did not always go smoothly (*Audubon and His Times*, ed. Audubon 1: 284). But his friendship with Sully remained firm.
126. *Correspondence of Allston*, ed. Wright, p. 324.
127. For Beard, see undated letter of introduction by Robert M. Bird (MS: HSP). For Frankenstein, see Sully, Journal [NYPL], Jan. 25, 1839, p. 195. For Corwine, see Sully, Journal [NYPL], March 29, 1829; July 11 and September 5, 1830, pp. 67, 76, 77. Under July 11 Sully noted that Corwine had died on the 4th.
128. For Frazer, see Dunlap 3: 301; for Bush, ibid., p. 198.
129. Floyd, in Jones and Weber, *The Kentucky Painter*, p. 15; Floyd, "Portraits of ante-bellum Kentuckians," in *Portrait Painting*, ed. Miles, pp. 165–74; Harris, *The Artist*, p. 116.
130. Pennington, *William Edward West*, pp. 5–6. Though we have few details concerning Sully's teacher–student relationship with West, West appears to have been close to Sully and his family (p. 6).
131. B & F claim the original is at West Point (p. 321). Bronson argues, convincingly, that the Academy holds West's slightly smaller copy (pp. 144–5). The Academy agrees, and dates the painting February–May 1815. Flanary thinks West left Philadelphia in 1816 ("William Edward West in New Orleans and Mississippi," p. 1010).
132. *BLJ* 9:17. West also painted Teresa Guiccioli and Edward John Trelawny.
133. On West and Byron see my two articles and Peach, pp. 106–12. A typescript on file at the Scottish National Portrait Gallery, which holds the original of West's *Byron*, lists several of the copies, of which Harrow School's is the best.
134. Noble, *Thomas Cole*, pp. xvii–xviii, 34–6; Goldstein, *Landscape with Figures*, p. 17, both drawing on Dunlap 3: 149–50.
135. See *Art and the Empire City. New York, 1825–1861*. It is possible that Murray, then vice president of the American Academy of Fine Arts, prompted Bruen to request a portrait of Byron. Murray did not acquire (for his own collection) Sully's *Byron* until about 1828. Why neither the *Byron* commissioned by Bruen nor a copy made it back to New York and why *Teresa*, even though Byron paid twice what West asked for, also remained in the artist's possession, remain puzzles yet unresolved.
136. Charles Turner (1826), John Taylor Wedgwood (1826), and Francis Engleheart (1827) did the first three engravings of West's portrait (Peach, p. 107). Others soon followed. Sully placed in one of his scrapbooks Engleheart's engraving, which appeared in the *Literary Souvenir* of 1827. When in 1830 Sully gave West's 1820 letter from Florence to his collector friend Robert Gilmor, Jr, the Baltimorean (presumably not having seen Sully's portrait) wrote on it: "This letter from West, the celebrated American artist who painted the best portrait of Lord Byron & the Countess Guiccioli, was given to me by Mr. Sully" (MS: HSP).

Chapter Four

1. Shakespeare, Sonnet 18, ll. 13–14.
2. Tscherny, "Likeness in Early Romantic Portraiture," p. 193, drawing upon Hazlitt, *Complete Works*, ed. Howe 18: 74–5.
3. Reynolds, *Discourses*, ed. Wark, p. 88.
4. S. West, "Thomas Lawrence's 'Half-history' Portraits," p. 228.
5. Williams, *Life of Lawrence*, 2: 430.
6. Upon returning in 1837, Sully saw both the original and Reynolds's copy.
7. Byron greatly admired Mrs. Siddons as an actress, and on the collage screen he put together he reserved the most prominent place for an engraving of Reynolds's portrait.
8. Williams, *Life of Lawrence*, 1: 197.
9. Lawrence, "On the Want of Encouragement for Historical Painting in this Country" [1829], cited from Blanshard, *Portraits of Wordsworth*, pp. 34, 198. When during 1818–20 Lawrence painted the major historical personages of post-Napoleonic Europe, he further gratified his desire for fame as a history painter.
10. Sully told Dunlap that during his first London visit he was too busy to take in any plays (2: 260–61). His journal is silent on the subject.
11. From Dunlap's various publications we learn much about Sully and his contemporaries. "Mr. Dunlap has passed many hours with me to collect notes for his biography of American artists," Sully wrote in his Journal ([NYPL], June 23, 1833, p. 93). The career of Dunlap (1766–1839), like that of Sully, illustrates the close connections between art and theater in Federal America.
12. Copybook 2 [Winterthur], pp. 137–8.
13. Levine, *Highbrow / Lowbrow*, pp. 16–18.
14. Ibid., p. 17.
15. Many of Sully's sketches are preserved in scrapbooks in the Philadelphia Museum of Art. The MM's scrapbook covering 1810–19 was not available for me to consult during the writing of this book.
16. Lavater, *Essays on Physiognomy* (1804), 1: vi.
17. Thus translated in the 1808 New York edition of *The Robbers* that Sully (and Wood) most likely used (Schiller, *The Robbers: A Tragedy in Five Acts* [New York: David Longworth, 1808]). Translations and editions differ greatly. In modern editions the scene depicted is in act 3, scene 2.
18. "When I read about great men in my Plutarch, then this ink-smudging age nauseates me" (act 1, scene 2).
19. Illustration of Mortimer's work in *Romantic Painting in Britain*, p. 109.
20. Boaden, *Memoirs of Kemble* 2: 279.
21. *BLJ* 3: 95.
22. *BLJ* 3: 229–30; Dunlap, 2: 357.
23. *Life of Ticknor* 1: 66.
24. Parry, *Last Days of Lord Byron*, p. 224. On his collage screen Byron placed on an adjoining panel to *Mrs Siddons* a large oval engraved portrait of Cooke as Richard III.
25. For Cooke's "abduction," see Skinner, "Madmen of the Theater: I: Cooke."
26. Hazlitt called Cibber's patched-together version of 1700 a "vile jumble," but Dunlap noted that it was Cooke himself who inserted the four lines from Gloucester's speech (*Cooke* 2: 399).
27. James, *Old Drury of Philadelphia*, p. 16.

28. Altick, *Paintings from Books*, pp. 281–3.
29. *Henry VI, Part 3*: 3.2.182–5.
30. James, "Yoricks of Yesteryear," p. 11; Johns, "Theater and Theory," p. 29; Gerdts, in *American Portraiture*, ed. Quick, pp. 33–4. Wood "vouched for the portrait as a true rendering of Cooke's costume and facial expression" (Fabian, *Portraits of the Stage*, p. 22).
31. John Walker, *Portraits*, p. 186.
32. Gerdts, in *American Portraiture*, ed. Quick, pp. 34–5.
33. Sully did several other portraits of Cooke, including a bust-sized version for Wilcocks of Cooke as Cardinal Richelieu.
34. Wood, *Personal Recollections*, pp. 156–7; Fabian, p. 57.
35. *Conférence de l'Académie Royale de peinture, et de sculpture pendant l'année 1667.*
36. Seznec, "Diderot and Historical Painting," p. 130.
37. Hautcoeur, *David*, p. 226.
38. Reynolds, *Discourses*, ed. Wark, p. 50.
39. Silverman, *Cultural History of the American Revolution*, pp. 24–5; Brewer, *Pleasures of the Imagination*, p. 307.
40. Austen, *Letters*, p. 273.
41. Daniel Fanshaw, reviewing the second exhibition held at the new National Academy of Design (cited by Gerdts in *American Portraiture*, ed. Quick, pp. 28–9).
42. Evans, in *The Portrait*, ed. Miles, p. 133.
43. Harris, *The Artist*, p. 84, drawing on comments by Horatio Greenough.
44. Vanderlyn's *View of Versailles* has been reinstalled in the MM's American Wing.
45. Miller, "John Vanderlyn," p. 33.
46. Tuckerman, p. 133.
47. Jaffe, *Trumbull: The Declaration of Independence*, p. 50.
48. Illustrated in Miller, *Rembrandt Peale*, p. 106.
49. Dunlap 2: 53; Miller, *Rembrandt Peale*, p. 113.
50. Richardson, *American Romantic Painting*, p. 10.
51. Bedell, *The Anatomy of Nature*, p. 27.
52. Williams, *Life of Lawrence*, 3: 6–7. By contrast, Lawrence never sold his major history painting *Satan Summoning his Legions*, regarded by him but by no one else as his masterpiece.
53. B & F say "as late as 1829" (p. 28); Bronson notes that Sully on tour often advertized himself as a portrait and history painter (p. 131n).
54. MS: HSP (January 29, 1820). Reproduced in Whitley, *Kentucky Ante-Bellum Portraiture*, pp. 776–7.
55. MS: HSP (January 19, 1817). Reproduced in Beal, *Jacob Eichholtz*, p. 377.
56. MS: HSP (February 23, 1817).
57. The painting has been variously named, but *Washington's Passage of the Delaware* is the most accurate title.
58. Kammen, *A Season of Youth*, pp. 87, 105, 77–8. Kammen's ch. 3 ("Revolutionary Iconography in National Tradition") is excellent.
59. Neal, pp. 12, 11. Poet, novelist, and critic, a controversial presence in every field into which he ventured, Neal weaves in and out of Sully's life. He merits a few words. Among Sully's contemporaries it is he who best understands his artistry. An impassioned critic of the arts, Neal first visited Sully's studio in 1820. He expressed his slash-and-burn opinions on all subjects with such vigor

that in 1823 he had to leave America for England. Returning four years later, he frequently visited Sully. Though repetitive, his analyses of the artist's character and work are often penetrating.

60. Sully confessed to Healy in the early 1830s "that he himself had always wanted to paint large murals of American life" (de Mare, *Healy*, p. 101). His name occasionally came up for major historical commissions. In the competition for panels in the Rotunda of the US Capitol, William Cullen Bryant in 1828 urged Gulian Verplanck, "Give one to Sully" (Callow, *Kindred Spirits*, p. 46). It did not happen. Most of the commissions went to New York artists, with Trumbull inevitably getting the lion's share.
61. Schwarz, *George Washington*, p. 2; Wick, *George Washington*, p. 168. On Weems's biography of Washington, see Leary, *The Book-Peddling Parson*, ch. 6.
62. Huntington, *Art and the Excited Spirit*, pp. 10–11; Bernier, *The World in 1800*, p. 128.
63. Hints [Winterthur], *c.* 1813. The passage occurs in the midst of pages of quotations from Northcote's *Life of Reynolds*. It may draw upon Reynolds, but it also reflects Sully's thinking.
64. Fast, *The Crossing*, pp. 9, 48. David Hackett Fischer's *Washington's Crossing* (Oxford and New York: Oxford University Press, 2004), now the definitive study of this battle, appeared after this volume had gone to press. I have been able to modify a few details in the light of Fischer's exhaustive research. My own interpretation of the scene is based on two visits in August 2001.
65. Sully showed Neal his own sketch (Neal, pp. 81–2).
66. Though Charles Willson Peale was present at Trenton, Fehl in his excellent study finds Trumbull's paintings more significant than Peale's ("*Washington's Passage*," p. 588).
67. Ibid., p. 592.
68. Some persons have found, Sully continued, "a resemblance to Mercer in the figure of the person next to the black servant of Washington," but that was "accidental, as I intended no other than those I have mentioned." I cite the copy of Sully's rare broadside in the Library Company of Philadelphia. Mentioned are Henry Knox, then still a colonel, who urges the men across with his sword and his stentorian voice; "General Greane" seems to be General Nathanael Greene. Unaccounted for by Sully is the personage on the extreme right next to Washington's black servant William Lee. Fehl, unaware of Sully's broadside, misidentifies several personages ("*Washington's Passage*," pp. 593, 589–92). Sully's source was James Wilkinson's *Memoirs of My Own Times* (Philadelphia: Abraham Small, 1816). Wilkinson, whose later career was unsavory, was present at the battle as a 19-year-old. His brief account of the crossing appears accurate.
69. MS: Library Company of Philadelphia. December 23 was presumably in 1818. Washington's Crossing is now a Pennsylvania State Park.
70. Neal, pp. 11, 12.
71. Sully to Daniel Peck, cited in Fehl, "*Washington's Passage*," p. 587; see also p. 597, document 22.
72. Cited from Fehl, "*Washington's Passage*," p. 591. The battle took place the morning of the 26th. Howard Fast, author of long the fullest account of the battle of Trenton, notes "that . . . between three and four o'clock, Washington's excitement disappeared and great calm replaced it" (*The Crossing*, p. 132).
73. Fast, *The Crossing*, p. 155. Wilkinson, Sully's source, notes "only two wounded, two were killed, and one frozen to death"; for the Hessians, 23

officers and almost 1000 non-commissioned officers and privates were captured (*Memoirs* 1: 131). John Ferling, perhaps Washington's best biographer, lists four American dead, and eight wounded, against 20 Hessian dead and 919 prisoners of war (*George Washington*, p. 186). As with all battles, estimates of casualties differ.

74. Clubbe, p. 276.
75. Nemerov, *The Body of Raphaelle Peale*, pp. 178–82. Nemerov seems unaware of Sully's careful preparations for his painting or of his explicatory broadside; nor did he examine, as had Sully, the terrain in which the crossing took place.
76. Fast, *The Crossing*, p. 119. Ferling also has Washington "one of the first to cross the Delaware" (*George Washington*, p. 184). Fehl is quite clear that the scene of Sully's painting is New Jersey ("*Washington's Passage*," pp. 588–9).
77. Nemerov, *Body of Raphaelle Peale*, pp. 179–80.
78. Fehl, "*Washington's Crossing*," p. 589.
79. Dunlap, *Diary*, 2: 524.
80. Nemerov, *Body of Raphaelle Peale*, p. 178.
81. Sully–Governor William Miller, June 3, 1817, cited from Fehl, "*Washington's Passage*," p. 596.
82. Nemerov, *Body of Raphaelle Peale*, pp. 179, 181; Neal, pp. 11, 12.
83. This *Self-portrait* (MM), the finest of his over twenty self-portraits, Sully painted as a gesture of thanks to his Baltimore host, the Englishman Henry Robinson.
84. Sully, Journal [NYPL], February 11, 1823, p. 28; Dunlap 2: 273. According to Neal, Sully had originally hoped to get $500 for the painting (a "paltry sum"), so in a way he came out even (p. 11). Several years later, Sully sold the original study, smaller and presumably less finished, for $400 (Journal [NYPL], December 15, 1825, p. 38).
85. Sully, Journal [NYPL], August 22, 1829, p. 69d.
86. Ibid., April 7, 1833, p. 92.
87. Ibid., [August 15, 1836], p. 111c and p. 113.
88. McGlinchee, *The First Decade of the Boston Museum*, especially pp. 28–9, 49.
89. Kammen, *A Season of Youth*, p. 82.
90. Neal, p. 11; Dunlap, *Diary* 2: 524; *Correspondence of Allston*, ed. Wright, p. 288; Jarves, *The Art-Idea*, p. 170.
91. A curator at the MFA assures me that when the museum completes its new wing in 2006 *Washington's Passage* will be hung prominently.
92. Groseclose, *Leutze*, p. 33.
93. Fast, *The Crossing*, pp. 119–20; *The Autobiography of Worthington Whittredge 1820–1910*, ed. John I. H. Baur (1942; New York: Arno Press, 1969), pp. 22–3.
94. *Henry James: Autobiography*, ed. Frederick W. Dupee (1913; New York: Criterion Books, 1956), p. 151.
95. Brown, *American Art to 1900*, p. 193.
96. *Godey's Lady's Book*, 29 (December 1844), 277–8, cited from Gerdts and Thistlethwaite, *Grand Illusions*, p. 82.
97. Sully, Journal [NYPL], August 15, 1836, p. 111c; May 3, 1841, p. 235; August 13, 1842, p. 253.
98. Peale, in an 1819 letter to Thomas Jefferson (Ellis, *After the Revolution*, p. 52).
99. Sully's sketch, *c.* 1810–12, of David's painting in his sketchbook at the MM is reproduced in *Thomas Sully 1783–1872* (Farmville, Virginia: Longwood College, 1973), p. 39.

100. The admiring David did not wish to place on such a lowly mount the presumed successor to Hannibal and Charlemagne. It was left for Paul Delaroche to depict Napoleon thus in 1838.
101. Sully, Journal [NYPL], November 26, 1842, p. 256; the artist valued *Washington at Trenton* at $2000.
102. Whiteman, *Paintings . . . at the Union League*, pp. 1–2, 54.
103. *Washington at Trenton*'s moment of fame came when it made the cover of *Life* (July 3, 1950) to publicize that magazine's lead article "The American Revolution. The Story as it Really Happened."

Chapter Five

1. Cited from Tscherny, "Likeness in Early Romantic Portraiture," p. 198.
2. Tuckerman, p. 158.
3. Evans, *Genius of Stuart*, p. 75, drawing upon John Neal.
4. S. West, "Portraiture: Likeness and Identity," p. 80.
5. Neal, p. 81.
6. Hazlitt, *Complete Works*, ed. Howe, 18: 152; 18: 19.
7. Not so in his person: even in old age Sully was described as a "man fond of manly society and manly pursuits" and "an excellent swordsman" (Budd, "Thomas Sully," p. 124).
8. *Don Juan*, canto 1, stanza 195. Though the words are Julia's, Byron ultimately defines the feminine brain through "mobility." See Jerome McGann, "'My brain is feminine': Byron and the Poetry of Deception" in *Byron: Augustan and Romantic*, ed. Andrew Rutherford (New York: St Martin's Press, 1990), especially pp. 41–2.
9. Finlay, *History of Greece*, cited from MacCarthy, *Byron*, pp. 35–6. Finlay may echo Faust's "two souls, alas, live in my breast" (I, l. 1112; "zwei Seelen wohnen, ach, in meiner Brust"). For Faust, each soul needs the other.
10. Knight, *The Golden Labyrinth* (London: Phoenix House, 1962), p. 230.
11. Joan Acocella, introduction to *The Diary of Vaslav Nijinsky* (New York: Farrar, Straus and Giroux, 1995), pp. xxxii–xxxiii. MacCarthy's *Byron* argues for Byron's essentially homosexual orientation. Anne Fleming in her review affirms that Byron was basically heterosexual (*TLS*, Nov. 8, 2002, pp. 6–7).
12. *Diary of Philip Hone*, p. 77.
13. Grimsted, *Melodrama Unveiled*, p. 57; Furnas, p. 119.
14. Wernick, "Glamorous actress found no glamor in Georgia slavery," *Smithsonian Magazine*, 5 (Nov. 1974), 75.
15. Fanny in her American *Journal* gave more space to Trelawny than to Butler, her husband-to-be. Butler was Sully's distant cousin by marriage.
16. Kemble, *Journal*, ed. Gough, p. 189.
17. Ibid., p. 187.
18. Ibid., p. 4. On Byron's impact upon the young Fanny, see her *Records of a Girlhood*, pp. 56–7.
19. Lease, *Anglo-American Encounters*, p. 154.
20. Furnas, p. 3.
21. Several American women expressed outrage at Fanny's outspoken admiration for *Childe Harold* (Clifford Ashby, "Fanny Kemble's 'Vulgar' Journal," p. 63).
22. Blainey, *Fanny and Adelaide*, p. 88.
23. Kemble, *Journal*, ed. Gough, p. 54.

24. Ibid., p. 60.
25. Furnas, p. 178; Geffen, *Philadelphia Unitarianism*, p. 204.
26. Her account also awakened Americans, Sidney Fisher among them (*A Philadelphia Perspective*, p. 456).
27. *Philadelphia*, ed. Weigley, p. 294ff. The small but close-knit Unitarian community in Philadelphia to which Sully belonged included an unusually high proportion of individuals associated with the arts.
28. Journal [NYPL], Aug. 30, 1840, pp. 224–5. Essential reading on Unitarianism's influence on the arts is Geffen's *Philadelphia Unitarianism 1796–1861*.
29. *Philadelphia's Cultural Landscape*, ed. Martinez and Talbott, p. 68. Sully painted at least two portraits of Blacks.
30. Another Longfellow sonnet, "Ah, precious evenings, all too swiftly sped!" expressed for Henry James the rapture elicited by Fanny Kemble's performances (*Essays on Literature*, p. 1083).
31. Ibid., p. 1079.
32. Downer, *The Eminent Tragedian*, pp. 283, 289. Macready no less than Fanny was "a lifelong student of Byron."
33. *A Philadelphia Perspective*, pp. 86, 153, 360, 533.
34. Leon Edel, introduction to *A Little Tour in France*, p. xii.
35. James, *Essays on Literature*, pp. 1079, 1085, 1094–5; Furnas, pp. 417–21.
36. James, *Essays on Literature*, p. 1075.
37. Woof says 23 (*Romantic Icons*, p. 52); John Walker, 50 (*Portraits*, p. 176); Cross, 28 (*A Striking Likeness*, p. 121).
38. For the whole sad story see Goldring, *Regency Portrait Painter*, chs. 8–10.
39. Baetjer, "British Portraits," p. 66
40. Kemble, *Records of a Girlhood*, p. 525; *Journal*, ed. Gough, pp. 45–6.
41. Marshall, *Fanny Kemble*, p. 49. Fanny often recalls Lawrence in *Records of a Girlhood.*
42. Kemble, *Journal*, ed. Gough, p. 169.
43. Armstrong, *Lawrence*, p. 47.
44 Ellis, *After the Revolution*, p. 132.
45. Kemble, *Journal*, ed. Gough, pp. 67, 69.
46. Ibid., pp. 71, 72.
47. Sully through Lawrence in London may have met Charles Kemble.
48. Sully–Audubon, Nov. 11, 1832. MS: Beinecke Library, Yale.
49. Journal [NYPL], Nov. 4, 1832, p. 88. This sketch, "painted from recollection," was begun October 30, 1832, and completed November 1.
50. Neal, p. 81. Henry Inman's 1837 portrait of Sully reveals him with a full head of curly black hair, still handsome (color reproduction in Barratt, p. 2).
51. He also went down to Baltimore to see the Kembles in *Romeo and Juliet*. On November 8–10, 1832 he made a sketch from memory – for an engraving by Cephas G. Childs – of Fanny in the play's last scene (B & F, p. 195; Journal [NYPL], Nov. 11, 1833, p. 89).
52. Kemble, *Journal*, ed. Gough, p. 31.
53. Copybook 1, p. 145 (February 14, 1838). MS: Winterthur.
54. James, *Essays on Literature*, p. 1094.
55. Kemble, *Journal*, ed. Gough, pp. 116 (Dec. 18), 125 (Dec. 29), 148 (Feb. 2). Sully's Journal entries tersely counterpoint Fanny's.
56. Journal [NYPL], March 10, 1833, p. 91.
57. So speculates Bronson (p. 212).

58. *Julia*, begun February 23, 1833, was completed on March 21, 1833; *Bianca*, begun on February 26, three days after *Julia*, was completed on April 23. *Lady Macbeth*, begun on February 25, was for reasons unknown "erased," that is, destroyed. Was it too difficult or too painful for Sully to conceive Fanny in this role? – or was the result insufficiently flattering? Sully valued the painting at $150, considerably more than his other portraits of Fanny Kemble in a role.
59. Medwin, p. 132.
60. Furnas, p. 96.
61. Neal, pp. 81, 5.
62. Furnas, pp. 5, 303.
63. James, *Essays on Literature*, p. 1080.
64. Kemble, *Records of a Girlhood*, p. 367. *Fanny as Beatrice* must also have been Sully's favorite. In the early 1860s he copied it three times.
65. *Fanny as Beatrice*, bought by Edward Carey, was left by him to his brother Henry C. Carey, who in turn bequeathed it to PAFA.
66. "Summer," ll. 1289–1370, in Thomson, *The Seasons*.
67. Von Erffa and Staley, *Paintings of Benjamin West*, pp. 229, 285.
68. Cooper, *Classical Taste in America 1800–1840*, p. 87; color reproduction, p. 56.
69. On this *Musidora*, see *American Paintings in the MM* 1: 347–8. Barratt discusses the painting in relation to *Victoria* and provides a color illustration (p. 40). She does not make the identification of *Musidora* with Fanny Kemble.
70. From 1833 until at least 1840, when the Pierce Butlers left for an extended stay in England, relations between the Sullys and the Butlers remained close. Sully's diary records numerous visits to the Butler estate in Germantown, and Fanny, sometimes accompanied by Butler, called frequently on the Sullys.
71. Sully began both these portraits on May 26, 1834, and finished them on June 17 and 18. At *c.* 27" x 36" (68.5 cm x 91.4 cm) they are slightly larger than the 30" x 25" (76 cm x 63.5 cm) format of most of the others. The portrait referred to by Fanny was purchased for the White House Collection in 1965.
72. Fabian, p. 88, citing Kemble, *Records of a Later Life*, 2 vols (London, 1882) 1: 132.
73. [Sully,] "Recollections of an Old Painter," (1869), p. 72; see also Sartain, *Reminiscences*, p. 103. Candid in self-analysis, Sully observed in 1838, in regard to his portraits of Fanny as Beatrice and as Isabella being exhibited at the British Institution, that "my pictures look dingy and vapid. I think more force and brightness in effect for an English atmosphere, than for our bright and clear skies. My own works, I see, are in too low a scale of color, and my usual fault of weakness of effect is *very* apparent here" (Hints [Winterthur], Feb. 15, 1838). Already in 1825 he had expressed dissatisfaction that he had "lost much of breadth and simplicity of manner that I once possessed" (Journal [NYPL], Aug. 6 and 14, 1825, p. 37). On both occasions Sully is overly self-critical. Portraitists alter their technique almost imperceptibly over the years, and though Sully's did change, it changed less than he thought. Gerdts notes a gradual relaxation in technique, but sees it beginning in the 1830s (in *American Portraiture*, ed. Quick, pp. 36–7, 46).
74. Budd, "Thomas Sully," p. 121.
75. Neal, p. 5.
76. Journal, 6.26.37, in Barratt, p. 77. Connoisseurs in Reynolds's day and for several decades after valued his subject paintings – that is, history paintings, allegories, and fancy subjects – more highly than his portraits. During his

second trip to England in 1839, Carey, upon viewing the British portraits at the Royal Academy, averred that nothing he had seen approached in quality Sully's work (Danly, "The Carey Collection," *Antiques*, 140 [Nov. 1991], 841).

77. Sully had belonged to the Society of the Sons of St George, a largely Unitarian organization, since 1818.

78. In letters home transcribed in two Copybooks preserved at Winterthur, Blanche and Sully provided the family with a running account of their day-to-day activities. Blanche's letters are full of infectious enthusiasm – her favorite ejaculation is "what a treat!" Once, introduced to the Belgian minister, she observes, "by the way he has the handsomest legs I ever saw" (Copybook 1, p. 80 [BS, 12.4.37]. Barratt spells her name "Blanch." Although Sully usually writes "Blanch," Blanche herself, who spelled her name both with and without the "e," seems to have preferred the "e" (Bronson, p. 202, n. 30). Most letters she signed "Blanche," and her name is thus on her gravestone in Laurel Hill Cemetery, Philadelphia.

For ease of reader reference I have quoted Sully's Journal for the period during which he was abroad (Sept. 19, 1837, to July 29, 1838) from Barratt rather than from the NYPL typescript. Barratt does not publish all passages in the NYPL typescript, which interpolates extracts from other Sully journals. By reproducing the Journal without reference to Sully and Blanche's often fuller and livelier letters Barratt presents a limited picture of Sully's time in England. I draw on the Copybooks extensively. Thus the foci and emphases of my narrative differ considerably from Barratt's.

79. Copybook 1, p. 6 (TS–SAS, Nov. 3 and 9, 1837).
80. Ibid., pp. 80 (11.16.37), 91 (12.14.37).
81. Ibid., p. 23 (TS, 11.11.37).
82. Ibid., pp. 69, 78, 79 (11.29.37, 12.4.37).
83. Ibid., p. 17 (11.6.1837).
84. Journal, in Barratt, *Queen Victoria*, pp. 80, 81.
85. "I have not yet seen Pickersgil[l], but Shee is the best *portrait* painter in oil that I have visited on this occasion. . . . Wilkie charmed me – not more in his simple unaffected kindness of manner, than in his noble and exquisite works" (Copybook 1, p. 45, [TS–Neagle, 11.22.37]). Sully preferred Wilkie's historical scenes to his portraits. Byron in *English Bards* associated Shee with "Genius," but Sully became disillusioned with him for paying him no attention during his residence in London. He later spoke positively about Pickersgill's portraits (Copybook 2, pp. 118–19, 3.24.38).
86. Copybook 1, pp. 134–5. Hitherto reserved in his response to Turner, Sully responded strongly to his work while in London. "What an artist! . . . What a nasty looking fellow he is[–]looks as though he had not an idea[.] beside that so careless and dirty is his dress I would not pick him out of the gutter – yet he can paint so magnificently" (Copybook 1, p. 41 [TS, 11.15.37]). He added a few days later, "Beechey – deplorably bad! – Turner is a Giant" (Copybook 1, p. 47 [TS–John Neagle, 11.27.37]). At the British Institution he saw Turner retouching "his large sea piece," presumably *The Fighting Temeraire*. "I cannot approve of the daring liberties he takes in coloring – a lemon colored boat, towed by the vessel, is outrageous" (Journal, 2.5.1838, Barratt, p. 117). Turner "grew upon" him; "there is much mind in his pictures" (Journal, 5.4.38, in Barratt, p. 160). He also found "the great Turner . . . extravagant beyond bounds" (Journal, 5.16.38, in Barratt, p. 165). How Turner earned the good living he did fascinated Sully: "Turner has sold enough to make him a

very rich man – although his money has been chiefly made from small works from the Booksellers and the profits arising from engravings of his works" (Copybook 1, pp. 47–8, [TS–Neagle, 11.27.37]). In appearance Turner was "a miniature likeness of the late G. F. Cooke. He is a peculiar man and chooses to indulge in eccentricity[.] The world as usual has the worst version of his character" (Copybook 2, p. 112 [TS, 3.24.38]).

87. Hints [Winterthur], June 17, July 25, 1838.
88. Copybook 1, p. 40 (TS–Neagle, 11.27.37). Sully does not mention further attendance.
89. Copybook 1, p. 133 (BS, after 1.28.38). "Captain Back": Sir George Back (1796–1878), noted Arctic explorer. James Smith and his brother Horace authored the famous *Rejected Addresses* (1812), much admired by Byron.
90. Copybook 2, p. 93 (March 28, 1838).
91. Ibid., p. 93 (3.28.1838). Everyone, recorded Sully, asked about Irving "who I find is beloved here" (ibid., p. 108 [TS, 3.24.1838]).
92. Copybook 1, p. 135 (2.5.1838).
93. Copybook 2, p. 38 (3.4.1838); p. 93 (3.28.1838). Virginia Murray informs me that there are no documents relating to Sully in the vast John Murray Byron archive.
94. Journal, in Barratt, p. 83; copybook 2, p. 53 (3.28.1838).
95. de Mare, *Healy*, p. 66.
96. Copybook 1, p. 92 (12.24.37).
97. Copybook 1, pp. 70–71 (BS, 12.1.37); Hints [Winterthur], December 1, 1837. In 1839 Sully made for Rogers a copy (now in the Royal Collection) of his original study of *Victoria*.
98. Copybook 1, p. 42 (BS, 11.15.37).
99. Ibid., p. 103 (12.28.1837).
100. Copybook 2, p. 60 (BS, 3.4.38).
101. Copybook 1, p. 98 (12.28.1837).
102. Although Wright's proposed volume does not seem to have materialized as such, some of the materials he collected may have made their way into the heavily annotated one-volume editions of Byron's poems issued by Murray.
103. Sully–Mrs Stith, Feb. 14, 1838. MS: Speck Collection, Beinecke Library, Yale. No great matter if Sully got details wrong – e.g., Byron's inscription became "marginal notes" – he had the essence of the encounter down pat. The story of Mrs Stith's encounter with Byron was current in various renderings.
104. Bancroft, "A Day with Lord Byron," in *History of the Battle of Lake Erie*, pp. 191–2. See also M. A. DeWolfe Howe, *The Life and Letters of George Bancroft*, 2 vols (New York: Scribner's, 1908) 1: 151–2.
105. Benson, "Catherine Potter Stith and Her Meeting with Lord Byron," p. 12. Major Stith, unwell at the time of meeting Byron, died in 1824 and was buried in Gibraltar. The next year, Sully in Philadelphia painted for his widow a portrait of the deceased.
106. *BLJ* 9: 171, even (sighed Byron) "with *more ceremony* than I am fond of" (ibid., p. 164).
107. Bancroft, "A Day," p. 193.
108. *BLJ* 9: 164. In 1806 Nicholas Biddle found American naval officers "clever sensible men" who were "much more temperate than the British" (*Nicholas Biddle in Greece*, ed. McNeal, p. 75).
109. Nathan, *Fugitive Pieces*, p. 137. C. 1815.
110. Forester, *The Age of Fighting Sail. The Story of the Naval War of 1812* (1956;

Sandwich, Mass.; Chapman Billies, [n.d.]). Byron's cousin and heir to the title, Captain George Anson Byron, later 7th Lord, could have told him much about naval happenings.

111. Huckel, "Thomas Sully in Philadelphia," p. 270.
112. *BLJ* 9: 162. *Faust* with Retzsch's illustrations, along with Byron's note, are now in the Beinecke at Yale.
113. Smith's famous quip in the *Edinburgh Review* drew an eloquent rebuttal from Washington Irving in *The Sketch-Book* (1819–20), which Byron and probably Sully had read. I cite Smith from Susan Manning's Introduction to the Oxford World's Classics edition of *The Sketch-Book*, p. ix.
114. Benson, "Catherine Potter Stith," p. 18. Mrs Stith is one of the few American women Byron met.
115. Copybook 2, p. 67 (BS, 3.15.38).
116. Copybook 1, p. 139 (2.14.38). Sully added, "There are some passable parts in it, but I do not like it altogether: it is too large and seems a woman of twenty-three or more – with somewhat of a care-worn expression. . . . " (Copybook 2, p. 3 [2.14.38]). Later, when asked by the Baroness Lehzen his opinion of Hayter's portrait, Sully felt "obliged to confess my disapproval, tho' I knew it would be unacceptable, but I must speak my opinion, even tho' it may displease Royalty. I could not be satisfied with a deception!" (Copybook 2, pp. 114–15 [4.2.38]).
117. Journal, in Barratt, p. 84.
118. Copybook 1, p. 33 (BS–SAS, 11.10.37).
119. Ibid. [Winterthur], p. 86 [12.4.37].
120. Ibid., p. 24 (11.11.37).
121. Ibid., p. 75 (12.4.37).
122. Ibid., p. 84 (12.4.37).
123. Ibid., p. 123.
124. Ibid., p. 143 (TS–J. Darley, 2.14.38).
125. Copybook 2, p. 35.
126. Copybook 2, p. 24 (TS, 2.26.38). Other examples abound. Sully often heard "expressions of censure against the Kemble family – all except Charles – and especially Fanny, with great pain."
127. Copybook 2, pp. 116–17 (3.24.38).
128. Vallone, *Becoming Victoria*, p. 230.
129. Journal, in Barratt, pp. 141–2.
130. Copybook 2, pp. 112, 114.
131. Ibid., p. 104 (TS, 3.24.38). Edward and William Finden had engraved *Finden's Illustrations of the Life and Works of Lord Byron*, 3 vols (London: John Murray, 1833).
132. Ibid. "Paul Pry," a busybody, in John Poole's comedy, *Paul Pry* (1825).
133. Ibid., p. 32. Blanche also posed in Victoria's state robes on May 22 and 23.
134. Weintraub, *Victoria*, p. 99.
135. Copybook 2, p. 117 (3.24.38).
136. "Queen Victoria as Seen by an American," arranged by William L. Royall, p. 463.
137. Copybook 1, p. 146, Copybook 2, p. 2: both TS–J. Darley (2.14.38). "Pall" in British pronunciation was pronounced "Pell" (as in "Pall Mall").
138. James, *Essays on Literature*, p. 1090.
139. Vallone, *Becoming Victoria*, pp. 153–4; Furnas quotes Victoria's words on p. 164. Fanny at Victoria's request was presented to her in 1841 (Furnas, pp. 248–9).

140. Journal, in Barratt, p. 141.
141. Bronson points out that Sully had the frame made to his specifications and that the portrait can only be fully understood in the context of its full title – *Her Majesty the Queen in her Robes of State Ascending the Throne in the House of Lords* (pp. 244, 245–6).
142. Budd, "Thomas Sully," pp. 111–18. Sully's copy eventually went to Charleston. In 1865 it burned in Columbia, South Carolina, where it had been moved for safekeeping, along with much of the rest of the city (Barratt, p. 60).
143. Journal, in Barratt, p. 149.
144. Tuckerman, p. 161.
145. Copybook 2, p. 110 (3.24.01), p. 80 (3.11.38).
146. An exception is Simon, *The Portrait in Britain and America.*
147. Alberts, *Benjamin West*, p. 340; see also Staley, *Benjamin West in Pennsylvania Collections*, p. 9. Rembrandt Peale informed Sully of David's opinion, and Sully retailed it to Daniel Wadsworth (letter of June 17, 1810, Connecticut State Library).
148. Dunlap 2: 51.
149. Sully, *Hints*, p. 45.

Chapter Six

1. Fisher, *A Philadelphia Perspective*, p. 158. Fisher thus assessed Biddle in 1844, after Biddle's death.
2. Burt, *First Families*, p. 173.
3. Burstein, *America's Jubilee*, pp. 193, 334.
4. Burt, *Perennial Philadelphians*, p. 47.
5. Conrad, "Nicholas Biddle," in *The National Portrait Gallery* 4: 3.
6. Burt, *Perennial Philadelphians*, p. 47.
7. Fisher, *A Philadelphia Perspective*, p. 154.
8. "Chestnut" in passport descriptions, 1804–5 (summarized by Govan in *Nicholas Biddle*, p. 12), "blue" in Conrad (*National Portrait Gallery* 4: 24), "grey" in Fisher (*A Philadelphia Perspective*, p. 154).
9. Fisher, *A Philadelphia Perspective*, p. 154.
10. A recollection of 1866, cited in Wainwright, "Nicholas Biddle in Portraiture," p. 149.
11. *Nicholas Biddle in Greece*, ed. McNeal, p. 179.
12. Biddle's Anacreonic "Ode to Bogle" (1829), a *jeu d'esprit* inspired by light Regency verse *à la* Thomas Moore, is his best-known effort (republished in Burt, *First Families*, pp. 464–7).
13. Woodhouse, "Nicholas Biddle in Europe," p. 16.
14. Laverty et al., *Monument to Philanthropy*, p. 156.
15. *Nicholas Biddle in Greece*, ed. McNeal, p. 164.
16. Woodhouse, "Nicholas Biddle in Europe," pp. 13, 15.
17. Zamoyski, *Holy Madness*, pp. 232–3.
18. *Nicholas Biddle in Greece*, ed. McNeal, p. 54.
19. *English Bards*, ll. 867–8 (*CPW* 1: 256).
20. Patrick Leigh Fermor, *Roumeli* (1966; London and New York: Penguin Books, 1983), p. 170.
21. *Nicholas Biddle in Greece*, ed. McNeal, pp. 1, 99n. The first was Joel Roberts Poinsett (1779–1850), who later held diplomatic posts in South America and

in 1825 was appointed minister to Mexico. He introduced the poinsettia to Philadelphians. Sully painted his portrait. One reason why Biddle made no effort to publish his journals may be that models for the new kind of travel writing he was engaged in did not yet exist. The first major *literary* account of Near Eastern travel experiences is Chateaubriand's *Itinéraire de Paris à Jerusalem et de Jerusalem à Paris* (1810).

22. *BLJ* 1: 173.
23. On *Anarcharsis* (which Biddle read in Italian) see McNeal, "Nicholas Biddle, *Anarcharsis*, and the Grand Tour" (1996), especially pp. 230 ff.
24. The lines from *Le Cosmopolite* begin, "L'univers est une espèce de livre, dont on n'a lu que la première page quand on n'a vu que son pays" (*CPW* 2: 3).
25. For a splendid overview, see David Roessel's *In Byron's Shadow. Modern Greece in the English and American Imagination* (2002).
26. Ziff, *Return Passages*, p. 15.
27. *Nicholas Biddle in Greece*, ed. McNeal, pp. 49, 88, 111, 137.
28. Ibid., p. 231. Herostratus burned the Temple of Diana at Ephesus – one of the Seven Wonders of the ancient world – solely to become famous.
29. The line quoted is from *Childe Harold*, canto 2, stanza 11 (*CPW* 2: 47).
30. *Nicholas Biddle in Greece*, ed. McNeal, pp. 107, 101, 194–5.
31. Wainwright, "Glimpses of Napoleon in 1804," p. 113.
32. So named by John Craig (Jane's father) because of business ties with that region of Spain.
33. Geffen, *Philadelphia Unitarianism*, p. 63. Moore also became a contributor to *The Port Folio*.
34. Woodhouse, "Nicholas Biddle in Europe," p. 29, citing *The Port Folio*, Jan. 1812, p. 134; July 1812, p. 36.
35. Leonard, *Byron and Byronism*, pp. 2, 3.
36. Accardo (1998), p. 6.
37. Ibid., p. 9; Leonard, *Byron and Byronism*, p. 23.
38. Ibid., p. 24. Though published after Biddle had resigned as editor, these words may well be his.
39. Govan, *Nicholas Biddle*, pp. 22, 36–7. Biddle's edition, standard for eighty years, influenced American thinking about "Manifest Destiny." Paul Russell Cutright praises Biddle's "rare literary ability" and notes that he worked without compensation (*A History of the Lewis and Clark Journals* [Norman: University of Oklahoma Press, 1976], pp. 53, 60, 66). As Biddle became active in the state legislature, he had no time to revise his manuscript of the journals. Paul Allen prepared it for the press. As with his Greek adventures, Biddle seemed indifferent to public recognition for his labors. His friends knew what he had done; as with the Greek journals, he did not seek popular acclaim.
40. *BLJ* 3: 229.
41. *Letters of the Lewis and Clark Expedition . . .*, edited by Donald Jackson, 2nd edn, 2 vols (Urbana: University of Illinois Press, 1979) 2: 547.
42. McMurtry, *Sacagawea's Nickname. Essays on the American West* (New York: Simon and Schuster, 2001), p. 139. Whitman, in Preface to *Leaves of Grass* (1855)
43. *Life of Ticknor* 1: 59. Byron probably read London editions of Barlow (1809) and of Lewis and Clark, *Travels to the Source of the Missouri River* (1814).
44. *Life of Ticknor* 1: 68.
45. *History of the Expedition . . . of Lewis and Clark*, ed. Elliot Coues (1893; New York: Dover, 1965), p. xi. Coues was the next editor of the journal after Biddle.

46. Clubbe, *Byron's Natural Man: Daniel Boone & Kentucky.*
47. Wainwright, "Glimpses of Napoleon in 1804," p. 106.
48. Biddle's *Oration Delivered before the Pennsylvania Society of the Cincinnati on the Fourth of July MDCCCXI* (Philadelphia, 1811), cited from Govan, *Nicholas Biddle*, p. 37.
49. Ibid.
50. Ibid., pp. 105, 104.
51. *An Address Delivered before the Alumni Association of Nassau Hall [in] . . . 1835* (1836), cited from Woodhouse, "Nicholas Biddle in Europe," p. 31.
52. Wainwright, citing a speech of 1835, in "Glimpses of Napoleon in 1804," p. 104. The phrase describing Napoleon as the "master spirit of the age," a commonplace, derives from Las Cases's *Mémorial de Sainte-Hélène* (1823).
53. *Nicholas Biddle in Greece*, ed. McNeal, p. 69.
54. Wordsworth's sonnet "To B. R. Haydon, on Seeing his Picture of Napoleon Buonaparte on the Island of St. Helena" is dated June 11, 1831. Haydon made 23 versions of *Napoleon Musing at St Helena.*
55. Biddle, "Joseph Bonaparte," reproduction opposite p. 216.
56. Wainwright, *Andalusia*, p. 65. Otis made at least four other copies.
57. Charles Lawrence depicted the estate at the time Joseph purchased it in *Point Breeze, the estate of Joseph Napoleon Bonaparte at Bordentown, New Jersey, 1817/1820* (Art Institute of Chicago; attributed). After a fire in January 1820, the house was rebuilt as an imposing three-story classical mansion, central block with wings, that Karl Bodmer depicted in 1832.
58. Fisher, *A Philadelphia Perspective*, p. 60. Fisher met Joseph only in 1838.
59. Biddle, "Joseph Bonaparte," p. 209.
60. May 10, 1816; June 18, 1831: ibid., pp. 210, 219, 221.
61. Ibid., p. 210.
62. Connelly, *The Gentle Bonaparte*, p. 250.
63. Ibid., p. 270.
64. Athenaeum of Philadelphia website description of ongoing (2002–) exhibition of Joseph's collection.
65. Connelly, *The Gentle Bonaparte*, p. 268; Rebora, "Sir Thomas Lawrence," p. 46, n. 80.
66. *Napoleon's Last Will and Testament* (New York and London: Paddington Press, 1977), p. 36. The emperor thought Lafayette "a political monomaniac."
67. Woodward, *Bonaparte's Park and the Murats*, p. 51.
68. Sully, Journal [NYPL], April 30, 1826, p. 41. Actually Joseph was also an early riser.
69. Sully, Hints [Winterthur], after April 24, 1826 (published in part by Dunlap [2: 277–8]).
70. Hall, *Travels in North America*, 2: 338.
71. [Mrs Basil Hall,] *The Aristocratic Journey*, p. 132. Sidney Fisher (in 1838) agreed with Hall: "Likeness to Napoleon very striking, particularly the profile" (*A Philadelphia Perspective*, p. 60).
72. MS: Frick Art Reference Library, New York (reverse photostat).
73. Mark Twain reassessed Hall's book tongue-in-cheek in "Appendix C" of *Life on the Mississippi* (1883).
74. Connelly, *The Gentle Bonaparte*, pp. 279–80. Disappointed in his hopes, Joseph returned twice to America, in 1835–36 and 1838–39. He died in Italy in 1844.
75. Govan, *Nicholas Biddle*, p. 79.

76. Smith, *Recollections*, cited from Wainwright, *Andalusia*, p. 22.
77. Laverty et al., *Monument to Philanthropy*, p. 105.
78. Unidentified individual, cited in Wainwright, *Andalusia*, p. viii.
79. Fisher, *A Philadelphia Perspective*, p. 154. Fisher also speaks of Biddle as "sensual, and much addicted to enjoyments not permitted to a husband & father" (p. 88). Apparently Biddle in 1839 fell in love with a "black-eyed, well-formed Italian lady" named Ameriga Vespucci (Govan, *Nicholas Biddle*, p. 347). Govan claims the relationship was chaste, but contemporaries were doubtful. Was Biddle also, like Byron, larger than life in his sexuality?
80. Burt, *Perennial Philadelphians*, p. 52.
81. *Diary of Philip Hone*, p. 577.
82. Wainwright, *Andalusia*, p. 46.
83. Burt, *Perennial Philadelphians*, p. 423.
84. *Nicholas Biddle in Greece*, ed. McNeal, p. 12.
85. Laverty et al., *Monument to Philanthropy*, p. 157.
86. Long-circulating rumors that Biddle influenced the Second Bank's design remain undocumented.
87. On this point, see Clubbe, "Interiors and the Interior Life in Edith Wharton's *The House of Mirth*," *Studies in the Novel*, 28 (Winter 1996), 548–9.
88. *Philadelphia*, ed. Weigley, p. 259; Biddle, *Proceedings on Laying the Cornerstone of the Girard College for Orphans*, cited from Woodhouse, "Nicholas Biddle in Europe," p. 28.
89. Laverty et al., *Monument to Philanthropy*, pp. 13, 79.
90. Ibid., pp. 72, 83. Biddle achieved an impressive, but not final, victory. Walter went on to plan and design the wings and dome of the US Capitol in Washington, but Greek Revival architecture gradually faded from the scene.
91. Laverty, in ibid., p. 89.
92. Burt, *Perennial Philadelphians*, p. 49.
93. Govan, *Nicholas Biddle*, pp. 71–2; Wainwright, *Andalusia*, pp. 27–38.
94. Woodhouse, "Nicholas Biddle in Europe," p. 28.
95. *Diary of Philip Hone*, p. 387.
96. *Nicholas Biddle in Greece*, ed. McNeal, p. 8.
97. Miles, "Sitters," in *Portrait Painting*, ed. Miles, p. 148.
98. Wainwright, "Nicholas Biddle in Portraiture," in ibid., p. 151.
99. Ibid., pp. 151–2.
100. Ibid., p. 155; Hensel, "Jacob Eichholtz, Painter," pp. 50, 51.
101. Sully's 1837 portrait of Biddle is an oval replica of an earlier portrait of 1831 (destroyed by fire) that Sartain had engraved.
102. By choosing a bust-sized portrait Biddle deflected allegations of ostentatious vanity. In 1844 Sully went to Biddle's funeral, one of only two funerals – the other that of his great patron, Benjamin Chew Wilcocks – at which he recorded his attendance (Sully, Journal [NYPL], May 13, 1809, p. 10; Sept. 27, 1838, p. 189; March 4, 1844, p. 273).
103. Such attire – Sully painted Rebecca Gratz similarly – implies that the sitter is in the vanguard of fashion.
104. Sully charged Biddle $75 for each portrait and an additional $25 for reworking *Biddle* in 1828.
105. Evans, *Genius of Stuart*, p. 65.
106. Danly, *Facing the Past*, p. 15.
107. Neal, p. 14.
108. Fisher, *A Philadelphia Perspective*, p. 158.

Chapter Seven

1. *Notions of the Americans*, 2 vols, intro. Robert E. Spiller (1828; New York: Frederick Ungar, 1963) 1: 61.
2. Burstein, *America's Jubilee*, p. 62.
3. Pennington, "Painting Lord Byron: An Account by William Edward West," p. 19.
4. Lease, *That Wild Fellow John Neal*, p. 20.
5. Vogel, *Cultural Connections*, p. 145.
6. In *The Case of the Greeks* (1826), cited from Bradsher, *Carey*, p. 77.
7. Roessel, *In Byron's Shadow*, p. 62. I am less certain.
8. "Navarin" in Hugo's *Les Orientales* (1829), cited from *Odes et Ballades / Les Orientales* (Paris: Editions Rencontre, 1968), pp. 332, 338.
9. As an instance of historical interconnections, consider a set of pistols brought by Lafayette from France to America in 1777. In 1778 he gave them to Washington. In 1824 William Robinson, a relation by marriage of the Washingtons and the man who had inherited them, gave them to Jackson on the ninth anniversary of his victory over the British at the Battle of New Orleans. Robinson told Jackson he was "the successor of Washington in the Military character of America." Jackson, who regarded the pistols as "sacred and holy relics," bequeathed them to Lafayette's son. They remained in the family until 1958. At a recent Christie's sale (January 18, 2002) they were expected to go for more than $1.5 million (Rita Reif, "Silent Witnesses to War and Fellowship," *The New York Times*, December 23, 2001, AR 38).
10. Lynes, *The Art-Makers*, p. 232.
11. This paragraph draws upon Miles's Introduction (unpaginated) to *Portrait Painting*, ed. Miles.
12. Burstein, *America's Jubilee*, p. 288.
13. B & F, pp. 186–7. Barber, *Andrew Jackson: A Portrait Study*, reproduces Sully's portrait on p. 55; Longacre's engraving, on the next page.
14. Torchia, in the National Gallery's *American Paintings of the Nineteenth Century* 2: 184, 186.
15. Burstein, *Jackson*, p. 139. This biography uses Sully's portrait for its dustjacket.
16. Sully, Journal [NYPL], Dec. 26, 1824, p. 33.
17. Sully, Journal [NYPL], June 30, 1834, p. 99d. A last-minute political complication prevented Jackson from attending.
18. Burstein, *America's Jubilee*, p. 291.
19. Burstein, *Jackson*, p. 125.
20. Miller, *Rembrandt Peale*, p. 143.
21. Burstein, *Jackson*, p. 169.
22. Ibid., p. 125. The comparison to Napoleon lasted well beyond Jackson's lifetime. After his death commentators compared him to celebrated commanders from Hannibal to Napoleon.
23. Kennett, "Le Culte de Napoléon," p. 149. My translation.
24. Guérard, *Reflections on the Napoleonic Legend*, p. 101.
25. In 1838 (Fisher, *A Philadelphia Perspective*, p. 60).
26. Kennett, "Le Culte de Napoléon," p. 152.
27. Alberts, *Benjamin West*, chs. 19–22 *passim*.
28. *Sir Thomas Lawrence's Letter-Bag*, ed. Layard, p. 38.
29. Farington, *Diary* 13: 4694 (Aug. 18, 1815).
30. *Sir Thomas Lawrence's Letter-Bag*, ed. Layard, pp. 92, 93.

31. Williams, *Life of Lawrence*, 2: 338–9.
32. Miller, *Rembrandt Peale*, ch. 6. Peale developed his essentially French portrait style in Paris.
33. Sellers terms Rembrandt "a hero-worshipper . . . of the romantic heroes, Napoleon, Byron, Scott, the idealized Washington, and his own spectre of genius" (*Charles Willson Peale*, p. 360).
34. Sellers, *Peale*, p. 360; Dunlap 2: 184–5n.
35. Neal, p. 18.
36. Barratt, *Queen Victoria*, pp. 107, 115; Journal [NYPL], April 6, 1828, p. 58.
37. Sully, Journal [NYPL], March 2, 1834, p. 98.
38. Princess Marie Liechtenstein, *Holland House*, 2 vols (London: Macmillan, 1874) 2: 155.
39. Journal, July 25, 1838, in Barratt, *Queen Victoria*, p. 195.
40. B & F, p. 238.
41. Sully, Journal [NYPL], December 31, 1825, pp. 38, 39.
42. *Lafayette, Hero*, p. 84.
43. Ibid., p. 92.
44. Ibid., pp. 141, 72.
45. Burstein, *America's Jubilee*, p. 8; *Lafayette, Hero*, pp. 11, 105.
46. *Lafayette, Hero*, p. 3.
47. Ibid., p. 6.
48. Neely, *Lafayette*, p. 41.
49. Ibid., p. 21.
50. Ibid., p. 11.
51. *Lafayette, Hero*, p. 50.
52. Ibid., p. 52.
53. Kramer, *Lafayette*, p. 186.
54. Thurlow Reed, writing half a century after the event (cited from Van Zandt, *Chronicles of the Hudson*, p. 155).
55. Ibid., p. 155; *Lafayette, Hero*, p. 106.
56. Burstein, *America's Jubilee*, p. 34.
57. *Lafayette, Hero*, p. 54.
58. Van Zandt, *Chronicles of the Hudson*, p. 155.
59. *Lafayette, Hero*, p. 148.
60. Sully, Journal [NYPL], July 21, 1825, p. 36.
61. *Lafayette, Hero*, p. 148.
62. For Greenough's sculpture, see *Lafayette, Hero*, pp. 173–5. Physiognomic approaches, when applied to political or social caricature, could also result in brilliant satire, e.g., the works in different mediums by Daumier.
63. *Lafayette, Hero*, pp. 122–6; Gilchrist, *Strickland*, p. 5 and pl. 50.
64. Henderson, *Pennsylvania Academy*, p. 321; *Lafayette, Hero*, p. 150.
65. *Lafayette, Hero*, p. 150.
66. Ibid., p. 145.
67. Byron's lyric "They say that hope is happiness" frames Burstein's excellent *America's Jubilee*, which has the second stanza as its epigraph and concludes with the entire poem (pp. 306–7). Poem and author serve as an integral motif in the book's argument, though Burstein does not point out that the poem was not published until *after* the 1826 Jubilee (*CPW* 3: 277–8, 461). Robinson also brings out Byron's importance for the Jubilee in "Byron and the Fourth of July," *passim*, esp., p. 25.
68. Zamoyski, *Holy Madness*, p. 239.

69. *BLJ* 7: 80 (4.22.1820). Byron refers to Lafayette's support of the French Revolution, but the application is broader.
70. *BLJ* 9: 20–21.
71. Medwin, p. 52.
72. Oueijan, "Byron's Notions of the American Revolution," in *Byronic Negotiations*, ed. Bachinger, p. 110.
73. Bancroft, "A Day with Lord Byron," pp. 195–6.
74. Accardo, "American Editions of Byron," p. 489, citing S. Austin Allibone, *A Critical Dictionary of English Literature*, 3 vols (Philadelphia: Childs and Peterson, 1858) 1: 323.
75. Parry, *The Last Days of Lord Byron*, p. 174.
76. Accardo, "Byron in America to 1830," p. 6. This paragraph owes much to Accardo's exhaustive research.
77. Accardo, "American Editions," p. 487.
78. Dumas, *Mes Mémoires*, cited from Zamoyski, *Holy Madness*, p. 243.
79. Field, *America and the Mediterranean World*, p. 121.
80. Justin Kaplan and Anne Bernays, *The Language of Names* (New York: Simon & Schuster/Touchstone, 1997), p. 42.
81. Vogel, *Cultural Connections*, p. 34.
82. Repousis, "The Cause of the Greeks," pp. 333–4n.
83. Lynes, *The Art-Makers*, p. 61. Throughout the nineteenth century Americans persistently drew analogies between the Greek Revolution and the American (Roessel, *In Byron's Shadow*, p. 94).
84. Larrabee, *Hellas Observed*, pp. 67, 55.
85. Bernier, *Lafayette*, p. 294; *Lafayette, Hero*, p. 52.
86. Repousis, "The Cause of the Greeks," pp. 334, 336, 339, 340, 341, 342.
87. Accardo, *Byron in Nineteenth-Century American Culture*, p. 35.
88. Repousis, "The Cause of the Greeks," p. 348.
89. *Lafayette, Hero*, p. 86; Loveland, *Emblem of Liberty*, pp. 113–17.
90. St Clair, *That Greece Might Still Be Free*, p. 176.
91. *Collected Letters of Thomas and Jane Welsh Carlyle* 3: 69–70 (5.20.1824); ibid., 68 (5.19.1824).
92. *Alfred Lord Tennyson. A Memoir*, ed. Hallam, Lord Tennyson, 2 vols (London: Macmillan, 1897) 1: 4.
93. *England and the English*, ed. Standish Meacham (1833; Chicago and London: University of Chicago Press, 1970), p. 280.
94. *The Miscellaneous Prose Works of Sir Walter Scott*, 28 vols (Edinburgh: Cadell, 1834–40) 4: 343–4. See also Clubbe, "Byron and Scott" and "After Missolonghi: Scott on Byron, 1824–32," The University of Pennsylvania *Library Chronicle*, 29 (Winter 1973): 18–33.
95. Ibid., p. 344, 348.
96. Ibid., pp. 347–8.
97. *The Letters of Sir Walter Scott*, ed. Herbert J. C. Grierson et al., 12 vols (London: Constable, 1932–37) 9: 199.
98. Zamoyski, *Holy Madness*, p. 243.
99. Mazzini, in *Byron: The Critical Heritage*, ed. Andrew Rutherford (London: Routledge & Kegan Paul, 1970), p. 340.
100. Lease, *Anglo-American Encounters*, pp. 152 ff.
101. Crozier, *The Novels of Harriet Beecher Stowe*, cited from *Critical Essays on Harriet Beecher Stowe*, ed. Elizabeth Ammons (Boston: G. K. Hall, 1980), pp. 195–6.

102. Hallock, *The American Byron: Homosexuality and the Fall of Fitz-Greene Halleck*, pp. 7, 98–9. Hallock's title misleads: Byron was bisexual, not homosexual; he was a major poet, Halleck was not.
103. "Marco Bozzaris," in *The Poetical Works of Fitz-Greene Halleck* (New York: D. Appleton and Company, 1865), pp. 10, 12. The poem is historically shaky.
104. Ch. 33. Hallock, *The American Byron*, pp. 96–7.
105. Brooks, *The World of Washington Irving*, pp. 191, 373. For over a century "Marco Bozzaris" was the bane of schoolboy declaimers.
106. Ellen M. Foshay and Barbara Novak, *Intimate Friends. Thomas Cole, Asher B. Durand, William Cullen Bryant* (New York: New-York Historical Society, 2000), p. 19.
107. Payne, in Roessel, *In Byron's Shadow*, p. 301, n.30; Longfellow, in manuscript journal (1829), cited in Accardo, *Byron in Nineteenth-Century American Culture*, p. 36. For this and other poems inspired by the Greek revolt, see Raizis and Pappas's excellent anthology *The Greek Revolution and the American Muse* (1972); also their *American Poets and the Greek Revolution 1821–1828. A Study in Byronic Philhellenism* [1971].
108. Accardo, "Byron in America to 1830," p. 32, citing Martineau's *Society in America*, 2 vols (New York: Saunders and Otley, 1837) 2: 311.
109. Ibid., pp. 32–3, citing Marryat's *Diary in America.*
110. Marryat, *Diary in America* (Bloomington: Indiana University Press, 1960), p. 125.
111. Reproduction in Burstein, *America's Jubilee*, p. 37.
112. Ibid., pp. 62–4.
113. Noble, *Cole*, p. 117. Byron's poems haunted Cole, who quoted them often in letters.
114. Hawthorne, *The Marble Faun*, ch. 17 ("Miriam's Trouble").
115. Patricia Junker, "Thomas Cole's *Prometheus Bound*: An Allegory for the 1840s," *American Art Journal*, 31 (2000), 50.
116. Raymund Fitzsimons, *Barnum in London* (New York: St Martin's Press, 1970), p. 155.
117. Jarves, *The Art-Idea*, p. 196.
118. Benjamin, in *Harper's New Monthly Magazine*, 59 (Sept. 1879): 492–3.
119. Turner, *Charles Eliot Norton*, p. 48.
120. Evans, *Genius of Stuart*, p. 71.

Chapter Eight

1. Praz, *The House of Life*, p. 146. He refers to his first book, *La fortuna di Byron in Inghilterra* (1925).
2. Saisselin, *Style, Truth and the Portrait*, p. 17.
3. Kleinfeld, "Infidel on Parnassus," p. 164.
4. Atop a cascade of flowing robes Friedel superimposed (and reversed) the head from Westall's 1813 portrait. The portrait is the frontispiece to St Clair's *That Greece Might Still Be Free.*
5. Huckel, p. 271.
6. The classic study is Altick, *Paintings from Books* (1985).
7. Budd, "Thomas Sully," p. 121. See the title page of volume 4 of the 1814 edition of Irving's *Works* (Irving, *Letters* 1: 381, 382).
8. Kirksey, in her study of Sully's *Crusoe* sketches, suggests that Crusoe appealed

to Sully not as a children's book but as "a serious work, stressing the need for personal industry and discipline and the rewards of Christianity" (p. 19).

9. Lockhart, *Memoirs of Scott*, p. 368.
10. Medwin, p. 7.
11. *Life of Ticknor*, 1: 58–9.
12. Guiccioli, *Recollections*, 1: 67. Captain Forrester, seeing Byron in 1824, thought he bore "as little resemblance to the pretended fac-simile, as I to Apollo" (Medwin, *Angler in Wales* 2: 200).
13. Accardo (1998), p. 10. In this instance, a bad engraving became a worse.
14. Walker, 1: 82.
15. Peach, citing an unpublished letter by Westall to Murray of January 11, 1814 (p. 44).
16. Walker 1: 82, citing Whitman, *Charles Turner*, p. 87. Evidently a favorite, Turner's engraving was reprinted on July 15, 1815, and reissued by Colnaghi in 1826.
17. Ibid., 1: 82; Peach, p. 44.
18. Piper, *Image of the Poet*, p. 133.
19. Peach, p. 44.
20. Neal, p. 40.
21. Though Walker dates the lithograph to 1825, Lillian Miller, Peale's biographer, thinks between January and May 1826 more likely. Either date would have allowed time for Sully to see, ponder, and draw upon Peale's pioneering work for his portrait.
22. Also reproduced in Mahey, "Lithographs by Rembrandt Peale," in *Portrait Painting*, ed. Miles, pp. 66–7.
23. Printed by Villain and published by Sazerac and Duval in Paris.
24. Navarino, a major sea battle between the Ottoman fleet and a combined Anglo-French force, did not take place until 1827, three years after Byron's death.
25. Hints (Winterthur).
26. Blake, "Proverbs of Hell," in *The Marriage of Heaven and Hell.*
27. Holmes, Thorwaldsen, and W. E. West have left accounts of Byron as sitter (see Kenyon Jones, in *Byromania*, ed. Wilson, pp. 124–5). One instance (Holmes): "When he was sitting for his portraits, he could seldom continue seated or be still for more than a minute or two at a time. He would be for ever moving about, now rising and going to the window, now suddenly taking up a stick and beginning to fence. When the artist remonstrated and said he could not paint while he was moving about like that, he would exclaim with a frown, 'O blood and guts, do get on!' and resume his seat for a brief space" (Kenyon Jones, "James Holmes and the Byron Circle," *Byron Journal*, 25 [1997], p. 83).
28. Evans, *Genius of Stuart*, p. 44. For a soul to emerge, as Harris puts it, the painter must turn his eye "inward and not outward: his hand must seek to embody not the outer forms of reality but the soul life which lay beneath" (*Artist in American Society*, p. 87).
29. Evans, in *The Portrait*, ed. Miles, p. 128.
30. McDermott, "Likenesses by Audubon," in *Portrait Painting*, ed. Miles, pp. 56–8.
31. Miles, *Saint-Mémin*, p. 51. Simple black silhouettes pleased Philadelphia Quakers. In 1825, upon graduating from Bowdoin College, Hawthorne could only afford a silhouette.

32. Sully in *Hints* (1873) quoted Lawrence's letter to Robert Gilmor Jr. urging him to let portraits "be so placed that the light may fall upon them from the *left* of the spectator" (p. 44).
33. Saltzman, *Portrait of Dr. Gachet*, p. xviii.
34. Lionel Trilling, *Sincerity and Authenticity* (Cambridge, Mass.: Harvard University Press, 1971).
35. Evans, in *The Portrait*, ed. Miles, p. 133; Evans, *Genius of Stuart*, p. 113.
36. Galt, *Life of Byron*, p. 61.
37. Hints (Winterthur), after March 27, 1826.
38. Unpublished paper, 29th Annual International Byron Seminar, Liverpool, August 2003. Byron, responsive to sculpture, characterized the Apollo Belvedere thus in stanza 161 of *Childe Harold* 4: "The God of life, and poesy, and light – / The Sun in human limbs arrayed" (*CPW* 2: 178).
39. *A Passion for Performance*, ed. Asleson, p. 128. Placing the sitter's illuminated head against a dark background became a hallmark of painterly Romantic portraiture. The practice lasted well into the nineteenth century.
40. Evans, *Genius of Stuart*, p. 26.
41. Cited from Patrick Noon et al., *Crossing the Channel. British and French Painting in the Age of Romanticism* (London: Tate Publishing, 2003), p. 112. The portrait is reproduced on p. 113. Christine Riding kindly called my attention to Lawrence's painting.
42. Burstein, *America's Jubilee*, pp. 242–3.
43. *Autobiography of Henry Taylor 1800–1875*, 2 vols (London: Longmans, Green, 1885) 1: 182.
44. Blessington, p. 5.
45. Coleridge, in *Quarterly Review* 16 (1816), 177; Jane Porter, cited from Praz, *The House of Life*, p. 148.
46. Lockhart, *Memoirs of Scott*, p. 368.
47. Langley Moore, "Byronic Dress," p. 7. The ideal (and era) of the golden tan lay decades in the future.
48. Hints (Winterthur), before Feb. 10, 1827.
49. John Murray III remembered "a handsome countenance, remarkable for the fine blue veins which ran over his pale, marble temples" (*A Publisher and His Friends*, ed. Smiles 1: 267).
50. Paley, *Portraits of Coleridge*, pp. 2–4.
51. Wordsworth, *Selected Poems and Prefaces*, ed. Jack Stillinger (Boston: Houghton Mifflin, 1965), p. 453.
52. Nathan, *Fugitive Pieces*, p. 35.
53. Ibid., pp. 118, 95.
54. Neal, p. 81.
55. Blessington, p. 5.
56. Only Medwin (who thought Byron's eyes "greyish brown") comes close (p. 8).
57. Captain Forrester, RN, as reprinted in Peach, *Portraits of Byron*, p. 16.
58. Hints (Winterthur), before Feb. 10, 1827.
59. Moore 2: 799.
60. *BLJ* 1: 119.
61. *His Very Self and Voice*, ed. Lovell, p. 42.
62. Moore 2: 799.
63. *Don Juan* attests to Byron's yearning for "thine 'incomparable oil,' Macassar" (*CPW* 5: 14, 675).
64. Neal, p. 5.

65. Hints (Winterthur).
66. Evans, *Genius of Stuart*, p. 113.
67. Torchia, *Neagle*, p. 8.
68. "My First Acquaintance with Poets" (1823), in Hazlitt, *Complete Works*, ed. Howe 17: 109. The shape of noses remains important for Hollywood. Nicole Kidman's digitally enhanced nose in *The Hours* (2002), the film based on Michael Cunningham's novel (itself drawing on Virginia Woolf's) was the work of one John Caglione Jr, who won the Oscar in 1991 for makeup for his work in the movie *Dick Tracy*.
69. *BLJ* 4: 79.
70. Blessington, p. 5.
71. Journal, cited from Barratt, pp. 141–2.
72. Hints (Winterthur).
73. De Quincey, *Reminiscences*, p. 104; Blessington, pp. 5–6.
74. *BLJ* 1: 227.
75. Paston and Quennell, "To Lord Byron," p. 65.
76. Piper, *Image of the Poet*, p. 135.
77. Langley Moore, "Byronic Dress," p. 1.
78. "A portrait – Lord Byron," *New Monthly Magazine*, 2nd series, 19 (1827), 382.
79. Medwin, p. 7; Trelawny in 1878 remembered the throat's "massiveness and length" (*Records* 1: 27).
80. Piper, *Image of the Poet*, p. 135.
81. Kenyon Jones, citing a correspondent in the *Literary Gazette*, May 1828 (*Byromania*, ed. Wilson, p. 113).
82. Dickens, *American Notes*, ch. 6, third paragraph.
83. Russell, *Aspects of British Art*, p. 143.
84. Brilliant, p. 101.
85. Friedländer, *Landscape, Portrait, Still-Life*, p. 112.
86. All three paintings discussed in this paragraph are reproduced in *The Collections of the Cincinnati Art Museum* (2000).
87. For instance, Sully provided detailed backgrounds for his portraits of Samuel Coates and Elizabeth Eichelberger Ridgely. Sully depicted *Miss Caroline Parsons as The Lady of the Lake*, inspired by the heroine of Scott's once enormously popular poem (1810), within a Romantic landscape meant to recall the poet's descriptions of the Scottish Highlands.
88. See last epigraph to Chapter 10.
89. Torchia, *Neagle*, p. 18. Verplanck had read his Reynolds.
90. A "Turnersque sky" may be seen in Sully's *William B. Wood*. Numerous oil sketches of mythological scenes in Sully's sketchbooks (Philadelphia Museum of Art) indicate his strong response to Fuseli's dramatic, mythmaking creativity, his fascination with dreams and the unconscious.
91. *Eloisa to Abelard*, ll. 163–5.
92. Susan L. Siegfried, *The Art of Louis-Léopold Boilly. Modern Life in Napoleonic France* (New Haven and London: Yale University Press, 1995), p. 107. The painting is reproduced on p. 109.
93. Peach, p. 43, citing *Childe Harold* 1: 27.
94. Piper, *Image of the Poet*, p. 134.
95. *Childe Harold* 3, stanza 78; "Alpine Journal" in *BLJ* 5: 102; Canto 4, stanza 20. Westall also uses the two trees in one of his illustrations to *Vathek*.
96. *Childe Harold* 3, stanzas 92–7. For Byron's note, see *CPW* 2: 311.

97. *Art and the Empire City*, p. 127.
98. S. G. W. Benjamin, "Fifty Years of American Art. 1828–1878," *Harper's New Monthly Magazine*, 59 (Sept. 1879), 488.
99. Tuckerman, in the 3rd edition of his *Italian Sketchbooks*, cited from ibid.
100. Sully also sketched landscapes. A clipping from *The New York Times* (February 23, 1946) reports that a "rare folio of landscape studies" by Sully had sold at Christie's London on February 22, 1946, and was bought by Colnaghi's (Artists' File, NYPL). Regarding landscape, see also Hints (Winterthur), after May 26, 1827.
101. Journal, Nov. 30, 1837, in Barratt, p. 93.
102. Sully to his sister Elizabeth ("Betsey") Smith in Charleston, Sept. 3, 1828 (MS: NYHS).
103. Leslie, *Autobiographical Recollections*, 2: 19–21. Perhaps Sully by sending Leslie to Westall's was testing his acuity.
104. I cite the opinions of Haydon and Hazlitt earlier. For Shaw's opinion see "The Authentic Portraits, Part I," p. 159.
105. Neal, p. 5.

Chapter Nine

1. *Love for Love* (1698), Act 2, ll. 272–3. Sir Sampson speaks to his brother Foresight about his son Valentine.
2. Lavater, *Essays* (abridged, 1800), p. 7.
3. Diderot, *Essai sur la peinture* in *Oeuvres complètes*, x, 484, cited by Tytler, *Physiognomy*, p. 105.
4. *Lavengro* (1851; London, etc.: T. N. Foulis, 1914), p. 156 (ch. 22).
5. *Lawrence's Letter-Bag*, ed. Layard, pp. 94–5.
6. No scholar has explored physiognomy's influence on Sully, though Bronson in discussing Fuseli's impact upon Sully mentions physiognomy in passing (p. 234).
7. The full title is *Physiognomische Fragmente zur Beförderung der Menschenkenntniss und Menschenliebe.*
8. The Latin phrase is from Juvenal, *Satires*, II, 8.
9. Shortland, p. 399.
10. Hegel, *Phenomenology of Spirit*, trans. A. V. Miller (Oxford: Oxford University Press, 1977), p. 198.
11. Lavater, introduction to *Essays on Physiognomy* (1804) 1: lxxxviii. Goethe and Chateaubriand expressed a like fear (Shortland, pp. 395–6).
12. Lavater, *Essays* (abridged, 1800), pp. 94–5.
13. Ibid., p. 84.
14. Napoleon in Las Cases, *Mémorial de Sainte-Hélène*, ed. Marcel Dunan, 2 vols (Paris: Flammarion, 1951) 2: 68; Staël, cited in Tytler, *Physiognomy*, p. 24.
15. Lavater, *Essays* (1804) 1: 10.
16. Ibid., pp. 3–4, 17; 34.
17. *Faust I*, 1. 2039 (trans. Philip Wayne).
18. *Nicholas Biddle in Greece*, ed. McNeal, p. 61; Woodhouse, "Nicholas Biddle in Europe," pp. 17, 23–4, 26.
19. Scholars often confuse the two. Paul Harvey's *Oxford Companion to English Literature* (3rd edn, 1946) has Lavater the inventor of phrenology, which he confuses with physiognomy. Margaret Drabble's revised 5th edition (1985)

repeats, with a slight addition, Harvey's brief note. A character in *War and Peace* attributes to Lavater a phrenological notion (Part I, ch. 1).

20. For Stuart, see Neal, pp. 72–3; for Lawrence, Goldring, *Regency Portrait Painter*, p. 241.
21. Hazlitt, *Table Talk* (cited in Barzun, *Berlioz and the Romantic Century*, 2 vols [Boston: Little, Brown, 1950] 2: 22); Blanshard, *Portraits of Wordsworth*, p. 46.
22. *Autobiography of Haydon*, ed. Taylor, 1: 210.
23. De Quincey, *Recollections*, p. 103. De Quincey was himself a determined phrenologist.
24. "Historic Survey of German Poetry" (1831), in Carlyle, *Works*, ed. H. D. Traill, 30 vols (London: Chapman and Hall, 1896–99) 27: 362.
25. Tytler, *Physiognomy*, pp. 114–15. All students of physiognomy owe much to this groundbreaking study.
26. Bryant, *Prose Writings*, ed. Parke Godwin, 2 vols (New York: D. Appleton, 1884) 2: 232. The quotation is from "The Academy of Design, an addressed delivered . . . in 1865."
27. David Cairns, *Berlioz. Servitude and Greatness 1832–1869*, 2 vols (Berkeley and Los Angeles: University of Califoria Press, 1999) 2: 191.
28. Berlioz, *Mémoires*, ed. Pierre Citron, 2 vols (Paris: Garnier-Flammarion, 1969) 1: 175.
29. Physiognomy in America lasted into the 1880s, indeed beyond. See, for example, Mary Olmstead Stanton, *Physiognomy. A Practical and Scientific Treatise*, 2nd edn (San Francisco: San Francisco News Co., 1881).
30. Tillyard, *The Elizabethan World Picture*, preface.
31. Epstein, *The Middle of My Tether*, pp. 75, 80.
32. Paul Theroux, *Sir Vidia's Shadow* (Boston and New York: Houghton Mifflin, 1998), p. 330.
33. New York: Ballantine Books, 1999.
34. "On Physiognomic Perception" in *Meditations on a Hobby Horse*, p. 47.
35. In "The Naked Face" Malcolm Gladwell surveys recent thinking about physiognomy (*The New Yorker*, August 5, 2002, 38–49).
36. Cooper, "Observations," p. 409.
37. *Physiognomics*, in *The Complete Works of Aristotle*, ed. Jonathan Barnes, 2 vols (Princeton/Bollingen: Princeton University Press, 1984) 1: 1237–50.
38. Cooper, "Observations," p. 417.
39. Lavater, *Essays* (abridged, 1800), p. 86.
40. *Macbeth* 1. iv. 11–12.
41. Wechsler, *A Human Comedy*, pp. 180–81.
42. Porter, "Making Faces," p. 393.
43. Clubbe, *Physiognomy* (1763), cited from his *Miscellaneous Tracts*, 2 vols (Ipswich: W. Jackson, for J. Shave [n.d., but early 1770s]) 1: 11.
44. Ibid., p. 14ff.
45. Ibid., p. 9.
46. Tytler, *Physiognomy*, p. 138.
47. Cooper, "Observations," p. 433.
48. *Sophie in London 1786*, p. 153.
49. Graham (1961a), pp. 566, 567.
50. Coxe, who visited Lavater in 1777 or 1778, typifies the responses: "the severest critics allow, that there is a fund of good sense and variety of fine observations dispersed throughout his treatise; and that it is one of those

works, which, to be admired, needs only to be read with attention" (*Sketches of . . . Swisserland*, 2nd edn [London: J. Dodsley, 1780], p. 88).

51. Porter, "Making Faces," p. 394.
52. *The Scots Magazine*, 63 (1801), 79, cited in Graham (1961a), p. 561.
53. *Gentleman's Magazine*, 71 (Feb. 1801), p. 123, cited in Graham (1961a), p. 561.
54. On Wollstonecraft's participation, see St Clair, *The Godwins and the Shelleys* (New York and London: Norton, 1989), p. 262. St Clair conflates physiognomy with phrenology, both subjects of interest to the Godwin circle.

    Lavater wrote in German, but outside the German-speaking world translations spread his ideas. He took an active role in various French and English editions, which often include material different from or omitted in the German. Forever revising, deleting, adding to both text and illustrations, Lavater always viewed his argument as an extended hypothesis and never established a final version in any language. The "chapters" in English editions are more accurately designated "fragments" in German and French editions.

    No standard edition or single authoritative text of Lavater's work exists in English. I have used the most complete English version – Thomas Holcroft's translation *Essays on Physiognomy*, 1st edn, 4 vols (London: G. J. & J. Robinson, 1789–93) – in its unrevised 2nd edn. of 1804. The abridgment cited reprints Robinson's abbreviated text of 1793 that, 15 times republished, the last time in 1878, served the English-speaking world throughout most of the nineteenth century. Translations and abridgements, notes Stemmler, often "reflected the private agendas of the translators." For example, Holcroft left out Lavater's frequent references to Christ, and researchers relying on his edition therefore "cannot fully understand Lavater's position" ("Physiognomical Portraits," pp. 152, 153). French editions contain far more of the religious passages (Shortland, p. 408, n. 99). For the complex textual history of Lavater's writings through 1810, see Shortland's essay and Graham (1961b). Both the abridged (1800) and the complete (1804) Holcroft editions that I have used appeared during the decade when Sully in America would have encountered ideas about physiognomy.
55. "Uber Physiognomik wider die Physionomen" (1777) and "Fragment von Schwanzen. Ein Beytrag zu den Physiognomischen Fragmenten" (1783), the latter, an eight-page pamphlet (Graham [1961a], p. 570).
56. Graham (1961a), p. 570.
57. Lavater, *Essays* (abridged, 1800), p. 258.
58. S. West names a few of the subscribers and examines why they found Lavater "indispensable" (*The Image of the Actor*, p. 139).
59. Graham (1966), pp. 212–18.
60. Tomory, *Fuseli*, p. 44; Frederick Antal, *Fuseli Studies* (London: Routledge and Kegan Paul, 1956), pp. 133, 165.
61. Tomory, *Fuseli*, p. 92, color illustration opposite p. 16.
62. *BLJ* 3: 253.
63. For references to Lavater, see *BLJ* 4: 167; *CPW* 1: 195, 386n (the note confuses physiognomy with phrenology); 2: 286n.
64. *BLJ* 4: 182.
65. *BLJ* 3: 239.
66. Wechsler, *A Human Comedy*, p. 8.
67. Lavater, *Essays* (1804) 2: 74.
68. Ray, *The Illustrator*, p. 21.

69. Lavater, *Essays* (abridged, 1800), p. 263.
70. Ibid., p. 3.
71. Ibid., pp. 259, 258.
72. Shortland, p. 394.
73. Lavater, *Essays* (abridged, 1800), pp. 256–7.
74. Ibid., p. 37.
75. Ibid., p. 260.
76. Quotations from Lawrence's description of Byron are not footnoted. The description was first published in D. E. Williams's 1831 biography of Lawrence, which Sully read and quoted from (Hints [Winterthur], *c.* Jan. 1833).
77. *Quarterly Review*, 16 (October 1816), 176–7.
78. Galt, *Byron*, p. 58.
79. Tomory, *Fuseli*, p. 117.
80. *A Handbook for Young Painters* (1855), cited in Tomory, *Fuseli*, p. 45.
81. Lavater, *Essays* (1804) 1: xxii.
82. Hazlitt's brilliant pen-portrait of Fuseli (upon which I draw) is republished in *The Mind of Fuseli*, ed. Mason, pp. 72–3.
83. Ray, *The Illustrator*, p. 21.
84. Allentuck, "Fuseli and Lavater," p. 97.
85. Gilchrist, *Life of Blake*, p. 63.
86. Blake, *Poetry and Prose*, ed. Erdman, pp. 572, 573, 589, 590.
87. Gilchrist, *Life of Blake*, p. 68.
88. Blake, *Poetry and Prose*, ed. Erdman, pp. 575, 37.
89. Miles, *Saint-Mémin*, p. 38.
90. Miller, *Rembrandt Peale*, p. 146. The elder Peale also left marginalia in his copy of Lavater's *Aphorisms on Man* (Dublin, 1790) (Evans, in Miles, *The Portrait*, p. 137, n. 14).
91. Danly, *Facing the Past*, p. 36.
92. Miles, *Saint-Mémin*, p. 38.
93. Gerdts and Burke, *American Still Life*, p. 30; Miles, *Saint-Mémin*, pp. 106–13.
94. Evans, *Genius of Stuart*, pp. 66, 67, and 143, n. 15.
95. Neal, p. 73.
96. Evans, *Genius of Stuart*, p. 67.
97. Ibid., p. 66.
98. Whitley, *Gilbert Stuart*, p. 95; Evans, *Genius of Stuart*, p. 66.
99. Stanley C. Arthur, *Audubon*, p. 194, cited from Dickson, "The Artist's Profession," p. 268.
100. Miller, *Rembrandt Peale*, p. 146.
101. Hevner, in ibid., pp. 281–2.
102. Hazlitt, in *Mind of Fuseli*, p. 72.
103. Haydon, *Autobiography*, ed. Elwin (1950), p. 25.
104. Todd, *Tracks in the Snow*, p. 74; *Mind of Fuseli*, ed. Mason, p. 75.
105. The other lectures did not appear until after 1820 and not in the order given. Though Fuseli included only limited discussion of physiognomy and Lavater, he infused his renderings of individual figures with physiognomical ideas.
106. Fuseli, *Lectures on Painting*, ed. Wornum, pp. 468, 500, 525.
107. Allentuck, "Fuseli and Lavater," p. 106.
108. Sully, Journal [NYPL], August 11, 1829, p. 69a.
109. Dunlap 2: 281.
110. Lavater, *Essays* (abridged, 1800), pp. 93–4.

111. Ibid., pp. 68, 25, 49 and 50, 51.
112. Trelawny, *Records* 1: 27; Blessington, p. 5. For Captain Forrester, however, "the head is rather large than otherwise" (Medwin, *Angler in Wales* 2: 210).
113. [John Galt], "Lord Byron's Conversations," *Blackwood's Edinburgh Magazine*, 16 (Nov. 1824), p. 535.
114. Lavater, *Essays* (abridged, 1800), p. 53.
115. *Life and Opinions of Tristram Shandy*, III, chapters xxvii–xxxviii. Slawkenbergius, an imagined author distinguished by the great length of his nose, was Sterne's authority on nose lore.
116. Rabelais, *Gargantua and Pantagruel*, Book 1, end of ch. 40.
117. De Quincey, *Recollections*, p. 103.
118. *The Love Letters of William and Mary Wordsworth*, ed. Beth Darlington (Ithaca, NY: Cornell University Press, 1981).
119. Tomory, *Fuseli*, pp. 163, 48.
120. Epstein, *The Middle of My Tether*, p. 80.
121. *The Autobiography of Charles Darwin 1809–1882*, ed. Nora Barlow (New York: Norton, 1958), p. 72.
122. Gollin, *Portraits of Hawthorne*, p. 13, n. 11.
123. Lavater, *Essays* (abridged, 1800), p. 60.
124. *The Age of Bronze*, 1. 535, in *CPW* 7: 17.
125. Lavater, *Essays* (abridged, 1800), p. 60.
126. Dunlap 2: 281.
127. Lavater, *Essays* (abridged, 1800), pp. 62, 63, 62. On the mouth Sully cited John Flaxman, also influenced by Lavater and one of Fuseli's circle, who believed it "that place where ignorance stops and knowledge triumphs" (Hints [Winterthur], Dec. 31, 1831).
128. Ibid., pp. 64, 93.
129. Ibid., p. 53.
130. Tytler, *Physiognomy*, p. 212.
131. Lavater, *Essays* (abridged, 1800), p. 53.
132. Sully, Journal, in Barratt, p. 141.
133. Lavater, *Essays* (abridged, 1800), p. 52.
134. Hints (Winterthur), after Jan. 19, 1827. Sully, who may be quoting an unidentified source, does not seem to be referring specifically to *Byron*.
135. Tytler, *Physiognomy*, p. 213.
136. Lavater, *Essays* (1804) 3. 242, 243, which develops from 3. 11–13.

Chapter Ten

1. Van Gogh, letter of June 3, 1890, to his sister Wil (*The Letters of Vincent Van Gogh*, sel. and ed. Ronald de Leeuw [London: Allen Lane/The Penguin Press, 1996], p. 492).
2. Hogarth, preface to *The Analysis of Beauty*, ed. Ronald Paulson (1753; New Haven and London: Yale University Press, 1997), p. 3.
3. *The Memoirs of Harriette Wilson*, 2 vols (London: Navarre Society, 1924) 2: 616, 617. The veracity of Wilson, a celebrated Regency courtesan, has often been questioned, but her seeing Byron at a ball, however fancifully depicted, has in essence if perhaps not in every detail a ring of authenticity.
4. Praz, *The House of Life*, p. 149.
5. Tscherny, "Likeness in Early Romantic Portraiture," p. 197.

6. Collingwood, *The Principles of Art*, p. 53.
7. Steiner, *Exact Resemblance to Exact Resemblance*, p. 6.
8. Blessington, p. 220.
9. Paley, *Portraits of Coleridge*, pp. 46, 45.
10. Keats, *Letters*, ed. Rollins 2: 88–9.
11. Bourrienne, cited from Wilson-Smith, *Napoleon and his Artists*, p. 68.
12. Cited from Gerhard von Breuning, *Memories of Beethoven*, ed. Maynard Solomon (Cambridge and New York: Cambridge University Press, 1992), pp. 110–111.
13. Wilfrid Mellers, *Beethoven and the Voice of God* (London: Faber & Faber, 1983), p. 20.
14. Picon, *The Birth of Modern Art*, p. 50.
15. Blanshard, *Portraits of Wordsworth*, p. 55.
16. Photography's limitations for portraiture were not immediately apparent. "Photographs, like statistics, often lie," observes Joseph Epstein, adding: "except in the hands of a photographer who is himself an artist, the camera generally misses what is most interesting in the human face" (*The Middle of My Tether*, p. 84).
17. Piper, *Image of the Poet*, p. 147.
18. Rick Lyman, "Movie Stars Fear Inroads By Upstart Digital Actors," *The New York Times*, July 8, 2001, pp. 1, 16.
19. Van Gogh, *Letters* (cited in note 1), p. 492.
20. Simon, *The Portrait*, p. 96.
21. Stoops, pp. 7, 36. Donna de Salvo, curating an earlier show of modern portraiture, claims that "the portrait has become a form in which issues of identity, especially as they relate to race and sexuality, are being defined." For her, it is "no surprise that portraiture, which is so directly related to how we see ourselves, should reemerge as a subject of aesthetic inquiry" (*Face Value: American Portraits* (Paris/New York: Flammarion, 1995), p. 22). This exhibit included work by, among others, Larry Rivers, Fairfield Porter, Elaine de Kooning, Alex Katz, Chuck Close, and Richard Avedon.
22. Brilliant, p. 59.
23. *Don Juan*, 17.11 (*CPW* 5: 660).
24. Gian Lorenzo Bernini quoted by his son, Domenico Bernini (Brilliant, p. 10).
25. So concludes Pointon, having studied Romney's sitters book, in "Portrait-Painting as a Business Enterprise," p. 197.
26. *A Passion for Performance*, ed. Asleson, p. 111. Reynolds might require as many as 16 sittings for a major full-length portrait.
27. Evans, *Genius of Stuart*, p. 113.
28. Vreeland, *Girl in Hyacinth Blue*, p. 202.
29. Piper, *The Image of the Poet*, p. 117.
30. Wilton, *The Swagger Portrait*, p. 50.
31. John Walker, *Portraits*, p. 173.
32. Aristotle, *On the Art of Poetry*, trans. Butcher, ed. Nahm, p. 20.
33. Leslie, *Autobiographical Recollections* 2: 21.
34. John Knowles, *The Life and Writings of Henry Fuseli, Esq.* 3 vols (London: Henry Colburn and Richard Bentley, 1831) 1: 333n; Levey, *Sir Thomas Lawrence*, p. 10.
35. Brooke, *Face to Face*, p. 16.
36. *CPW* 1: 289, 326.
37. *BLJ* 3: 224.

38. *CPW* 5: 79. Canto 1, stanza 218.
39. Evans, *Genius of Stuart*, pp. 59, 49.
40. Sully, *Hints*, pp. 30–31. The conversation with Wilkie took place in London on June 8, 1838. For another version see Sully's Journal under that date in Barratt, p. 171. The text there misreads "completion" for "complexion."
41. Ibid., p. 31.
42. Pointon, "Portrait-Painting as a Business," p. 195. Copying of course means different things in different cultures. Chinese artists have for generations copied and recopied revered works, and some of the copies have established themselves in their own right as masterpieces.
43. Reynolds, *Discourses*, ed. Wark, p. 106.
44. Coleridge, *Collected Letters*, ed. Griggs, 3: 501; Woodring, "What Coleridge Thought of Pictures," in Karl Kroeber and William Walling, *Images of Romanticism: Verbal and Visual Affinities* (New Haven and London: Yale University Press, 1978), p. 95.
45. Inès Murat, *Napoleon and the American Dream* (1976; Baton Rouge and London: Louisiana State University Press, 1981), p. 220; Clubbe, in *British Romantics as Readers*, pp. 283–5.
46. Jacques Henric, in Tony Scherman, *Forensic Portraits. Chasing Napoleon* (Moffat, Dumfriesshire: Cameron & Hollis/Thames and Hudson, 1999), p. 103.
47. Brilliant, pp. 72–4.
48. Goldring, *Regency Portrait Painter*, p. 212.
49. Piper, *Image of the Poet*, p. 155. One of the best known icons of London's National Portrait Gallery – Phillips's *Byron in Albanian Dress* – is a copy made by the artist in 1835, more than twenty years after he completed the original (British Embassy, Athens).
50. Evans, *Genius of Stuart*, pp. 61, 63.
51. Stuart's words, cited in ibid., p. 53.
52. Marc H. Miller, in *Lafayette, Hero*, ed. Idzerda, p. 161.
53. *American Paintings* (Philadelphia: Schwarz Gallery, [2000]), number 19. The catalogue entry by Carol Eaton [Hevner] Soltis offers the most comprehensive discussion of the origin and evolution of Rembrandt's porthole portraits.
54. Miller, *Rembrandt Peale*, p. 144 (color reproduction, p. 174).
55. For a good overview of the Stuart-Peale contest see Verheyen.
56. Jordanova, *Defining Features*, p. 36.
57. Recently the skull of a man buried in Jerusalem two thousand years ago has resulted in a computer-generated image of a face of what (experts think) Jesus may have look liked.
58. Groseclose, *Leutze*, p. 38.
59. Journal (NYPL), Nov. 21, 1836, p. 114. See also Dunlap, *Diary* 3: 694.
60. On Bache, see Fabian, p. 121; on Shakespeare, see B & F, p. 270; on Westall, B & F, p. 391 and Journal (NYPL), October 9, 1828, p. 63.
61. The 1983 Sully exhibition at the National Portrait Gallery included several copies to show how he modified his style when he "adapted the work of other painters" ("Foreword" by Alan Fern to Fabian).
62. Edited by James Soderholm (Cambridge: Cambridge University Press, 2002). Lorenz Eitner, a leading Géricault scholar, considers the portrait, in the Musée Fabre, Montpellier, "a total misattribution" (Hyman, p. 235).
63. One reviewer of McGann's volume describes it, wittily and allusively, as "of a swarthy man in shadow, forefinger to temple, a surprisingly modern face, more

like the chairman of an international conglomerate than the poet he was supposed to represent" (Roddy Cavaliero, *Keats–Shelley Review*, 17 [2003], 161).

64. Schrade, *Beethoven in France. The Growth of an Idea* (New Haven: Yale University Press, 1942), p. 176.
65. Austin, *1812* (*The March on Moscow, Napoleon in Moscow, The Great Retreat*) (London: Greenhill Books, 1993–96).
66. Barlow, in *Portraiture*, ed. Woodall, pp. 228, 232.
67. Ibid., p. 233.
68. Hints (Winterthur), entry after Jan. 16, 1827.
69. Moore 2: 798.
70. Browne, "Voyage from Leghorn," p. 56; Shaw, "The Authentic Portraits, Part I," p. 156.
71. Moore 2: 798; *Life of Ticknor* 1: 59; Blessington, p. 5; Forrester, in Medwin, *Angler in Wales* 2: 208.
72. As noted earlier, only Medwin agrees (in part), describing Byron's eyes as "greyish brown" (p. 8).
73. De Quincey, *Reminiscences*, p. 103.
74. Peach, pp. 49, 60.
75. Ibid., pp. 108, 111. Regarding these divergences, Peter Graham, in a private communication, observes: "The common sense way would be to conclude that Byron's eyes were of a mixed or middling hue that can be described variously ("hazel," "gray," "dark blue" – all can be semantic differences) and also that can look different in different lights, or according to what colors the person is wearing or surrounded by. What we know is that Byron did not have pale blue eyes (the pure watery kind that red-haired Scots often have) or deeply dark brown eyes (common among Mediterranean types)."
76. Paley, *Portraits of Coleridge*, p. 93.
77. De Quincey, *Reminiscences*, p. 103.
78. Selden Rodman, *The Heart of Beethoven* (New York: Shorewood, 1962), p. 57.
79. Gollin, *Portraits of Hawthorne*, p. 1.
80. Moore 2: 798–9. I omit features in Moore's description irrelevant to consideration of Sully's *Byron*, e.g., the teeth, visible in no painting.
81. Dunlap 2: 276.
82. Ibid., 2: 248.
83. *Lectures 1808–1829 on Literature*, ed. R. A. Foakes, 2 vols (Princeton: Princeton University Press, 1987) 1: 275, cited from Paley, *Portraits of Coleridge*, p. 1.

Select Bibliography

The most comprehensive bibliography of Sully scholarship is that appended to Steven Bronson's 1986 dissertation on Sully. Bronson writes knowledgeably about Sully's voluminous manuscripts, most of which remain unpublished, as does David M. Robb, Jr, in the bibliography to his unpublished 1967 M.A. thesis on Sully. I build on these discussions and attempt to bring them up-to-date. Few of Sully's letters have been published, and those that survive, not a great number, are in widely scattered depositories. They are cited in the notes from manuscript.

The chief Sully texts (many still held by his descendants) are:

Sully's *Hints to Young Painters*
This is a severe redaction of a manuscript that exists in several states. The published version, prepared for the press posthumously in 1873 by Sully's grandson, Francis Thomas Sully Darley, contains only a small portion of Sully's several texts; the 1965 edition I have used, with an introduction by Faber Birren, reprints the 1873 edition.

Sully assembled the manuscript of Hints in 1851, revised it in 1871, and Darley published his abridgment in 1873. The Winterthur Museum holds the 1851 version: "Memoirs of the Professional Life of Thomas Sully Dedicated to his brother Artists," a manuscript of 66 pages dated by Sully "November 1851." Yale holds the 1871 version: "Thomas Sully's 'Hints for Painters' 1809–1871." Either is to be preferred to the published version.

A typed version of *Hints* entitled "Thomas Sully's Hints for Pictures, 1809–1871 . . . " was made in August–September 1921 from the original manuscript in the possession of Mrs M. H. Sully, 102 Cambridge Place, Brooklyn. Xerox copies of the typed version, generally accurate and serviceable, are at Winterthur and the New York Public Library. I have used that in the former. If the material from *Hints* has been published, I cite the published version of 1965; if not, I cite the typed version of Hints by date of entry followed by page number.

A 1991 note in the Winterthur catalogue states that a shorter, edited version of *Hints*, possibly close to the 1873 version, was "discovered" in a safe deposit box maintained by a descendant of Sully's and subsequently sold at auction. I have not discovered the present location of this manuscript.

Sully's Journal
"Incidents in the Life of Thomas Sully, chiefly of Painting" exists in manuscript in the Frick Art History Reference Library, which lists it as "Philadelphia 1871, 2 volumes." A typescript made in the 1920s – "Journal of Thomas Sully's Activities May 1792–1793, 1799–December 1846" – has

been in the New York Public Library since 1949. It incorporates material from Sully's travel journals, which he called his "Waste Books." I have found the New York Public Library (NYPL) typescript generally accurate. Carrie Rebora Barratt in *Queen Victoria and Thomas Sully* has published the entries from September 19, 1837 through July 29, 1838. Except for these entries, I have for convenience cited the typescript as "Journal (NYPL)," followed by date of entry and page number.

A further volume (or volumes) of the Journal chronicling Sully's activities after 1846 has not yet surfaced and may be lost.

Sully's List of Portraits

Sometimes referred to as Sully's "Register" or "Account of Pictures." The manuscript, in the Historical Society of Pennsylvania (HSP), has had two publications: (1) *A Register of Portraits Painted by Thomas Sully 1801–1871*, arranged and edited with an introduction and notes by Charles Henry Hart. Philadelphia: [no publisher], 1909. Limited edition of 110 copies; (2) a more comprehensive edition, arranged alphabetically by sitter and with new information added whenever possible, by Edward Biddle and Mantle Fielding in 1921. Despite many omissions, the latter remains the standard published source of information about Sully's work. I cite it as "B & W."

Sully's Letters from England

These are copies of letters made by Sully's daughter Jane (Darley) that Sully and his youngest daughter Blanche wrote home in 1837–38 to Sarah Annis Sully and other family members, including Sully's son-in-law John Neagle, in Philadelphia. They describe meetings with various artists, dining out, and art exhibitions, and provide valuable information about the progress of Sully's portrait of Queen Victoria.

These letters are in two Copybooks held at Winterthur. I have cited them as Copybook 1 and Copybook 2. The second copybook ends with Blanche's letter of April 13, 1838. Father and daughter would be abroad another three months, but no other letters from this period seem to have survived. When ascertainable, I have given the author and date of the letter and the intended recipient.

The following bibliography of articles, reviews, and books used expands the brief references in the notes. Omitted are most encyclopedia articles and the like as well as citations in the text to materials deemed less important. Also omitted are articles, reviews, and books fully cited in a note or in the Abbreviations. Rather than dividing the bibliography into sections such as "Exhibition Catalogues," "Unpublished Materials," "Articles and Books," and so on, I have listed all works in alphabetical order.

Abrams, Ann Uhry. *The Valiant Hero. Benjamin West and Grand-Style History Painting*. Washington, DC: Smithsonian Institution Press, 1985.

Adkins, Nelson Frederick. *Fitz-Greene Halleck. An Early Knickerbocker Wit and Poet.* New Haven: Yale Univeristy Press, 1930.

Alberts, Robert G. *Benjamin West. A Biography*. Boston: Houghton Mifflin, 1978.

Allentuck, Marcia. "Fuseli and Lavater: physiognomical theory and the Enlightenment." *Studies on Voltaire and the Eighteenth Century*, ed. Theodore Besterman. Vol, 55. Genève: Institut et musée Voltaire, 1967.

[Allston, Washington.] *The Correspondence of Washington Allston*. Nathalia Wright, ed. Lexington: The University Press of Kentucky, 1993.

Altick, Richard. "Faces of the People." *London Review of Books*, 19 August–2 September 1982, pp. 22–4.

———. *Paintings from Books. Art and Literature in Britain, 1760–1900*. Columbus: Ohio State University Press, 1985.

———. *The Presence of the Past. Topics of the Day in the Victorian Novel*. Columbus: Ohio State University Press, 1991.

———. *The Shows of London*. Cambridge, MA and London: Harvard University Press, 1978.

American Art : 1740–1950. Towards Independence, general eds, Charles F. Montgomery and Patricia E. Kane. Boston: New York Graphic Society, 1976.

American Paintings before 1945 in the Wadsworth Atheneum, ed. Elizabeth Mankin Kornhauser et al. 2 vols. New Haven and London: Yale University Press, 1996.

American Paintings in the Metropolitan Museum of Art, Vol. 1. Text by John Caldwell and Oswaldo Rodriguez Roque. New York: MM of Art in association with Princeton University Press, 1994.

The American Paintings in the Pennsylvania Academy of Fine Arts, compiled by Nancy Fresella-Lee. Philadelphia: PAFA/ Seattle and London: University of Washington Press, 1989.

American Paintings of the Nineteenth Century, Part II. *The Collections of the National Gallery*, text by Robert Wilson Torchia. National Gallery of Art, Washington, DC/New York and Oxford: Oxford University Press, 1998.

[Anonymous.] "Cochran Collection of Presidential Portraits Assured of Permanent Home." *Scenic and Historic America*, 1 (Sept. 1929): 3–21.

Aristotle, *On Poetry and Music*, trans. S. H. Butcher, ed. Milton Nahm. New York: The Liberal Arts Press, 1948.

[Aristotle?] *Physiognomics* in *The Complete Works of Aristotle*, ed. Jonathan Barnes. 2 vols. Bollingen Series lxxi.2. Princeton, NJ: Princeton University Press, 1984. Vol. 1: 1237–50.

Armstrong, Walter. *Lawrence*. London: Methuen, 1913.

Art and the Empire City. New York, 1825–1861, ed. Catharine Hoover Voorsanger and John K. Howat. New York: MM of Art/New Haven and London: Yale University Press, 2000.

Ashby, Clifford. "Fanny Kemble's 'Vulgar' Journal." *Pennsylvania Magazine of History and Biography*, 98 (1974): 58–66.

Asleson, Robyn, ed. *A Passion for Performance. Sarah Siddons and Her Portraits*. Los Angeles: The J. Paul Getty Museum, 1999.

[Audubon, John James.] *The 1826 Journal of John James Audubon*, ed. Alice Ford. University of Oklahoma Press, 1967.

———. *Audubon and his Journals*, ed. Maria R. Audubon. 2 vols. New York: Scribner's, 1897.

———. *Selected Journals*, ed. Ben Forkner. New York: Penguin Books, 1996.

———. *Writings and Drawings*. New York: The Library of America, 1999.

[Austen, Jane.] *Jane Austen's Letters*, ed. Deirdre Le Faye. Oxford and New York: Oxford Univeristy Press, 1995.

Ayres, William, ed. *Picturing History in American Painting 1770–1930*. New York: Fraunces Tavern Museum/Rizzoli, 1993.

Baetjer, Katharine. "British Portraits in the Metropolitan Museum of Art." *The Metropolitan Museum of Art Bulletin*, LVII (Summer 1999): 1–72.

Bainbridge, Simon. "From Nelson to Childe Harold: The Transformations of the Byronic Image." *The Byron Journal*, 27 (1999): 13–25.

Bakeland, Frederick. "Collectors of American Paintings, 1813–1913." *American Art Review*, 3 (Nov.–Dec. 1976): 120–66.

Ballantyne, Andrew. *Architecture, Landscape and Liberty: Richard Payne Knight and the Picturesque*. Cambridge: Cambridge University Press, 1997.

Baltzell, E. Digby. *Puritan Boston and Quaker Philadelphia*. New York: The Free Press, 1979.

Bancroft, George. *History of the Battle of Lake Erie and Miscellaneous Papers*. 1860; New York: Robert Bonner's Sons, 1891.

Barker, Virgil. *American Painting. History and Interpretation*. New York: Bonanza Books, 1960.

Barlow, Paul, "Facing the Past and Present: The [British] National Portrait Gallery and the Search for 'Authentic Portraiture.'" In *Portraiture: Facing the Subject*, ed. Joanne Woodall. Manchester and New York: Manchester University Press, 1997, pp. 219–38.

Barratt, Carrie Rebora. "Faces of a New Nation. American Portraits of the 18th and Early 19th Centuries." *The Metropolitan Museum of Art Bulletin*, LXI (Summer 2003): 1–56. *See also* under Rebora, Carrie.

Barrett, Walter [pseudonym of Joseph Alfred Scoville?]. *The Old Merchants of New York*, 5 vols. New York: Carleton, 1870.

Bates, William N., ed. "Nicholas Biddle's Journey to Greece." *Proceedings of the Numismatic and Antiquarian Society of Pennsylvania*, 28 (1919): 167–83.

Beal, Rebecca J. *Jacob Eichholtz. Portrait Painter of Philadelphia*. Philadelphia: HSP, 1969.

Bedell, Rebecca. *The Anatomy of Nature. Geology & American Landscape Painting, 1825–1875*. Princeton and Oxford: Princeton University Press, 2001.

Benson, Adolph B. "Catherine Potter Stith and Her Meeting with Lord Byron." *South Atlantic Quarterly*, 22 (1923): 10–22.

Bernier, Olivier. *Lafayette. Hero of Two Worlds*. New York: E. P. Dutton, 1983.

———. *The World in 1800*. New York: John Wiley, 2000.

Bernstein, Aline. *An Actor's Daughter*. New York: Alfred A. Knopf, 1941.

Biddle, Edward, ed. "Joseph Bonaparte in America as Recorded in the

Private Journal of Nicholas Biddle." *Pennsylvania Magazine of History and Biography*, 55 (1931): 208–24.

[Biddle, Nicholas.] *Nicholas Biddle in Greece. The Journals and Letters of 1806*, ed. R. A. McNeal. University Park, PA: Pennsylvania State University Press, 1993.

Blainey, Ann. *Fanny and Adelaide. The Lives of the Remarkable Kemble Sisters*. Chicago: Ivan R. Dee, 2001.

[Blake, William.] *The Poetry and Prose of William Blake*, ed. David B. Erdman. 1965; Garden City, New York: Doubleday, 1970.

Blanshard, Frances. *Portraits of Wordsworth*. London: George Allen & Unwin, 1959.

Boaden, James. *Memoirs of the Life of John Philip Kemble*, 2 vols. London: Longman, etc., 1825.

Boime, Albert. "The Iconography of Napoleon," in Boime, *Art in an Age of Bonapartism 1800–1815*. Chicago and London: University of Chicago Press, 1991, pp. 35–95.

Bradsher, Earle Lockridge. *Mathew Carey, Editor, Author and Publisher; a Study in American Literary Development*. New York: Columbia University Press, 1912.

Brewer, John. *The Pleasures of the Imagination. English Culture in the Eighteenth Century*. New York: Farrar Straus Giroux, 1997.

Brilliant, Richard. *Facing the New World. Jewish Portraits in Colonial and Federal America*. New York: Jewish Museum, 1997.

Brooks, Ianthe. *Face to Face. Three Centuries of Artists' Self-Portraiture*. Liverpool: National Museums & Galleries on Merseyside, [1994].

Brooks, Van Wyck. *The World of Washington Irving*. New York: E. P. Dutton, 1944.

Brown, Milton W., et al. *American Art to 1900*. New York: Harry N. Abrams, 1979.

———. *One Hundred Masterpieces of American Painting in . . . Washington, D.C.* Washington, DC: Smithsonian Institution Press, 1983.

Broughton, Lord [John Cam Hobhouse]. *Recollections of a Long Life*, ed. Lady Dorchester. 6 vols. New York: Charles Scribner's Sons, 1909–11.

Browne, James Hamilton. "Voyage from Leghorn to Cephalonia with Lord Byron . . ." *Blackwood's Edinburgh Magazine*, 55 (Jan. 1834): 56–67; 55 (Sept. 1834): 392–407.

Budd, Henry. "Thomas Sully." *Pennsylvania Magazine of History and Biography*, 42 (1918): 97–126.

Bulwer-Lytton, Edward. *England and the English*, ed. with an introduction by Standish Meacham. Chicago and London: University of Chicago Press, 1970.

Burke, Russell, and Gerdts, William H. *American Still-Life Painting*. New York: Praeger, 1971.

Burnham, Patricia M. and Giese, Lucretia Hoover, eds. *Redefining American History Painting*. Cambridge: Cambridge University Press, 1995.

Burstein, Andrew. *America's Jubilee*. New York: Alfred A. Knopf, 2001.

———. *The Passions of Andrew Jackson*. New York: Alfred A. Knopf, 2003.

Burt, Nathaniel. *First Families, The Making of an American Aristocracy.* Boston: Little, Brown, 1970.

———. *The Perennial Philadelphians. The Anatomy of an American Aristocracy.* Boston: Little, Brown, 1963.

Bush, Alfred L. *The Life Portraits of Thomas Jefferson.* Charlottesville, VA: 1962; Thomas Jefferson Memorial Foundation, 1987 (revised edn).

Butcher, Fanny. *Many Lives – One Love.* New York: Harper & Row, 1972.

[Byron, Lord]. *His Very Self and Voice. Collected Conversations of Lord Byron*, ed. Ernest J. Lovell, Jr. New York: Macmillan, 1954.

———. *Lady Blessington's Conversations of Lord Byron*, ed. Ernest J. Lovell, Jr. Princeton, NJ: Princeton University Press, 1969.

———. *Medwin's Conversations of Lord Byron*, ed. Ernest J. Lovell, Jr. Princeton, NJ: Princeton University Press, 1966.

Callow, James T. *Kindred Spriits. Knickerbocker Writers and American Artists, 1807-1855.* Chapel Hill: University of North Carolina Press, 1967.

Carlyle, Thomas. *The Collected Letters of Thomas and Jane Welsh Carlyle*, ed. Charles Richard Sanders et al. 30 vols. Durham, NC: Duke University Press, 1970–.

Champlin, John Denison. *Cyclopedia of Painters and Painting.* New York: Scribner, 1913.

Chew, Samuel. "Byron in America." *American Mercury*, 1 (March 1924): 335–44.

Churchill, Winston and Clementine. *Speaking for Themselves. The Personal Letters of Winston and Clementine Churchill*, ed. Mary Soames. New York: Doubleday, 1988.

Cikovsky, Nicolai, Jr and Quick, Michael. *George Inness.* Los Angeles: Los Angeles County Museum of Art; New York: Harper & Row, 1985.

Clarke, Eliot. *History of the National Academy of Design.* New York: Columbia University Press, 1954.

Clarke, Michael and Penny, Nicholas, eds. *The Arrogant Connoisseur.* Manchester: Manchester University Press, 1982.

Clarke, Thomas B. *Early American Portraits.* New York: American Art Association, 1919.

———. *Portraits by Early American Artists of the Seventeenth, Eighteenth and Nineteenth Centuries.* Fairmount: Philadelphia Museum of Art, 1928.

Clubbe, John. "Physiognomy," in *Miscellaneous Tracts of the Rev. John Clubbe.* 2 vols. Ipswich: W. Jackson, for J. Shave, London: J. Dodsley, 1763. Vol. 1, iii–xi, 1–84.

Clubbe, John. "Byron and Scott." *Texas Studies in Literature and Language*, 15 (Spring 1973): 67–91.

———. *Byron's Natural Man. Daniel Boone & Kentucky.* Lexington: King Library Press, 1980 [1982].

———. "Portrait of Teresa Guiccioli." *The Byron Journal*, 7 (1979): 22–30.

———. "The West Portrait of Byron." *The Byron Journal*, 8 (1980): 76–87.

[Coleridge, Samuel Taylor.] *The Collected Letters of Samuel Taylor Coleridge*, ed. Earl Leslie Griggs. 6 vols. Oxford: Clarendon, 1956–71.

Collingwood, R. G. *The Principles of Art*. Oxford: Clarendon, 1938.
Connelly, Owen. *The Gentle Bonaparte. A Biography of Napoleon's Elder Brother*. New York: Macmillan, 1968.
Constable, W. G. *Art Collecting in the United States of America*. London: Nelson, 1964.
[Cooper, James Fenimore]. *The Letters and Journals of James Fenimore Cooper*, ed. James Franklin Beard. Vol. 1. Cambridge, MA: Harvard University Press, 1960.
———. *Notions of the Americans*. 2 vols. Introduction by Robert C. Spiller. 1828; New York: Frederick Ungar, 1963.
Cooper, John. *National Portrait Gallery. A Visitor's Guide*. London: National Portrait Gallery, 2000.
Cooper, Thomas. "Observations respecting the History of Physiognomy." *Memoirs of the Literary and Philosophical Society of Manchester*, 3 (1790): 408–62.
Conrad, R. T. "Nicholas Biddle." *The National Gallery of Distingushed Americans*. Vol. 4. Philadelphia: D. Rice & A. N. Hart, 1859.
Cooper, Wendy A. *Classical Taste in America 1800–1840*. New York: Abbeville Press, 1993.
[Corcoran Gallery.] *A Catalogue of American Paintings in The Corcoran Gallery of Art*. Vol. 1. 1966; Washington, DC: The Corcoran Gallery of Art, 1974.
Cosentino, Andrew J. *The Paintings of Charles Bird King (1785–1862)*. Washington: Smithsonian Institution Press, 1977.
Cowdrey, M. B., ed. *The American Academy of Fine Arts and American Art-Union*. 2 vols. New York: New York Historical Society, 1953.
Crompton, Louis. *Byron and Greek Love. Homophobia in 19th Century England*. Berkeley, Los Angeles: University of California Press, 1985.
Cross, David A. *A Striking Likeness. The Life of George Romney*. Aldershot: Ashgate, 2000.
Crozier, C. Alice. [Harriet Beecher Stowe and Byron], in *Critical Essays on Harriet Beecher Stowe*, ed. Elizabeth Ammons. Boston: G. K. Hall, 1980.
Cunningham, Allan. *The Lives of the Most Eminent British Painters, Sculptors, and Artists*. 2nd edn. 6 vols. London: John Murray, 1830–33.
Dallas, Robert Charles. *Recollections of the Life of Lord Byron*. London: Charles Knight, 1824.
Danly, Susan. "The Carey Collection at the Pennsylvania Academy of Fine Arts." *Antiques* (Nov. 1991): 838–48.
———. *Facing the Past. Nineteenth-Century Portraits from the Collection of the Pennsylvania Academy of the Fine Arts*. Philadelphia: Pennsylvania Academy of the Fine Arts, 1992.
Deák, Gloria. "Fanny Kemble's New York." *Antiques* (Oct. 2001): 536–45.
———. *Picturing New York. The City from its Beginnings to the Present*. New York: Columbia University Press, 2000.
Dearinger, David B. *Rave Reviews. American Art and its Critics, 1826–1925*. New York: National Academy of Design, 2000.
de Mare, Marie. *G. P. A. Healy. American Artist*. New York: David McKay, 1954.

De Quincey, Thomas. *Reminiscences of the English Lake Poets*, introduction and notes by John E. Jordan. London: J. M. Dent, 1961.

De Salvo, Donna. *Face Value: American Portraits*. Southampton, NY: Parrish Art Museum, 1995.

Dickson, H. E. "The Artist's Profession in the Early Republic." *Art Quarterly*, 8 (Autumn 1945): 261–80.

———. *Arts of the Young Republic. The Age of William Dunlap*. Chapel Hill: University of North Carolina Press, 1968.

Diderot, Denis. *Salon de 1765/Essais sur la peinture*, ed. Else Marie Bukdahl, Annette Lorenceau, and Gita May. Paris: Hermann, 1984.

Downey, Cleta H. *Lithography: The First Hundred Years*. Albuquerque: University of New Mexico, 1977.

Dunlap, William. *Diary of William Dunlap (1766–1839)*. 3 vols. New York: New York Historical Society, 1930.

———. *Memoirs of George Frederick Cooke*. 2 vols. London: Henry Colburn, 1813.

Egbert, Donald Drew. "Two Portraits by Thomas Sully." *Record of the Art Museum. Princeton University*, xix (1960): 11–16.

Encylopedia of American Art before 1914, edited by Jane Turner. London: Macmillan, 2000.

Ellis, Joseph J. *After the Revolution. Profiles of Early American Culture*. New York/London: Norton, 1979.

Epstein, Joseph. *The Middle of My Tether. Familiar Essays*. New York: Norton, 1983.

Evans, Dorinda. *Benjamin West and His American Students*. Washington: Smithsonian Institution Press, 1980.

———. *The Genius of Gilbert Stuart*. Princeton, NJ: Princeton University Press, 1999.

Fabian, Monroe. *Portraits of the American Stage 1771–1971*. Washington, DC: Smithsonian Institution Press, 1971.

Farington, Joseph. *The Diary of Joseph Farington*, ed. Kenneth Garlick and Angus Macintyre, then by Kathryn Cave. Index by Evelyn Newby. 17 vols. New Haven and London: Yale University Press, 1978–98.

Fast, Howard. *The Crossing*. 1971; Newark: New Jersey Historical Society, 1984.

Fehl, Philipp P. "Thomas Sully's *Washington's Passage of the Delaware*: The History of a Commission." *Art Bulletin*, 15 (March 1973): 584–9.

Feigen, Richard. *Tales from the Art Crypt*. New York: Alfred A. Knopf, 2000.

Ferling, John F. *The First of Men. A Life of George Washington*. Knoxville, TN: University of Tennessee Press, 1988.

Field, James A. *America and the Mediterranean World 1776–1832*. Princeton, NJ: Princeton University Press, 1969.

Fink, Lois Marie. "Rembrandt Peale in Paris." *Pennsylvania Magazine of History and Biography*, 110 (Jan. 1986): 71–90.

[Fisher, Sidney George.] *A Philadelphia Perspective. The Diary of Sidney George Fisher Covering the Years 1834–1871*, ed. Nicholas B. Wainwright. Philadelphia: Historical Society of Pennsylvania, 1967.

Flanary, Sara E. Lewis. "William Edward West in New Orleans and Mississippi." *Antiques* (Nov. 1983): 1010–15.
Floyd, William Barrow. *Matthew Harris Jouett. Portraitist of the Ante-Bellum South*. Lexington, KY: Mitchell Fine Arts Center, 1980.
Foshay, Ellen M. *Mr. Luman Reed's Picture Gallery. Pioneer Collection of American Art*. New York: Harry N. Abrams, 1990.
Frank, Robin Jaffee. *Love and Loss. American Portrait and Mourning Miniatures*. New Haven and London: Yale University Press, 2000.
Friedländer, Max J. *Landscape. Portrait. Still-Life. Their Origin and Development*. New York: Philosophical Library, [n.d.].
Friedman, Winifred H. *Boydell's Shakespeare Gallery*. New York: Garland, 1976.
Furtwangler, Albert. *Acts of Discovery. Visions of America in the Lewis and Clark Journals*. Urbana and Chicago: University of Illinois Press, 1993.
[Fuseli, Henry] *Lectures on Painting by the Royal Academicians. Barry, Opie, and Fuseli*, ed. Ralph N. Wornum. London: Henry G. Bohn, 1848.
Henry Fuseli 1741–1825. London: Tate Gallery, 1975.
[Fuseli, Henry] *The Mind of Henry Fuseli. Selections from his Writings with an Introductory Study*, ed. Eudo C. Mason. London: Routledge & Kegan Paul, 1951.
Galt, John. *The Life of Lord Byron*. London: Henry Colburn and Richard Bentley, 1830.
Gardner, Albert Ten Eyck. "Queen Victoria and Mr. Sully." *Metropolitan Museum of Art Bulletin*, 5, n.s. (January 1947): 144–8.
Gareau, Michel. *Charles Le Brun. First Painter to King Louis XIV*. New York: Abrams, 1992.
Garlick, Kenneth. *Sir Thomas Lawrence*. London: Routledge & Kegan Paul, 1954.
———. *Sir Thomas Lawrence*. 1963: Bristol: Purnell and Sons, 1965. The Masters 18.
Garraty, John and Carnes, Mark C., eds. *American National Biography*. 24 vols. New York: Oxford University Press, 1999.
Garrett, Wendell C. et al. *The Arts in America. The Nineteenth Century*. New York: Scribner, 1969.
Garvan, Beatrice B. *Federal Philadelphia, 1785–1825. The Athens of the Western World*. Philadelphia: Philadelphia Museum of Art, 1987.
Gasier, Manuel. *Self-Portraits from the Fifteenth Century to the Present Day*. 1961; New York: Appleton-Century, 1963.
Gaull, Marilyn. *English Romanticism. The Human Context*. New York and London: Norton, 1988.
Geffen, Elizabeth M. *Philadelphia Unitarianism 1796–1861*. Philadelphia: University of Pennsylvania Press, 1961.
Gerdts, William H. *Painting and Sculpture in New Jersey*. Princeton, NJ: D. Van Nostrand, 1964.
———. "National Aristocrats in a Democracy: 1810–1870," in *American Portraiture in the Grand Manner: 1720–1920*, ed. Michael Quick.

——— and Rebora, Carrie. *The Art of Henry Inman*. Washington, DC: National Portrait Gallery, 1987.

——— and Stebbins, Theodore E. *"A Man of Genius": The Art of Washington Allston 1779–1843*. Boston: Museum of Fine Arts/ Charlottesville: University Press of Virginia, 1979.

——— and Thistlethwaite, Mark. *Grand Illusions. History Painting in America*. Fort Worth, TX: Amon Carter Museum, 1988.

Gilbert, Martin. *"Never Despair": Winston S. Churchill 1945–1965*. London: Heinemann, 1988.

Gilchrist, Agnes Addison. *William Strickland. Architect and Engineer. 1788–1854*. Philadelphia: University of Pennsylvania Press, 1950.

Gilchrist, Alexander. *The Life of William Blake*. 2nd edn. 1863; London: John Lane, [1906].

Goldberg, Michael. "'A Physiognomic Reader': Carlyle and the Art of Portraiture." *Mosaic*, 13 (1979): 1–15.

Goldring, Lawrence. *Regency Portrait Painter. The Life of Sir Thomas Lawrence, P.R.A.* London: Macdonald, 1951.

Goldstein, Jonathan. *Philadelphia and the China Trade 1682–1846. Commercial, Cultural, and Attitudinal Effects*. University Park and London: Pennsylvania State University Press, 1978.

Goldstein, Malcolm. *Landscape with Figures. A History of Art Dealing in the United States*. New York: Oxford University Press, 2000.

Gollin, Rita. *Portraits of Nathaniel Hawthorne. An Iconography*. DeKalb: Northern Illinois University Press, 1983.

Gombrich, E. H. *Meditations on a Hobby-Horse*. 1963; New York and London: Phaidon, 1978.

Goodrich, Lloyd. *Winslow Homer*. New York: Macmillan, 1944.

Goodyear, Frank H., Jr. *Some Thoughts on Painting in Pennsylvania*. Philadelphia: PAFA, 1976.

Govan, Thomas Payne. *Nicholas Biddle. Nationalist and Public Banker 1786–1844*. Chicago: University of Chicago Press, 1959.

———. "Nicholas Biddle at Princeton." *Princeton University Library Chronicle*, 9 (Feb. 1948): 49–63.

Groseclose, Barbara S. *Emanuel Leutze, 1816–1868. Freedom Is the Only King*. Washington: Smithsonian Institution Press, 1975.

Guérard, Albert Leon. *Reflections on the Napoleonic Legend*. New York: Charles Scribner's Sons, 1924.

Guiccioli, Teresa. *My Recollections of Lord Byron*. 2 vols. London: Richard Bentley, 1869.

Hall, Captain Basil. *Travels in North America in the Years 1827 and 1828*. 3 vols. Edinburgh: Cadell and Co., 1829.

[Hall, Mrs. Basil.] *An Aristocratic Journey. Being the Outspoken Letters of Mrs. Basil Hall. . .*, prefaced and ed. by Una Pope-Hennessey. New York and London: G. P. Putnam's Sons, 1931.

[Halleck, Fitz-Greene.] *The Poetical Works of Fitz-Greene Halleck*. New edn. New York: Appleton, 1865.

Hallock, John W. M. *The American Byron. Homosexuality and the Fall of*

Fitz-Greene Halleck. Madison, WI and London: University of Wisconsin Press, 2000.

Hansen, Harry. *North of Manhattan. Persons and Places of Old Westchester*. New York: Hastings House, [n.d.].

Harding, Anneliese. *John Lewis Krimmel. Genre Artist of the Early Republic*. Winterthur, DE: Winterthur, 1994.

Harris, Neil. *The Artist in American Society. The Formative Years 1790–1860*. New York: George Braziller, 1966.

Hartley, Lucy. *Physiognomy and the Meaning of Expression in Nineteenth-Century Culture*. Cambridge: Cambridge University Press, 2001.

Hautcoeur, Louis. *Louis David*. Paris: La Table Ronde, 1954.

Haydon, Benjamin Robert. *The Autobiography and Memoirs of Benjamin Robert Haydon*. 2 vols, ed. Tom Taylor. Introduction by Aldous Huxley. New York: Harcourt, Brace, 1926.

———. *The Diary of Benjamin Robert Haydon*. 5 vols, ed. Willard Bissell Pope. Cambridge, MA: Harvard University Press, 1960.

———. *Invisible Friends. The Correspondence of Elizabeth Barrett Browning and Benjamin Robert Haydon 1842–1845*, ed. Willard Bissell Pope. Cambridge, MA: Harvard University Press, 1972.

Hayes, John. *British Paintings of the Sixteenth through Nineteenth Century*. Washington, DC: National Gallery of Art/Cambridge University Press, 1992.

———. *The Portrait in British Art*. London: National Portrait Gallery, 1991.

[Hazlitt, William.] *The Complete Works of William Hazlitt*, ed. P. P. Howe. 21 vols. London: J. M. Dent, 1930–34.

Henderson, Helen W. *The Pennsylvania Academy of the Fine Arts*. Boston: Page, 1911.

Hennessey, William John. *The American Portrait. From the Death of Stuart to the Rise of Sargent*. Worcester, MA: Worcester Art Museum, 1973.

Hensel, W. U. *Jacob Eichholtz, Painter. An Address*. Lancaster, PA: Brecht Printing Co., for Lancaster County Historical Society, [1912].

———. "Jacob Eichholtz, Painter," *The Penn Germania*, 2 (February 1913): 81–96.

———. "Jacob Eichholtz, Painter," *The Penn Germania*, 3 (March 1913): 161–75.

Hevner, Carol Eaton. *Rembrandt Peale 1778–1860. A Life in the Arts*. Philadelphia: HSP, 1985.

Holmes, Richard. *The Romantic Poets and Their Circle*. London: National Portrait Gallery, 1997.

——— and Crane, David et al. *Romantics & Revolutionaries. Regency Portaits from the National Portrait Gallery*. London: National Portrait Gallery, 2002.

Homer, William Innes and Goodrich, Lloyd. *Albert Pinkham Ryder. Painter of Dreams*. New York: Abrams, 1989.

[Hone, Philip.] *The Diary of Philip Hone*, ed. Allan Nevins. New and enlarged edn New York: Dodd, Mead, 1936.

Honour, Hugh. *Neo-Classicism*. Harmondsworth: Penguin, 1968.

Hough, Richard. *Winston and Clementine The Triumphs and Tragedies of the Churchills*. New York: Bantam Books, 1991.

Huckel, Earle W. "Thomas Sully in Philadelphia." *Antiques* (Oct. 1948): 270–71.

Hughes, Robert. *Nothing If Not Critical. Selected Essays on Art and Artists*. New York: Alfred A. Knopf, 1991.

Huizinga, J. H. *Dutch Civilisation of the Seventeenth Century with Other Essays*. New York: Frederick Ungar, 1968.

Huntington, David C. *Art and the Excited Spirit. America in the Romantic Period*. Ann Arbor: University of Michigan Museum of Art, 1972.

Hutchison, Sidney C. *The History of the Royal Academy 1768–1986*. London: Robert Royce, 1986.

Idzerda, Stanley J., Loveland, Anne C., Miller, Marc H. *Lafayette, Hero of Two Worlds. The Art and Pageantry of His Farewell Tour of America, 1824–1825*. Hanover and London: University Press of New England, 1989.

Ingamells, John. *The Wallace Collection* 1990; London: Scala Books, 1994.

In This Academy. The Pennsylvania Academy of Fine Arts, 1805–1976. Philadelphia: Pennsylvania Academy of Fine Arts, 1976.

[Irving, Washington.] *Letters*. Volume 1 1802–23, ed. Ralph M. Aderman et al. Boston: Twayne, 1978.

Irwin, David. *English Neoclassical Art. Studies in Interpretation and Taste*. New York: New York Graphic Society, 1966.

Isham, Samuel. *The History of American Painting*. New York: Macmillan, 1905.

Jackson, Donald. *Letters of the Lewis and Clark Expedition*. 2 vols. 1962; Urbana: Univeresity of Illinois Press, 1978.

Jaffe, Irma B. *John Trumbull. Patriot-Artist of the American Revolution*. Boston: New York Graphic Society, 1975.

———. *Trumbull: The Declaration of Independence*. London: Allen Lane (Penguin Books), 1976.

James, Henry. *Essays on Literature. American Writers. English Writers*. New York: The Library of America, 1984.

———. *A Little Tour in France*, introduction by Leon Edel. New York: Farrar, Straus and Giroux, 1983.

———. *The Painter's Eye*, ed. John L. Sweeney. 1956; Madison: University of Wisconsin Press, 1989.

James, Reese Davis. *Cradle of Culture. The Philadelphia Stage, 1800–1810*. Philadelphia: University of Pennsylvania Press, 1957.

———. *Old Drury of Philadelphia. A History of the Philadelphia Stage, 1800–1835*. Philadelphia: University of Pennsylvania Press, 1932.

———. "Yoricks of Yesteryear." *The Philadelphia Forum Magazine*. Undated clipping [after 1932] in author's possession.

Jarvis, James Jackson. *The Art-Idea*, ed. Benjamin Rowland, Jr. 1864; Cambridge, MA: Harvard University Press, 1960.

Johns, Christopher M. S. "A Study of a Theatrical Portrait by Thomas Sully:

George Frederick Cooke as Richard III." M.A. thesis, University of Delaware, 1980.

———. "Theater and Theory: G. F. Cooke as Richard III." *Winterthur Portfolio*, 18 (1983): 27–38.

Jones, Arthur F. and Weber, Bruce. *The Kentucky Painter. From the Frontier to the Civil War*. Lexington: University of Kentucky Art Museum, 1981.

Jones, Christine Kenyon. "James Holmes and the Byron Circle." *The Byron Journal*, 25 (1997): 83–8.

———. "Fantasy and Transfiguration: Byron and his Portraits." In *Byromania. Portraits of the Artist in Nineteenth- and Twentieth-Century Culture*, ed. Frances Wilson. London: Macmillan, 1999.

Jordanova, Ludmilla. *Defining Features. Scientific and Medical Portraits 1660-2000*. London: National Portrait Gallery/Reaktion Books, 2000.

———. "Reading Faces in the Nineteenth Century" [review essay of Mary Cowling, *The Artist as Anthropologist*]. *Art History*, 13 (Dec. 1990): 570–75.

Kammen, Michael. *A Season of Youth. The American Revolution and the Historical Imagination*. New York: Knopf, 1978.

[Keats, John.] *The Letters of John Keats 1814–1821*. 2 vols, ed. Hyder Edward Rollins. Cambridge, MA: Harvard University Press, 1958.

Kemble, Frances Ann. *Records of a Girlhood*, 2nd edn. New York: Henry Holt, 1879.

———. *Fanny Kemble. The American Journals*, ed. Elizabeth Mavor. London: Weidenfeld and Nicolson, 1990.

———. *Fanny the American Kemble. Her Journals and Unpublished Letters*, ed. with annotations by Fanny Kemble Wister. Tallahassee, Florida: South Pass Press, 1972.

———. *Fanny Kemble. Journal of a Young Actress*, ed. Monica Gough. New York: Columbia University Press, 1990.

———. *Journal of a Residence on a Georgian Plantation in 1838–1839*, ed. John A. Scott. New York: Alfred A. Knopf, 1961.

Kennedy, Roger G. *Architecture, Men, Women and Money in America 1600–1860*. New York: Random House, 1985.

Kennett, Lee. "Le culte de Napoléon aux Etats-Unis jusqu'à la guerre de sécession." *Revue de l'Institut Napoléon*, 125 (1972): 145–56.

Kimmelman, Michael. *Portraits. Talking with Artists at the Met, the Modern, the Louvre and Elsewhere*. New York: Random House, 1998.

Kirksey, Kristal. "Thomas Sully's Sketches for *Robinson Crusoe* in the Museum of Fine Arts, Houston." M.A. thesis, Rice University, 1989.

Kleinfeld, H. W. "Infidel on Parnassus: Lord Byron and the *North American Review*." *New England Quarterly*, 32 (June 1960): 164–85.

Kloss, William, ed. *Art in the White House. A Nation's Pride*. New York: Harry N. Abrams, 1992.

Kramer, Lloyd. *Lafayette in Two Worlds. Public Cultures and Personal Identities in an Age of Revolutions*. Chapel Hill and London: University of North Carolina Press, 1996.

Lamb, Caroline. *Glenarvon*, ed. Frances Wilson. London: J. M. Dent, 1995.

Larkin, Oliver. *Art and Life in America*, rev. and enlarged edn. New York: Holt, Rinehart and Winston, 1960.

———. *Samuel F. B. Morse and American Democratic Art*. Boston/Toronto: Little, Brown, 1954.

Larrabee, Stephen A. *English Bards and Grecian Marbles*. 1943; Port Washington, New York: Kennikat Press, 1964.

———. *Hellas Observed. The American Experience of Greece. 1775–1865*. New York: New York University Press, 1957.

Laverty, Bruce, Lewis, Michael J., and Taylor, Michelle Taillon. *Monument to Philanthropy. The Design and Building of Girard College 1832–1848*. Philadelphia: Girard College, 1998.

[Lawrence, Thomas] *Sir Thomas Lawrence's Letter-Bag*, ed. George Somes Layard. London: George Allen, 1906.

Lease, Benjamin. *Anglo-American Encounters. England and the Rise of American Literature*. Cambridge: Cambridge University Press, 1981.

———. *That Wild Fellow. John Neal and the American Literary Revolution*. Chicago and London: University of Chicago Press, 1972.

Leonard, William Ellery. *Byron and Byronism in America*. 1907; New York: Gordian Press, 1965.

Leslie, Charles Robert. *Autobiographical Recollections*. 2 vols, ed. Tom Taylor, new intro. by Robin Hamlyn. 1860; Wakefield, UK: E. P. Publishing, 1978.

Levey, Michael. *Sir Thomas Lawrence. 1769–1830*. London: National Portrait Gallery, 1979.

Levine, Lawrence W. *Highbrow/Lowbrow. The Emergence of Cultural Hierarchy in America*. Cambridge, MA and London: Harvard University Press, 1988.

Lindsay, Kenneth C. *The Works of John Vanderlyn*. Binghamton, NY: University Art Gallery, 1970.

Lockhart, John Gibson. *Memoirs of the Life of Sir Walter Scott, Bart*, new edn. Edinburgh: Robert Cadell, 1842.

———. *Peter's Letters to His Kinsfolk*, 2nd edn, 3 vols. Edinburgh: William Blackwood, 1819.

London, Hannah. "Portraits of Rebecca Gratz by Thomas Sully." In *Portrait Painting in America*, ed. Ellen Miles. New York: Main Street/Universe Books, 1977, pp. 162–4.

Longacre, James B. and Herring, James. *The National Portrait Gallery of Distinguished Americans*, 3 vols. New York, etc.: Henry Perkins, 1836.

Loveland, Anne C. *Emblem of Liberty. The Image of Lafayette in the American Mind*. Baton Rouge: Louisiana State University Press, 1971.

Lynes, Russell. *The Art-Makers of Nineteenth Century America*. New York: Atheneum, 1970.

———. *The Taste-Makers*. New York: Harper, 1955.

McAllister, A. "Physiognomy." *Encyclopedia Britannica*, 11th edn. Vol. 21. Cambridge: Cambridge University Press, 1911.

MacCarthy, Clarence Edward and Dorrance, Gordon. *The Bonapartes in America*. Philadelphia: Doran, 1939.

MacCarthy, Fiona. *Byron. Life and Legend*. London: John Murray, 2002.

McGlinchee, Claire. *The First Decade of the Boston Museum*. Boston: Bruce Humphries, 1940.

McNeal, R. A. "Nicholas Biddle, Anarcharsis, and the Grand Tour." *Pennyslvania Magazine of History and Biography*, 120 (July 1996): 217–47.

[Macready, William.] *The Diaries of William Charles Macready 1833–1851*, ed. William Toynbee. 2 vols. London: Chapman and Hall, 1912.

Madeira, Edward. "Thomas Sully's 'Queen Victoria.'" *The American Collector*, 3 (Feb. 1927): 189–91.

Marshall, Dorothy. *Fanny Kemble*. London: Weidenfeld and Nicolson, 1977.

Martinez, Katharine and Talbott, Page. *Philadelphia's Cultural Landscape. The Sartain Family Legacy*. Philadelphia: Temple University Press, 2000.

Marzio, Peter. *The Democratic Art. Pictures for a Nineteenth Century America*. Boston: Godine, 1979.

Master Paintings form the Butler Institute of American Art, ed. Irene S. Sweetkind. New York: Harry N. Abrams, 1994.

Matson, Cathy. *Merchants and Empire. Trading in Colonial New York*. Baltimore, MD and London: Johns Hopkins University Press, 1998.

May, Henry F. *The Enlightenment in America*. New York: Oxford University Press, 1976.

Maynard, W. Barksdale. *Architecture in the United States 1800–1850*. New Haven, CT and London: Yale University Press, 2003.

Meeker, Arthur, Jr. *Chicago, With Love. A Polite and Personal History*. New York: Alfred A. Knopf, 1955.

Meeker, Arthur, Mrs. "The First Church Wedding in Chicago." In Kirkland, Caroline, ed. *Chicago Yesterdays. A Sheaf of Reminiscences*. Chicago: Daughaday, 1919, pp. 41–6.

Mellor, Ann. "Physiognomy, Phrenology, and Blake's Visionary Heads." In *Blake in His Time*, ed. Robert N. Essick and Donald Pearce. Bloomington and London: Indiana University Press, 1978.

Miles, Ellen G. *Saint-Mémin and the Neoclassical Profile Portrait in America*. Washington: National Portrait Gallery/Smithsonian Institution Press, 1994.

———, ed. *The Portrait in Eighteenth-Century America*. Newark: University of Delaware Press, 1993.

———. *Portrait Painting in America. The Nineteenth Century*. New York: Main Street/Universe Books, 1977.

Miller, Lillian B. *In Pursuit of Fame. Rembrandt Peale 1778–1860*. Washington: National Portrait Gallery/Seattle and London: University of Washington Press, 1992.

———. "John Vanderlyn and the Business of Art." *New York History*, 26 (Jan. 1951): 33–44.

———. *Patrons and Patriotism. The Encouragement of the Fine Arts in the United States 1790–1860*. Chicago and London: University of Chicago Press, 1966.

———, ed. *The Peale Family. Creation of a Legacy 1770–1870*. New York: Abbeville Press, [1996].

Mitnick, Barbara J., general ed. *George Washington American Symbol*. New York: Hudson Hills Press, 1999.

Moore, Doris Langley. "Byronic Dress." *Costume*, 5 (1971): 1–13.

———. *The Late Lord Byron. Posthumous Dramas*. Philadelphia and New York: J. B. Lippincott, 1961.

[Moran, Lord.] *Churchill. Taken from the Diaries of Lord Moran. The Struggle for Survival 1940–1945*. Boston: Houghton Mifflin, 1966.

Motion, Andrew. *Keats*. London: Faber and Faber, 1997.

Mott, Frank Luther. *A History of American Magazines 1741–1850*. 1930; Cambridge, MA. Harvard University Press, 1957.

Murray, Sarah S. *In the Olden Time. A Short History of the Descendants of John Murray, the Good*. New York: Stettiner, Lambert & Co., 1894.

[Napoleon Bonaparte.] *Napoleon's Last Will and Testament*, trans. by Alex de Jonge. New York and London: Paddington Press, 1977.

Nathan, Isaac. *Fugitive Pieces and Reminiscences of Lord Byron*. London: Whittaker, Treacher, 1829.

Neely, Sylvia. *Lafayette and the Liberal Ideal 1814–1824. Politics and Conspiracy in an Age of Reaction*. Carbondale and Edwardsville: Southern Illinois University Press, 1991.

Nemerov, Alexander. *The Body of Raphaelle Peale. Still Life and Selfhood, 1812–1824*. Berkeley, Los Angeles and London: University of California Press, 2001.

Noble, Louis Legrand. *The Life and Works of Thomas Cole*, ed. Elliot B. Vesell. 1853; Cambridge, MA: Harvard University Press, 1964.

Nye, Russell Blaine. *Society and Culture in the United States*. New York: Harper & Row, 1974.

Ormond, Richard. *Early Victorian Portraits*. 2 vols. London: National Portrait Gallery, 1973.

Ormsbee, Thomas Hamilton. *The Sully Portraits at the United States Military Academy*. A pamphlet reprinted from the *American Collector* (September 1940).

Oueijan, Naji B. "Byron's Notions of the American Revolution." In *Byronic Negotiations*, ed. Katrina Bachinger. Frankfurt am Main: Peter Lang, 2002.

Paley, Morton D. *Portraits of Coleridge*. Oxford: Clarendon Press, 1999.

Parry, William. *The Last Days of Lord Byron*. London: Knight and Lacey, 1825.

Paston, George, and Quennell, Peter, ed. *"To Lord Byron": Feminine Profiles Based upon Unpublished Letters 1807–1824*. London: John Murray, 1939.

Peach, Annette. "'San Fedele alla mia Biondetta': A Portrait of Lord Byron formerly belonging to Lady Caroline Lamb." *Bodleian Library Record*, 14 (1993): 285–95.

———. "Byron and Romantic Portrayal." In *Lord Byron. A Multidisciplinary Open Forum*, ed. Thérèse Tessier. Versailles: Société Française des Etudes Byroniennes, 1999.

Pennington, Estill Curtis. "Painting Lord Byron: An Account by William Edward West." *Archives of American Art Journal*, 24 (1984), 16–21.

———. *William Edward West, 1788–1857. Kentucky Painter.* Washington, DC: National Portrait Gallery, 1985.

Pevsner, Nikolaus. *Studies in Art, Architecture and Design.* 2 vols. Princeton, NJ: Princeton University Press, 1968.

Piper, David. *The English Face.* London: Thames and Hudson, 1957.

———. *The Image of the Poet. British Poets and their Portraits.* Oxford: Clarendon Press, 1982.

Pointon, Marcia. *Hanging the Head. Portraiture and Social Formation in Eighteenth-Century England.* New Haven, CT and London: Yale University Press, 1993.

———. *Milton & English Art.* Toronto: University of Toronto Press, 1970.

———. "Portrait-Painting as a Business Enterprise in London in the 1780s." *Art History*, 7 (June 1984): 187–205.

Porter, Roy. "Making Faces: Physiognomy and Fashion in Eighteenth-Century England." *Etudes Anglaises*, 38 (Oct.–Dec. 1985): 385–96.

Powell, Edith W. "An American 'Old Master.'" *International Studies*, 75 (June 1922): 237–41.

Praz, Mario. *The House of Life*, trans. Angus Davidson. 1958; New York: Oxford University Press, 1964.

Prown, Jules David. "Two Manuscript Notebooks of Thomas Sully." *Yale University Library Gazette*, 39, no. 2 (Oct. 1964): 73–9.

Raizis, Marios Byron and Papas, Alexander. *American Poets and the Greek Revolution 1821–1828. A Study in Byronic Philhellenism.* Thessaloniki: Institute for Balkan Studies, [1971?].

———. *Greek Revolution and the American Muse. A Collection of Philhellenic Poetry, 1821–1828.* Thessaloniki: Institute for Balkan Studies, 1972.

Ray, Gordon. *The Illustrator and the Book in England. From 1790 to 1914.* New York: Dover, 1976.

Rebora, Carrie. "Sir Thomas Lawrence's *Benjamin West* for the American Academy of Fine Arts." *American Art Journal*, 21, no. 3 (1989): 18–47. *See also* under Barratt, Carrie Rebora.

Redgrave, Richard and Samuel. *A Century of British Painters.* 1866; Ithaca, NY: Cornell University Press, 1981.

Reynolds, Sir Joshua. *Discourses on Art*, ed. Robert R. Wark. New Haven, CT and London: Yale University Press, 1975.

Ribeiro, Aileen. *The Art of Dress. Fashion in England and France 1750 to 1820.* New Haven, CT and London: Yale University Press, 1995.

———. *The Gallery of Fashion.* Princeton, NJ and Oxford: Princeton University Press, 2001.

Richardson, Edgar P. *American Romantic Painting.* New York: E. Weyhe, 1944.

———. *Jacob Eichholtz, 1776–1842, Pennsylvania Painter. A Retrospective Exhibition.* PAFA, 1969.

———. *Painting in America. From 1502 to the Present.* New York: Crowell, 1965.

———. "Portraits by Jacob Eichholtz." *Art in America and Elsewhere*, 27 (Jan. 1939): 14--22.

———. *Washington Allston. A Study of the Romantic Artist in America.* Chicago: University of Chicago Press, 1948.

Richardson, John. *The Sorcerer's Apprentice. Picasso, Provence, and Douglas Cooper.* New York: Alfred A. Knopf, 1999.

Robb, David M. "Thomas Sully: The Business of Painting." M.A. thesis, Yale University, 1967.

Roberts, George and Mary. *Triumph on Fairmount. Fiske Kimball and the Philadelphia Museum of Art.* Philadelphia and New York: Lippincott, 1959.

Robinson, Charles E. "Byron and the Fourth of July." *Newstead Byron Society Review* (January 2001): 19–28.

———. "The Influence of Byron's Death on America." *The Byron Journal*, 5 (1977): 50–66.

Roessel, David. *In Byron's Shadow. Modern Greece in the English and American Imagination.* Oxford and New York: Oxford University Press, 2002.

Romantic Art in Britain, Paintings and Drawings 1760–1860. Catalogue: Frederick Cummings, Allen Staley. Philadelphia: Philadelphia Museum of Art, 1968.

Rosenblum, Robert. *Transformations in Late Eighteenth Century Art.* 1967; Princeton, NJ: Princeton University Press, 1989.

Rossheim, Beth N. "Thomas Sully (1783–1872): Beginning Portraitist in Norfolk." M.A. thesis, Old Dominion University, 1981.

Royall, William L. "Queen Victoria as Seen by an American. Being the Letters of Mrs. Sallie Coles Stevenson, wife of the American Minister in London, 1836–1841." *Century Illustrated Monthly Magazine*, 77 (Nov. 1908): 453–69. Further installments through April 1909.

Rotberg, Robert I. and Rabb, Theodore K., eds. *Art and History. Images and their Meaning.* New York and Cambridge: Cambridge University Press, 1982.

Rubin, William, ed. *Picasso and Portraiture. Representation and Transformation.* New York: Harry N. Abrams (Museum of Modern Art), 1997.

Russell, John. "British Portrait Painters," in *Aspects of British Art*, ed. W. J. Turner. London: Collins, 1947.

Rutledge, Anna Wells. "Dunlap Notes." *Art in America*, 39 (Feb. 1951): 36–43.

Saarinen, Aline B. *The Proud Possessors.* London: Weidenfeld and Nicolson, 1959.

St Clair, William. *The Godwins and the Shelleys. A Biography of a Family.* New York and London: Norton, 1989.

———. *That Greece Might Still Be Free. The Philhellenes in the War of Independence.* London: Oxford University Press, 1972.

Saisselin, Rémy G. *Style, Truth, and the Portrait.* New York: Harry N. Abrams, [1963].

Saltzman, Cynthia. *Portrait of Dr. Gachet. The Story of a Van Gogh Masterpiece*. New York: Viking, 1998.

Sartain, John. *The Reminiscences of a Very Old Man. 1808–1897*. New York: D. Appleton, 1899.

Saslow, James M. *Pictures and Passions. A History of Homosexuality in the Visual Arts*. New York: Penguin Books, 1999.

Saunders, Richard H. "The Eighteenth-Century Portrait in American Culture of the Nineteenth and Twentieth Centuries." In *The Portrait in Eighteenth-Century America*, ed. Ellen G. Miles. Newark: University of Delaware Press, 1993.

Scenic and Historic America, 1 (1929), 5–7: "Cochran Collection of Presidential Portraits Assured of Permanent Home."

Schama, Simon. *Dead Certainties (Unwarranted Speculations)*. New York: Alfred A. Knopf, 1989.

Schmutz, Thomas. "Between Instruction Manuals and Studio Practice: *Thomas Sully's Notebooks*." *Archives of American Art Journal*, 39, nos 3–4 (1999): 21–31.

Schwartz, Barry. *George Washington: The Making of an American Legend*. New York: The Free Press, 1987.

[Schwarz Gallery.] *American Paintings*. Philadelphia: Schwarz Gallery, 2001.

Scott, Walter. "Death of Lord Byron" (1824). In *Miscellaneous Prose Works*, 28 vols, 1834–40; Edinburgh: Adam and Charles Black, 1851–55: 4: 343–50.

———. [Review article on *Childe Harold's Pilgrimage*, canto III, *The Prisoner of Chillon*, etc.] *Quarterly Review*, 16 (October 1816): 172–208.

———. *The Letters of Sir Walter Scott*. 12 vols, ed. Sir Herbert J. C. Grierson et al. London: Constable, 1932–37.

———. *Notes and Index to Sir Herbert Grierson's Edition of The Letters of Sir Walter Scott*, ed. James C. Corson. Oxford: Clarendon Press, 1979.

Sellers, Charles Coleman. *Charles Willson Peale*. New York: Charles Scribner's Sons, 1969.

Severens, Martha R. and Wyrick, Charles L., Jr. *Charles Fraser of Charleston*. Charleston, SC: Carolina Art Association/Gibbes Art Gallery, 1983.

Seznec, Jean. "Diderot and Historical Painting." In *Aspects of the Eighteenth Century*, ed. Earl R. Wasserman. Baltimore, MD: Johns Hopkins University Press, 1965.

Scharf, J. Thomas and Westcott, Thompson. *History of Philadelphia, 1609–1884*. 3 vols. Philadelphia: L. H. Everts, 1884.

Shaw, William A. "The Authentic Portraits of Byron." Part 1: *The Connoisseur*, 30 (July 1911): 155–61.

Silverman, Kenneth. *A Cultural History of the American Revolution*. New York: Thomas Crowell, 1976.

Simon, Robin. *The Portrait in Britain and America*. Oxford: Phaidon, 1987.

Simpson, Marc. *The Rockefeller Collection of American Art at the Fine Arts Museums of San Francisco*. New York: Harry N. Abrams, 1994.

Skalet, Linda. "Thomas B. Clarke, American Collector." *Archives of American Art Journal*, 15 (1975), 2–7.

Skinner, Otis. "Three Madmen of the Theatre." *Scribner's Magazine*, 30 (Nov. 1926): 478–88.

Smiles, Samuel. *Memoir and Correspondence of the Late John Murray*. 2 vols. London: John Murray, 1891.

Soames, Mary. *Clementine Churchill. The Biography of a Marriage*. New York: Paragon House, 1979.

[Society of the Sons of St George.] *The Original Painting of Queen Victoria*. [A copy of this rare pamphlet, *c*. 1838, is in the American Philosophical Society.]

Staiti, Paul. "Character and Class: The Portraits of John Singleton Copley." In *Reading American Art*, ed. Marianne Doezema and Elizabeth Milroy. New Haven, CT and London: Yale University Press, 1998, pp. 12–37.

Staroblinski, Jean. *1789. The Emblems of Reason*. 1973; Charlottesville: University Press of Virginia, 1982.

———. *The Invention of Liberty. 1700–1789*. Geneva: Skira; Cleveland, OH: World, 1964.

Steiner, Wendy. *Exact Resemblance to Exact Resemblance: The Literary Portraiture of Gertrude Stein*. New Haven, CT and London: Yale University Press, 1978.

Stemmler, Joan K. "The Physiognomical Portraits of Johann Caspar Lavater." *Art Bulletin*, 75 (March 1993): 151–68.

Stevenson, Warren. *Romanticism and the Androgynous Sublime*. Madison, NJ and London: Fairleigh Dickinson University Press, 1996.

Stewart, Robert G. *Henry Benbridge (1743–1812). American Portrait Painter*. Washington: Smithsonian Institution Press for the National Portrait Gallery, 1971.

———. *A Nineteenth-Century Gallery of Distinguished Americans*. Washington: Smithsonian Institution Press, 1969.

Stewart-Smith, Elizabeth. *Lord Byron's Screen*. Mansfield, UK: Reliance Press, 1995.

Stoops, Susan L. *Mask or Mirror? A Play on Portraits*. Worcester, MA: Worcester Art Museum, 2002.

Strong, Sir Roy, introduction. *The British Portrait 1660–1960*. Woodbridge, Suffolk: Antique Collectors Club, 1991.

Stroud, Patricia Tyson. *The Emperor of Nature. Charles-Lucien Bonaparte and His World*. Philadelphia, PA: University of Pennsylvania Press, 2002.

[Stuart, Gilbert.] *Gilbert Stuart. Portraitist of the Young Republic 1755-1828*. Museum of Art, Rhode Island School of Design, 1967.

Studing, Richard. *Shakespeare in American Painting. A Catalogue from the Late Eighteenth Century to the Present*. London and Toronto: Associated University Presses, 1993.

[Sully, Thomas.] *Catalogue of the Memorial Exhibition of Portraits by Thomas Sully*. Philadelphia, PA: Pennsylvania Academy of Fine Arts, 1922.

———. *A Register of Portraits Painted by Thomas Sully 1801–1871*,

arranged and edited with an introduction and notes by Charles Henry Hart. Philadelphia, PA: [no publisher], 1909.
———. "Recollections of an Old Painter." *Hours at Home*, 10 (Nov. 1869): 69–74.
———. *Thomas Sully, 1783–1872*. Farmville, VA: Longwood College, 1973.
Swan, Mabel Munson. *The Athenaeum Gallery, 1827–1873. The Boston Athenaeum as an Early Patron of Art*. Boston: [n.p.] 1940.
Swenson, E. B. "An Early Theatrical Portrait by Sully – *William B. Wood as Charles de Moor*." *Corcoran Gallery of Art Bulletin*, 3 (Jan. 1951): 6–12.
Tatham, David. *Winslow Homer in the Adirondacks*. Syracuse, NY: Syracuse University Press, 1996.
Thorpe, James. *Henry Edwards Huntington. A Biography*. Berkeley, Los Angeles and London: University of California Press, 1994.
[Ticknor, George.] *Life, Letters, and Journals of George Ticknor*. 2 vols. 9th edn. Boston: James R. Osgood, 1878.
Tomory, Peter. *The Life and Art of Henry Fuseli*. London: Thames and Hudson, 1972.
Torchia, Robert W. *John Neagle. Philadelphia Portrait Painter*. Philadelphia, PA: HSP, 1989.
Torrey, Raymond H. "Philipse Manor Hall, Yonkers." *Scenic and Historic America*, 4 (Feb. 1935): 3–28.
Towner, Wesley. *The Elegant Auctioneers*. New York: Hill and Wang, 1970.
[Trelawny, Edward John.] *The Last Days of Shelley and Byron*, ed. J. E. Morpurgo. New York: Philosophical Library, 1952.
Trollope, Frances. *Domestic Manners of the Americans*, ed. Donald Smalley. New York: Alfred A. Knopf, 1949.
Tscherny, Nadia. "Likeness in Early Romantic Portraiture." *Art Journal*, 46 (1987): 193–9.
Three Hundred Years of American Painting. The Montclair Art Museum Collection, ed. Marilyn S. Kushner et al. New York: Hudson Hills Press/Montclair Art Museum, 1989.
Turner, James. *The Liberal Education of Charles Eliot Norton*. Baltimore, MD and London: Johns Hopkins University Press, 1999.
Tytler, Graeme. *Physiognomy in the European Novel. Faces and Fortunes*. Princeton, NJ: Princeton University Press, 1981.
Vallone, Lynne. *Becoming Victoria*. New Haven, CT and London: Yale University Press, 2001.
Van Devanter. Ann C. "*Anywhere So Long as There Be Freedom*": *Charles Carroll of Carollton, His Family & His Maryland*. Baltimore, MD: Baltimore Museum of Art, 1975.
[Van Gogh, Vincent.] *The Letters of Vincent Van Gogh*, selected and ed. by Ronald de Leeuw. London: Allen Lane/Penguin Press, 1996.
Van Zandt, Roland. *Chronicles of the Hudson. Three Centuries of Travelers' Accounts*. New Brunswick, NJ: Rutgers University Press, 1971.
Varnedoe, Kirk. "The Self and Others in Modern Portraits." *Art News*, 75, no. 8 (Oct. 1976): 64–70.

Vaughan, William. *British Painting. The Golden Age from Hogarth to Turner*. London: Thames and Hudson, 1999.

Velázquez in New York Museums. New York: The Frick Collection, 1999.

Verheyen, Egon. "'The most exacting representation of the Original': Remarks on Portraits of George Washington by Gilbert Stuart and Rembrandt Peale." In *Retaining the Original. Multiple Originals, Copies, and Reproductions*. Hanover, NH and London: University Press of New England, 1989.

Viola, Herman J. *The Indian Legacy of Charles Bird King*. Washington and New York: Smithsonian Institution Press/Doubleday, 1976.

Vogel, Morris J. *Cultural Connections. Museums and Libraries of Philadelphia and the Delaware Valley*. Philadelphia, PA: Temple University Press, 1991.

von Erffa, Helmut, and Staley, Allen. *The Paintings of Benjamin West*. New Haven and London: Yale University Press, 1986.

Vose, Robert C. "Boston's Vose Galleries: A Family Affair." *Archives of American Art Journal*, 21 (1981): 8–20.

Vreeland, Susan. *Girl in Hyacinth Blue*. Denver, CO: MacMurray & Beck, 1999.

Wainwright, Nicholas B. *Andalusia. Country Seat of the Craig Family and of Nicholas Biddle and his Descendants*. Philadelphia, PA: Historical Society of Pennsylvania, 1976. [Rev. edn with color photographs, 2002.]

———. "Nicholas Biddle in Portraiture." In *Portrait Painting in America. The Nineteenth Century*, ed. Ellen Miles. New York: Main Street/Universe Books, 1977.

———. *Philadelphia in the Romantic Age of Lithography*. Philadelphia, PA: Historical Society of Pennsylvania, 1958.

Walker, John. *Portraits. 5000 Years*. New York: Harry Abrams, 1983.

Walters, Charles Thomas. "Sculpture and the Expressive Mechanism." In Wrobel, Arthur, ed. *Pseudo-Science and Society in Nineteenth-Century America*. Lexington, KY: The Univerity Press of Kentucky, 1987, pp. 180–204.

Wark, Robert R. *Ten British Painters 1740–1840*. San Marino, CA: Huntington Library, 1971.

Waterhouse, Ellis. *Painting in Britain 1530—1790*. 1953; New Haven, CT and London: Yale University Press, 1994.

Watkin, David. *Thomas Hope 1769–1831 and the Neo-Classical Idea*. London: John Murray, 1968.

Watson, Peter. *Wisdom and Strength. The Biography of a Renaissance Masterpiece*. New York: Doubleday, 1989.

Watts, Harvey. "Thomas Sully – A Revaluation of His Art." *Arts & Decoration* (June 1922): 104–5.

Weber, Bruce. *American Paintings XI*. New York: Berry-Hill, 2000.

Wechsler, Judith. *A Human Comedy. Physiognomy and Caricature in 19th Century Paris*. Chicago: University of Chicago Press, 1982.

Weigley, Russell L., ed. *Philadelphia. A 300-Year History*. New York and London: Norton, 1982.

Weinberg, H. Barbara. "Thomas B. Clarke: Foremost Patron of American Art from 1872 to 1899." *American Art Journal*, 8 (May 1976): 52–83.
———. *Thomas Eakins and The Metropolitan Museum of Art*. Reprinted from *The Metropolitan Museum of Art Bulletin* (Winter 1994–95).
Weintraub, Stanley. *Victoria. An Intimate Biography*. New York: E. P. Dutton, 1987.
Wernick, Richard. "Glamorous actress [Fanny Kemble] found No glamor in Georgia slavery." *Smithsonian Magazine*, 5, 8 (Nov. 1974): 74–81.
West, Alyn Pennington. "Thomas Sully's Visit to London: Motives and Results." M.A., University of Delaware, 1995.
[West, Benjamin.] *Benjamin West in Pennsylvania Collections*, text by Allen Staley. Philadelphia: Philadelphia Museum of Art, 1986.
West, Shearer. *The Image of the Actor. Verbal and Visual Representation in the Age of Garrick and Kemble*. New York: St Martin's Press, 1991.
———. "Portraiture: Likeness and Beauty." In *The Bullfinch Guide to Art History*, ed. Shearer West. Boston, etc.: Little, Brown, 1996, pp. 71–83.
———. "Thomas Lawrence's 'Half-History' Portraits and the Politics of the Theatre." *Art History*, 14 (June 1991): 225–49.
Westall, Richard J. "The Westall Brothers." *Turner Studies*, 4 (Summer 1984): 23–38.
White, Newman Ivey. *Shelley*. 2 vols. New York: Alfred A. Knopf, 1940. Appendix 5, "The Portraits and Busts of Shelley." Vol. 2, pp. 518–38.
Whiteman, Maxwell. *Paintings and Sculpture at the Union League of Philadelphia*. Philadelphia, PA: The Union League, 1978.
Whitley, William T. *Art in England 1800–1820*. Cambridge: Cambridge University Press, 1928.
———. *Gilbert Stuart*. Cambridge, MA: Harvard University Press, 1932.
Whitman, Alfred. *Charles Turner*. London: G. Bell, 1907.
Wick, Wendy C. *George Washington. An American Icon. The Eighteenth-Century Graphic Portraits*. Washington, DC: Smithsonian Institution, 1982.
Wilburn, Jean Alexander. *Biddle's Bank. The Crucial Years*. New York: Columbia University Press, 1967.
Williams, D. E., ed. *The Life and Correspondence of Sir Thomas Lawrence*. 4 vols. London: Henry Colburn and Richard Bentley, 1831. Extra illustrated edition. Pagination may be different from 2 vol. edn.
Willis, Eola. *The Charleston Stage in the XVIII Century*. Columbia, SC: The State Company, 1924.
Wills, Garry. *Cincinnatus. George Washington and the Enlightenment*. Garden City, NY: Doubleday, 1984.
Wilmerding, John. *Compass and Clock. Defining Moments in American Culture. 1800. 1850. 1900*. New York: Harry N. Abrams, 1999.
———. *Thomas Eakins (1844–1916) and the Heart of American Life*. London: National Portrait Gallery, 1993.
———, ed. *The Genius of American Painting*. New York: William Morrow, 1973.
Wilson, Frances, ed. *Byronmania. Portraits of the Artist in Nineteenth and Twentieth-Century Culture*. London: Macmillan, 1999.

Wilson-Smith, Timothy. *Napoleon and His Artists*. London: Constable, 1996.

Wilton, Andrew. *The Swagger Portrait: Grand Manner Portraiture in Britain from Van Dyck to Augustus John 1630–1930*. London: Tate Gallery, 1992.

Wimsatt, W. K. *The Portraits of Alexander Pope*. New Haven, CT and London: Yale University Press, 1965.

Wolf, Edwin, 2nd and Whiteman, Maxwell. *The History of the Jews of Philadelphia from Colonial Times to the Age of Jackson*. Philadelphia, PA: The Jewish Publication Society of America, 1957.

Wood, William B. *Personal Recollections of the Stage*. Philadelphia, PA: Henry Carey Baird, 1855.

Woodall, Joanne, ed. *Portraiture: Facing the Subject*. Manchester and New York: Manchester University Press, 1997.

Woodhouse, Anne Felicity. "Nicholas Biddle in Europe, 1804–1807." *The Pennsylvania Magazine of History and Biography*, 103 (1979): 3–33.

Woodward, E. M. *Bonaparte's Park and the Murats*. Trenton, NJ: MacCrellish and Quigley, 1879.

Woodward, Roland H., introduction. *Bass Otis: Painter, Portraitist & Engraver*. Wilmington, DE: Historical Society of Delaware, 1976.

Woof, Robert, and Hebron, Stephen. *Romantic Icons*. The Wordsworth Trust, 1999.

Wright, Frances. *Views of Society and Manners in America*. Ed. Paul R. Baker. 1821; Cambridge, MA: Harvard University Press, 1963.

Zamoyski, Adam. *Holy Madness. Romantics, Patriots and Revolutionaries 1770–1871*. New York: Viking, 2000.

Ziff, Larzer. *Return Passages. Great American Travel Writing 1780–1910*. New Haven, CT and London: Yale University Press, 2000.

Index[1]

1 Key references given in *italics*. Black and white illustrations indicated in **bold**. Color plates are not indexed.